Making Sovereign Financing and Human Rights Work

Edited by

Juan Pablo Bohoslavsky

and

Jernej Letnar Černič

·HART·
PUBLISHING

OXFORD AND PORTLAND, OREGON

2016

Published in the United Kingdom by Hart Publishing Ltd
16C Worcester Place, Oxford, OX1 2JW
Telephone: +44 (0)1865 517530
Fax: +44 (0)1865 510710
E-mail: mail@hartpub.co.uk
Website: http://www.hartpub.co.uk

Published in North America (US and Canada) by
Hart Publishing
c/o International Specialized Book Services
920 NE 58th Avenue, Suite 300
Portland, OR 97213-3786
USA
Tel: +1 503 287 3093 or toll-free: (1) 800 944 6190
Fax: +1 503 280 8832
E-mail: orders@isbs.com
Website: http://www.isbs.com

First published in hardback 2014
Paperback edition, 2016

Hart Publishing is an imprint of Bloomsbury Publishing plc.

British Library Cataloguing in Publication Data
Data Available

ISBN: HB: 978-1-84946-438-3
PB: 978-1-50990-924-7

Typeset by Hope Services, Abingdon
Printed and bound in Great Britain by
Lightning Source UK Ltd

MAKING SOVEREIGN FINANCING AND HUMAN RIGHTS WORK

Poor public resource management and the global financial crisis curbing fundamental fiscal space, millions thrown into poverty, and authoritarian regimes running successful criminal campaigns with the help of financial institutions are all phenomena that raise fundamental questions around finance and human rights. They also highlight the urgent need for more systematic and robust legal and economic thinking about sovereign finance and human rights.

This edited collection aims to contribute to filling this gap by introducing novel legal theories and analyses of the links between sovereign finance debt and human rights from a variety of perspectives. These chapters include studies of financial complicity, UN sanctions, ethics, transitional justice, criminal law, insolvency proceedings, millennium development goals, global financial architecture, corporations, extraterritoriality, state of necessity, sovereign wealth and hedge funds, project financing, state responsibility, international financial institutions, the right to development, UN initiatives, litigation, as well as case studies from Africa, Asia and Latin America. These chapters are then theorised by the editors in an introductory chapter.

In July 2012 the UN Human Rights Council finally issued its own guidelines on foreign debt and human rights, yet much remains to be done to promote better understanding of the legal and economic implications of the interface between finance and human rights. This book will contribute to that understanding as well as help practitioners in their everyday work. The authors include world-renowned lawyers and economists, experienced practitioners and officials from international organisations.

To Mariana and León, my accomplices.

JPB

To my grandparents, Ivan and Ivanka.

JLC

*Foreword by Philip Alston**

This book should have been written a long time ago. The extent to which gross human rights violations are frequently underpinned by international financial structures was convincingly demonstrated in the 1970s, particularly in the cases of apartheid South Africa, and Chile. And some of the New International Economic Order debates of the same era were also premised on the assumption that international markets controlled by and in the interests of the North were incompatible with meaningful development in the South. But the intervening decades have seen all too little sustained pursuit of these insights, especially in terms of examining the ways in which the rules governing sovereign financing arrangements and those applying to human rights can be made more complementary.

The present volume of essays is thus especially welcome because it reflects the engagement of an impressive and diverse group of contributors with a broad range of issues under the rubric of sovereign financing and human rights. It is to be hoped that its publication marks the beginning of a new scholarly phase in which more sophisticated, financially literate, critical and informed analyses of the impacts of international economic and financial systems will be brought to bear upon efforts to promote respect for human rights by financial and other actors who have long been highly resistant to such concerns.

It must be said, however, that the financial community has hardly been under much pressure from the sources that one might expect to be in the forefront of insisting upon such linkages. Those sources would include, as a minimum, international lawyers, international development practitioners and international human rights bodies. It is instructive to note the extent to which each of these groups has avoided playing such a role.

Public international lawyers for their part have historically succeeded in carving out a space for themselves that did not require engagement in any systematic or meaningful way with the impact that the norms that they promoted and defended might have upon the private sphere, whether at the micro or macro levels. At the micro-level, the failure of states to reign in death squads or to respond to plagues of violence against women, could be ignored since these were matters that were within the *domaine reservé* of states. In such areas, international law shored up sovereignty and strengthened the hands of governments. And at the macro-level, international economic norms (private international law) and institutions and the conduct of private economic actors, were for the most part kept very separate from the mainstream of international law.

Many examples could be cited, but one will suffice to make the point. International law has, as any international lawyer will know, played a central role throughout the history of the Congo Free State (1884–1908), the Belgian Congo (1908–1960), the Republic of the Congo (1960–1971), Zaire (1971–1997), and the Democratic Republic of the Congo (1997–today). The issues that emerge from international law accounts of this evolving situation range from the annexation of territory, decolonization, self-determination and the succession of states, to the use of force, development and humanitarian assistance,

* John Norton Pomeroy Professor, New York University School of Law.

the multiple roles of the United Nations and of its peacekeepers and litigation in the International Court of Justice. But the deeper story underlying this entire period is one of unremitting foreign economic exploitation of the vast mineral and other forms of wealth of the territory. On the international law balance sheet this dimension remains curiously neglected, or at least somehow separate, despite the fact that international legal norms and institutions variously facilitated, shielded, or approved much of what was going on, or alternatively provided support for claims that there was little that could be done about any activities which were clearly contrary to existing norms. The predations of the colonial powers, the massive foreign debt incurred by President Mobutu Sese Seko, and the continuing connivance by neighbouring states and other foreign actors to illegally exploit the DRC's resources – all accompanied by, and often contributing to, massive human rights abuses – are somehow matters to be addressed in other contexts and perhaps by other actors. The recent work of the expert group created by the Security Council's Sanctions Committee stands as a rare exception to the failure to explore some of the international law implications of this siloing of concerns.[1]

The international development sector is another source which we might expect to have generated sustained pressure on the sovereign financing community to reconcile their activities with professed adherence to human rights standards. But, as many of the contributors to this volume demonstrate, there has been an extraordinary dissonance in this area. In a nutshell, one could say that the UN, the World Bank, the International Monetary Fund and others seem to have been endlessly prescriptive about what actors in the South should do in terms of resource transparency, the rule of law, anti-corruption measures and so on, while being wondrously permissive in terms of what typically (although increasingly less so) Northern corporate interests are expected to do to contribute to achieving the same goals. Recent efforts under the auspices of UNCTAD, such as the adoption of the Principles on Responsible Sovereign Lending and Borrowing, have begun to redress part of the imbalance, but there is a long way to go.

Finally, it might reasonably have been assumed that international human rights bodies could be counted upon to have taken up these crucial linkages in a systematic manner, and to have identified measures that ought to be taken to promote a more constructive relationship. But in fact, all too little has been done. The major historical exception was the struggle against apartheid, in relation to which a range of United Nations bodies successfully linked various forms of sovereign financing and related arrangements to the ongoing repression in the country and helped to compel deep political change. But the case of Chile is perhaps more revealing. Because of the ready availability of abundant evidence pointing to the deep complicity of western financial interests in the overthrow of the democratically elected government of Salvador Allende in 1973, the UN's Sub-Commission on human rights launched a study in 1976 on 'the impact of foreign economic aid and assistance on respect for human rights in Chile'. The task was entrusted to Antonio Cassese who was later to become one of the key architects of the international criminal justice regime. In July 1978 he submitted a massive dossier which was highly critical of the role played by the financial sector in Chile.[2] Subsequently summing up his

[1] In its 2014 report, for example, the committee documented the extent to which 'minerals – particularly tin, tungsten and tantalum – continued to be smuggled from eastern Democratic Republic of the Congo through neighbouring countries, undermining the credibility and progress of international certification and traceability mechanisms'. UN Doc S/2014/42 (23 Jan 2014), pp 3–4.

[2] UN Doc E/CN/4/Sub.2/412, Vols I–IV (1978).

findings, he concluded that 'economic assistance to a very great extent permits the perpetuation [sic] of violations of human rights, and such violations, in turn, bring about the necessary conditions to obtain economic assistance'.[3] The study broke important new ground and the response from Western governments was prompt and efficient: Cassese failed in his bid for re-election to the Sub-Commission and the study disappeared from sight.

In 2000, the UN Commission on Human Rights signalled a change of direction by appointing an 'Independent Expert on the effects of foreign debt and other related international financial obligations of States on the full enjoyment of all human rights, particularly economic, social and cultural rights.' This in turn led to the Human Rights Council's endorsement in 2012 of a set of Principles on Foreign Debt and Human Rights, proposed by the Independent Expert. But the utility of such ambitious and abstract formulations, especially when adopted over the dissenting votes of many of the key states, is limited.

There is, of course, no simple remedy by which to achieve a more constructive and mutually reinforcing approach between sovereign financing arrangements and respect for human rights. What is required is a broad range of measures, some of which are admittedly unlikely to become politically palatable to global elites any time soon, along with many more limited measures which are already well within reach of effective global advocacy campaigns.

Two examples might be cited in relation to responses to gross human rights violations. They involve the increasing resort to the establishment of truth and reconciliation commissions at the national level and the creation of commissions of inquiry at the international level. While these mechanisms have become more professional and systematic in their approaches, they continue to be extraordinarily reluctant to 'follow the money' when it comes to reporting on and seeking to understand egregious human rights violations. The assumption appears to be that it is safer to leave those dimensions to others who will not draw uncomfortable human rights links, and who will confine themselves to expressing concern about the security or viability of the investment climate in a given country and suggest prudential measures to protect investors. This is not to suggest that all truth commissions and all commissions of inquiry should necessarily include a focus on the role of financial actors, but it is at least an option that should be pursued when it is clearly of major relevance.

The great merit of this volume is that its contributors place the spotlight on many of the measures that are available and argue that they are both feasible and essential.

[3] Antonio Cassese, 'Foreign Economic Assistance and Respect for Civil and Political Rights: Chile – A Case Study,' (1979) 14 *Texas International Law Journal* 251, at 263.

Acknowledgements

We wish to thank the contributors of this book for their commitment, innovative ideas, hard work, courage and patience.

We also would like to thank Philip Alston for providing in the foreword his systemic and in perspective insights on human rights, finance and international politics.

In addition, we would like to acknowledge Tom Adams and Charlotte Austin from Hart who made invaluable edits to this book.

Contents

Table of Cases

African Commission on Human and Peoples' Rights

Arbitration awards

Argentina

Belgium

European Committee of Social Rights

European Court of Human Rights

European Court of Justice

Germany

List of Contributors

Robert Bejesky is attorney in Michigan, USA. He has published works involving international law and US constitutional law.

Nadia Bernaz is Senior Lecturer in Law at Middlesex University London.

Giuseppe Bianco is a PhD Fellow in International Economic Law at the University of Oslo and Université Paris 1 Panthéon-Sorbonne.

Christina Binder is Associate Professor of International Law at the University of Vienna.

Juan Pablo Bohoslavsky is Sovereign Debt Expert at the United Nations Conference on Trade and Development.

Jernej Letnar Černič is an Assistant Professor of Human Rights Law at the Graduate School of Government and European Studies (Kranj, Slovenia), where he serves as a Vice-Dean.

Angela Cummine is a sovereign investment analyst for Investec and Editor of *Global Public Investor* for the Official Monetary and Financial Institutions Forum (London).

Surya Deva is Associate Professor at the School of Law of City University of Hong Kong.

Abel Escribà-Folch is an Assistant Professor in the Department of Political and Social Sciences at the Universitat Pompeu Fabra.

Andreas Follesdal is Professor of Philosophy, affiliated with the Department of Philosophy, University of Tromsø, Norway. He directs the ERC Advanced Grant 269841 MultiRights, on the Legitimacy of Multi-Level Human Rights Judiciary; and a Research Council of Norway Centre of Excellence project number 223274, PluriCourts: The Legitimacy of the International Judiciary.

Filippo Fontanelli is Lecturer in Law at the University of Surrey.

Matthias Goldmann is a Senior Research Fellow at the Max Planck Institute for Comparative Public Law and International Law and a Postdoc Researcher at the Cluster of Excellence 'Normative Orders' at Goethe University Frankfurt.

Ingrid Gubbay is head of human rights and environmental law at the law firm Hausfeld & Co LLP.

Nicola Jägers holds the Chair in International Human Rights Law at the Law School of Tilburg University in the Netherlands. She is also Commissioner at the Netherlands Human Rights Institute, the official NHRI.

Dan Kuwali is a post doctoral fellow at the Centre for Human Rights, Faculty of Law, University of Pretoria and an associate professor of law, Centre for Security Studies, Mzuzu University, Malawi.

Rosa Lastra is Professor of International Financial and Monetary Law at the Centre for Commercial Law Studies, Queen Mary University of London.

Sheldon Leader is Professor of Law in the University of Essex and Director of the Essex Business and Human Rights Project.

Fozia Nazir Lone is Assistant Professor in Law at City University of Hong Kong.

Cephas Lumina is UN Independent Expert on foreign debt and human rights and Extra-Ordinary Professor of Human Rights Law at the University of Pretoria.

Patricia Pinto Soares is Human Rights Officer at the United Nations Organization Stabilization Mission in the Democratic Republic of Congo.

Kunibert Raffer is Associate Professor at the Department of Economics, University of Vienna, and Honorary Professor of the Universidad Nacional de Rio Negro.

August Reinisch is Professor of International and European Law at the University of Vienna.

Dustin Sharp is Assistant Professor of Peace Studies at the University of San Diego.

International Court of Justice

ICTY

ICTR

ICSID

International Monetary Fund

International Tribunal for the Law of the Sea

Italy

Permanent Court of Arbitration

Permanent Court of International Justice

Portugal

Netherlands

Nuremberg Military Tribunals

Mexico

Slovenia

South Africa

United States

United Kingdom

Table of Legislation

International instruments

International resolutions

International guidelines and declarations

National legislation

1

Placing Human Rights at the Centre of Sovereign Financing

JUAN PABLO BOHOSLAVSKY AND JERNEJ LETNAR ČERNIČ*

I OBSERVING THE INTERLINKS BETWEEN SOVEREIGN DEBTS AND HUMAN RIGHTS

SOVEREIGN DEBT is one of the most effective tools to implement domestic economic and social policy: public debt can fund human capital development and physical infrastructure projects, provision of basic goods such as water and food, education and social security transfers. It can mitigate the effects of temporary economic downturns and bad loans of state-owned banks and redistribute resources from future generations to the current one.[1] However, it can also facilitate large-scale, systematic and serious human rights violations, such as exacerbating global financial crises, throwing millions of people into poverty while sustaining celebrity lifestyles of narrow elites (not only, but particularly, in undemocratic regimes)[2] and consolidating authoritarian regimes running successful criminal campaigns.

How is this link between sovereign financing and human rights generally established? What are the most relevant cases in which sovereign debt can negatively affect human rights? Should international and domestic human rights law be applied in the sovereign debt realm? If so, under what conditions? Do non-state financial actors have any human rights obligations when they give out loans or is the provision of basic services a responsibility of the borrower state only? If so, what are these obligations and where do they derive from? Which forum can enforce these obligations and how? These are the central questions that contributors in this book deal with.

While political institutions (parliaments and ministries of finance, for example) shape sovereign borrowing, lending to sovereigns also shapes their political institutions and, transitively, the states' capacity to respect, protect and fulfil human rights. At the same time, and in more legalistic language, given the *erga omnes* effect of human rights obligations, the impact of sovereign debts over states' capacities to respect, protect and fulfil

* The views and conclusions reflected in this chapter are solely those of the authors and are in no way intended to reflect the views of any of the institutions with which the authors are affiliated. The authors wish to thank Sabine Michalowski for comments on drafts of this chapter.

[1] E Borensztein et al, *Living with Debt: How to Limit Risks of Sovereign Finance* (Washington DC, Inter-American Development Bank, 2006) 6.

[2] See, for instance, Human Rights Watch, 'World Report 2013, Equatorial Guinea': www.hrw.org/world-report/2013/country-chapters/equatorial-guinea, accessed 2 September 2013.

human rights is not something legally strange to lenders: they should look at the consequences of their loans in terms of affecting the state capacity (and will) to face human rights demands.

There are cases in which sovereign financing is closely linked to human rights violations, such as the cases of funding death squads[3] and death camps.[4] And there are some other cases in which this connection is less direct, such as the case of derivatives and their role in financial crises and poverty.[5] Falling into one or other category mainly relies on one factor: how much the human rights fulfilment depends on these funds (or how much other factors interact with these same rights). This variable is important in terms of allocating responsibilities.

Let us see some more examples of how sovereign financing can harm human rights. The current high debt-to-GDP ratio of a number of developed economies,[6] as a consequence and also as an aggravation of the financial crisis, has led to a slow-down in economic activity and consumer demand and more recently to a significant reduction in labour demand, particularly in North America and Europe. On the other hand, while it is true that extreme poverty levels have been significantly reduced in the south,[7] there are still millions of people living in these extreme conditions.[8] The poor usually suffer the most since they do not have the proper means to protect themselves against adverse income, employment shocks, inflation, currency depreciation and public expenditure cuts. What is more, most often they are left without any judicial recourse to effectively protect their rights. All this typically perpetuates income inequality and lack of respect for basic rights.[9] Financial decisions, poor public financial resources management, debt management and the ways in which crises are channelled and solved therefore have a notable impact on attaining the Millennium Development Goals (MDGs),[10] which translated into law means that all this has a serious impact in terms of economic and social rights.

Financial institutions and corporations play an important role in the realisation of the civil, political, economic, social and cultural rights of the society as a whole; particularly in the current scenario in which private lending to sovereigns plays an overwhelming role

[3] The original funding of Operation Bandeirante (OBAN), the Brazilian multi-agency military operation in charge of repressing people during the dictatorship in Brazil, mostly came from private business people of the state of Paulo who had given political support to the coup in 1964, supporting institutional and economic reforms promoted by the regime, see T Skidmore, *The Politics of Military Rule in Brazil, 1964–1985* (Oxford, Oxford University Press, 1988) 127–28; M Weichert, 'O financiamento de atos de violação de direitos humanos por empresas durante a ditadura brasileira' (2008) 21(2) *Acervo* 186.

[4] For example, Deutsche Bank provided loans to construction and chemical (IG Farben for instance) companies with contracts for facilities at Auschwitz, see H James, *The Nazi Dictatorship and the Deutsche Bank* (Cambridge, Cambridge University Press, 2004) 215.

[5] M Dowell-Jones and D Kinley, 'Minding the Gap: Global Finance and Human Rights' (2011) 25 2 *Ethics and International* Affairs 183–210.

[6] UNCTAD, 'Trade and Development Report, 2012', 2012, New York and Geneva, 23. See also Eurostat, Euro area government debt up to 92.2% of GDP, News release 114/2013, 22 July 2013, http://epp.eurostat.ec.europa.eu/cache/ITY_PUBLIC/2-22072013-AP/EN/2-22072013-AP-EN.PDF, accessed 30 July 2013.

[7] See '2013 Human Development Report', Unided Nations Development Programme, http://hdr.undp.org/en/reports/global/hdr2013/, accessed 30 July 2013.

[8] United Nations, 'Millennium Development Goal 8. The Global Partnership for Development: Making Rhetoric a Reality', MDG Gap Task Force Report, New York, 2012; UNCTAD (n 6) 61.

[9] See decomposition of world income inequality in UNCTAD (n 6) 64.

[10] United Nations Millennium Declaration, GA Res 55/2, UN GAOR, 55th Sess, Supp No 49, at 4, UN Doc A/55/49 (2000).

in financial markets.[11] They can become violators of economic, social and cultural rights, for example where the policies they support and facilitate lead to denial of access to water, food, housing, health and education. The primary responsibility for realising human rights remains with states. Yet, given the powerful position that financial institutions and corporations increasingly have and the consideration they should pay to human rights, as is argued in several chapters in this volume, they should carry an additional responsibility under human rights law.[12]

Another example of how lenders are crucial in terms of securing enjoyment of human rights: to remain in power and carry out a massive campaign of human rights violations a criminal regime has to be capable of facing economic constraints that secure a minimum political support (buying loyalties) and/or enable the bureaucratic (military particularly) machinery to function efficiently in order to control and repress. Reliable financial sources are necessary to support this policy for a certain period, coupled with disregard of basic needs of populations in these countries. Therefore, financial providers facilitate regimes' goal achievements.

All the aforementioned cases pose a great methodological challenge to human rights legal theory, which has historically used micro criteria to observe and understand the causal link between finance and human rights abuses, focusing almost exclusively on human rights as individual legal entitlements with all the requirements and conditions that this implies,[13] which usually entails a rigid and narrow view of the same causal link. This micro perspective needs to be integrated into and complemented by a macro approach, carrying out a holistic and interdisciplinary study of the link considering the broad context and driving forces operating over sovereign debts and human rights in a concrete case. Otherwise, cases such as financial derivative products generating more poverty or financial assistance consolidating criminal regimes would inevitably fall off of the radar of human rights law.

Contributors in this book have sought to explain how private, official and multilateral loans and financial aid can affect human rights in a broad range of causal scenarios. In some of them, such as project financing, a micro criterion can be used to isolate the link between the funds and, for example, the flood provoked by the dam financed. In some others a macro criterion is mandatory because only the economic, political and social backdrop helps us to understand interactions and outcomes, such as the case of debt restructurings or global financial architecture.

Once the causal link between sovereign financing and human rights has been identified – by using a macro or a micro approach – the next challenge is defining its legal implications. At this point the backwardness and underdevelopment of the legal theory addressing this link becomes evident. There is a notable gap, which obviously overlaps with the one that also characterises international finance more generally (capital adequacy, liquidity, risk

[11] In emerging market economies in 2011, private financial inflows (therefore excluding equity investment – which in any case reached US$598 billion) amounted US$548 billion while official inflows (bilateral and multilateral lenders) amounted only US$61 billion, *see* Institute of International Finance, 'Capital Flows to Emerging Market Economies', *IIF Research Note*, 26 June 2013.

[12] Special Representative of the Secretary-General on the Issue of Human Rights and Transnational Corporations and Other Business Enterprises, Guiding Principles on Business and Human Rights: Implementing the United Nations 'Protect, Respect and Remedy' Framework, UN Doc A/HRC/17/31 (21 March 2011) (by John Ruggie); 2011 Update of the OECD Guidelines for Multinational Enterprises, www.oecd.org/document/33/0,3746,en_2649_34889_44086753_1_1_1_1,00.html, accessed 30 July 2013.

[13] Dowell-Jones and Kinley (n 5) 187.

management, derivatives, financial modelling, ratings, and supervision are also issues in which human rights law has played an extremely marginal role).[14] In the next section the reasons for this gap and why it should be filled will be studied.

A Filling the Gap: Human Beings First

Even though it is politically, socially and economically relevant and timely, and intellectually challenging, not much has so far been written on the relationship between sovereign debt and human rights. Despite the growing attention paid to sovereign debt due to the recent crises in Greece, Ireland, Portugal, Slovenia and Spain, there has been little examination of the impact of sovereign debt crises on enjoyment of human rights. The majority of the literature tends to focus on either human rights or sovereign debt as unconnected concepts, or focus on specific kinds of lenders, or financial instruments or human rights abuses rather than studying common features of the link between debt and human rights generally.[15] One of the few probable exceptions reflecting on this issue from a comprehensive perspective is an article by Dowell-Jones and Kinley examining the inter-connection between these two fields.[16]

The reasons for this gap are multifaceted. First, this topic requires interdisciplinary examination from the perspective of political science, economics, sociology, law, history and other social sciences. Sovereign financing and human rights have historically been analysed in two separate boxes, without much interdependence and interrelation. Second, the relationship between sovereign financing and debt does not fall within politically correct topics and historically it has been neglected. It is obvious why it does not attract attention from financial centres of power. Moreover, besides the Equator Principles,[17] the political weight of the financial sector has managed to block the entrance of a minimum set of standards, which have already been accepted for other corporations. Third, there is the historical argument that considering human rights when taking decisions on loans or aid would be tantamount to unduly politicising financial decisions.[18] Fourth, there is an inherent difficulty in tracing money and then assessing its impact on a given human rights context, aggravated in part because international law has historically dealt exclusively with the nation state system and corporations have largely evaded oversight given their status in the cracks of that particular legal regime.[19] And fifth, only recently studies have showed that sovereign financing strongly affects the enjoyment of human rights.[20]

As seen, taking advantage of interdisciplinary approaches, the political momentum on the social dimension of the economic crisis and its growing academic interest, make the

[14] ibid.

[15] See D Bradlow, 'The World Bank, the IMF, and Human Rights' (1996) 6 *Journal of Transnational Law and Contemporary Problems* 47–90; S Michalowski, 'Sovereign Debt and Social Rights – Legal Reflections on a Difficult Relationship' (2008) 8 *Human Rights Law Review* 35–68; C Tan, 'Life, Debt, and Human Rights: Contextualizing the International Regime for Sovereign Debt Relief' in K Nadakavukaren Schefer (ed), *Poverty and the International Economic Legal System. Duties to the World's Poor* (Cambridge, Cambridge University Press, 2013).

[16] Dowell-Jones and Kinley (n 6) 184.

[17] See in detail at www.equator-principles.com/, accessed 30 July 2013.

[18] See this discussion in the context of international financial institutions in Bradlow (n 15) 81.

[19] See N Jägers, Chapter 12 in this volume.

[20] See J Letnar Černič, Chapter 10 in this volume.

goal of this book of reducing the gap between human rights and sovereign debt as much timely as relevant.

This book makes two fundamental claims: first, that human rights law helps to understand, unravel, denounce and recompose asymmetric power relations that operate underneath sovereign debts that produce and reproduce human suffering; and second, that human rights law applies and offers solutions in sovereign debt contexts and can prevent human rights abuses and provide judicial and/or non-judicial relief to victims. Behind these claims there is a conception that the outcome of sovereign debt should benefit the population not the privileged, undemocratic elites.[21] This argument is translated into legal language in the following way: valid debt contracts should be in the interest of the sovereign and as human rights play an important role in defining popular sovereignty,[22] sovereign debt that will presumably and potentially translate into serious damage for the borrower's population potentially violates human rights law,[23] which includes social, economic, political or civil rights, as it requests that at least a core of every right should be respected in all situations, while recognising the limitations and pitfalls of the concept of a core of human rights.[24]

States are traditionally asked to protect human rights within their territory. And international law protects sovereign states' rights in their territory and at international level.[25] However, states cannot convincingly justify violations of human rights on the basis of state sovereignty. Actually, human rights violations may form one of the reasons which would justify the lifting of an absolute sovereign paradigm.

International human rights law particularly requests states and other actors to ensure respect for the core of every human right. The United Nations Committee on Economic, Social and Cultural Rights (ESCR) developed in General Comment number 3 the doctrine of a minimum core of each economic and social right, which every individual should enjoy. It argued that 'a minimum core obligation to ensure the satisfaction of, at the very least, minimum essential levels of each of the rights is incumbent upon every State party'.[26] States are therefore obliged to provide minimum levels of food, water, housing, education and healthcare.[27] Though not perfect, particularly in relation to positive

[21] Arbitration *Tinoco Case (Gr. Britain v Costa Rica)* (1923) 1 *R Int'l Arb Awards*, 369, reprinted in (1924) 18 *American Journal of International Law*, 147. See comments on this award in O Lienau, 'Who is the "Sovereign" in Sovereign Debt?: Reinterpreting a Rule-of-Law Framework from the Early Twentieth Century' (2008) 33(1) *Yale Journal of International Law* 63.

[22] M Reisman, 'Sovereignty and Human Rights in Contemporary International Law' (1990) 84 *American Journal of International Law* 866.

[23] See generally O Lienau, *Rethinking Sovereign Debt: Debt and Reputation in the Twentieth Century* (Cambridge, MA, Harvard University Press, forthcoming).

[24] P Alston, '"Core Labour Standards" and Transformation of International Labour Rights Regime' (2004) 15(3) *European Journal of International Law* 457–521.

[25] Max Huber in the capacity of arbitrator at the Permanent Court of Arbitration noted in the *Island of Palmas* case that 'the development of the national organization of States during the last few centuries and, as a corollary, the development of international law, has established [the] principle of the exclusive competence of the State in regard to its own territory in such a way as to make it the point of departure in settling most questions that concern international relations', *Island of Palmas Case (or Miangas), United States v Netherlands*, Award (1928) II RIAA 829, ICGJ 392 (PCA 1928), 4 April 1928, Permanent Court of Arbitration.

[26] Committee on Economic, Social and Cultural Rights, General Comment 3, The Nature of States Parties' Obligations (Fifth session, 1990) UN Doc E/1991/23, annex III at 86 (1991), para 10.

[27] KG Young, 'The Minimum Core of Economic and Social Rights: A Concept in Search of Content' (2008) 33 *Yale Journal of International Law* 113. See also P Alston and G Quinn, 'The Nature and Scope of States Parties' Obligations under the International Covenant on Economic, Social and Cultural Rights' (1987) 9 *Human Rights Quarterly* 156, and K Tomaševski, 'Has the Right to Education a Future within the United

obligations,[28] the minimum core model can, jointly with the 'reasonableness test' developed by the South African Constitutional Court in the *Grootboom* case,[29] effectively address the obligations of public and private lenders in the sovereign financing field. Yeshanew observes that the minimum core model 'more or less concentrates on the content of the rights to identify minimum obligations', while the reasonableness test 'focuses on the obligations of states or measures to realize rights'.[30] The two-tiered approach can effectively address deficiencies of both approaches. In the same way, courts and human rights bodies can apply such an approach towards negative and positive obligations under social and economic rights.[31] At the same time, a robust list of international conventions[32] requires that bilateral, multilateral and private lenders pay due attention to the fundamental civil and political rights externalities of their decisions when lending to sovereigns.

Sovereign debt has deep intergenerational and global redistributive implications, which lead us to the problem of global distribution of political authority and economic growth. As international human rights law can (and should)[33] contribute to understanding and transforming the global political economy, it is not surprising that the link between finance and human rights is becoming increasingly relevant on a global scale. One piece of evidence of this is offered by the fact that the United Nations Human Rights Council endorsed in 2012 the report elaborated by the Independent Expert on the Effects of Foreign Debt and Other Related International Financial Obligations of States on the Full Enjoyment of All Human Rights, Particularly Economic, Social and Cultural Rights.[34] Yet, this resolution was mostly endorsed by developing countries, whereas so-called developed states ignored it.[35]

Nations? A Behind-the-Scenes Account by the Special Rapporteur on the Right to Education 1998–2004' (2005) 5 *Human Rights Law Review* 205. However, it should be noted that there have been disagreements on whether the Committee's views are binding or not. For comprehensive discussion see M Sepúlveda, *The Nature of the Obligations under the International Covenant on Economic, Social and Cultural Rights* (Cambridge, Intersentia, 2003).

[28] S Lienberg, 'Socio-Economic Rights: Revisiting the Reasonableness Review/Minimum Core Debate' in SC Woolman and M Bishop (eds), *Constitutional Conversations* (PULP, Pretoria, 2008) 303.

[29] *Government of the Republic of South Africa and Others v Grootboom and Others* (CCT11/00) [2000] ZACC 19; 2001 (1) SA 46; 2000 (11) BCLR 1169 (4 October 2000).

[30] SA Yeshanew, *The Justiciability of Economic, Social and Cultural Rights in the African Regional Human Rights System* (Cambridge, Intersentia, 2013) 294.

[31] ibid.

[32] See eg Charter of the International Military Tribunal, 82 UNTS 280, Article 6; Convention against Torture and Other Cruel, Inhuman or Degrading Treatment or Punishment, UN Doc A/39/51 (1984), Article 4; International Convention on the Suppression and Punishment of the Crime of Apartheid, UN Doc A/9030 (1974), Article III(b); Supplementary Convention on the Abolition of Slavery, the Slave Trade, and Institutions and Practices Similar to Slavery, 226 UNTS 3, Article 6; Convention on the Prevention and Punishment of the Crime of Genocide, 78 UNTS 277, Article 3e; Convention on Combating Bribery of Foreign Public Officials in International Business Transactions, available at: www.oecd.org/dataoecd/4/18/38028044.pdf, Article 1(2); United Nations Convention Against Transnational Organized Crime, UN Doc A/45/49 (Vol I) (2001), Article 5(1)(b); International Convention for the Suppression of the Financing of Terrorism, UN Doc A/54/49 (Vol I) (1999), Article 2(5)(a); International Convention for the Suppression of Terrorist Bombing, UN Doc A/52/49 (1998), Article 2(3)(a); Rome statute of the International Criminal Court, 2187 UNTS 90, Article 25(3); and Statutes of the International Criminal Tribunals for Rwanda, 33 ILM 1598, Article 6; and for the former Yugoslavia, UN Doc S/25704 at 36, annex (1993) and S/25704/Add 1 (1993), Article 7. These conventions do not pay much attention to whether the accomplice is a human being or a legal entity, be it private or State.

[33] D Kennedy, 'Law and the Political Economy of the World' (2013) 26(1) *Leiden Journal of International Law* 7–48.

[34] A/HRC/RES20/10, 18 July 2012. See in detail Lumina's Chapter 16 in this volume.

[35] ibid.

This book seeks to contribute to enhancing the dialogue and interaction between both human rights and sovereign debt dimensions. A better understanding of the conditions under which international human rights law can operate effectively[36] is based, in turn, on a better understanding of the ways in which sovereign financing impacts on human rights. This helps to design a more nuanced toolkit to deal with debt issues in the light of human rights commitments. Painting a clearer picture of how sovereign financing affects human rights also offers those working on debt issues a more compelling, sophisticated and complete set of data that can be incorporated into their reasoning and financial decisions so that they fulfil international human rights law without being exposed to major legal risks.[37]

B A Bottom-up Approach

This book seeks a better understanding of the causal link between sovereign debt and human rights in a variety of financial scenarios, and to enhance the discussion on how public debt and human rights can be adequately integrated so that human rights always benefit most in this encounter. In this latter regard, making sovereign debt have a positive (or at the very least neutral) impact in terms of human rights asks for a novel approach, one that necessarily takes into consideration not only rights of sovereign debtors and their creditors, but also human rights of ordinary people, who are living ordinary lives, but are affected by a causal chain in which sovereign debt is a determinant link. In order to achieve this, it is pertinent to consolidate the change of the paradigm of traditional international law, which is created by states for state and non-state actors, and take a thorny road of creating international law also through legal sources more receptive to a broad range of stakeholders' views and interests, including, centrally, those of the citizens. Here it is clear how representation, consultation and deliberation are able to foster the normative legitimacy and acceptance of international human rights law in sovereign financing.

In order to promote a link between sovereign financing and human rights that is in line with a human-being-based sovereign financing approach, a bottom-up strategy would be appropriate, which would take into account mainly the needs of the ordinary people. Levit notes that 'bottom-up lawmaking at once debunks the perceived hegemony of official, top-down international lawmaking – lawmaking that often occurs beyond the physical and metaphysical reach of its subjects – and showcases an alternative route to law that is inherently grounded and pluralist',[38] namely law that is not created far away from

[36] R Goodman, D Jinks and A Woods, '*Social Science and Human Rights*' in Goodman, Jinks and Woods (eds), *Understanding Social Action, Promoting Human Rights* (Oxford, Oxford University Press, 2012).

[37] See, elaborating on this but from a broader perspective of international finance, M Dowell-Jones, 'International Finance and Human Rights: Scope for a Mutually Beneficial Relationship' (2012) 3(4) *Global Policy* 467–70.

[38] J Koven Levit, 'Bottom-Up International Lawmaking: Reflections on the New Haven School of International Law' (2007) 32 *Yale Journal of International Law* 393, 409. See also B Rajagopal, *International Law from Below: Development, Social Movements and Third World Resistance* (Cambridge, Cambridge University Press, 2003); KW Danish 'International Environmental Law and the "Bottom-Up" Approach: A Review of the Desertification Convention' (1995) 3(1) *Indiana Journal of Global Legal Studies*. See also J Koven, 'A Bottom-Up Approach to International Lawmaking: The Tale of Three Trade Finance Instruments' (2005) 30 *Yale Journal of International Law* 125.

ordinary people's lives in different ivory towers, but which arises from the participation in various private and public initiatives.

What may appear problematic, or at least highly complex, in adopting a bottom-up approach to legalisation at the international level[39] of the link between human rights and sovereign debt is that stakeholders of sovereign financing and human rights are not only different and fall into a variety of categories, but they also operate in different arenas and speak different languages. Human rights stakeholders most often include states, non-governmental organisations, public interest groups, victims' organisations, trade unions, student organisations, consumer groups, academics and also international organisations. They work in a broad range of fora (national and international courts, education, national and international non-governmental organisations, culture, mass media) and speak a common and plain human rights language. On the other hand, sovereign financing organisations include – besides sovereign borrowers – organisations of creditors, being multilateral organisations, states or private creditors. They interact and negotiate in rather closed frames and organisations (ministries of finance, Bretton Woods institutions, Paris Club, London Club, G20) while communicating through a self-contained and financially sophisticated language.

The bottom-up approach can bridge the abyss between stakeholders from financial and human rights sectors by bringing human rights considerations to the often aloof and highly technical field of sovereign financing by offering (and forcing when necessary) communication in a common language. This approach has implications in terms of legitimacy and effectiveness.

On the one hand, input and output legitimacy of the normative outcomes of this dialogue is reinforced twice. First, adopting a broader representation, consultation and deliberation will enhance the legitimacy of the law-making process, which interprets and produces the legal meaning of the link between sovereign debt and human rights.[40] Second, considering that sovereign debt should be contracted in the citizens' interest,[41] giving special consideration to human rights law when dealing with debt issues reinforces the substantive legitimacy of this normative outcome.[42]

On the other hand, this approach would enhance the respect for human rights, first, because it should allegedly lead to a change in the benefits and costs rational calculations of business operations of potential financial human rights abusers. Financial profits at the expense of human suffering would not be as easily justified as it used to be; and second, because a better understanding of, and making more visible, the link between

[39] This means 'a process of adding to, changing or subtracting from the body of law and the legal system over time': K Abbott and D Snidal, 'Law, Legalization and Politics: An Agenda for the Next Generation of IR-IL Scholars' in J Dunoff and M Pollack (eds), *Interdisciplinary Perspectives on International Law and International Relations: The State of the Art* (Cambridge, Cambridge University Press, 2012).

[40] H Keller, 'Codes of Conduct and their Implementation: the Question of Legitimacy' in R Wolfrum and V Röben (eds), *Legitimacy in International Law* (Heidelberg, Springer, 2008) 297.

[41] JP Bohoslavsky and M Sudreau, 'Does Legitimacy Matter in Sovereign Debt Governance? The Case of The UNCTAD's Principles on Responsible Sovereign Financing' paper presented at the conference on 'The Legitimation and Delegitimation of Global Governance Organizations', 11–13 September 2013, University of Bremen.

[42] A Bogdandi and M Goldmann, 'Sovereign Debt Restructurings as Exercises of International Public Authority: Towards a Decentralized Sovereign Insolvency Law' in Esposito et al (eds), *Sovereign Financing and International Law: The UNCTAD Principles on Responsible Sovereign Lending and Borrowing* (New York, Oxford University Press, 2013) 39.

sovereign financing and human rights would compel financial actors to behave under more commonly agreed beliefs and values underpinning the concept of human rights.

There are at least three United Nations initiatives tackling some of the problems arising from the encounter of human rights and sovereign financing that have adopted the bottom-up approach presented here: first, the Guiding Principles on Foreign Debt and Human Rights mentioned earlier;[43] second, the Principles on Responsible Sovereign Lending and Borrowing elaborated in the context of the United Nations Conference on Trade and Development, which explicitly link sovereign lending and borrowing to the feasibility of the MDGs;[44] and finally, the Guiding Principles on Business and Human Rights,[45] which have been developed from the bottom up or at least with some involvement of civil society and provide in paragraph 11 that corporations should respect human rights, which 'means that they should avoid infringing on the human rights of others and should address adverse human rights impacts with which they are involved'.[46]

To a lesser or greater extent, these three initiatives took seriously the notions of representation, consultation and deliberation as catalysts of international law legitimacy, so that stakeholders (civil society, labour unions, affected people, etc)[47] had their say during the formation of those standards.

Some may argue that a bottom-up approach could create problems of enforcement. However, as Deva answers, 'if norms of international law can be developed "bottom-up" by the participation of non-state actors, the same could be said about the enforcement of such norms by informal means and by using social sanctions'.[48] Such actions could include internal and external pressure on sovereign borrowers but also on lenders in the form of demonstrations, boycotts, media campaigns, pressure through social media, civil disobedience, lobbying in the public administration structures and other forms of social pressures: it is a concrete, practical and pragmatic strategy to implement human rights in the field of sovereign financing.[49]

Some examples of this kind of enforcement are worth mentioning:

[43] Guiding Principles on Foreign Debt and Human Rights (n 34).

[44] See the preamble of these Principles at www.unctad.info/en/Debt-Portal/News-Archive/Our-News/UNCTAD-Releases-Consolidated-Principles-on-Responsible-Sovereign-Financing-310112/, accessed 30 July 2013.

[45] Special Representative of the Secretary-General on the Issue of Human Rights and Transnational Corporations and Other Business Enterprises, Guiding Principles on Business and Human Rights: Implementing the United Nations 'Protect, Respect and Remedy' Framework, UN Doc A/HRC/17/31 (21 March 2011) (by John Ruggie).

[46] ibid, para 11.

[47] H Keller, 'Codes of Conduct and their Implementation: the Question of Legitimacy' in *Wolfrum and* Röben *(eds) (n 40) 297.*

[48] S Deva, 'Keynote Address, Multinationals, Human Rights and International Law: How to Deal with the Elephant in the Room?' in J Letnar Černič and Tara Van Ho (eds), *Direct Human Rights Obligations of Corporations* (The Hague, Wolf Legal Publishers, forthcoming 2014) 14.

[49] On how to make law and power work in tandem in the context of human Rights, see generally E Hafner-Burton, *Making Human Rights a Reality* (Princeton, Princeton University Press, 2013).

- mass claims processes before governmental commissions and courts particularly in the context of Holocaust litigation in Austria,[50] Belgium,[51] France,[52] Germany,[53] the Netherlands[54] and the United States;[55]
- the social, media and political pressure around the claims filed by victims of Nazi Germany;[56]
- the crucial role played by international and American NGOs in denouncing human rights abuses in Latin American dictatorships during the Carter administration and the enactment of legislative financial initiatives to curtail those abuses;[57]
- influential role of civil society organisations in Central and Eastern Europe in pressuring governments to compensate the victims of communist regimes, particularly the return of nationalised property, including banks, and their attempts to reconcile divided societies;[58]
- the participation of civil society in the administration and monitoring of sovereign wealth funds;[59]
- the civil society (Jubilee 2000) campaign in the 1990s, which eventually led to adoption and implementation of the International Monetary Fund and World Bank Heavily Indebted Poor Countries (HIPC) Initiative;[60]

[50] See cases under the Austrian General Settlement Fond, http://de.nationalfonds.org/, accessed 3 September 2013.

[51] See Belgian Jewish community Indemnification Commission, www.combuysse.fgov.be/en/index.html, accessed 3 September 2013.

[52] French Commission for the Compensation of Victims of Spoliation Resulting from the Anti-Semitic Legislation in force during the Occupation, www.civs.gouv.fr/, accessed 3 September 2013.

[53] See German Foundation 'Remembrance, Responsibility and Future', www.stiftung-evz.de/start.html, accessed 3 September 2013.

[54] See The Netherlands' Foundation for Individual Bank Claims Shoah, www.ushmm.org/information/exhibitions/online-features/special-focus/holocaust-era-assets/the-netherlands, accessed 3 September 2013.

[55] *Bodner v Banque Paribas*, 114 F. Supp. 2d 117 (EDNY 2000) (settled); *In re Holocaust Victim Assets Litigation*, 105 F. Supp. 2d 155–57 (settled). See also the official website of the Swiss Banks Settlement: *In re Holocaust Victim Assets Litigation*, www.swissbankclaims.com/, accessed 30 July 2013. See also MT Allen, 'The Limits of Lex Americana: The Holocaust Restitution Litigation as a Cul-de-Sac of International Human-Rights Law' (2011) 17 *Widener Law Review* 1; and MJ Bazayler, *Holocaust Justice: The Battle for Restitution in America's Courts* (New York: New York University Press, 2003). See further SA Bilenker, 'In Re Holocaust Victms' Assets Litigation: Do the US Courts Have Jurisdiction Over the Lawsuits Filed by Holocaust Survivors Against the Swiss Banks?' (1997) 21 *Maryland Journal of International Law & Trade* 251; and L Bilsky, 'Transnational Holocaust Litigation' (2012) 23(2) *European Journal of International Law* 349–75; MJ White, 'Asbestos and the Future of Mass Torts' (2004) 18(2) *Journal of Economic Perspective* 183–204. See also the International Bureau of the Permanent Court of Arbitration (ed), *Redressing Injustices through Mass Claims Processes* (Oxford, Oxford University Press, 2006).

[56] S Eizenstat, *Imperfect Justice: Looted Assets, Slave Labor, and the Unfinished Business of World War II* (Cambridge, Perseus Books Group, 2003).

[57] JM Griesgraber, 'Implementation by the Carter Administration of Human Rights Legislation Affecting Latin America' (1983) PhD thesis, Georgetown University (on file with authors).

[58] Central and Eastern European countries introduced after democratisation in the 1990s policies of denationalisation, which aimed to return nationalised, confiscated and robbed property, including financial property (banks and financial corporations), to its rightful owners. The denationalisation process is yet to be concluded in most of the CEE countries. See, for instance, concurring opinion of judge of the Constitutional Court of Slovenia, Lovro Šturm, in case U-I-121-97, 23 May 1997. See also P Jambrek (ed), *Crimes Committed by Totalitarian Regimes*, (Brussels, Ljubljana Slovenian Presidency of the Council of the European Union, 2008) 11–85. www.crce.org.uk/lessons/Articles/eu_hearing.pdf, accessed 30 July 2013.

[59] See A Cummine, Chapter 11 in this volume.

[60] 'The Birth of Jubilee 2000', Jubilee Debt Campaign, 16 May 1998, available at www.jubileedebtcampaign.org.uk/The3720birth3720of3720Jubilee37202000+282.twl, accessed 3 September 2013.

- the audit carried out in 2007–08 by Ecuador to verify the details of its sovereign debt portfolio with broad civil participation;[61]
- the participation of taxpayers and public employees in the debt restructuring process of US municipalities under chapter 9 of the Bankruptcy Code, seeking debt agreements that protect both creditors' rights and the public interest;[62]
- Iceland's referendum (and eventually rejection) in 2010 on a plan to repay Britain and the Netherlands $5 billion from a bank crash.[63]

At a later stage, informal methods or collaborative enforcement, which started at the bottom close to ordinary people, could gradually turn into more formalised domestic and international procedures and institutions. However, once formalised, it cannot be guaranteed that those mechanisms will adequately address individual rights.[64] That is why broad citizenship participation in the processes of designing sovereign debt policies and enforcing human rights should always be an available tool to make sure that debt and human rights work together.

Contributing to the discussion on how sovereign financing can be incorporated into the field of human rights and/or how human rights can be included in sovereign financing is one objective of this book. It is argued here that rules (and their interpretation) touching upon sovereign debt and human rights should be developed bottom-up instead of top-down as they have actually been developed in the last decades. As sovereign financing is usually conceived, negotiated and executed at a very high political level, far away from daily human rights concerns of ordinary people, an approach that promotes and facilitates a serious legal and political consideration of state borrowers' and their lenders' human rights obligations in sovereign financing should be adopted.[65] In terms of legal interpretation and development, the bottom-up approach would provide arguments to employ systemic integration of human rights in the sovereign financing field or vice versa in order for the rights of individuals to be acknowledged and respected.[66]

II PRESENTATION OF THE CONTENTS OF THE BOOK

Contributors of this book include well-known professors, practitioners, international experts and vigorous young scholars from around the world coming from a variety of academic and professional backgrounds including human rights law, financial law, international law, corporate law, international organisations, economics and history, and a geographical background, covering all continents. This interdisciplinary and pluralistic approach of the book allows the borrowing of questions from different disciplines in

[61] See information available at www.auditoriadeuda.org.ec, accessed 10 September 2013.

[62] See cases in J Spiotto et al, 'Municipalities in Distress? How States and Investors Deal with Local Government Financial Emergencies' (Chapman and Cutler LLP attorneys, Chicago, 2012).

[63] S Lyall 'Iceland Voters Set to Reject Debt Deal', *New York Times*, 5 March 2010, available at www.nytimes.com/2010/03/06/world/europe/06iceland.html?_r=0, accessed 15 September 2013.

[64] LM Carzola Prieto, 'La articulación jurídica del gobierno de la globalización financiera' in F Gómez Isa, A I Herrán, Alberto Atxabal (eds), *Retos del Derecho ante una economía sin fronteras* (Bilbao, Universidad de Deusto, 2012) 199–54.

[65] See the Maastricht principles on Extraterritorial Obligations of States in the area of Economic, Social and Cultural Rights, 29 February 2013, www.fian.org/fileadmin/media/publications/2012.02.29_-_Maastricht_Principles_on_Extraterritorial_Obligations.pdf, accessed 30 June 2013.

[66] See, for example, B Simma, 'Foreign Investment Aribitration: A Place for Human Rights?' (2011) 60(3) *International Law and Comparative Law Quaterly* 584.

order to forge a legal theory more receptive to the complex financial context in which human rights law is supposed to work.

Besides this introductory chapter, the book is divided into five parts. Part A deals with sovereign financing and gross violations of political and civil human rights. In Chapter 2 Juan Pablo Bohoslavsky and Abel Escribà Folch argue that more funds to criminal regimes are usually translated into their consolidation. They explain this link by providing statistical data and using a rational choice approach based on incentives of authoritarian governments and private and official lenders. Then they study the current (rudimentary) response provided by international law to financial complicity, and discuss the policy and legal implications of the empirical findings. In Chapter 3 Patricia Pinto Soares analyses how UN sanctions can safeguard and/or undermine human rights. She reviews the limitations of the Security Council when imposing economic (specifically financial) sanctions, using Iran as a case study to show that these sanctions can also have negative externalities in terms of human rights. She proposes guidelines aimed at reconciling different demands and interests, promoting human rights and at the same time ensuring that the necessary leeway for the achievement of sanctions' purposes and their recognised utility is left open. In Chapter 4 Dustin Sharp discusses the implications of sovereign debt of countries in transition. He explains that problems created by high levels of sovereign debt are typically addressed through a prism of debt management and sustainability, while neglecting human rights and social justice consideration. He first explores the linkages between sovereign debt and human rights, paying special attention to debt forgiveness. He then looks at the role to be played by transitional justice mechanisms in bringing questions of economic violence and sovereign financing into the policy foreground. In Chapter 5 Nadia Bernaz explores establishing criminal liability for complicity of financial corporations in international crimes at the international level. She first examines the potential legal basis for prosecution of corporate complicity in international crimes and thereafter turns specifically to financial complicity, drawing examples from the Nuremberg trials. Finally, she draws upon experience and insight from international law on financing of terrorism.

Part B deals with debt crises and social and economic rights. In Chapter 6 Matthias Goldmann studies the relevance of human rights law in the context of sovereign insolvencies. He starts by highlighting the historical (and current) asymmetry in the relationship between the rights of citizens in the insolvent state and the rights of creditors. Then he explains the impact of sovereign insolvencies on human rights, particularly economic and social rights, and explores the avenues for reconciling human rights with adjustment policies. He also discusses which lenders are bound by human rights law and finally discusses how human rights impact assessments, among other procedural tools, might help in reconciling the rights and interests of people living in insolvent states with creditors' rights and interests. In Chapter 7 Kunibert Raffer explores the links between sovereign debt, human rights and the MDGs. The main argument is that unsustainable debt burden compromises the full enjoyment of human rights, in particular economic, social and cultural rights. In the case of state insolvency, the MDGs can and should play an important role protecting the debtor, human rights and human dignity. In Chapter 8 August Reinisch and Christina Binder analyse the state of necessity defence when dealing with debts. They state that such a defence is already available for economic emergencies (even vis-à-vis non-state actors), and discuss the complexities of its prerequisites and implementation, concluding that it might be preferable for states to aim at sovereign debt restructuring as a durable – and not just temporary – solution. In Chapter 9 Rosa Lastra discusses the need to take human rights into account in the shaping of the evolving international financial architecture. The author explains that even though financial law has grown exponentially in recent years and its regulations are highly technical and specialised, general principles of law and function within an ethical framework of accepted values and principles do need to be considered. She then also argues that the interplay between hard law and soft law in international financial law can provide a fundamental key to improve the attention of the global financial architecture to human rights issues. The IMF and other international financial institutions, and non-state lenders as well, should recognise and protect human rights. In Chapter 10 Jernej Letnar Černič addresses emerging corporate responsibility for economic and social rights in the sovereign debt context, noting that not only states but also financial corporations have obligations to respect, protect and fulfil those rights. More specifically, he argues that financial corporations must primarily ensure that they will not violate the reasonable minimum core of economic and social rights of individuals during the whole period of the debt cycle. He proposes a bottom-up approach in establishing accountability of corporate actors.

Part C deals with specific financial actors and instruments, and novel approaches as well. In Chapter 11 Angela Cummine examines the relationship between sovereign wealth funds and human rights. She argues that sovereign wealth funds should be obliged to observe human rights in their operations and discusses the form and content of such obligations. Finally, she examines ethical sovereign fund investments in practice and provides the example of New Zealand as a potential role model of sovereign investors considering human rights. Part D of the book presents several chapters dealing with particular financial actors and instruments in connection to human rights. In Chapter 12 Nicola Jägers studies finance and human rights obligations of non-state actors. She makes the case that the emerging framework (soft law, standards and regulations) on corporate human rights responsibilities is relevant in the context of adverse human rights effects of sovereign financing, even though she highlights some of the challenges in terms of operationalisation. In Chapter 13 Sheldon Leader discusses the interaction between project financing and human rights, examines their advantages and disadvantages and proposes how notions of project financing and human rights can at first be reconciled. Further, he studies the place of corporate social responsibility in the management of project financing risks and examines the example of the Chad–Cameroon oil pipeline and the health of local populations. He concludes that project financing can offer valuable insights for the field of human rights and business. In Chapter 14 Giuseppe Bianco and Filippo Fontanelli explore the potential accountability of the IMF's compliance with human rights. They focus on its role as protector of global public goods and in doing so analyse its accountability *within*, but also its accountability in relation to, its external policies, particularly giving out loans on the basis of a policy of conditionality and argue that some of the steps towards greater compliance with human rights are encouraging, although the Fund is not responsible for its activities yet. In Chapter 15 Fozia Lone analyses the implications of extraterritorial human rights violations when they are associated with irresponsible sovereign financing. She argues that the *mother states* of financial corporations should be responsible for regulating and monitoring the activities of companies registered on their territories which may incur liability if this responsibility is not fulfilled. In Chapter 16 Cephas Lumina presents and analyses the link between sovereign debt and human rights from the unique perspective of the United Nations Independent Expert on the effects of foreign debt and other related international financial obligations of states on the full enjoyment of all human rights, particularly economic, social and cultural rights. His chapter discusses the practice of the UN Human Rights Council and human rights treaty bodies, paying special attention to the UN Guiding Principles on Foreign Debt and Human Rights. He argues that sovereign debt directly affects the ability of states to respect, protect and fulfil human rights.

Part D presents several case studies describing in detail how, in different contexts and referring to a diversity of financial instruments, human rights have been negatively affected by sovereign debt. In Chapter 17 Dan Kuwali explores interactions between foreign (especially sovereign) finance and armed conflicts in Africa. He explores what impact finance has on armed conflicts in this region and the belligerent parties. In this way, he recommends steps to limit financial profiteering from armed conflict in Africa. In Chapter 18 Surya Deva analyses the likely negative consequences of the investment/finance-driven model of development, from an Indian perspective. He discusses two case studies: the Enron corporation's power project in Dabhol (Maharashtra) and the Vendata corporation's activities in the state of Orissa. He argues that current private financing of development projects is not human rights compliant and therefore a more holistic approach is needed to both financial and human rights considerations. In Chapter 19 Robert Bejesky and Juan Pablo Bohoslavsky describes the Carter administration's efforts to elicit human rights improvements from the authoritarian governments in Uruguay, Chile and Argentina. The US government curtailed financial (bilateral and multilateral) aid to these states because of the human rights situation. The authors explain how these historical facts meaningfully contribute to the current debate on financial complicity. In Chapter 20 Andreas Follesdal offers insights in the operations of the Norwegian government pension fund as a model of socially responsible investment and argues that its disinvestment approach has showed great promise in terms of promoting human rights in the countries receiving their financial support. In Chapter 21 Ingrid Gubbay studies lessons learnt from the apartheid litigation in the US using the Alien Torts statute based on the notion that financial complicity with the apartheid regime signals prospects for future claims of foreign plaintiffs. She examines different approaches to establishing complicit liability of commercial lenders for atrocities committed by state actors and provides some proposals for alternative avenues.

As shown by the chapters described above, the book seeks to cover a wide, but not comprehensive, range of possible interlinks between sovereign financing and human rights. A variety of actors, financial instruments and human rights are studied by the contributors, but in all of them the red thread is there: sovereign financing negatively affecting human rights. With the expectation of finding common roots, patterns and characteristics in the problems illustrated by the contributors, this book offers an in-depth starting point for future discussions while seeking to contribute to a better understanding of the colossal encounter of sovereign financing and human rights, dilemmas that such a relationship triggers and proposals for discussion of conceptual tools to make this relationship work in favour of the human beings, always.

Part I

Debt and Gross Violations of Political and Civil Rights

2

Rational Choice and Financial Complicity with Human Rights Abuses: Policy and Legal Implications

JUAN PABLO BOHOSLAVSKY AND ABEL ESCRIBÀ-FOLCH*

I INTRODUCTION: WHY THIS INTERDISCIPLINARY APPROACH?

DESPITE THE FACT that political science and international law have for years been exchanging and mutually enriching their own scientific knowledge and methods, these two fields are still notable for their distance. Basically, political science literature sees international law (or *legal institutions*) as just one of many forces at work, while international lawyers focus on the content of law and judicial decisions and interpretations.[1]

Two ways in which these two fields have been shrinking this gap are, on the side of political scientists, by paying more attention to how law works;[2] and on the side of international lawyers, by doing more empirical research. This chapter is another brick in this interdisciplinary effort for integrating both disciplines. The challenge here is even bigger since, in addition, human rights law not only needs interdisciplinary insights to close the gap between its aspirations and achievements, but also brings its own expansive toolkit of norms, knowledge and goals.[3]

In particular, this interdisciplinary collaborative exercise discusses the implications of financing authoritarian governments. If sovereign financing is alone a very complex issue, when crossed with human rights abuses on a large scale, the factual complexities that these encounters provoke largely surpass what international law has to offer in terms of interpreting this causal link and the forces behind it. At the same time, behavioural change (improvement) from the side of the lenders that support a criminal regime needs more than empirical research and analyses around power, cooperation or domestic politics; it actually needs the elaboration of sophisticated legal tools to protect human rights.

* The authors wish to extend their gratitude for the comments to the drafts of this chapter received from Robert Bejesky, Jo Marie Griesgraber, Kunibert Raffer and Dustin Sharp. The views and conclusions reflected in this chapter are solely those of the authors and are in no way intended to reflect the views of any of the institutions with which the authors are affiliated.

[1] E Hafner-Burton, D Victor and Y Lupu, 'Political Science Research on International Law: The State of the Field' (2012) 106 *American Journal of International Law* 47, 48.

[2] ibid.

[3] On the relevance of social science in the context of human rights, see R Goodman, D Jinks and A Woods, '*Social Science and Human Rights*' in J Goodman and A Woods (eds), *Understanding Social Action, Promoting Human Rights* (Oxford, Oxford University Press, 2012).

Hence, the aim of this chapter is to link two so-far unrelated literatures and approaches regarding financial complicity, namely political science and international law, by focusing on the political and legal implications of foreign funds accruing to authoritarian regimes. To do so, we first analyse how access to foreign income affects the survival strategies and the durability of autocracies, and discuss the mechanisms explaining such impact. Second, we study the current and very limited response provided by international law to financial complicity. Finally, we discuss the policy and legal implications that the rational-choice approach may have for those providing regimes with essential financial resources.

This chapter will first in Section II discuss, departing from a rational-choice approach, the link between foreign revenue and other financial resources and autocratic survival and repression. Reviewing the specialised political science literature on authoritarianism and showing some empirical evidence we stress that foreign revenue sources have an important impact on the decisions and the durability of dictators in power. These findings, based on both rational-choice theoretical approaches as well as large-N quantitative analyses, set the ground for the policy and legal discussion on financial complicity. In turn, Section III will describe the rudimentary answer that international law offers to financial complicity. In Section IV, this chapter will present for discussion concrete policy and legal implications of the findings described in Section II. Finally, Section V will assess whether those same implications are grounded in recent institutional and legal developments.

II FINANCIAL COMPLICITY IN POLITICAL SCIENCE: FOREIGN INCOME AND AUTHORITARIAN RESILIENCE

Authoritarian regimes have much worse human rights records than democracies. They not only place enormous or total restrictions on economic and social rights, but also show much lower levels of respect for physical integrity rights.[4] As a result, any factor allowing for the duration and stability of such regimes in principle contributes to the prolongation of human rights violations. What role does foreign income play in this?

To survive in power, authoritarian rulers rely on two basic tools between which, it is argued, a trade-off exists: political loyalty and repression.[5] Mobilising and buying the political support of some individuals and groups is as crucial to autocracies as coping with opposition groups and internal challengers. Both instruments of survival require that governments have sufficient economic resources. Public employment, appointments, kickbacks, contracts and other economic benefits ensure that cliques remain loyal. On the other hand, military spending and other funds devoted to the security apparatus must ensure these groups' capacity to cope with internal and external threats, but also serve their corporate interests to prevent coups.[6]

[4] C Davenport, 'Human Rights and the Democratic Proposition' (1999) 43(1) *Journal of Conflict Resolution* 92–116; C Davenport, 'The Promise of Democratic Pacification: An Empirical Assessment' (2004) 48(3) *International Studies Quarterly*, 539–60; C Davenport and D Armstrong II, 'Democracy and the Violation of Human Rights: A Statistical Analysis from 1976 to 1996' (2004) 48(3) *American Journal of Political Science*, 538–54; S Poe, C Tate and L Keith, 'Repression of the Human Right to Personal Integrity Revisited: A Global Cross-National Study Covering the Years 1976–1993' (1999) 43(2) *International Studies Quarterly* 291–313.

[5] R Wintrobe, *The Political Economy of Dictatorship* (New York, Cambridge University Press, 1998).

[6] P Collier and A Hoeffler, 'Military Spending and the Risks of Coups d'État' (2007) manuscript, Centre for the Study of African Economies, Oxford University; G Rivero, 'Oligopoly of Violence: Civilian Control of a Heterogeneous Military' (2011) manuscript, New York University.

However, the general picture that there is a trade-off between loyalty and repression needs a more nuanced and sophisticated interpretation for one particular reason: both loyalty creation and repression can be further divided into alternative instruments. To obtain support, autocratic regimes have two instruments: patronage and policy/rights concessions. Dictators divert public resources to fund patronage networks and deliver targeted public goods. Since dictatorships have smaller support coalitions relative to democracies, they rely heavily on private goods to reward political support of insiders.[7] These economic benefits can consist, for example, of transfers, subsidies, credits, contracts, licences, tariff protections, regulations that guarantee profits, employments, appointments, consumption and local public services.[8] The skewed expenditures associated with these forms of governance often result in forms of economic violence to those excluded from patronage networks.[9] Resources are extracted from some social sectors through abusive and biased taxation, predatory behaviour, extortion, and state monopolies in order to favour other politically relevant groups.[10]

As for repression (and so, human rights violations), although generally seen as a homogeneous type of state behaviour, Davenport claims that it has two basic components: (i) violent repression in the form of violations of personal integrity and (ii) less (or non-) violent activities consisting of the restriction of individuals' civil and political rights.[11] The latter is strongly related to the concessions for obtaining support. Violent repression entails targeted measures including physical abuses, torture, imprisonment, extra-judicial killings, and disappearances. Restrictions on civil and political rights serve to mould citizens, ban certain challenging behaviours, and prevent contentious collective action.

To some extent a sort of trade-off might be present between these sub-types of coercive instruments as well. In brief, the availability of rents to allocate economic benefits and buy off support reduces the need to obtain it through the extension and concession of certain civil and political rights and other public goods. In contrast, regimes with poorer endowments of resources to fund spoil distribution must grant rights and policy concessions.[12] Likewise, the hindering of collective action through rights restrictions often prevents the need to resort to the extensive use of violent repression. In other words, dictators increase political terror and torture when they face more organised (especially, party and legislative) opposition.[13]

Foreign revenues have a profound influence on authoritarian regimes' politics. They influence regime structure and stability as well as the autocratic elites' choices between survival instruments.[14] First, from a revenue perspective, countries with access to foreign

[7] B Bueno de Mesquita et al, *Logic of Political Survival* (Cambridge, MIT Press, 2003).

[8] On how these economic instruments were used by the Uruguayan military regime, see J Notaro, *La política económica en el Uruguay (1968–1984)* (Montevideo, Ediciones de la Banda Oriental, 1984) 94.

[9] On this see broadly D Sharp (ed), *Justice and Economic Violence in Transition* (New York, Springer, 2013).

[10] R Bates, *Markets and States in Tropical Africa: The Political Basis of Agricultural Policies* (Berkeley, University of California Press, 1981); G Padró-i-Miquel, 'The Control of Politicians in Divided Societies: The Politics of Fear' (2007) 74(4) *Review of Economic Studies* 1259–74.

[11] Davenport (n 4), 539–60; C Davenport, 'State Repression and Political Order' (2007) 10 *Annual Review of Political Science* 1–23.

[12] C Conrad, 'Constrained Concessions: Beneficent Dictatorial Responses to the Domestic Political Opposition' (2011) 55(4) *International Studies Quarterly* 1167–87; J Gandhi and A Przeworski, 'Cooperation, Cooptation, and Rebellion under Dictatorships' (2006) 18(1) *Economics and Politics* 1–26; R Desai, A Olofsgard and T Yousef, 'The Logic of Authoritarian Bargains' (2009) 21(1) *Economics and Politics* 93–125.

[13] Conrad (n 12) 1167–87; J Vreeland, 'Political Institutions and Human Rights: Why Dictatorships Enter into the United Nations Convention Against Torture' (2008) 62(1) *International Organization* 65–101.

[14] Gandhi and Przeworski (n 14) 1–26. Desai, Olofsgard and Yousef (n 12) 93–125; Conrad (n 12) 1167–87.

income rely much less on citizens' taxes to obtain resources. This gives political elites little or no incentive to grant representation or political openings to citizens in exchange for their economic compliance in the form of paid taxes.[15] In addition, citizens have fewer incentives to control government officials and demand representation in order to influence decisions concerning how their money is spent and to prevent abusive tax rises. From a spending perspective, abundant foreign income in the hands of authoritarian governments allows them to buy support through the distribution of spoils, targeted public goods, and increased public spending. Thus, such funds serve to reward the members of the support coalition, co-opt potential opponents, and provide public goods to appease revolutionary threats, thereby reducing the likelihood of an ouster led by either regime insiders or outsiders.[16] Even those funds which cannot be diverted or directly used to fund patronage and repression may be helpful due to their fungibility. That is, foreign income received to fund specific projects in practice augments the revenues available to the regime as it frees up government resources, which can be devoted to strengthening the regime.

In sum, according to the framework developed above, such funds have a persistent long-term effect on authoritarian regimes, making it possible for them to consolidate rule, to perpetuate political exclusion and human rights violations, and to reduce the need for political concessions.[17] Restricting access to these funds would increase autocracies' vulnerability by reducing their ability to fund patronage and the coercive apparatus. A cut in the control of and access to such resources may thus jeopardise regimes' exchanges bringing about splits and defections within the ruling coalition or forcing it to substitute rights concessions for patronage and, so, to liberalise. Such adjustments, though, may come at a cost in the short run. Given the trade-off between survival strategies, a fall in revenues may lead autocrats to rely more heavily on the other instrument of power, namely violent repression.[18]A situation of intensive reliance on violent repression may be useful in the short run but it is sustainable in the mid to long run. Such a strategy is likely to lead to escalation effects, radicalisation of opposition groups, and to defections from the security forces, as the recent events of the Arab Spring clearly illustrate.[19] Further, difficulties in access to foreign income may weaken the regime's ability to pay the security forces, potentially causing resentment and splits among personnel.

[15] M Ross, 'Does Taxation Lead to Representation?' (2004) 34(2) *British Journal of Political Science* 229–49. On the different levels of compliance required to collect different types of taxes see: E Lieberman, 'Taxation Data as Indicators of State–Society Relations: Possibilities and Pitfalls in Cross-National Research' (2002) 36(4) *Studies in Comparative International Development* 89–115.

[16] B Bueno de Mesquita and A Smith, 'Leader Survival, Revolutions, and the Nature of Government Finance' (2010) 54(4) *American Journal of Political Science* 936–50; M Ross, 'Does Oil Hinder Democracy?' (2001) 53(3) *World Politics* 325–61; A Smith, 'The Perils of Unearned Income' (2008) 70(3) *Journal of Politics* 780–93; Gandhi and Przeworski (n 12) 1–26; K Remmer, 'Does Foreign Aid Promote the Expansion of Government?' (2004) 48(1) *American Journal of Political Science* 77–92.

[17] Some recent evidence also suggests that oil and other natural resources, such as diamonds, increase the likelihood of a country experiencing a civil war, which leads to a dramatic deterioration in (already poor) human rights conditions. M Ross, 'A Closer Look at Oil, Diamonds, and Civil War' (2006) 9 *Annual Review of Political Science* 265–300.

[18] For example, it is found that economic sanctions tend to be associated with increases in the levels of violent repression, especially in some types of autocracies more vulnerable to economic pressure. A Escribà-Folch, 'Authoritarian Responses to Foreign Pressure: Spending, Repression, and Sanctions' (2012) 45(6) *Comparative Political Studies* 683–713. D Peksen, 'Better or Worse? The Effect of Economic Sanctions on Human Rights' (2009) 46(1) *Journal of Peace Research* 59–77. RM Wood, 'A Hand upon the Throat of the Nation: Economic Sanctions and State Repression, 1976–2001' (2008) 52(3) *International Studies Quarterly* 489–513.

[19] A Escribà-Folch, 'Repression, Political Threats, and Survival under Autocracy' (2013) 34(5) *International Political Science Review*.

Political scientists have primarily focused on two types of foreign income and their consequences for democracy: oil revenues and foreign aid. Generally, the cross-national empirical literature has found that non-tax revenue decreases the likelihood of authoritarian regime breakdown.[20] In particular, oil and natural resources are shown to be a regime- and leader-stabilising factor and to hurt democracy levels.[21] Similarly, foreign aid has been empirically shown to help autocrats retain power, to impede democratisation (during the Cold War period),[22] and to boost military expenditures.[23]

The source of that foreign income may exert a powerful political impact. As Wright points out:

> [O]il revenue accrues to authoritarian governments directly from the revenue-generating operations of state oil companies. In some cases, oil revenue also arrives in the coffers of the government via taxes on international firms or the sale of concessions to exploit oil reserves.[24]

In contrast, aid is given by donors' official aid agencies bilaterally and/or by multilateral organisations (eg, the World Bank), which may attach conditions to disbursements or reward some particular reforms. Indeed, most democratic donors started to attach political conditions after the end of the Cold War, when geostrategic considerations became less dominant in aid allocation decisions. Aid from democratic donors has been found to encourage democratisation in this particular period.[25]

Besides these well-studied windfalls, numerous notorious dictators, such as Haiti's Duvaliers, Zaire's Mobutu Sese Seko, and the Philippines' Ferdinand Marcos, have also been able to obtain substantial loans from multilateral agencies and other financial actors and, as a result, accumulate huge debt burdens. However, while the impact on democracy of natural resource rents and official development assistance (ODA) has been well studied, the potential consequences of foreign borrowing (ie, external debt) and foreign direct investment (FDI) have received little or no attention in the political science literature.

In addition to well-known contextual and economic motivations, the accumulation of debt has been found to have profound political determinants, being autocratic regimes more prone than democracies to borrow from foreign lenders.[26] Despite facing higher

[20] K Morrison, 'Oil, Non-Tax Revenue, and the Redistributional Foundations of Regime Stability' (2009) 63(1) *International Organization* 107–38.

[21] Ross (n 16), 325–61; B Smith, 'Oil Wealth and Regime Survival in the Developing World: 1960–1999' (2004) 48(2) *American Journal of Political Science* 232–46; J Ulfelder, 'Natural-Resource Wealth and the Survival of Autocracy' (2007) 40(8) *Comparative Political Studies* 995–1018; L Omgba 'On the Duration of Political Power in Africa: The Role of Oil Rents' (2009) 42)(3) *Comparative Political Studies* 416–36; K Tsui, 'More Oil, Less Democracy: Evidence from Worldwide Crude Oil Discoveries' (2011) 121(551) *Economic Journal* 89–115; S Aslaksen, 'Oil and Democracy: More than a Cross-country Correlation?' (2011) 47(4) *Journal of Peace Research* 421–31; J Wright, E Frantz and B Geddes, 'Oil and Autocratic Regime Survival' (2013) manuscript.

[22] D Kono and G Montinola, 'Does Foreign Aid Support Autocrats, Democrats, or Both?' (2009) 71(2) *Journal of Politics* 704–18; A Licht, 'Coming into Money: The Impact of Foreign Aid on Leader Survival' (2010) 54(1) *Journal of Peace Research* 58–87; S Djankov, J Montalvo and M Reynal-Querol, 'The Curse of Aid' (2008) 13(3) *Journal of Economic Growth* 169–94; T Dunning, 'Conditioning the Effects of Aid: Cold War Politics, Donor Credibility, and Democracy in Africa' (2004) 58(2) *International Organization* 409–23.

[23] P Collier and A Hoeffler, 'Unintended Consequences: Does Aid Promote Arms Races?' (2007) 69(1) *Oxford Bulletin of Economics and Statistics* 1–27.

[24] J Wright, 'Curses and Conditionality: Do Oil and Aid Affect Democracy Differently?' (2011) manuscript.

[25] S Bermeo, 'Foreign Aid and Regime Change: A Role for Donor Intent' (2011) 39(11) *World Development* 2021–31; J Wright, 'How Foreign Aid Can Foster Democratization in Authoritarian Regimes?' (2009) 53(3) *American Journal of Political Science* 552–71.

[26] T Oatley, 'Political Institutions and Foreign Debt in the Developing World' (2010) 54(1) *International Studies Quarterly* 175–95.

interest rates and worse access to credit markets,[27] autocrats have powerful political incentives to borrow. As Nooruddin highlights, '[i]n developing countries, tax bases are typically narrow and the state's ability to extract taxes is notoriously limited. Therefore, governments utilise their ability to sell loans internationally to generate revenue needed to fund domestic spending projects'.[28] Yet, these public spending projects have clear political objectives, especially under dictatorship, including rewarding the loyalty of regime insiders, self-enrichment, and financing the coercive apparatus. Additionally, access to foreign credit can be particularly important during times when regimes are under fiscal distress due to shrinking tax revenues caused by economic crises, or, similarly, due to decreasing prices of commodities on which the country is highly dependent. All in all, public spending is a key instrument of political survival as explained above.

As Ames clearly puts it, 'political survival must be actively pursued by manipulating public policy to construct support coalitions. Public expenditures are central to survival coalitions'.[29] In particular, Easterly claims that in developing countries 'debt was accumulated not to finance productive investments, but to finance the government's patronage employment and large military and police forces'.[30] Indeed, military expenditures, used to strengthen the coercive capacity of the regime and its stability,[31] have been found to strongly contribute to a country's external debt burden.[32] For example, a recent report by the Jubilee Debt Campaign[33] revealed that UK Export Finance-backed loans allowed Mugabe (Zimbabwe's president) and Mubarak (Egypt's former president), among others, to acquire military equipment.[34] A parliamentary inquiry on international corporate responsibility is now starting with the aim of shedding light on these proceedings involving a public agency and British firms.

In sum, borrowed funds may have a direct impact on regimes' resilience if they are used to finance spending programmes aimed at buying support and enhancing the coercive capacity of the regimes. Nevertheless, foreign borrowing may also have indirect effects that reinforce its potential stabilising impact due to its fungibility. For instance, even those loans that apparently are given as part of aid programmes and, hence, aimed at funding development projects, may have pernicious consequences. First, such inflows of income, albeit allegedly directed to investment projects, free up government resources which can be devoted to strengthening clientelistic networks and the regime's repressive capacity,

[27] E Beaulieu, G Cox and S Saiegh, 'Sovereign Debt and Regime Type: Reconsidering the Democratic Advantage' (2012) 66(4) *International Organization* 709–38.

[28] I Nooruddin, 'The Political Economy of National Debt Burdens, 1970–2000' (2008) 34(2) *International Interactions* 156–85.

[29] B Ames, *Political Survival: Politicians and Public Policy in Latin America (*Berkeley, University of California Press, 1987) 7.

[30] W Easterly, 'How Did Heavily Indebted Poor Countries Become Heavily Indebted? Reviewing Two Decades of Debt Relief' (2002) 30(1)0 *World Development* 1677.

[31] M Albertus and V Menaldo, 'Coercive Capacity and the Prospects for Democratization' (2012) 44(2) *Comparative Politics* 151–69.

[32] See, among others R Looney, 'The Influence of Arms Imports on Third World Debt' (1989) *Journal of Developing Areas* 221–32; J Dunne, S Perlo-Freeman and A Soydan, 'Military Expenditure and Debt in Small-Industrialised Economies: A Panel Analysis' (2004) 15(2) *Defence and Peace Economics* 125–32; R Smyth and P Narayan, 'A Panel Data Analysis of the Military Expenditure-External Debt Nexus: Evidence from Six Middle Eastern Countries' (2009) 46(2) *Journal of Peace Research* 235–50.

[33] See www.jubileedebtcampaign.org.uk/REPORT373A3720The3720Department3720for3720Dodgy3720 Deals+6700.twl, accessed 2 September 2013.

[34] R Neate, 'MPs to Ask Firms to Explain How UK Taxes Helped Dictators Build Arsenals', *The Guardian*, 7 May 2012. Available at www.guardian.co.uk/world/2012/may/07/mps-bae-uk-taxes-dictators-arsenals, accessed 2 September 2013.

and to enriching elite members. Second, loans given to fund development projects also enable substantial resources to be diverted for other purposes and funds to be channelled to companies with close ties to the regime, thus still benefiting regimes' allies.[35]

In regard to FDI, its impact on democracy levels is largely understudied. There are contradicting arguments concerning its potential impact on regime change and democracy.[36] Some argue it may indirectly enhance democratisation by fostering investment and economic development, and by increasing pressure for market liberalisation and other institutional reforms. Conversely, it is also claimed that FDI may facilitate revenue collection, especially when directed to natural resource sectors and other state-controlled sectors, and so help stabilise incumbent regimes. FDI may also enhance corruption by providing regimes with rents and bribes from foreign firms willing to get access to protected sectors and obtain favourable regulations. Further, foreign investment may also improve economic performance in the short term, which contributes to regime entrenchment. The existing empirical evidence is very limited and far from being conclusive though. Some findings suggest that portfolio investment inflows may hurt democracy levels, while FDI seems to improve them slightly.[37] Others find no relationship between these financial flows and democracy for the Third Wave period.[38]

In addition to the (public finance) mechanisms outlined above, obtaining credits from international institutions and investments from multinational corporations may also strengthen autocracies by legitimising them. Foreign finance may be interpreted as a form of international recognition by relevant multilateral institutions, states, or private actors. As a result, it can be domestically viewed as a source of international legitimacy, thereby strengthening the ruling elite vis-à-vis the opposition.[39]

Do external borrowing and investment stabilise dictatorships and so contribute to continued human rights violations? Some preliminary evidence is provided here that suggests they indeed do so. Figure 2.1 portrays the impact of net transfers on public and publicly guaranteed[40] external debt and net inflows of FDI on the predicted likelihood that an autocracy transits to democracy in a given year for the period 1970–2006.[41] The predictions are calculated from the estimates of a logistic regression that includes several control variables normally used in the extant comparative literature on democratisation.[42]

[35] See, eg, the case of the government of Suharto in Indonesia channelling loans through the national oil company (Pertamina), in C *Caufield, Masters of Illusion: The World Bank and the Poverty of Nations* (New York, Henry Holt, 1997) 246.

[36] See, for a review, Q Li and R Reuveny, *Democracy and Economic Openness in an Interconnected System: Complex Transformations* (Cambridge, Cambridge University Press, 2009).

[37] ibid.

[38] J Teorell, *Determinants of Democratization: Explaining Regime Change in the World, 1972–2006* (Cambridge, Cambridge University Press, 2010).

[39] The cover page of the Argentinean newspaper *Clarín* on 27 March 1976 illustrates this. It puts together and so relates two international decisions: the US recognising the Junta and the concession of an IMF credit.

[40] Public debt is an external obligation of a public debtor, including the national government, a political subdivision (or an agency of either), and autonomous public bodies. Publicly guaranteed debt is an external obligation of a private debtor that is guaranteed for repayment by a public entity. Net transfers are net flows minus interest payments during the year.

[41] Both are measured in constant (2000) dollars per capita. Data compiled from the Word Bank's *World Development Indicators*. Our sample includes 158 different authoritarian regimes in 91 countries.

[42] These controls include: religious fractionalisation index, economic growth (two-year moving average), GDP per capita (logged), ongoing armed intrastate and interstate conflict, past coups (logged), oil rents (logged), a variable indicating if the regime was previously a democracy, and democratic transitions in neighbour countries. Time effects are controlled including a Cold War period dummy, and duration dependence including regime duration polynomials. Standard errors are clustered on country. The dependent variable is a

The results in Figure 2.1 clearly show the negative impact that foreign debt and investment have on the likelihood of a transition to democracy.[43] These effects are statistically significant at conventional levels, thereby confirming that foreign loans and investment contribute to the perpetuation of authoritarian regimes.[44] It can also be observed that the impact of foreign borrowing is slightly stronger than that of FDI. Moving from the minimum to the maximum value of the debt variable brings about a 1.65 per cent decrease in the probability of democratisation.[45] FDI causes a total decrease of 1.5 per cent in the likelihood of a transition.[46] Some additional tests also reveal that, as anticipated, foreign borrowing is of special relevance in times of economic downturn, which usually lead to severe shrinkages in state revenues

Loans have different sources. One distinction of particular relevance is that between official and private creditors. The former include loans from international organisations (multilateral loans) and loans from governments (bilateral loans); while the latter include commercial bank loans from private banks and other private financial institutions, other private credits from manufacturers, exporters, and other suppliers of goods, as well as bank credits covered by a guarantee of an export credit agency. Since our focus is on financial complicity, we in turn explore whether loans from private economic agents or

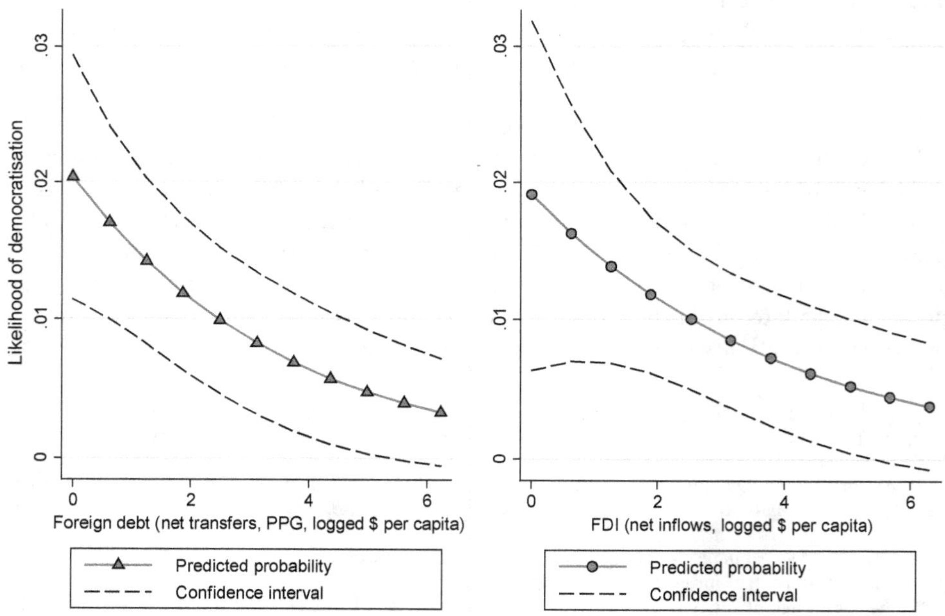

Figure 2.1. The impact of foreign debt and FDI on the likelihood of democratisation (1970–2006)

binary variable coded 1 if a regime change that results in democracy takes place in a given year and 0 otherwise. See B Geddes, J Wright and E Frantz, 'New Data on Autocratic Regimes' (2012) manuscript.

43 To estimate these probabilities the rest of the variables have been held constant at their means.

44 The average marginal effect of the public debt variable is −.0077, while that of FDI is −.0067.

45 The results remain largely unaltered if one controls for trade (imports plus exports as a percentage of GDP).

46 To give some perspective to these figures, note that the gross probability of a transition to democracy in our sample is 2.2%.

official creditors do have a stronger impact on the durability of autocracies. To this end, we have rerun the regime survival model detailed above, but we now distinguish between net transfers on external debt (PPG) from official creditors and those from private ones. Again we present the results with the help of a graph showing the relation between the predicted probability of democratic transition and the two variables of debt measured in constant per capita dollars.

The results reveal that, although both sources of funds have helped authoritarian regimes last longer, the negative impact of loans from private creditors has actually been stronger than that of official ones in stabilising autocracies.[47] Despite some exceptions, on average debt from both official as well as private creditors prolongs authoritarian rule and so permits the perpetuation of poor human rights conditions – especially the latter. These differences might be partially explained by the fact that official creditors, especially bilateral ones, are subject to (limited) political accountability.[48] Governments are controlled by voters and civil society organisations, who may resent money from taxpayers being used to support dictators.[49] Similarly, albeit largely criticised for their lack of

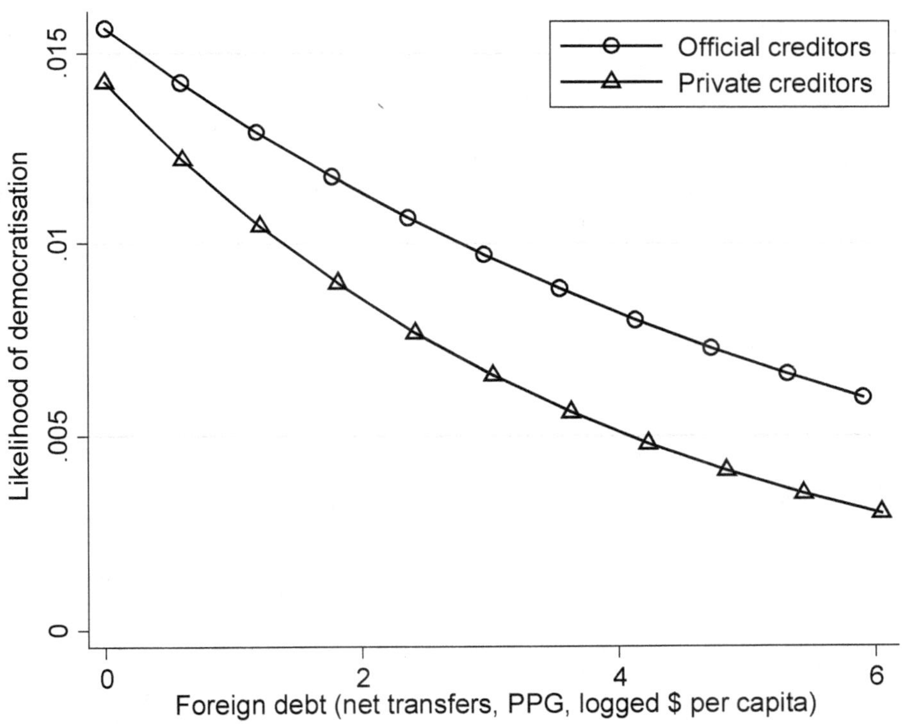

Figure 2.2. The impact of foreign debt from private and official creditors on the likelihood of democratisation (1970–2006)

[47] In fact, while the coefficient of the former is significant, the one for the latter is not.

[48] See for example how the US government (financially) reacted when civil society denounced the crimes perpetrated in Argentina, L Schoultz, *Human Rights and United States Policy toward Latin America* (Princeton, Princeton University Press, 1981).

[49] Numerous campaigns and organisations, such as the Jubilee Debt Campaign UK, Jubilee Australia, Jubilee USA Network, CATDM, EURODAD, among others, highlight the growing concern of civil society on the topic of illegitimate debt.

transparency,[50] international organisations are subject to the scrutiny of public opinion, NGOs, and member states (under pressure from their own voters). In contrast, even when civil society is increasingly monitoring corporations,[51] states and voters do not effectively exert a political control over private lenders' practices.[52]

Despite the existence for some creditors of potential political accountability mechanisms, money has been flowing to dictatorships anyway. Given that political mechanisms of control have not been very effective and, further, given that some creditors are not even subject to such political accountability, the question is, thus, should creditors of regimes that violate human rights be held legally accountable for contributing directly or indirectly to the survival of such regimes?

III LEGAL DIMENSION: A RUDIMENTARY ANSWER

Even though its origin can be traced back to the jurisprudence of the Nuremberg Military Tribunal,[53] it is in recent years that responsibility for economic complicity with human rights abuses has been growing robustly and coherently, as the International Commission of Jurists has exposed.[54] In parallel with the increasing relevance of corporations in the economic, social and political lives of countries, in recent years human rights duties of those same actors have been becoming stricter.[55] As other contributors in this book explain, jurisprudence, soft law instruments, legal doctrines, UN initiatives and human rights law generally have evolved in the last 15 years towards a more consistent legal framework to tackle corporations' complicity.

States can also be held responsible for their assistance in an internationally wrongful act of another state.[56] This kind of derivative responsibility is recognised by the Articles on Responsibility of States for Internationally Wrongful Acts elaborated by the International Law Commission (ILC) in 2001.[57] International financial institutions are

[50] W Easterly and C Williamson, 'Rhetoric versus Reality: The Best and Worst of Aid Agency Practices' (2011) 39(11) *World Development* 1930–49.

[51] Information available at the Business & Human Rights Resource Center, at www.business-humanrights.org/, accessed 2 September 2013.

[52] In 1978, the chairman of Lloyds Bank in London responded to criticism for granting loans to the Chilean dictatorship, admitting that this regime was repressive, but also alleging that lending money to Chile was not banned. See 'Lloyds Bounces Chile Protest', *The Guardian*, 31 March 1978. See also Bejesky and Bohoslavsky, Chapter 19 in this volume.

[53] J Bush, 'The Prehistory of Corporations and Conspiracy in International Criminal Law: What Nuremberg Really Said' (2009) 109 *Columbia Law Review* 1094.

[54] See broadly ICJ, 'Corporate Complicity & Legal Accountability' (2008) Vols I–III, Geneva, available at www.icj.org/default.asp?nodeID=349&sessID=&langage=1&myPage=Legal_Documentation&id=22851, accessed 2 September 2013.

[55] UN Human Rights Council, 'Guiding Principles on Business and Human Rights for Implementing the UN 'Protect, Respect and Remedy' Framework', Resolution A/HRC/RES/17/4, 16 June 2011, available at www.ohchr.org/Documents/Publications/GuidingPrinciplesBusinessHR_EN.pdf, accessed 2 September 2013.

[56] See H Aust, *Complicity and the Law of State Responsibility* (Cambridge, Cambridge University Press, 2011); V Lanovoy, 'Responsibility for Complicity in an Internationally Wrongful Act: Revisiting a Structural Norm' in A Nollkaemper and I Plakokefalos (eds), *Principles of Shared Responsibility* (Cambridge, Cambridge University Press, forthcoming 2014).

[57] ICJ, *Case Concerning the Application of the Convention of the Prevention and Punishment of Genocide (Bosnia and Herzegovina v Serbia and Montenegro)*, judgment, 26 February 2007, para 420.

under an obligation not to violate or become complicit in the violation of general rules of human rights law,[58] as is explained elsewhere in this book.[59]

Even when hermeneutical efforts can be made to adjust classical international law rules to the sophisticated features of financial complicity,[60] this is one of the most underdeveloped areas in the general trend towards increasing accountability of economic actors in authoritarian contexts,[61] as it will be explained in the next paragraphs.

A Conventions and Customary International Law

No international convention deals specifically with responsibility for financial complicity with human rights violations. However, there is a long and robust list of international instruments generally prohibiting complicity, without being specific on the type of accomplice and contribution.[62]

As juridical persons are not excluded from the scope of these norms,[63] the universal application (by international and national courts, and through national legislations) of these norms that prohibit certain acts irrespective of the perpetrator,[64] specifically those that compromise *jus cogens* definitions, crystallise responsibility for complicity in customary international law.[65]

Even so, these conventions and customs do not provide specific or technical standards to assess responsibility for financial complicity with authoritarian governments.

B Jurisprudence

International jurisprudence has applied the notion of responsibility for complicity to those persons who contributed to the perpetration of the crimes.[66] In the Nuremberg Tribunal there were two contradictory decisions involving individuals engaged in corporate activities. On the one hand, in the *Ministries Case*, the Tribunal stated that loans to be used in unlawful enterprises may well be condemned from a moral standpoint but the

[58] C Tomuschat, 'International Law: Ensuring the Survival of Mankind on the Eve of a New Century. General Course on Public International Law' (1999) 281 *Receuil des cours* 138–39.

[59] See in this volume, Lastra, Chapter 9, and Bianco and Fontanelli, Chapter 14.

[60] J Bohoslavsky, 'Tracking Down the Missing Financial Link in Transitional Justice' (2012) 1 *International Human Rights Law Review* 54–92.

[61] Sharp (n 9); S Michalowski (ed), *Corporate Accountability in the Context of Transitional Justice* (New York, Routledge, 2013).

[62] See Bohoslavsky (n 60).

[63] W Dodge, 'Corporate Liability Under Customary International Law' (2012) 43 *Georgetown Journal of International Law* 1045; M Kelly, 'Prosecuting Corporations for Genocide Under International Law' (2012) 6(2) *Harvard Law & Policy Review* 339.

[64] B Stephens, 'Are Corporations People? Corporate Personhood Under the Constitution and International Law' (2013) 44(1) *Rutgers Law Journal* 1.

[65] Bohoslavsky (n 60) 71–82.

[66] *Prosecutor v Vasiljevic*, Case No IT-94-32-A, Judgment, paras 94–95, 102 (25 Feb 2004); *Prosecutor v Furundzija*, Case No IT-95-17/1-T, Judgment, paras 187–90 (10 Dec 10 1998); *Prosecutor v Akayesu*, Case No ICTR 96-4-T, Judgment, paras 471–91 (2 Sep 1998); Trials of War Criminals Before the Nuremberg Military Tribunals Under Control Council Law, No 10, Volumes VI (*Flick*), VII and VIII (*IG Farben*), IX (*Krupp*), Nuremberg, October 1946–October 1949, Washington, DC, United States, Government Printing Office, 1953.

transaction can hardly be said to be a crime.[67] On the other hand, two German industrialists were convicted in *Flick* even though the prosecution could not show that any part of the money the two had donated to the Schutzstaffel (SS) was directly used for criminal activities: they nonetheless gave Himmler, the Reich Leader SS, a blank cheque.[68]

South African victims sued several corporations in the US courts (among them banks) that contributed to the apartheid regime. In 2002 they refined their approach, explicitly linking financial assistance, macroeconomic indicators of the country, and general and military budgets.[69] Eventually, in 2009[70] the Court – using the 'inherent quality' of the commodities as its criterion – made a distinction between an agent such as poison gas being provided to a regime (referring to the 1946 *Zyklon B* case before a post-World War II British Military Court)[71] and a fungible resource, such as finance or investment (referring to the *Ministries* case defendant Karl Rasche[72]), which it felt did not meet the legal standards for responsibility in this case. The Court decided when analysing the *actus reus* component that loans could not empirically be sufficiently connected to the crimes in question.[73] Ironically, the Court simultaneously allowed the case to go forward and be heard against IBM[74] for providing computers and software to the apartheid regime, charging that it had helped to implement a 'de-nationalisation' policy against black South Africans.[75]

US courts have also decided on responsibility for financing terrorism.[76] Cases like *Boim*[77] and *Almog*[78] confirmed and strengthened the idea that lenders can be held responsible for facilitating crimes.[79]

As explained, there have been only a handful cases that have dealt with financial complicity specifically, which, in any case, have not established a consistent criterion in this field. Political and economic implications of granting financial support to criminal regimes were absent in these cases.

[67] *United States v Von Weizsaecker* (*The Ministries Case*), Case No 11, 14, Trials of War Criminals Before the Nuremberg Military Tribunals Under Control Council Law No 10, 622, (1952) (Nuremberg Mil Trib 1949).

[68] *United States v Flick (The Flick Case)*, Case No 5, 6, Trials of War Criminals Before the Nuremberg Military Tribunals Under Control Council Law No 10, 1217-23 (1952) (Nuremberg Mil Trib 1947).

[69] Khulumani complaint, 11 November 2002, paras 393 ff, available at www.khulumani.net/attachments/259_Khulumani%20Complaint.pdf, accessed 2 September 2013.

[70] *In re South African Apartheid Litigation*, 617 F. Supp. 2d 228, 257 (S.D.N.Y. 2009).

[71] Trial of Bruno Tesch and Two Others (*The Zyklon B Case*), 1 *Law Reports of Trials of War Criminals* (1947) 93–103.

[72] See n 67.

[73] *Apartheid Litigation*, (n 70) 70.

[74] Nonetheless, this claim was also dismissed at later stage.

[75] *Apartheid Litigation*, (n 70) 265. *Criticising* the criterion used in this decision, S Michalowski and J Bohoslavsky, 'Ius Cogens, Transitional Justice and other Trends of the Debate on Odious Debts. A Response to the World Bank Discussion Paper on Odious Debts' (2010) 48 *Columbia Journal of Transnational Law* 95.

[76] See D Bulloch, 'Tracking Terrorist Finance: The "Swift" Program and the American Anti-Terrorist Finance Regime' (2011) 3(4) *Amsterdam Law Forum* 74.

[77] *Boim v Holy Land Found for Relief and Development*, 549 F. 3d 685 (7th Cir. 2008).

[78] *Almog v Arab Bank* (471 F. Supp. 2d 257, E.D.N.Y. 2007).

[79] On this jurisprudence and its connection to liability for financial complicity with human rights violations, see S Michalowski, 'No Complicity Liability for Funding Gross Human Rights Violations? (2012) 30 *Berkeley Journal of International Law* 484.

IV POLICY AND LEGAL IMPLICATIONS OF THE FINDINGS IN THE CONTEXT OF COMPLICITY

The classical causal criterion in international law consisting of the normal, natural and reasonable foreseeable consequences[80] is under the pressure of the empirical finding that sovereign financing stabilises authoritarian regimes. There is a strong presumption that lending to a criminal regime helps it to remain in power. Should this presumption have a say in the discourse of international politics, finance and human rights law?

From a technical point of view, when assessing the potential liability of a lender for financial complicity, the presumption that providing funds consolidates the regime (with all the human suffering that this entails) will have an influence in the *actus reus* and *mens rea* standards. For example, it will help to answer questions such as whether the financial assistance provided must be considered substantial in its connection to the strengthening of the regime and its human rights abuses, and whether the wrongful effect of this assistance was reasonably foreseeable.

In this vein, odious debt debates would be enriched if they incorporated empirical data on the link between finance and fundamental human rights abuses and a rational-choice explanation of this interaction. This would probably lead to more realistic and sophisticated legal doctrines on the (in)validity of loans to criminal regimes.

The United Nations Security Council has also connected sovereign lending and human rights abuses when applying economic sanctions.[81] As the effectiveness of these sanctions is still the subject of heated debate,[82] the costs of not stopping capital flowing into criminal regimes might be reassessed in the light of the findings presented for discussion in this chapter.

Multilateral and bilateral lenders' calculations of the foreseeable effects of their loans and grants could be enriched if they incorporated the high probability that their funds will strengthen the borrower/recipient regime. This exercise should allegedly have an influence in the criteria to provide official funds. This would not be novel in international finance: the US and other governments used this argument to refuse granting financial assistance to dictatorships, both bilaterally[83] and multilaterally.[84] The argument made in this piece could also help in negotiations with creditors to reduce or reschedule debt,[85] as happened in the recent Iraqi case.[86]

As the ways in which borrowed funds are spent can, to a certain extent, be contractually conditioned, debt contracts could set mechanisms to ensure that monies reach needy people without reinforcing the regime. Specific and clear goals aiming at improving

[80] B Cheng, *General Principles of Law as Applied by International Courts and Tribunals* (Cambridge, Cambridge Grotius Publications Limited, 1987) 251.

[81] UN Security Council, Res No 757, 30 May 1992, Article 5.

[82] D Peksen, 'Better or Worse? The Effect of Economic Sanctions on Human Rights' (2009) 46(1) *Journal of Peace Research* 59.

[83] Foreign Assistance and Related Programs Appropriations for Fiscal Year 1978: Hearing Before the Subcomm. on Foreign Operations of the S Comm on Appropriations, 95th Cong 9 (1977) (testimony of Cyrus Vance, US Secretary of State).

[84] Act of May 31, 1976, Pub L No 94-302, § 211, 90 Stat 591, 595; Act of Oct 3, 1977, Pub L No 95-118, § 701, 91 Stat 1067, 1069–71.

[85] See Sharp, Chapter 4 in this volume.

[86] R Bejesky, 'Currency Cooperation and Sovereign Financial Obligations' (2012) 24(1) *Florida Journal of International Law* 99–104.

citizens' life conditions are of course important, but they are also crucial in empowering their participation in the development of projects as well as improving their organisation capacity (all of which means that it is the citizens who benefit from the loans, not the government, as its control capacity over the economic system is weakened while access to public goods is improved), and post-disbursement monitoring of the likely effects of the projects is a contractual option that could be implemented.

Increasing pressure on both official and private lenders for greater accountability would not simply have the effect of pushing authoritarian regimes into the arms of other type of lenders or donors (specially those that do not attach human rights conditionalities) as all of them can be held responsible for complicity.[87]

The transitional justice field might also potentially be receptive to the argument made here. As economic factors are gaining relevance in the transitional agenda,[88] the fact that sovereign financing in principle strengthens authoritarian regimes should be a reason for designing and implementing adequate transitional justice mechanisms to address this financial dimension.[89]

V ASSESSING THE VERISIMILITUDE OF THE IMPLICATIONS

Is there any institutional or legal signal indicating that responsibility for financial complicity is becoming a relevant standard in sovereign financing? Would international relations and international law even consider the potential policy and legal implications of the link between finance and human rights showed in this chapter?

As is explained in another chapter in this volume,[90] the United Nations Independent Expert on foreign debts and human rights has been elaborating during recent years a set of guiding principles.[91] However, for the purpose of this chapter, as these guiding principles focus on debt and the enjoyment of economic, social and cultural rights they do not provide many technical tools to tackle financial complicity issues.

The same can be said regarding the UNCTAD Principles on Responsible Sovereign Lending and Borrowing. They basically deal with debt crisis prevention, restructurings and the Millennium Development Goals.[92] There is only one principle that is partially connected to financial complicity: in instances of serious misconduct where United Nations sanctions are deemed to be necessary, lenders should not participate in financial transactions that violate, evade or hamper such sanctions (principle 6). It is also worth recalling that the UN Secretary General approved in 2011 a due diligence policy on

[87] See Bohoslavsky (n 60) 71–82.

[88] Sharp (n 9); Michalowski (n 61).

[89] See Sharp, Chapter 4 in this volume.

[90] See Lumina, Chapter 16 in this volume.

[91] 'Report of the Independent Expert on the effects of foreign debt and other related international financial obligations of States on the full enjoyment of all human rights, particularly economic, social and cultural rights', Cephas Lumina, Human Rights Council, 10 April 2011, A/HRC/20/23, available at http://daccess-dds-ny.un.org/doc/UNDOC/GEN/G12/128/80/PDF/G1212880.pdf?OpenElement, accessed 2 September 2013. This document was endorsed by the United Nations Human Rights Council in July 2012, see Human Rights Council, 18 July 2012, Resolution, A/HRC/RES/20/10, available at http://daccess-dds-ny.un.org/doc/RESOLUTION/GEN/G12/162/01/PDF/G1216201.pdf?OpenElement, accessed 2 September 2013.

[92] See consolidated version of the UNCTAD Principles, 12 January 2012, available at www.unctad.info/upload/Debt%20Portal/Principles%20drafts/SLB_Principles_English_Doha_22-04-2012.pdf, accessed 2 September 2013.

preventing UN financial support of non-UN security forces engaged in human rights violations.[93]

In the context of transitional justice, only a few truth commissions (El Salvador, Chad and South Africa) addressed the issue of financial complicity, and they did it marginally and without significant political or legal outcomes. In the context of the recently established Brazilian Truth Commission, the Brazilian Secretary of Justice stated that 'the Truth Commission must investigate the corporations that financed the dictatorship'. [94] In March 2014, the Brazilian Truth Commission started investigating the role of the corporations that financed the repression.[95] In recent civil lawsuits in Argentina based on responsibility for financing criminal regimes, victims have sued the banks that financed the military junta between 1976 and 1983.[96] In March 2014, the legislature of the province of Rio Negro (Patagonia, Argentina) established a Truth Commission to investigate the economic dimension of the Argentinean dictatorship, with special reference to the contributions of the banks.[97] In April 2014, the majority party in the Argentinean congress presented a bill to establish a National Truth Commission on Economic Complicity.[98] In this same vein, the prosecutor of the International Criminal Court, Fatou Bensouda, stated in July 2012 that:

> [I]n general terms, when crimes against humanity are judged, all the elements must be considered and all the actors involved must be observed: political and military leaders, executioners and also those who financed these crimes. In principle, they are also responsible and must be held accountable for the civilian casualties to which they contributed with their support for systematic plans against the civilian population (authors' translation)[99]

All these recent developments in the field of human rights and sovereign financing seem to indicate that this interlink is gradually gaining significance in both global and domestic arenas.[100] However, more nuanced and interdisciplinary work is necessary to face the challenge. And innovative approaches for developing adequate jurisdictional and procedural avenues for victims should also be proposed for discussion.

Responsibility for financial complicity presents a notable backwardness compared to the responsibility arising from providing other types of goods and services. The explanation

[93] Secretariat of the United Nations, Note Verbale of 25 October 2011 on 'Human Rights Due Diligence Policy on UN Support to Non-UN Security Forces', New York.

[94] 'Paulo Abrão: Comissão da Verdade deve investigar empresas que financiaram a ditadura', 17 October 2011, available at www.viomundo.com.br/politica/paulo-abraocomissao-da-verdade-deve-investigar-empresas-que-financiaram-a-ditadura.html, accessed 2 September 2013. And see more recently http://www.cartacapital.com.br/sociedade/comissao-da-verdade-quer-responsabilizar-empresas-que-colaboraram-com-a-ditadura-8874.html, accessed 18 March 2014.

[95] 'Comissão da Verdade quer responsabilizar empresas que colaboraram com a ditadura', 15 March 2014, available at http://www.cartacapital.com.br/sociedade/comissao-da-verdade-quer-responsabilizar-empresas-que-colaboraram-com-a-ditadura-8874.html, accessed 3 April 2014.

[96] *Ibañez Manuel Leandro y otros casos/Diligencia Preliminar*, Juzgado Nacional de 1° Instancia en lo Civil 34, Buenos Aires, N° 95.019/2009; *Garramone, Andrés c. Citibank NA y otros*, 2010, Juzgado Nacional en lo Contencioso Administrativo Federal N° 8, Buenos Aires, N° 47736/10.

[97] 'Avalan la creación de la comisión Especial Investigadora por la Memoria, Verdad y Justicia', 28 March 2014, available at http://www.legisrn.gov.ar/lrn/?p=10077, accessed 3 April 2014.

[98] 'Derecho a la defensa contra la amnesia', 8 April 2014, available at http://www.pagina12.com.ar/diario/elpais/1-243635-2014-04-08.html, accessed 9 April 2014.

[99] F Barrio, 'Aquellos que financiaron crímenes de lesa humanidad deben rendir cuentas', *Perfil*, 22 July 2012 available at http://www.perfil.com/ediciones/2012/7/edicion_696/contenidos/noticia_0077.html, accessed 2 September 2013.

[100] On the evolution of the *outcome orientation* in sovereign contracting see O Lienau, *Rethinking Sovereign Debt: Debt and Reputation in the Twentieth Century* (Cambridge, MA, Harvard University Press, 2013).

for this phenomenon is rooted in the conceptual gap between sovereign finance and human rights: there is an inherent difficulty in tracing money and then linking it to human rights abuses. One way to tackle this shortage is to undertake more empirical and interdisciplinary research[101] in order to better understand whether and how financing has an impact on human rights abuses perpetrated on a large scale.

Recent qualitative empirical research on Latin American authoritarian governments and their lenders,[102] the aforementioned civil lawsuit filed by victims of the Argentinean military junta, the investigative work that is currently carried out by a few Truth Commissions, and the seminal report written by Antonio Cassese in 1978,[103] contribute to confronting the challenge of better understanding and adequately dealing with sovereign financing in contexts of criminal regimes.

The argument that more funds to criminal regimes are usually translated into their consolidation can be explained from a rational-choice perspective and is empirically grounded. This explanation hopefully improves our understanding of the role played by sovereign financing in authoritarian contexts and, correlatively, intensifies the political and institutional interest in developing and enforcing adequate legal standards.

[101] G Shaffer and T Ginsburg, 'The Empirical Turn in International Legal Scholarship' (2012) 106 *American Journal of International Law* 1–46.

[102] See, eg, J Bohoslavsky and M Torelly, 'Financial Complicity: The Brazilian Dictatorship Under the "Macroscope"' in D Sharp (ed), *Justice and Economic Violence in Transition* (New York, Springer, 2013).

[103] A Cassese, 'Study of the Impact of Foreign Economic Aid and Assistance on Respect for Human Rights in Chile' (1978) E/CN.4/Sub.2/412, Vols I–IV.

3

*UN Sanctions that Safeguard, Undermine, or Both, Human Rights**

PATRICIA PINTO SOARES

I INTRODUCTION

SANCTIONS ENTAIL THREATS or inducements for states to comply with binding rules or to follow determinate policies or lines of conduct. They may be imposed multilaterally or unilaterally.[1] The former are stronger from a legitimacy viewpoint and may trigger a cascade effect, by which states and/or international and regional organisations develop and adopt stricter regimes in respect of the target state. Among the different categories of sanctions, the one most relevant for this analysis, in view of the negative impact it has upon human rights, is that of economic sanctions.[2] These may be subdivided into three sub-categories, that is (i) limiting exports to a country; (ii) limiting imports from that country; and (iii) imposing financial sanctions. The latter comprises the 'blocking of government assets held abroad, limiting access to financial markets and restricting loans and credits, restricting international transfer payments and restricting the sale and trade of property abroad, [together with the] . . . freezing of development aid'.[3]

After its inception and until the Cold War, the UN passed economic sanctions against Rhodesia, in 1966, and South Africa, in 1977. Afterwards, the world assisted in a proliferation of these instruments, with sanctions being imposed on Iraq, the former Yugoslavia, Haiti, Somalia, Liberia, Libya, Angola, Rwanda, Sudan and Iran.

Mostly in the 1990s, humanitarian institutions started pointing out the adverse effects economic sanctions might involve for the population of the targeted state, precisely the people whom they ultimately aimed to protect.[4] Accordingly, it is important to assess the

* The author wrote this article in her personal capacity. The views expressed are her own and are not to be taken as the views of her present or previous employers.

[1] As early as 1979, after the Iranian Revolution, the United States banned Iran's oil imports and froze approximately $11 billion of its assets. See S Maloney, 'The Revolutionary Economy', United States Institute of Peace, 2010, www.iranprimer.usip.org/resource/revolutionary-economy, accessed 2 September 2013. See also, for example, K Kessler, 'U.S. Links Iranian Bank To Fifth Avenue Building', *Washington Post*, 18 December 2008, available at www.washingtonpost.com/wp-dyn/content/article/2008/12/17/AR2008121703844_pf.html, accessed 2 September 2013.

[2] Other categories include travel sanctions, military sanctions, diplomatic sanctions and cultural sanctions. See M Bossuyt, 'The Adverse Consequences of Economic Sanctions on the Enjoyment of Human Rights', UN Document E/CN.4/Sub.2/2000/33, United Nations Economic and Social Council, 21 June 2000, 5.

[3] ibid, 6.

[4] For an analysis of the situations in Iraq, Burundi and Cuba, see Bossuyt (n 2), paras 58–100. It is explained, for example, how in Burundi, following the imposition of comprehensive economic sanctions by a number of states as a response to the 1996 *coup d'Etat*, '[d]evelopment assistance, approximately $250 million annually, was cut off and foreign currency reserves were exhausted. Burundi's health infrastructure was heavily hit, and the inability to obtain even emergency medical supplies led to severe shortages of medicines and vaccines.

legal framework governing the imposition of sanctions, the practical challenges to their effectiveness, and the harmful consequences they entail for civilians. Likewise, an effort is in order to try to develop a consistent set of guidelines that might assist both the UN and states in the responsible implementation of such measures.

Thus, the chapter starts by reviewing the limitations by which the United Nations (UN), and very specifically the Security Council (SC), are bound to abide in deciding on the passing of economic sanctions, followed by an assessment of their practical consequences in Iran. Finally, an effort is made to propose some guidelines towards the development of an operational model aimed at reconciling different demands and interests in the hope of assisting in the unrelenting promotion of human rights and well-being of individuals, whilst at the same time leaving the necessary leeway for the achievement of sanctions' purposes and their recognised utility.

II UN SANCTIONS: LEGAL FRAMEWORK

Economic collective sanctions find their immediate legal basis in Article 41 UN Charter,[5] which is included under Chapter VII. This is to say, it may be resorted to if a threat to the peace, breach of the peace, or act of aggression has been previously determined under Article 39.[6] In accordance with this provision, the determination by the SC of a threat to peace, breach of the peace, or act of aggression is an essential condition for the exercise of the binding powers provided for in Chapter VII. The *travaux préparatoires* of Article 39 reveal the intent of states to ensure the possible intervention of the SC in a plethora of situations and not to submit its performance to a large range of limitations. Accordingly, the SC enjoys a high level of discretion: Articles 40–42 restate the wide discretion of the SC regarding the choice of measures to respond to threats to peace and security. Article 41 allows for measures 'not involving the use of armed forces', such as economic sanctions; were these to be insufficient to neutralise the threat to, or stop the breach of, international peace and security, Article 42 enables the SC to adopt measures involving military action as may be necessary to maintain or restore peace. Against this background, and in view of Article 103 UN Charter – in the terms of which 'in the event of a conflict between the obligations of the Members of the United Nations under the present Charter and their obligations under any other international agreement, their obligations under the present Charter shall prevail' – one could argue that the SC enjoys unfettered powers when deciding upon the measures to address a breach of Article 39. In support of this view one could eventually invoke Articles 24 and 25. This view is, however, unsustainable.

Sanitation and water programmes were scaled down or eliminated. Humanitarian aid agencies were left helpless in the face of escalating need and increasingly difficult working conditions – the World Food Programme (WFP) alone was distributing emergency food assistance to an average of 218,000 people each month in 1998' (reference omitted), para 80.

[5] 'The Security Council may decide what measures not involving the use of armed force are to be employed to give effect to its decisions, and it may call upon the Members of the United Nations to apply such measures. These may include complete or partial interruption of economic relations and of rail, sea, air, postal, telegraphic, radio, and other means of communication, and the severance of diplomatic relations'.

[6] 'The Security Council shall determine the existence of any threat to the peace, breach of the peace, or act of aggression and shall make recommendations, or decide what measures shall be taken in accordance with Articles 41 and 42, to maintain or restore international peace and security'.

It would amount to the SC being bound by no human rights or humanitarian principles and in the position of overriding treaty commitments without particular constraints in doing so, which is per se inconsistent with the wording and spirit of the Charter. Indeed, the SC is immediately bound by Articles 1(1) and 24(2) of the Charter, especially by the 'duty to act in accordance with the Purposes and Principles of the Organisation'. The Purposes of the Organisation are referred to in the Preamble and enshrined in Article 1 of the Charter, providing guiding principles for UN organs.[7] Their systemic position and the peculiarity of a provision and a Preambular paragraph with the same content support the argument that the Purposes of the UN give rise to legal obligations as opposed to constituting mere programmatic directives.[8] In line with this view, each decision taken by an organ of the UN must reflect the Purposes of the Charter. The most relevant paragraph of Article 1 to the present study is the first, determining the commitment of the UN in maintaining international peace and security 'in conformity with the principles of justice and international law . . .'. With a view to giving more concrete insight into this wording, it must be noted that fundamental principles of human rights law integrate international law and basic considerations of justice. By the same token, one should recall the terms of Article 55(c) UN Charter, according to which:

> [T]he creation of conditions of stability and well-being which are necessary for peaceful and friendly relations among nations based on *respect for the principle of equal rights and self-determination of peoples, the United Nations shall promote . . . universal respect for, and observance of, human rights and fundamental freedoms for all without distinction* (emphasis added).

Paragraph 4 of Article 1 is equally worthy of attention, determining the UN aims '[t]o be a centre for harmonizing the actions of nations in the attainment of these common ends'. It establishes the need for agreement within the organisation, highlighting how the consensus of members is *conditio sine qua non* for each decision. It is true that the five powers (P-5) enjoy the privilege of veto, meaning their consent is particularly relevant. However, if the SC can do nothing with the express opposition of the permanent members, even the agreement of the all P-5 is not sufficient to permit the political body to issue any kind of decision.[9] With this it is aimed to draw attention to the fact that economic sanctions adopted by UN organs should reflect the consensus of, at least, the majority of the members as the latter are the legitimating vector of the binding obligation to abide by Chapter VII resolutions. Economic sanctions should not be used as tools to obtain economic benefits for one state (or a small group of states) independently of a realistic concern regarding the maintenance of peace and security. Nor can they be motivated by strictly politically divergent viewpoints (eg 'East–West', 'left–right'). In this evaluation, it

[7] The Purposes are 'the *raison d'être* of the Organization . . . the aggregation of the common ends . . . the cause and object of the Charter to which member states collectively and severally subscribe', Report of the Committee I71, UNCIO VI, p 447, Doc 944.

[8] The legal importance of the Purposes was affirmed by the General Assembly. See, for example, Resolution 1301 (XIII), 10 December 1958, in which the GA stressed that the observance of the 'Purposes and Principles' would allow states to assist one another, in mutual tolerance and understanding for the interests of all. See also GA Resolution 377 (V), 3 November 1950, which affirmed that the 'Purposes' as a whole provide one of the constitutional bases for its decisions. In its Declaration on Principles of International Law concerning Friendly Relations and Co-operation among States in Accordance with the Charter of the United Nations, the GA affirmed that 'the adoption of the declaration . . . would contribute to the strengthening of world peace and constitute a landmark in the development of international law and of relations among States, in promoting the rule of law among nations and particularly the universal application of the Principles embodied in the Charter', Resolution 2625 (XXV), 24 October 1970.

[9] See Chapter X.2.

must be borne in mind that the consensus of the international community is expressed in different manners, one of which is undoubtedly through treaties broadly ratified, such as the International Covenant on Civil and Political Rights (ICCPR) and , which are considered to crystallise international customary law.[10]

Consistently with the above considerations, Articles 24[11] and 25[12] can hardly be conceived of as a black hole entitling the SC to unlimited powers.[13] Paragraph 1 attributes to the SC the primary responsibility regarding the maintenance of international peace and security. States have endorsed the far-reaching powers of the SC because they expected it to act on their behalf. Paragraph 2 specifically highlights that in exercising the powers awarded by Chapter VII it 'shall act in accordance with the Purposes and the Principles of the United Nations'. Accordingly, the SC only exercises the powers provided by Chapter VII on behalf of member states if it respects the Purposes and Principles of the Charter. When those parameters are disregarded the action of the SC is no longer in accordance with the provision. Its enactments are thus ultra vires and states' obligation to comply with them is far from absolute.[14]

Hence, that economic sanctions may not lower the standard of living of a significant segment of the population to levels below the subsistence level appears to be a convincing argument.[15] By the same token, they may not violate people's basic right to life and survival. As noted earlier, the deference of the Charter to human rights is unquestionable, though specific references to human rights are scarce and generic.[16] The exact extent of the SC's limitations when passing sanctions thus demands further analysis.

International humanitarian law does not specifically refer to economic sanctions nor does it deal with the impact thereof on civilian populations. Yet, general rules on the protection of civilians continue to apply as *lex generalis* whenever sanctions are applied in war time. This is to say, a legitimate sanctions regime shall take into consideration international humanitarian law, in particular by establishing humanitarian exceptions that will permit

[10] This is all the more important since the argument can be made that Article 103 UN Charter applies exclusively to conflicts between the UN Charter and other treaty agreements, thus excluding customary law. A considerable parcel of human rights and humanitarian principles are considered to pertain to customary rather than conventional law.

[11] '1. In order to ensure prompt and effective action by the United Nations, its Members confer on the Security Council primary responsibility for the maintenance of international peace and security, and agree that in carrying out its duties under this responsibility the Security Council acts on their behalf. 2. *In discharging these duties the Security Council shall act in accordance with the Purposes and Principles of the United Nations* . . .' (emphasis added).

[12] 'The Members of the United Nations *agree to accept and carry out the decisions* of the Security Council in accordance with the present Charter' (emphasis added).

[13] See G Arangio-Ruiz, 'On the Security Council's "Law-Making"' (2000) 83 *Rivista di Diritto Internazionale* 609. Against, J Delbruck, 'Article 24' in B Simma (ed), *The Charter of the United Nations, A Commentary*, vol I (Oxford, Oxford University Press, 2002) 404.

[14] Article 25 explicitly establishes that member states are only compelled to 'accept and carry out . . . decisions of the Security Council [which are] in accordance with the . . . Charter'.

[15] See L Damrosch, 'The Civilian Impact of Economic Sanctions' in L Damrosch (ed), *Enforcing Restraint: Collective Intervention in Internal Conflicts* (New York, Council on Foreign Relations Press, 1993) 274. See also A Segall, 'Economic Sanctions: Legal and Policy Constraints' (1999), *International Review of the Red Cross*, www.icrc.org/eng/resources/documents/misc/57jq73.htm, accessed 2 September 2013.

[16] Article 1(1) UN Charter reads as follows: 'To maintain international peace and security, and to that end: . . . to bring about by peaceful means, and in conformity with the *principles of justice and international law*, adjustments or settlements of international disputes or situations which might lead to a breach of the peace' (emphasis added). Article 55(c) establishes that the organisation's mandate is to promote 'universal respect for, and observance of, human rights'. Article 56 provides that 'All Members pledge themselves to take joint and separate action in co-operation with the Organization for the achievement of the purposes set forth in Article 55'.

and facilitate medical and food supplies.[17] From international humanitarian law are derived also the prohibition on starvation of the civilian population,[18] and the obligation to allow for relief supplies in naval and air blockades as well as occupied territories.[19]

When faced with sanctions imposed in peacetime, human rights law – as opposed to international humanitarian law – offers the framework of reference for distinguishing the fundamental principles the violation of which should be avoided at all costs. All human rights instruments generally recognise, inasmuch as relevant for this chapter, the right to life, right to an adequate standard of living, including food, clothing, housing and medical care, and freedom from hunger.[20] These texts conversely impose on states positive obligations demanding the adoption of measures necessary to ensure, or at least promote, the full enjoyment thereof. That these rights must be taken into account in any sanctions regime may seem self-evident. Yet, from a legal standpoint, the issue has not been clear cut or unchallengeable. Some argue that the right to life prohibits only the arbitrary deprivation of life through execution, disappearance, torture and others similar acts, thus not comprising deprivation of life by means of starvation, or the fulfilment of basic needs such as food, water and basic health and medical care.[21] This view has, nonetheless, been clearly contested by the Human Rights Committee, in its first General Comment on Article 6 ICCPR:

> [It] notes that the right to life has too often been narrowly interpreted. The expression 'inherent right to life' in Article 6 [ICCPR] cannot properly be understood in a restrictive manner, and the protection of this right requires that States adopt positive measures.[22]

Equally important, the right to food imposes on states an obligation to adopt measures so as to allow and facilitate, to the extent possible and within the available resources, individuals' access to the necessary goods to fulfil the right. It clearly entails a duty not to act in such a manner that will deliberately deprive a person of his or her life, including by starvation.

[17] Fourth Convention, Article 23, and Protocol I, Article 70.

[18] Protocol I Additional to the Geneva Conventions, Articles 54, 69 and 70; Protocol II Additional to the Geneva Conventions, Article 14.

[19] Fourth Geneva Convention, Articles 23, 55, 59; Protocol I Additional to the Geneva Conventions, Articles 69(1) and 70.

[20] Article 11 ICESCR reads as follows: '1. The States Parties to the present Covenant recognize the right of everyone to an adequate standard of living for himself and his family, including adequate food, clothing and housing, and to the continuous improvement of living conditions. The States Parties will take appropriate steps to ensure the realization of this right, recognizing to this effect the essential importance of international co-operation based on free consent. 2. The States Parties to the present Covenant, recognizing the fundamental right of everyone to be free from hunger, shall take, individually and through international co-operation, the measures, including specific programs, which are needed : (a) To improve methods of production, conservation and distribution of food by making full use of technical and scientific knowledge, by disseminating knowledge of the principles of nutrition and by developing or reforming agrarian systems in such a way as to achieve the most efficient development and utilization of natural resources ; (b) Taking into account the problems of both food-importing and food- exporting countries, to ensure an equitable distribution of world food supplies in relation to need'. See also Articles 12, 13 ICESCR; Articles 3, 5, 25 UDHR; Articles 6, 7 ICCPR.

[21] See Y Dinstein, 'The Right to Life, Physical Integrity and Liberty' in L Henkin (ed), *The International Bill of Rights* (New York, Columbia University Press, 1981) 115.

[22] HRC, General Comment No 06: The right to life (art 6), 30 April 1982, www.unhchr.ch/tbs/doc.nsf/%28Symbol%29/84ab9690ccd81fc7c12563ed0046fae3?Opendocument, accessed 2 September 2013.

Notably, the Genocide Convention protects a 'collective right to life',[23] in the terms of which the deliberate starvation of a national, ethnic, racial or religious group, if committed with intent to destroy the group, would amount to genocide.[24] It is worth recalling that the Convention applies in both times of war and peace.[25]

III IMPACT ON HUMAN RIGHTS: THE IRANIAN CASE

After a brief assessment of the relevant legal framework when appraising the imposition of economic sanctions, it is in order to analyse the practical consequences these mechanisms involve in practice. To this effect, there follows an overview of how Iran's human rights situation has been affected by sanctions.

Iran is under a number of UN sanctions,[26] which generally bar nuclear, missile and certain military exports to Iran; investments in oil, gas and petrochemicals; exports of refined petroleum products; business dealings with the Iranian Republican Guard Corps; banking and insurance transactions, including with the Central Bank of Iran; and shipping. Through Resolution 1929 (2010), the UN political body banned Iran from participating in any activities related to ballistic missiles. For that purpose, it tightened the arms embargo and imposed travel bans on individuals involved with the programme, and froze the funds and assets of the Iranian Revolutionary Guard and Islamic Republic of Iran Shipping Lines. Importantly, it further recommended states to prohibit the servicing of Iranian vessels involved in forbidden activities; prevent the provision of financial services used for sensitive nuclear activities; closely watch Iranian individuals and entities; ban the opening of Iranian banks on their territory and prevent Iranian banks from entering into relationships with national banks if it might contribute to the nuclear program; and not allow financial institutions operating in their territory to open offices and accounts in Iran.[27] In keeping with this view, some states have adopted harder approaches. This is the case for the United States and the members of the European Union.[28]

As noted earlier, sanctions are a tool – as opposed to a policy as such – aiming therefore at the achievement of specific targets.[29] Sanctions on Iran are intended to force Tehran to halt nuclear enrichment, which Western powers and their allies fear will be used to further develop nuclear weapons. Tehran denies the claim, arguing its atomic work is directed at improving medicine and generating electricity. Be that as it may, sanctions' impact on the

[23] See, for example, B Kandoch, 'The Limits of Economic Sanctions under International Law: the Case of Iraq' in M Bothe and B Kandoch (eds), *International Peacekeeping: The Yearbook of International Peace Operations* (Leiden, Martinus Nijhoff Publishers, 2002) vol 7, 289.

[24] Convention on the Prevention and Punishment of the Crime of Genocide, Article 3(c).

[25] ibid, Article 1.

[26] See UN SC Resolutions 1696 (2006), 1737 (2006), 1747 (2007), 1803 (2008), 1929 (2010), 1984 (2011) and 2049 (2012).

[27] SC Resolution 1929 (2010), 9 June 2010. See, in particular, para 23.

[28] Council of the European Union, *Council Conclusions on Iran*, 3191st Foreign Affairs Council Meeting, Luxembourg, 15 October 2012, www.consilium.europa.eu/uedocs/cms_data/docs/pressdata/EN/foraff/132833.pdf, accessed 2 September 2013. See also R Gladstone, 'US Acts with Europe to Strengthen Iran Penalties', *The New York Times*, 21 December 2012, www.nytimes.com/2012/12/22/world/middleeast/penalties-on-iran-strengthened-by-us-and-europe.html?_r=0, accessed 2 September 2013. See also J Pawla, 'EU Sanctions Target Iran Oil, Gas, Banker Companies', *Reuters*, 16 October 2012, www.reuters.com/article/2012/10/16/us-iran-nuclear-eu-idUSBRE89F08N20121016, accessed 2 September 2013.

[29] On the objectives of sanctions see G Hufbauer, J Schott and K Elliot, *Economic Sanctions Reconsidered: History and Current Policy* (Washington, DC, Institute for International Economics, 1985) 23–28.

civilian population has been highly distressing[30] while the achievement of the envisaged goal is far from being on the horizon.

Indeed, pharmaceuticals and medical products and equipment, for instance, are exempt from the scope of sanctions but still Iran is facing shortages of drugs for the treatment of 30 illnesses, including cancer, heart and breathing problems, thalassaemia and multiple sclerosis, because the country is not allowed to use the international payment systems.[31] In late 2012, an Iranian boy died due to a lack of essential medicines as a result of sanctions blockades:

> This is against human rights . . . Even in wars, women and children and patients are protected by some impunity based on international treaties . . . But sanctions hitting medicine in Iran are causing a silent death and are a ploy to hurt the health of Iranian people.[32]

It has been reported that 85,000 cancer patients in Iran require chemotherapy and radiotherapy, which it is now extremely difficult to deliver. A considerable number of Iranians – mostly those in need of chemotherapy treatment and blood-clotting agents – are under imminent risk, an unwarranted side-effect of sanctions. To be fair, the international community has endeavoured to address the concerning situation and make sure essential medicines get through, but the waivers established are not effective since there is an inherent clash with blanket restrictions on banking and bans on 'dual-use' chemicals that might be used for military and nuclear purposes. As pointed out by UN Secretary General Ban Ki Moon, '[e]ven companies that have obtained the requisite license to import food and medicine are facing difficulties in finding third-country banks to process the transactions'.[33] Due to the shortage of anti-clotting medicines, 40,000 haemophiliacs are under serious threat, with operations having been almost entirely suspended due to the associated risks.[34] Likewise, an estimated 23,000 people infected with HIV/AIDS have extreme difficulty in accessing life-supporting drugs. Individuals suffering from thalassaemia, an estimated population of 8,000, have started to die due to the scarcity of deferoxamine, the drug used to control the iron content in the blood. Furthermore, Iran is facing serious problems in purchasing medical equipment such as autoclaves (sterilising machines), which are essential for the production of many drugs, because some of the principal Western suppliers refuse to do business given the image damage that may arise therefrom.[35]As a consequence of this precarious situation, a medical and pharmaceutical black market is developing, fed by a local population desperate to gather life-saving

[30] 'Report of the UN Secretary General to the General Assembly on the Situation on Human Rights in the Islamic Republic of Iran', 22 August 2012, 16, in particular Section G, www.unhcr.org/refworld/country,,, COUNTRYREP,IRN,,50a107f02,0.html, accessed 2 September 2013.

[31] G Esfandiari, 'Iran Sanctions Result in Shortages of Cancer Drugs, Heart Medicine', *Payvand Iran News*, 5 June 2012, http://payvand.com/news/12/may/1062.html, accessed 30 January 2013.

[32] S Ghavidel, Director of Iran's Haemophilia Society, 'Blood Sanctions: Iranian Boy Dies from Medicine Shortage', *Question More*, 16 November 2012, http://rt.com/news/iranian-boy-dies-sanctions-880/, accessed 2 September 2013. See also S Dehghan, 'Haemophiliac Iranian Boy Dies After Sanctions Disrupt Medicine Supplies', *The Guardian*, 14 November 2012, www.guardian.co.uk/world/2012/nov/14/sanctions-stop-medicines-reaching-sick-iranians, accessed 2 September 2013.

[33] Report of the UN Secretary General on the Situation on Human Rights in Iran (n 30), para 43.

[34] M Sahimi, 'The Unfolding Human Rights Catastrophe in Iran – Sanctions Imposed on Iran's Banks and Financial Institutions Could Lead to a Humanitarian Crisis', *Aljazeera*, 28 October 2012, www.aljazeera.com/indepth/opinion/2012/10/20121023101710641121.html, accessed 2 September 2013.

[35] J Borger and S Dehghan, 'Iran Unable to Get Life-saving Drugs Due to International Sanctions', 13 January 2013, www.guardian.co.uk/world/2013/jan/13/iran-lifesaving-drugs-international-sanctions, accessed 2 September 2013.

goods. Of course, the associated health and economic costs are unquestionable.[36] Given that some states continue to trade with Iran, eg China and India, this only means that Iran ill be forced to purchase more, if not all, medical products from these countries. Consequently, the high-quality Western products are replaced with lower-quality products and, once again, the standard of living is undermined. Drugs imports from the United States and Europe decreased by roughly 30 per cent in 2012 and this percentage is set to increase. The pharmaceutical patents regime often makes it impossible to replace advanced medicines, particularly for very serious diseases such as cancer and multiple sclerosis.[37]

Delivery of some agricultural products to Iran has also been affected for the same reasons.[38] Scott Lucas, a specialist in Iranian affairs at Birmingham University, explains:

> If you are talking about the number of deals needed for a country of 75 million . . . you do not have an organized overall strategy for *finance*, purchase and distribution. I do not think they can cope with the challenge. Even if the sanctions were lifted, which is a huge if, the problems in the system are now so endemic I think they face real serious structural problems.[39]

Even though foodstuffs are not covered by the sanctions prohibition, importers are reluctant to trade with Iran due to the instability of the rial currency. Likewise, many foreign banks avoid engaging in, and financing, even those deals exempted from the sanctions owing to the political and public perception this might entail.

IV TOWARDS AN OPERATIONAL METHODOLOGY

Against this background, it is submitted that the assessment of whether to impose sanctions on a specific state, and if so, what sanctions, will follow a structured path that starts by considering two sets of fundamentals: (i) effectiveness-related elements and (ii) human rights implications. With regard to the former, it must be borne in mind that sanctions do not have a purely retributive nature, rather aiming at neutralising a breach of, or threat to, peace and security, where dialogue, dispute-settlement mechanisms or diplomacy have failed to do so. Therefore, it is imperative to ponder the nature of the harm as well as the likelihood of the sanction envisaged truly being able to remedy it. The most obvious way of judging the effectiveness of sanctions is in terms of their capacity to alter the conduct of the target state. Another relevant factor is the potential destabilising effect of the sanction in the government, economic, social and political context of the besieged state. As a second step, and on the basis of the results of the context assessment, the extent of the harm inflicted on the rights of the population must not be neglected. Likewise, it must be ensured that humanitarian assistance will find its way through, in other words, any legitimate sanctions regime must provide for humanitarian exceptions, in law but also in

[36] N Karimi, 'Iran's Medical Crisis Deepens as Economy Sputters', *Associated Press*, 8 January 2013, bigstory.ap.org/article/irans-medical-crisis-deepens-economy-sputters, accessed 2 September 2013.

[37] S Namazi, 'Sanctions and Medical Supply Shortage in Iran', *Wilson Center – Viewpoints No 20*, February 2013, www.wilsoncenter.org/sites/default/files/sanctions_medical_supply_shortages_in_iran.pdf, accessed 2 September 2013.

[38] J Saul and M George, 'Sanctions Side Effect Hits Iran's Food System', *Reuters*, 28 November 2012, www.reuters.com/article/2012/11/28/us-iran-food-idUSBRE8AR0DG20121128, accessed 2 September 2013.

[39] ibid.

practice.[40] This is to say, there must not be an excessively bureaucratic and administratively overwhelming procedure that nullifies the very nature and scope of urgent humanitarian missions. In line with this view, the Committee on Economic, Social and Cultural Rights (CESCR) noted, in its General Comment 8, that entities applying economic sanctions must always take full account of the provisions of the ICESC.[41] The Committee emphasised that attention should be focused on the impact of sanctions on vulnerable groups, such as women, children, and the elderly, and that human rights protection must be incorporated into the design and monitoring of all sanctions regimes. There must be an open and transparent discussion procedure so that the international community may be aware of the corresponding costs.

Indeed, once it is decided to adopt a specific sanction, an effective monitoring system must be put in place to ensure that the intent the sanction was to serve is still feasible, and that the means used to achieve the goal are not disproportionate to the suffering caused to civilians.[42] In short, the SC must adopt a precautionary approach to the adoption and imposition of economic sanctions. Nothing prevents the SC from concluding that what was initially seen as an appropriate response to a breach of Article 39 UN Charter no longer remains as such. It may even decide that military action is the appropriate course of action, or that peace talks or diplomatic sanctions better serve the purpose pursued. Of course, when states adopt unilateral sanctions or further harden the sanctions regime passed by the SC they are equally bound to abide by human rights principles and humanitarian considerations. This may be all the more important in the face of situations similar to that undergone by the Iranian people, where foreign companies refuse to do business with Iran and Iranian companies even if the deal does not fall under the scope of sanctions.

Certainly, the considerations above may seem overly simplistic since the application of sanctions is likely to entail different – and even opposing – consequences. For instance, bans on credit and bank dealings will probably strain the economic situation of the country, leading to the worsening of debt, cuts in public spending, inflation escalation, and, hence, further breaches of people's rights (eg, to healthcare, education, food). In turn, the population is expected to react and rebel against the hardening conditions of life, thus contesting the ruling powers. As in a vicious circle, it is easily conceivable that the government, often a repressive one, will adopt measures to tighten individual freedoms so as to protect the regime from any potential threats. Accordingly, one would be assisting another wave of human rights violations, prospectively civil and political ones, such as freedom of expression, assembly and association, right to life, freedom from arbitrary arrest and illegal detention, etc. One may question as well whether it is not preferable to be intransigent in the application of sanctions for a relatively short period, even at the cost of human

[40] General Comment 12: 'States Parties should refrain at all times from food embargoes or similar measures which endanger conditions for food production and access to food in other countries. Food should never be used as an instrument of political or economic pressure'.

[41] UN Committee on Economic, Social and Cultural Rights, General Comment No. 8 : *The relationship between economic sanctions and respect for economic, social and cultural rights*, E/C 12/1997/8, 4 December 1997.

[42] UNCTAD's Principles on Responsible Sovereign Lending and Borrowing propose the principles of due diligence and responsible management as well as the establishment of a robust monitoring system as guidelines for a more transparent, reliable and fair international financial system. With due adaptations, the same principles may be extremely useful in accommodating human rights promotion with economic sanctions' primary objectives. See M Goldmann, 'Responsible Sovereign Lending and Borrowing: The View from Domestic Jurisdictions', UNCTAD – Max Planck Institute For Comparative Public Law and International Law, February 2012.

rights protection, if this meant that the targeted government would soon fall, instead of loosening coercive measures that could mean a long-term deprivation of fundamental guarantees for the people.[43] Decision makers on the passing of economic sanctions thus face a difficult choice. But it does not mean that the aforementioned criteria are not suitable. To the contrary, it only signifies that one must not have the pretension of assuming that imposing sanctions is a one-pack deal. It is a continuing commitment as much as an ongoing endeavour until the sanction is lifted, either because it is replaced by a more suitable alternative, or because the underlying goal has been achieved and therefore the fundamentals for its imposition no longer persist. It is worth noting that situations where a state or international institution might be called to reassess its policy on loans and economic assistance provided to repressive states[44] presents considerable differences vis-à-vis the framework this chapter focuses on, that is coercive measures that prevent, ban and curtail financial dealings and economic assistance or cooperation, which are fundamental pillars for most repressive regimes. In the former scenario it appears easier to evaluate the impact of foreign aid or cooperation because the usage given to funds will usually already be known, as well as the normal behaviour of the state under such circumstances (eg, whether it employs foreign aid in social policies aimed at improving living conditions). In the latter, the manner in which a government may react to sanctions is not evident at the moment of their adoption, which makes the assessment of the adequacy of specific sanctions much more complicated. There will hardly ever be significant confidence as to whether the sanction will be effective. For as much as previous sanctions might have been unsuccessful, the next one might fairly be the 'last straw' for the targeted regime. Common to both situations is the need to delineate a coherent decision-making methodology founded on rational criteria, leading to effect-driven choices. No kind of aprioristic or settled path to decide upon the imposition of sanctions is proposed here. Whatever the decision might be, it will likely entail costs for the population. The moment when such costs became disproportionate to the aim envisaged cannot be detected without a robust monitoring system which, as previously mentioned, rigorously takes into account the suffering of the people, and the potential for altering the state's behaviour. In the case of Iran, it is important to bear in mind that it has been the subject of sanctions for roughly 30 years. No major advancements in its nuclear policies have been achieved. However, as noted earlier, the negative impact of sanctions on human living conditions seems to be increasing. Another element to bear in mind is the profile of the target state. When deeply ingrained ideologies are at stake as well as claims or fears of an existence under threat (as in Iran, and whether founded or unfounded), it is unlikely that the government will be sensible to economic sanctions unless its internal conjuncture (*rectior*, its financial and institutional capabilities rather than the human rights situation) provides no alternative. It was earlier proposed that economic sanctions be re-adapted so as to provide for the necessary waiver required for alleviating human rights conditions in the targeted state. Were, for example, certain loans or financial deals to start being allowed with Iran and Iranian banks and companies, it would be necessary, again, to design a rigorous supervising mechanism that would make sure funds are employed in a manner that directly or reflexively benefits the population

[43] Bohoslavsky refers, in this context, to a 'trade-off' between loyalty and repression which is visible in authoritarian regimes. See JP Bohosvavsky, 'Tracking Down the Missing Financial Link in Transitional Justice' (2012) 1 *International Human Rights Law Review* 63, and references cited therein.

[44] On this scenario, see Bohoslavsky, ibid, 63–71. See also A Cassese, 'Foreign Economic Assistance and Respect for Civil and Political Rights: Chile - A Case Study' (1979) 14 *Texas International Law Journal* 251–56.

rather than being diverted to further enhance the potential of the regime to follow its internationally rejected agenda. To summarise, it is submitted that a robust system for the passing and implementation of economic sanctions requires three main items: (i) a capable 'preventive' toolbox, which is to focus on the study and assessment of the profile of the state and its vulnerability to external pressure as well as on the likely impact of sanctions on the population; (ii) a strong monitoring kit, to scrutinise whether the initial analysis reveals itself to be realistic; and (iii) a resourceful 'reactive' kit, that allows for flexibility and permits re-adapting or replacing sanctions with due caution and well-grounded information, without creating loopholes that might open the leeway for interests other that international peace and security to take the lead in the decision-making process.

But an effective approach to the responsible management of economic sanctions may not focus exclusively on the UN, and specifically the SC. As mentioned earlier, the SC acts on behalf of the international community. It is the approval and consensus of the majority of states that bestows legitimacy upon its decisions. Certainly, as of today, the action of the SC is extremely difficult to control due to its structure, dynamic, composition and voting system. Still, it is for states to ensure that the decisions of the SC, even when adopted under Chapter VII, do not fly in the face of fundamental human rights principles, either in theory or in practice. While this approach is indeed rare, it is not unknown. Nor are states entirely oblivious to the possibility.[45] In the *Kadi* case, the Court of First Instance of the European Communities (CFI), admitting the supremacy of the UN Charter and the submission of EU members to Article 103 of the Charter, held that the matter under appreciation – the alleged violation of fundamental human rights by the UN's so-called terrorist lists – called into question the entire framework of human rights guarantees established in Europe since the end of World War II and found an exception to the purportedly non-reviewable nature of SC decisions. It ruled:

> [T]he Court is empowered to check, indirectly, the lawfulness of the Resolutions of the Security Council in question with regard to Jus Cogens, understood as a body of higher rules of public international law binding on all subjects of international law, including the bodies of the United Nations, and from which no derogation is possible.[46]

The Court further affirmed that the Charter itself 'presupposes the existence of mandatory principles of international law, in particular, the protection of the fundamental rights of the human person'.[47] The Court referred to 'the mandatory provisions concerning the universal protection of human rights, from which neither the member States nor the UN bodies may derogate because they constitute intransgressible principles of international customary law'.[48] This decision was reversed by the European Court of Justice (ECJ), which refused to accept the competence of the courts of the EC/EU to review the

[45] While discussing the adoption of a controversial decision under Chapter VII – Resolution 1422 (2002) – Canada's Representative noted that the 'adoption of the Resolution currently circulating could place Canada and, we expect, others in the unprecedented position of having to examine the legality of a Security Council Resolution', Statements of States' Representatives to the United Nations at the meeting on 10 July 2002, available online at www.iccnow.org, accessed 2 September 2013. The representatives of the Netherlands, Jordan, Samoa and Germany, Costa Rica, Liechtenstein, Brazil, Switzerland, Mexico, Venezuela, Fiji, Ukraine, Colombia, Malaysia, Syria, Argentina and Cuba presented similar declarations. See Docs S/PV. 4568 and S/PV. 4568 (Resumption I).

[46] Case T-351/01 *Yassin A Kadi v Council of the EU and Commission of the* EC, para 5, section 5.

[47] Ibid, para 228.

[48] Ibid, para 231, referring to 'Advisory Opinion of the International Court of Justice of 8 July 1996, *The Legality of the Threat or Use of Nuclear Weapons,* Reports 1996, p 226, para 79.

decisions of the SC.[49] Rather, it was of the view that the Community judicature was entitled to assess the compatibility of an act of the Community aimed at enforcing or implementing a resolution of the SC adopted under Chapter VII with higher norms of the legal order of the Community.[50] This understanding seems, however, to be based on an unwanted dualist conception of national and international law which does not reflect the reality of the contemporary international legal order.[51] Furthermore, in other parts of the ruling, the ECJ acknowledges that the acts of organs of the UN produce effects within the Community.[52] Obviously, though, in order for those effects to be recognised, the decisions of the UN need to be consistent with procedural and substantive legal standards. Therefore, the powers to assess whether decisions of international bodies have complied with the legal requirements that allow them to fully operate within the Community must necessarily be conferred on the courts of the EC/EU. In reality, when the ECJ admits that the Community judicature is competent to examine the compatibility of domestic enforcing laws with higher norms, it is implicitly admitting its competence to indirectly revisit, as a preliminary matter, the validity of the act intended to be enforced by the domestic provisions challenged.[53] In *Kadi II*, the ECJ considered that even after the establishment of the Office of the Ombudsperson, the Sanctions Committee still could not be deemed to comply with fundamental human rights.[54] This case shows that while states are not in a position to directly review, like a court of appeal, decisions adopted under Chapter VII, they are entitled to do so indirectly; or in other words, to assess the implementation of SC resolutions, eventually adopting supplementary measures so as to complement and refine the judgment of the UN political arm. This proposal is daring, to be sure, but otherwise one may be accepting that the SC may impose a 'duty to do wrong',[55] in clear contradiction of the UN Charter. Again, examples of judicial approaches similar to the

[49] For a comprehensive analysis of the *Kadi* Judgment see M Cremona, F Francioni and S Poli (eds), 'Challenging the EU Counter-Terrorism Measures Through the Courts', EUI Working Papers, AEL 2009/10, Academy of European Law, Badia Fiesolana, 2009.

[50] ECJ, Judgment (Grand Chamber), Joined Cases C-402/05 P and C-415/05 P, *Yassin Abdullah Kadi and Al Barakaat International Foundation v Council of the European Union and Commission of the European Communities*, nyr, 3 September 2008. Paragraphs 286–88 read as follows: 'It must be emphasized that . . . the review of lawfulness thus to be ensured by the Community judicature applies to the Community act intended to give effect to the international agreement at issue, and not to the latter as such. With more particular regard to a Community act which, like the contested regulation, is intended to give effect to a resolution adopted by the Security Council under Chapter VII of the Charter of the United Nations, it is not, therefore, for the Community judicature . . . to review the lawfulness of such a resolution adopted by an international body, even if that review were to be limited to the examination of the compatibility of that resolution with *jus cogens*. However, any judgment given by the Community judicature deciding that a Community measure intended to give effect to such a resolution is contrary to a higher rule of law in the Community legal order would not entail any challenge to the primacy of that resolution in international law'.

[51] See, eg, L Van de Erik and N Schrijver, 'Eroding the Primacy of the UN System of Collective Security: The Judgment of the European Court of Justice in the Cases of Kadi and Al Barakaat' (2008) 5 *International Organizations Law Review* 336. For a critique, see also F Francioni, 'Kadi and the Vicissitudes of Access to Justice' in Cremona, Francioni and Poli (eds) (n 49) 19.

[52] ECJ, Judgment (Grand Chamber), Joined Cases C-402/05 P and C-415/05 P, *Yassin Abdullah Kadi and Al Barakaat International Foundation v Council of the European Union and Commission of the European Communities*, nyr, 3 September 2008, para 203.

[53] E Cannizzaro, 'Security Council Resolutions and EC Fundamental Rights: Some Remarks on the ECJ Decision in the Kadi Case' in Cremona, Francioni and Poli (eds) (n 49) 44.

[54] ECJ, *Yassin Abdullah Kadi v Commission*, Case C-85/09, 30 September 2010, paras 126, 128.

[55] See also Article 2 2001 ILC's Draft Articles on the Responsibility of States for Internationally Wrongful Acts, in the terms of which 'There is an internationally wrongful act of a State when *conduct consisting of* an action or *omission*: (a) Is attributable to the State under international law; and (b) Constitutes a breach of an international obligation of the State' (emphasis added).

one crystallised in the *Kadi* decisions are not common. Indeed, the rulings are historic for their innovative and progressive stance. Yet their importance is not reserved to the space of the European Union. That is to say, they paved the way – more precisely, the juridical and legal methodology – for other institutions, and eventually states, to follow an analogous path.

The purpose of recalling the *Kadi* rulings in the context of this work is that of underlining that the rights capable of being affected by economic sanctions – as shown by the case of Iran – are widely accepted and broadly recognised by the majority of states.[56] They are crystallised under international customary law, the prohibition on violating some of them is of peremptory nature, and many are incorporated into widely ratified treaties that mirror customary law and or *jus cogens*.[57] They may very well be considered as fundamental pillars of democratic states abiding by the rule of law. Accordingly, the application of the *Kadi* fundamentals to adjust SC sanctions (eg, by establishing waivers in imports and exports, as well as in financial trades and banking activities that serve the purpose, well monitored, of improving individuals' rights) is not out of the question.

V CONCLUSION

The chapter does not aim to claim that economic sanctions have no purpose or utility. South Africa is an illustrative example of the persuasive power these tools may have.[58] In reality, their objective may be to directly improve the human rights situation in the country. As a matter of fact, sanctions against Iran were also imposed, at least until a certain point, as a deterrent against its averred support for terrorist activities as well as a coercive response to the daunting human rights situation faced by its people.[59] This notwithstanding, the real effect of sanctions may be, as noted earlier, that of further diminishing the living conditions of individuals. Where sanctions were not directly triggered by human rights concerns, the pressing question arises: at what cost? At what cost are financial or economic or political interests to be pursued? Or, at what cost is the international community going to accept stepping back – even though all attempts might have failed to protect individuals from massive human rights violations – for the sake of not undermining economic, financial or political interests? Mostly when under international law, the responsibility-to-protect doctrine allows – if not demands – action.[60]

[56] See above, Section II.

[57] In this context, see Article 41(1) 2001 ILC's Draft Articles on State Responsibility, above n 55: 'States shall cooperate to bring to an end through lawful means any serious breach within the meaning of Article 40. 2.'

[58] See, for example, J Davis, 'Squeezing Apartheid: Economic Sanctions against South Africa' (1993) 49(9) *Bulletin of the Atomic Scientists* 16; R Kinloch Massie, *Loosing the Bonds - The United States and South Africa in the Apartheid Years* (New York, Nan A Talese/Doubleday, 1997) 623.

[59] After the so-called Iranian Hostage Crisis, the US adopted sanctions against Iran on the basis that the latter was supporting international terrorism, engaging in human rights violations and breaching cooperation with IAEA. On the topic, see, for example, R Caswell, 'Economic Sanctions and the Iran Experience' (1981) *Foreign Affairs*, www.foreignaffairs.com/articles/35846/robert-caswell/economic-sanctions-and-the-iran-experience, accessed 2 September 2013.

[60] While scrutiny of the responsibility-to-protect doctrine is beyond the scope of this work, it could be argued that given that the responsibility of the international community progressively increases in view of the failure of the state concerned to ensure human rights and the gross violation thereof such that the use of force might be legitimated, there seems to be *a fortiori* a strong argument to maintain that, if for the sake of human rights of the population of targeted states sanctions must be reversed or re-adapted, nothing prevents this. By the same token, it is not out of the question that the degradation of living conditions might achieve such levels as to

There is no unsolvable contradiction between economic sanctions and respect for human rights. To the contrary, the former may be a powerful tool to pursue and ensure respect for the latter. Still, a conscious and committed effort to accommodate human rights, on the one hand, and financial and political interests, on the other, seems to be lacking, when the reconciling path does not appear unbearably arduous. Were one to be willing to engage in such an effort, it is submitted that a rational path towards effectiveness calls upon three 'musts': (i) a capable 'preventive' toolbox that operates to create informed options based on in-depth knowledge of the context and profile of the target state and the likely impact of sanctions on people's fundamental rights; (ii) a robust monitoring system; and (iii) a ready-to-be-triggered 'reactive' kit that may permit legitimate re-adaptation or replacement of sanctions in accordance with the applicable legal framework. This notwithstanding, as mentioned before, whatever the decision may be, it is likely to have undesirable consequences for human beings. Severing or maintaining hard economic sanctions might in time weaken the regime and assure a more stable and enduring human rights situation in the mid and long term, even if it means neglecting human rights imperatives in the short term. Conversely, loosening sanctions by waiving restrictions on imports, exports and financial dealings might ease living conditions but might also allow more time and opportunity for the regime to strengthen itself and plan how to resist. It may well leave loopholes that may permit the regime to divert funds and resources to purposes other than those that the waivers were intended to serve. There are no 'one size fits all' solutions or automatic responses. Nor are economic sanctions the only available mechanism to address threats to, or breaches of, international peace and security. It is submitted that economic sanctions should be resorted to in the context of a 'complementary appeal' to existing avenues. That is to say, economic sanctions are unlikely to be effective if not coupled with other mechanisms, such as diplomatic, cultural, and eventually military sanctions. Likewise, from the moment the SC adopts economic sanctions it is making a statement that the targeted state is engaging in some practice that amounts to a breach of Article 39 UN Charter. Accordingly and logically, any state that cooperates in that practice is itself breaching or threatening to breach international peace and security. In such case, a more active SC, capable and willing to react to such situations, independent of who and how powerful the 'abetting' and 'accomplice' state might be, would be most desirable. Indeed, no state may survive completely isolated from the world for a long time. The 'reactive' kit should thus also be applied to states that breach UN sanctions and consequently assist in undermining human rights conditions.

demand stronger international intervention, including that of a military nature, mostly if *jus cogens* norms are affected.

4

The Significance of Human Rights for the Debt of Countries in Transition

DUSTIN SHARP

HIGH LEVELS OF sovereign debt can create a thorny moral, political and legal problem for many of the world's countries. What should a government do when it is not possible to meet debt service obligations while at the same time providing for a bare minimum of essential services in areas such as healthcare and education? If the contractual rights of creditors are respected and the debt serviced as required, there will be less money in the national budget to address the basic economic and social rights of the population, potentially leading to schools that are understaffed, hospital cabinets that are empty, and the lowering or cancelling of social security transfers. On the other hand, the risk of alienating creditors and capital markets needed for future economic development must also be considered. Historically, human rights, particularly economic and social rights, have been on the losing side of this conundrum in all too many cases.

This dilemma is particularly poignant for new regimes transitioning from conflict or dictatorship to democracy where many of the debts in question were taken out by a predecessor regime that may have used the money for authoritarian or repressive purposes inconsistent with the basic will and human rights of the population. The money associated with the loans in question may have been embezzled, hindering a government's ability to progressively realise economic and social rights.[1] In other cases, it may have helped to facilitate or make possible the perpetration of human rights abuses against the very population now expected to make good on the debt by providing fiscal breathing space and longevity to a repressive regime.[2] Historically, payment of these debts has often been seen as legally required, yet seems morally repugnant, especially considering that it will have further negative human rights impacts going forward as a successor regime's ability to meet basic needs is reduced.

Despite the strong linkages between debt and human rights evident in this dilemma, at the level of international financial institutions and other lenders, the problems created by high levels of sovereign debt are typically addressed through a prism of debt management and sustainability, rather than one of human rights and social justice, of abstract poverty reduction, rather than individual rights fulfilment. At the same time, the so-called

[1] For a discussion of the linkages between corruption and violations of economic and social rights, see C Albin-Lackey, 'Corruption, Human Rights, and Activism: Useful Connections and their Limits' in D Sharp (ed), *Justice and Economic Violence in Transition* (New York, Springer, 2014) 139.

[2] For an example of how this worked in the Brazilian context, see JP Bohoslavsky and M Torelly, 'Financial Complicity: The Brazilian Dictatorship Under The "Macroscope"' in Sharp (ed) (n 1) 233.

'odious' and 'illegitimate' debts[3] of predecessor regimes have only rarely featured in transitional justice processes, which have tended to foreground civil and political rights – particularly violations of physical integrity such as murder, rape, torture and disappearances – while pushing economic crimes and economic violence to the margins. The result is that questions of debt have not always been considered from a human rights perspective.

Yet viewing the tough questions created by high levels of sovereign debt through a human rights lens is important, not because it provides the answers to some of the seemingly intractable dilemmas of poverty and debt, but because such a perspective calls upon policymakers to ask some of the right questions. Since it would require participants in the system to think through the linkages between debt and concrete human rights impacts to a greater extent than has historically been the case, such a perspective has important policy implications for lenders and borrowers alike. In the particular context of countries in transition, greater attention to the linkages between debt and human rights could also lead to the mobilisation of important practical tools for both grappling with what went wrong in the past and promoting policy and accountability frameworks that could help to prevent recurrence going forward.

This chapter will proceed in three parts. I begin by exploring the linkages between sovereign debt and human rights generally. In so doing, I also examine whether debt forgiveness has the potential to increase respect for human rights. In the second part of the chapter, I look at sovereign debt in the particular context of countries in transition from conflict or dictatorship, with a particular eye towards the role that transitional justice mechanisms could play in helping to bring questions of economic violence into the policy foreground. Finally, I conclude the chapter by reflecting upon the policy relevance of bringing a human rights perspective to bear on questions relating to the debt of countries in transition.

I LINKAGES BETWEEN DEBT AND HUMAN RIGHTS

High levels of sovereign debt have the potential to undermine human rights in a number of overlapping ways. Perhaps the simplest and most straightforward impact can be seen in the area of economic and social rights. Under a number of international legal instruments, mostly notably the International Covenant on Economic, Social and Cultural Rights, individuals have a right to, among other things, food, shelter, basic education, and the highest attainable standard of health.[4] A state's duties with regard to such rights are varied, and include the duty (1) to respect (refraining from actively or directly interfering with enjoyment of the right); (2) to protect (preventing third parties from interfering with enjoyment of the right); and (3) to fulfil (ensuring that enjoyment of the right is gradually advanced in correspondence with a state's available resources).[5]

[3] A brief history and definitions of these terms are provided below.

[4] International Covenant on Economic, Social and Cultural Rights, 16 December 1966, 993 UNTS 3, arts 11 (rights to adequate standard of living and to food), 12 (right to the highest attainable standard of health), 13 (right to education). International commitments to economic and social rights can also be found in the Convention on the Rights of the Child, and regional instruments such as the African Charter on Human and Peoples Rights.

[5] See, eg, UN Committee on Economic, Social and Cultural Rights, *General Comment No 12: The Right to Adequate Food (art 11)*, 12 May 1999, E/C.12/1999/5, para 15. For a discussion of the origins and a critique of this tripartite typology of state obligations, see I Koch, 'Dichotomies, Trichotomies, or Waves of Duties' (2005) 5 *Human Rights Law Review* 81.

Linkages between debt and human rights are perhaps most pertinent with respect to the third category, the duty to fulfil, which requires governments to do the maximum possible to achieve economic and social rights based on the resources available at any given time, with no backsliding. This requirement, often known as 'progressive realisation', uses a sliding-scale legal standard that clearly lacks some precision as it can be difficult to determine in a given instance when non-enjoyment of economic and social rights can be attributed to genuine resource constraints or some other factor, yet all economic and social rights are generally understood to have a minimum core.[6] Falling below this minimum standard would be considered a prima facie violation of the right in question.[7] In matters of basic food, health, education and shelter, a state that falls below these minimum thresholds 'must demonstrate that every effort has been made to use all resources that are at its disposition in an effort to satisfy, as a matter of priority, those minimum obligations'.[8] Thus, where a government does not have enough money to pay creditors and at the same time give adequate protection to economic and social rights, it must make a choice between the contractual rights of creditors and the basic human rights of its population. At the heart of the clash between debt and human rights is the stark fact that while creditors' contractual rights are generally legally enforceable, the same cannot often be said for economic and social rights under international law, meaning that in practice when faced with the dilemma, creditors' rights often take precedence.[9]

In cases where a highly indebted state spends a significant portion of its budget on debt servicing, it stands to reason that less money will generally be available to progressively realise rights to things like health and education, and in many instances it will be hard for the state to satisfy core minimum obligations. There are a number of cases that help to illustrate this connection. For example, in 2000, Tanzania spent *nine times* more on debt service than on health at a time when 1.6 million of its citizens lived with AIDS.[10] In 1998 Mauritania spent more on debt service than on health and education combined, and nearly five times more than on health care alone.[11] In more recent years, Jamaica, a country considered too wealthy to benefit from debt-forgiveness programmes, similarly spent more on debt servicing than education and health combined.[12]

Though there is a tendency to focus on debt-related impacts on economic and social rights, it is worth noting that debt servicing may also result in difficult tradeoffs implicating civil and political rights. Well-functioning court and prison systems, for example, are not cheap. And yet a failure to pay prison guards or to provide adequate resources to courts can lead to prolonged pre-trial detention and other egregious human rights abuses.[13] Consider in this regard that in 1994 Malawi spent more on debt servicing than on health, education *and* its police and judicial system combined.[14]

[6] UN Committee on Economic, Social and Cultural Rights, *General Comment No 3: The Nature of States Parties' Obligations*, 14 December 1990, E/1991/23, para 10.

[7] ibid.

[8] ibid.

[9] The enforceability of economic and social rights varies greatly at the national level, with South Africa being a notable example of a country that has enshrined such protections in its domestic constitution.

[10] C Barry, 'Sovereign Debt, Human Rights, and Policy Conditionality' (2011) 19 *The Journal of Political Philosophy* 282, 284.

[11] C Okeke, 'The Debt Burden: An African Perspective' (2001) 35 *The International Lawyer* 1489, 1495.

[12] Jubilee Debt Campaign UK, *Country Information: Jamaica*, www.jubileedebtcampaign.org.uk/Jamaica+4109.twl, accessed 2 September 2013.

[13] See, eg, Human Rights Watch, *The Perverse Side of Things; Torture, Inadequate Detention Conditions, and Excessive Use of Force by Guinean Security Forces* (New York, HRW, August 2006).

[14] Okeke (n 11) 1495.

Beyond potential impacts inherent in the tension between debt servicing and the progressive realisation of economic and social rights, high debt burdens raise human rights concerns in other, less direct ways. Historically, lenders, especially the international financial institutions (IFIs), the World Bank and the International Monetary Fund (IMF), have been able to wield enormous influence over highly indebted countries based on conditions set for lending, debt restructuring and debt forgiveness. In previous decades, such influence was often wielded though strict loan conditionalities and structural adjustment programmes, which mandated, among other things, that indebted countries cut subsidies, privatise state-owned companies, and slash public sector spending, resulting in some instances in deep cuts to the health and education sectors.[15] It has been argued that such policies had negative impacts not just on economic and social rights to health and education, but even on some physical integrity rights.[16]

The extent of the influence wielded by such institutions has often meant that debtor governments' scope of freedom to address poverty issues through a broad range of policies has been drastically curtailed, with implications for sovereignty, self-determination and basic principles of democracy. Thus, a high debt burden not only affects a government's ability to progressively realise economic and social rights, but it also creates dependence on institutions that limit citizens' ability to exercise meaningful control over their own policies and institutions relating to questions of poverty, among other things. While conditionalities have arguably become less onerous in recent years than under the Washington-consensus-inspired structural adjustment programmes of the 1980s and 1990s, the liberal policy prescriptions inherent in the debt-forgiveness efforts associated with the Highly Indebted Poor Countries Initiative (HIPC), the primary framework for debt forgiveness today, raise similar concerns, even if HIPC also conditions debt relief on spending intended to reduce poverty.[17]

A Debt Forgiveness and Human Rights

The fact that a highly indebted country spending several times more on debt servicing than on health and education *could* in theory devote more resources to the realisation of economic and social rights if given the chance does not necessarily mean that it *would* do so in practice. A government suddenly relieved of its debt might, for example, choose to spend the newly liberated portion of the budget on military procurement or other policy objectives not directly related to fulfilment of economic and social rights. Some of the money that would have gone to debt servicing might instead find its way into the pockets of corrupt elites. To be sure, a government that shirked its responsibilities in this regard might violate international law, particularly where the money was not used to bring healthcare and other basic service delivery up to core minimums. Yet given the general lack of enforcement mechanisms for economic and social rights, we must consider the concrete human rights impacts of debt and debt forgiveness not just in theory, but in practice as well.

[15] A Pettifor, 'Global Economic Justice: Human Rights for Debtor Nations' (2001) 2 *Journal of Human Development* 47.

[16] M Abouharb and D Cingranelli, 'IMF Programs and Human Rights, 1981–2003' (2009) 4 *The Review of International Organizations* 47.

[17] S Michalowski, 'Sovereign Debt and Social Rights – Legal Reflections on a Difficult Relationship' (2008) 8 *Human Rights Law Review* 35, 42.

In this regard, evaluation of the HIPC initiative becomes important. Since its creation in 1996, the HIPC initiative, supplemented by the Multilateral Debt Relief Initiative (MDRI) has led to debt reduction packages for 36 countries, and has included the cancellation of $76 billion in debt.[18] In theory, such debt cancellation ought to be a boon to service delivery in the affected countries as funds formerly tied up in debt servicing can now be shifted to things like health and education. Indeed, both the IMF and various NGOs routinely tout the poverty-alleviating effects of such debt relief. Oxfam, for example, reports that Zambia has used money from debt cancellation to eliminate user fees that had made healthcare inaccessible to many rural poor.[19] The Jubilee Debt Campaign reports that debt relief has led to a free childhood immunisation programme in Mozambique.[20] The IMF states that the HIPC initiative has allowed governments to 'increase[] markedly their expenditures on health, education, and other social services'.[21]

Despite these rosy assessments, the broader literature is mixed in its evaluation of the effects of debt cancellation on social spending. Thus, for example, a study recently published in *The Lancet* concludes that debt relief has no detectable effect on domestic government health spending.[22] Similarly, in a review of 62 countries, Chauvin and Kraay find 'little evidence that debt relief has affected the level and composition of public spending in recipient countries'.[23] In contrast, Hinchliffe concludes that in the 20 countries reviewed, health expenditures as a share of total government expenditures increased on average between 6.2 and 8.1 per cent.[24] Such contradictory results make definitive conclusions difficult. Nevertheless, one might deduce that while basic maths – comparing money spent on debt servicing with funds budgeted for public health programmes, for example – suggests that debt relief has great potential to help governments progressively realise economic and social rights, the reality is far more complicated. It may be that debt relief accomplishes little in the absence of strong political will to progressively realise economic and social rights in the first place, or without the existence of suitable policy and institutional frameworks, including robust measures to minimise corruption.

Yet all of this leads to further human rights tensions and questions. Should lenders make debt relief even more conditional on having stricter 'good governance' policies in place, even if this has the anti-democratic effect of actually reducing a government's scope of freedom to address poverty issues? And if the answer is 'yes', why should we expect conditions associated with debt relief to be any more successful in bringing about enlightened policy and respect for human rights than the structural adjustment conditionalities of the past?[25] Resolving this conundrum is beyond the scope of this chapter. What can be fairly said, however, is that it will take more than debt relief to generate

[18] International Monetary Fund, 'Factsheet, Debt Relief Under the Heavily Indebted Poor Countries (HIPC) Initiative', 26 June 2012, www.imf.org/external/np/exr/facts/hipc.htm, accessed 30 August 2012.

[19] Oxfam International, *Zambia Uses G8 Debt Cancellation to Make Health Care Free for the Poor*, press release, 31 March 2006, www.oxfam.org/en/news/pressreleases2006/pr060331_zambia, accessed 30 August 2012.

[20] Jubilee Debt Campaign, *Debt and Health, Briefing/07*, www.jubileedebtcampaign.org.uk/download.php?id=589, accessed 30 August 2012.

[21] International Monetary Fund (n 18).

[22] C Lu et al, 'Public Financing of Health in Developing Countries: A Cross-National Systemic Analysis' (2010) 375 *The Lancet* 1375.

[23] N Chauvin and A Kraay, 'What Has 100 Billion Dollars Worth of Debt Relief Done for Low-Income Countries?' (2005) Research Paper Draft, Princeton University/Inter-American Development Bank/World Bank (2005).

[24] K Hinchliffe, 'Notes on the Impact of the HIPC Initiative on Public Expenditures in Education and Health in African Countries' (2004) *Africa Region Human Development Working Paper Series*, World Bank.

[25] W Easterly, 'Think Again: Debt Relief' (November 2001) *Foreign Policy*.

significant improvements to economic and social rights, and yet the space created by debt relief may be a necessary condition for success, together with broader national institutional strengthening.[26]

II TRANSITIONAL JUSTICE AND ECONOMIC VIOLENCE

While the relationship between debt and human rights can be troublesome even in the best of times, the implications of the dynamics discussed above are particularly acute in transitional contexts where a post-conflict or post-dictatorial government may have inherited the debts of a predecessor regime that were used to fuel corruption or repression. In such circumstances, forcing a state to pay down debts that were taken out without regard to the benefit or consent of the people expected to pay them – the payment of which will impact the enjoyment of the rights of the same people – is problematic from the perspective of human rights and social justice. This section looks to the relevance of transitional justice mechanisms to the difficult questions that debt raises in transitional contexts.

In many transitional situations, predecessor regimes have been notorious for large-scale human rights violations, including murder, torture and disappearances, as examples from Argentina, Chile, South Africa and elsewhere vividly illustrate. The field of transitional justice emerged in the 1980s and 1990s as transitional regimes attempted to grapple with these legacies of violence, while at the same time managing a political transition from an illiberal and autocratic past to something resembling a Western liberal democracy.[27] While some of the practices associated with transitional justice go back centuries if not millennia, in the last 25 years, use of transitional justice mechanisms has exploded, becoming a truly global phenomenon.[28] Kathryn Sikkink has traced a crescendo of human rights prosecutions, both national and international, spanning recent decades, and argues that they signal an emerging global norm of accountability for human rights violations, or a 'justice cascade'.[29] Beyond prosecutions, Priscilla Hayner has documented the existence of some 40 truth commissions that have been created since the early 1980s, with new truth commissions created nearly every year.[30] Other mechanisms from the transitional justice 'toolbox' – ranging from reparations, to the vetting of abusive officials, to efforts centred on memory and memorials – have also gained currency.[31] More and more, the question is not whether there will be some kind of justice in times of transition, but what the scope, sequencing and modalities should be.[32]

[26] D Dömeland and H Kharas, 'Debt Relief and Sustainable Financing to Meet the MDGs' in C Braga and D Dömeland (eds), *Debt Relief and Beyond: Lessons Learned and Challenges Ahead* (Washington, DC, The World Bank, 2009).

[27] See P Arthur, 'How "Transitions" Reshaped Human Rights: A Conceptual History of Transitional Justice' (2009) 31 *Human Rights Quarterly* 321, 325–26.

[28] See generally J Elster, *Closing the Books: Transitional Justice in Historical Perspective* (Cambridge, Cambridge University Press, 2004).

[29] K Sikkink, *The Justice Cascade: How Human Rights Prosecutions Are Changing World Politics*, 2nd edn (New York, WW Norton, 2011).

[30] P Hayner, *Unspeakable Truths: Transitional Justice and the Challenge of Truth Commissions* (New York, Routledge, 2011). In 2011 alone, new truth commissions were created in Brazil and Côte d'Ivoire.

[31] See United Nations Secretary General, *The Rule of Law and Transitional Justice in Post-conflict Societies*, UN Doc S/2004/616, 23 August 2004, para 8 (outlining the various tools and mechanisms of transitional justice).

[32] See R Nagy, 'Transitional Justice as a Global Project: Critical Reflections' (2008) 29 *Third World Quarterly* 275, 276.

As transitional justice emerged and evolved in its first two decades, notions of justice and reconciliation in transition largely focused on violations of physical integrity, as well as violations of civil and political rights more generally. While addressing these legacies of *physical violence* was and remains critical, it must not be forgotten that in many instances predecessor regimes also leave devastating legacies of *economic violence* in their wake, including widespread corruption, plunder of natural resources for personal or political gain, and other violations of economic and social rights. Thus, for example, Zaire accumulated over $12 billion in debt under the dictator Mobutu Sese Seko with new loans being made even after Zaire had virtually stopped paying its debts and in the face of massive and flagrant corruption.[33] In all, Mobutu is estimated to have embezzled some $4 billion of his nation's wealth.[34] When Philippine dictator Ferdinand Marcos was ousted from power in 1986, he went into exile with over $5 billion, having stolen one-third of the Philippines' foreign loans.[35] The apartheid government in South Africa amassed $21 billion in debt even as it brutally repressed much of its population.[36] Under the Argentinean military junta that killed some 30,000 people, foreign debt rose from $8 billion to $46 billion, and the proceeds from many of the loans never even made it to Argentina, but stayed in bank accounts in London.[37]

In sum, it is a rare despotic regime that manages to brutally repress its people without at the same time feeling at liberty to steal from them as well. Despite this, with few exceptions, the first decades of transitional justice are characterised by an almost exclusive focus on physical violence – murder, rape, torture, etc – while questions of economic justice and economic violence have largely been pushed to the margins, or treated as mere context to help understand why the violations of physical integrity took place.[38] Thus, for example, Latin American truth commissions in Argentina, Uruguay and Chile largely focused on violations of civil and political rights, passing over the role of economic crimes in the violence that was perpetrated.[39] The much-lauded South African truth commission focused on murder, torture and other egregious acts of bodily harm, but placed less emphasis on the economic and structural violence of the apartheid system itself, and only those who had suffered 'gross violations of human rights, including killing, abduction, torture, or ill-treatment' qualified as 'victims'.[40]

There are certainly exceptions to this trend, and in recent years an increasing number of truth commissions have in fact begun to pay attention to legacies of economic violence. For example, in Sierra Leone the truth commission took a close look at the relationship between corruption, conflict and natural resources, issuing a number of recommendations keyed to the reduction of potential economic violence in the future.[41] In

[33] J Hanlon, '"Illegitimate" Loans: Lenders, Not Borrowers, are Responsible' (2006) 27 *Third World Quarterly* 211, 215.

[34] Okeke (n 11) 1500.

[35] Hanlon (n 33) 215.

[36] ibid, 218.

[37] ibid, 216.

[38] See Z Miller, 'Effects of Invisibility: In Search of the "Economic" in Transitional Justice' (2008) 2 *International Journal of Transitional Justice* 266.

[39] J Cavallaro and S Albuja, 'The Lost Agenda: Economic Crimes and Truth Commissions in Latin America and Beyond' in K McEvoy and L McGregor (eds), *Transitional Justice from Below, Grassroots Activism and the Struggle for Change* (Oxford, Hart Publishing, 2008).

[40] P De Greiff and R Duthie, 'Repairing the Past: Reparations for Victims of Human Rights Violations' in P De Greiff (ed), *The Handbook on Reparations* (Oxford, Oxford University Press, 2006) 8.

[41] See generally *Witness to Truth, Report of the Sierra Leone Truth and Reconciliation Commission*, vol II (2004) 27.

East Timor, the Commission for Reception, Truth, and Reconciliation, often known by its Portuguese acronym CAVR, explored in some depth violations of economic and social rights, including the rights to an adequate standard of living, health and education, under the Indonesian occupation.[42] Truth commissions in Chad, Ghana, Liberia, Kenya and the Solomon Islands have also looked at various facets of economic violence under predecessor regimes.[43] This small bedrock of practice has been accompanied by a growing interest among both scholars and practitioners in grappling with the legal and policy dilemmas inherent in using transitional justice tools to address legacies of economic violence.[44]

A Odious and Illegitimate Debt

Even with the growing interest in using the tools of transitional justice to address different facets of economic violence, the question of so-called 'odious' and 'illegitimate' debts has only rarely been addressed by formal transitional justice mechanisms and institutions.[45] Under the classic doctrine of odious debt as articulated by legal scholar Alexander Sack in the 1920s, a state may unilaterally repudiate debts that were (1) not consented to by a state's people, (2) were not used for the benefit of the people, and (3) where the regime's creditors had knowledge of the aforementioned facts.[46] The Sackian conception of odious debt would therefore not include a debt simply because it was incurred by an abusive regime unless the other conditions are met. The question of whether this traditional definition should be extended to cover *all* of the debts incurred by repressive regimes is a topic of some debate in the literature, with some arguing that 'because of fungibility, all loans to odious regimes and dictators should be classed as odious, even if the ostensible purpose was permissible'.[47] Other scholars and activists have also spoken of 'illegitimate debt', a far broader category of debt that attempts to bring into focus the responsibility of the lender rather than just the borrower. It has been argued to include loans that broadly support dictatorships and even loans for failed development projects that caused social or environmental damage.[48] This chapter does not take a position on this broader definitional debate except to note that, as a practical matter in the transitional justice context, those instances where the debt–human rights violations nexus is tightest, involving the most simple causal chain, will probably provide the source of the most promising work for pioneering transitional justice mechanisms.

[42] *Chega!, The Report of the Commission for Reception, Truth and Reconciliation in Timor Leste (CAVR), Final Report* (2005) part 7.9.

[43] I have elsewhere explored the work of these pioneering truth commissions in greater detail. See D Sharp, 'Economic Violence in the Practice of African Truth Commissions and Beyond' in Sharp (ed) (n 1) 79.

[44] See, eg, L Arbour, 'Economic and Social Justice for Societies in Transition' (2007) 40 *New York University Journal of International Law and Politics* 1, 4; the entire volume of 2 *International Journal of Transitional Justice* (2008); P De Greiff and R Duthie (eds), *Transitional Justice and Development: Making Connections* (New York, Social Science Resource Council, 2009); Sharp (ed) (n 1).

[45] One striking exception is that of the South African Truth and Reconciliation Commission, which recommended that the government repudiate its apartheid-era debts.

[46] See A Gelpern, 'What Iraq and Argentina Might Learn from Each Other' (2005–06) 6 *Chicago Journal of International Law* 391, 403.

[47] Hanlon (n 33), 221; cf D Gray, 'Devilry, Complicity, and Greed: Transitional Justice and Odious Debts' (2007) 70 *Law and Contemporary Problems* 137 (arguing against an expansion of the odious debt doctrine to cover all debts of odious regimes).

[48] See Hanlon (n 33) 218.

Despite the long pedigree of the concept of odious debt, there are but few examples of its application in practice.[49] Indeed, after some scholarly interest in the 1920s, the concept languished for decades until it was revived in the late 1990s with the Jubilee 2000 movement,[50] receiving a further boost after the US-led ouster of Saddam Hussein when some scholars and policymakers suggested that Iraq should not have to pay Saddam-era debts.[51] Nevertheless, even with increasing attention in activist, academic and policy circles, the concept has failed to gain firm traction as a matter of international law, which provides that, as a general matter, states are legally responsible for repaying past debts.[52] Moreover, even in those states that would undoubtedly have had a very strong argument for the repudiation of debt accumulated under a previous regime, South Africa, Iraq and Nigeria, for example, successor regimes have generally chosen to either continue payment and/or renegotiate with creditors rather than repudiate. It appears that in practice, fear of alienating capital markets and the relative success of attempts to renegotiate often trump any moral aversion to repayment of at least some of the loans.[53]

Thus, even while both are ultimately tied to fundamental human rights and questions of economic justice, formal transitional justice mechanisms such as trials and truth commissions and procedures for addressing odious and illegitimate debt have largely operated on separate tracks in the post-conflict context. Insofar as the tools of transitional justice might prove useful for grappling with the moral, political and legal dilemmas created by debt, this separate-tracks approach represents a lost opportunity. While transitional justice is not equipped to fully resolve questions of sovereign debt, transitional justice tools could nevertheless be mobilised in ways that would meaningfully advance the dialogue and discourse on debt and human rights in transitional contexts, help establish a degree of accountability for the practices that helped to produce odious and illegitimate debts in the first place, and possibly even help to set a fruitful policy agenda for moving forward.

To begin, transitional justice is intimately associated with discourses and practices of accountability. Prosecutions are often said to be necessary to end impunity and thereby deter future abusers. Prosecuting those responsible for things like widespread murder and torture before a tribunal while failing to take similar steps in cases of corrupt leaders responsible for odious debts and other economic crimes can therefore only serve to reinforce impunity for economic violence. At a minimum, therefore, accountability for odious debts should be pursued by prosecuting officials responsible. At the same time, accountability for economic crimes that can be traced to the creation of odious and illegitimate debt should not be limited to prosecutions alone. In some transitional contexts, vetting procedures have been employed to minimise the number of former rights abusers who end up in positions of power in the new regime. In the context of odious and illegitimate debts, vetting could be used to make sure that officials who committed economic

[49] See L Buchheit et al, 'The Dilemma of Odious Debts' (2007) 56 *Duke Law Journal* 1201, 1208–20 (reviewing the history of the application of the doctrine).

[50] M Kremer and S Jayachandran, 'Odious Debt: When Dictators Borrow, Who Repays the Loan?' (2003) 21(2) *The Brookings Review*.

[51] C Ochoa, 'From Odious Debt to Odious Finance: Avoiding the Externalities of a Functional Odious Debt Doctrine' (2008) 49 *Harvard Human Rights Journal* 109, 119.

[52] One possible exception to this default rule may be debts that violate *jus cogens* norms. See S Michalowski and JP Bohoslavsky, 'Ius Cogens, Transitional Justice and Other Trends of the Debate on Odious Debts: A Response to the World Bank Discussion Paper on Odious Debts' (2009) 48 *Columbia Journal of Transnational Law* 59, 61.

[53] See Gelpern (n 46) 407.

crimes in connection with odious and illegitimate debts are excluded from new governmental positions.

Extending the scope of accountability mechanisms from physical to economic violence would of course cost money. In this regard, it is worth noting that transitional regimes have occasionally pursued asset recovery schemes in an attempt to return to state coffers money that was embezzled by former regime members. While not all money squirreled away in the proverbial Swiss bank account will be traceable to the accumulation of odious sovereign debt, it has been argued that asset recovery schemes might generally help newly established regimes to pay for the broader range of accountability mechanisms that are required under the rubric of transitional justice.[54]

Beyond the formal accountability of the courtroom, transitional justice initiatives have also employed a variety of mechanisms relating to the need for truth telling and fact finding. In this regard, truth commissions could play a useful role when it comes to questions of odious and illegitimate debt. Though still more the exception than the rule, an increasing number of truth commissions have begun to delve into the world of economic crimes. An early example of this, Chad, had a dedicated economic crimes section tasked with examining corrupt practices of former president Habré and his entourage.[55] While the Chadian Commission appeared to lack the time, money and expertise in forensic accounting to properly unravel the maze of presidential accounts used to embezzle public money for private gain, properly resourced commissions may have better success in the future. As a more recent example, in Liberia, the truth commission drew up a list of those individuals suspected of corruption and other economic crimes and recommended further investigation and, if warranted, prosecution by the new government.[56] The efforts of commissions in Chad and Liberia were not, of course, focused on economic crimes relating to odious and illegitimate debt per se, but there is no a priori reason why a truth commission might not play a useful fact-finding role in this regard. In so doing, a commission might also help establish whether certain debts were in fact odious, in the sense that the money involved was not used for the benefit of the people now expected to pay it back, or only debts that happen to have been incurred by odious regimes.

The work of a truth commission in establishing facts and a narrative of conflict bears an important relationship to broader projects of history and memory. Because the work of truth commissions is often tightly circumscribed by time, work relating to public memory and memorials that builds upon a commission's work can play an important role in furthering the goals of transitional justice. In this regard, the 'External Debt Museum' of Argentina[57] provides a pioneering example of how future generations might come to understand historical connections between debt and a number of social justice issues.

Beyond establishing a public record of the facts, the work of a truth commission in regard to odious and illegitimate debt could pay dividends in other meaningful ways. For example, even if, as in the case of South Africa or Iraq, a regime chooses not to repudiate its debt, fact finding carried out by a truth commission tending to establish that certain tranches of debt are associated with nefarious activities might help in negotiations with

[54] See R Carranza, 'Plunder and Pain: Should Transitional Justice Engage with Corruption and Economic Crimes?' (2008) 2 *International Journal of Transitional Justice* 310.

[55] See generally Commission d'enquête nationale du ministère Tchadien de la justice, *Les crimes et détournements de l'ex-président Habré et de ses complices* (Paris, L'Harmattan, 1993).

[56] Liberian Truth Commission, *Truth and Reconciliation Commission, Consolidated Final Report* (2009).

[57] See details on the museum at www.museodeladeuda.com/index2.php, accessed 30 August 2012.

creditors to reduce or reschedule debt. Even if linking specific debts to specific illegitimate activities is not always possible, the painstaking work of a truth commission in this general area might increase the extent to which renegotiation of debt occurs within the shadow of the odious debt doctrine. While a truth commission would not likely have the ability to sanction external actors associated with the problem of odious or illegitimate debt, fact finding done in this regard might be used to 'name and shame' complicit lenders, which could lead to policy changes. The downside to these approaches is that they would likely involve slow, time-consuming work, and truth commissions often take years to get up and running. At the same time, the issue of debt is often one of immediate and pressing urgency for new regimes in the early phases of the transition.

Truth commissions may also play a useful role in terms of establishing a platform for key institutional and policy reforms under the new regime. In many contexts, truth commissions have a large soapbox on which to stand. This can be used to issue recommendations relating to the creation or reform of anti-corruption commissions, transparency initiatives and the like, with the work of truth commissions in Liberia and Sierra Leone serving as two examples. Using this same soapbox, truth commissions might also play an important role in providing an impetus for the creation of reparations programmes, whereby lenders and corporate actors complicit in the misdeeds of a previous regime would pay monies into a reparations fund for victims.[58] Of course, it is a sad fact that in all too many countries even the best recommendations issued by truth commissions often go unheeded by the new government, to say nothing of relevant members of the international community. It therefore bears emphasising that establishing a degree of truth and accountability for the practices that led to odious and illegitimate debt will ultimately require not just the political will and action of national actors, but of international lenders and multilateral institutions as well.

In many instances, it may often prove difficult for transitional justice mechanisms to link actions related to the creation of odious and illegitimate debt with specific violations of human rights.[59] Such work will require different sorts of expertise, and forms of evidence beyond the victim testimony and forensic data upon which truth commissions have traditionally relied. That said, the pioneering work of some NGOs linking government corruption with a failure to progressively realise economic and social rights might serve as a useful precedent.[60] And given that international accountability regimes for corruption and other financial crimes are generally more robust than those relating to economic and social rights, it may be possible to hold officials responsible for offences related to corruption even where accountability for human rights crimes proves problematic.[61] Yet even if the full scope and complexity of odious and illegitimate debt remains out of reach, to the extent that transitional justice mechanisms can shed some light on economic crimes

[58] See Bohoslavsky and Torelly (n 2).

[59] For an example of just how casually complex this may be, see ibid.

[60] Human Rights Watch has published a number of reports looking at the linkages between natural resources, corruption and violations of economic and social rights. See, eg, Human Rights Watch, *Chop Fine: The Human Rights Impact of Local Government Corruption and Mismanagement in Rivers State, Nigeria* (New York, HRW, January 2007) (contending that the local government in Rivers State, Nigeria has violated its duty to progressively realise rights to health and education through widespread and flagrant corruption and mismanagement of oil revenues); Human Rights Watch, *Some Transparency, No Accountability: The Use of Oil Revenue in Angola and Its Impact on Human Rights* (New York, HRW, January 2004) (arguing that, due at least in part to mismanagement and corruption, the government of Angola has impeded Angolans' ability to enjoy their economic and social rights, including healthcare and education).

[61] C Albin-Lackey (n 1) 154.

involving the misuse of proceeds from loans, this would be an important step forward in helping to understand the linkages between corruption, economic crimes and violations of economic and social rights under international law.

III THE POLICY RELEVANCE OF A HUMAN RIGHTS PERSPECTIVE

While there are important actual and potential linkages between sovereign debt, human rights and transitional justice, international discourse on questions of sovereign debt frequently fails to consider these connections. There are small signs that this is changing, with some efforts at normative development within the United Nations, though there is much work to be done.[62] Development of a stronger human rights-based perspective in matters of sovereign debt is nevertheless critical as it would serve to further establish justice and individual rights as an important ground for understanding and addressing the debt problem. In so doing, we move away from simple and abstract considerations of debt management and sustainability and towards a focus on individual human harms and impacts. A human rights perspective is therefore important because it asks us to consider not just the formal rights of creditors and the obligations of sovereign borrowers in matters of lending, repayment and forgiveness, but also the fundamental human rights and dignity of those very individuals who are supposed to benefit from the loans in the first place.

Ex ante, this means that lenders and borrowers alike need to think about the potential human rights impact of new loans, including the realistic chances that a loan will contribute to improvement of human rights standards, or at a minimum, will not actively contribute to their worsening. If taken seriously, this might lead to the conduct of human rights impact assessments at the outset that look to the likelihood that any given loan will help a government realise human rights.[63] Such forward-looking preventative efforts would go a long way towards ensuring that the tools of transitional justice do not need to be marshalled in transitional contexts to address the economic crimes that have led to situations of odious and illegitimate debt.

To be sure, a human rights perspective does not serve to cut the Gordian knot of all of the many policy dilemmas created by both high levels of debt and the understandable desire to prevent contributing to odious debt in the future. For example, does a human-rights approach favour, as has been argued, greater use of loan conditionalities in an attempt to mitigate negative human rights impacts going forward?[64] Or does a human rights approach demand that governments be given the breathing room to develop locally grown solutions to poverty even where these do not meet the policy expectations and best practices of the IFIs? While lenders should, as a moral and policy matter, refrain from providing assistance that will foreseeably impact human rights in a negative way or prop up corrupt autocrats, experience also shows that internationals

[62] See, eg, Human Rights Council, Report of the Independent Expert on the Effects of Foreign Debt and other Related International Financial Obligations of States on the Full Enjoyment of all Human Rights, Particularly Economic, Social and Cultural Rights, Cephas Lumina, A/HRC/20/23, 10 April 2011.

[63] I have elaborated upon this idea in the context of World Bank-sponsored extractives projects. See D Sharp, 'Requiem for a Pipedream: Oil, the World Bank, and the Need for Human Rights Assessments' (2011) 25 *Emory International Law Review* 379.

[64] See, eg, Barry (n 10) (arguing that objections advanced against conditionality are unconvincing and that conditionality warrants serious exploration).

cannot substantially alleviate issues of poverty by imposing reforms from the outside. This is a difficult needle to thread, and in many ways a human rights perspective only serves to complicate matters.

Rather than provide answers to such questions, the value of a human rights perspective in matters of sovereign debt is that it forces us to ask the right questions. In so doing, it can be hoped that a human rights perspective would help participants throughout the system to strike a better and more equitable balance than has been the case in the past, and achieve a greater degree of accountability and truth in those instances where past efforts have failed. To this extent, a human rights perspective would be a useful tool in helping to address the failures of governance that contribute to crushing poverty in many of the world's most indebted nations.

5

Establishing Liability for Financial Complicity in International Crimes

NADIA BERNAZ

I INTRODUCTION

TAKING THE STATUTE of the International Criminal Court (ICC) as representing a consensus on the issue, states have agreed on the definitions of four distinct international crimes: genocide, crimes against humanity, war crimes and the crime of aggression.[1] International criminals, usually individuals, may be prosecuted by international bodies, such as the ICC or ad hoc tribunals such as the International Criminal Tribunals for the Former Yugoslavia and Rwanda or the Special Court for Sierra Leone; or by domestic courts on the basis of domestic statutes incorporating internationally defined law and principles. A glance at the case law of international criminal tribunals shows that international crimes are generally committed by state (or state-like organisation) agents, or members of rebel groups. State involvement is not an element of the definition of international crimes, except for the crime of aggression which can only be committed 'by a person in a position effectively to exercise control over or to direct the political or military action of a State'.[2] In practice most of these crimes are committed in the context of conflicts, international or non-international, or civil unrest where at least one state is involved. Because of the contextual element they require, such as a 'widespread or systematic attack against a civilian population' for crimes against humanity, and although the number of victims does not formally form part of the elements of the crimes, international crimes tend to be large scale.

Therefore, from a purely practical point of view, the commission of crimes of that magnitude necessarily requires finance to pay for the equipment and human resources international crimes entail. The perpetrators who actually kill or torture victims are usually paid and need food, shelter, vehicles and weapons. The highest-ranked officials who plan operations also need salaries or compensation of some sort, as well as intelligence and surveillance equipment. In short, international crimes cannot be committed without capital.[3] At a time when funds circulate from one country to another in an instant, and states borrow on financial markets, funds used to finance international crimes can come from virtually anywhere, and the lenders may be both public and private entities and

[1] Statute of the ICC, Articles 6, 7, 8 and 8*bis*.

[2] Statute of the ICC, Article 8*bis*.

[3] As noted, for example, in the Final Report of the South African Truth and Reconciliation Commission (1998) vol 4, ch 2, para 161.

even, although more rarely, mere individuals. Dowell-Jones and Kinley point to the necessity, when looking at the broad subject of global finance and human rights, to depart from the 'traditional human rights approaches to the global economy'.[4] They consider that:

> Exploring these deeper, more technical macro-level linkages within and between the financial markets and human rights necessitates moving away from thinking about rights solely in the narrow terms of individual entitlements and direct causality or reasonably proximate complicity to examining the structural conditions that play a role in the ability of responsible agents to fulfill their human rights obligations.[5]

Looking at the issue of financial liability, however, primarily implies following the traditional approach which consists in linking a violation to acts or omissions of an entity or individual, to explore the micro-level and not the macro-level linkages. This is because establishing liability before a court requires a high degree of certainty and loose connections by themselves cannot be enough. While this micro-level approach is imperfect and perhaps ill-adapted to the area of finance and human rights, for the time being it is the only one acceptable when it comes to legal consequences. In other words, for a human rights lawyer, discussing liability for financial complicity can be done while remaining within one's comfort zone. This is not to say that the macro level is irrelevant to the discussion. If nothing else, it provides much needed context. However, ascertaining the precise role of macro-level linkages in the determination of liability is an area in which more research is needed.

Furthermore, public finance is not the only source of funding for conflicts and gross human rights violations. Going even further upstream, the companies that provide equipment and services to regimes committing international crimes also have financial backing. Therefore in an inquiry as to who funds these crimes attention should also be directed to corporate finance. From a purely factual point of view, investigating the origins of the funds that make international crimes possible in a wide sense leads to a virtually endless list of potential legal and natural persons who would be 'responsible'.

Establishing liability in law, civil or criminal, is a different matter which requires first and foremost a careful examination of causation. For example, in order to be deemed to have *caused* the eventual criminal conduct, actions or omissions of the actor in question have to pass strict tests, such as the 'but for' test. Other key elements that have to be present include knowledge or at least foreseeability, and proximity.[6] Financial complicity in international crimes is extremely difficult to establish and to complicate matters further the case law is still scarce: there is no international case law as such and in theory, just as for corporate (and not specifically financial) complicity in international crimes, 'different courts in different jurisdictions could reach different conclusions on similar fact situations'.[7] It must also be noted that those who provide the funds necessary for the commission of international crimes are not necessarily corporations. They can be states, groups or individuals. State responsibility for international crimes, however, is outside the scope of this chapter. This is because the mechanisms pertaining to state responsibility are distinct from the mechanisms pertaining to corporate or individual liability. Moreover, state

[4] M Dowell-Jones and D Kinley, 'Minding the Gap: Global Finance and Human Rights' (2011) 25 *Ethics & International Affairs* 183, 189.

[5] ibid.

[6] International Commission of Jurists, *Corporate Complicity and Legal Accountability* (2008) vol 1, 8.

[7] ibid, 10.

criminal responsibility does not exist under current international law.[8] That said, this does not exclude the possible liability of state or even international financial institution (IFI) officials. Similarly, while the substantial sums involved make it more likely that corporations can be financially complicit, this does not necessarily exclude liability of senior management staff. As will be seen below, individuals have been prosecuted for their financial contribution to criminal regimes.

When discussing corporate involvement in international crimes one usually refers to complicity. As indicated above, it is the nature of international crimes to be primarily committed by state or state-like agents, or members of rebel groups. In this context, corporations trading with, or financial sponsors of, these states or groups are not the main perpetrators but are complicit in the crimes committed. They make them possible and they also gain capital in the process but they generally are not the masterminds behind international crimes.

To fully grasp the complexity of this area of law, it is useful to recall that to a large extent corporate complicity in human rights violations in general is a new area of law with currently very few cases to point to, as will be discussed in Section II. Corporate complicity in international crimes, in other words for especially gross human rights violations, is a narrower area. As pointed out by van den Herik and Černič:

> International criminal law has a rather succinct area of application. With its three [now four] core crimes of genocide, crimes against humanity and war crimes, the vertical or modern international criminal law is rather concise in scope. Human rights law in turn spans a whole array of different rights, civil and political rights, economic, social and cultural rights, as well as group rights.[9]

Moreover, within the area of corporate complicity, financial complicity in international crimes, which entails providing the funds that made the crimes possible, is even narrower. Nevertheless, interrogations about the liability of financiers and lenders of criminal regimes are not new. For example, following the Second World War, Rasche, the chairman of Dresdner Bank, and Puhl, deputy to the president of the German Reichsbank, were prosecuted for their financial support of the Nazi regime.[10] These cases are explored in some detail in Section III as they provide an entry point to the following fundamental question: whether lending money and providing commodities can be distinguished for the purpose of establishing complicity. In other words, when it comes to lenders, should financial complicity be distinguished from corporate complicity in general, or should money be treated as any other commodity?

Because the law on financial complicity in international crimes is in its infancy, it is of use to look at developments in other areas in order to see the direction in which the law could go in the future. Indeed, while there is still no consensus on mechanisms by which financial backers of international criminals could be held liable for the crucial role they play, there is now a robust set of rules to establish liability in the context of financing terrorist activities. The final section considers the lessons that can be learnt from such

[8] See L van den Herik, 'Corporations as Future Subjects of the International Criminal Court: An Exploration of the Counterarguments and Consequences' in C Stahn and L van den Herik (eds), *Future Perspectives on International Criminal Justice* (The Hague, TMC Asser Press, 2009) 354–56.

[9] L van den Herik and JL Černič, 'Regulating Corporations under International Law: from Human Rights to International Criminal Law and Back Again' (2010) 8 *Journal of International Criminal Justice* 725, 741.

[10] *Trials of War Criminals Before the Nuernberg Military Tribunals Under Control Council Law No. 10*, vols XII–XIV, 'The Ministries Case' (Washington, United States Government Printing Office, 1952).

developments and explores the appropriateness of calling for international legislation on financial complicity in international crimes, for example in the form of a treaty.

II CORPORATE COMPLICITY IN INTERNATIONAL CRIMES

The involvement of business entities in international crimes may give rise to two distinct forms of liability: the liability of the legal person, the company; or the liability of natural persons, company officials, senior managers, directors or possibly lower-level employees of the company in question. Whether the company itself or individuals working for the company are held liable depends on whether corporate liability is recognised by the jurisdiction in which the facts are being examined. By and large international criminal tribunals do not have jurisdiction over legal persons and only individuals can be held criminally liable for international crimes before such tribunals.[11] The situation is much different with regards to the domestic law of a variety of countries which, additionally, offers both criminal and civil law routes to hold business liable for international crimes.[12]

A No Recognition of Corporate Complicity before International Criminal Tribunals

The exclusion of legal persons as entities who may be prosecuted by the ICC is not a simple omission but rather the result of intense negotiations. Article 23 of the final Draft Statute produced by the Preparatory Committee before the start of the Rome Conference in 1998 contained these two bracketed paragraphs:

> [5. The Court shall also have jurisdiction over legal persons, with the exception of States, when the crimes committed were committed on behalf of such legal persons or by their agencies or representatives.
> 6. The criminal responsibility of legal persons shall not exclude the criminal responsibility of natural persons who are perpetrators or accomplices in the same crimes.][13]

The document also contains this comment:

> There is a deep divergence of views as to the advisability of including criminal responsibility of legal persons in the Statute. Many delegations are strongly opposed, whereas some strongly favour its inclusion. Others have an open mind. Some delegations hold the view that providing for only the civil or administrative responsibility/liability of legal persons could provide a middle ground. This avenue, however, has not been thoroughly discussed. Some delegations, who favour the inclusion of legal persons, hold the view that this expression should be extended to organizations lacking legal status.

Early on in the negotiations in Rome and well aware of this divergence of views, the French delegation submitted a watered down version of Article 23(5), aiming at going 'at least as far as the Nuremberg Charter, which had provided for the criminal responsibility

[11] The Statute of the Special Court for Sierra Leone does not explicitly exclude legal persons from its jurisdiction and therefore seems to have jurisdiction over them. That said, this has never materialised and only natural persons have been prosecuted before the Court.

[12] A Ramasastry and R Thompson, 'Commerce, Crime and Conflict. Legal Remedies for Private Sector Liability for Grave Breaches of International Law' (2006) FAFO Institute for Applied International Studies.

[13] UN Doc A/CONF.183/2/Add.1, 49.

of "criminal organizations"'.[14] The proposal read as follows: '5. When the crime was committed by a natural person on behalf or with the assent of a group or organization of every kind, the Court may declare that this group or organization is a criminal organization'.[15] This version gave rise to interesting discussions among the delegates. Some were clearly opposed to any form of liability for anything other than natural persons. Others supported the French proposal but doubted that a compromise could be reached in the limited time available. Tanzania actually favoured the initial draft and not the more general French proposal in those terms:

> To take a specific example, one of the allegations concerning the genocide in Rwanda was that there had been companies in whose warehouses arms bought with the profits of those companies had been stored and from which they had been distributed, with the full knowledge of the representatives of those companies. Tanzania believe[s], therefore, that not only should criminal responsibility be attributed to representatives in their individual capacity, but that the entity itself should be held criminally liable, if only by paying fines or by being liquidated.[16]

A later working paper further elaborated on the practicalities of recognising the responsibility of legal persons as well as natural persons. By this point, it was made clear that what was meant by 'juridical person' was 'a corporation whose concrete and real objective is private ends'.[17] Hence what was at stake from then on was the inclusion of corporate liability for international crimes in the Rome Statute establishing the International Criminal Court. Eventually, and after discussions during which no consensus emerged either in favour of the inclusion of corporate liability in the Statute or of the introduction of the notion of criminal organisations, the idea was dropped altogether and the bracketed draft paragraphs of Article 23 on jurisdiction over legal persons were deleted.[18] The ICC would have jurisdiction over individuals only and this is reflected in the final version of Article 23.

This does not mean that corporate crimes cannot be examined by the ICC. Indeed nothing prevents corporate officials, who are natural persons, from being prosecuted. However, due to the nature of international crimes discussed above, corporations and therefore corporate officials are often only complicit in the commission of international crimes, as opposed to being the main perpetrators, those who are said to be the masterminds behind the crimes. With this in mind, and because the ICC is meant to prosecute only those who bear the greatest responsibility in the commission of crimes, it is unlikely that corporate officials will ever face trial at the ICC.[19] For all practical purposes and as the law stands, domestic legal systems alone deal with corporate involvement in international crimes.

[14] UN Doc A/CONF.183/C.1/SR.1, 5.

[15] UN Doc A/CONF.183/C.1/L.3, 1.

[16] UN Doc A/CONF.183/C.1/SR.1, 8.

[17] UN Doc A/CONF.183/C.1/WGGP/L.5/Rev.1, 2.

[18] UN Doc A/CONF.183/C.1/L.58, 10. See D Stoitchkova, *Towards Corporate Liability in International Criminal Law* (Antwerp, Intersentia, 2010) 16–17.

[19] Although international criminal tribunals may sanction accomplices, it is unlikely that the ICC would trigger its jurisdiction against a presumed accomplice on this basis only.

B The Notion of Corporate Complicity before Domestic Courts

Under domestic law, corporate complicity in international crimes can be established under civil law or criminal law. Under the latter, prosecutions may target individuals who have held positions of authority within the company and/or the company itself, which may depend on whether the concept of criminal responsibility of legal persons exists in the jurisdiction in question. At first sight it may seem surprising that international crimes, which are widely viewed as the worst crimes possible, may be dealt with through a civil lawsuit, since civil claims are essentially about financial compensation for damage incurred by the claimant. It feels somehow inappropriate that a company held responsible for complicity in such atrocities could escape criminal prosecution. Certainly, this would not be acceptable for individuals, yet most cases involving corporate complicity in international crimes have been civil cases. As such, both criminal law and the law of civil remedies deserve to be looked at.

In a 2008 report the International Commission of Jurists summarised the elements that need to be present for a company to be held complicit in international crimes. Their analysis is relevant both for criminal and civil law. They broke down the elements into three categories: causation or contribution; knowledge and foreseeability; and proximity.[20] In turn, causation or contribution is broken down into three sub-categories depending on the degree of contribution. The most straightforward contribution is when the company is said to have 'enabled' the crimes

> if the specific abuses carried out by the principal actor would not have happened without the company's contribution. There are always many causes that contribute to a particular outcome, but in this situation, the company's conduct must be at least one such crucial ingredient – a necessary, though usually not the only, factor in the perpetration of the abuses.[21]

In the context of financial complicity, this can cover, for example, the act of granting a loan to perpetrators to buy military equipment, which is later used to commit war crimes, and which could not have been purchased without the loan.

The second form of contribution is when the company 'exacerbates' the abuses. In other words,

> the principal perpetrator would still have carried out the human rights abuses, but the company's conduct either increased the range of human rights abuses committed by the principal actor, the number of victims, or the severity of the harm suffered by the victims (ie exacerbated or aggravated the harm).[22]

This can cover the act of granting a loan to buy new military equipment, which makes the abuse worse due to the fact, for example, that it allows the perpetrators to cover larger distances and thus to commit abuses against a larger number of people.

The third and final form of contribution is when the company 'facilitates' the abuses. These are circumstances where

> the human rights abuses would still have occurred without the assistance or encouragement of the company, but where the company's contribution made it easier to carry out the abuses or

[20] International Commission of Jurists (n 6) 8.
[21] ibid, 11.
[22] ibid, 12.

> changed the way in which the abuses were carried out, even if it did not aggravate or exacerbate the harm.[23]

Going back to our example, this could cover the act of granting a loan allowing the perpetrators to buy weapons or equipment, when otherwise they could have used their resources to fund other types of projects. In that way, the loan 'facilitates' the abuses even though it could be difficult to prove with the required degree of certainty that this necessarily aggravated the harm.

The report then proceeds to discuss three types of situations which generally do not amount to contribution to the abuses in the legal sense. These are 'silent presence', 'receiving an economic benefit', and 'paying taxes'. Silent presence refers to a situation where companies 'have business operations in countries where gross human rights abuses are occurring and they fail to intervene with the authorities to try to stop or prevent the abuses'.[24] Receiving an economic benefit usually goes hand in hand with silent presence. As is explained in the report,

> There are at least two situations in which this might arise. First, a company might earn a profit from buying or selling goods or services to or from an actor that is committing gross human rights abuses. Second, a company might benefit commercially from a favourable business environment created in a country by another actor, enabling it to establish lucrative operations in the country. For example, a government might commit gross human rights abuses that provide the company with an infrastructure or access to resources.

Receiving an economic benefit is generally not enough to be held legally responsible for complicity in international crimes. Similarly, paying taxes to a government or a levy to a rebel group is usually not enough to entail legal responsibility.

In cases where there is sufficient evidence that a company contributed to the abuses, the next step is to prove that they wished for the abuses to occur. Alternatively, it must be established that they knew or should have known that their acts or omissions would bring about the abuses. These are referred to as 'knowledge' and 'foreseeability'. On this point criminal law and the law of civil remedies differ but, importantly, neither area of law 'require[s] a desire to cause harm on the part of a company'.[25]

Once causation and knowledge or foreseeability have been established, the final element necessary to establish corporate complicity both in criminal and civil law is proximity, which means that 'the closer – or more proximate – a company is, in time and space and relationship, to those who carry out the human rights abuses or those who suffer the abuses, the more likely it is that the company could be held legally responsible when it is complicit'.[26] The factors that may be used to establish proximity include 'geographical proximity', 'economic and political relationships', 'legal relationships', and the 'intensity, duration and texture of relationships'.[27]

Despite the relative clarity surrounding the elements necessary to establish corporate complicity in international crimes, as discussed in detail in the International Commission of Jurists' report, the legal proceedings that have actually resulted in a company being held liable for such crimes, either criminally or under the law of civil remedies, are few.

[23] ibid.
[24] ibid, 14.
[25] ibid, 19.
[26] ibid, 24.
[27] ibid, 25.

There are several reasons for this. First, as mentioned above, it is a relatively new area of the law, which concerns crimes of exceptional gravity which occur much less frequently than more traditional human rights violations such as violations of labour rights, even when they are of a serious nature. Second, despite extensive research on these questions in the past years, the law remains uncertain as exemplified by the judicial saga surrounding the *Kiobel v Royal Dutch Shell* case in the United States. Third, establishing liability often comes only after complex questions of jurisdiction have been dealt with. In other words, in a large number of cases courts never get to look into the issue of complicity and the cases are dismissed on jurisdictional grounds rather than on the merits. This is due to the fact that international crimes are generally not committed on the territory of the state where the claim or complaint has been filed, which means that courts are faced with the complex and multifaceted notion of extraterritoriality.[28] Numerous cases did not pass the hurdle of the jurisdictional stage.[29] Other cases, such as the complaint brought against the French companies Amesys and Qosmos for complicity in torture with the Gadaffi and al-Assad regimes respectively, are still ongoing.[30] Finally, one cannot ignore the political influence of the corporate and financial sectors, which may not look positively at the development of clear legal obligations and ensuing lawsuits, and may prefer to develop non-binding guidelines, such as the Equator Principles, instead.[31]

These difficulties are not limited to the process of establishing corporate liability for complicity in international crimes, but extend to the narrower notion of financial complicity as well. The next section focuses on financial complicity as a sub-form of corporate complicity in international crimes.

III FINANCIAL COMPLICITY IN INTERNATIONAL CRIMES

At the outset, it must be noted that the case law on financial complicity in international crimes is scarce and unsettled. As pointed out in the introduction, a company, a bank, an individual or a group of individuals may contribute financially to the commission of international crimes, directly or indirectly, in a variety of ways. This section explores these different ways using past or ongoing cases as illustrations, and attempts to establish the conditions under which liability for financial complicity may or should arise. Financial support may come in the form of a donation. However, and this is by far the most common occurrence, the financial contribution usually comes in the form of loans to the entity committing the crimes – usually a state – or to a company which, in turn, is selling goods or services to the entity committing the crimes. In these types of scenarios, lenders are selling money for a profit – interest – which raises questions about whether one should distinguish between money and commodities for the sake of establishing liability for financial complicity. Indeed, from a moral point of view it seems that there is little difference between those who granted loans to the Nazis to build concentration camps and

[28] For a detailed analysis of extraterritoriality, see N Bernaz, 'Enhancing Corporate Accountability for Human Rights Violations: Is Extraterritoriality the Magic Potion?' (2013) 117 *Journal of Business Ethics* 493.

[29] See, eg, *Jota v Texaco, Inc.*, 157 F.3d 153 (2d Cir. 1998); *Aguinda v Texaco, Inc.*, 142 F. Supp. 2d 534 (SDNY 2001).

[30] See the press releases of the FIDH (in French) on the Amesys case (www.fidh.org/La-justice-francaise-saisie-du, accessed 15 January 2013) and on the Qosmos case (www.fidh.org/La-FIDH-et-la-LDH-demandent-a-la, accessed 15 January 2013).

[31] The Equator Principles (2006), www.equator-principles.com/, accessed 15 January 2013.

those who sold them Zyklon B gas, which was used to kill over six million people in Auschwitz alone. However, in terms of establishing liability the law seems to distinguish between the two, a point vigorously challenged below.

The first judgment of significance on financial complicity in international crimes is the *Flick* judgment. The *Flick* trial was one of the subsequent Nuremberg trials conducted in Germany by the Allies in their respective zones of occupations under Control Council Law No 10. The trial was conducted by the United States against Friedrich Flick and five other leading officials of the Flick Concern or its subsidiary companies.[32] The Flick Concern was 'a large group of industrial enterprises . . . including coal and iron mines and steel producing and fabricating plants'. Two of the defendants, Friedrich Flick himself and Otto Steinbrinck, were members of the same group alternately called 'Friends of Himmler', 'Freundeskreis' (Circle of Friends), or the 'Keppler Circle'. This group,

> throughout the period of the Third Reich, worked closely with the SS, met frequently and regularly with its leaders, and furnished aid, advice, and support to the SS, financial and otherwise. This organization was composed of about thirty German business leaders, and a number of SS leaders, including Heinrich Himmler, head of the entire SS from 1929 to 1945.[33]

The indictment describes the scale of the financial support as follows:

> Each year from 1933 to 1945, the circle contributed about one million marks to Himmler to aid in financing the activities of the SS. During this period, the defendants Flick and Steinbrinck made and procured contributions by Flick and the Flick Concern to the SS through the circle, aggregating at least one hundred thousand marks annually for many years. Flick and the Flick Concern, by the action and procurement of Flick and Steinbrinck, also contributed substantial additional amounts to the SS over the years 1933 to 1945. Steinbrinck also procured substantial contributions by Vereinigte Stahlwerke A.G. and affiliated enterprises to the SS through the circle in the years 1940 through 1944.[34]

Flick and Steinbrinck were charged under count 4 of the indictment for, 'as members of the Keppler Circle or Friends of Himmler, with knowledge of its criminal activities, [having] contributed large sums to the financing of Die Schutzstaffen der Nationalsozialistischen Deutschen Arbeiterpartei [the SS]'. The SS had been declared a criminal organisation by the International Military Tribunal at Nuremberg. Therefore, the key element of this count is that the defendants knew of the criminal activities of the organisation they were directly funding, the SS. As the tribunal asserted in the *Flick* judgment, speaking about the SS,

> an organization which on a large scale is responsible for such crimes can be nothing else than criminal. One who knowingly by his influence and money contributes to the support thereof must, under settled legal principles, be deemed to be, if not a principal, certainly an accessory to such crimes.[35]

The question of knowledge was therefore central. The tribunal shows that at least initially the defendants may not have been fully aware of the extent of the crimes committed by the SS and might have viewed their financial contributions 'with some thought of cur-

[32] *Trials of War Criminals Before the Nuernberg Military Tribunals Under Control Council Law No 10*, vol VI 'The Flick Case' (Washington, United States Government Printing Office, 1952).

[33] ibid, 23.

[34] ibid, 24.

[35] ibid, 1217.

rying favor with a powerful State official with whom from time to time these industrialists might have to deal'.[36] Later, however, the crimes were well known and the financial support continued. This support enabled the SS to commit various atrocities. As the tribunal put it,

> It remains clear from the evidence that each of . . . [the defendants] gave to Himmler, the Reich Leader SS, a blank check. His criminal organization was maintained and we have no doubt that some of this money went to its maintenance. It seems to be immaterial whether it was spent on salaries or for lethal gas. So we are compelled to find from the evidence that both defendants are guilty on count four.[37]

Perhaps unsurprisingly, and although the International Commission of Jurists' template described above concerns corporate liability and not individual liability, the three elements the Commission have highlighted in their report are present in the *Flick* judgment. First, it was proved that the donations were substantial and as such clearly enabled the crimes, so causation is established. As pointed out by Bohoslavsky and Opgenhaffen, 'the key challenge is always to determine whether, without this contribution, the chain of causality would have been interrupted or whether the contribution had a substantial effect on the development of the financed activity'.[38] As seen above, Flick and Steinbrinck were contributing 10 per cent of the overall donations by the 'Friends of Himmler' and, according to the tribunal, 'a hundred thousand Reichsmarks even to a wealthy man was not then a trifling but a substantial contribution'.[39]

Second, the defendants knew of the criminal nature of the SS's activities, so knowledge or at the very least foreseeability is established. Third, the tribunal describes in detail the relation between the defendants and the Reich Leader SS Himmler, whom the defendants regularly met at dinners and other events. It seems to have been enough to convince the tribunal of the existence of sufficient proximity between the defendants and the crimes.

Interestingly, the tribunal points out that the defendants need not know the precise destination of the funds. What mattered was the fact that they contributed. This is a recurrent and central question when one looks at financial complicity in large-scale human rights violations, whether or not they amount to international crimes. Requiring the proof that the precise funds donated were used to commit a precise crime or human rights violation, which amounts to tracking the funds, is onerous for the claimants, can come up against bank secrecy and may bring most proceedings to an end.

The second case of significance in the area of financial complicity in international crimes is the *Ministries* case, which was also one of the subsequent Nuremberg trials conducted by the Americans.[40] Among the 21 defendants in the *Ministries* case were Karl Rasche, chairman of Dresdner Bank, and Emil Puhl, deputy to the president of the Reichsbank. Whereas in the *Flick* case the fact of donating money was deemed enough for criminal liability to be established, in the *Ministries* case the Court held firstly that Rasche's donations to Himmler's Circle of Friends could not give rise to his criminal liability. Arguably,

[36] ibid, 1220.

[37] ibid, 1221.

[38] JP Bohoslavsky and V Opgenhaffen, 'The Past and Present of Corporate Complicity: Financing the Argentinean Dictatorship' (2010) 23 *Harvard Human Rights Journal* 157, 172–73.

[39] The Flick Case (n 32), 1220.

[40] *Trials of War Criminals Before the Nuernberg Military Tribunals Under Control Council Law No 10*, vols XII–XIV, 'The Ministries Case' (Washington, United States Government Printing Office, 1952).

this is because of his lack of knowledge of the criminal acts committed by the SS.[41] In other words, while the tribunal inferred knowledge from the circumstances in *Flick*, it did not do so with regards to Rasche. It is rather difficult to ascertain whether this is due to different elements of evidence or whether the tribunal actually used a different test.[42]

Second, the Court held that providing loans could not be considered a criminal act either. After having established the role of Dresdner Bank's loans in enabling some of the SS slave labour programmes, the court begins by asserting that Rasche, an experienced banker, would not have lent money without knowledge of what it was for and that therefore he knew that his financial contribution was going to enable the commission of crimes.[43] The Court continues as follows:

> The real question is, is it a crime to make a loan, knowing or having good reason to believe that the borrower will use the funds in financing enterprises which are employed in using labor in violation of either national or international law? . . . A bank sells money or credit in the same manner as the merchandiser of any other commodity. It does not become a partner in enterprise, and the interest charged is merely the gross profit which the bank realizes from the transaction, out of which it must deduct its business costs, and from which it hopes to realize a net profit. Loans or sale of commodities to be used in an unlawful enterprise may well be condemned from a moral standpoint and reflect no credit on the part of the lender or seller in either case, but the transaction can hardly be said to be a crime. Our duty is to try and punish those guilty of violating international law, and we are not prepared to state that such loans constitute a violation of that law, nor has our attention been drawn to any ruling to the contrary.[44]

This conservative reasoning has since been criticised, notably by Ramasastry[45] and Bohoslavsky and Opgenhaffen, who argue that there should be liability 'for knowing that this money would contribute to the financial support of a particular state machinery through which crimes against humanity would be openly perpetrated, and yet granting the loans despite these highly probable consequences'.[46]

Despite various criticisms, more contemporary decisions have essentially followed the tribunal's reasoning with regards to Rasche. For example, in the *South African Apartheid Litigation* case before the United States federal courts, which is part of a larger case brought by South African claimants against a number of companies and banks for their role in enabling the crimes of the apartheid regime in South Africa, Scheindlin J distinguished between the provision of goods specially designed to kill, such as poisonous gas, and other goods which can be said to be 'fungible', such as building material and money.[47] She concluded:

> [S]upplying a violator of the law of nations with funds – even funds that could not have been obtained but for those loans – is not sufficiently connected to the primary violation to fulfil the *actus reus* requirement of aiding and abetting a violation of the law of nations.[48]

[41] ibid, vol XIV, 621–22.

[42] S Michalowski, 'No Complicity Liability For Funding Gross Human Rights Violations?' (2012) 30 *Berkeley Journal of International Law* 451, 478–79.

[43] The Ministries Case (n 40) 622.

[44] ibid.

[45] A Ramasastry, 'Corporate Complicity: From Nuremberg to Rangoon, An Examination of Forced Labor Cases and Their Impact on the Liability of Multinational Corporations' (2002) 91(20) *Berkeley Journal of International Law* 113.

[46] Bohoslavsky and Opgenhaffen (n 38) 175.

[47] *In re South African Apartheid Litigation*, 617 F. Supp. 2d 228 (SDNY 2009) 44.

[48] ibid, 70.

Professor Michalowski criticises this approach, which consists in 'automatically shield[ing] from liability'[49] some types of business at the *actus reus* stage, without even looking into the specific circumstances of each case and, crucially, without even looking into *mens rea*. She concludes that the reasoning adopted in the *Apartheid* litigation 'has the effect of absolving commercial lenders from all complicity liability, no matter what effect the loans might have on the commission of gross human rights violations and regardless of the *mens rea* of the financier'.[50] *Mens rea*, however, really should play a crucial role in the establishment of liability and as such should 'be established on a case-by-case basis, both where the goods are inherently harmful and where they are not, as what gives rise to liability is the mental state of the corporation in relation to the usage of the goods'.[51]

She also suggests that it is incorrect to consider the decision in the *Ministries case* as authority for the existence of a clear-cut distinction between the provision of money and the provision of other commodities. She argues that it can be inferred from other parts of the judgment that Rasche's liability under another count, but also for lending money to the SS, was in fact envisaged and only rejected by the tribunal for lack of evidence.[52] She concludes as follows: 'Looking at the decision against Rasche in its entirety, the judgment does not suggest that complicity liability for commercial loans is always excluded. At best, the decision lends limited support to the approach in *South African Apartheid Litigation*'.[53] Finally, it is also of relevance that the Nuremberg cases were about individual criminal liability when the contemporary US Alien Tort Statute cases on these issues are about civil corporate liability, for which a lesser burden of proof is required.[54]

In sum, the current case law is both strikingly scarce and unclear and test cases are much needed. It seems that under current US law financial complicity is even harder to establish than other forms of corporate complicity in international crimes. This is an unfortunate state of affairs since, as long as the three elements of causation, knowledge or foreseeability and proximity can be present, the distinction rests on unsure theoretical grounds. Moreover, international law does recognise the key role of financiers in a specific area, that of financing terrorism. As the next section shows, there exists a sophisticated legal framework in this area, which could provide a solid basis for developments in the field of financial complicity in international crimes outside terrorist activities.

IV LESSONS FROM INTERNATIONAL LAW ON FINANCING TERRORISM

There exist a number of international treaties aiming to criminalise financing of terrorism.[55] However, there is no international treaty criminalising financing of international crimes as defined in the Statute of the ICC, and even domestic law is still in its infancy, as

[49] Michalowski (n 42) 451, 469.
[50] ibid, 470.
[51] ibid, 469.
[52] ibid, 473–74.
[53] ibid, 474.
[54] ibid, 482.
[55] United Nations International Convention for the Suppression of the Financing of Terrorism, UN Doc A/RES/54/109, 9 December 1999; Council of Europe Convention on Laundering, Search, Seizure and Confiscation of the Proceeds from Crime and on the Financing of Terrorism, CETS No 198, 16 May 2005; Organization of American States, Inter-American Convention Against Terrorism, AG/RES 1840, 3 June 2002.

shown above. This section aims to briefly review the law on terrorism to see if it could be used as a basis for the development of international rules criminalising the funding of international crimes, for example in a proposed International Convention on the Suppression of the Financing of International Crimes. The main treaty on financing of terrorism is the 1999 International Convention on the Suppression of the Financing of Terrorism. Article 2 of the Convention reads as follows:

> 1. Any person commits an offence within the meaning of this Convention if that person by any means, directly or indirectly, unlawfully and wilfully, provides or collects funds with the intention that they should be used or in the knowledge that they are to be used, in full or in part, in order to carry out:
>
> (a) An act which constitutes an offence within the scope of and as defined in one of the treaties listed in the annex; or
>
> (b) Any other act intended to cause death or serious bodily injury to a civilian, or to any other person not taking an active part in the hostilities in a situation of armed conflict, when the purpose of such act, by its nature or context, is to intimidate a population, or to compel a government or an international organization to do or to abstain from doing any act.

Taking this definition as a model, one could imagine the definition of an offence which would entail providing or collecting funds 'with the intention that they should be used or in the knowledge that they are to be used, in full or in part, in order to carry out' international crimes as defined in the Statute of the ICC. The first point of interest in this definition is the fact that there must be intention or knowledge on the part of the perpetrator and that consequently negligence, recklessness or 'should have known' standards are excluded.[56] Such strict *mens rea* requirements would necessarily exclude the criminal liability of those financiers, bankers or investors whose money contributes to the crimes but who are just looking for a good financial deal and do not share the objectives of those who commit the crimes themselves. In other words, the vast majority of those who have financially contributed to the commission of international crimes would not be covered by the definition. In the context of terrorism, the aim of the offence is therefore to catch those who wilfully provide funds to terrorists and who, to some extent, share their ideas and goals and approve their actions. In the context of international crimes, keeping this type of *mens rea* could probably be seen as a first step but would not tackle the core issue, which is that international law does not provide for any clear obligation for banks and investors to run some basic checks about where their money goes and what it will be spent on.

Secondly, Article 2 mentions that providing or collecting funds must be done 'unlawfully' to constitute an offence. The *travaux* of the Convention suggest that the word 'unlawfully' was retained in the definition 'since it added an element of flexibility by, for example, excluding from the ambit of application of the . . . convention legitimate activities, such as those of humanitarian organizations and ransom payments'.[57] This is where, perhaps, the comparison between financing terrorist activities and financing international crimes as defined in the ICC Statute reaches its limits. Any transfer of funds, even

[56] M Pieth, 'Criminalising the Financing of Terrorism' (2006) 4 *Journal of International Criminal Justice* 1074, 1081–82.

[57] UN Doc A/C.6/54/L.2, 26 October 1999, Annex III, Informal summary of the discussions in the Working Group, para 67.

in the form of a loan, to a terrorist group must be seen as a clear form of support to the organisation, except if it falls under the exceptions mentioned in the *travaux*. This is because terrorist groups are in themselves criminal groups. Their *raison d'être* is to intimidate and terrorise. One of the traditional difficulties about the funding of terrorism is that an organisation defined by some as terrorist may be seen as a freedom fighting organisation by others. This, it has been argued, is 'the problem'.[58] It is indeed a major issue since *all* funds transferred to such organisations, save the above-mentioned exceptions in the *travaux*, are deemed to constitute an offence.

Terrorism must therefore by distinguished from international crimes, which are committed by state agents, or non-state actors engaged in different types of activities. While these individuals may commit crimes in the process, the organisations they belong to are not necessarily criminal in nature. In fact, they mostly are not. From this point of view, it is much easier to criminalise the financing of terrorism than it is to criminalise the financing of international crimes. The offence of financing a terrorist group does not have to be linked to a specific terrorist attack. The very fact of transferring funds to the group is criminal because it is expected that the funds will inevitably be used to pursue unlawful goals. By contrast, the offence of financing international crimes would have to be linked, even if loosely, to the commission of specific crimes. Indeed, even funds transferred to a so-called 'criminal state' may be used for legitimate purposes, such as funding schools or hospitals.

Speaking about the confiscation of assets, which is yet another way of dealing with the issue of financing of terrorism, one author has argued that 'the fact that the concept was not automatically adapted to other forms of crime, including the financing of underground armies, who use excessive and brutal violence against civilians, clearly stems from the political difficulties in drawing a clear line between "freedom fighters" and "terrorists"'.[59] In other words, it would be politically difficult to intervene, through freezing of assets (or prosecuting those who fund terrorist activities), since the groups may not be terrorist after all but, rather, freedom fighters. It is argued here that this argument is unconvincing. No matter how legitimate a movement is, international crimes can never be justified. 'Brutal violence against civilians' does not become acceptable because the perpetrators fight for their freedom or for the rights of the wider population. In other words, the endless debates about which organisations are terrorist, and the ensuing discussions about whether or not those who fund them should be prosecuted, are irrelevant when it comes to funding international crimes. What matters is the fact that gross human rights violations have been perpetrated.

In sum, international law on the financing of terrorism is informative on several grounds. First, it shows that when states have the political will to act, measures can be taken to tackle the transfer of funds which can be used to unlawfully kill civilians. Second, it shows that for an offence to be constituted, intention or at least knowledge is required, which means the onus is on the prosecution to prove that such intention of enabling the crimes, or knowledge of the likely consequences of the fund transfer is present. Whether or not intention or knowledge will be established may depend on whether intention to commit, or knowledge of, the precise crimes is required or whether the foreseeable consequences of funding a criminal regime, in general, would be deemed sufficient. Requiring

[58] A Cassese, 'The Multifaceted Criminal Notion of Terrorism in International Law' (2006) 4 *Journal of International Criminal Justice* 933, 934.

[59] Pieth (n 56) 1076.

knowledge of the precise crimes committed would stand in the way of establishing liability for financial complicity due to the fact that in practice, in a lot of cases, bankers and investors do not know precisely where their money goes, despite the development of non-binding guidelines on this issue.[60] Introducing rules, under domestic law, forcing them to obtain more information about this could be a first step to overcome the issue, even if it falls short of criminalising the financing of international crimes. Such rules could be introduced as part of the series of measures states are expected to adopt to implement the UN Guiding Principles on Business and Human Rights, endorsed by the Human Rights Council in 2011.[61] In parallel, one could imagine the adoption of a treaty criminalising the financing of international crimes, even one that would require intention or knowledge. It would be a clear sign to the finance industry that they are expected to introduce checking processes prior to lending funds.

V CONCLUSION

Current international law does not specifically criminalise the financing of international crimes by corporations or individuals. Rather international law, for example in the Statute of the ICC, criminalises the perpetration of certain gross human rights violations and provides for complicity liability. Moreover, the fact that corporate liability was excluded from that Statute does not mean that corporate liability is excluded from the scope of international law or, for that matter, that individuals – state officials or business people – involved in financial complicity in international crimes cannot be prosecuted by the Court.

As shown by the International Commission of Jurists, under the domestic law of a range of countries, establishing liability for complicity in international crimes entails strict tests that are unlikely to be passed in the case of financial complicity. Moreover, at the international level, the comparison with the emerging law on the financing of terrorism is uneasy due to the fact that the organisations, state or non-state, whose members and leaders commit international crimes are not necessarily criminal in nature. The catch-all approach of the 1999 International Convention on the Suppression of the Financing of Terrorism, which criminalises any transfer of funds to terrorist organisations, is therefore ill-adapted to the financing of international crimes.

The deliberate funding, through donations or loans, of organisations committing international crimes should of course be prosecuted, as any form of corporate complicity in international crimes. Yet the main issue remains the fact that banks and corporate investors may not know what the funds transferred will be used to do, despite developing international guidelines and expectations in the area.[62] There are two ways to address this issue. One way would be to steer clear of criminal liability for financial complicity in international crimes when intention and knowledge are not established and to focus instead on the development of corporate *accountability* in the area, as opposed to corporate *liability*.[63] As the International Commission of Jurists put it in their report:

[60] The Equator Principle (n 31).
[61] UN Human Rights Council, UN Doc A/HRC/RES/17/4, 6 July 2011.
[62] The Equator Principle (n 31).
[63] When intention or knowledge are present, then liability should of course be established.

> [T]here are company acts and omissions that may be currently beyond legal sanction, but that may nonetheless be criticised publicly by different actors as unacceptable behaviour as a matter of morality or ethics, or that may give rise to market-place or public image implications for companies.[64]

Accountability can be developed through disclosure obligations and increased scrutiny by certain actors. Informed actors may bring about more behavioural changes than cumbersome criminal law procedures, which may be too difficult to apply in practice due to the nature of the offences at stake.

The other way would be to criminalise the conduct, or to develop mechanisms for establishing civil liability, even when knowledge of the commission of specific crimes, let alone intent, is not established. This would constitute a significant step towards an effective prevention of atrocity crimes since, as was shown in this chapter, crimes cannot be committed without capital. This could be encouraged by the drafting and adoption of an international treaty. Although treaties do not constitute a panacea and are not necessarily the best way to bridge gaps in human rights protection, a treaty criminalising the financing of international crimes and requiring states to make the necessary changes in their domestic law would be a step in the right direction. This would have to be progressively introduced and financial institutions which are genuinely not supportive of the crimes would have to be strongly advised to run checks before lending money in order to avoid prosecutions.

[64] International Commission of Jurists (n 6), 7.

Part II

Debt Crises and Social and Economic Rights

6

Human Rights and Sovereign Debt Workouts

MATTHIAS GOLDMANN*

I THE ASYMMETRY BETWEEN DEBT AND HUMAN RIGHTS ENFORCEMENT: LEGAL AND DISCURSIVE HISTORY

FOR MOST OF the time during the last two centuries, the needs and interests of the citizens in debtor states hardly played a role in the efforts to resolve sovereign debt crises. In the nineteenth and early twentieth centuries, sovereign lenders were usually private investors. In sovereign debt crises, they negotiated a settlement with the insolvent states, either directly or through creditor associations which received at best implicit government support.[1] A robust idea of state sovereignty demanded that the consequences of restructurings for citizens in the debtor state were to be left to the discretion of the government of the latter – and were nothing the creditors needed to worry about. Thus, a private law paradigm prevailed in the resolution of sovereign debt workouts which emphasised the idea of *pacta sunt servanda* and did not recognise overarching public interests such as the socio-economic situation of the population in the debtor state, especially of those depending on public services.[2] However, at that time, it was quite difficult for creditors to enforce their claims from abroad due to a largely intact doctrine of state immunity, the flip side of sovereignty. 'Gunboat diplomacy' remained the exception.

This pattern has undergone fundamental changes since the end of the Second World War. Two developments account for this. First, beginning with the Universal Declaration of Human Rights, both civil and economic interests of individual citizens came to be recognised as rights which set a standard for states and prevented them from hiding behind the veil of sovereignty. The Covenants adopted within the framework of the United Nations on Civil and Political Rights (ICCPR), and on Economic, Social and Cultural Rights (ICESCR) followed suit, as did a number of regional human rights instruments. Second, sovereign lending and the resolution of debt crises underwent enormous transformations. The emergence of an international regime for sovereign lending and sovereign debt workouts replaced the idea of unfettered state sovereignty. Instead of

* For valuable advice I am indebted to Armin von Bogdandy, Franz Ebert and Mateja Steinbrück Platise. Thanks to Silvia Steininger for research assistance.

[1] WN Eskridge, 'Les Jeux Sont Faits: Structural Origins of the International Debt Problem' (1984–85) 25 *Virginia Journal of International Law* 281, 307–12; Y Wong, *Sovereign Finance and the Poverty of Nations. Odious Debt in International Law* (Cheltenham, Edward Elgar, 2012) 40–41.

[2] Characterising this tension as one between two diverging concepts of sovereignty: O Lienau *Rethinking Sovereign Debt* (Cambridge MA, Harvard University Press, 2014) 34 ff.

private bondholders, states and international organisations became the main lenders in the immediate post-war period, increasing their volumes significantly during the 1960s in order to satisfy the financial needs of newly independent states. Sovereign lending by foreign private lenders became significant again in the 1970s when Western banks saw an inflow of petrodollars in search of attractive investment opportunities. This established the International Monetary Fund (IMF) and the Paris Club, an informal group of bilateral lenders from the West, as key players in the resolution of sovereign debt workouts, besides venues of private creditors such as the London Club.[3] With the onset of the Latin American debt crisis in the 1980s, the IMF developed its policy of concessional long-term lending to countries experiencing debt crises, sometimes even though they had accumulated arrears to private creditors.[4] Lending has been tied to conditionalities which usually include structural adjustment policies designed to stimulate growth and help the country regain access to capital markets and service its debt.[5]

Compared to the situation prevailing during the nineteenth and early twentieth centuries, these developments led to an asymmetry in the relationship between the rights of citizens in the defaulting state and the rights of creditors. On the one hand, human rights, and especially socio-economic rights, are often hard to enforce. While some complaint mechanisms exist for civil and political rights, the Optional Protocol to the ICESCR establishing a complaint and inquiry mechanism only entered into force in May 2013 and so far has only 10 states parties. Complaints, although only collective ones, may also be lodged before the European Committee of Social Rights under the European Social Charter. However, the international financial institutions, above all the IMF, hold the view that they are not bound by human rights obligations, and no court or committee has ever held them accountable despite allegations that adjustment measures violate human rights.[6] Only in the last few years have international organisations begun to recognise the human rights impact of adjustment measures. In 1999 the UN Human Rights Commission pointed out that adjustment cannot ignore human conditions.[7] Most recently, the Human Rights Council adopted Guiding Principles on foreign debt and human rights,[8] but most developed states and some emerging economies voted against the adoption, or abstained.[9]

[3] For an analysis of the authority exercised by these institutions, see A von Bogdandy and M Goldmann, 'Sovereign Debt Restructurings as Exercises of International Public Authority: Towards a Decentralized Sovereign Insolvency Law' in C Esposito, JP Bohoslavsky, and Y Li (eds), *Sovereign Financing and International Law: The UNCTAD Principles on Responsible Sovereign Lending and Borrowing* (Oxford, Oxford University Press, 2013) 39–70.

[4] B Eichengreen and R Portes, 'After the Deluge: Default, Negotiation, and Readjustment During the Interwar Years' in B Eichengreen and PH Lindert, *The International Debt Crisis in Historical Perspective* (1989) 12, 13 ff; R Swaminatham, 'Regulating Development: Structural Adjustment and the Case for National Enforcement of Economic and Social Rights' (1998–99) 37 *Columbia Journal of Transnational Law* 161–214, 171.

[5] For current lending policies see IMF, *Sovereign Debt Restructuring – Recent Developments and Implications for the Fund's Legal and Policy Framework*, 26 April 2013.

[6] eg Swaminatham (n 4) especially at 177–78. See below, section IV.B.

[7] UN Commission on Human Rights, *Effects on the full enjoyment of human rights of the economic adjustment policies arising from foreign debt and, in particular, on the implementation of the Declaration on the Right to Development*, Resolution 1999/22, 23 April 1999, UN Doc E/CN.4/RES/1991/13.

[8] The Guiding Principles are annexed to the *Report of the Independent Expert on the effects of foreign debt and other related international financial obligations of States on the full enjoyment of all human rights, particularly economic, social and cultural rights*, Cephas Lumina, UN Doc A/HRC/20/23, 10 April 2011. See C Lumina, 'Sovereign Debt and Human Rights: The UN Approach', see Ch 16 in this chapter.

[9] Human Rights Council, *The effects of foreign debt and other related international financial obligations of States on the full enjoyment of all human rights, particularly economic, social and cultural rights*, UN Doc A/HRC/RES/20/10, 18 July 2012, operative para 2.

Also, the discussion about extraterritorial human rights obligations of states, including bilateral creditors, has received new momentum with the adoption of the Maastricht Principles by a group of experts in 2011.[10] It remains to be seen whether state practice will follow their line of reasoning.

On the other hand, for creditors, enforcement of their claims has become a more promising option with the emergence of a regime for sovereign debt workouts. First, IMF conditionality regularly includes debt repayment. Indeed, the goal of the growth strategy pursued by the international financial institutions is to assist countries in regaining market access in order to roll over their debt.[11] Second, the opportunities for creditors to enforce their judgments have increased. Sovereign debt instruments nowadays regularly contain broad waivers of immunity. Domestic courts have allowed creditors to enforce their claims, especially by intercepting payments to other creditors which participated in a restructuring geared towards reducing debt to a sustainable level.[12] The *Abaclat* case will show to what extent international investment tribunals set up under the International Convention on the Settlement of Investment Disputes will offer a new avenue for creditors seeking enforcement of their claims against sovereign debtors.[13]

The resulting asymmetry between human rights protection and the enforcement of creditors' claims is the subject of this chapter. It first analyses the impact of sovereign debt workouts on human rights (Section II); subsequently, it explores avenues for the justification of measures affecting human rights with a view to reconciling human rights with adjustment policies and rectifying the present structural disadvantage of the former (Section III); in the following, it discusses which actors besides the debtor state are bound by human rights (Section IV). The concluding section discusses how human rights impact assessments, among other procedural tools, might help reconcile the rights and interests of people living in debtor states with creditors' rights and interests and cure the present asymmetrical relationship (Section V).

II HUMAN RIGHTS AFFECTED IN SOVEREIGN DEBT WORKOUTS

A Economic, Social and Cultural Rights of People in the Debtor State

i Potentially Affected Rights

Although the origin of economic, social and cultural rights (ESC rights) does not date back as far as that of civil and political rights, they emerged as a result of bitter economic experiences. The experience of industrialisation in the West showed that liberal rights

[10] Maastricht Principles on Extraterritorial Obligations of States in the Area of Economic, Social and Cultural Rights (Maastricht Principles), www.fian.org/fileadmin/media/publications/2012.02.29_-_Maastricht_Principles_on_Extraterritorial_Obligations.pdf, accessed 20 September 2013.

[11] C Lichtenstein, 'Aiding the Transformation of Economies: Is the Fund's Conditionality Appropriate to the Task?' (1994) 62 *Fordham Law Review* 1943, 1948; S Michalowski, 'Sovereign Debt and Social Rights – Legal Reflections on a Difficult Relationship' (2008) 8 *Human Rights Law Review* 35–68, 38.

[12] eg US Court of Appeals, Second Circuit, *NML Capital Ltd et al v Argentina*, case no 12-105(L), 26 October 2012; Brussels Court of Appeals, 8th Chamber, *Elliott Associates v Peru*, case no 2000/QR/92, decision of 26 September 2000.

[13] *Abaclat v Argentine Republic*, ICSID Case ARB/07/5, Decision on Jurisdiction and Admissibility, 14 November 2011. In this case, more than 180,000 mostly Italian holders of defaulted Argentinean bonds sued Argentina for compensatory damages.

alone do not guarantee a 'decent life' to large parts of the population. ESC rights are therefore necessary not just as roadblocks against excessive market forces impinging upon individuals, but as trumps against governments and other wielders of public authority which show little interest in the fate of their citizens.[14] The core of ESC rights is guaranteed by the Universal Declaration of Human Rights, which contains, among other guarantees, in its Art 22 the entitlement of everyone to 'realization . . . of the economic, social and cultural rights indispensable for his dignity and the free development of his personality'.[15] The main international instrument guaranteeing ESC rights is the ICESCR. It enjoys almost universal ratification, with the notable exceptions of the United States and South Africa. Sovereign debt crises and the ensuing structural adjustments might affect many of the guarantees of the ICESCR, such as the right to social security (Art 9), to special protection for families, mothers and children (Art 10), to an adequate standard of living and to food (Art 11), to the highest attainable standards of health (Art 12) and to education (Art 13), but also the right to form trade unions and their right to function freely, or the right to strike (Art 8, see also Art 22 ICCPR). Other international instruments such as the Conventions on the Rights of the Child or on the Rights of Persons with Disabilities or regional instruments like the European Social Charter corroborate these guarantees. The right to property guaranteed by Art 1 of the First Protocol to the European Convention for the Protection of Human Rights and Fundamental Freedoms (ECHR) comprehensively protects welfare benefits.[16] However, the chapter will focus on the ICESCR due to its comprehensive character and near-universal acceptance.

In order to assess the impact of sovereign debt workouts and in particular of structural adjustment measures on ICESCR rights, it is important to keep in mind that ESC rights usually entail three different obligations for states, the obligations to respect, to protect and to fulfil.[17] With respect to the latter, Art 2 ICESCR obliges each member state to take steps 'to the maximum of its available resources, with a view to achieving progressively the full realisation of the rights recognised in the present covenant'. This idea of progressive realisation does not make ESC rights completely indeterminate,[18] but gives them the character of process requirements.[19] In order to further concretise this process, the Committee has developed the so-called IBSA procedure: the Committee on Economic, Social and Cultural Rights (CESCR) defines indicators for measuring the level of ESC rights enjoyment, the state defines the benchmarks which it plans to attain, the Committee reviews these benchmarks ('scoping') and later assesses the performance of the state.[20] These obligations also apply in times of economic emergency or sovereign debt crisis.

[14] cf Swaminatham (n 4) 162.

[15] Other ESC rights guaranteed in the Universal Declaration of Human Rights are the right to social security (Art 22), the right to work and equal pay (Art 23), the right to an adequate standard of living (Art 25), the right to education (Art 26), and the right to freely participate in the cultural life of the community (Art 27).

[16] C Grabenwarter, *European Convention on Human Rights* (Munich, Beck, 2014) 369–70.

[17] CESCR, General Comment No 12, 12 May 1999, para 15; A Eide, 'Economic, Social and Cultural Rights as Human Rights' in A Eide, C Krause and A Rosas (eds), *Economic, Social and Cultural Rights. A Textbook*, 2nd edn (Dordrecht, Nijhoff, 2001) 9–28, 23–4; M Sepúlveda, *The Nature of the Obligations Under the International Covenant on Economic, Social and Cultural Rights* (Antwerpen, Intersentia, 2003) 157 ff.

[18] See, however, Swaminatham (n 4) 162.

[19] P Alston and G Quinn, 'The Nature and Scope of States Parties' Obligations under the International Covenant on Economic, Social and Cultural Rights' (1987) 9 *Human Rights Quarterly* 156–229, 180.

[20] E Riedel, 'Measuring Human Rights Compliance – The IBSA Procedure as a Tool of Monitoring' in A Auer et al (eds), *Les droits de l'homme et la constitution – Etudes en l'honneur du Professeur Giorgio Malinverni* (Geneva, Schulthess, 2007) 251–71; M Duchstein, *Das internationale Benchmarkingverfahren und seine Bedeutung für den gewerblichen Rechtsschutz* (Heidelberg, Springer, 2010) 217 ff.

Such events might only reduce the amount of 'available resources' of that state for the fulfilment of ESC rights. Besides the duty of progressive realisation, the CESCR has argued that the enjoyment of a minimum core of all ESC rights is non-discretionary and needs to be ensured at all times, including during crisis periods.[21] States need to seek to obtain the resources necessary for this purpose.[22] This has priority over other tasks, such as debt service. Some of the general comments relating to specific ESC rights define the content of the minimum core. Further, Art 3 ICESCR prohibits gender discrimination with regard to the realisation of ESC rights.

ii Modalities of Affection: Structural Adjustment Programmes

In case of a sovereign debt crisis, ESC rights might be affected, first, by using 'available resources' for debt service instead of the realisation of ESC rights,[23] and second, by structural adjustment programmes which require states to take certain measures affecting the level of ESC rights enjoyment.[24] Usually, sovereign debt workouts consist in the negotiation of package deals which include IMF loans, whose conditionalities specify the debt service expected by the debtor state, and structural adjustment programmes. Therefore, both issues are closely interrelated, and it might suffice to focus on an analysis of the human rights impact of structural adjustment programmes.

Before the IMF began with long-term concessional lending, it lent its resources at market rates and for shorter periods. By virtue of Art 1(v) of its Articles of Agreement, these loans had to include conditionalities. They usually focused on macroeconomic figures such as exchange rates and interest rates and left it otherwise to the discretion of the debtor states to develop their policies in matters concerning ESC rights, such as the provision of public services. Some exceptions confirm the rule. A case in point is Argentina, which received several loans during the decades following the Second World War. Their conditionalities included, besides macroeconomic benchmarks, policy measures such as the imposition of wage controls. This had severe consequences for the right of trade unions to function freely, and unions were at times even put under military control.[25] Nevertheless, the IMF did not specify in its conditionalities how budget cuts should be carried out. Thus, it was the government which chose that budget cuts should target public and social services and their employees, instead of, for example, military expenses.[26]

Since the beginning of concessional lending, conditionalities have regularly included measures aiming at the structural adjustment of economic and social policies.[27] On the recommendation of the IMF, debtor states set out those measures in letters of intent and memoranda of understanding. Only if they satisfy the IMF, will the Executive Board approve a loan. Conditionalities should therefore not be considered as voluntary, despite

[21] CESCR, General Comment No 3, 14 December 1990, para 10. On the intricate difficulties of determining the minimum content: KG Young 'The Minimum Core of Economic and Social Rights: A Concept in Search of Contents' (2008) 33 *Yale Journal of International Law* 113–75.

[22] M Ssenyonjo, *Economic, Social and Cultural Rights in International Law* (Oxford, Hart Publishing, 2009) 66–68.

[23] Michalowski (n 11) 46.

[24] S Skogly, *Human Rights Obligations of the World Bank and the International Monetary Fund* (London, Cavendish, 2001) 751–78, 752.

[25] M Conklin and D Davidson, 'The IMF and Economic and Social Human Rights: A Case Study of Argentina, 1958–1985'(1986) 8 *Human Rights Quarterly* 227–69, 237–38, 254–57.

[26] ibid, 251–52.

[27] IMF, *Guidelines on Conditionality* (2002) para 7.

the fact that the legal instruments used for their stipulation are formally non-binding.[28] The structural measures comprise issues such as the privatisation of public enterprises or services. This has at times increased the costs for the citizens depending on them, or led to a reduction in the quality of service. Cuts in fuel subsidies, another recurrent example, affect especially the poorer parts of society. In the case of the recent Greek debt crisis, the IMF and other players involved went as far as to request the sale of pharmaceuticals outside pharmacies.[29] In certain African states, conditionalities made a deficient and unfair health system even more precarious. The lack of funds immediately led to a scarcity of drugs, most of which needed to be imported. The requirement to make people pay for health services rendered them effectively unavailable to more and more people, while it did not solve the financial problems of the health sector due to staggering inflation rates.[30]

Certainly, one might always argue that the expected long-term benefits might outweigh the short-term structural disadvantages. This position is contested.[31] But even if it were true, adjustment measures must not lead to discrimination. In a report for the UN Human Rights Commission, Danilo Türk stated that structural adjustment made women, children and the poor suffer disproportionately.[32] Also, one might ask whether certain adjustment measures reduced the level of ESC rights realisation below the respective minimum requirements.

In light of such contestations, the 1990s saw a rising concern of international financial institutions for the social and economic implications of conditionalities. The IMF therefore began to establish so-called social safety nets. They consist of specific measures ensuring that disenfranchised groups do not suffer disproportionately from adjustment and are not deprived of essential services. They might comprise the distribution of essential pharmaceutical drugs, public work programmes and labour market incentives.[33] Further, the IMF began requesting developing states to set up Poverty Reduction and Growth Strategies which focus not only on macroeconomic variables, but also on socio-economic well-being, and might qualify a country for debt relief under the Highly Indebted Poor Countries initiative.

B Civil and Political Rights of People in the Debtor State

i Right to Political Participation

Besides ESC rights, sovereign debt workouts might also affect the political rights of people living in the country afflicted by a sovereign debt crisis. Article 25 ICCPR guarantees the right to political participation. However, this right is of limited reach. While struc-

[28] See von Bogdandy and Goldmann (n 3).

[29] IMF, *Greece: Memorandum of Economic and Financial Policies*, 17 July 2013, 20.

[30] This and much further data is contained in S Ogoh Alubo, 'Debt Crisis, Health and Health Services in Africa' (1990) 31 *Social Science Med* 639–48, 642–45.

[31] eg M Lucas, 'The International Monetary Fund's Conditionality and the International Covenant on Economic, Social and Cultural Rights: An Attempt to Define the Relation' (1992) 25 *Revue Belge de droit international* 104–35, 113.

[32] UN ECOSOC, *Realization of Economic, Social and Cultural Rights*, Second progress report prepared by Mr Danilo Türk, Special Rapporteur, 18 July 1991, E/CN.4/Sub.2/1991/17, paras 148 ff.

[33] IMF, *Social Policy Issues in IMF-Supported Programs: Follow-Up on the 1995 World Summit for Social Development*, 16 March 2000. See also B Ghazi, *The IMF, the World Bank Group and the Question of Human Rights* (Ardsley, Transnational Publishers, 2005) 75.

tural adjustment measures do put external constraints on the domestic political process, they neither completely eliminate legislative or executive discretion, nor do they prohibit the participation of the people in the formulation of policy. In fact, the IMF nowadays emphasises that conditionalities should be based on the idea of ownership of the affected population.[34] Whether and to what extent specific conditionalities in fact reflect the idea of ownership might be debated. But this does not affect the right to vote, unless one reads Art 25 ICCPR in a similar way as the German Constitutional Court read the right to vote guaranteed by the German Basic Law, namely as a right to effective control over any public authority on the federal or supranational level through the elections to the national parliament.[35] In any case, the question whether and how the citizens of the debtor state should have a say in the development of conditionalities might more adequately be conceptualised as an issue of legitimacy, not of individual rights. It affects the capacity of those citizens to exercise collective self-determination and to organise their community according to their views. To remedy any deficits in this regard, one would need a political decision devising ways to rearrange the international structures and institutions charged with the negotiation of sovereign debt workouts in appropriate ways, not just a decision establishing the violation of rights without specifying apposite remedies.[36]

ii Other Civil and Political Rights

Although adjustment measures usually do not target other civil and political rights directly, in principle, each of them might be affected indirectly. Empirical data suggests that austerity leads to decreases in human security, including torture, extrajudicial killings, disappearance and imprisonment of political opponents.[37] Such consequences might derive from overly harsh reactions of governments to protests and civil unrest in response to austerity measures.[38] In extreme cases, debt crises might even trigger wars or civil conflicts.[39] However, for such violations to happen there need to be additional, intervening causes. Restructurings, debt repayments or adjustment measures are not their proximate cause. They might only worsen the economic and social situation to an extent which triggers additional causal chains. Therefore, the impact of sovereign insolvency on ESC rights should be the main focus. Civil and political rights should be considered to the extent that they are immediately affected by austerity. An example would be trouble with the provision of paper for newspapers arising as a consequence of economic adjustment.[40]

C Human Rights of Creditors

Creditors might also see their human rights violated in the course of sovereign debt workouts. First, their financial claims against the debtor states might be protected by guarantees

[34] IMF (n 27) para 3.

[35] German Constitutional Court, *Maastricht Case*, 12 October 1993, BVerfGE 89, 155.

[36] On the legitimacy of restructurings, see von Bogdandy and Goldmann (n 3).

[37] M Rodwan Abouharb and DL Cingranelli, 'IMF Programs and Human Rights' (2009) 4 *Review of International Organizations* 47–72.

[38] Ghazi (n 33) 48–49.

[39] On these implications see M Goldmann, 'Sovereign Debt Crises as Threats to the Peace: Restructuring Under Chapter VII of the UN Charter?' (2012) 4 *Goettingen Journal of International Law* 153–75.

[40] Skogly (n 24) 771.

of the right to property. The European Court of Human Rights (ECtHR) adopted a wide definition of the term 'possession' stipulated in Art 1 of the First Protocol to the ECHR which also comprises claims in respect of which the claimant has a 'legitimate expectation' that they will be realised.[41] The ICCPR does not comprise a right to property. For other human rights instruments, the situation is sometimes controversial just because creditors' claims are only expectations and do not have an inherent value.[42]

But even assuming that creditors' claims against sovereign debtors are covered by international guarantees of the right to property, the question arises whether debt restructurings violate this right. Usually, debt exchanges are voluntary and consensual and would not violate the right to property, whether it covers such claims or not. However, sometimes states refuse to repay their debts and unilaterally default on them in full or partially, or change their legislation in the case of domestic debt. The private sector involvement in the Greek crisis of 2012 prompted some holdout creditors to consider suing Greece.[43] But in such a case, it has to be considered that claims against a debtor that is effectively insolvent might hardly give rise to legitimate expectations that the debt will be repaid. Rather, insolvency is one of the risks inherent in any investment. Still, non-consensual sovereign debt restructurings require the intervention of the state or of an international organisation by which the outstanding debt is explicitly or implicitly repudiated. Such an act might raise eyebrows from a human rights perspective, but primarily because it might violate due process rights rather than the right to property. In particular, delays in the implementation of debt workouts on the part of the debtor state might give rise to successful human rights litigation.[44]

III JUSTIFICATION OF MEASURES AFFECTING HUMAN RIGHTS

A Retrogressive Measures Affecting Economic, Social and Cultural Rights

In order to manage a debt crisis, and in particular as part of structural adjustments, states might need to take retrogressive measures which reduce the level of ESC rights enjoyment. For this eventuality, General Comment No 3 provides:

> *Any deliberately retrogressive measures in that regard would require the most careful consideration and would need to be fully justified by reference to the totality of the rights provided for in the Covenant and in the context of the full use of the maximum available resources.*

The Guiding Principles adopted by the Human Rights Council approach this issue in even stricter terms, providing that '[s]tates have an obligation to avoid retrogressive measures . . .'.[45] But a contextualised reading of these passages reveals that the Guiding Principles, seeking to strike a balance between creditors' legitimate interests and the human rights of the population of the defaulting state, provide that states should make best efforts to

[41] ECtHR, *Pressos Compania Naviera SA and Others v Belgium*, judgment of 20 November 1995, Series A No 332.

[42] M Waibel, *Sovereign Defaults before International Courts and Tribunals* (Cambridge, Cambridge University Press, 2011) 183.

[43] L Thomas, 'Hedge Funds May Sue Greece If It Tries to Force Loss', *New York Times*, 18 January 2012, B1. Currently potential applicants have not yet exhausted local remedies. A case has been filed with an ICSID tribunal, see *Poštova banka as and Istrokapital SE v Hellenic Republic*, ICSID Case ARB/13/8.

[44] eg ECtHR, *Fomin an others v Russia*, App no 34703/04, judgment of 26 February 2013.

[45] Guiding Principles (n 8) paras 19 and 20.

avoid retrogressive measures.[46] This is in line with voices from the literature which claim that there is a presumption of unreasonableness applying to retrogressive measures and that states have to provide reasons for their justification.[47]

This raises the question how the presumption of the unreasonableness of retrogressive measures may be rebutted. As regards the ICESCR, the focus instrument of this chapter, two articles may guide the rebuttal. Article 4 ICESCR permits limitations to the rights of the Covenant 'determined by law only in so far as they are compatible with the nature of the rights and solely for the purpose of promoting the general welfare in a democratic society'. By contrast, according to Art 2(1) ICESCR, states only need to deploy the 'maximum of [their] available resources'. Traditionally, Art 2(1) has been understood as addressing the issue of the scarcity of resources and the limitations it imposes on the realisation of ESC rights in general, while Art 4 regulates the admissibility of specific limitations to generally realised ESC rights, which do not necessarily apply for all right holders in all situations.[48] Such limitations might be justified by policy considerations, such as modifications in the conditions for access to social services motivated by the desire to stimulate growth.[49] Structural adjustment programmes in the first line are necessary in order to remedy an imminent scarcity of resources. Yet they also pursue longer-term growth strategies which are not necessarily motivated by the scarcity of resources, but also driven by the desire to accumulate more resources in the long term. This makes it difficult to tell with precision which of the two cited articles provides the standard by which structural adjustment programmes should be measured. Therefore, both articles should be applied cumulatively.[50]

Besides Arts 2(1) and 4 ICESCR, the provisions of General Comment No 3 quoted above might provide useful guidance for the admissibility of retrogressive measures, as well as other General Comments and statements on specific ESC rights which address retrogressive acts,[51] and a letter by the chairperson to the States Parties of 2012 specifying that adjustment should be temporary, proportionate, non-discriminatory and respect the minimum core obligations.[52] They enable the proposal of a checkbox list for the assessment of retrogressive measures, which should not be used in a mechanical fashion, but rather be considered as a framework to guide deliberations. The framework might be divided into formal and procedural criteria on the one hand, and substantive criteria on the other.

Formal and procedural criteria:

- Retrogressive measures should be prescribed by law (Art 4);

[46] cf *Report of the Independent Expert* (n 8) Introduction, 10.

[47] Michalowski (n 10) 52; M Krajewski, 'Human Rights and Austerity Programmes', manuscript, on file with the author, 14–15.

[48] Alston and Quinn (n 19) 205–06.

[49] ibid, 194.

[50] See also A Müller, 'Limitations to and Derogations from Economic, Social and Cultural Rights' in M Ssenyonjo (ed), *Economic, Social and Cultural Rights* (Farnham, Ashgate, 2011) 113–57, 140–41; see, however, A Nolan, 'Putting ESR-Based Budget Analysis into Practice: Addressing the Conceptual Challenges' in A Nolan, R O'Connell and C Harvey (eds), *Human Rights and Public Finance* (Oxford, Hart Publishing, 2013) 41–57, 49.

[51] eg General Comment No 19 on the Right to Social Security; CESCR Statement: 'An Evaluation of the Obligations to Take Steps to the "Maximum of Available Resources" under an Optional Protocol to the Covenant', 21 September 2007, para 10.

[52] Letter from the Chairperson of CESCR to all States Parties to the ICESCR, 16 May 2012, http://www2.ohchr.org/english/bodies/cescr/docs/LetterCESCRtoSP16.05.12.pdf.

- The decision-making process should give due consideration to available alternatives, especially low-cost options;
- The decision-making process should ensure the genuine participation of affected groups in examining both the measures and possible alternatives (Art 4 – 'democratic society');[53]
- The measures should be accompanied by a reasonable justification;
- The measures should be subject to review at the national level.

Substantive criteria:

- Measures need to be non-discriminatory, cf Art 2(2);
- The minimum requirement for each ESC right must always be guaranteed, even for short-term adjustment measures.[54] In this respect, General Comment No 2 provides in para 9:

  > *A matter which has been of particular concern to the Committee in the examination of the reports of States parties is the adverse impact of the debt burden and of the relevant adjustment measures on the enjoyment of economic, social and cultural rights in many countries. The Committee recognizes that adjustment programmes will often be unavoidable and that these will frequently involve a major element of austerity. Under such circumstances, however, endeavours to protect the most basic economic, social and cultural rights become more, rather than less, urgent. States parties to the Covenant, as well as the relevant United Nations agencies, should thus make a particular effort to ensure that such protection is, to the maximum extent possible, built-in to programmes and policies designed to promote adjustment. Such an approach, which is sometimes referred to as 'adjustment with a human face' or as promoting 'the human dimension of development' requires that the goal of protecting the rights of the poor and vulnerable should become a basic objective of economic adjustment.*

  Adjustment programmes respectful of the minimum requirements usually comprise social safety nets, ie specific measures providing guarantees and services for disenfranchised groups. However, this has not always produced the expected results.[55] Human rights impact assessments might further this goal.[56]
- Measures need to be proportional at all times. The principle of proportionality is recognised as an important element of human rights law.[57] In the context of retrogressive measures, the principle of proportionality is invoked by General Comment No 3, in a statement by the CESCR,[58] as well as by the Guiding Principles adopted by the Human Rights Council.[59] Certainly, applying the principle of proportionality is not an objective craft, but involves weighting and balancing. The outcomes might depend on whether the underlying economic approach is more neoclassical or more Keynesian.[60] In order to rationalise the application of this principle, one might distinguish two tests of proportionality for retrogressive measures: *first*, the available alternatives need to be compared and weighted according to their impact on ESC rights. This follows from

[53] On the importance of proceduralisation: P O'Connell, 'Let Them Eat Cake: Socio-Economic Rights in an Age of Austerity' in A Nolan et al (n 50) 59–76, 73ff.

[54] Michalowski (n 11) 49, 53; Ssenyonjo (n 22) 67–68.

[55] For negative examples drawn from Indian labour market reforms: see Swaminatham (n 4) 206.

[56] See section V below.

[57] Müller (n 50) 139.

[58] CESCR Statement (n 52) para 10.

[59] Guiding Principles (n 8) para 2.

[60] D Elson, R Balakrishnan and J Heintz, 'Public Finance, Maximum Available Resources and Human Rights' in A Nolan et al (n 50) 13–39, 18 ff.

the term 'by reference to the totality of rights' in para 19 of General Comment No 3. This exercise includes establishing the degree to which the competing rights are affected by each alternative. The alternatives examined should not be limited to structural adjustment only, but should rather put structural adjustment into a wider perspective. Sometimes tax increases or further debt relief might be required in order to avoid disproportionate effects on ESC rights, thereby increasing the 'available resources'.[61] *Second*, the short-term disadvantages caused by retrogressive measures need to be weighted with the expected long-term benefits.[62] This requirement follows in particular from Art 4 ICESCR, which permits limitations to ESC rights only for the promotion of the general welfare. Such an assessment requires careful analysis and research, since retrogressive measures such as, to name an example, cuts in public services might cause not only long-term benefits because of their positive fiscal effects, but also potential long-term losses as an effect of reduced public service. Thus, cuts in primary healthcare might result in poorer health of large parts of the population, which might not remain without economic repercussions besides the social cost. In this respect, the temporary nature of a measure might be decisive.

This checkbox list is geared towards the ICESCR, but might also be applied to other international instruments. For some of them, the admissibility of retrogressive measures has not been defined yet with the same degree of precision. The European Committee of Social Rights stated in 2009 that the crisis provided no excuse for states not to fulfil their obligations.[63] In a decision regarding a complaint against Greece from 2012, however, it accepted that retrogressive measures concerning labour law were permissible if they do not 'excessively destabilise the situation of those who enjoy the rights enshrined in the Charter'.[64] This resembles the minimum requirements under the ICESCR. In another decision regarding a complaint against Greece from 2012, the Committee recognised the need to consolidate public finances in a crisis, but emphasised that this should not 'undermine the core framework of a national social security system or deny individuals the opportunity to enjoy the protection it offers against serious social and economic risk'.[65] This decision seems to endorse a proportionality test, especially since the Committee weighted the short-term losses in protection by the social security system with the potential long-term benefits of the measure under review.

B Measures Affecting Property Rights and Due Process Rights

In order to justify infringements upon creditors' property or due process rights, debtor states frequently have recourse to the concept of necessity or state emergency.[66] These

[61] cf General Comment No 2, para 9: 'Similarly, international measures to deal with the debt crisis should take full account of the need to protect economic, social and cultural rights through, *inter alia*, international cooperation. In many situations, this might point to the need for major debt relief initiatives'.

[62] A McBeth, *International Economic Actors and Human Rights* (London, Routledge, 2010) 191; Michalowski (n 11) 53.

[63] European Committee of Social Rights, Conclusions XIX-2 (2009) on the repercussions of the economic crisis on social rights.

[64] European Committee of Social Rights, Complaint No 65/2011, Decision on the merits, 23 May 2012, para 18.

[65] European Committee of Social Rights, Complaint No 66/2011, Decision on the merits, 23 May 2012, para 47.

[66] On necessity, see A Reinisch and C Binder, 'Debts and State of Necessity', Ch 8 in this volume.

concepts are highly controversial and lend themselves to greatly diverging interpretations by domestic and international courts. Thus, in the *Galli* case, the Argentine Suprema Corte decided that the unilateral transformation of dollar bonds into bonds of local currency had not been arbitrary because it had been justified by a state of emergency.[67] By contrast, the German Constitutional Court did not recognise the applicability of the concept of necessity between states and private citizens,[68] and investment tribunals held widely diverging views regarding the burden of proof for a state of necessity.[69]

The ECtHR has recourse to the more general concept of public interests in order to justify restructurings infringing creditors' rights. In *De Dreux-Brézé v France*, France had concluded a settlement with Russia concerning debt incurred by the Tsarist regime. Bondholders considered the payment obligations of Russia under the settlement as too low. The ECtHR emphasised that Art 1 of the First Additional Protocol did not give a right to full repayment. Rather, public interest might require a reduction of the repayments, or even their complete suspension. It granted the French government wide discretion regarding the settlement with Russia. Since negotiations had experienced severe delays, the French government had not exceeded its discretion by finally settling on the terms of the agreement. The court did not, however, consider the fact that Russia was also under an obligation to fulfil its citizens' ESC rights, something which might have tipped the scales even further in the direction of Russia.[70] In *Malysh v Russia*, the ECtHR finally recognised the need to progressively realise ESC rights as a defence against creditors' claims. The court decided that it was legitimate to defer debt repayment while prioritising expenditures for social issues.

Due process rights are indeed crucial to the success of sovereign insolvency law.[71] In emergency situations calling for an urgent solution such as IMF emergency lending, due process rights might not be respected to the same extent as expected in other situations. States should therefore seek to take preliminary measures in the first place in order to mitigate due process rights violations, and enter into inclusive negotiations with all affected parties as soon as the situation permits.

IV RESPONSIBILITY

A Debtor State

Besides customary human rights obligations, the debtor state is bound by the human rights instruments to which it is a state party, as well as by its own constitutional guarantees.[72] In case of a worsening financial situation, the principle of proportionality demands that a state is granted debt relief. One might infer from this that the debtor state is obliged to 'file' for insolvency, ie to extend an invitation to her creditors to negotiate a restructuring, as soon as the debt burden becomes unsustainable. Delays in getting negotiations off

[67] Case *Galli, Hugo Gabriel y otro c/ PEN*, La Ley 2005-C, 27.

[68] German Federal Constitutional Court, Decision of 8 May 2007, 2 BvM 1-5/03.

[69] Reinisch and Binder (n 66).

[70] In this direction see already Michalowski (n 11) 58 ff.

[71] cf von Bogdandy and Goldmann (n 3).

[72] Finding violations of, among others, the right to equality: Italian Constitutional Court, cases no 223/2012, 241/2012 and 116/2013; Portuguese Constitutional Tribunal, cases 353/2012, 187/2013 and 862/2013.

the ground have been frequent, and they usually render a bad situation worse.[73] Still, the indebted state would have to be granted a wide margin of appreciation with respect to this decision, making it very difficult for human rights bodies to review it.

In order for a state to be responsible for human rights violations, there needs to be a causal link between state action and the human rights violation (or, in case of omissions, between hypothetical state action and the prevention of human rights violations). The ECtHR does not hold states responsible for acts by which they seek to comply with international obligations deriving from a transfer of power to an international organisation presumed to ensure an equivalent standard of fundamental rights protection, unless the state enjoys discretion in implementing such obligation.[74] Working out a solution for a debtor state is sometimes a complex process involving many actors, including the IMF, the Paris Club and private creditors. Structural adjustment programmes are usually an important element of this process, and the promise to implement them might not be so voluntary after all. However, this does not relieve the debtor state of its responsibility for adjustment measures. Conflicting international obligations may not claim primacy over human rights obligations, but they might have an impact on the application of the proportionality principle, since they define the goals of the measures that need to be justified as proportional. In an ideal situation, the state might be able to figure out a solution which gives optimal weight to each of its countervailing obligations. In practice, one might have to grant governments a reasonable degree of discretion in defining that solution. In two decisions regarding public sector employment conditions, the ECtHR held that adjustment measures were proportionate and that Greece had not overstepped its discretion.[75]

B International Organisations

The imposition of conditionalities in the frame of IMF lending constitutes an exercise of public authority.[76] Whether the memoranda defining the conditionalities are legally binding or not, as soon as the IMF grants the debtor state access to its resources, the state is factually bound to follow the programme set out for the resolution of its debt crisis. Access to the Fund's resources also constitutes a condition for restructurings facilitated by the Paris Club or by venues of private creditors. They want the debtor state to participate in an IMF programme in order to make sure that it follows a growth strategy enabling it to service at least the restructured debt. According to virtually any contemporary political theory for liberal societies, the exercise of public authority needs to respect human rights guarantees. Respect for human rights thus constitutes an essential aspect of such authority's legitimacy.[77] It therefore seems apposite to examine whether and to what extent international organisations, and in particular the IMF, are bound by human rights obligations.[78]

[73] C Trebesch, 'Delays in Sovereign Debt Restructurings', working paper (2010).

[74] ECtHR, *Bosphorus v Ireland*, App no 45036/98, judgment of 30 June 2005, paras 155–57.

[75] ECtHR, *Mateus et al v Greece*, App nos 57725/12 and 62235/12, decision of 8 October 2013; *Koufaki et al v Greece*, App nos 57665/12 and 57657/12, decision of 7 May 2013.

[76] Extensively on this: von Bogdandy and Goldmann (n 3).

[77] ibid.

[78] cf G Bianco and F Fontanelli, 'Enhancing the International Monetary Fund's Compliance with Human Rights – The Issue of Accountability', see Ch 14 in this volume.

i Legal Basis of Responsibility

An obligation to observe human rights might, first, follow from the statute of the IMF. The Articles of Agreement do not explicitly mention human rights. Traditionally, the IMF saw itself as responsible for economic development, not for social policy, and cultivated the idea of its political neutrality.[79] For example, it declined to participate in the drafting of the ICESCR.[80] As recently as 2001, the Fund still explicitly rejected the application of human rights to its activities,[81] and to date it has no strategy or policy for ensuring their respect. In practice, however, the IMF has not always managed to stay out of social policy. Rather, as described in Section II, its adjustment programmes had severe consequences for social security, labour markets, healthcare and other fields where ESC rights apply.[82] This role for the IMF was probably not intended by the drafters of its Articles of Agreement, but it came to exercise it due to the evolution of international economic relationships in the post-war period.[83] It therefore seems apposite to interpret the Articles of Agreement dynamically, in line with the evolution of the Fund's mandate.[84] Article 1(v) of the Articles of Agreement, the legal basis for the imposition of conditionalities, refers to 'national and international prosperity'. If prosperity is understood as a concept that endorses the idea of development, and there is reason for this assumption since the IMF has recognised the need for development on many occasions, especially by designing specific policies for developing states, then a dynamic interpretation of this provision should recognise that the IMF is bound by human rights. For there is increasingly a conviction that development and human rights go hand in hand.[85] Danilo Türk argued already in 1991 that '[t]he link between human rights and development has become inseparable'.[86] In 1993, the Vienna Declaration and Programme of Action stipulated that '[d]emocracy, development and respect for human rights and fundamental freedoms are interdependent and mutually reinforcing'.[87] It is a matter of systemic coherence to interpret the Articles of Agreement accordingly. Interestingly, the IMF's own Guidelines on Conditionality urge the Fund 'to pay due regard to domestic social and political objectives',[88] which comprise their human rights commitments.[89] Certainly, such an interpretation of the Articles of Agreement does not amount to establishing a duty for the IMF to actively fulfil ESC rights and transform it into a development agency. But it follows that the IMF should at least respect human rights, and especially ESC rights, when car-

[79] J Gold, 'Political Considerations Are Prohibited by Articles of Agreement When the Fund Considers Requests for Use of Resources' (1983) 12 *IMF Survey* 146.

[80] UN ECOSOC, *Co-Operation Between the Commission on Human Rights and the Specialised Agencies and other Organs of the United Nations in the Consideration of Economic, Social and Cultural Rights*, UN Doc E/CN.4/534, 28 March 1951, Annex.

[81] *Economic, Social and Cultural Human Rights and the International Monetary Fund* (prepared by F Gianviti), UN Doc E/C.12/2001/WP.5, 7 May 2001, para 56.

[82] cf also R Swedberg, 'The Doctrine of Economic Neutrality of the IMF and the World Bank' (1986) *Journal of Peace Research* 377–90.

[83] See Section I above.

[84] Eg McBeth (n 62) 176–78.

[85] A Sen, *Development as Freedom* (Oxford, Oxford Unviersity Press, 1999) 35 ff; C Janik, *Die Bindung internationaler Organisationen an internationale Menschenrechtsstandards* (Tübingen, Mohr Siebeck, 2012) 369–80.

[86] Türk (n 32) para 53.

[87] Vienna Declaration and Programme of Action, adopted by the World Conference on Human Rights in Vienna on 25 June 1993, ch I, para 8.

[88] IMF Guidelines on Conditionality (2002), para 4.

[89] See Conklin and Davidson (n 25) 247–48.

rying out its activities. Also, it may not frustrate the efforts of its member states to realise ESC rights.[90] Retrogressive measures requested in adjustment programmes always need to be justifiable in accordance with the criteria set out above. The IMF already tries to live up to this obligation by its policy on social safety nets designed to mitigate the effects of austerity for the most vulnerable groups.

A second line of argument as to why the IMF is bound by human rights emphasises its character as a specialised agency of the United Nations. Articles 55 and 56 of the UN Charter make reference to human and economic rights as well as social and cultural concerns; they are understood as obliging the United Nations to obey these standards.[91] Article 59 envisages the United Nations as an overarching framework for the architecture of international law and the creation of specialised agencies following the same standards. The IMF became one of these specialised agencies, even though only after its creation.[92] Since the IMF is responsible for economic prosperity, it can be argued that the human rights obligations of the United Nations apply to it, too.[93] As membership of the IMF and the United Nations is by and large universal, one could also consider Arts 55, 56 and 59 of the UN Charter as relevant rules of international law in the sense of Art 31(3)(c) of the Vienna Convention on the Law of Treaties and interpret the IMF Articles of Agreement accordingly. The duties deriving from the character of the IMF as a specialised agency do not differ from the duties that follow from a dynamic interpretation of the Articles of Agreement. In particular, the ICESCR is addressed to states. International institutions therefore have a duty to refrain from interference and protect against it, but not necessarily a duty to fulfil.

Several arguments have been advanced against such interpretative strategies.[94] First, the relationship agreements between the United Nations and the IMF as well as the World Bank do not refer to human rights.[95] However, since the United Nations Charter contains such a reference, should the authors of the relationship agreement have wished to exclude any human rights obligations for the IMF, one might perhaps have expected a specific provision to that effect. Second, Gianviti interprets Art 24 of the ICESCR as an impediment to the application of the Covenant to the IMF. Article 24 stipulates that '[n]othing in the present Covenant shall be interpreted as impairing the provisions of the Charter of the United Nations and of the constitutions of the specialised agencies which define the respective responsibilities of the various organs of the United Nations . . .'.[96] Remarkably, the relative clause at the end of this quote is omitted in Gianviti's text. Only this makes his interpretation tenable. However, the relative clause clarifies that Art 24 addresses only the internal repartition of competencies among the various organs of both the United Nations and the specialised agencies. Third, it has been argued that the relationship agreement provides for a loose cooperation among equals and that it intends that the IMF

[90] Krajewski (n 47) 8.

[91] E Riedel and K Arend, 'Art 55(c)' in B Simma et al (eds), *The Charter of the United Nations*, vol II, 3rd edn (2012) 1565–602, margin no 8.

[92] Skogly (n 24) 101; P Alston, 'The IMF and the Right to Food'(1987) 30 *Howard Law Review* 473, 479; D Bradlow, 'The World Bank, the IMF, and Human Rights' (1996) 6 *Transnational Law & Contemporary Problems* 47–90, 63 (with respect to the World Bank); Lucas (n 31) 119 ff.

[93] McBeth (n 62) 170–71.

[94] Overview in F Gianviti, 'Economic, Social and Cultural Rights and the International Monetary Fund' in P Alston (ed), *Non-State Actors and Human Rights* (Oxford, Oxford University Press, 2005) 113–38, 119–20; Gianviti (n 81) para 15.

[95] Janik (n 85) 344.

[96] Gianviti (n 94) para 12.

remain an independent organisation.[97] But the independence of the IMF is manifested first and foremost in the fact that it is not subject to the instructions of the United Nations, unlike other specialised agencies. Imposing on the IMF those human rights obligations by which the United Nations are bound themselves does not compromise the Fund's independence vis-à-vis the United Nations. Fourth, recourse has been taken to Art X of the relationship agreement, which stipulates that the latter may not modify the Articles of Agreement.[98] But Art X can also be understood as referring to formal amendments. In that way its function would be to signify that the relationship agreement is not of the same normative quality as the Articles of Agreement. In such an understanding, Art X does not stand against interpreting the Articles of Agreement in light of the UN Charter and its provisions on human rights.

Similar to the previously discussed line of argument, a third view argues that the IMF is subordinated to the United Nations and the human rights provisions of its Charter by virtue of Art 103 of the UN Charter.[99] However, this provision only applies to the UN Member States. It does not bind other international organisations or subject them to the human rights provisions of the Charter.[100] At most, Art 103 might serve as a guide to the interpretation of other agreements such as the Articles of Agreement, which should not be presumed to violate other international duties of their member states. However, it does not directly bind the organisation based on such agreement.

According to a fourth view, the human rights obligations of the IMF derive from those of their member states.[101] Article 2 ICESCR obliges developed states parties to assist developing states; something which they should also observe when they carry out international interactions through the IMF.[102] However, such 'mortgage theories', which transfer the obligations of states to international organisations, fail to account for the difference between a state acting for itself and a state acting in the frame of an international organisation as one of its members, over which it does not have control.[103] International organisations are separate legal entities which develop their own dynamics, and the organisation as such remains unaffected by other international obligations of some or all of its members.

Finally, the IMF needs to respect customary human rights obligations. Although custom is created by state practice, international organisations are generally considered to be bound by customary international law.[104] However, the scope of customary human rights norms is probably small and controversial, especially with respect to ESC rights. The rights enumerated in the Universal Declaration of Human Rights might have acquired the character of customary norms,[105] but certainly not all of the guarantees contained in

[97] Janik (n 85) 341; the text of the relationship agreement is quoted in Skogly (n 22) 103.

[98] Gianviti (n 94) para 16.

[99] Skogly (n 24) 101; Ssenyonjo (n 20) 131–32.

[100] cf ECJ, *Yassin Abdullah Kadi and Al Barakaat International Foundation v Council of the European Union and Commission of the European Communities*, Joined Cases C-402/05 P and C-415/05 P, Judgment of 3 September 2008.

[101] eg Ssenyonjo (n 22) 117–18; Skogly (n 22) 106–08.

[102] Michalowski (n 11) 46.

[103] Note that General Comment No 18 para 33, referred to by Ssenyonjo (n 22, 117–18) in support of his view, does not address the exercise of voting rights in international organisations.

[104] CF Amerasinghe, *Principles of the Institutional Law of International Organizations*, 2nd edn, (2005) 20–21; Ghazi (n 33) 133–34; Janik (n 85) 449.

[105] Some voices in the older literature recognised customary status only for core civil and political rights, cf Lucas (n 31) 117; Gianviti (n 81) paras 18–20. Others argue that only a small core of ESC right has customary status, such as the prohibition of forced labour, eg Krajewski (n 47) 8.

the ICESCR since it does not enjoy universal ratification and an equally universal practice respecting all the rights contained therein. Support for the view that at least the core of ESC rights forms part of customary law might be derived from a number of international soft law instruments, such as the Copenhagen Declaration on Social Development, which envisages social development and social justice as goals that cannot be attained without respect for human rights;[106] the CESCR's General Comment No 8, which stipulates that international organisations are bound by at least a core of ESC rights;[107] and the recent General Principles of the Human Rights Council.[108] The modifications in the IMF's policies such as social safety nets in order to prevent the most egregious consequences of adjustment policies for the most vulnerable groups of society might serve as examples for the practice that brings such customary law into existence. But be that as it may, compared to the statutory and UN Charter-based lines of argument, the argument from customary law seems to be weaker and fraught with uncertainty.

ii Causality and Attribution

It would be an overstatement to derive from the preceding considerations that international financial institutions are responsible for negative effects of adjustment policies on ESC rights. Rather, adjustment policies are always implemented by the member state, not by the IMF itself. This raises the question when ESC rights infringements are attributable to the IMF.[109]

In principle, the IMF bases conditionality on the idea of ownership.[110] But it is questionable whether and to what extent this discharges the IMF from its responsibility. Indeed, there are good reasons not to discharge the IMF too quickly. In the implementation of structural adjustment programmes, the margin of appreciation of the debtor state is sometimes rather small. Although those programmes are formally considered as voluntary commitments, the IMF influences their development and implementation in many important respects. First, the IMF's Debt Sustainability Analysis (DSA) sets the preconditions for any structural adjustment programme. States will only receive loans if their adjustment programme enables them to reach with a high probability medium-term debt sustainability as defined by the DSA.[111] In fact, the IMF even insists on keeping control over the DSA. In response to requests from the private sector to be formally included in the drafting of DSAs, the IMF maintained that this would compromise its independence and credibility.[112] Second, the fact that many adjustment programmes contain similar, almost standardised conditions demonstrates the influence of the IMF in their drafting.[113] Indeed, the adjustment programmes usually reflect (or at least reflected in the past) what has been termed the Washington Consensus, ie supply-oriented economic policies geared towards increasing a country's competitiveness.[114] Those policies are (or at least were) favoured by the IMF

[106] Copenhagen Declaration on Social Development, UN Doc A/CONF.166/9 (1995), para 5.

[107] CESCR, General Comment No 8 on the relationship between economic sanctions and respect for economic, social and cultural rights, 12 December 1997, para 7.

[108] General Principles (n 8) para 9.

[109] Bradlow (n 92) 72; Michalowski (n 11) 43.

[110] See n 34.

[111] See IMF (n 5) 9; IMF, *Staff Guidance Note for Public Debt Sustainability Analysis in Market-Access Countries*, 9 May 2013, 11–17.

[112] IMF (n 5) 40.

[113] Skogly (n 24) 756.

[114] Bradlow (n 92) 71.

and its most important member states, but not necessarily by the debtor states. By setting the general conditions for adjustment measures which violate ESC rights, one might attribute responsibility to the IMF at least for aiding and abetting in accordance with Art 14 of the Draft Articles on the Responsibility of International Organizations.[115]

Depending on the case, the IMF might even incur responsibility for the violation of ESC rights by virtue of its effective control over an adjustment programme, in accordance with Art 15 of the Draft Articles on the Responsibility of International Organizations. Most structural adjustment programmes are probably not specific enough for such responsibility to arise because they grant the debtor state considerable leeway for implementation. At times, however, the IMF might insist on the inclusion of very specific measures in adjustment programmes, leaving the debtor state with no effective choice in order to avoid human rights violations, or just with a choice between different options which all violate human rights in one way or another. The wage cuts and layoffs for public service employees provided for in the recent Greek Memorandum of Understanding might constitute an example.[116] By contrast, with respect to certain adjustment measures such as the introduction of taxes on property and luxury goods, the memorandum envisages the establishment of a framework for avoiding cases of hardship.

Poverty Reduction Strategy Papers should give the country concerned a greater voice in the formulation of adjustment policies and put the idea of ownership into practice. They enable participation to a greater degree, which should in theory have consequences for the responsibility of the IMF in case of human rights infringement. But in practice, the programmes devised by Poverty Reduction Strategy Papers still reflect the Washington Consensus.[117] If human rights violations arise in such a case, establishing the responsibility of the IMF would require a difficult examination of the effective impact of the country on the formulation of its strategy paper.

C Paris Club

The legal basis of the Paris Club's responsibility is more difficult to establish. Legally speaking, it is only an informal network of governments with important roles in bilateral lending, although in fact it has the role of an international organisation. The Paris Club does not have statutes, nor is it an agency of the United Nations. Indeed, the question is whether the Paris Club has legal personality at all. Since the Paris Club acts as an entity with rules on membership, established decision-making processes, a framework of material rules for debt restructurings, and a secretariat borrowed from the French ministry of finance, one might indeed argue that it has some kind of legal capacity of its own, even though it lacks a founding treaty. In that case, the Paris Club would at least be bound by customary human rights law. Should one deny any proper legal capacity to the Paris Club, each of its member states would have to bear responsibility for the human rights impact of Paris Club decisions and would have to have them measured by the human rights

[115] Previously, scholars drew analogies to Art 16 of the ILC Articles on State Responsibility: Ghazi (n 33) 192–93; Janik (n 85) 119.

[116] IMF (n 29) 9. Other examples from troika negotiations in the euro area confirm this impression, see M Ioannidis, 'EU financial assistance Conditionality after "Two Pack"' (2014) 74 *Zeitschrift für ausländisches öffentliches Recht und Völkerrecht* 61–104, 95.

[117] cf UNDP, *Review of the Poverty Reduction Strategy Paper (Bangladesh)*, December 2001.

standards to which it subscribed. While the legal basis of the latter line of argument might be more solid, it adds the complication that each member might have different extraterritorial human rights commitments. This brings us to the next section.

D Bilateral Lenders

While the duties arising for states under the ICCPR are by no means limited to the territory of a state,[118] there has been a lively debate as to whether the obligation to respect, to protect and to fulfil ESC rights might extend beyond the territory of member states of the ICESCR. Some base this view on a dynamic interpretation of the ICESCR.[119] Some passages in several General Comments indicate that the CESCR assumes that such extraterritorial duties have emerged.[120] This view has been corroborated by principles developed by renowned legal experts in the field. The Maastricht Principles on Extraterritorial Obligations of States in the Area of Economic, Social and Cultural Rights assume at least a procedural duty of the member states of international organisations to 'use their influence' for the realisation of ESC rights.[121] While some consider this as a purely moral duty,[122] one might derive a corresponding legal duty from the universal, *erga omnes* character of human rights obligations which finds recognition, inter alia, in Art 55 of the UN Charter.[123] This confirms a view expressed by the drafters of the Tilburg Guiding Principles.[124] In support of this position, it might be argued that the globalisation of the economy, which has certainly provided many people, companies and states with great opportunities, has also created economic interdependencies which reduce the capacity of states to realise ESC rights independently. In accordance with a purposive interpretation of ESC rights, which considers their codifications as living instruments, the emergence of economic interdependencies must not come at the expense of ESC rights. Rather, the scope and content of ESC rights needs to change in accordance with the transformation of the economic, legal and political framework which sets the precondition for their realisation. Therefore, the deliberate creation of economic interdependencies affecting the realisation of ESC rights entails the recognition of *legal* interdependencies among states in the form of extraterritorial ESC rights obligations as their necessary legal corollary. As with the human rights obligations of the IMF, this is a matter of systemic coherence in international law.

This situation raises the question as to the extent of states' extraterritorial obligations to respect, protect or fulfil ESC rights. The most obvious case is the obligation to respect. It would prohibit deliberate efforts to infringe ESC rights in other states, whether in the frame of structural adjustment programmes or not.[125] The obligation to protect amounts to a duty to prevent persons and companies, such as private creditors, from taking measures which endanger the realisation of ESC rights in third states. An excellent example

[118] eg Human Rights Committee, General Comment No 31, para 10.

[119] cf Krajewski (n 47) 9; Janik (n 85) 147–49.

[120] See CESCR General Comment No 8, para 7; General Comment No 13, para 56; General Comment No 15, para 33; General Comment No 17, para 56.

[121] Maastricht Principles (2011), paras 19 and 20.

[122] Janik (n 85) 150.

[123] O de Schutter et al, 'Commentary to the Maastricht Principles on Extraterritorial Obligations of States in the Area of Economic, Social and Cultural Rights' (2012) 34 *Human Rights Quarterly* 1084–169, 1127; McBeth (n 62) 51.

[124] Tilburg Guiding Principles on World Bank, IMF and Human Rights, October 2001, April 2002, para 8.

[125] Ssenyonjo (n 22) 72–73.

for how states might comply with this duty in practice was set by the United Kingdom Debt Relief (Developing Countries) Act of 2010. It came after some 'vulture funds' tried to profit from debt relief granted to low-income developing countries in order to improve the provision of essential public services.[126] The most difficult aspect is certainly the extraterritorial dimension of the obligation to fulfil ESC rights. Applying *mutatis mutandis* the effective control test stipulated in Art 9 of the Articles on State Responsibility, states will normally not have an obligation to realise ESC rights in third states except if they are under their domination like occupied territories. Otherwise, states are only under an obligation to cooperate pursuant to Art 2(1) ICESCR. In the context of sovereign debt workouts, this might amount to a duty to enter into negotiations about the restructuring of unsustainable debt.[127]

E Private Creditors

The human rights obligations of private creditors depend on whether they exercise public authority, or participate in the exercise thereof, or not. Some creditor 'clubs' convened for the purpose of negotiating sovereign debt restructurings (like the London Club or the Institute of International Finance in the case of the recent Greek debt restructuring) act in such close cooperation with the IMF, the Paris Club, and other international organisations such as the European Union, and according to the standards required by them, that one might consider them as exercising public authority delegated to them by those organisations.[128] In such a case, one might assume that the (implicit) delegation includes the duty to respect the human rights obligations of the principal.

However, such acts of delegation may not be presumed lightly. If private actors such as funds or even retail investors through their representatives participate in debt restructurings, the question arises as to what extent they are bound by human rights obligations. The rise of globalisation and with it of powerful, transnational actors has triggered a discussion whether the latter are bound by human rights. Some point out the universal character of human rights and argue that at least a minimum of them should apply to private actors.[129] Recently, the Guiding Principles confirmed this view.[130] Most importantly, the 2011 update of the OECD Guidelines for Multinational Enterprises stipulates that '[e]nterprises should respect the internationally recognised human rights of those affected by their activities'.[131] Although non-binding, the OECD Guidelines comprise a quasi-judicial enforcement mechanism which allows for a human rights review of private economic activities upon request by individuals or associations.[132] Such horizontal human

[126] eg *Donegal Int'l Ltd v Zambia* [2007] EWHC (Comm) 197.

[127] On different possible legal bases of such a duty, see von Bogdandy and Goldmann (n 3).

[128] von Bogdandy and Goldmann (n 3).

[129] A Reinisch, 'The Changing International Legal Framework for Dealing with Non-State Actors' in Alston (ed) (n 94) 71, 72; McBeth (n 62) 59–60.

[130] Guiding Principles (n 8) para 9.

[131] OECD Guidelines for Multinational Enterprises (2011), Part II, Guiding Principles, A.2; see also Part IV on human rights.

[132] See, eg, M Goldmann, 'OECD Guidelines for Multinational Enterprises: The Aker Kvaerner Case – Corporate Social Responsibility and Human Rights at Guantanamo Bay' in S Cassese et al (eds), *Global Administrative Law: The Casebook*, 3rd edn (Rome, Istituto di Ricerche sulla Pubblica Amministrazione, 2012) vol VII, 131–36.

rights effects, which are rare, but not unknown in domestic constitutional law,[133] find theoretical support in the very idea of human rights as the expression of the minimum of mutual respect which individuals owe each other in a society.[134]

V RECTIFYING ASYMMETRIES THROUGH HUMAN RIGHTS IMPACT ASSESSMENTS

Certainly, the deployment of human rights in sovereign debt workouts cannot prevent hardship in economic and financial crises. But it might trigger a process of reflection and deliberation, which would ultimately provide a counterweight to the asymmetry which currently exists between creditors' rights and the rights of the people most affected by sovereign debt workouts. Human rights as argumentative burdens in the justification of adjustment measures might make stakeholders think twice when imposing structural adjustment and search for less severe alternatives, or provide more safeguards for the most vulnerable groups of society.[135] Respect for human rights does not amount to denying the validity of contractual commitments (*pacta sunt servanda*), or to abolishing conditionalities and structural adjustment. It would only make debt workouts fairer and prevent cases of excessive hardship. But the government of the debtor state would still have to pay a political price for debt workouts, which should prevent moral hazard. On the other hand, fairer, more balanced structural adjustment programmes might be easier to implement and therefore amount to more effective debt workouts enabling the state to resume debt service earlier.

Discourse about the human rights effects of debt workouts should take place, first and foremost, within the international institutions charged with the negotiation and implementation of debt workouts. As this chapter has demonstrated, most of them are bound by at least a core of ESC rights as well as civil and political rights. In addition, investment tribunals should include such considerations in the interpretation of the fair and equitable treatment standard.[136] The same applies for National Contact Points erected pursuant to the OECD Guidelines for Multinational Enterprises. And of course, the new Optional Protocol of the ICESCR provides new opportunities for human rights discourse and enforcement in this context.

Beyond the mechanisms which are already available, it might be useful to include a human rights impact assessment as a routine procedure in sovereign debt restructuring negotiations and in particular in the drafting of structural adjustment programmes.[137] It should explore potential risks ensuing from structural adjustment programmes such as resettlements, unemployment, wage cuts, cuts in public services, and discriminatory effects. The statutory powers of the IMF should allow it to carry out such an assessment. It would help the Fund to respect 'domestic social and political principles' of its members, as required by Art IV(3)(b) of the Articles of Agreement. Those principles also

[133] German Federal Constitutional Court, *Lüth*, judgment of 15 January 1958, BverfGE 7, 198.

[134] J Habermas, *Between Facts and Norms* (Cambridge, Polity Press, 1998) ch 3, I (on the common origin of human rights and democracy); J Rawls, *A Theory of Justice* (Oxford, Oxford University Press, 1971) 52 ff.

[135] Krajewski (n 47) 17.

[136] D Desierto, 'Human Rights and Investment in Economic Emergencies: Conflict of Treaties, Interpretation, Valuation Decisions', working paper, SSRN.

[137] Skogly (n 24) 759, 775; Bradlow (n 83) 83–84.

include member states' human rights obligations.[138] Such an impact assessment would require the participation of potentially affected individuals and groups, either directly or through representatives. This might also enhance the legitimacy of structural adjustment programmes. Certainly, the impact of structural adjustments is notoriously difficult to assess.[139] Human rights impact assessments should not amount to mere checkbox-style examinations based on a few highly aggregate indicators.[140] Rather, their point is to retrieve information on the ground and provide valuable input into a complex decision-making process without being capable of determining its outcome. That will always remain a political question.

[138] cf Skogly (n 24) 761; Bradlow (n 92) 81.

[139] Designing indicators and measuring attribution constitute particular challenges, see BA Andreassen and H-O Sano, 'What's the Goal? What's the Purpose? Observations on Human Rights Impact Assessment' (2007) 11 *International Journal of Human Rights* 275–92.

[140] J Harrison and M-A Stephenson, 'Assessing the Impact of the Public Spending Cuts: Taking Human Rights and Equality Seriously' in A Nolan et al (n 50) 219–41, 234ff.

7

A Sovereign Debt Overhang, Human Rights and the MDGs: Legal Problems through an Economist's Lens

KUNIBERT RAFFER

I INTRODUCTION

AN UNSUSTAINABLE DEBT burden compromises the full enjoyment of human rights. Financial crises have routinely affected opportunities to enjoy these rights – economic, social and cultural rights in particular. They might not impact on civil and political rights barring the government from concrete actions (such as torturing people) in the same way. Nevertheless, the capacity of the state to fulfil obligations under international human rights laws, such as guaranteeing a fair trial, or sufficient supervision of the police to prevent torture, may suffer. The problem is complicated further in the case of countries because the debtor having unsustainable debts is a legal personality of its own – not being human these entities do not enjoy human rights. Nevertheless its debt overhang directly affects and usually compromises the full enjoyment of all human rights by its population.

The need to protect human rights and the human dignity of debtors has meanwhile been recognised by all civilised municipal laws.[1] Debt slavery, indenture and debt prisons are things of the past, not least for economic reasons. Cutting out the proverbial pound of flesh may delight perverted creditors but does not yield worthwhile financial results. A minimum of resources is exempt and immune, even bona fide creditors cannot attach or seize them, such as the debtor's last winter coat in Austria. Technically, these exempt objects could be sold (even though at modest prices usually) and cover part of legitimate creditor claims. Debtors cannot be forced to starve themselves or their children to be able to pay. Human rights and human dignity are given unconditional priority over repayment, even though insolvency only deals with claims based on solid and proper legal foundations.

[1] eg USC Title 11 Section 522 and USC Title 11, Chapter 9 or in Austria www.ris.bka.gv.at/Dokumente/Justiz/JJR_19880427_OGH0002_009OBA00087_8800000_010/JJR_19880427_OGH0002_009OBA00087_8800000_010.pdf on exemptions, accessed 3 March 2013. An example from Germany: www.zeit.de/2012/40/Schulden-Reform-Insolvenzrecht, accessed 3 March 2013.

Neither insolvency protection granted to individual debtors nor the total isolation of owners of joint-stock or limited liability companies from any consequences of the bankruptcy of their companies (beyond losing their shares in this company) are available to the inhabitants of a sovereign debtor. They are the only ones denied any protection when (rather than if) a state defaults. Official creditors in particular still relish 'their' pound of flesh when it comes to the population of sovereign debtors in default.

Traditionally, there exists a divide between civil and political human rights and economic, social and cultural rights that have to be realised by state actions. Regarding sovereign debt crises, however, there seems to be a bridge. Demanding that governments abstain from policies destroying economic, social and cultural rights may be seen as similar to requesting governments not to torture, though more difficult to achieve in practice. Focusing on economic and social rights, the human rights obligations of governments and key human rights principles in connection with budget cuts are definitely new territory, in economics as well as in law.[2] Examining such cuts – typical in debt overburdened countries – in the UK under a human rights perspective, Elson[3] concludes that 'there is evidence to suggest noncompliance with the human rights obligations of the UK government'.

Similar to economic, social and cultural rights, the Millennium Development Goals (MDGs) aim at ensuring minimum, humane standards.[4] In contrast, though, the MDGs fall short of guaranteeing everyone this standard. They aim at improving the standard of living of the poor, without guaranteeing full enjoyment of human rights to everyone. The 2003 *Human Development Report* subtitled *Millennium Development Goals: A compact among nations to end human poverty* describes the relation between the two:

> The Goals also reflect a human rights agenda – rights to food, education, healthcare and decent living standards, as enumerated in the Universal Declaration of Human Rights. The need to ensure all these rights – economic, social and cultural – confers obligations on the governments of countries both rich and poor.[5]

The Report's Box 1.1[6] elaborates further on this relation. One has to agree that MDGs reflect human rights or that both concepts 'share a common motivation'. They 'also mirror the fundamental motivation for human rights'. While permitting gradual improvements, both concepts rule out retrogression. Nevertheless, in spite of shared interests between the MDGs and human rights there exists 'relative reluctance of both sides' to 'embrace one another'.[7]

This chapter will show that in the case of state insolvency the MDGs can and should play an important role in protecting human rights and human dignity, even though this protection falls short of full implementation of human rights. Retrogression, though, would be excluded or at least reduced. Reality being as it is, substantial improvements of

[2] International law tries to elaborate minimum standards, though not connected to state insolvency, by the concept of minimum core; cf K Young, 'The Minimum Core of Economic and Social Rights: A Concept in Search of Content' (2008) 33(1) *Yale Journal of International Law* 113–75.

[3] D Elson, 'The Reduction of the UK Budget Deficit: A Human Rights Perspective' (2012) 26 *International Review of Applied Economics* 177.

[4] This mainly refers to MDGs 1–6.

[5] UNDP, *Human Development Report 2003, Millennium Development Goals: A compact among nations to end human poverty* (New York, Oxford University Press, 2003) 29.

[6] ibid, 28.

[7] P Alston, 'A Human Rights Perspective on the Millennium Development Goals' (undated), paper prepared as a contribution to the work of the Millennium Project Task Force on Poverty and Economic Development, 9.

the lot and the rights of the poor by debtor protection are worth establishing even if these fail to comply with ideals.

II HUMAN RIGHTS OBLIGATIONS AND UNPAYABLE DEBTS

The Universal Declaration of Human Rights, generally seen as the foundation of international human rights law, contains 'the right to social security . . . and in accordance with the organization and resources of each State, of the economic, social and cultural rights indispensable for his dignity and the free development of his personality'.[8] It also contains the right to work (Article 23), 'to a standard of living adequate for the health and well-being of himself and of his family' (Article 25), and education (Article 26). Clearly, all these rights and the entitlement 'to a social and international order in which the rights and freedoms set forth in this Declaration can be fully realized' (Article 28) are infringed upon by unsustainable debts and in debt crises. Unfortunately, they are by no means guaranteed during boom eras either. Hunger and poverty as well as joblessness have persisted, especially in the South. Due to the same set of 'debt management' policies they are spreading to Europe too.

These declared rights have become part of international treaties, such as the International Covenant on Economic, Social and Cultural Rights (ICESCR), which entered into force in 1976. It expressly contains obligations of signatory states. Its Article 6, for example, obliges the 'States Parties to the present Covenant' to 'take appropriate steps to safeguard'[9] the right to work. The Committee on Economic, Social and Cultural Rights monitors its implementation. Although generally difficult to enforce, these rights are not totally deprived of legal protection. Elson recalls that 'legal procedures can be invoked and governments can be taken to court for non-compliance'[10] in many countries having constitutions or municipal laws that safeguard these rights.[11] In the UK a women's rights organisation brought an unprecedented court case asking for a judicial review of the budget because a gender equality impact assessment had not been published.[12] The court did not grant a judicial review of the budget, but made clear that government budgets are subject to equality law, and a 'permission hearing' took place. Represented by the Treasury, the government appeared, conceding that they had not met all the requirements of the gender equality duty when drawing up the budget, expressing regret and pledging to take a different approach in future.[13]

In practice these rights have routinely been infringed by debt management. One essential feature from 'Structural Adjustment', under whichever name, from the late 1970s to Greece nowadays is austerity policies lemon-squeezing foreign exchange in favour of creditors. A larger slice of Gross National Income (GNI) has to go to debt service at the expense of fighting poverty and of financing expenditures securing rights such as education. This stress on repayment and creditor interest was a fundamental change in the

[8] UN, The Universal Declaration of Human Rights (1948), www.un.org/en/documents/udhr/index.shtml#atop, accessed 20 November 2012.

[9] International Covenant on Economic, Social and Cultural Rights, www2.ohchr.org/english/law/cescr.htm, accessed 20 November 2012.

[10] Elson (n 3) 179.

[11] ibid. Elson mentions South Africa and India as examples of where this happened.

[12] ibid, 184.

[13] ibid.

1970s. During the McNamara years the International Bank for Reconstruction and Development (IBRD) had advocated helping the poor, although with debatable results on the ground. It did not, for instance, reach the poorest 20 per cent.[14] With debt problems increasing, and eager to assume the role of a debt manager, the Bank changed its views radically. Even before 1982, the year the debt crisis 'officially' started, the IBRD[15] put its new approach succinctly into a nutshell, describing the 'major drawback' of efficient food subsidies as costly, often using up 'scarce foreign exchange or aid'.[16] Money that could be used to pay creditors was used up to feed the hungry. In plain English: no money to be wasted on expenditures necessary to protect the rights enumerated by the Universal Declaration of Human Rights or – formulated in a more instrumental and modern way – the MDGs. Austerity measures cut down social expenditure, causing misery and economic decline in debtor economies. The Bretton Woods Institutions (BWIs) insisted that carrying on 'Structural Adjustment' had positive impacts and was in the very interest of the poor. Special measures to protect them would thus be superfluous if not harmful. Emphasising human needs might obstruct needed reforms.[17] Basically, this view was held until the famous UNICEF study *Adjustment with a Human Face*[18] was published in 1987, although the BWIs had been confronted with the effects of their debt management before.

BWI staff at the highest level explicitly and clearly connected Structural Adjustment with highly negative effects on the poor, recognising a causal link between the two. In 1987 the IMF's Managing Director, Michel Camdessus, admitted at the UN Economic and Social Council (ECOSOC) that the poorest 'too often . . . carried the heaviest burden of adjustment'.[19] Obviously, this was not seen as a reason to provide more protection to them in line with human rights covenants. Quite the contrary, the IBRD's Senior Vice President, Ernest Stern, praised 'Structural Adjustment' as the response to a 'feasible . . . call for increased sacrifices'[20] by the population, which the IBRD had to back and ensure by a 'firm understanding' of monitoring.

The term 'Structural Adjustment' is used with inverted commas because the BWIs monopolised it to mean their own specific ideas, or whatever they were doing. While there is an evident need for reform in countries on the brink of default or which have already defaulted – or for structural adjustment – this does not mean that the specific set of BWI prescriptions is indicated. Empirical outcome so far rather suggests the opposite. Early attempts to prove success by econometric results were short lived.[21] Empirical evidence remained, at best, inconclusive. Usually there was no statistically significant difference between 'adjusters' and 'non-adjusters'. Statistical methods, such as country groupings, were repeatedly attacked as purpose serving.[22] One of the extremely few statistically

[14] K Raffer, *Debt Management for Development – Protection of the Poor and the Millennium Development Goals* (Cheltenham, Edward Elgar, 2010) 117.

[15] IBRD (International Bank for Development and Reconstruction), *World Development Report 1980* (Washington DC, IBRD, 1980) 62.

[16] ibid.

[17] cf K Raffer, 'Structural Adjustment, Liberalisation, and Poverty' (1994) X(4) *Journal für Entwicklungspolitik* (Special issue: 'Structural Adjustment' edited by K Raffer) 431–41.

[18] GA Cornia, R Jolly and F Stewart (eds), *Adjustment with a Human Face* (Oxford, Oxford University Press, 1987).

[19] *IMF Survey*, 29 June 1987, 195.

[20] E Stern, 'World Bank Financing and Structural Adjustment' in J Williamson (ed), *IMF Conditionality* (Washington DC, IIF and MIT, 1983) 91.

[21] Raffer (n 14) 119.

[22] ibid, 118–23.

significant results was published by Khan,[23] an IMF econometrician, in the IMF Staff Papers: a predicted reduction in growth rates of at least 0.7 per cent of GDP each year countries had an IMF programme. Others found adverse effects of 'Structural Adjustment' on growth, particularly in countries with low slippage on conditionality, and declining shares of investment in GDP. Eventually, the IBRD[24] itself acknowledged that 'Structural Adjustment' lending had achieved some success regarding the improvement of the balance of payments (largely due to import compression, critics rightly pointed out) but did not encourage investments nor enable debtors to grow out of debts. The GATT (General Agreement on Tariffs and Trade) noted that 'adjustment has involved mostly import contraction rather than export expansion', which threatened to result in a 'vicious circle of reduced imports and reduced export potential'.[25] The GATT[26] observed import cuts 'large enough to affect the future productive capacity of these countries'. Obviously, 'Structural Adjustment' did impair future production capacity and growth and thus the economic base for financing goals such as the MDGs.

Empirical evidence found a serious deterioration of living standards and living conditions in debtor countries. May it suffice to quote SAPRIN,[27] a global network established after a group of NGOs approached the then new IBRD president, James Wolfensohn, proposing that the Bank and civil society jointly assess the impact of 'Adjustment' programmes in 1995. This led to the Structural Adjustment Participatory Review Initiative (SAPRI), officially launched in July 1997, designed as a tripartite exercise bringing together organisations of civil society, debtor governments and the IBRD in a joint review of Structural Adjustment Programmes and an exploration of new policy options. This exercise soon produced evidence of devastating consequences of adjustment measures on production, employment and social services in debtor countries. Unsurprisingly, the IBRD's bureaucracy opposed SAPRI. Little of the analysis made its way into country programming. Influence on the Bank's own adjustment assessments and operations also remained limited at best. This joint learning exercise eventually ended with two separate final reports, reportedly at the IBRD's insistence: one rather formal and vacuous produced by the IBRD, the other by NGOs.[28]

More recently, the Independent Expert on the effects of foreign debt and other related international financial obligations of states on the full enjoyment of all human rights, particularly economic, social and cultural rights of the UN,[29] concluded in his report that 'apart from undermining obligations on economic, social and cultural rights, excessive debt burdens pose major obstacles for some countries in achieving the Millennium Development Goals'.[30] In debtor countries of the Eurozone similar mechanisms are at

[23] M Khan, 'The Macroeconomic Effects of Fund-Supported Adjustment Programs' (1990) 37(2) *IMF Staff Papers*, 195–231.

[24] IBRD, *Adjustment Lending: Ten Years of Experience* (Washington DC, IBRD, 1990).

[25] GATT, *International Trade 1985–86*, 1986, 95.

[26] ibid, 95.

[27] SAPRIN (Structural Adjustment Participatory Review International Network), *Structural Adjustment: The SAPRI Report The Policy Roots of Economic Crisis, Poverty and Inequality* (London, Zed Books, 1994) or www.saprin.org/global_rpt.htm, accessed 20 November 2012; see also Raffer (n 14).

[28] cf Raffer (n 14) 122.

[29] On this initiative see Lumina's Chapter 16 in this volume.

[30] C Lumina, 'Report of the Independent Expert on the effects of foreign debt and other related international financial obligations of States on the full enjoyment of all human rights, particularly economic, social and cultural rights', General Assembly 10 April 2011, A/HRC/20/23, http://daccess-dds-ny.un.org/doc/UNDOC/GEN/G12/128/80/PDF/G1212880.pdf?OpenElement, accessed 20 November 2012.

work. Thus, the Memorandum of Understanding on Specific Economic Policy Conditionality between the Troika and Cyprus contains obligations to cut wages and expenditure on education, health, and social transfers as well as to increase regressive VAT rates, to introduce fees for medical services, and to abolish educational allowances. The existing cost of living adjustment of wages and salaries is to be halved to only half the official price increases in the previous year unless negative growth was registered for this year. Then wages and salaries are frozen. Pensions are to be frozen, welfare expenditures to be cut. The Global South has finally arrived in Southern Europe.

In spite of these reversals, quite substantial change has occurred in debt management since the early 1980s. Under pressure from civil society, most notably the international Jubilee Movement, supported by findings such as those of the UNICEF study, some form of debtor protection was first accepted by the Enhanced Highly Indebted Poor Countries Initiative (HIPC II). An official anti-poverty focus was introduced, eventually at least accepting the idea of debtor protection, not necessarily always fully honoured by practice, but with visible improvements. Anti-poverty measures, namely a Poverty Reduction Strategy, were made part and parcel of HIPC II.[31] Poverty Reduction Strategy Papers (PRSP) are prepared through a participatory process involving civil society and a Poverty Reduction and Growth Facility (PRGF) was officially established. In reality, the PRGF is just what was 'formerly known as the Enhanced Structural Adjustment Facility (ESAF)',[32] as the IMF itself explains: ESAF renamed, to emphasise the new, official anti-poverty focus. This does not indicate a fundamental reorientation of thinking. Nevertheless, it was an important change allowing debtor countries to spend more on providing basic health services or education to their inhabitants. The IMF's proposal of a Sovereign Debt Restructuring Mechanism (SDRM) again failed to incorporate any form of protection of people in indebted countries.[33] 'Debt management' in Southern euro-countries does not even respect and guarantee the minimum of debtor protection established by HIPC II, falling severely behind even this relatively low standard.

Naturally, anti-poverty measures as such do not satisfy the standard set by human rights. As long as there remain people whose social and economic rights are not fully safeguarded and realised, the human rights of some continue to be violated – which unfortunately had also been the case before default. One cannot expect a solution to state insolvency also to overcome all previously existing problems and shortcomings. But these measures improve the lives of many – though not all – people.

This also applies to the MDGs. Not all Goals and Targets even aim at eliminating living conditions that violate social, economic and cultural human rights. It may be argued that MDG 2 ('Achieve universal primary education'), for example, realises the right to education pursuant to Article 26 of The Universal Declaration of Human Rights. However, as it does not demand technical and professional education to be made generally available, nor make higher education equally accessible to all on the basis of merit (Article 26(1)), one may also say that it falls short of Article 26.

[31] See Raffer (n 14) 29.

[32] IMF, 'IMF Financial Activities – Update January 15, 2009', 2009, www.imf.org/external/np/tre/activity/2009/011509.htm, accessed 22 November 2012.

[33] cf K Raffer, 'The IMF's SDRM – Simply Disastrous Rescheduling Management?' in C Jochnick and FA Preston (eds), *Sovereign Debt at the Crossroads – Challenges and Proposals for Resolving the Third World Debt Crisis* (Oxford, Oxford University Press, 2006) 246–67.

Other MDGs, MDG 1 in particular, cannot by any stretch of the imagination be interpreted as attempting to safeguard human rights for all. In spite of its wording – 'Eradicate extreme poverty and hunger' – Goal 1 only intends to halve the proportion of the extremely poor (Target 1) and the proportion of people suffering from hunger. Targets 10 and 11 (Goal 7) are to halve the proportion of people without sustainable access to safe drinking water, and to 'achieve significant improvement in the lives of at least 100 million slum dwellers, by 2020'[34] respectively. One critique from human rights advocates is therefore that '[t]he MDGs' preparedness to settle for half measures (e.g. halving poverty, instead of eliminating it) is incompatible with the HR commitment to the right of every individual and the need to seek comprehensive solutions'.[35] Economically, though, it is a Paretian improvement if some people are better off without anyone being worse off, and thus preferable to the initial (pre-improvement) situation. Technically, it would also be in line with Article 2 of the ICESCR[36] requesting each signatory to take steps 'to the maximum of its available resources, with a view to achieving progressively the full realization of the rights recognized in the present Covenant by all appropriate means'. Without any doubt, much still needs to be done to bring about the full realisation of human rights. One has to concur with Sen regarding human rights: 'if they cannot be realized because of inadequate institutionalization, work for institutional expansion or reform can be part of the obligations generated by recognition of these rights'.[37] Logically this means that funding for such expansion must be provided.

The genesis of Goal 1, no doubt one of the most important MDGs, is also highly interesting. Pogge points out that the Rome Declaration of the UN's Food and Agriculture Organization on World Food Security adopted earlier (in 1996) demanded halving the number of undernourished people by 2015, while MDG 1 only sets out to halve the proportion of people suffering from hunger.[38] Due to population growth, MDG 1 puts up with more people going hungry. It is less ambitious. Economically it is less costly, which appears to be the reason for that change. After all, the MDGs come with concrete indices (called Indicators) to be checked regularly. Progress or lack of progress has been widely published. Easier goals might be less embarrassing.

The Rome Declaration stipulated the 'political will and our common and national commitment to achieving food security for all and to an ongoing effort to eradicate hunger in all countries', as Pogge points out.[39] The text of the Millennium Declaration signed by 189 countries at the UN Millennium Summit in September 2000 even goes beyond this commitment. UN members (including creditor nations) pledged:

> We will spare no effort to free our fellow men, women and children from the abject and dehumanizing conditions of extreme poverty . . . we are committed to making the right to development a reality for everyone and to freeing the entire human race from want.[40]

[34] The MDGs are listed at UN Millennium Development Goals 2012, www.un.org/millenniumgoals/, accessed 22 November 2012, or see Raffer (n 14) 113–71.

[35] Alston (n 7) 14.

[36] International Covenant on Economic, Social and Cultural Rights.

[37] A Sen, 'Elements of a Theory of Human Rights' (2004) 32(4) *Philosophy and Public Affairs* 320.

[38] T Pogge, 'The First UN Millennium Development Goal: A Cause for Celebration?' (updated version; original 2003) www.etikk.no/globaljustice/, 1–2, accessed 23 November 2012.

[39] ibid.

[40] UN 55/2. United Nations Millennium Declaration, www.un.org/millennium/declaration/ares552e.htm, point 11, accessed 4 March 2013.

MDG 1, however, already falls short of this pledge unless one interprets the word 'eradication' benignly as the indication that further steps after 2015 are implicitly included. Nevertheless, MDG 1 is an important step towards reaching a world free of hunger and improving the lot of millions of the poorest and is thus worth achieving. Achieving all MDGs would be a huge improvement. Even massive improvements for the poor short of actually achieving the MDGs would be substantial changes for the better. Such improvements became especially necessary due to the severe setbacks suffered by debtor countries because of policies forced upon them by official creditors during the early phases of debt management. To some extent they just repair the damage official creditors caused in the first place.

III SOVEREIGN DEBTS AND DEBTOR PROTECTION

A debt overhang is essentially characterised by the conflict between legitimate creditor rights and the human right that no one must be forced to fulfil contracts if that causes inhumane distress, endangers one's life or health or violates human dignity. Generally, human rights and human dignity enjoy unconditional preference over *pacta sunt servanda*.

The principle of debtor protection is firmly established in all debt relations except in the case of the inhabitants of sovereigns, where the pound-of-flesh approach still survives. Although unconditional priority of human life and human dignity is one main principle of any civilised legal system, debtor protection has remained totally absent in international debt management so far. Globalisation has not replicated the structures of domestic civilised legal and political systems – considered useless at best to creditors and speculators. For a sovereign debt overhang no crisis resolution procedure with proper debtor protection exists yet.

The pertinent question is whether and how debtor protection can be introduced in the case of sovereigns overburdened by debts. HIPC II finally accepted this idea, although still in a rudimentary form. Nevertheless its anti-poverty programmes are a move in the right direction and a change from the position held immediately before HIPC II. Then it was claimed in discussions on my proposal[41] that debtor protection would be impossible. Sadly, both the IMF's SDRM proposal and present debt management by the EU and the Fund in EU countries fell way behind the standard of HIPC II.

The problem is how to adapt debtor protection from the individual level to entities with governmental powers, be they sovereigns or governmental entities without sovereignty, such as cities or counties. Surprisingly, very few insolvency mechanisms for debtors with governmental powers exist worldwide, although quite a few municipalities, cities and even federal states (such as, prominently, the *Land* of Berlin) have experienced payment difficulties. The US was farsighted enough to introduce an insolvency mechanism for municipalities (Chapter 9, Title 11 USC) during the Great Depression of the last century, a measure virtually no other country copied in spite of defaults and debt service problems by local authorities in many countries. Hungary is one, maybe the only, exception, introducing such a mechanism after the downfall of communism on the advice of

[41] See K Raffer, 'Applying Chapter 9 Insolvency to International Debts: An Economically Efficient Solution with a Human Face' (1990) 18(2) *World Development*; Raffer (n 14) 78–113.

private consultants. Its features are so specific, though, that it does not lend itself to international adaptation.

Introducing an insolvency mechanism for a 'political subdivision or public agency or instrumentality of a State' (§101(34) 11 USC), the US had to cope with two generally relevant problems: governmental powers (highly relevant for sovereigns and the protection of sovereignty) and the extent to which the population (legally different from their municipality) must enjoy debtor protection. It did so brilliantly.

Chapter 9 is the only procedure protecting governmental powers, and thus applicable to sovereigns. Section 904, titled 'Limitation on Jurisdiction and Powers of Court', states with utmost clarity that the court depends on the debtor's volition and must not interfere with any of the political and governmental powers of the debtor; any of the property or revenues of the debtor; or the debtor's use or enjoyment of any income-producing property. This strong legal position is, of course, qualified by economic facts. The debtor needs a solution, and must therefore propose a plan acceptable to a creditor majority. Protecting everything sovereignty protects, §904 also proves how suitable the essential features of Chapter 9 are for sovereigns.

The court's jurisdiction depends on the municipality's volition, beyond which it cannot be extended, similar to the jurisdiction of international arbitrators. Unlike in other bankruptcy procedures, liquidation of the debtor or receivership are not possible. No trustee can be appointed (§926, avoiding powers, if seen as an exception, is very special and justified). Section 902(5) explicitly confirms: '"trustee", when used in a section that is made applicable in a case under this chapter . . . means debtor'. A US municipality cannot go into receivership and change of 'management' (ie removing elected officials) by courts or creditors is not possible – nor should this be possible in the case of sovereigns.

While §904 is debtor protection too, although in an unusual way because insolvency laws are usually made for non-governmental entities, Chapter 9 does not stop here. It also stipulates the protection of the municipality's inhabitants. The principle of debtor protection demands exempting resources necessary to finance humane minimum standards for the poor, and a sustainable economic recovery.

There exists a public interest in the functioning of the debtor, which safeguards a minimum of municipal activities. US municipalities are allowed to maintain basic social services essential to the health, safety and welfare of their inhabitants. In the 1930s, some creditors insisted on financing higher payments by the City of Asbury Park by further tax increases and refused to agree to the plan. The US Supreme Court stated clearly: 'the notion that a city has unlimited taxing power is, of course, an illusion. A city cannot be taken over and operated for the benefit of its creditors, nor can its creditors take over the taxing power'.[42]

Naturally, approval of the plan has to be denied if the municipality has the means to honour all its obligations. In *Fano v Newport Heights Irrigation District* this was done, because the district had assets greatly exceeding its liabilities and 'there was no sufficient showing why the district's tax rate should not have been increased either'.[43] To be confirmed, the plan presented by a municipality has to be reasonable and also, pursuant to §943(b)(7), in the best interest of creditors, who must be provided the 'going concern value'[44] of their claims. Briefly, US Chapter 9 is rule-of-law based, transparent and fair.

[42] A Malagardis, *Ein Konkursrecht für Staaten? Zur Regelung von Insolvenzen souveräner Schuldner in Vergangenheit und Gegenwart* (Baden-Baden, Nomos, 1990).

[43] §943, note 3, USCA.

[44] Raffer (n 14) 103.

Public interest in the US extends beyond municipal insolvency. In the case of railroad reorganisation (Subchapter IV of Chapter 11, Title 11 USC) §1165 protects public interest 'in addition to the interests of the debtor, creditors, and equity security holders'. Section 1170(a)(2) permits courts to abandon railway lines only if this is 'consistent with the public interest'. Public interest in the preservation of rail transportation mandates finding a balance between various interests, which economically means that creditors may have to lose more than without such balancing. The plan can only be confirmed (§1173(a)(4), 11 USC) if consistent with the public interest. No creditor government has shown a similar public interest in avoiding debt service increasing infant mortality in debtor countries or in whether hospitals can still afford basic hygiene, like surgery gloves (as in Greece), nor whether essential medications remain available.

But Chapter 9 does not stop there. If any regulatory or electoral approval are necessary under non-bankruptcy law in order to carry out a provision of the plan, §943(b)(6) requests that it must be obtained before the court can confirm the plan, a point clearly adaptable to sovereigns. This norm contrasts most vividly with the approach of the EU. Brussels abhors referenda in spite of receiving the Nobel Price for allegedly fostering democracy, the very democracy the EU is presently busily rolling back by curtailing the essential right of parliaments to vote on their national budgets. The announcement that the Greeks would vote on the conditions imposed by official creditors caused panic in Brussels and the referendum was foiled. Massive creditor pressure forced Prime Minister George Papandreou to cancel it. Democracy and decisions by people are to be avoided at any cost in EU-type 'democracy', a Greek word literally meaning that the people – not 'leaders' – have the sovereign right to decide.

Naturally, the policies imposed on debtors by official creditors would not be possible if the people, constitutionally the sovereign in most countries, had a say. Iceland had referenda on whether to socialise all losses. 'Private creditors ended up shouldering most of the losses relating to the failed banks, and today Iceland is experiencing a moderate recovery.'[45] Iceland introduced capital controls, and did not tighten her fiscal policy during the first year of the programme. Legal and official investigations of the behaviour of decision makers followed. 'Iceland set an example by managing to preserve, and even strengthen, its welfare state during the crisis.'[46] She returned to capital markets in 2011.

Determining debtor protection poses problems when it comes to the people living in a municipality or in a sovereign debtor country. While a standard of protection has been developed over decades in the US for insolvent municipalities, such standard still has to be elaborated for sovereigns. The problem is further complicated by the fact that the inhabitants of poor countries had normally not enjoyed all their economic, social and cultural rights before the debt crisis. With some justification, creditors can argue that a sovereign insolvency mechanism cannot resolve all development problems of a debtor country that existed independently of debt problems, in other words substitute development policy. Poverty, for example, existed before the crisis and one cannot demand that crisis solutions do more than solve problems caused by debt. Economically, one has to point out that even a 100 per cent haircut is unlikely to resolve all development problems and shortcomings in poor countries. Debts would be gone – which is good – but development problems and poverty will continue to exist.

[45] IMF, 'Iceland's Unorthodox Policies Suggest Alternative Way Out of Crisis', IMF Survey online, November 03 2011, www.imf.org/external/pubs/ft/survey/so/2011/car110311a.htm, accessed 29 November 2012.

[46] ibid.

In search for an international standard the MDGs are thus the solution. Determining debtor protection the MDGs prove useful and predestined to serve as the measuring rod. The MDGs are an internationally accepted standard capable of preventing excessive debt service from constituting an obstacle to the realisation of human rights. Resources necessary to finance the MDGs can provide a measuring rod and make things much easier, although the MDGs do not aim – strictly speaking – at establishing the standard of debtor protection usual and accepted in all other cases. Many people, for instance, would still go hungry.

The MDGs have been accepted by virtually all countries. Creditor governments, too, promised to 'spare no effort' to free people from 'the abject and dehumanizing conditions of extreme poverty', and 'committed' themselves to realising the right to development for everyone as well as to 'freeing the entire human race from want'.[47] If that is a true statement rather than a political truth, important creditor governments cannot but enthusiastically embrace the MDGs as an acceptable standard for debtor protection. The proof of the pudding is always in the eating.

Debtor protection in line with US Chapter 9 was demanded by affected people early on. In a letter to the Paris Club dated 10 September 2000 the Confederación de Nacionalidades Indigenas del Ecuador (CONAIE), an organisation that was also part of the government for a short period of time, stated that fundamental human rights had been violated by debt management denying otherwise customary debtor protection to the poorest. The letter demanded debt-to-development swaps of all existing debts, and international arbitration to solve problems of future overindebtedness in line with the Raffer Proposal.[48] Debt service should be replaced by payments into a Fondo Social y Ecológico to finance social, cultural and ecological programmes (including education), essentially the same demand as the counterpart fund proposed by Jubileo 2000 Red Guayaquil in a joint study with the United Nations Development Programme (UNDP) and UNICEF. Referring specifically to US municipalities, CONAIE's demand for arbitration also seconded Jubileo 2000 Red Guayaquil. Quite rightly, CONAIE pointed out that such arbitration procedures result from the very fundamental base of the rule of law that no one must be permitted to be judge in their own cause. The document also stated with clarity that this essential base of the rule of law had been violated by creditors being 'judge and party'. CONAIE demanded that creditor governments respect the rule of law and human rights. This letter went unanswered.

The example of Malawi illustrates the importance of debtor protection. The BWIs were accused of having forced Malawi to sell maize from its National Food Reserve to repay debts. The IBRD encouraged the country 'to keep foreign exchange instead of storing grain'.[49] In a BBC interview Malawi's president said the government 'had been forced [to sell maize] in order to repay commercial loans taken out to buy surplus maize in previous years'. The IMF and IBRD had insisted on it.[50] Malawi sold a substantial amount of maize. After harvest problems in 2002 famine struck, and 7 million of a population of 11 million were severely short of food according to Action Aid. Creditor interest was given priority over survival.

[47] See n 40.

[48] See nn 41 and 53.

[49] A Pettifor, 'Debt is Still the Lynchpin: The Case of Malawi', 2002 (mimeo), version 2003. Cf also Raffer (n 14) 85.

[50] ibid.

Confronted with facts in the House of Commons' Treasury Select Committee,[51] the IMF's Managing Director, Horst Köhler, insisted that this advice had been given by the IBRD and the EU Commission, so 'it is just plain wrong to accuse the Fund that it advised and made even a conditionality out of this . . . I want to underline: this is an issue in the responsibility of the World Bank and the EU Commission'. He admitted

> that the IMF was part of, say, the kind of international advice and the IMF may, again, not have been attentive enough how they exercised how to run this maize stock, but it was not the responsibility of the Fund to implement the advice.

Obviously, while being 'part of the kind of advice' that resulted in starving people, the IMF did not give this advice at all. In any case, the IMF is innocent. What is important to the argument, though, is that repayment was preferred over the right to life. This would no longer be possible if the Raffer Proposal were implemented and the MDGs were established as the norm for debtor protection.

Exempting resources necessary to finance minimum standards of basic health services, primary education etc can only be justified if that money is demonstrably used for its declared purpose. Not without reason creditors as well as NGOs are concerned that this might not always be guaranteed. The solution is quite simple: a transparently managed fund as proposed by Pettifor,[52] financed by the debtor in domestic currency. Naturally, this would be money that could alternatively be paid to creditors but which debtor protection exempts from being seized by creditors. So-called 'phantom debts'[53] cannot finance anything. These are debts existing exclusively on paper because creditors refuse to acknowledge reality, without any economic base whatsoever. They cannot be cashed, they are technically irrecoverable. Creditors record money already lost as though it were still encashable, eagerly calculating and adding interest on this money already lost, and declare such phantom claims as 'costs' of debt reduction. Money already lost is officially lost again.

This fund's management could be monitored by an international board or advisory council consisting of members from the debtor country as well as from creditor countries. They could be nominated by NGOs and by governments (including the debtor government). As this fund is a legal entity of its own, checks and discussions of its projects would not concern the government's budget, which is an important part of a country's sovereignty. Additionally, aid could be channelled through the fund, changing its character of money just set apart from the ordinary budget towards a normal fund for the poor.

In analogy to domestic Chapter 9 this fund would finance basic social services essential to the health, safety and welfare of inhabitants, and finance a fresh start of the debtor economy. Necessary environmental protection measures could be funded. While this idea was severely attacked when first presented as part of my sovereign Chapter 9,[54] HIPC II incorporates anti-poverty measures. The Multilateral Debt Reduction Initiative (MDRI)

[51] Treasury Select Committee, House of Commons, 'Treasury – Uncorrected Evidence', Thursday, 4 July 2002, paras 158, 160, at www.publications.parliament.uk/pa/cm200102/cmselect/cmtreasy/uc868-iii/uc86802.htm, accessed 5 December 2012.

[52] A Pettifor, 'Concordats for Debt Cancellation: Making Debt Relief Work Twice – First, as Money to the Poor; Second, For Empowering the Poor', New Economics Foundation, Jubilee Research, 2001 (mimeo).

[53] cf Raffer (n 14) 191–93.

[54] K Raffer, 'International Debts: A Crisis for Whom?' in HW Singer and S Sharma (eds), *Economic Development and World Debt* (London, Macmillan/St Martin's, 1989) 51 ff (Papers of a Conference held at Zagreb University in 1987) 59; Raffer (n 41) 305–06.

officially declared providing additional support to HIPCs to reach the MDGs as its goal.[55] Although actual positive pro-poor effects lag perceptibly behind official declarations, the principle is accepted. The SDRM and the EU presently in Europe are rolling this progress back.

Nevertheless, debtor protection is slowly gaining ground. Argentina's President Kirchner quoted the needs of the population as a reason for the debt reduction demanded from creditors. The Caracas Declaration by Ministers of the G-24 in February 1998 called for 'domestic social safety-nets as integral elements of stabilization and adjustment programs to protect the most vulnerable elements of the population of crisis affected countries'.[56]

As the EU illustrates so abundantly clearly, however, creditor interests and violation of debtor rights and human rights still prevail. The piece of bread that could feed a few hungry is forced to go to speculators as well as to official creditors whose lending has aggravated the crisis and is delaying the eventually necessary, final haircut.[57] While violating human rights, pushing millions into misery and distress by insisting on their pound of flesh, the EU gets the Nobel Peace Prize, not least for its alleged record in securing human rights. Sadly, and presumably against poor Alfred Nobel's intentions, this will encourage official creditors to go on rolling back human rights and democracy.

IV CONCLUSIONS

Exempting resources needed to finance the MDGs is the advisable and analogous way of implementing debtor protection in a sovereign debt context. Technically, it can be implemented easily and promptly once political resistance is overcome. Unfortunately, it cannot be expected to solve all development problems. Introducing fair, transparent insolvency proceedings modelled after the basic principles of the US Chapter 9, Title 11 USC, aka the Raffer Proposal, would safeguard human rights and make economic, juridical and ethical sense. Like all civilised insolvency laws it implements the principle of debtor protection and the basic human right that people must not be forced to starve their children to service their debts in line with the general principle that human rights and human dignity must enjoy unconditional preference over *pacta sunt servanda*. It is a stark contrast to present 'debt management'. Using the MDGs as the standard for debtor protection would improve the situation substantially and dramatically, even though falling short of the full realisation of human rights.

[55] Cf eg IBRD, 'HIPC At-A-Glance Guide, Spring 07', 2007, http://siteresources.worldbank.org/INTDEBTDEPT/Resources/Debt_PocketBroch_Spring07.pdf?resourceurlname=Debt_PocketBroch_Spring07.pdf, 2, accessed 5 March 2013.

[56] Raffer (n 14) 86.

[57] This practice is abusive lending; see JP Bohoslavsky, 'Lending and Sovereign Insolvency: A Fair and Efficient Criterion to Distribute Losses among Creditors' (2010) 2(1) *Göttingen Journal of International Law* 387–412.

8

Debts and State of Necessity

AUGUST REINISCH AND CHRISTINA BINDER

I INTRODUCTION

EACH ERA CONSIDERS that its pressing problems are unique and that they require new solutions. A glimpse at history demonstrates, however, that often this is not the case. The phenomenon of sovereign insolvency is not a new one,[1] nor are various attempts trying to cope with it.[2] Likewise the possible negative effects of sovereign debts for the economic and social rights of a state's population are well known.[3] This contribution will show that also the idea of justifying the non-performance of a state's obligations by invoking state of necessity, *force majeure* or related legal concepts is not totally new. It will do so by initially answering in the affirmative the preliminary question whether there is a state of necessity defence available for economic emergencies.

Subsequently, it will turn to one of the main practical issues concerning the application of the necessity defence for modern debtor states, the question whether this state responsibility concept developed by international jurisprudence as a rule of customary international law (see only the ICJ's characterisation in the *Gabčíkovo-Nagymaros*[4] case as well as in the *Wall* opinion[5]) and codified by the ILC in its Articles on State Responsibility (ILC

[1] See S Szodruch, *Staateninsolvenz und private Gläubiger–Rechtsprobleme des Private Sector Involvement bei staatlichen Finanzkrisen im 21. Jahrhundert* (Berlin, Bwv Berliner-Wissenschaft, 2008); M Waibel, *Sovereign Debt before International Courts and Tribunals* (Cambridge, Cambridge University Press, 2011).

[2] See K Rogoff and J Zettelmeyer, 'Bankruptcy Procedures for Sovereigns: A History of Ideas, 1976–2001' (2002) *IMF Staff Papers No 3*; K Berensmann and A Herzberg, 'Sovereign Insolvency Procedures – A Comparative Look at Selected Proposals' (2009) 23 *Journal of Economic Surveys* 856; RP Buckley, 'The Bankruptcy of Nations: An Idea Whose Time Has Come' (2009) 43 *International Lawyer* 1189; S Hagan, 'Designing a Legal Framework to Restructure Sovereign Debt' (2005) 36 *Georgetown Journal of International Law* 299.

[3] See eg S Michalowski, 'Sovereign Debt and Social Rights – Legal Reflections on a Difficult Relationship' (2008) 34 *Human Rights Law Review* 1; see also the Open Letter by the Chairperson of the UN Committee on Economic, Social and Cultural Rights to the States Parties to the Covenant on Economic Social and Cultural Rights in relation to the protection of Covenant rights in the context of the economic and financial crisis of 16 May 2012, available at www2.ohchr.org/english/bodies/cescr/docs/LetterCESCRtoSP16.05.12.pdf, accessed 2 September 2013; Sharp, Ch 4 in this volume; NG Villavoram, 'Debt Servicing and its Adverse Impact on Economic, Social and Cultural Rights in Developing Countries' (2010) 9 *Journal of Human Rights* 487.

[4] See *Gabčíkovo-Nagymaros Project (Hungary/Slovakia)*, ICJ Reports 1997, 7, para 51: 'The Court considers . . . that the state of necessity is a ground recognized by customary international law for precluding the wrongfulness of an act not in conformity with an international obligation'. See also *M/V Saiga (No 2) Case*, International Tribunal for the Law of the Sea, 1 July 1999 (1999) 38 *ILM* 1323, para 134.

[5] In its Advisory Opinion the Court spoke of 'a state of necessity as recognized in customary international law'. *Legal Consequences of the Construction of a Wall in the Occupied Palestinian Territory*, ICJ, Advisory Opinion, 9 July 2004 (2004) 43 *ILM* 1009, para 140.

Articles)[6] can also be invoked vis-à-vis non-state actors, ie private creditors.

It will then address the main prerequisites needed to successfully invoke necessity and analyse in particular whether human rights considerations play a role in this regard.

Finally, it will assess to what extent the necessity defence is a useful tool for indebted states to alleviate their debt burden.

II IS THERE A STATE OF NECESSITY DEFENCE AVAILABLE FOR ECONOMIC EMERGENCIES?

When we speak of sovereign insolvency or states on the brink of insolvency, our associations are with Argentina in the wake of its financial crisis 2001/2002, the European victims of the financial crisis since 2008 like Greece, Portugal, Spain or Cyprus and possibly other casualties. In fact, however, states or more often their sovereign rulers have become bankrupt throughout history and it is no surprise that on various occasions they have tried to excuse their inability to perform their financial obligations by invoking circumstances beyond their control.

What we now consider relatively neatly described as state of necessity in Article 25 of the ILC Articles,[7] has in fact been invoked under various guises, such as *force majeure* or the like, in order to justify the non-performance of a state's financial obligations. While in the wording of today's Article 25 it is not clear whether the concept encompasses the notion of financial necessity, past practice demonstrates that it may indeed be possible to successfully invoke the necessity defence also for situations of extreme economic emergencies.

In fact, the state of financial necessity is probably one of the oldest forms of the state of necessity defence recognised in international jurisprudence. The *locus classicus* is the *Russian Indemnity* case or Ottoman debt arbitration in which the Ottoman Empire unsuccessfully invoked *force majeure* in order to justify its refusal to honour outstanding debts vis-à-vis Czarist Russia.[8] However, the arbitral tribunal called upon to adjudicate the Russian repayment claim did not reject the availability of the defence as such. Rather, it found that the situation of the Ottoman Empire did not amount to such an extreme form of financial emergency that it would amount to a state of necessity. Though the tribunal used the terminology of *force majeure*, it in effect developed criteria for state of necessity,[9] when it held that 'the obligation for a state to execute treaties may be weakened if the very existence of the State is endangered, if observation of the international duty is . . . *self-destructive*'.[10] Thus, the Ottoman debt arbitration is an important precedent confirming that states can in fact rely on situations of extreme economic hardship in order to justify their non-performance of financial obligations.

This outcome was affirmed in a number of cases throughout the twentieth century. In

[6] *Commentaries to the draft articles on Responsibility of States for internationally wrongful acts*, adopted by the International Law Commission at its fifty-third session (2001), Report of the International Law Commission on the work of its Fifty-third session, *Official Records of the General Assembly, Fifty-sixth session, Suiepplement No 10* (A/56/10), chp.IV.E.2 (in the following: ILC Commentary).

[7] See n 37 below for the text of Art 25.

[8] *Affaire de l'Indemnité Russe* (*Russian Indemnity Case*) (1912) XI *UNRIAA* 431.

[9] The ILC Commentary rightly characterises what the tribunal refers to as *force majeure* as an incident of necessity. ILC Commentary (no 6) 197.

[10] 'l'obligation pour un Etat d'exécuter les traités peut fléchir "si l'existence même de l'Etat vient à être en danger, si l'observation du devoir international est [..] *self destructive*."' (*Russian Indemnity Case* (n 8) 443).

the *Serbian Loans* case the PCIJ only briefly touched upon the issue under the heading of *force majeure*.[11] The same Court did not explicitly address the issue in the *Socobel* case,[12] but it appeared that the parties recognised economic necessity.[13] Finally, in the *Oscar Chinn* case,[14] Judge Anzilotti reflected upon the possibility to invoke the economic dislocations after World War I as a justification for the non-performance of international obligations.[15] However, it was not until the recent Argentine crisis that international tribunals had the opportunity to reaffirm the availability of the state of necessity defence in situations of economic turmoil.

In a number of investment cases brought against Argentina, tribunals were faced with the Argentine argument that various emergency measures it adopted were in fact justified by a state of necessity as codified in the ILC Articles. Though individual arbitral panels disagreed over whether the situation prevailing in Argentina during the financial crisis was severe enough to amount to such a state of necessity, they were unanimous in holding that, as a matter of principle, economic emergencies may amount to a state of necessity.[16]

III DOES THE STATE OF NECESSITY OPERATE ONLY ON THE INTER-STATE LEVEL OR CAN IT ALSO BE INVOKED VIS-À-VIS PRIVATE CREDITORS?

On a practical level, it appears important to look at the current structure of external debt incurred by states in order to assess the potential relevance of the necessity defence. There has been a remarkable shift from inter-state loans to financing through private banks and

[11] '*Force majeure*. – It cannot be maintained that the war itself, despite its grave economic consequences, affected the legal obligations of the contracts between the Serbian Government and the French bondholders. The economic dislocations caused by the war did not release the debtor State . . .' (*Serbian Loans*, 1929, PCIJ, Series A, No 20, 39/40).

[12] *Société Commerciale de Belgique*, 1939, PCIJ Series A/B, No 78.

[13] 'Doctrine recognizes in this matter that the duty of a Government to ensure the proper functioning of its essential public services outweighs that of paying its debts.' Pleadings of the Greek representative before the PCIJ, cited according to Ago Report (Addendum to Eighth Report on State Responsibility by Mr Roberto Ago, UN Doc A/CN.4/318/ADD.5-7, in [1980] YBILC vol II, part one, 25).

[14] '[T]he economic depression was an important or even decisive factor . . .' *Oscar Chinn* (*UK v Belgium*) 1934, PCIJ, Series A/B, No 63, 65, 113 (Separate Opinion Judge Anzilotti).

[15] All these cases have been regarded by the ILC and its Special Rapporteur Roberto Ago as confirming that also economic difficulties may give rise to a state of necessity. Ago Report (n 13) 24–25.

[16] See eg *CMS v Argentine Republic*, ICSID Case No ARB/01/8, Award, 12 May 2005, para 214; *LG&E v Argentine Republic*, ICSID Case No ARB/02/1, Decision on Liability, 2 October 2006, paras 226 ff; *Sempra v Argentine Republic*, ICSID Case No ARB/02/16, Award, 28 September 2007, para 374; *Enron v Argentine Republic*, ICSID Case No ARB/01/3, Award, 22 May 2007, para 339; *Suez v Argentine Republic*, ICSID Case No ARB/03/17, Decision on Liability, 30 July 2010, paras 236 ff; *Continental Casualty Company v Argentine Republic*, ICSID Case No ARB/03/9, Award, 5 September 2008, para 173; *Impregilo SpA v Argentine Republic*, ICSID Case No ARB/07/17, Award, 21 June 2011, 75 ff; *El Paso Energy International Company v Argentina*, ICSID Case No ARB/03/15, Award, 31 October 2011, 203 ff. The *Enron* and *Sempra* awards were subsequently annulled. *Enron Creditors Recovery Corp v Argentina*, ICSID Case No ARB/01/3, Decision on the Application for Annulment of the Argentine Republic, 30 July 2010; *Sempra Energy International v Argentina*, ICSID Case No ARB/02/16, Decision on the Argentine Republic's Application for Annulment of the Award, 29 June 2010. For further literature on the initial ICSID 'necessity' cases also see inter alia A Reinisch, 'Necessity in International Investment Arbitration – An Unnecessary Split of Opinion in Recent ICSID Cases? Comments on CMS and LG&E' (2007) 8 *Journal of World Investment and Trade* 191; M Waibel, 'Two Worlds of Necessity in ICSID Arbitration: CMS and LG&E' (2007) 20 *Leiden Journal of International Law* 637; C Binder, 'Changed Circumstances in Investment Law: Interfaces between the Law of Treaties and the Law of State Responsibility with a Special Focus on the Argentine Crisis' in C Binder et al (eds), *International Investment Law for the 21st Century. Essays in Honour of Christoph Schreuer* (Oxford, Oxford University Press, 2009) 608. See also Section IV for further reference.

increasingly through bond issuances over the last decades.[17] This implied that, for instance, in the Argentine case most of the external debt was incurred vis-à-vis private bondholders. When Argentina announced its inability to repay its debt, a number of these bondholders sued according to the terms of the bond issuances before German and Italian courts. The Italian Supreme Court of Cassation cut off these cases on a preliminary issue; it held that the Argentine emergency measures were of a *iure imperii* character and thus prevented any lawsuit for the redemption of the bonds,[18] disregarding the fact that the initial bond issuance was not only generally considered to be a *iure gestionis* or commercial activity[19] but also ignoring the express waivers of immunity in the bond issuance conditions.[20] German bondholders were more successful; German courts did not permit the state immunity defence raised by Argentina. However, on the merits of the German bondholder claims some courts had doubts whether the Argentine defence of state of necessity would justify non-performance. They thus availed themselves of a procedural device open to them: they made a reference to the Constitutional Court in order to ascertain whether a norm of customary international law existed which permitted the invocation of a state of necessity in case of economic emergencies. Though ample evidence of such a rule was presented to the Karlsruhe Court by one co-author of this contribution,[21] the Court basically avoided the issue by adopting a very narrow reading of the availability of the customary necessity defence in principle. The Court's majority held that a state of necessity could only be invoked on the inter-state level and not vis-à-vis private bondholders.[22] This ruling was widely criticised, not only by an outspoken dissenter on the Court itself,[23] but also by many commentators.[24]

[17] Compare Figure 3.7 'Bank Holdings of Government Debt in Selected Economies' from the latest IMF World Economic Outlook (April 2013), available at www.imf.org/external/pubs/ft/gfsr/2013/01/pdf/text.pdf, accessed 2 September 2013.

[18] Corte di Cassazione, order of 27 May 2005, n 11225, *Borri v Republic of Argentina*. See F Bassan, *The Law of Sovereign Wealth Funds* (Cheltenham, Edward Elgar Publishing, 2011) 96 for further reference.

[19] See eg the US Supreme Court in *Republic of Argentina v Weltover Inc*, 504 US 607 (1992); But as PJ Power shows, even before *Weltover*, courts generally held that sovereign borrowing constituted a commercial activity: *e Shapiro v Republic of Bolivia*, 930 F.2d 1013, 1018–19 (2d Cir 1991); *Carl Marks & Co v Union of Soviet Socialist Republics*, 841 F.2d 26, 27 (2d Cir), cert denied, 487 U.S. 1219 (1988); *West v Multibanco Comermex*, 807 F.2d 820, 825–26 (9th Cir), cert denied, 482 U.S. 906 (1987); *Callejo v Bancomer*, 764 F.2d 1101, 1109 (5th Cir. 1985); *Wolf v Banco Nacional de Mexico*, 739 F.2d 1458, 1460 (9th Cir 1984); *Schmidt v Polish People's Republic*, 579 F. Supp. 23, 26 (S.D.N.Y. 1984); *Allied Bank Int'l v Banco Credito Agricola de Cartago*, 566 F. Supp. 1440, 1443 (S.D.N.Y. 1983), aff'd, 733 F.2d 23 (2d Cir. 1984), vacated and rev'd on other grounds, 757 F.2d 516 (2d Cir), cert dismissed, 473 U.S. 934 (1985). See also his further discussion on the matter: PJ Power, 'Sovereign Debt: The Rise of the Secondary Market and its Implication for Future Restructurings' (1996) 64 *Fordham Law Review* 2701, 2730 ff.

[20] See for a critical assessment of this case BI Bonafè, 'State Immunity and the Protection of Private Investors: The *Argentine Bonds* Case before Italian Courts' (2006) 16 *Italian Yearbook of International Law* 165; S Dorigo, 'The Italian Jurisprudence Facing Argentina's Financial Crisis: Some Critical Remarks from the Perspective of International Law', in S Wittich and A Reinisch/A Gattini (eds), *Kosovo – Staatsschulden – Notstand – EU-Reformvertrag – Humanitätsrecht. Beiträge zum 33. Österreichischen Völkerrechtstag in Conegliano* (Frankfurt am Main, Peter Lang, 2009) 51.

[21] A Reinisch, 'Sachverständigengutachten zur Frage des Bestehens und der Wirkung des völkerrechtlichen Rechtfertigungsgrundes "Staatsnotstand"' (2008) 68 *Zeitschrift für ausländisches öffentliches Recht und Völkerrecht* 3.

[22] German Federal Constitutional Court, Decision of 8 May 2007, 2 BvM 1-5/03; NJW 2007, 2610. While the Court accepted that necessity was recognised as a circumstance precluding the wrongfulness of a breach of international law, it held that 'currently no rule of general international law can be ascertained entitling a State, vis-à-vis private individuals, to suspend the performance of due obligations for payment arising under private law by invoking necessity based on an inability to pay.' (ibid, author's translation).

[23] Judge Lübbe-Wolff, ibid, paras 75–95.

[24] See eg SW Schill, 'Der völkerrechtliche Staatsnotstand in der Entscheidung des BVerfG zu Argentinischen Staatsanleihen – Anachronismus oder Avantgarde?' (2008) 68 *Zeitschrift für ausländisches öffentliches Recht und Völkerrecht* 45, 45.

Indeed, it is hard to understand why the German Constitutional Court adopted such a narrow reading which cast serious doubt on the practical viability of the necessity defence. The ILC Articles on State Responsibility have certainly been drafted mainly with inter-state relations in mind, however they do not exclude that their grounds precluding wrongfulness be invoked vis-à-vis private parties.[25] It seems in fact difficult to conceive why a state would not be allowed to suspend the fulfilment of its payment obligations to the extent necessary to protect elementary concerns of the *bien commun*, such as the protection of the life and health of its citizens, also towards investors.[26] This view is also shared by the ILA Committee on International Monetary Law, which affirms the availability of the defence in its 1988 Report along similar lines.[27] The availability of the defence in such cases corresponds to the growing importance of the individual in contemporary international law. This change of paradigms is most visible in sub-regimes such as international human rights law and international criminal law but also in ICJ findings concerning diplomatic protection.[28] Likewise doctrine supports the availability of the necessity defence against private persons, inter alia investors.[29]

The possible availability of the defence in private–state relationships is furthermore confirmed in jurisprudence, as already in the *Serbian Loans*[30] and *French Company of Venezuela Railroads* cases.[31] Although these are inter-state cases brought in the exercise of the individuals'/companies' home states' diplomatic protection, they clearly indicate a possible relevance of necessity (*force majeure*) towards private persons as in effect it is their rights that are at stake.[32] It was also amply demonstrated by the Argentine cases before numerous investment tribunals. For them, the fact that the claimants were private investors did not play any role. They generally proceeded to a discussion of the fulfilment

[25] For instance, the fact that the ILC Commentary clearly states that '[the Articles on State Responsibility] apply to the whole field of the international obligations of States, whether the obligation is owed to one or several States, to an individual or group, or to the international community as a whole', supports the conclusion that rights and interests of individuals may have to be balanced against the interests of the state taking necessity measures. See for further reference Reinisch (n 16) 201.

[26] In this sense, eg, Reinisch (n 21) 27.

[27] ILA Committee on International Monetary Law, 'The International Law of External Debt Management. Some Current Aspects', *ILA-Report*, 1988, 418. The ILA Committee also states that 'it would be surprising if an individual or institution were to receive a higher degree of protection than a state. In general, aliens will enjoy only a minimum standard of protection, whereas the rules on the relationship between States reflect the principle of sovereign equality' (ibid, 432). More recently, Schill supports the availability of the necessity defence also towards investors in his discussion of a judgment of the German Constitutional Court (n 24) 45.

[28] See eg ICJ, *Case concerning Ahmadou Sado Diallo* (*Republic of Guinea v Democratic Republic of the Congo*), Judgment, 24 May 2004, paras 49–96. See also Schill (n 24) 55–56. Such approach finds support in a generally accepted line of jurisprudence that states are entitled to unilaterally modify or terminate contracts with private investors in the public interest, provided that they pay adequate compensation. (See ibid, 60 ff for further reference).

[29] Paparinskis for instance affirms: 'those circumstances precluding wrongfulness that do not require an anterior breach (like necessity, distress and *force majeure*) can in principle also apply to obligations owed to investors. Consequently, the application of law of necessity to obligations owed under US–Argentina BIT is in principle uncontroversial: the protection of essential interests of the State is a circumstance that could preclude wrongfulness of an obligation owed also to individuals' (M Paparinskis, 'Investment Arbitration and the Law of Countermeasures' (2009) 79 *British Yearbook of International Law* 264, 342).

[30] *Serbian Loans* (n 11) 39–40.

[31] *French Company of Venezuelan Railroads Case*, 31 July 1905, X *RIAA* 285, 353–54.

[32] See also the *Russian Indemnity* case where the Permanent Court of Arbitration stated explicitly that *force majeure* was available in international as well as in private law. 'L'exception de la *force majeure* . . . est opposable en droit international public aussi bien qu'en droit privé . . .' (*Russian Indemnity Case* (n 8) 443).

of the criteria demanded by Article 25 of the ILC Articles on State Responsibility without pausing to assess whether the nature of the claimants permitted such invocation.[33]

IV WHAT ARE THE CRITERIA FOR A SUCCESSFUL INVOCATION OF THE NECESSITY DEFENCE? IS THERE ANY ROOM FOR HUMAN RIGHTS CONSIDERATIONS?

Having confirmed the general availability of the necessity defence for economic emergencies and also vis-à-vis private investors, a closer scrutiny of the main requirements for successfully invoking necessity – and in particular whether human rights considerations play a role in this regard – seems warranted.

A The Elements of the Necessity Defence According to Article 25 of the ILC Articles

The obvious starting point for any inquiry into the criteria governing a reliance on necessity is Article 25 (former Article 33[34]) of the ILC Articles on State Responsibility which was recognised as the defence's authoritative codification of customary law in literature[35] and jurisprudence.[36] Article 25 of the ILC Articles subjects reliance on necessity to strict limitations.[37] Numerous detailed and narrowly defined conditions must be cumulatively satisfied for reliance on necessity to be permissible. Non-performance of international (here: treaty) obligations is only justifiable when the non-performance is the *only way* for the state to safeguard an *essential* interest against a *grave* and *imminent* peril. The ILC's Commentary explicates that the danger must be objectively established and not merely apprehended as possible,[38] that reliance on necessity is precluded if there are other (lawful) means available, even if they are more costly or less convenient,[39] and that any measures going beyond the strictly necessary will not be covered.[40] In addition, in accordance with Article 25(1.b) of the ILC Articles, the conduct in question must not seriously impair

[33] See eg *CMS* (n 16); *LG&E* (n 16); The *BG* tribunal avoided taking a clear position on the availability of the defence. See *BG Group Plc v Republic of Argentina*, UNCITRAL, Final Award, 24 December 2007, paras 408 ff.

[34] Art 33 was adopted by the ILC in the first reading. Art 25 differs slightly from Art 33 as it omits the qualifying addendum 'of the State' after 'essential interest' and denies reliance on necessity when interests of the 'international community as a whole' would be impaired.

[35] See eg C Tietje, 'Die Argentinienkrise aus rechtlicher Sicht: Staatsanleihen und Staateninsolvenz' (2005) 37 *Beiträge zum Transnationalen Wirtschaftsrecht* 17; T Christakis, 'Nécessité n'a pas de loi?' in Société Française pour le Droit International (ed), *Colloque de Grenoble. La nécessité en droit international* (Paris, Pedone, 2007) 11, 34 ff; see also S Heathcote, 'Circumstances Precluding Wrongfulness in the ILC Articles on State Responsibility: Necessity' in J Crawford, A Pellet and S Olleson (eds), *The Law of International Responsibility* (Oxford, Oxford University Press, 2010) 491, 494.

[36] See above nn 4 and 5.

[37] Art 25 of the ILC Articles: '1. Necessity may not be invoked by a State as a ground for precluding the wrongfulness of an act not in conformity with an international obligation of that State unless the act: (a) Is the only way for the State to safeguard an essential interest against a grave and imminent peril; and (b) Does not seriously impair an essential interest of the State or States towards which the obligation exists, or of the international community as a whole. 2. In any case, necessity may not be invoked by a State as a ground for precluding wrongfulness if: (a) The international obligation in question excludes the possibility of invoking necessity; or (b) The State has contributed to the situation of necessity.'

[38] ILC Commentary(n 6) 'Article 25', para 15 (Crawford, 183–84).

[39] ibid.

[40] ibid.

the interest of the state(s) to which the obligation is owed or of the international community as a whole. According to the ILC Commentary 'the interest relied on must outweigh all other considerations, not only from the point of view of the acting State but on a reasonable assessment of the competing interests'.[41] Respectively, and although not explicitly stated in Article 25(1.b), weighty arguments support the view that the balancing test should also take the interests of individual(s) (investors) into account.[42] Two additional general limits are likewise imposed by Article 25: reliance on necessity is prevented, even if the above-mentioned conditions are fulfilled, when the international obligation in question excludes (explicitly or implicitly) the invocation of necessity, or when the state has contributed to the situation of necessity.

B The Criteria for a Successful Invocation of Necessity in International Jurisprudence

As argued, economic emergencies are generally considered a permissible ground for reliance on the necessity defence.[43] So are serious threats to a state's population, although some, including Special Rapporteur Ago, put the threshold for invocation as high as the 'survival of a sector of a population'.[44] Other examples given were the breakdown of a state's infrastructure, of its administration, its schools or the police.[45] These examples touch upon human rights considerations (and more particularly upon compliance with economic and social rights) in the context of economic crisis situations. However, states rarely explicitly referred to human rights as justification for reliance on necessity; even less was the issue addressed in the jurisprudence of international tribunals.

The cases brought against Argentina in the context of the country's economic crisis in the early 2000s are most instructive, since Argentina also referred to the human rights of its population to support its reliance on the necessity defence. In *CMS*, Argentina held that 'as the economic and social crisis that affected the country compromised basic human rights, no investment treaty could prevail as it would be in violation of such constitutionally recognized rights'.[46] Likewise in *National Grid*, Argentina invoked

[41] ibid, para 17 (Crawford, 184).

[42] See eg the ILC's reference to individual interests in the *Barcelona Traction* case where the ICJ speaks of 'obligations concerning the treatment to be afforded' to 'foreign investments or foreign nationals' and distinguishes between 'obligations of a State towards the international community as a whole, and those arising vis-à-vis another State in the field of diplomatic protection' (ICJ, *Barcelona Traction Light and Power Company Limited, Second Phase* (*Belgium v Spain*) 5 February 1970, ICJ Rep 1970, 3, para 33). See furthermore A Reinisch: 'Also the fact that the ILC Commentary clearly states that "[the Articles on State Responsibility] apply to the whole field of the international obligations of States, whether the obligation is owed to one or several States, to an individual or group, or to the international community as a whole", supports the conclusion that rights and interests of individuals may have to be balanced against the interests of the state taking necessity measures' (Reinisch (n 16) 201).

[43] See Section II above.

[44] Ago Report (n 13) 13, 14 (para 2).

[45] 'No state is required to execute, or to execute in full, its pecuniary obligation if this jeopardizes the functioning of its public services and has the effect of disorganizing the administration of the country.' (ibid, 25 (para 28)). See also the statement of the South African government: 'A State cannot, for example, be expected to close its schools and universities and its courts, to disband its police force and to neglect its public services to such an extent as to expose its community to chaos and anarchy merely to provide the money wherewith to meet its moneylenders, foreign or national' (ibid, 24 (para 25).

[46] *CMS* (n 16) para 114.

social and economic rights as a matter of constitutional law.[47] In *Impregilo*, Argentina maintained more generally that 'the regulatory actions taken by the Province and Argentina were lawful and proportionate. In this case, the regulatory powers of the State were particularly important in order to guarantee its inhabitants the human right to water'.[48] Also in *Suez*, Argentina argued with the human right to water of its population and asserted that, given the fundamental role of water in sustaining life and health, it should be granted a broader margin of discretion than in cases involving other commodities and services.[49]

However, the investment tribunals avoided dealing in detail with the necessity defence's preconditions and limits in cases of threats to the human rights of Argentina's population. The *Suez* tribunal was most explicit when stating that BIT obligations and human rights obligations had to be fulfilled. But also the *Suez* tribunal stopped short there, since it held that on the facts of the case, Argentina had failed to show its inability to discharge both obligations at the time of the 2001/02 crisis.[50] Thus, jurisprudence is inconclusive on the role of human rights considerations for reliance on necessity.[51]

What is more, the cases brought against Argentina evidence the problems relating to reliance and application of the necessity defence in economic emergencies. Notwithstanding the largely identical fact situations and the frequently similar applicable law – many of the cases were brought under the US-Argentina BIT[52] – the tribunals reached fundamentally different conclusions. The *LG&E* and *Continental Casualty*[53] tribunals accepted Argentina's reliance on necessity and found that the economic crisis constituted a state of necessity precluding the wrongfulness of BIT violations.[54] *CMS*[55] and, later, *Enron*,[56] *Sempra*,[57] *BG Group*,[58] *National Grid*,[59] *Suez*,[60] *Impregilo*[61] and *El Paso*[62] oppositely concluded that the

[47] *National Grid PLC v Argentina*, Award of 3 November 2008, UNCITRAL para 78; *see also* paras 89 and 90.

[48] *Impregilo* (n 16) para 228; see also Argentina's reference to the fact 'that human life was endangered in the crisis' in *Enron* (n 16) para 315.

[49] *Suez* (n 16) para 232.

[50] ibid, para 238. See for further reference, D Desierto, 'Calibrating Human Rights and Investment in Economic Emergencies: Prospects of Treaty and Valuation Defenses' (2012) 9 *Manchester Journal of International Economic Law* 162, 165.

[51] More generally, Reiner and Schreuer found that '[w]hen states have used human rights as defenses to investment claims, arbitral tribunals have preferred to 'dismiss the issues raised on a procedural basis rather than dealing with the substantive arguments themselves'. See C Reiner and C Schreuer, 'Human Rights and International Investment Arbitration' in P-M Dupuy, F Francioni and E-U Petersmann (eds), *Human Rights in International Investment Law and Arbitration* (Oxford, Oxford University Press, 2009) 82, 89–90.

[52] *Treaty between the United States of America and the Argentine Republic Concerning the Reciprocal Encouragement and Protection of Investments*, signed on 14 November 1991, entered into force on 20 October 1994. Two of the cases (*BG* and *National Grid*) were brought under the 1990 Argentina–UK BIT; *Metalpar* was brought under the 1995 Argentina–Chile BIT (*Metalpar SA and Buen Aire SA v Argentina*, ICSID Case No ARB/03/5, Award, 6 June 2008); *Suez* and *Total* under the 1991 Argentina–France BIT (1728 UNTS 298) and *Impregilo* under the 1988 Argentina–Italy BIT.

[53] *Continental Casualty* (n 16).

[54] To be precise, both tribunals accepted the applicability of the BIT's emergency exception (Art XI of the US–Argentina BIT), but drew heavily, in their interpretation of Art XI, on the elements of the customary law necessity defence; see eg ibid, paras 160–236.

[55] *CMS* (n 16).

[56] *Enron* (n 16).

[57] *Sempra* (n 16).

[58] *BG* (n 33).

[59] *National Grid* (n 47).

[60] *Suez* (n 16).

[61] *Impregilo* (n 16).

[62] *El Paso* (n 16).

Argentine situation could not justify the abrogation of investment obligations under the applicable BIT.[63] Again another approach was adopted by the *Total* tribunal,[64] which took account of Argentina's economic emergency in its examination of the respective BIT provisions. As it did not find a violation of the 'fair and equitable treatment' standard of Article 3 of the 1991 France–Argentina BIT during the core times of the crisis,[65] the examination of Article 25 of the ILC Articles became to a large extent unnecessary.

The tribunals' divergent approaches presented a particularly problematic issue: given the various methods of addressing economic emergencies, it proved difficult to assess whether Argentina's measures to handle the economic crisis were the 'only way' of safeguarding the interest of the state in the meaning of Article 25(1.a) of the ILC Articles. The *CMS* tribunal held that Argentina had a choice of measures and declared that '[t]he necessity plea is excluded if there are other (otherwise lawful) means available, even if they may be more costly or less convenient'.[66] The *Sempra* and *Enron* tribunals followed the same approach.[67] The *LG&E* tribunal, to the contrary, stated that an economic response was needed and that 'an economic recovery package was the only means to respond to the crisis'.[68] As such, the tribunal implied that even if the measures adopted were wholly inadequate to respond to the crisis, it still would have exempted Argentina from its responsibility vis-à-vis the foreign investors. The *Continental Casualty* tribunal chose a different approach again by maintaining that even another economic policy would not have put the claimant in a better position.[69] The tribunals' diverging reasons evidence the challenges presented in determining whether the measures employed were the 'only way' of dealing with the crisis.

Likewise, the limitations introduced by Article 25(2) of the ILC Articles, which exclude reliance on the necessity defence, pose difficulties in times of economic emergencies. The jurisprudence of the investment tribunals points to problems especially regarding the defence's 'contribution' element by which a state invoking necessity must not have contributed to the situation of necessity (Article 25(2.b) of the ILC Articles). While all tribunals concurred that a state's contribution to a state of necessity excluded the possibility of invoking it, they disagreed considerably on the level of state contribution needed to bar reliance on the necessity defence. The *CMS* tribunal stated that 'government policies and their shortcomings significantly contributed to the crisis and the emergency and while exogenous factors did fuel additional difficulties they do not exempt the Respondent from its responsibility in the matter'.[70] The *Enron* and *Sempra* tribunals closely followed this approach,[71] and the *National Grid* tribunal rejected Argentina's reliance on necessity largely because Argentina's contribution to the crisis had been substantial.[72] So did the

[63] In *Metalpar*, the tribunal did not consider it necessary to examine the elements of Argentina's necessity defence more closely because the claimants could not prove in any case that their investments were negatively affected by Argentina's measures (*Metalpar*, n 52, para 211).

[64] *Total SA v Argentina*, ICSID Case No ARB/04/1, Decision on Liability, 27 December 2010.

[65] ibid, para 184.

[66] *CMS* (n 16) para 323.

[67] *Enron* (n 16) para 309; *Sempra* (n 16) para 350.

[68] *LG&E* (n 16) para 257.

[69] *Continental Casualty* (n 16) para 230. The *BG* tribunal does not deal in detail with the different elements of Art 25 of the ILC Articles including the contribution element, arguing inter alia that the restrictive elements of the defence impeded reliance in any case; *BG* (n 33) paras 407–12.

[70] *CMS* (n 16) para 329.

[71] *Enron* (n 16) paras 311–12; *Sempra* (n 16) paras 353–54.

[72] *National Grid* (n 47) para 262.

Impregilo and the *El Paso* tribunals.[73] The *LG&E* tribunal, on the other hand, concluded that there was 'no serious evidence in the record that Argentina contributed to the crisis resulting in the state of necessity'.[74] However, the *LG&E* tribunal arrived at this conclusion only by relying on a doubtful burden of proof rule that shifted the burden of proof to the claimant. Likewise rejecting the claimant's contribution argument, the *Continental Casualty* tribunal held that Argentina had not contributed to the emergency in a way which would bar it from relying on the necessity defence, arguing that Argentina's economic policy had been praised by outside experts and previously benefited the country.[75]

Consequently, numerous problems relate to the defence's substantive criteria for application notwithstanding the general availability of the defence in economic crisis situations. What is more, and as will be shown next, even a successful reliance on necessity merely grants limited relief.

V WHAT IS THE EFFECT OF A SUCCESSFUL INVOCATION OF THE NECESSITY DEFENCE?

While past experience has demonstrated that a state of necessity may form a potential defence available to debtor states unable to service their debts, it remains questionable whether its successful invocation presents a useful tool for states.

The ILC Articles, codifying custom,[76] are explicit in stating the consequences of a state of necessity. A state of necessity brings temporary relief in the form of a suspension of the wrongfulness of non-payment, but not cancellation or partial cancellation of the original obligation.[77] Also international tribunals corroborate the defence's temporary nature which was, for instance, prominently affirmed by the ICJ in the *Gabčíkovo-Nagymaros* case. When considering Hungary's argument that the wrongfulness of its conduct in discontinuing the work on the project was precluded by a state of necessity, the Court stated that '[a]s soon as the state of necessity ceases to exist, the duty to comply

[73] *Impregilo* (n 16) para 358; *El Paso* (n 16) para 665.

[74] *LG&E* (n 16) para 257.

[75] *Continental Casualty* (n 16) paras 234–36. The *BG* tribunal did not examine the issue in detail.

[76] The consequences flowing from the reliance on a circumstance precluding wrongfulness are dealt with – in a 'one fits all approach' – in Art 27 of the ILC Articles (Consequences of invoking a circumstance precluding wrongfulness). Especially jurisprudence provides ample evidence that Art 27 codifies customary international law: for instance, Art 27 is referred to by the *CMS* tribunal as establishing 'the appropriate rule on the issue' (*CMS* (no 16) para 390). See also *LG&E* (no 16) paras 225, 260, 264; *Patrick Mitchell v Democratic Republic of the Congo*, ICSID ARB/99/7, Decision on the Application for Annulment of the Award, 1 November 2006, para 57.

[77] Art 27 of the ILC Articles outlines the temporary functioning of the circumstances precluding wrongfulness as follows: 'The invocation of a circumstance precluding wrongfulness in accordance with this chapter is without prejudice to: (a) Compliance with the obligation in question, if and to the extent that the circumstance precluding wrongfulness no longer exists; . . .'. The ILC Commentary confirms the temporary effect: 'Paragraph (a) of article 27 addresses the question of what happens when a condition preventing compliance with an obligation no longer exists or gradually ceases to operate. It makes clear that Chapter V has merely preclusive effect. When and to the extent that a circumstance precluding wrongfulness ceases . . . The obligation in question (assuming it is still in force) will again have to be complied with . . .' (ILC Commentary, n 6, 'Article 27', para 2 (Crawford, 189)). See also Szurek: 'These circumstances [precluding wrongfulness] authorize the temporary non-observance of the rule or non-performance of obligations, but the non-observance or non-performance is no longer acceptable once the reasons which justified it cease to exist' (S Szurek, 'The Notion of Circumstances Precluding Wrongfulness' in J Crawford, A Pellet and S Olleson (eds), *The Law of International Responsibility* (Oxford, Oxford University Press, 2010) 427, 434).

with treaty obligations revives'.[78] Likewise, investment tribunals have referred to the temporary nature of the defence. In the context of the Argentine crisis the investment tribunals agreed that reliance on necessity had to be temporary, ie only as long as the emergency situation persisted. The *CMS* tribunal held, in the form of an *obiter dictum*, that '[e]ven if the plea of necessity were accepted, compliance with the obligation would re-emerge as soon as the circumstance precluding wrongfulness no longer existed, which is the case at present'.[79] Similarly, the *LG&E* tribunal affirmed that Argentina's obligations under the BIT would revive after the end of the state of necessity.[80]

In view of this merely temporary relief from obligations, reliance on necessity may thus be of limited value for debtor states seeking to return to economic viability. Still, what about other means of debt reduction, like currency devaluation or bondholder haircuts in reliance on necessity? Could a state invoke necessity vis-à-vis investors in these situations to escape liability for alleged expropriations or violations of the fair and equitable treatment standard?

This ultimately depends on whether there is a state obligation to compensate foreign investors for measures taken in (successful) reliance on necessity after the emergency's end. The ILC Articles do not resolve the question. Formulated as 'non-prejudice clause', Article 27 of the ILC Articles deliberately avoids a final determination as to whether compensation is to be paid.[81] The ILC's open approach may be explained, inter alia, by the fact that Article 27 applies to circumstances precluding wrongfulness as diverse as self-defence, countermeasures or necessity.[82] Still, certain arguments militate in favour of compensation in cases of necessity. Arguments for such a duty may first be derived from drafting history.[83] Also the current ILC Commentary affirms that the burden of reliance on necessity should not be shifted to an innocent third state and approvingly refers to Hungary's willingness to compensate Slovakia in the *Gabčíkovo-Nagymaros* case.[84] Doctrine favours a duty of compensation in case of necessity as well.[85]

[78] *Gabčíkovo-Nagymaros* (n 4) 63 (para 101). See also *Rainbow Warrior* (*New Zealand v France*) 30 April 1990, 20 *RIAA* 217, 254.

[79] *CMS* (n 16) para 382.

[80] *LG&E* (n 16) para 263.

[81] Art 27 of the ILC Articles states that '[t]he invocation of a circumstance precluding wrongfulness in accordance with this chapter is without prejudice to: . . . (b) The question of compensation for any material loss caused by the act in question'. In so doing, Art 27 is, in Christakis' words, a 'clause de non dire' with the only purpose of keeping the door open for possible compensation (T Christakis, 'Les "circonstances excluant l'illicéité": une illusion optique?' in *Droit du pouvoir, pouvoir du droit – Mélanges offerts à Jean Salmon* (Brussels, Bruylant, 2007) 223, 236).

[82] The range of situations covered by Art 27 of the ILC Articles made it inappropriate to lay down a detailed compensation regime. See ILC Commentary, n 6, 'Article 27', para 6 (Crawford, 190).

[83] Whereas draft Art 35 of the first reading 1980 left open the possibility of compensation for consent, *force majeure*, necessity and distress, no such possibility was foreseen for self-defence or countermeasures. In his draft proposal for the second reading, Special Rapporteur Crawford limited the possibility of compensation to necessity and distress. Among the reasons given for this limitation were, amongst other things, the element of free choice of the state relying on necessity (or distress) and the need to balance the positions of the state acting in a situation of necessity and that of the other state(s) whose rights were encroached upon (J Crawford, *Second Report on State Responsibility* (1999) A/CN.4/498/Add 2, para 356. See also the Special Rapporteur's comments on draft Art 35 (Report of the ILC on the Work of its 51st Session (1999) *YBILC*, vol II/2, 84–85 (paras 402 ff)).

[84] 'As the Court noted, "Hungary expressly acknowledged that, in any event, such a state of necessity would not exempt it from the duty to compensate its partner"' (ILC Commentary, no 6, 'Article 27', para 5 (Crawford, 190)). In this sense also V Lowe, 'Precluding Wrongfulness or Responsibility: a Plea for Excuses' (1999) 10 *European Journal of International Law* 405, 410 (Lowe refers to the comparable situation of distress).

[85] Christakis (n 35) 51 ff. According to Christakis: 'il y a un prix à payer pour l'Etat qui choisit de violer les droits d'un Etat tiers pour conjurer un danger qui menace ses propres intérêts. . . . Si, en revanche, l'Etat lésé est "innocent", le Juge peut, en fonction de la situation, décider de maintenir en partie une obligation de réparation

Such obligation is furthermore generally confirmed in jurisprudence. To exemplify, in 1905 the *Umpire* held in the *Company General of the Orinoco* case[86] that Venezuela might annul the concessions of a French company in order to avoid an armed conflict with Colombia; this, however, notwithstanding a duty of compensation.[87] Also some of the investment decisions rendered in the context of the Argentine crisis confirmed a duty of compensation. The *CMS* tribunal stated, by way of *obiter dictum*, that '[t]he plea of state of necessity may preclude the wrongfulness of an act, but it does not exclude the duty to compensate the owner of the right which had to be sacrificed'.[88] Overall, it seems safe to conclude that a state will generally have to compensate investors even in cases of a successful reliance on necessity.

True, the amount of compensation is reduced. Article 27 of the ILC Articles refers only to compensation for losses which have actually occurred.[89] The compensation in cases of a successful invocation of necessity is thus diminished as compared to the concept of damage in cases of breach, with the latter also including lost profit.[90] Special Rapporteur Crawford contrasts the concept of *actual losses* in cases of reliance on the circumstances precluding wrongfulness with that of *full reparation* as follows:

> Rather [*draft* Article 35] is concerned with the question whether a State relying on a circumstance precluding wrongfulness should nonetheless be expected to make good any actual losses suffered by any State directly affected by that reliance. That is a perfectly proper condition, in principle, for allowing the former State to rely on a circumstance precluding wrongfulness. . . . Under the secondary rules of responsibility, which are the proper subject of the present draft articles, a State would normally be required to make full reparation to an injured State for conduct which . . . is not in compliance with its international obligations. If the draft articles define circumstances in which the putatively injured State is not so entitled, it is perfectly proper that they should do so subject to the proviso that any actual losses suffered by that State, and for which it is not itself responsible, should be met by the invoking State.[91]

ne retenant l'excuse de l'état de nécessité comme une simple *circonstance atténuante*' (ibid, 54). See also Szurek, n 77, 436. Generally in favour of compensation likewise R Dolzer and C Schreuer, *Principles of International Investment Law* (Oxford, Oxford University Press, 2008) 170; A Bjorklund, 'Emergency Exceptions: State of Necessity and *Force Majeure*' in P Muchlinski et al (eds), *Oxford Handbook of International Investment Law* (Oxford, Oxford University Press, 2008) 459, 510 ff.

86 *Company General of the Orinoco Case*, 31 July 1905, X RIAA, 184. Although labelled '*force majeure*' the constitutive elements of the defence are rather those of necessity.

87 'It [the Government of Venezuela] considered the peril superior to the obligation and substituted therefore the duty of compensation' (ibid, 280). The ILC refers to it as follows: '[The *Umpire*] ruled that, in the exceptional circumstance of the case, it was lawful under international law . . . to rescind the concessions, although he agreed that the company was entitled to compensation for the consequences of an act which had been internationally lawful' (Report of the ILC, 32nd Session (1980) *YBILC*, vol II(2), 40, para 17). See also *Properties of Bulgarian Minorities in Greece case* (1926) SDN, JO, 7e année, No 2, February 1926, Annex 815 and the reference made in Ago Report (n 13) 26, para 32; (1979) *YBILC*, vol II/1, 53, para 115.

88 *CMS* (n 16) para 388.

89 In the words of the ILC Commentary: 'Article 27 concerns only the adjustment of losses that may occur when a party relies on a circumstance covered by Chapter V' (ILC Commentary, n 6, 211 (para 4)).

90 See the pertinent Art 36 of the ILC Articles: 'Compensation. 1. The State responsible for an internationally wrongful act is under an obligation to compensate for the damage caused thereby, insofar as such damage is not made good by restitution. 2. The compensation shall cover any financially assessable damage including loss of profits insofar as it is established.'

91 Comments of Special Rapporteur Crawford on *draft* Art 35, n 83, 84–85).

What is more, the compensation is only due after the end of the economic emergency, and also the interests in case of default start to run only then.[92] Thus, there are certain advantages for the state relying on necessity. These notwithstanding, even a successful reliance on necessity remains an incomplete means for a state in economic emergency given its merely temporary relief and the – albeit reduced – duty to compensation.

VI TOWARDS AN ORDERLY SOVEREIGN DEBT RESTRUCTURING?

It consequently appears warranted to look for alternatives. The most obvious – which is also frequently alluded to in literature[93] – is sovereign debt restructuring. Sovereign debt restructuring ultimately entails states' permanent relief. At the same time, if done in a fair and orderly way, also creditors have certain advantages: namely (relative) legal security, equity and the receipt of at least parts of their claims.[94]

Not surprisingly, the *UNCTAD Principles on Promoting Sovereign Lending and Borrowing*[95] (UNCTAD Principles) put central emphasis on the possibility of debt restructuring when states are 'manifestly unable to service their debts':

> Principle 7 – Debt Restructurings:
>
> In circumstances where a sovereign is manifestly unable to service its debts, all lenders have a responsibility to behave in good faith and with cooperative spirit to reach a consensual rearrangement of those obligations. Creditors should seek a speedy and orderly resolution to the problem.
>
> Principle 15 – Restructuring:
>
> If a restructuring of sovereign debt obligations becomes unavoidable, it should be undertaken promptly, efficiently and fairly.[96]

[92] See Art 38 of the ILC Articles: 'Interest. . . . 2. Interest runs from the date when the principal sum should have been paid until the date the obligation to pay is fulfilled'.

[93] See M Waibel, 'The Two Worlds of Necessity in ICSID Arbitration: CMS and LG&E' (2007) 20 *Leiden Journal of International Law* 637, 648. See also A von Bogdandy and M Goldmann, 'Sovereign Debt Restructurings as Exercise of International Public Authority: Towards a Decentralized Sovereign Insolvency Law', February 2013, available at SSRN: http://papers.ssrn.com/sol3/papers.cfm?abstract_id=2089480, accessed 2 September 2013; A Krueger, 'Sovereign Debt Restructuring: Messy or Messier?' (2003) 93(2) *The American Economic Review* 70; B Eichengreen, 'Restructuring Sovereign Debt' (2003) 17(4) *The Journal of Economic Perspectives* 75; RK Rasmussen, 'Sovereign Debt Restructuring, Odious Debt, and the Politics of Debt Relief' (2007) 70(4) *Law and Contemporary Problems* 249.

[94] Sovereign debt restructuring is generally understood to mean 'an exchange of outstanding sovereign debt instruments, such as loans or bonds, for new debt instruments or cash through a legal process'; for this definition and a general overview of how such a restructuring mechanism should work and to what standards it should adhere, see US Das, MG Papaioannou and C Trebesch, 'Sovereign Debt Restructurings 1950–2010: Literature Survey, Data, and Stylized Facts', IMF Working Paper WP/12/203 (2012) 7.

[95] *UNCTAD Principles on Promoting Responsible Sovereign Lending and Borrowing*, 10 January 2012, available at: www.unctad.info/upload/Debt%20Portal/Principles%20drafts/Principles%20consolidated_jan%2010.pdf, accessed 2 September 2013. The Principles are the outcome of a joint initiative including experts from academia, civil society and international financial institutions, with additional input form governments and other stakeholders. They aim at building consensus on the rules to be applied to debt crises. For further reference see M Goldmann, 'Responsible Sovereign Lending and Borrowing: The View from Domestic Jurisdictions' (UNCTAD, MPI for Comparative Public Law and International Law, February 2012) 7.

[96] See also the explanation of Principles 7 and 15: 'Under current international law, in the absence of any formalized, legally binding restructuring mechanism, sovereign borrowers as well as sovereign lenders may opt for holdouts and prevent timely, efficient, equitable and sustainable restructurings. Collective action clauses are used in order to reduce the likelihood of lender holdouts. Market discipline should ideally prevent borrower

A comparative study on the *UNCTAD Principles*' reflection as general principles of law in domestic jurisdictions observes a wide recognition especially of the principles concerning debt restructuring:

> *Restructurings, Principles 7 and 15:* Certain general principles of insolvency law seem to enjoy virtually universal acceptance. Those principles include the automatic stay of other proceedings, the equality of borrowers with respect to payments, the priority of creditors holding collateral or privileges which are in the public interest, and majority decision-making by creditors. These principles could also be applied to international negotiations about, and procedures for, the rescheduling of sovereign debt. The increasing use of Collective Action Clauses and the exclusion of sovereign debt in some recent BITs points towards a consolidation of sovereign debt restructuring mechanisms on an international level.[97]

Thus, rather than placing too much emphasis on the necessity defence, it might be preferable for states to aim at sovereign debt restructuring as a durable – and not just temporary – solution. To achieve lasting debt relief should also be the best option for the economic and social rights of a country's population. *De lege ferenda*, for reasons of stability and predictability, the enactment of binding international rules for sovereign debt restructuring appears desirable.[98]

holdouts, i.e. the refusal of governments to enter into negotiations about consolidation measures in exchange for restructurings or debt relief. Holdouts may also be less likely if restructurings are perceived as fair and equitable. In this respect, some of the items in the questionnaire aim at investigating whether it is appropriate to distil certain general principles of law from the practice of domestic legal orders' (Goldmann (n 95) 39).

[97] ibid, 5. Conversely, economic emergencies rarely count as defence at domestic level. While an according Principle 9 was included in the UNCTAD Principles and reads as follows: 'A sovereign debt contract is a binding obligation and should be honored. Exceptional cases nonetheless can arise. A state of financial necessity can prevent the borrower's full and/or timely repayment. Also, a competent judicial authority may rule that circumstances giving rise to legal defense have occurred . . .', it is not met with widespread acceptance. See in this sense Goldmann: '*Defenses, Principle 9:* . . . economic deteriorations rarely count as a defense. Although there are some notable cases, mostly based on the *clausula rebus sic stantibus*, the materialization of economic risks usually does not count as a reason for the modification of contractual terms. This strict rule, however, is generally justified by the possibility to file for bankruptcy. Such filing usually requires the inability of a debtor to make due payments' (ibid, 5).

[98] A number of different proposals regarding the introduction of binding international rules on sovereign defaults, ranging from suggestions of application of domestic bankruptcy proceedings (in particular based on 'Chapter 9' (K Raffer, 'International Debts: A Crisis for Whom?' in HW Singer and S Sharma (eds), *Economic Development and World Debt* (London, Macmillan Press, 1990) 52) or 'Chapter 11' (SL Schwarcz, 'Sovereign Debt Restructuring: A Bankruptcy Reorganization Approach' (2000) 85 *Cornell Law Review* 980) of the US Bankruptcy Act) to statutory proposals (Krueger (n 93)) or its implementations by means of institutionalisation (CG Paulus and S Kargman, 'Reforming the Process of Sovereign Debt Restructuring: A Proposal for a Sovereign Debt Tribunal' (2008) *Workshop on Debt, Finance and Emerging Issues in Financial Integration*); also see on this issue von Bogdandy and Goldmann (n 93). Specifically on the virtues of a non-binding approach see A Gelpern, 'Hard, Soft, and Embedded: Implementing Principles on Promoting Responsible Sovereign Lending and Borrowing', UNCTAD Working Paper, 2012.

9

Global Financial Architecture and Human Rights

ROSA M LASTRA

Whereas recognition of the inherent dignity and of the equal and inalienable rights of all members of the human family is the foundation of freedom, justice and peace in the world,

Whereas disregard and contempt for human rights have resulted in barbarous acts which have outraged the conscience of mankind, and the advent of a world in which human beings shall enjoy freedom of speech and belief and freedom from fear and want has been proclaimed as the highest aspiration of the common people,

Whereas it is essential, if man is not to be compelled to have recourse, as a last resort, to rebellion against tyranny and oppression, that human rights should be protected by the rule of law,

THE GENERAL ASSEMBLY proclaims THIS UNIVERSAL DECLARATION OF HUMAN RIGHTS as a common standard of achievement for all peoples and all nations.

Preamble to the UDHR, 1948

THIS CHAPTER DISCUSSES the need to take human rights into account in the shaping of the evolving international financial architecture. A basic premise in my argumentation is that any institution – national, supranational or international, private or public – needs to respect the dignity of human beings. This dignity is embedded in the concept of human rights. Financial law has grown exponentially in recent years and the myriad of prescriptive rules, statutes and regulations may erroneously lead us to believe that somehow the law related to financial markets and institutions – nationally and internationally – is so technical and specialised that the consideration of general principles of law (fairness, transparency, good faith, non-discrimination) is not really necessary. But those principles are the crystallisation of the accepted values that underlie the rules that govern society.[1] Financial law, this chapter contends, needs to function within an ethical framework of accepted values and principles. The recognition and protection of human rights is a fundamental part of those accepted principles.[2] Any positive

[1] The primary sources of international law are conventional law (treaty law), customary law and the general principles of law, as recognised by Article 38 of the Statute of the International Court of Justice. Customary international law results when states follow certain practices generally and consistently. Customary law, however, can evolve into conventional law. Indeed, important principles of customary international law have become codified in the Vienna Convention of the Law of Treaties, thus acquiring the characteristic of 'conventional law'.

[2] That rights were grounded in principle was one of the arguments espoused by Richard Dworkin. See R Dworkin, *Taking Rights Seriously* (Cambridge, MA, Harvard University Press, 1977) and *Justice for Hedgehogs* (Cambridge, MA, Harvard University Press, 2011).

law that is not rooted in the respect for human dignity can be at its very extreme (think Nazi regime) profoundly anti-human. Linkages between the discourse on economic law and the discourse on human rights can be dismissed on the basis that the former is 'scientific' while the latter is 'moralistic'.[3] However, though the discussion about human dignity and human rights undoubtedly has an ethical dimension, the incorporation of such rights into legal documents creates obligations for individuals, corporations, states and international organisations.[4]

I HUMAN RIGHTS AND INTERNATIONAL LAW

'The concept of human rights derives primarily from international law, which in turn took it from the philosophy of natural law'.[5] In a revisionist account of the history of human rights, Freeman persuasively argues that the seventeenth-century concept of natural rights developed by Grotius, Hobbes and Locke derived from late-medieval controversies and from the Spanish thinkers of the sixteenth century,[6] particularly from the so-called 'School of Salamanca'.[7] According to their understanding, 'natural rights were what were commanded by natural law'.[8] Domingo de Soto and Francisco de Vitoria in particular developed the association between right and freedom.[9] Freeman uses this revisionist account to show that the concept of natural rights – anchored in the Christian tradition of respect for the dignity of human beings[10] – pre-dated by a few centuries the concept of capitalism and that the concept of human rights has 'transcended the debate between capitalism and socialism to become a post-socialist instrument for the critique of capitalism'.[11] Indeed, in his opinion, on the one hand international human rights embody

[3] M Freeman, 'Beyond Capitalism and Socialism' in J Dine and A Fagan (eds), *Human Rights And Capitalism: A Multidisciplinary Perspective on Globalisation* (Northampton, Edward Elgar Publishing, 2006) 4: 'Historically . . . the discourse of rights was moralistic, whereas that of capitalism was "scientific"'.

[4] As explained in Section 1, the theory of human rights was first developed by the 'School of Salamanca' – the first school of International Law – in the sixteenth century. Modern human rights law developed out of customs and theories that established the rights of the individual in relation to the state. These rights were expressed in legal terms in documents such as the English Bill of Rights of 1688, the US Declaration of Independence of 1776, the .S Bill of Rights added to the US Constitution in 1789, and the French Declaration of the Rights of Man and the Citizen added to the French Constitution in 1791. The Universal Declaration of Human Rights of 1948 is the first international legal document that states that human rights should be protected by the rule of law.

[5] Freeman (n 3) 3.

[6] ibid, 7–26.

[7] The 'School of Salamanca' is the name applied to a group of Spanish jurists, theologians and philosophers who created a body of doctrine on natural, international and economic law, rooted in the intellectual work of Francisco de Vitoria, who started teaching in Salamanca in 1526 on the *catedra de prima*, the most important chair of theology at the University. Other distinguished members of this school were Domingo de Soto, Fernando Vázquez de Menchaca, Diego de Covarrubias, Luis de Molina, Juan Ginés de Sepúlveda and Francisco Suárez. The role of the School of Salamanca in the development of early monetary theory has been documented in the work of Marjorie Grice-Hutchinson. While at the LSE, Marjorie came under the influence of Friedrich von Hayek, who urged her to study the manuscripts of this group of Spanish scholars from the sixteenth and early seventeenth centuries. Her monograph, *School of Salamanca. Reading in Spanish Monetary Theory, 1544–1605*, was published by Clarendon Press, Oxford in 1952.

[8] Freeman (n 3) 9

[9] ibid, 10. Freeman also argues (13) that '[t]he historical record of the liberal-democratic West . . . has given inordinate emphasis to individual property rights'. He argues that medieval debates about property (24–25) can aid understanding of the current debate about the relationship between rights, property and justice.

[10] These Christian origins can actually be traced back to St Augustine, ibid, 23.

[11] ibid, 6–7.

some of the most important concessions capitalism has made and, on the other hand, they signify an erosion of the concept of state sovereignty.[12]

In the aftermath of the Great Financial Crisis, discontent with the inequitable distribution of the fruits of economic development has highlighted the anger that many feel about the human and social dimension of the consequences of the economic and financial crisis, in particular the lack of opportunities for many, effectively a deprivation of some basic human rights. The Occupy movement in New York's Zucotti Park and its spread to other cities (London, Madrid) signified a frustration not so much with markets' capitalism per se, but with the 'social injustice' many feel associated with what has been aptly described as the 'privatisation of gains and socialisation of losses' in banking and finance. This together with the inter-generational issues triggered by excessive debt and what has been referred to as 'a two-tier labour market that too often obliges younger workers to suffer job insecurity, while preserving for older workers a significant degree of protection'[13] brings a new light to the study of human rights.

Amartya Sen in his acclaimed book *Development as Freedom* sees the expansion of freedoms as both the primary end and the principal means of development.[14] His focus on human freedoms contrasts with other narrower views of development:

> Development requires the removal of major sources of un-freedom: poverty as well as tyranny, poor economic opportunities as well as systematic social deprivation, neglect of public facilities as well as intolerance of over-activity of repressive states.[15]

He considers the empirical link that exists between different rights or freedoms:

> Political freedoms (in the form of free speech and elections) help to promote economic security. Social opportunities (in the form of education and health facilities) facilitate economic participation. Economic facilities (in the form of opportunities for participation in trade and production) can help to generate personal abundance as well as public resources for social facilities. Freedoms of different kinds can strengthen one another.[16]

Sen views individual freedoms as social commitments. The connection between the individual and the social dimension of human rights is indeed at the core of their modern understanding.

The thirty articles of the Universal Declaration of Human Rights (UDHR)[17] establish the civil, political, economic, social and cultural rights of all people and constitute the

[12] ibid, 25–26.

[13] See *Financial Times* editorial, 24 October 2011, 'Capitalism and its Global Malcontents. Politicians in the West Ignore the Indignants at their Cost'.

[14] See A Sen, *Development as Freedom* (Oxford, Oxford University Press, 1999).

[15] ibid, 3. Sen considers that markets are not sufficient for the fulfilment of human freedoms.

[16] ibid, 11.

[17] See The Universal Declaration of Human Rights (UDHR) adopted by the United Nations General Assembly on 10 December 1948, The 'International Bill of Human Rights' is formed by the UN General Assembly, Universal Declaration of Human Rights, 10 December 1948, GA res 217 A (III), www.unhchr.ch/udhr/lang/eng.htm, accessed 30 June 2013, the International Covenant on Civil and Political Rights, New York, 16 December 1966, 999 UNTS 171, www.ohchr.org/english/law/ccpr.htm, accessed 30 June 2013 and the International Covenant on Economic, Social and Cultural Rights, New York, 16 December 1966, 993 UNTS 3, www.ohchr.org/english/law/cescr.htm, accessed 30 June 2013. Basic social standards are defined in the ILO Declaration on Fundamental Principles and Rights at Work, 18 June 1998, at www.ilo.org/dyn/declaris/DECLARATIONWEB.static_jump?var_language=EN&var_pagename=DECLARATIONTEXT, accessed 30 June 2013, and further developed in the various ILO Conventions, which are based upon the economic and social rights guaranteed in Arts 23 and 24 of the UDHR and the UN Covenant on Economic, Social and Cultural Rights (Preamble and Arts 6–8), www.ilo.org/ilolex/english/index.htm, accessed 30 June 2013.

foundation of the international system for the recognition and protection of human rights. Articles 3–21 refer to the rights of individuals to life, liberty, security and property, freedom of expression, freedom from torture, right to due process, equality before the law and others (avoiding the arbitrary interference by government), while Articles 22–27 set forth economic, social and cultural rights whose progressive accomplishment sets the path for development, such as the right to education, work and an adequate standard of living. Articles 28–30 deal with the promotion, protection and fulfilment of the UDHR.[18]

II THE GLOBAL FINANCIAL ARCHITECTURE

While the concept of human rights is well understood[19] the definition of global financial architecture lacks precise contours and refers to a variety of issues.[20] Some authors focus on the normative or rule-making function, such as Giovanoli:

> This concept is generally understood as encompassing the rules, guidelines and other arrangements governing international financial relations as well as the various institutions, entities and bodies through which such rules, guidelines and other arrangements are developed, monitored and enforced.[21]

Other definitions emphasise the framework for the prevention and resolution of international financial crises:

> While there is no agreed definition of what constitutes international financial architecture, it refers broadly to the framework and set of measures that can help prevent crises and manage them better in the more integrated international financial environment. Several aspects of the agenda for crisis prevention and crisis resolution deal with weaknesses in the international financial system that potentially contribute to the propensity and magnitude of global instability, hence requiring collective action at the international level. But there is widespread recognition that global financial stability also rests on robust national systems and hence requires enhanced measures at the country level as well.[22]

The common element of the various definitions is the consensus that surrounds the need to ensure financial stability, increasingly regarded as an international public good in the aftermath of the Great Financial Crisis.

The actors in the international financial architecture are international financial institutions, regional financial institutions, (informal) international standard setters such as the Financial Stability Board, the Basel Committee on Banking Supervision or the International Organization of Securities Commissions, 'informal' international groupings where inter-

[18] There are several taxonomies of human rights. According to the 'nature' of the human rights, there are civil rights, political rights and social, economic and cultural rights. According to the 'recipient' of the human rights, there are individual rights such as the rights to life, education, health, work; and collective rights, such as women's rights, children's rights, indigenous people's rights and others.

[19] As explained above, human rights are universal legal guarantees protecting individuals and groups against actions which interfere with fundamental freedoms and human dignity.

[20] See generally ch 14 of R Lastra, *Legal Foundations of International Monetary Stability* (Oxford, Oxford University Press, 2006) and R Lastra (ed), *The Reform of the International Financial Architecture* (Alphen aan den Rijn, Kluwer Law International, 2001).

[21] See M Giovanoli, 'A New Architecture for the Global Financial Markets: Legal Aspects of International Financial Standard Setting' in M Giovanoli (ed), *International Monetary Law. Issues for the New Millennium* (Oxford, Oxford University Press, 2000) 9.

[22] See www.worldbank.org/ifa/ifa_more.html, accessed 30 June 2013.

national financial issues are discussed (such as the Group of Seven, G-7 now G-10, G-22 etc), national central banks and ministries of finance or treasuries (which can play a role individually or collectively, meeting in an international forum of a formal or informal character) and private financial institutions acting on a global scale, including their professional associations (market entities). This multiplicity of actors creates a very complex structure.

'Formal' international financial institutions, whose existence is formally recognised by a treaty, fall mainly into two groups: multilateral organisations (with a global scope) and regional institutions (with a regional focus). The main multilateral organisations are the International Monetary Fund, the World Bank Group (comprising the International Bank for Reconstruction and Development, IBRD; the International Development Association, IDA; the Multilateral Investment Guarantee Agency, MIGA; and the International Centre for the Resolution of Investment Disputes), the Bank for International Settlements (BIS), the Organisation for Economic Co-operation and Development and the World Trade Organization (WTO) (with regard to trade in financial services). The regional institutions are a broad and expanding category that includes the European Bank for Reconstruction and Development (EBRD) and other regional development banks (Inter-American Development Bank, African Development Bank, Asian Development Bank), the European System of Central Banks and the European Investment Bank.

With a few exceptions (notably, the Articles of Agreement of the IMF), most of the international standards, codes of conduct, and other arrangements governing cross-border financial relations are 'soft law'.[23]

Soft law can be defined as rules that are not legally binding, but which in practice are adhered to by those to whom they are addressed or by those who subscribe to them, for a variety of reasons (moral suasion, fear of adverse action and other 'incentives' to observe the rules).[24] The essential feature of 'soft law' is that it cannot be enforced by formal legal means because it is not legally binding. Soft law is informal law. Its main problem is enforcement. Its main drawback is legitimacy. Its greatest advantage is flexibility. Hard law is formal law, enforceable and legitimate. It is also rigid and this rigidity can be problematic with regard to the regulation of money and financial markets. Soft law fills a need, a legal vacuum in regulation of cross-border banking activities and in other areas (eg, in the context of this chapter, UN principles on external debt and human rights, and the UNCTAD Principles on sovereign lending and borrowing). It cannot therefore be dismissed.

While most of the entities involved in the process of international financial standard-setting are inter-governmental or official entities, and their principles or recommendations can be characterised as 'top down' rules (typically 'public law'), the work done by professional associations and market entities[25] (uniform rules and standards, voluntary

[23] See Giovanoli (n 21) 33. For a recent study on soft law see Ch Brummer, *Soft Law and the Global Financial System: Rule Making in the 21st Century* (Cambridge, Cambridge University Press, 2012).

[24] See R Goode, *Commercial Law*, 2nd edition (London, Penguin Books, 1995) 20–21.

[25] The International Accounting Standards Committee, the Emerging Markets Trade Association, the International Chamber of Commerce, ICC, and its various commissions and working groups, think tanks such as the Group of Thirty and others also contribute to this process. The ICC has 16 commissions of experts which cover every specialised field of concern to international business. Subjects range from banking techniques and financial services to taxation, trade policy, competition policy, telecommunications, intellectual property, information technology and others. Self-regulation is a common thread running through the work of the

'codes of conduct', 'codes of practice', etc) can be characterised as 'bottom up' rules, an exercise in self-regulation. The success of standardised clauses and model rules in private contracts developed by trade and financial industry associations (such as the rules developed by the International Swaps and Derivatives Association, ISDA, governing derivative contracts) has demonstrated that markets are capable of spreading existing standards across jurisdictions and developing common rules (self-regulation).[26]

From a 'private law' perspective, the work of the organisations concerned with the harmonisation of transnational commercial law, such as UNCITRAL (United Nations Commission on International Trade Law),[27] UNIDROIT (the International Institute for the Unification of Private Law)[28] and the Hague Conference on International Private Law,[29] is also relevant[30] (albeit of a different character from those rules that emanate from professional associations).

The dynamic interplay between hard law and soft law[31] can provide a fundamental key to improve the attention of the global financial architecture to human rights issues. This architecture is work in progress, an evolving reality. Though states remain key actors,[32] they are not the only actors, as just outlined. This suggests a reassessment of the normative powers and of the limitations of states in the design of the international financial architecture. It is no longer enough for states to advance human rights law. Other actors – in particular international organisations – also need to advance this cause.

III GLOBAL FINANCIAL ARCHITECTURE AND HUMAN RIGHTS

Article 28 of the UDHR says: 'Everyone is entitled to a social and international order in which the rights and freedoms set forth in this Declaration can be fully realized'. The present global financial architecture does not meet the requirements of this provision. Why is this so and what can we do to remedy this deficiency? Let us start with the 'why', recalling the origins of the IMF, the institution at the centre of the global financial architecture.

commissions. The ICC has direct access to national governments all over the world through its national committees. The ICC's Paris-based international secretariat feeds business views into intergovernmental organisations on issues that directly affect business operations. See www.iccwbo.org/id93/index.html, accessed 30 June 2013.

[26] See also Giovanoli (n 21) 10, n 20.

[27] www.uncitral.org, accessed 30 June 2013.

[28] www.unidroit.org, accessed 30 June 2013.

[29] www.hcch.net/index_en.php, accessed 30 June 2013.

[30] See R Goode, 'Rule, Practice and Pragmatism in Commercial Law' (2005) 54 *International Comparative Law Quarterly* 553. Goode refers to the UNIDROIT Principles of International Commercial Contracts. Goode points out (ibid, 539) that transnational commercial law is the product of various means: 'international conventions, model laws, contractually incorporated uniform rules, international restatements and conscious or unconscious legislative or judicial parallelism, which lead to the harmonization of commercial law at the international level'. He also points out (ibid) that his concern 'is primarily with the private law governing cross-border transactions, not with international economic law or regulatory law'.

[31] Though the word 'compliance' is a term typically used in the case of hard law and 'observance' (or adherence to) in the case of soft law, sometimes the word compliance is also used in references to soft law.

[32] In the *Lotus* case, the Permanent Court of International Justice described the international legal system as follows: 'International law governs relations between independent states. The rules of law binding upon states therefore emanate from their own free will as expressed in conventions or by usages generally accepted as expressing principles of law and established in order to regulate the relations between these coexisting independent communities or with a view to the achievement of common aims'. See *The Case of the 'SS Lotus'*, 1927 PCIJ, Series A, No 10, 18.

The IMF was established following the conclusion of the International Monetary and Financial Conference of the United and Associated Nations, commonly referred to as the Bretton Woods conference, in 1944. The Articles of Agreement of the IMF were adopted on 22 July 1944 came into force on 27 December 1945.[33] The IMF began operations in Washington DC in May 1946.[34]

The IMF is a specialised agency of the United Nations (as the World Bank). This status was obtained through an agreement entered into with the Economic and Social Council of the United Nations Charter in accordance with Articles 63 and 57[35] of the United Nations Charter.[36] Though the IMF functions as an independent international organisation (so does the World Bank), this agreement has legal significance, including the way human rights come into play (or should come into play) in the policies of the Fund (and in the policies of the Bank).[37] The IMF likes to remind its members that it is an international monetary institution, rather than a development organisation (even though some of its policies have a development angle and influence human rights issues). However, as Bradlow puts it:

> The IMF as a subject of international law, has some responsibility to help protect the citizens in its Member States from human rights abuses. It cannot be indifferent to situations in which human rights abuses have become so serious as to cause monetary consequences.[38]

Though the IMF Articles of Agreement say nothing about human rights, the IMF as a juridical person cannot ignore the UDHR. In 1941–42 when Harry Dexter White and John Maynard Keynes wrote the proposals that eventually led to the establishment of the IMF in Bretton Woods in 1944, the UDHR had not yet been adopted. The IMF Articles of Agreement were therefore signed before the United Nations adopted the UDHR. In my opinion, however, human rights law should bind the IMF as much as it should bind any other national or international organisation that pre-dates the adoption of the UDHR.

[33] 'Bretton Woods constituted the first formal international agreement applicable for economic transactions among the countries that had subscribed to it'. See M Guitián, 'The Unique Nature of the Responsibilities of the International Monetary Fund', IMF Pamphlet Series No 46, Washington DC, 1992, 2.

[34] For a history of the IMF see generally Lastra (n 20) ch 12.

[35] The Charter of the United Nations, www.un.org/en/documents/charter/chapter9.shtml, accessed 30 June 2013.

> Article 57 reads as follows:
> '1. The various specialized agencies, established by intergovernmental agreement and having wide international responsibilities, as defined in their basic instruments, in economic, social, cultural, educational, health, and related fields, shall be brought into relationship with the United Nations in accordance with the provisions of Article 63.
> 2. Such agencies thus brought into relationship with the United Nations are hereinafter referred to as specialized agencies'.
> Article 63 reads as follows:
> '1. The Economic and Social Council may enter into agreements with any of the agencies referred to in Article 57, defining the terms on which the agency concerned shall be brought into relationship with the United Nations. Such agreements shall be subject to approval by the General Assembly.
> 2. It may co-ordinate the activities of the specialized agencies through consultation with and recommendations to such agencies and through recommendations to the General Assembly and to the Members of the United Nations'.

[36] See Agreement Between the United Nations and the International Monetary Fund, art IV(2), 16 U.N.T.8. 328, 332 (1948).

[37] See generally, S Skogly, *Human Rights Obligations of the World Bank and the IMF* (London, Cavendish Publishing, 2001) 27 and ch 5. See also D Bradlow, 'The World Bank, the IMF, and Human Rights' (1996) 6 *Journal of Transnational Law and Contemporary Problems* 47–90.

[38] Bradlow (n 38) 72–73.

'Modern' organisations such as the EU or the EBRD show deference towards human rights. As for the WTO, the issues have been examined elsewhere.[39]

Human rights, democracy and the rule of law are core values of the European Union.[40] Embedded in the founding treaty, they were reinforced when the EU adopted the Charter of Fundamental Rights in 2000, and strengthened still further when the Charter became legally binding with the entry into force of the Lisbon Treaty in 2009. Countries seeking to join the EU must respect human rights. And all trade and cooperation agreements with third countries contain a clause stipulating that human rights are an essential element in relations between the parties.[41]

As for the EBRD, according to the Preamble of the EBRD Agreement[42] of 1991:

> The contracting parties, committed to the fundamental principles of multiparty democracy, the rule of law, respect for human rights and market economics; recalling the Final Act of the Helsinki Conference on Security and Cooperation in Europe, and in particular its Declaration on Principles; welcoming the intent of Central and Eastern European countries to further the practical implementation of multiparty democracy, strengthening democratic institutions, the rule of law and respect for human rights and their willingness to implement reforms in order to evolve towards market-oriented economies; . . . Have agreed to establish hereby the European Bank for Reconstruction and Development . . ..

International organisations must evolve. The IMF should support – through the exercise of its functions – the efforts countries make to improve their human rights performance, even though such performance is not part of the obligations of members, according to Article IV and Article VIII of the IMF Articles of Agreement.

The main functions performed by the IMF in relation to its members are surveillance (Article IV), financial assistance (Article V, Section 3) and technical assistance (Article V Section 2 b). These are the tools that the IMF uses to accomplish its objectives or purposes as defined in Article I of the Articles of Agreement. From the point of view of the member states, they constitute the main 'services' that the Fund provides to them.[43]

[39] The WTO, though a modern institution, has inherited the legacy of the Bretton Woods framework for understanding international economic relations and is not designed to promote human rights per se. However, many of the trade rules are anchored – as Petersmann reminds us – in the same values as human rights law: 'individual freedom and responsibility . . .; non-discrimination; rule of law; access to courts and adjudication to disputes; promotion of social welfare through peaceful cooperation among free citizens'. Petersmann argues that 'like the EC, the WTO can and should become an advocate not only of economic freedom, but of human freedom more generally'. See generally E-U Petersmann, 'The WTO Constitution and Human Rights' (200) 3(1) *Journal of International Economic Law* 19–25. See also T Cottier, J Pauwelyn and E Bürgi (eds), *Human Rights and International Trade* (Oxford, Oxford University Press, 2005) and S Joseph, D Kinley and J Waincymer (eds), *The World Trade Organization and Human Rights: Interdisciplinary Perspectives* (Cheltenham, Edward Elgar, 2009). G Marceu, in 'WTO Dispute Settlement and Human Rights' (2002) 3(4) *European Journal of International Law* 753–814, suggests that WTO law must evolve and be interpreted consistently with human rights law.

[40] http://eeas.europa.eu/human_rights/index_en.htm, accessed 30 June 2013 and http://europa.eu/pol/rights/index_en.htm, accessed 30 June 2013. The European Union sees human rights as universal and indivisible. It actively promotes and defends them both within its borders and when engaging in relations with non-EU countries.

[41] See also www.consilium.europa.eu/uedocs/cms_data/docs/pressdata/EN/foraff/131173.pdf, accessed 30 June 2013.

[42] The Agreement Establishing the European Bank for Reconstruction and Development was signed in Paris on 29 May 1990. The Agreement entered into force on 28 March 1991. An Amendment to Article 1 of the Agreement was approved by Resolution of the Board of Governors adopted on 30 January 2004, and entered into force on 15 October 2006.

[43] From the Fund's perspective, its powers can be broken down into three categories: (i) regulatory (jurisdiction), comprising Article VIII Section 2 and Article IV; (ii) financial (Article V, Section 3), and (iii) advisory (technical assistance, Article V Section 2 b). For an extensive analysis of IMF surveillance, conditionality and technical assistance, see Lastra (n 20), ch 13.

IMF surveillance has evolved significantly over the last decades (thanks to the ample room for interpretation granted to the Fund in the exercise of surveillance), with the increased attention to financial sector issues and policies being the most significant development. Bilateral surveillance is typically exercised through the so-called Article IV consultations. While surveillance in the past was typically focused on the jurisdiction over the exchange arrangements of members and macroeconomic policies, surveillance nowadays also takes into account other issues, often involving the workings of the private sector, such as good governance (both political and corporate governance), legal and institutional reform, labour market reform, social safety nets, bank resolution, restructuring, financial reform, etc. The remit of Article IV consultations is not fixed; indeed the experience over the past two decades suggests that such remit is like an expanding accordion. According to Bradlow, '[t]he broad scope of the Article IV consultations suggests that the IMF can exert influence over the human rights situations in Member States';[44] '[t]he Articles do not . . . preclude the IMF from raising serious human rights issues in its Article IV consultations'.[45]

Surveillance provides the Fund with a picture of what goes wrong (or right) in a country and, given the empirical connection, to which Amartya Sen referred, between different types of rights and the positive impact on development that their expansion triggers, the IMF is in a position to recommend reforms that can improve the human rights situations of its members.

In addition to surveillance, the IMF has a powerful tool to influence economic and social developments (including human rights performance) in a country, namely the provision of conditional financial assistance.[46] Conditionality refers to the policies and procedures developed by the Fund to govern the access to and the use of its resources by member countries.

Countries in need of balance of payments support subject themselves to conditionality (as well as to surveillance and technical assistance) as the price that must be exacted to obtain financial support. Members are not necessarily keen to tighten their belts or the belts of their citizens to obtain the resources they need to address balance of payments difficulties, but they are well aware that non-observance of their financial obligations with the Fund will lead them into further trouble.

The use of IMF conditionality acts as a very powerful official incentive, when the country's adherence to a particular set of standards is made a 'condition' for the disbursement of IMF funds under a stand-by or extended arrangement. Conditionality thus provides a unique platform to exert influence upon members' policies. Structural reforms – of the kind the IMF has been preaching over recent decades – have economic, as well as social, cultural and political, consequences over time.[47] The Fund has also been promoting transparency, accountability and the rule of law in recent years.[48] All this suggests that the Fund can and should do more to develop a human rights policy.

[44] See Bradlow (n 38) 70.

[45] ibid, 72.

[46] For an extensive analysis of conditionality see Lastra (n 20), ch 13.

[47] Bradlow (n 38) n 126, 77: 'Since it tends to focus its attention on the Finance Ministries and the Central Banks in its Member States, the IMF is also able to make policies without necessarily consulting all interested line ministries in the country's government'.

[48] ibid, 72–73: 'The IMF, as a subject of international law, has some responsibility to help protect the citizens in its Member States from human rights abuses. It cannot be indifferent to situations in which human rights abuses have become so serious as to cause monetary consequences. For example, during the 1980s the IMF was forced to recognize that the systematic abuses caused by South Africa's apartheid policy had adverse effects on its ability to meet its obligations as a Member of the IMF. As result the IMF was forced to limit South Africa's access to the resources and services of the IMF'.

IV CONCLUSIONS

The recognition and protection of human rights should be an obligation for individuals, corporations, states, NGOs and international organisations. The IMF and other international financial institutions need to evolve in this direction. One of the lessons of the Great Financial Crisis is that finance should not be dissociated from ethics. In order to reconnect the interests of bankers with the interests of society, finance needs to go back to being an instrument directed towards improved wealth creation and development. This is fundamental when it comes to sovereign debt markets.[49]

The link between development and freedoms/rights can no longer be ignored. The respect for human dignity and the rule of law are universal values that should underlie the global financial architecture.

[49] In his speech at the Cass Business School on 17 March 2010, Lord Turner stated: 'A critical issue is . . . whether this increased financial intensity has delivered value added for the real economy – whether it has improved capital allocation, increased growth or increased human welfare and choice . . . And whether it has made the economy more or less volatile to shocks'. See also www.vatican.va/holy_father/benedict_xvi/encyclicals/documents/hf_ben-xvi_enc_20090629_caritas-in-veritate_en.html, accessed 30 June 2013. See generally R Lastra and G Wood, 'The Crisis of 2007–2009: Nature, Causes and Reactions' 2010 13(3) *Journal of International Economic Law* 531–50.

10

Sovereign Financing and Corporate Responsibility for Economic and Social Rights

JERNEJ LETNAR ČERNIČ*

I INTRODUCTION

SOVEREIGN FINANCING HAS most often been connected to one sovereign state lending financial resources to another sovereign state, and in the process rights of ordinary people have mostly been forgotten. However, with the diminishing role of states, other global actors such as financial corporations have become more influential and taken dominant positions in the global financial markets, assuming a large proportion of sovereign debt in the secondary markets. Several states spend large proportions of their annual revenue to repay sovereign debt. For instance, in 2010 Gambia spent 13.9 of its annual revenues on debt repayment, Bhutan 26.6 per cent, El Salvador 25.8 per cent and the Philippines 27.1 per cent,[1] thereby undermining capabilities of those states to provide even basic social security, education, health, food, housing and water services to their populations. Whereas the impact of corporations in sovereign financing has expanded in past decades, development of their normative human rights obligations has been much slower.[2]

Corporations can as a result of sovereign financing directly affect economic and social rights of individuals. For example, provision of water services in Dar es Salaam substantially deteriorated after Tanzania was pressured to privatise its water supply system and sell the rights to City Water Services Limited, a subsidiary of the British corporation, Biwater.[3] Human rights can also be affected through sovereign financing more indirectly.

* The views and conclusions reflected in this chapter are solely those of the author and are in no way intended to reflect the views of any of the institutions with which the author is affiliated. The author wishes to thank Wouter Vandenhole and Juan Pablo Bohoslavsky for comments on earlier drafts of this chapter.

[1] Jubilee Debt Campaign, Tim Jones, *State of Debt 2012*, 43–45.

[2] See, for instance, W Vandenhole, *Emerging Normative Frameworks on Transnational Human Rights obligations*, 2012, EUI Working Papers RSCAS, 2012/17, 1.

[3] Food and Water Watch, *Biwater : A civil society perspective*, www.foodandwaterwatch.org/global/africa/tanzania/biwater-a-civil-society-perspective/, accessed 30 April 2013. See also Business and Human Rights Resource Centre, Biwater-Tanzania arbitration, www.business-humanrights.org/Categories/Lawlawsuits/Lawsuits regulatoryaction/LawsuitsSelectedcases/Biwater-Tanzaniaarbitration, accessed 30 April 2013. See also A Seager, 'Tanzania Wins £3m Damages from Biwater Subsidiary', 11.1.2008, www.theguardian.com/business/2008/jan/11/worldbank.tanzania, accessed 30 April 2013. See ICSID case No ARB/05/22 *Biwater Gauff (Tanzania) Ltd v United Republic of Tanzania*, 24 March 2008.

More specifically, recent examples illustrate that financial and non-financial corporations have been refusing to participate in debt restructuring, and claiming the full amount of the owned debt or benefiting from sovereign financing can thereby potentially directly or indirectly affect the enjoyment of economic and social rights of individuals. For instance, on 2 October 2012 the Commercial Court in Accra seized Argentine vessel *ARA Libertad* on the request of NML Capital, a global equity investment company, which purchased part of Argentina's debt on secondary sovereign debt marked before the country defaulted[4] in 2001 because of more than 100 billion US dollars of sovereign debt.[5] Later, the International Tribunal on the Law of the Sea ordered the release of the vessel.[6] The majority of this debt was later discounted and restructured, however a few private financial corporations refused to take part in the debt restructuring.[7] Since then they have sought a legal forum which would hear their claims against Argentina to repay this part of its sovereign debt.[8] In this way, NML Capital brought a claim in 'the "trial of the century" in sovereign debt restructuring'[9] before the Southern District Court of New York against Argentina to repay 1.33 billion US dollars of its outstanding sovereign debt.[10] As a result, the US Federal District Court ordered Argentina on 21 November 2012 to repay 1.33 billion dollars.[11] The US Court of Appeals for the Second Circuit (New York) on 23 August 2013 affirmed the District Court orders.[12] What is more worrying is that the decision against Argentina 'would expose it to $43 billion in additional claims it can't pay and trigger a new default'.[13] If such a scenario were realised, it is not far off to claim that Argentina would encounter major difficulties in securing even a reasonable minimum level of economic and social rights. On the other hand, it should be noted that Belgian and German courts dismissed similar claims.[14]

Consider another example. In 2007 the High Court in London delivered a decision against Zambia ordering it to repay $15 million US to Donegal International, a hedge

[4] The Guardian, 'Argentinean Naval Ship Stranded at Ghanaian Port as Vulture Fund Circles', 10 October 2012, www.guardian.co.uk/world/2012/oct/10/argentinian-naval-ship-ghanaian-port, accessed 10 January 2013.

[5] JF Hornbeck, 'Argentina's Defaulted Sovereign Debt: Dealing with the "Holdouts"', 6 February 2013, www.fas.org/sgp/crs/row/R41029.pdf, 1, accessed 15 May 2013.

[6] International Tribunal for the Law of the Sea, the 'ARA LIBERTAD' case, Order, 15 December 2012, www.itlos.org/fileadmin/itlos/documents/cases/case_no20/C20_Order_15_12_2012.pdf, accessed 10 January 2013. See M Waibel, 'ITLOS order Ghana to release Argentine navy ship', 17 December 2012, www.ejiltalk.org/itlos-order-ghana-to-release-argentine-navy-ship/, accessed 10 January 2013.

[7] ibid. See also M Warren, 'Argentina Offers to Pay Debts With Cash & Bonds', Yahoo News, 30 March 2013, http://news.yahoo.com/argentina-offers-pay-debts-cash-bonds-040817493--finance.html, 15 April 2013.

[8] See Reinisch and Binder, Ch 8 in this volume.

[9] *Financial Times*, http://ftalphaville.ft.com/tag/pari-passu-saga/, accessed 10 April 2013. See also Jubilee USA www.jubileeusa.org/vulturefunds/argentina.html, accessed 11 April 2013.

[10] *NML Capital Ltd v Republic of Argentina*, 08-cv-06978, US District Court, Southern District of New York (Manhattan).

[11] Fundsupermart, 'A New Argentine Debt Crisis – Background And Impacts', www.fundsupermart.com.my/main/research/viewHTML.tpl?articleNo=3067, accessed 13 January 2013.

[12] *NML Capital Ltd v Republic of Argentina*, 12-00105, US Court of Appeals for the Second Circuit (New York), 23 August 2013, 25 www.ieco.clarin.com/economia/Fallo-Corte-Apelaciones-Nueva-Argentina_CLAFIL20130823_0001.pdf, accessed 15 September 2013. See also B Van Voris, 'Argentina "Greek Tragedy" Nears End as Debt Ruling Looms', Argentina, 1 October 2013, www.bloomberg.com/news/2013-03-31/argentina-greek-tragedy-nears-end-as-debt-ruling-looms.html, accessed 5 April 2013.

[13] B Van Voris, 'Argentina "Greek Tragedy" Nears End as Debt Ruling Looms, Argentina', 1 October 2013.

[14] *Buenos Aires Herald*, 'German Court Rules in Argentina's Favour Against "Vulture Funds"', 11 July 2013, www.buenosairesherald.com/article/135798/german-court-rules-in-argentina-favour-against-vulture-funds-, accessed 30 August 2013.

fund.[15] Further, several private banks lent substantial funds to the Argentinean government during the rule of the military junta between 24 March 1976 and 9 December 1983.[16] In this way, they may have contributed to the violations of civil, political, economic and social rights during the years of dictatorship but also beyond.[17] What is more, the 1978 United Nations Study on the impact of foreign economic aid and assistance on the respect for human rights in Chile during Pinochet's totalitarian dictatorship, prepared by Antonio Cassese, the rapporteur at that time, illustrates the negative effects of economic aid and assistance on enjoyment of economic and social rights.[18]

The above examples illustrate a clear connection between sovereign financing and corporate responsibility for economic and social rights. One can define sovereign debt as financial obligations owned by a sovereign state. Sovereign debt can undermine the financial ability of a country to fully implement even the reasonable minimum core of economic and social rights of its population. If a state is obliged to repay its sovereign debt to private corporations, international organisations or states, it will be less likely to be financially capable of providing the reasonable minimum core of economic and social rights.[19] This is exacerbated by the examples from current and former totalitarian regimes, whose governments often take out vast loans to finance their military activities and their exuberant lifestyles and/or impose economic policies against the majority's interests.[20] All in all, not only states but also corporations are obliged to uphold individuals' economic and social rights in the sovereign financing context.[21]

The remainder of this chapter is therefore devoted to exploring corporate responsibility for economic and social rights in the context of sovereign financing. It will attempt to explore the nature, value and scope of corporate obligations under economic and social

[15] BBC World, 'Zambia loses "vulture fund" case', 15 February 2007, http://news.bbc.co.uk/2/hi/business/6365433.stm, accessed 9 April 2013.

[16] See, for example, case of *Ibañez Manuel Leandro and others v Undetermined Financial Institutions* by the Essex Transitional Justice Network and the Essex Business' and Human Rights Project of the University of Essex (United Kingdom) and by the Centro de Estudios Legales y Sociales (CELS), www.essex.ac.uk/tjn/documents/Amicus%20Banks%20%28final-English%20version%29March24.pdf, accessed 20 March 2013. See also H Verebitsky, Los prestamos de la muerte, 16 March 2009, www.pagina12.com.ar/diario/elpais/1-121607-2009-03-16.html, accessed 30 March 2013. See also JP Bohoslavsky and V Opgenhaffen, 'Pasado y Presente de la Complicidad Corporativa: Responsabilidad Bancaria por Financiamiento de la Dictadura Militar Argentina' (2009) *Revista Jurídica de la Universidad de Palermo* 241, 258–69. Re Uruguay, see JP Bohoslavsky, 'El eslabon financiero en la justicia transicional uruguaya' (2012) 21(2) *Revista Uruguaya de Ciencia Política*, 153–79.

[17] World Bank Study, Foreign bank commercial credit accounted for roughly two thirds of Argentina's external debt in 1982, World Bank, A World Bank Country Study: Economic Memorandum on Argentina, (Washington, 1985) 12.

[18] A Cassese, United Nations, 'Economic and Social Council Study on the Impact of Foreign Economic Aid and Assistance on the Respect for Human Rights in Chile', E/CN.4/Sub.2/412, 20 July 1978, paras 88–249.

[19] M Dowell-Jones and D Kinley, 'Minding the Gap: Global Finance and Human Rights' (2011) 25(2) *Ethics and International Affairs* 184.

[20] S Michalowski and JP Bohoslavsky, 'Ius Cogens, Transtional Justice and Other Trends of the Debate on Odious Debts: A Response to the World Banks Discussion Paper on Odious Debts' (2009) 48 *Columbia Journal of Transnational Law* 61–121. See also JP Bohoslavsky and V Opgenhaffen, 'The Past and Present of Corporate Complicity: Financing the Argentinean Dictatorship' (2010) 23 *Harvard Human Rights Journal* 157–204.

[21] The Castan Centre of Human Rights notes that 'it does not follow that from additional sites of responsibility comes a corresponding reduction of the State's liability in respect of human rights protection and promotion'. R Chambers, D Kinley and S Joseph, Submission to the UN Office of the High Commissioner's review of the UN's Human Rights Norms for Corporations 'Responsibilities of Transnational Corporations and Related Business Enterprises with Regards to Human Rights', the Castan Centre for Human Rights Law, Monash University, Melbourne, Australia, www.law.monash.edu.au/castancentre/publications/ohchr-sub-final.pdf, accessed 30 June 2013.

rights and to answer whether there are uniform international or national legal standards concerning corporate responsibility for economic and social rights. The task will be divided into five steps. Section II discusses sovereign financing and the enjoyment of economic and social rights. Section III examines the role of financial corporations in sovereign financing and their impact on individuals' enjoyment of economic and social rights in borrowing states. Section IV discusses and analyses sources of corporate obligations concerning economic and social rights and their nature and scope. Section V examines the enforcement of corporate obligations in the context of sovereign financing. It does so in three steps: first, by discussing and analysing enforcement of corporate responsibility before US courts on the basis of the Alien Torts Claims Act; second, by examining enforcement mechanisms under international and regional human rights law; and third, by examining enforcement of economic and social rights against corporations in national legal orders. On the basis of this analysis, the conclusion in Section VI assesses corporate responsibility for economic and social rights in the sovereign debt context and how such rights could be better implemented in the future. Overall, the chapter argues that financial corporations have obligations to respect, protect and fulfil the reasonable minimum core of economic and social rights stemming from both national legal orders and international law.

II SOVEREIGN FINANCING AND ENJOYMENT OF ECONOMIC AND SOCIAL RIGHTS

The International Covenant on Economic, Social and Cultural Rights (ICESCR) provides in Article 2(1) that states shall undertake

> steps, individually and through international assistance and co-operation, especially economic and technical, to the maximum of its available resources, with a view to achieving progressively the full realization of the rights recognized in the present Covenant by all appropriate means, including particularly the adoption of legislative measures.[22]

This provision includes most common characteristics of economic and social rights including that their full realization is to be achieved *progressively* depending on the available financial resources of a state.[23] However, the phrase 'maximum available resources' does not refer only to financial capabilities of a state, but also to those of the international community on the basis of obligations of 'international assistance and co-operation'.[24] Positive obligations under economic and social rights are most often connected with financial resources. Therefore, insisting on the immediate realization of the core of economic and social rights in every situation may impose an unjustified burden on states that have been facing systematic and long-term public resources shortages. For instance, some states and even some corporations can provide free elementary education, whereas others, even the least developed states, must charge for attending primary school simply due to lack of available public financial resources even though charging fees

[22] International Covenant on Economic, Social and Cultural Rights, GA res 2200A (XXI), 21 UNGAOR Supp (No 16) at 49, UN Doc A/6316 (1966), 993 UNTS 3, entered into force 3 January 1976.

[23] RE Robertson, 'Measuring State Compliance with the Obligation to Devote the "Maximum Available Resources" to Realizing Economic, Social and Cultural Rights' (1994) 16 *Human Rights Quarterly* 694.

[24] General Comment No 3, para 13. See M Sepulveda, The Nature of the Obligations under the International Covenant on Economic, Social and Cultural Rights (Antwerp, Hart/Intersentia, 2003) 370–77.

is often counterproductive and the obligation to provide free education falls within core obligations under the ICESCR and is therefore not dependent on available resources.[25] Some commentators claim that international human rights law therefore traditionally places only obligations of conduct on states, not obligations of result. However, the views of the ESCR Committee and scholarship on immediate obligations of result challenge such an assumption.[26]

Economic and social rights have for a long time been considered as secondary and even nowadays in practice both sets of rights are still not placed on an equal footing. Economic, social and cultural rights include rights to housing, food, education, water and health.[27] This set of rights complements the so-called civil and political rights.[28] As Scheinin notes, 'there is no water-tight division between different categories of human rights'.[29] However, despite claims that both sets of rights are of equal importance and interdependent, civil and political rights are more solidly established under international and national law.[30] Economic, social and cultural rights generally have a programmatic nature and are not always directly justiciable to the same extent that civil and political rights are.[31] Victims have therefore enforced their economic and social rights through the creative interpretation of civil and political rights before various human rights forums, particularly before the European Court of Human Rights. Such problems with enforcement of economic and social rights are most often ascribed to their distinctive legal nature and scope.[32] Yeshanew defines justiciability as rights being 'subjected to a judicial or quasi-judicial procedure of enforcement.[33] Scheinin argues that 'the problem relating to the legal nature of economic and social rights does not relate to their validity but rather to their applicability'.[34] The central question of economic and social rights therefore lies in their enforcement or justiciability. However, the Optional Protocol to the ICESCR entered into force on 5 May 2013, thereby recognising the political acceptance by states of their justiciability.[35] Further, the European Committee of Social Rights examines more and more collective

[25] Committee on Economic, Social and Cultural Rights, General Comment 11, Plans of action for primary education (Twentieth session, 1999) UN Doc E/C.12/1999/4 (1999), para 7.

[26] P Alston and G Quinn, 'The Nature and Scope of States Parties' Obligations under the International Covenant on Economic, Social and Cultural Rights' (1987) 9 *Human Rights Quarterly* 156–229. See also Sepulveda (n 24).

[27] A Eide, 'Economic, Social and Cultural Rights as Human Rights' in A Eide, C Krause and A Rosas (eds), *Economic, Social and Cultural Rights: A Textbook* (Dordrecht, Martinus Nijhoff Publishers, 2001) 21, 22; See also Amnesty International, *What are Economic, Social and Cultural Rights*? www.amnesty.org/en/economic-and-social-cultural-rights/what-are-escr, accessed 30 April 2013.

[28] M Scheinin, 'Human Rights Committee: Not Only a Committee on Civil and Political Rights' in M Langford (ed), *Social Rights Jurisprudence: Emerging Trends in International and Comparative Law* 540, (Cambridge, Cambridge University Press, 2008).

[29] ibid.

[30] M Scheinin 'Economic and Social Rights as Legal Rights' in Eide, Krause and Rossas (eds) (n 27) 41, 53.

[31] Eide (n 27) 22.

[32] F Coomans (ed), *Justiciability of Economic, Social and Cultural Rights* (Antwerp, Intersentia, 2006). See also M Langford, 'Justiciability of Social Rights: From Practice to Theory' in M Langford (ed), *Social Rights Jurisprudence: Emerging Trends in International and Comparative Law* (Cambridge, Cambridge University Press, 2008).

[33] SA Yeshanew, *The Justiciability of Economic, Social and Cultural Rights in the African Regional Human Rights System* (Cambridge, Intersentia, 2013) 37.

[34] Scheinin (n 30) 41; see also C Courtis, 'Standards to Make ESC Rights Justiciable: A Summary Exploration' (2009) 2 *Erasmus Law Review* 379.

[35] Optional Protocol to the International Covenant on Economic, Social and Cultural Rights, Doc.A/63/435; C.N.869.2009.TREATIES-34, 11 December 2009, http://treaties.un.org/Pages/ViewDetails.aspx?src=TREATY&mtdsg_no=IV-3-a&chapter=4&lang=en, accessed 15 May 2013.

complaints. What is more, the body of case law in domestic jurisdictions is growing substantially.[36]

The enjoyment of economic and social rights and sovereign financing are directly intertwined and correlated.[37] The state's obligations to repay its sovereign debt may even result in armed conflict, which could potentially also undermine economic and social rights.[38] The enjoyment of economic and social rights is highly correlated to the state's GDP. For instance, a recent study shows that education years and level of students in a state are closely correlated to the level of state GDP.[39]

The repayment of sovereign debt directly affects individuals' enjoyment of human rights, particularly economic and social rights. Previous research illustrates that heavily indebted states are less likely to ensure an adequate level of protections of economic and social rights.[40] Further, there exists growing evidence from the sovereign debt crises of Southern Europe that suggests that the repayment of sovereign debt directly undermines the level of economic and social rights. In particular, the examples of Greece,[41] Portugal[42] and Spain[43] illustrate how damaging an effect restructuring of sovereign debt can have on state resources to provide economic and social rights. Cephas Lumina, the United Nations independent expert on foreign debt and human rights, eloquently summarises that the repayment of sovereign debt triggers 'diversion of scarce national resources from fundamental public services of education, health, water, sanitation, housing and infrastructure to debt servicing' and undermines 'the conditions for the realization of . . . economic, social and cultural rights'.[44] Several states spend annually more on the repayment of debt than on provision of basic social services.[45] Such practice has not gone unnoticed by the

[36] M Craven and M Langford, *The International Covenant on Economic, Social and Cultural Rights*, revised edn (Oxford, Oxford University Press, forthcoming 2014). K Young and J Lemaitre, 'The Comparative Fortunes of the Right to Health: Two Tales of Justiciability in Colombia and South Africa' (2013) 26 *Harvard Human Rights Journal*; F Coomans, 'Justiciability of the Right to Education' (2009) 2(4) *Erasmus Law Review* 427–43.

[37] See generally S Michalowski, 'Sovereign Debt and Social Rights – Legal Reflections on a Difficult Relationship' (2008) 8(1) *Human Rights Law Review* 35–68. See also C Barry, 'Sovereign Debt, Human Rights, and Policy Conditionality' (2011) 19(3) *The Journal of Political Philosophy* 282–305.

[38] M Goldmann, 'Sovereign Debt Crises as Triggers of Armed Conflict: Restructuring under Chapter VII of the UN Charter?' (2012) 4 *Goettingen Journal of International* Law 153–75. See also N Kim and P Conceição, 'The Economic Crisis, Violent Conflict, and Human Development' (2009) UNDP/ODS Working Paper.

[39] EL Glaeser, 'Education Last Century, and Economic Growth Today', *New York Times*, 20 October 2009. http://economix.blogs.nytimes.com/2009/10/20/education-last-century-and-economic-growth-today/, accessed 20 March 2013.

[40] E Borenzstein and U Panizza, 'The Costs of Sovereign Default' (2008) IMF Working Paper, No 238, 8.

[41] J Kulpa, 'Why Is Sovereign Debt Restructuring a Challenge? The Case of Greece' (2012) Bruges European Economic Policy Briefings BEEP no 24, www.coleurope.eu/sites/default/files/research-paper/beep24.pdf, accessed 20 March 2013.

[42] See the Constitutional Court of Portugal, case 187/2013, 5 April 2013, www.tribunalconstitucional.pt/tc/acordaos/20130187.html, accessed 15 April 2013. EV Rodrigues, 'O Estado e as Políticas Sociais em Portugal Sociologia' (2010) *Revista do Departamento de Sociologia da FLUP*, vol XX, 191–230, http://ler.letras.up.pt/uploads/ficheiros/8794.pdf, accessed 15 April 2013.

[43] Informe Conjunto al Comité de Derechos Económicos, Sociales y Culturales, Examen del 5° Informe Periódico de España, 48° sesión del CESCR, mayo 2012, www2.ohchr.org/english/bodies/cescr/docs/ngos/JointSubmission19NGOs_Spain_CESCR48_sp.pdf, accessed 15 March 2013; GO Aguilar, Derechos sociales; el otro déficit, El Pais, 7 May 2012, http://elpais.com/elpais/2012/05/03/opinion/1336056886_000607.html, accessed 15 March 2013.

[44] C Lumina, Report of the Independent Expert on the effects of foreign debt and other related international financial obligations of States on the full enjoyment of all human rights, particularly economic, social and cultural rights, Guiding principles on foreign debt and human rights, A/HRC/20/23, 10 April 2011.

[45] S Mandel, *Debt Relief as if Justice Mattered: A Framework for a Comprehensive Approach to Debt Relief that Works* (London, New Economics Foundation, 2008); T Mutazu, 'African Debt Crisis: A Human Rights Perspective Balancing Human Rights and the Need for Debt Cancellation in Africa', African Forum and

international human rights bodies. The UN ESCR Committee observed in its 2012 Concluding Observations on Spain that the implementation of economic and social rights '[has] been reduced as a result of the austerity measures'[46] and expressed its concern that 'one in four minors is living below the poverty line',[47] and that 'pensions are in many cases below subsistence level, so that pensioners are at risk of falling into poverty'[48] as well as at 'the situation of individuals and families who find themselves overwhelmed by housing costs'[49] and 'the regressive measures adopted by the State party that increase university tuition fees'.[50] The UN ECSR Committee therefore asked Spanish authorities to ensure that 'all the austerity measures adopted reflect the minimum core content of all the Covenant rights and that it take all appropriate measures to protect that core content under any circumstances, especially for disadvantaged and marginalized individuals and groups'.[51] The 2012 Concluding Observations on Spain are illustrative of any state attempting to restructure its growing sovereign debt which was caused by poor public and private sector management, at the expense of economic and social rights. In this way, the public resources available for social expenditure decline substantially. This can lead to a decrease in the level of effective protection of economic and social rights.[52] As a consequence, states cannot provide equal level access to health care, social housing, water and food. Access to university education is thereafter often subjected to increasing tuition fees, whereas there are in primary and secondary education more pupils per class. Having examined the potential impact of denial of economic and social rights, it is now necessary to consider normative obligations to observe economic and rights.

The UN ESCR Committee developed in General Comment no 3 the concept of a minimum core of each economic and social right, which every individual should enjoy. It argued that:

> a minimum core obligation to ensure the satisfaction of, at the very least, minimum essential levels of each of the rights is incumbent upon every State party. Thus, for example, a State party in which any significant number of individuals is deprived of essential foodstuffs, of essential primary health care, of basic shelter and housing, or of the most basic forms of education is, prima facie, failing to discharge its obligations under the Covenant. If the Covenant were to be read in such a way as not to establish such a minimum core obligation, it would be largely deprived of its raison d'être.[53]

Network on Debt and Development 2009; D Millet and E Toussaint, 'Figures Relating to the Debt for 2009', Committee for the Abolition of Third World Debt (CADTM). See similarly Dowell-Jones and Kinley (no 19) 190.

[46] Committee on Economic, Social and Cultural Rights, Concluding Observations on Spain, E/C.12/ESP/CO/5, 6 June 2012, http://daccess-dds-ny.un.org/doc/UNDOC/GEN/G12/433/06/PDF/G1243306.pdf?OpenElement, accessed 20 February 2013, para 8.

[47] ibid, para 17. See also the 2012 Annual Report of the EU Fundamental Rights Agency, 'Safeguarding Fundamental Rights in Times of Crisis, http://fra.europa.eu/sites/default/files/annual-report-2012-focus_en.pdf, accessed 2 September 2013.

[48] ibid, para 20.

[49] ibid, para 21.

[50] ibid, para 28.

[51] ibid, para 8. See also statement by MS Carmona, UN Special Rapporteur on extreme poverty and human rights, 'Impact of austerity measures on the enjoyment of human rights', www.ohchr.org/EN/Issues/Poverty/Pages/ImpactofausteritymeasuresontheenjoymentHR.aspx, accessed 20 February 2013.

[52] AG Pillay, Open letter to state parties, 16 May 2012, www2.ohchr.org/english/bodies/cescr/docs/LetterCESCRtoSP16.05.12.pdf, accessed 25 February 2013.

[53] Committee on Economic, Social and Cultural Rights, General Comment 3, The nature of States parties' obligations (Fifth session, 1990) UN Doc E/1991/23, annex III at 86 (1991) para 10.

The concept of the minimum core identifies minimum core obligations to respect, protect and fulfil economic and social rights. It has been illustrated that sovereign financing often affects the ability of states to comply even with this minimum core obligation to provide economic and social rights.[54] In this way, state and other actors are obliged to provide a minimum level of food, water, housing, education and health care.[55] For the minimum core concept to have practical relevance, it must be employed together with the 'reasonableness test' developed by the South African Constitutional Court in the *Grootboom* case[56] to effectively address the obligations of private lenders in the sovereign financing field.[57]

However, states also often invoke increasing sovereign debt obligations in order to justify the adoption of the austerity measures which affect economic and social rights. In a private law setting, a debtor would be obliged to repay her debt to the creditor, unless she declares insolvency. In a sovereign financing context, a state is also liable to repay its debt to a creditor, being another state, international organisation or corporation. However, states are often faced with multiple obligations they need to address. What is more, the ranking of repayment of such obligations is not clear.[58] Dowell-Jones and Kinley aptly noted that 'human rights are intimately tied up with the economic health of the state, as well as, of course, much else besides'.[59] In answering these questions, a dilemma arises: should a state give priority to repayment of its sovereign debt or should it first ensure that it observes, at the very least, a reasonable minimum essential level of every economic and social right. Respect for economic and social rights and sovereign financing obligations illustrates the dilemma encountered by many states in reconciling two conflicting values. This is whether the sovereign debt repayment would undermine the protection of economic and social human rights, and whether the protection of fundamental human rights may impede the repayment of, or terminate, state sovereign debt obligations. In this respect, the UN ESCR Committee states that

> In order for a State party to be able to attribute its failure to meet at least its minimum core obligations to a lack of available resources it must demonstrate that every effort has been made to use all resources that are at its disposition in an effort to satisfy, as a matter of priority, those minimum obligations.[60]

What 'every effort' is remains unclear. On the other hand, states must show their willingness to repay their debt in order to be able to borrow further on the international credit markets.[61]

[54] See C Espósito, Y Li and JP Bohoslavsky (eds), *Sovereign Financing and International Law, The UNCTAD Principles on Responsible Sovereign Lending and Borrowing* (Oxford, Oxford University Press, 2013). See also LC Buchheit and G Mitu Gulati, 'Responsible Sovereign Lending and Borrowing', *UNCTAD Discussion Papers* No 198, April 2010, http://unctad.org/en/Docs/osgdp20102_en.pdf, accessed 5 April 2013.

[55] KG Young, 'The Minimum Core of Economic and Social Rights: A Concept in Search of Content' (2008) 33 *Yale Journal of International Law* 113, 113.

[56] *Government of the Republic of South Africa and Others v Grootboom and Others* (CCT11/00) [2000] ZACC 19; 2001 (1) SA 46; 2000 (11) BCLR 1169 (4 October 2000).

[57] S Lienberg, 'Socio-Economic Rights: Revisiting the Reasonableness Review/Minimum Core Debate' in SC Woolman and M Bishop (eds), *Constitutional Conversations* (Pretoria, PULP, 2008) 303.

[58] A Gelpern, 'Building a Better Seating Chart for Sovereign Restructurings' (2004) 53 *Emory Law Journal* 1119–62.

[59] Dowell-Jones and Kinley (n 19) 184.

[60] UN ESCR Committee, General Comment 3, para 10 (n 53). See also CESCR, General Comment No 19: The right to social security (Art 9 of the Covenant), 4 February 2008, E/C.12/GC/19, paras 59–61.

[61] ES Phelps and A Bhide, 'The Root of All Sovereign-Debt Crises', Project Syndicate www.project-syndicate.org/commentary/the-root-of-all-sovereign-debt-crises#sfMuDj1OX9mB1mRT.99, accessed 15 March 2013. The authors provide that: 'governments offer no collateral, and their principal incentive to repay – the fear of being cut off by international credit markets – derives from a perverse addiction'.

Traditionally, the protection of human rights has always concentrated on balancing the interests of the individual with those of society as whole, which include its international obligations to repay its debt to creditors. It is very easy to claim that debt repayment violates economic and social rights.[62] However, without repayment of sovereign debt, the financial markets and lenders will most probably not be willing to lend further to a state in need, thereby in the worst case scenario leaving it without necessary resources to secure the reasonable minimum of economic and social rights. Joyce argues that 'in the end, governments must raise cash both on the markets . . . People might not like the idea of secondary debt, but would any lender lend unless they had scope to sell on bad debt in the event of a default?'[63] All of this calls for a middle approach where not only individuals' reasonable minimum core of social and economic rights, but also rights of lenders will be heeded. However, such a solution is often difficult to achieve.

Nonetheless, the practice of financial markets and investment arbitration panels illustrates that economic and social rights are not only underrated but that they do not play any slightly significant role. However, it is argued that the reasonable minimum core of every human right, even economic and social rights, is untouchable. In the context of sovereign financing only a false dilemma arises as states are obliged to non-discriminatorily provide at least a reasonable minimum core of economic and social rights. Raffer, similarly, argues that

> the right of creditors to interest and repayments collides and the principle recognized generally (not only in the case of loans) by all civilized legal systems that no one must be forced to fulfil contracts if that leads to inhumane distress, endangers one's life or health, or violates human dignity.[64]

All in all, states, but also corporations, must guarantee at least the reasonable minimum core of economic and social rights, at the same time heeding their obligations deriving from sovereign financing.

III CORPORATIONS, SOVEREIGN FINANCING, AND ECONOMIC AND SOCIAL RIGHTS

Corporations play an important role in sovereign financing either as primary or secondary loan providers. They can commit direct human rights violations, they act in complicity with a state or another state actor or they are not directly involved in violations but they fail to speak or act against human rights violations in the country where they do business.[65] Financial corporations mostly commit violations of economic and social rights indirectly. Sovereign states nowadays owe much of their debt to private creditors. For instance, 'the debt share of non-residents accounted for more than 31.5% of the

[62] Michalowski (n 37) 46–50.

[63] E Joyce, 'Congo's victory against a "vulture fund" is hollow', *The Guardian*, 19 July 2012.

[64] K Raffer, 'Solving Sovereign Debt Overhang by Internationalizing Chapter 9 Procedures', University of Klagenfurt (2002) http://www.jahrbuch2002.studien-vonzeitfragen.net/Weltfinanz/RAFFER_1/raffer_12.HTM, accessed 20 March 2013.

[65] See, for example, A Clapham and S Jerbi; 'Categories of Corporate Complicity in Human Rights Abuses' (2001) 24 *Hastings International and Comparative Law Review* 339–49.

general government debt in 21 EU Member States'.[66] Financial actors held 38.4 per cent of government debt in Euro countries in 2010.[67]

Private corporations include hedge funds, corporations, insurance corporations and other corporate bondholders. States can issue debt in the form of either loans or bonds. Direct loans have been common practice since the Second World War. However, Davies notes that 'since the 1980's, the composition of privately held sovereign debt has shifted from syndicated bank loans to bondholders'[68] and therefore most debt owned by private creditors is nowadays placed in bonds. The size of global bond markets in 2011 was estimated at $157 trillion.[69] States usually issue debt on the primary market, whereas bonds are freely sold or purchased in the secondary market. In recent decades much of the state-owned sector, predominantly banks, has caused much of the foreign debt by giving non-guaranteed, corrupt and excessive loans to the private sectors, for which states are held liable. The 2012 IMF Study on Sovereign Debt Restructurings 1950–2010 reports of '186 debt exchanges with foreign private creditors'.[70] Even more telling, the IMF Study illustrates that '57 involved a cut in face value (debt reduction), while 129 implied only a lengthening of maturities (debt rescheduling). However, both types of debt operations can involve a "haircut," i.e., a loss in the present value of creditor claims'.[71] Private creditors include commercial banks, hedge funds and other private bondholders. They often buy sovereign debt on the secondary market at the discounted prices and thereafter ask the governments for full repayment, often ignoring, for example, the Heavily Indebted Poor Countries Initiative.[72]

A 2012 IMF Working Paper argues that this strategy is 'an attractive business model for a small number of investor funds who have specialized in suing sovereign debtors to make a profit'.[73] As attractive as such an industry may be, it directly jeopardises the ability of states to provide economic and social rights as they have to repay or restructure their debt. However, human rights obligations have not so far played a very important role, if any, in the field of sovereign financing. A particular problem is posed by increasing interest rates. Cash-strapped states can by issuing sovereign bonds finance provision of economic and social rights.[74] Another instance where private financial corporations may interfere with enjoyment of economic and social rights is hedge or equity funds. Such funds are often called vulture funds.[75] They pray on weak states and decrease sovereign states' ability to provide social and economic rights. However, some commentators argue 'sovereign creditors are not all out for quick and easy "windfall" on distressed sovereign debt' and

[66] Eurostat, 'Structure of Government Debt in Europe in 2011', Statistics in Focus 34/2012, 3.

[67] D Hartwig Lojsch, M Rodríguez-Vives and M Slavík, 'The Size and Composition of Government Debt in Euro Area' European Central Bank, Occasional paper series, no 132, October 2011, 33–34.

[68] K Davis, 'Sovereign Debt – Background', www.iilj.org/courses/FDSovereignDebtBackground.asp, accessed 25 March 2013.

[69] Size of Global Stock and Bond Markets, http://qvmgroup.com/invest/2012/04/02/world-capital-markets-size-of-global-stock-and-bond-markets/, accessed 13 March 2013.

[70] US Das, MG Papaioannou and C Trebesch, 'Sovereign Debt Restructurings 1950–2010: Literature Survey, Data, and Stylized Facts' (2012) IMF Working Paper WP/12/203, www.un.org/esa/ffd/ecosoc/debt/2013/IMF_wp12_203.pdf, accessed 30 March 2013, 5.

[71] ibid, 6.

[72] International Monetary Fund, Debt Relief Under the Heavily Indebted Poor Countries (HIPC) Initiative, www.imf.org/external/np/exr/facts/hipc.htm, accessed 15 April 2013.

[73] Das, Papaioannou and Trebesch (n 70) 51.

[74] Dowell-Jones and Kinley (n 19) 190.

[75] JE Fisch and CM Gentile, 'Vultures or Vanguards?: The Role of Litigation in Sovereign Debt Restructuring' (2004) 53 *Emory Law Journal*, 1047, 1082–84.

emphasise the importance of the ancient principle of *pacta sunt servanda*.[76] Vulture funds buy sovereign debt at heavily discounted prices, thereafter refuse to participate in debt restructuring and claim the debt at its initial price. It is estimated that they 'averaged recovery rates of about 3 to 20 times their investment'.[77] Lumina argues that 'vulture funds erode the gains from debt relief for poor countries and jeopardize the fulfilment of these countries' human rights obligations'.[78] Dowell-Jones and Kinley observe that 'far-reaching economic consequences of bond market dynamics that have a critical impact on human rights by influencing the capacity of states to deliver on their human rights obligations'.[79]

The banking sector is also an important factor in providing loans to sovereign states. Several plaintiffs identified the questionable role of banks in providing loans to authoritarian regimes during past decades in South America,[80] Africa[81] and Europe.[82] Questions arise whether private lenders carry any obligations and responsibility to observe human rights in lending states, particularly with respect to economic and social rights, which depend to a large extent on available financial resources of a respective state.[83] All in all, financial corporations can impact on economic and social rights in a variety of ways and should therefore also assume responsibility. The next section thus addresses sources, nature and scope of corporate obligations with respect to economic and social rights.

IV CORPORATE HUMAN RIGHTS OBLIGATIONS: FROM THEIR SOURCES AND NATURE TO THEIR SCOPE

Whereas the previous section showed that sovereign debt affects economic and social rights, this section examines the nature and scope of corporate obligations concerning economic and social rights in the context of sovereign borrowing. That corporations have human rights obligations is no longer heavily disputed,[84] even though some states and

[76] P Wautelet, 'Vulture Funds, Creditors and Sovereign Debtors: How to Find a Balance?' in M Audit (ed), *Insovabilite des états et dettes souveraines* (Paris, LGDJ, November 2011).

[77] African Development Bank Group, 'Vulture Funds in the Sovereign Debt Context', www.afdb.org/en/topics-and-sectors/initiatives-partnerships/african-legal-support-facility/vulture-funds-in-the-sovereign-debt-context/, accessed 30 April 2013.

[78] C Lumina, 'Report of the independent expert on the effects of foreign debt and other related international financial obligations of States on the full enjoyment of all human rights, particularly economic, social and cultural rights', UN Human Rights Council, 29 April 2010, A/HRC/14/21, at 12, para 33.

[79] Dowell-Jones and Kinley (n 19) 190.

[80] Bohoslavsky and Opgenhaffen (n 16) 22.

[81] G Handl, 'In Re South African Apartheid Litigation and Beyond: Corporate Liability for Aiding and Abetting under the Alien Tort Statute' (2010) *German Yearbook of International Law* 53, 425–61.

[82] *In re Austrian and German Bank Holocaust Litig*, No 98 Civ 3938 (SDNY 7 March 2001); *In re Holocaust Victim Assets Litig*, No 96 Civ 4849 (EDNY 22 November 2000), *Bodner v Banque Paribas*, 114 F. Supp. 2d 117 (EDNY 2000). See also R Alford, 'The Claim Resolution Tribunal and Holocaust Claims Against Swiss Banks' (2002) 20 *Berkeley Journal of International Law* 250. See JP Bohoslavsky and J Letnar Černič, introductory chapter of this volume.

[83] See, for example, J Hanlon, '"Illegitimate" Loans: Lenders, Not Borrowers, are Responsible' (2006) 27 *Third World Quarterly* 211.

[84] S Ratner, 'Corporations and Human Rights: A Theory of Legal Responsibility' (2001) 111 *Yale Law Journal* 443–545. D Kinley and J Tadaki, 'From Talk to Walk: The Emergence of Human Rights Responsibilities for Corporations under International Law' (2004) 44(4) *Virginia Journal of International Law* 931–1023; A Clapham, *Human Rights Obligations of non-State Actors* (Oxford, Oxford University Press, 2006); L Van den Herik and JL Černič, 'Regulating Corporations under International Law: from Human Rights to International Criminal Law and Back Again' (2010) 8 *Journal of International Criminal Justice* 725; J Letnar Černič, *Human Rights Law and Business* (Groningen, Europa Law Publishing, 2010). See also J Nolan and L Taylor, 'Corporate Responsibility for Economic, Social and Cultural Rights: Rights in Search of a Remedy?' (2009) 44(4) *Journal of Business Ethics* 433–51.

international organisations are only slowly moving towards such recognition. What is questionable is the nature and the scope of corporate human rights obligations. This section first examines sources of corporate human rights obligations in national legal orders and international law.

The normative thrust of corporate human rights obligations derives from the international and national levels. National legal orders provide a primary layer of corporate obligations to observe economic and social rights. The majority of national constitutions provide protection for economic and social rights. Such protections apply also to legal persons such as banks, financial funds and corporations. More specifically, some jurisdictions have adopted domestic legislation directly aimed at corporations which are active in sovereign debt markets. For instance, the United Kingdom adopted the Developing Country Debt (Restriction of Recovery) Bill, which provides in section 2 that 'a court may not award a creditor of the defaulted sovereign debt of a Low or Middle Income country the right to recover in excess of the maximum recovery amount'.[85] This statute defines 'maximum recovery amount' as '(a) the amount paid by a creditor to acquire the interest the creditor has in the defaulted sovereign debt (excluding any legal fees or other fees and costs associated with collection)' and '(b) interest, calculated as simple interest only, on the amount the creditor paid to acquire the interest in the defaulted sovereign debt . . .'.[86] Similarly, several countries adopted national legislation prohibiting the conduct of vulture funds. For instance, Belgium introduced legislation combating activities of vulture funds.[87] The Isle of Man introduced the Heavily Indebted Poor Countries (Limitation on Debt Recovery) Act 2012.[88] The matter was discussed also in the Parliament of Australia.[89] In the same context, the Paris Club, an informal organisation of sovereign creditors, noted that 'Paris Club creditors have confirmed that they are committed to avoid selling their claims on HIPCs to other creditors who do not intend to provide debt relief under the HIPC initiative, and urged other creditors to follow suit'.[90] What is more, a number of domestic courts have protected enjoyment of economic and social rights against the activities of corporations.

The international level provides an additional layer of support for corporate human rights obligations. A number of international legal instruments such the OECD Guidelines for Multinational Enterprises,[91] the UN Global Compact[92] and the ILO Tripartite Declaration[93] provide growing support for corporate human rights obligations. Such obligations may not have reached the status of direct obligations in international law,

[85] Developing Country Debt (Restriction of Recovery) Bill 2009, s 2.

[86] ibid, s 3.

[87] Act of 6 April 2008, cited in Wautelet (n 76) 21.

[88] Act 11 of 2012 (Isle of Man).

[89] Parliament of Australia, 25 June 2012, http://parlinfo.aph.gov.au/parlInfo/search/display/display.w3p;db=CHAMBER;id=chamber/hansardr/7503935a-ef9f-47a5-9ab8-7a228d52f809/0283;query=Id:%22chamber/hansardr/7503935a-ef9f-47a5-9ab8-7a228d52f809/0283%22, accessed 30 March 2013.

[90] Paris club, www.clubdeparis.org/sections/themes-strategiques/2009-8217-action-du-club, accessed 30 March 2013.

[91] 2011 Update of the OECD Guidelines for Multinational Enterprises, www.oecd.org/document/33/0,3746,en_2649_34889_44086753_1_1_1_1,00.html, accessed 30 March 2013.

[92] UN Global Compact, www.unglobalcompact.org/, accessed 30 March 2013.

[93] ILO, Tripartite Declaration of Principles concerning Multinational Enterprises and Social Policy, 204th Sess, 83 ILO. Official Bulletin (2000) para 8. For a critical discussion see J Letnar Černič, 'Corporate Responsibility for Human Rights: Analyzing the ILO Tripartite Declaration of Principles Concerning Multinational Enterprises and Social Policy' (2009) 6(1) *Miskolc Journal of International Law* 24–34.

however there is strong evidence of the commitments corporations must obey.[94] What is more, Deva notes that 'if norms of international law can be developed "bottom-up" by the participation of non-state actors, the same could be said about the enforcement of such norms. . .'.[95] All in all, international human rights bind corporations even if there exists so far no international mechanism for enforcing them.[96]

This paragraph briefly explains a tripartite typology of human rights obligations, including corporate human rights obligations, which apply also in the sovereign debt context. The tripartite obligations to respect, protect and fulfil economic and social human rights apply universally to all rights and entail a combination of negative and positive duties.[97] This tripartite typology of human rights obligations refers, under traditional human rights doctrines, to state obligations.[98] However, the fact that the state is the bearer of human rights obligations does not imply that only the state has such obligations.[99] Shue notes in this regard that 'for every basic right – and many other rights as well – there are three types of duties, all of which must be performed if the basic right is to be fully honoured but not all of which must necessarily be performed by the same individuals or institutions'.[100] This includes also obligations of corporations to observe the reasonable minimum core of economic and social rights.

[94] See, for example, Glothro workshop on direct human rights obligations of corporations in international law, Bled, 17–19 January 2013, Bled, www.glothro.org/main.aspx?c=.GLOTHRO&n=105963, accessed 30 April 2013.

[95] S Deva, 'Multinationals, Human Rights and International Law: How to Deal with the Elephant in the Room?' in J Letnar Černič and T Van Ho (eds), *Direct Human Rights Obligations of Corporations* (The Hague, Wolf Legal Publishers, forthcoming 2014), 14.

[96] See Clapham (n 84) 91.

[97] See generally African Commission on Human and Peoples' Rights, Decision Regarding Communication 155/96 (*Social and Economic Rights Action Centre and the Centre for Economic and Social Rights v Nigeria*) 44, ACHPR/COMM/AO44/1 (17 May 2002) (reporting that the Commission interpreted the African Charter for Human and Peoples' Rights and developed a four-fold typology of human rights obligations in the case of *Social and Economic Rights Action Centre and the Centre for Economic and Social Rights v Nigeria*, (Communication 155/96, 27 May 2002)). The Commission held that 'internationally accepted ideas of the various obligations engendered by human rights indicate that all rights – both civil and political rights and social and economic – generate at least four levels of duties for a State that undertakes to adhere to a rights regime, namely the duty to respect, protect, promote, and fulfil these rights'. ibid.

[98] See International Commission of Jurists (ICJ), Maastricht Guidelines on Violations of Economic, Social and Cultural Rights, 6 (26 January 1997), available at http://www.uu.nl/faculty/leg/NL/organisatie/departementen/departementrechtsgeleerdheid/organisatie/onderdelen/studieeninformatiecentrummensenrechten/publicaties/simspecials/20/Documents/20-01.pdf, accessed 30 March 2013 (requiring states responsible for violating international legal obligations to establish mechanisms for investigating, prosecuting and correcting such violations); UN Comm on Economic, Social and Cultural Rights, General Comment No 12: The Right to Adequate Food (Art 11) para 15 (12 May 1999) (explaining that the obligation to 'respect' imposes on states a duty not to take any measures that in any way deprive protected parties of the right concerned); H Shue, *Basic Rights: Subsistence, Affluence, and U.S. Foreign Policy* (Princeton, Princeton University Press, 1980) observing the tripartite typology of duties to include (1) duties to avoid the deprivation of the right concerned, (2) duties to protect rights holders from deprivation, and (3) duties to aid rights holders who have been deprived).

[99] See A Rosas and M Scheinin, 'Categories and Beneficiaries of Human Rights' in R Hanski and M Suksi (eds), *An Introduction to the International Protection of Human Rights: A Textbook*, 2nd edn (Turku, Åbo Akademi University, 1999) 57–58.

[100] Shue (n 98) 76; see also A Eide, 'Realization of Social and Economic Rights and the Minimum Threshold Approach' (1989) 10 *Human Rights Law Journal* 35, 37 (arguing that the tripartite typology of duties bestows on states a negative obligation to abstain from acts contrary to human rights principles and a positive obligation as a 'protector and provider' of rights).

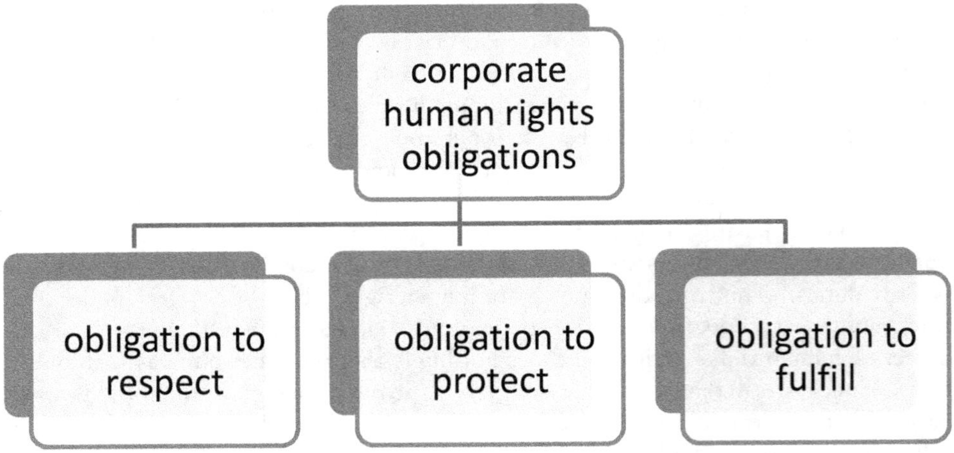

Figure 10.1. Corporate tripartite human rights obligations

Corporate Obligation to Respect

Corporate obligation to respect means that financial corporations shall refrain from interfering in the enjoyment of the reasonable minimum essential level of economic and social rights.[101] This rule derives from the ancient Roman principle *sic utere tuo ut alterum non laedes*.[102] This obligation to respect also obliges the corporations to effectively recognise economic and social rights of individuals. The obligation to respect means that corporations must undertake due diligence, ensuring not only that they comply with human rights obligations concerning economic and social rights, but also that they do everything possible to avoid causing harm to economic and social rights. *Mutatis mutandis*, a corporation would need to ensure that 'every effort has been made to use all resources that are at its disposal in an effort to satisfy, as a matter of priority, these minimum obligations'.[103]

More specifically, the Guiding Principles on foreign debt and human rights state that creditors have

> the obligation to perform due diligence on the creditworthiness and ability to repay of the borrower as well as the duty to refrain from providing a loan in circumstances where the lender is aware that the funds will be used for non-public purposes or for a non-viable project.[104]

Similarly, the Guiding Principles on business and human rights note in paragraph 11 that corporations 'should respect human rights', which 'means that they should avoid infring-

[101] See International Human Rights Instruments, Compilation of General Comments and General Recommendations Adopted by Human Rights Treaty Bodies, at 158, at 7, UN Doc HRI/GEN/1/Rev.1 (12 May 1994).

[102] See EE Ruddick, 'The Continuing Constraint of Sovereignty: International Law, International Protection, and the Internally Displaced' (1997) 77 *Boston University Law Review* 429, 471 n 231 (citing *Black's Law Dictionary*, which defines the term as requiring one to use his or her own property 'in such a manner as not to injure that of another').

[103] General Comment No 19 (n 60) para 60.

[104] Guiding Principles on foreign debt and human rights, para 23.

ing on the human rights of others and should address adverse human rights impacts with which they are involved'.[105] Paragraph 11 does not include the word 'shall', whereas, for instance, the 2008 Ruggie report recognised that 'the baseline responsibility of companies is to respect human rights'.[106] Vandenhole therefore convincingly argues that 'the Guiding Principles evoke a weak corporate responsibility to respect human rights'.[107] In contrast, as noted above, several international documents, national legal orders and scholars argue that corporations already have human rights obligations. For instance, the United Nations Guiding Principles on extreme poverty state that 'business enterprises, have, at the very minimum, the responsibility to respect human rights'.[108]

Further, the OECD Guidelines for Multinational Enterprises noted that both states and enterprises that lend to sovereign states 'should' respect human rights 'within the framework of internationally recognized human rights, the international human rights obligations of the countries in which they operate', including domestic human rights obligations.[109] Whereas the text of the Guidelines employs the verb *should*, the Commentary on the Guidelines suggests that enterprises have an obligation to respect human rights because 'respect for human rights is the global standard of expected conduct for enterprises'.[110] The nature of obligations to respect requires that corporations avoid causing harm.[111] However, financial enterprises should only respect human rights 'within the context of their own activities'.[112] They should 'avoid causing or contributing to adverse human rights impacts and address such impacts when they occur'.[113] Further, the Guidelines oblige enterprises to conduct due diligence 'as appropriate to their size, the nature and context of operations and the severity of the risks of adverse human rights impacts'.[114] Similarly, the UNCTAD Principles on Responsible Sovereign Lending and Borrowing state in principle 4 that 'a lender is responsible to make a realistic assessment of the sovereign borrower's capacity to service a loan based on the best available information and following objective and agreed technical rules on due diligence and national accounts'.[115] Further, these Principles oblige lenders to 'perform their own ex ante investigation into and, when applicable, post-disbursement monitoring of, the likely effects of the project, including its financial, operational, civil, social, cultural, and environmental

[105] Special Representative of the Secretary-General on the Issue of Human Rights and Transnational Corporations and Other Business Enterprises, Guiding Principles on Business and Human Rights: Implementing the United Nations 'Protect, Respect and Remedy' Framework, UN Doc A/HRC/17/31 (21 March 2011) (by John Ruggie).

[106] 'Protect, Respect and Remedy: a Framework for Business and Human Rights', Report of the Special Representative of the Secretary-General on the issue of human rights and transnational corporations and other business enterprises, John Ruggie, A/HRC/8/5, 7 April 2008, para 54.

[107] Vandenhole (n 2) 12.

[108] The United Nations guiding principles on extreme poverty and human rights, submitted by the Special Rapporteur on extreme poverty and human rights, Magdalena Sepúlveda Carmona, A/HRC/21/39, 18 July 2012, para 100.

[109] OECD Guidelines (n 91) 31 (Human Rights).

[110] Commentary on the Implementation Procedures of the OECD Guidelines for Multinational Enterprises, 37.

[111] OECD Guidelines, (n 91) 31 (Human Rights).

[112] ibid.

[113] ibid.

[114] ibid.

[115] UNCTAD Principles on Responsible Sovereign Lending and Borrowing, 22 April 2012, Principle 4, www.unctad.info/upload/Debt%20Portal/Principles%20drafts/SLB_Principles_English_Doha_22-04-2012.pdf, accessed 20 March 2013. See M Goldmann, 'Responsible Sovereign Lending and Borrowing : The View from Domestic Jurisdictions', UNCTAD, February 2012, www.unctad.info/upload/Debt%20Portal/RSLB_MGoldmann_02-2012.pdf, accessed 30 March 2013.

implications'.[116] The measures that financial corporations can adopt to ensure respect for the economic and social rights of the population of borrowing states include acknowledging the human rights in internal policies and their codes of conduct, constantly and consistently examining human rights situations where economic and social rights are at stake, effectively monitoring policies that protect the reasonable minimum core economic and social rights of individuals in the borrowing state, and implementing an effective monitoring system to ensure that human rights policies relating to economic and social rights are being implemented. Financial corporations are also obliged to prevent and investigate violations, address complaints brought by victims, and potentially provide reparations for harm and injuries caused.[117] Another legal source which is relevant for activities of financial corporations is the Principles on Responsible Investment developed by the group of international investors.[118] What is more, the Equator Principles (soft law principles of the financial industry) provide in their preamble that 'we will not provide loans to projects where the borrower will not or is unable to comply with our respective social and environmental policies and procedures that implement the Equator Principles'.[119] All in all, corporations are obliged to refrain from violating at the very least, the reasonable and minimum core of economic and social rights in the sovereign debt context.

Corporate Obligation to Protect

A financial corporation's obligation to protect economic and social rights includes the obligations to protect the individual's enjoyment of economic and social rights, particularly of their reasonable minimum core, and to support the protection of economic and social rights by employing its expertise and resources to protect. Obligation to protect means not only that private financial corporations must not interfere with economic and social rights of individuals of the borrowing state, but it must request that its business partners throughout their supply chain also comply with them. This means that private lenders which sell sovereign debt of a state on secondary financial markets to other private financial entities have obligations to ensure that such buyers ensure the respect of at least a reasonable minimum core of economic and social rights. In order to ensure that private lenders ensure such commitment a due diligence or human rights impact assessment should be conducted prior to adopting a decision to proceed with project.[120] Insistence on such a procedure may seem at first illusionary, but it is necessary to make sure that private lenders do not eye only potential profits and totally disregard social and economic rights when purchasing sovereign debt in secondary markets. The economists often emphasise that financial markets function on the basis of the credibility of borrowing states, but it is equally significant to look at the other side of the coin and ask for the credibility of private lenders to comply with minimum human rights norms. The corpo-

[116] ibid, Principle 5.

[117] Guiding Principles on Business and Human Rights (n 105) 15 and 22.

[118] Principles on Responsible Investment, www.unpri.org, accessed 15 April 2013. See also the Monterrey Consensus of the International Conference on Financing for Development, www.un.org/esa/ffd/monterrey/MonterreyConsensus.pdf, accessed 15 January 2013, 18–22 March 2002, UN DocA/Conf.198/11.

[119] Equator Principles, preamble, www.equator-principles.com/resources/equator_principles.pdf, accessed 30 March 2013.

[120] Guiding Principles on Business and Human Rights (n 105) 15 and 17.

rate obligation to protect also includes a commitment on the side of the lender to devote the necessary human resources to complying with the reasonable minimum core of the economic and social rights.

Obligation to Fulfil

The third category of corporate obligations concerning economic and social rights includes the obligation to fulfil, which is defined as a positive obligation. It is further divided into obligations to facilitate, provide and promote.[121] It depends on the available financial resources of the corporation, but not only this. It requires that the corporation takes active measures to ensure the availability, accessibility and affordability of economic and social rights.[122] Corporations are therefore obliged to work towards abolition of obstacles for the enjoyment of human rights.[123] For instance, the Maastricht Principles on Extraterritorial Obligations of States in the area of Economic, Social and Cultural Rights note in principle 28 that '[a]ll States must take action, separately, and jointly through international cooperation, to fulfil economic, social and cultural rights of persons within their territories and extraterritorially . . .'.[124] Such obligations apply under the qualifying condition under Principle 31, which argues that 'a State has the obligation to fulfil economic, social and cultural rights in its territory to the maximum of its ability'.[125] *Mutatis mutandis*, the obligation to fulfil of the private lenders would mean that financial corporations must contribute to the enjoyment of economic and social rights of the individuals in a borrowing state when lending financial resources and strive to abolish obstacles to the enjoyment of economic and human rights. This could be done in several ways. The most straightforward, but also the least likely, would be that a corporation cancels part of the sovereign debt or that it accepts favourable write-off in a debt restructuring programme which would not totally strip off economic and social rights.[126] However, it must be noted that the obligation to fulfil exists also before a problem arises. In this context, Principle 1 of the UNCTAD Principles on Responsible Sovereign Lending and Borrowing notes that 'lenders should recognize that government officials involved in sovereign lending and borrowing transactions are responsible for protecting public interest (to the State and its citizens for which they are acting as agents)'.[127] The implications of that principle note that 'agents (the government officials directly involved in the borrowing process) . . . owe responsibility to the State and its citizens for which they act' and that 'any attempt by a lender to suborn a government official to breach that duty is wrongful (for example,

[121] Committee on Economic, Social and Cultural Rights, General Comment 12, Right to adequate food (Twentieth session, 1999) UN Doc E/C.12/1999/5 (1999) para 15.

[122] See generally 'Economic, Social, and Cultural Rights: Norms on the Responsibility of Transnational Corporations and Other Business Enterprises with Regard to Human Rights', Economic and Social Council, UN Doc E/CN.4/Sub.2/2003/12/Rev.2, 4 (2003). The Maastricht principles on Extraterritorial Obligations of States in the area of Economic, Social and Cultural Rights, 29 February 2013, www.fian.org/fileadmin/media/publications/2012.02.29_-_Maastricht_Principles_on_Extraterritorial_Obligations.pdf, accessed 30 June 2013.

[123] QUB Budget Analysis Project, *Budgeting for Economic and Social Rights: A Human Rights Framework* (Belfast, QUB School of Law, 2010) 43.

[124] The Maastricht principles on Extraterritorial Obligations of States in the area of Economic, Social and Cultural Rights, 29 February 2013, 28.

[125] ibid, 31.

[126] See M Goldmann's Ch 6 in this volume.

[127] UNCTAD Principles on Responsible Sovereign Lending and Borrowing, 22 April 2012, Principle 1.

instances of bribes or corruption)'.[128] Another way would involve the corporation providing its own financial resources in order to guarantee reasonable minimum economic and social rights, for instance in a particular geographical area or with regard to particular social rights. However, a reasonable approach should be employed when examining the corporate obligation to fulfil economic and social rights. Financial corporations are not expected to take the role of the state, but to do what they can. States are and should be primarily responsible for fulfilling this obligation. However, a corporation, such as Royal Dutch Shell in Ogoniland, may become the primary holder of an obligation to fulfil economic rights in the context of a failed state where there is no governmental control or no efficient authority to protect economic and social rights and where corporations were asked to provide public functions on behalf of state.[129] A financial corporation may assume some of such obligations when the borrowing state cannot anymore guarantee economic and social rights. The size and availability of corporate financial resources will play a large role in meeting these standards to protect economic and social rights. While the resources available for fulfilling human rights obligations may not be as plentiful in small corporations as in large corporations, corporations may adopt such policies to the maximum extent given their available resources. Given the above, such obligations also have implications beyond the legal sphere in the field of ethical and moral obligations.

This section has shown that financial corporations have tripartite obligations to respect, protect and fulfil the reasonable minimum core of economic and social rights of individuals in the borrowing state.

V CORPORATE RESPONSIBILITY FOR ECONOMIC AND SOCIAL RIGHTS IN SOVEREIGN FINANCING

The right to a remedy for victims of human rights violations as an individual or group is a tenet of every functioning judicial system. The effectiveness of all other rights rests on access to an effective legal remedy. This section discusses and analyses three different potential avenues allowing individuals to enforce economic and social rights against financial corporations. The Basic Principles and Guidelines on the Right to a Remedy and Reparation for Victims of Gross Violations of International Human Rights Law and Serious Violations of International Humanitarian Law identify the state's obligation in relation to the due diligence standard also with respect to economic and social rights.[130] The Basic Principles suggest that states are required to 'take appropriate legislative and administrative and other appropriate measures to prevent violations';[131] 'investigate violations effectively, promptly, thoroughly, impartially and, where appropriate, take action

[128] ibid.

[129] The Maastricht Principles (n 122) 12 (providing that non-state actors are responsible for fulfilling the obligations of the state when they are acting in the capacity of the state). See also Report of the Special Representative of the Secretary- General on the Issue of Human Rights and Transnational Corporations and Other Business Enterprises, UN GAOR, Human Rights Council, 17th Sess, Agenda item 3, principles 2, 3–10, UN Doc A/HRC/17/31 (2011) (John Ruggie). A Nolan, 'Addressing Economic and Social Rights Violations by Non-State Actors through the Role of the State: A Comparison of Regional Approaches to the "Obligation to Protect"' (2009) *Human Rights Law Review* 225.

[130] Basic Principles and Guidelines on the Right to a Remedy and Reparation for Victims of Gross Violations of International Human Rights Law and Serious Violations of International Humanitarian Law, GA Res 60/147, UN Doc A/RES/60/147, 21 March 2006.

[131] ibid, para 3(a).

against those allegedly responsible in accordance with domestic and international law';[132] 'provide those who claim to be victims of a human rights or humanitarian law violation with equal and effective access to justice . . . irrespective of who may ultimately be the bearer of responsibility for the violation';[133] and 'provide effective remedies to victims, including reparation'.[134] Taken together, states have an international legal obligation to comply with the due diligence standard relating to economic and social rights.[135] This section therefore now discusses in more detail the enforcement of corporate obligations to respect, protect and fulfil economic and social rights. It does so in three steps: first, by discussing and analysing enforcement of corporate responsibility before US courts on the basis of the Alien Torts Claims Act; second, by examining the enforcement mechanism under international and regional human rights law; and third, by examining the enforcement of economic and social rights against corporations in national legal orders.

Alien Tort Claims Act

The Alien Tort Claims Act (ATCA) provides a forum to bring cases against financial corporations before civil courts in the United States as direct perpetrator or accessory to a state actor either by having knowledge of or directly assisting human rights violations. The US Congress enacted the ATCA as part of section 9 of the Judiciary Act of 1789. The relevant section provides as follows: 'The district courts shall have original jurisdiction of any civil action by an alien for a tort only, committed in violation of the law of nations or a treaty of the United States'.[136] US Courts have so far dealt with more than 100 ATCA cases that have been brought against corporations. Several claims are currently pending against several corporations for, inter alia, alleged involvement in crimes against humanity, war crimes, torture and forced labour, all of them at least indirectly connected with economic and social rights. To date, 13 claims against corporations have been settled.[137] In two cases victims were successful.[138] US Courts have dealt with a number of cases against financial corporations, particularly banks. However, most of them have not resulted in positive outcomes for the victims.[139] This avenue will be even more limited after the April 2013 decision of the Supreme Court of the United States in *Kiobel v Royal Dutch Petroleum*,[140] where it confirmed presumption against extraterritoriality of ATCA, except regarding claims that 'touch and concern the territory of the United States with sufficient force to displace the presumption against extraterritorial application'.[141]

[132] ibid, para 3(b).

[133] ibid, para 3(c).

[134] ibid, para 3(d).

[135] Basic Principles and Guidelines (n 130).

[136] Alien Torts Claims Act of 1789, 28 USC § 1350. Judiciary Act of 1789, ch 20, § 11, 1 Stat 73, 78. Human rights claims against corporations can also be brought in the United States under the Torture Victims Protection Act, 28 USC, section 1350.

[137] MD Goldhaber, 'Corporate Human Rights Litigation in Non-U.S. Courts: A Comparative Scorecard' (2013) 3 *UC Irvine Law Review* 127, 128–29.

[138] *Licea v Curacao Drydock Co*, 584 F. Supp. 2d 1355 (S.D.Fla. 2008), *Aguilar v Imperial Nurseries*, No 3-07-cv-193 (JCH), 2008 WL 2572250. See Goldhaber (n 138) 128.

[139] See *Khulumani v Barclay Nat. Bank Ltd*, United States Court of Appeals, Second Circuit, October 12, 2007, 2007 WL 2985101.

[140] *Kiobel v Royal Dutch Petroleum Co*, No 10-1491, slip op at 5 (US Sup Ct 17 April 2013).

[141] ibid, at 12–13.

However, it remains to be seen what will be the consequences of this decision for future plaintiffs.[142]

International Human Rights Law

International human rights law currently does not provide an effective mechanism whereby individuals could effectively protect their economic and social rights against corporate activities within or outside the sovereign debt context. The European Social Charter provides at regional level the only quasi-judicial complaints mechanism.[143] However, there is no right to an individual complaint and the European Social Charter issues only non-binding recommendations. However, the European Committee for Social Rights has dealt with some collective complaints arising from sovereign debt crises and has confirmed that state and non-state actors shall guarantee the enjoyment of economic and social rights.[144] However, the Charter offers the only avenue of complaint against states and therefore might not be that strong a tool for alleged corporate violations. All in all, individuals are largely excluded from international forums when seeking to enforce their economic and social rights. If monitoring mechanisms exist, they are at best ineffective and at worst only hold symbolic significance for the enforcement of economic and social rights against financial corporations in the context of sovereign debt. Some commentators have already argued for a world court of human rights, which would also hear cases against corporations.[145]

National Jurisdictions

National enforcement mechanisms play a vital role in protecting human rights both in a borrowing and lending state. Private lenders tend to seek protection of their rights before arbitration proceedings or national jurisdictions if a state refuses to pay off or restructure its debt.[146] They are often successful.[147] However, national courts have in some instances dismissed often exaggerated claims of private financial funds.[148] For instance, the Jersey

[142] J Letnar Černič, 'Business and Human Rights after *Kiobel*, *Dignitas*' (2013) 2 *Dignitas - Slovene Journal of Human Rights*, 445–53.

[143] European Social Charter, ETS No 35, Turin, 18 October 1961, revised on 3 May 1996.

[144] European Committee of Social Rights, complaint No 66/2011, *General Federation of employees of the national electric power corporation (GENOP-DEI)/Confederation of Greek Civil Servants' Trade Unions (ADEDY) v Greece*; Decision on the merits, 23 May 2012, para 47. European Committee of Social Rights, Complaint No 65/2011 *General Federation of employees of the national electric power corporation (GENOP-DEI)/Confederation of Greek Civil Servants' Trade Unions (ADEDY) v Greece*, 23 May 2012, para 17. *Panhellenic Federation of Public Service Pensioners v Greece* No 76/2012 *Federation of employed pensioners of Greece ((IKA –ETAM) v Greece*, Decision on merits, 12 December 2012.

[145] See, eg, M Scheinin, 'Towards a World Court of Human Rights: Research Report Within the Framework of the Swiss Initiative to Commemorate the 60th Anniversary of the Universal Declaration of Human Rights' (30 April 2009), www.eui.eu/Documents/DepartmentsCentres/Law/Professors/Scheinin/WorldCourtReport30April2009.pdf, accessed 30 March 2013. For a critical account of this proposal see P Alston, 'Against a World Court for Human Rights', (2014) *Ethics and International Affairs* 13–71.

[146] See, for instance, M Waibel, *Sovereign Defaults before International Courts and Tribunals* (Cambridge, Cambridge University Press, 2011).

[147] See, for example, *Elliott Associates LP v Banco de la Nacion and the Republic of Peru*, 194 F.3d 363 (2d Cir 1999).

[148] See Section I.

Court of Appeal delivered on 14 July 2011 a decision against the Democratic Republic of Congo, providing that it had to pay off a debt owed to FG Hemisphere Associates LLC, a hedge fund, in the amount of more than $100 million US. However, the UK Privy Council later reversed this decision and dismissed the claims.[149] What is more, national constitutional courts have in the past reaffirmed the importance of economic and social rights,[150] also against corporations.[151] What is more, some national human rights commissions have upheld economic and social rights against corporations.[152]

The National Contact Points (NCPs) under the OECD Guidelines for Multinational Enterprise may provide an avenue for enforcement of some economic and social rights against financial corporations. NCPs monitor compliance of business enterprises with the Guidelines. Under the new provisions, the NCPs are 'composed and organised such that they provide an effective basis for dealing with the broad range of issues covered by the Guidelines' and must 'enable the NCP to operate in an impartial manner while maintaining an adequate level of accountability to the adhering government'.[153] When an NCP is not complying with procedural obligations in specific instances under the OECD Guidelines, an adhering country, an advisory body, or OECD Watch can send 'a substantiated submission' that will be considered by the OECD Committee.[154] A number of cases against corporations have so far been brought before respective NCPs, however their efficiency varies from country to country.[155]

All in all, it appears that there is only some effective judicial protection of the reasonable minimum core economic and social rights against private financial corporations. Where a corporation fails to meet its obligations, adequate and effective remedies must be available to victims whose human rights have been violated. In the future, the United Nations Human Rights Council may consider establishing complaints mechanisms to receive the complaints of individuals. Another option would be to consider a holistic approach to corporate responsibility for human rights violations, which suggests that responsibility can be established against corporations, an individual director or employee and against the state at the same time. The concurrence between individual and corporate (criminal) responsibility is already possible in some national legal orders.[156]

[149] M Jones, 'Vulture fund's $100m DR Congo claim blocked', 18 July 2012, www.bbc.co.uk/news/business-18894874, accessed 30 March 2013. See also *Elliott Associates LP v The Republic of Peru* 194 F.3d 63 (2d Cir 1998).

[150] *Minister of Health and Others v Treatment Action Campaign and Others (No 1)* (CCT9/02) [2002] ZACC 16; 2002 (5) SA 703; 2002 (10) BCLR 1075 (5 July 2002); *Government of the Republic of South Africa and Others v Grootboom and Others* (CCT11/00) [2000] ZACC 19; 2001 (1) SA 46; 2000 (11) BCLR 1169 (4 October 2000); *Certification of the Constitution of the Republic of South Africa*, 1996 (CCT 23/96) [1996] ZACC 26; 1996 (4) SA 744 (CC); 1996 (10) BCLR 1253 (CC) (6 September 1996).

[151] *Mazibuko and Others v City of Johannesburg and Others* (CCT 39/09) [2009] ZACC 28; 2010 (3) BCLR 239 (CC); 2010 (4) SA 1 (CC) (8 October 2009).

[152] See, for example, Comision Estatal Derechos Humanos, Nuevo Leon, Mexico CEDH/242/2011, 31.12.2012.

[153] OECD Guidelines (n 91) 71 (Procedural Guidance).

[154] Commentary (n 110) 47.

[155] European Centre for Constitutional and Human Rights, 'A comparison of National Contact Points – Best practices in OECD complaints procedures', Berlin, November 2011, www.ecchr.de/index.php/ecchr-publications/articles/a-comparison-of-national-contact-points-best-practices-in-oecd-complaints-procedures-1333.html, accessed 20 March 2013.

[156] See, for example, *Public Prosecutor v Van Anraat*, LJN: BA4676, Court of Appeal, The Hague, 2200050906-2, 9 May 2007. For a detailed discussion, see H van der Wilt, *Public Prosecutor v Van Anraat*, Judgment of The Hague Court of Appeal, LJN BA4676, 2200050906-2, *Oxford Reports on International Law in Domestic Courts*; ILDC 753 (NL2007), 9 May 2007, www.oxfordlawreports.com/, accessed 10 February 2013.

However, giving real meaning to sovereign financing and human rights asks for a novel approach, an approach which would not only take the rights of corporations and their owners and executives into consideration, but also the human rights of ordinary people living ordinary lives. It is therefore advisable to develop human rights obligations of corporations and their accountability, from the point closest to human beings. In order to develop the right medicine for the relationship between business and human rights, one has to look at the bottom and employ a bottom-up approach as well as taking the needs of ordinary people into account.[157]

VI CONCLUSIONS

The enjoyment of economic and social rights is crucial for the survival and well-being of an individual. Not only states but also financial corporations have obligations to respect, protect and fulfil them. They should not infringe the reasonable minimum core of economic and social rights, not only when requiring states to repay their sovereign debt but also before a loan is granted. Sovereign debt has often undermined not only economic and social rights, but also civil and political rights.[158] The overall aim of this chapter was to examine the responsibility of financial corporations for economic and social rights in the sovereign debt context. While it can be concluded that economic and social rights are well incorporated into some national legal orders, it is also evident that they could be generally better protected, implemented and enforced, particularly against private actors. Corporations must be accountable for the failure to meet their obligations under economic and social rights. Yet it appears that those corporate obligations concerning economic and social rights are more or less without teeth as they do not provide clear sanctions in the event of violations. Financial corporations must primarily ensure that they will not violate the reasonable minimum core of economic and social rights, not only when pressuring a borrowing state to repay its debts, but also throughout the whole debt cycle and even before the agreement is signed. All in all, economic and social rights must be taken into consideration when evaluating the extent of private creditors' property rights against sovereign borrowers.

[157] See JP Bohoslavsky and J Letnar Černič, introductory chapter of this volume and S Deva, *Regulating Corporate Human Rights Violations* (Oxford, Routledge, 2012).

[158] A Cassese (n 18). He argues that dictatorship in Argentina illustrated that economic and social rights are inherently linked with civil and political rights.

Part III

Specific Financial Actors and Instruments, and Novel Approaches

11

Ethical Sovereign Investors: Sovereign Wealth Funds and Human Rights

ANGELA CUMMINE

> The Future Fund . . . is public money invested and it is a public institution. That fact alone obliges us to consider the implications of its actions. . . It should seek profits only in so far as they help to balance the ledger. If we cannot do that without causing harm in other countries, how can we endorse this enterprise?
>
> Senator Di Natale, *Parliamentary Statement*, Australia (2012)[1]

I INTRODUCTION

SOVEREIGNS PARTICIPATE IN financial markets as borrowers and investors. Both activities – borrowing and investing – have potential human rights implications, many of which are explored throughout this volume. This chapter focuses on the links between government financial *investment* and human rights, through the prism of one significant public investment vehicle.[2] Sovereign Wealth Funds (SWFs), government-sponsored funds that invest public capital in financial markets, are now major players in the international economy[3] with over US$5 trillion in assets making them the world's 'wealthiest investors'.[4] Despite this high-profile status, the growing literature on the human rights impact of global finance has not yet turned its gaze upon SWFs.[5] Equally, scholarly treatment of sovereign funds fixates on their investment behaviour and

[1] Senator R Di Natale, 'Government Investment Funds Amendment (Ethical Investment) Bill 2011', *Second Reading Speech*, 13 September 2012 (Canberra, The Commonwealth of Australia Senate, 2012) 6845, 6848.

[2] According to Kimmit, states may invest public funds in one of four key ways including through SWFs, but also through international reserves, public pension funds and state-owned enterprises. See R Kimmit, 'Public Footprints in Private Markets: Sovereign Wealth Funds and the World Economy' (2008) 87 *Foreign Affairs* 119.

[3] See 'Introduction' in E Truman, *Sovereign Wealth Funds: Threat or Salvation* (Washington DC, Peterson Institute for International Economics, 2010).

[4] A 2013 study by *TheCityUK* estimated global SWF assets at $5.2 trillion by 2012 year end. S Rau, 'Sovereign Wealth Funds to Hit Record $5.6 Trln by Year-end Study', *Reuters Business News*, 12 March 2013 www.uk.reuters.com/article/2013/03/12/financial-funds-sovereign-idUKL6N0C45T220130312, accessed 30 September 2013. Some projections forecast growth of up to $12 trillion in SWF assets by 2015. See Preqin Equity, 'Sovereign Wealth Funds: SWFs Total Assets Continue to Grow', *Prequin Special Report May 2010* (New York, Prequin).

[5] Curiously, a recent attempt to survey the impact of the finance industry on human rights in the wake of the financial crisis did not mention sovereign funds, despite the high-profile role SWFs played in bailing out struggling blue chip firms in America and Britain. See M Dowell-Jones and D Kinley, 'Mind the Gap: Global Finance and Human Rights' (2011) 25 *Ethics and International Affairs* 183. There are some exceptions to this oversight of SWFs' impact on human rights. See n 22 below.

geopolitical significance, but very rarely their ethical footprint. This chapter redresses that oversight by identifying potential links between SWF investment and human rights and suggesting how current frameworks for guiding sovereign fund behaviour may better recognise and regulate those links.

After first framing the discussion with the growing importance of SWFs in international finance, Section III reviews potential connections between sovereign fund investment and human rights. It shows how existing normative frameworks for governing SWF behaviour do not adequately acknowledge the potential links. In response, Section IV suggests a method for improving those frameworks that draws upon fiduciary theory. A fiduciary conception of the state holds that government must act solely in the interests of its principal, the people. It is not unprecedented for the citizen–state relationship *generally* or sovereign finance *in particular*,[6] however, it has not enjoyed specific application to sovereign funds. Yet, as captured in the opening quote to this chapter, SWFs are 'public institutions' investing 'public money' on behalf of and with ramifications for their citizen-beneficiaries. Viewing sovereign funds in fiduciary terms offers a useful foundation for exploring the duties and rights that may attach to states and citizens through SWF activity. Section V argues that one crucial implication of the fiduciary approach to SWFs is that government sponsors, as part of their duty of loyalty to their principal, must shield citizens' ethical agency in the course of SWF investment activity. To fulfil this duty, a legal obligation to invest ethically should be imposed on SWFs, which includes a commitment to protect and promote human rights.

Moving from theory to practice, Section VI assesses the extent to which sovereign funds already comply with this demand, examining the pursuit of ethical (or responsible)[7] investment among SWFs. This section concludes with a closer look at the ethical investment mandate and behaviour of New Zealand's sovereign fund, one of only two sovereign funds globally to boast a legally entrenched ethical investment mandate. The other fund, Norway's Government Pension Fund Global (GPFG), already receives substantial attention in ethical investment analyses, warranting a fresh focus on New Zealand here. In scrutinising a lesser-known role model investor for its effectiveness in shielding citizens from complicity in morally objectionable investment, including human rights violations, this chapter seeks to advance our practical understanding of how to regulate the impact of sovereign finance on human rights.

[6] For a fully developed fiduciary theory of the state, see E Fox-Decent, *Sovereignty's Promise: The State as Fiduciary* (Oxford, Oxford University Press, 2011). This work builds on a series of articles that develop the fiduciary state concept as a formal theoretical framework for understanding legal and moral norms governing state power. See EJ Criddle, 'Mending Holes in the Rule of (Administrative) Law' (2010) 104 *Northwestern University Law Review* 1271; E Fox-Decent and EJ Criddle, 'The Fiduciary Constitution of Human Rights' (2009) 15 *Legal Theory* 301; EJ Criddle and E Fox-Decent, 'A Fiduciary Theory of Jus Cogens' (2009) 34 *Yale Journal of International Law* 331; EJ Criddle, 'Fiduciary Foundations of Administrative Law' (2006) 54 *UCLA Law Review* 117; and E Fox-Decent, 'The Fiduciary Nature of State Legal Authority' (2005) 31 *Queen's Law Journal* 259.

[7] I use the terms 'ethical' and 'responsible' investment interchangeably. For a discussion on the evolution of terminology in the ethical investment space covering the phrases 'ethical', 'responsible', 'socially responsible' and most recently 'extra financial' investing, see J Solomon, *Corporate Governance and Accountability*, 3rd edn (Chichester, Wiley, 2010) 304–07.

II THE SIGNIFICANCE OF SOVEREIGN WEALTH FUNDS AS GOVERNMENT INVESTORS

In the past decade, governments have become prominent investors through the seemingly new entity of the sovereign wealth fund. Best described as government owned and controlled (directly or indirectly) investment funds that have no outside beneficiaries or liabilities (beyond the government or the citizenry in abstract) and that invest their assets, either in the short or long term, according to the interests and objectives of the sovereign sponsor,[8] the majority of the world's more than 50 funds[9] came into existence this century.[10] The recent establishment surge saw 'some 30 new sovereign wealth funds . . . created since 1999, compared with just 16 in the preceding half century',[11] fuelling a perception of SWFs as 'new'. However, the sovereign fund phenomenon far pre-dates this recent exponential growth.[12] The world's earliest funds date back to the nineteenth century, while the 1953 establishment of the Kuwait Investment Authority (KIA) marks the twentieth-century establishment wave, which resulted in nearly 20 funds.[13] All this occurred prior to the birth of the term 'Sovereign Wealth Fund' as official moniker for the investor group in 2005,[14] a development that signals sovereign funds' emergent status, rather than their newness in the twenty-first century.

The rapid expansion in the number of sovereign funds is also being accompanied by an impressive escalation in asset levels, leading to SWFs' characterisation as a new 'power broker' in the global economy.[15] Estimates of SWF assets under management range from conservative valuations of around US$3 trillion to upper end projections of more than

[8] A Monk, 'Recasting the Sovereign Wealth Fund Debate: Trust, Legitimacy, and Governance' (2009) 14 *New Political Economy* 451, 452.

[9] The number of SWFs in the world is the subject of constant dispute given the lack of consensus on the definition of 'sovereign wealth fund'. See A Rozanov, 'Definitional Challenges of Dealing with Sovereign Wealth Funds' (2011) 1 *Asian Journal of International Law* 249. Estimates range from between 50 and 80 funds depending on whether pension funds are included in the definition. Most studies cite figures of between 50 and 60 sovereign funds. For a methodology producing an upper estimate of almost 80 funds, see Truman (n 3).

[10] Another study of the rise of SWFs finds that '50% of global Sovereign Funds are less than seven years old'. See Y Selfin et al, *Sovereign Wealth Funds – the Key to Economic Success* (London, PWC, 2011).

[11] L Adamson, 'Riding a New Wave of Wealth', *Institutional Investor Magazine*, 25 September 2012, www.institutionalinvestor.com/Article/3088148/Riding-a-New-Wave-of-Wealth.html, accessed 30 September 2013.

[12] France's 1816 establishment of the Caisse des Dépots et Consignations (CDC) following Napoleon's depletion of the public coffers rivals the 1863-founded Texas Permanent School Fund for oldest SWF, depending on the definition of sovereign fund adopted: The Corner House, 'Sovereign Wealth Funds: Some Frequently Asked Questions', *Corner House Briefing* 38 (London, Corner House, 2008) 4.

[13] According to Miracky et al: 'The oldest [funds](in Kuwait and what is now Kiribati) were set up in the 1950s to manage surplus foreign reserves and offset the eventual decline of natural resource endowments. Another wave in the 1970s and 1980s reflected a spike in energy prices and the rise of the Asian tiger economies. Large funds were established in these decades in Abu Dhabi (the first of several in the UAE), Norway (which later converted into a pension fund), and Singapore (Temasek Holdings [1974] and Government Investment Corporation [GIC, 1981]). Another wave in the 1990s brought smaller funds in Asia, Africa, and the Middle East. The major wave, starting in 2000, has led to the formation of nearly 20 funds, most of which are funded by capital inflows based either on high energy prices (especially in the Middle East but also in Russia) or continued large trade surpluses (eg, in China). Thus the most recent group includes not only funds originating in small, wealthy nations but also in major geopolitical powers'. See W Miracky et al, 'Assessing the Risk: The Behaviours of Sovereign Wealth Funds in the Global Economy' (London, Monitor Group, 2008) 14–15.

[14] The term 'Sovereign Wealth Fund' first appeared in a 2005 article in which the author refers to these institutional investors as 'Sovereign Wealth Managers'. See A Rozanov, 'Who Holds the Wealth of Nations' (2005) 15 *Central Banking Journal* 52.

[15] D Farrell et al, *The New Power Brokers: How Oil, Asia, Hedge Funds, and Private Equity Are Shaping Global Capital Markets* (San Francisco, McKinsey Global Institute, 2007).

US$5 trillion.[16] Although these asset levels are dwarfed by the holdings of public and private pension funds, even today's lower SWF estimates still eclipse the US$2.1 trillion in global hedge funds and match those of private equity.[17] Moreover, with forecasts predicting that SWF assets will more than double to $12 trillion as soon as 2015,[18] and a further 20 SWFs to be created in the next five years,[19] commentators unsurprisingly suggest that 'the global significance of this diverse group of investors is poised to expand significantly'.[20] States as varied as Tanzania, Cyprus, India, Western Australia, Mozambique, Israel, Panama, Angola, Peru, South Africa, Columbia and Papua New Guinea have recently established or announced an intention to establish a sovereign fund, substantially widening the global presence of these entities.[21]

III SOVEREIGN FUND INVESTMENT AND HUMAN RIGHTS

Despite the growing reach and influence of this investor class, the ethical consequences of SWF investment have not featured prominently on the analytical agenda.[22] Instead, the SWF debate has been consumed by 'whether [sovereign funds] represented a threat of foreign government control over important national industries, or, during the financial crisis in 2007–2008, if they could be suppliers of necessary capital to financial institutions in difficulties'.[23] Even scholarship explicitly focused on 'how better to integrate the objects and practices of global finance and human rights' has overlooked the role of sovereign funds in human rights investing.[24]

Yet, as investors across the full asset spectrum, sovereign funds risk complicity in human rights violations through exposure to traditional assets like equities and debt, where the majority of the world's sovereign wealth sits,[25] as well as alternative assets like commodities, currencies, property, derivatives and private equity, which are attracting a growing proportion of SWF portfolio allocations as sovereign funds seek more aggressive returns.[26] The link between alternative assets and human rights is the least developed of

[16] Adamson (n 11).

[17] In 2011, pension funds in the world's 13 largest markets held $27.5 trillion in assets. See Adamson ibid.

[18] Truman (n 3) 1.

[19] Rau (n 4); Adamson (n 11). Many of the new funds will be in Africa with at least 7 African funds slated for establishment in 2013. See A Monk, 'Mapping the Growth of Sovereign Funds in Africa', *Institutional Investor Blog*, 11 December 2012, www.institutionalinvestor.com/blogarticle/3129981/Blog/Mapping-the-Growth-of-Sovereign-Funds-in-Africa.html.

[20] Adamson (n 11).

[21] ibid; Monk (n 19).

[22] There are some notable exceptions including B Demeyere, 'Sovereign Wealth Funds and (Un)ethical Investment: Using "Due Diligence" to Avoid Contributing to Human Rights Violations Committed by Companies in the Investment Portfolio' in G Nystuen, A Follesdal and O Mestad (eds), *Human Rights, Corporate Complicity and Disinvestment* (Cambridge, Cambridge University Press, 2011); S Ghahramani, 'Governments, Financial Markets, and International Human Rights: The State's Role as Shareholder' (2011) 85 *Yale Journal of International Affairs* 85–95; P Keenan and C Ochoa, 'The Human Rights Potential of Sovereign Wealth Funds' (2009) 40 *Georgetown Journal of International Law* 1151; S Chesterman, 'The Turn to Ethics: Disinvestment from Multinational Corporations for Human Rights Violations – The Case of Norway's Sovereign Wealth Fund' (2008) 23 *American University International Law Review* 577.

[23] 'Introduction' in Nystuen et al (n 22) 5.

[24] Dowell-Jones and Kinley (n 5) 204.

[25] Preqin Ltd, *The 2012 Preqin Sovereign Wealth Fund Review* (London, Preqin, 2012) (the 'Preqin Review').

[26] ibid.

all the asset classes.[27] The potential links are far better understood and regulated in the case of equities, with high-profile equity divestments by sovereign funds already having occurred on human rights grounds, most notably by Norway's GPFG.[28] Norway has also acted on human rights-violating debt assets,[29] and is developing a clearer policy for how SWF investment in bonds, particularly sovereign bonds, should be regulated. This move follows a 2009 report that revealed an inconsistency in the GPFG's ethical guidelines where equity assets were subject to the guidelines but not investment in government bonds.[30] Nor was Norway's debt investing covered by any rules for responsible lending or investment,[31] despite the fact that acquisition of government bonds amounts to loaning other sovereigns' money and thus a direct investment in that particular regime. Indeed, the only restriction on debt investing to which the GPFG is subject is a ban on purchasing bonds from countries that are subject to international sanctions that Norway support. So far, this has only covered Burma, despite calls for the GPFG to divest its bonds in other dubious regimes with poor human rights records.[32] Recognising this inconsistency between the treatment of equity and debt assets, in August 2012 Norway became the first country to commit to undertaking a 'debt audit' to determine the legitimacy of much of its international debt, including that held by its sovereign fund.[33] Norway's GPFG has outstanding loans totalling about 600 billion NOK, spread across 44 different countries, all in the form of government bonds. The conclusion of the debt audit is likely to offer clearer guidance on how sovereign funds should think about their lending activities to other governments through sovereign bonds.[34]

SWFs' potential impact on human rights is also neglected at the level of regulatory norms. Sovereign funds come under the auspices of two recently developed normative frameworks for guiding the investment behaviour of financial actors.[35] The first relates to the responsible investment obligations of market participants generally. The United

[27] Understanding of the connection between investor complicity and human rights in these asset classes is in its embryonic stages. See Dowell-Jones and Kinley (n 5). Some sovereign funds are acknowledging the need for expanded coverage of responsible investment principles beyond traditional asset classes. For instance, in 2008 the NZ Auditor-General recommended that the country's sovereign fund expand its screening process beyond equity positions and sovereign bonds to include corporate bonds as the current approach left the fund at risk of holding an excluded entity. Auditor-General (2008) para 3.74. In response, the NZSF participated in creating a guide for responsible investment in private equity under the auspices of the PRI, reflecting a commitment to shifting focus beyond pursuing RI in the traditional asset classes of equities and bonds and has since created its own specific guidelines for Private Equity and Public Markets RI investing. See NZSF, *Guardians Response to Independent Review* (2010) June 2010, 2.

[28] Consider, for instance, the high-profile divestments by Norway's SWF from investments in both equity and bond assets on human rights grounds. By 2010, the GPFG had divested multiple equity holdings on human rights grounds, including Wal-mart, Monsanto, Total and Vedanta. See 'Introduction' in Nystuen et al (n 22) 9.

[29] The GPFG has also divested from bonds. In 2007, the fund excluded sovereign bonds issued by the Burmese government from its portfolio on human rights grounds.. See Norwegian Ministry of Finance, 'Prudent and Long-term Asset Management', *Press Release* (2008) 4 April 2008, www.regjeringen.no/en/dep/fin/press-center/press-releases/2008/prudent-and-long-term-asset-management.html?id=506651, accessed 30 September 2013.

[30] SLUG (The Norwegian Coalition for Debt Cancellation), *Borrow My Pension – The Norwegian Government Pension Fund – Global: A Responsible Lender?* (Oslo, Norway, SLUG, 2009) 5.

[31] SLUG, *Ethical Deficit – Lending by the Norwegian Sovereign Wealth Fund*, 23 November 2012, www.slettgjelda.no/no/english/Ethical+Deficit+-+Lending+by+the+Norwegian+Sovereign+Wealth+Fund.b7C_wlDQXf.ips, accessed 30 September 2013.

[32] SLUG (n 30) 36–37.

[33] SLUG (n 31).

[34] For one possible approach, see L Du Toit, *Ethical Deficit* (Oslo, SLUG, 2012) where the author explores the possibility of conditioning government bond investments on a certain degree of transparency in the bond-issuing country.

[35] The present discussion is confined to normative *contra* legal frameworks for regulating investor behaviour.

Nations Principles for Responsible Investment (PRI) were launched in 2006 by a group of institutional investors. Containing six principles on how asset owners, investment managers and other finance industry actors should pursue responsible investment, the PRI had 1,175 signatories as at March 2013.[36] Only three of the 273 asset owner signatories are sovereign funds – the New Zealand Superannuation Fund (NZSF), the Norwegian GPFG and the French Caisse des Dépots et Consignations (CDC).[37] Given these principles are considered 'the most important developed initiative' with regard to responsible investment,[38] the lack of sovereign fund adherence is troubling.

That said, the effectiveness of the PRI as a framework for governing the human rights impact of investment activity is questionable. Some have observed that while the PRI requires signatories to integrate 'economic, social and governance' (ESG) issues into their investment analysis and decision making, human rights considerations are not explicitly mentioned in the PRI. Instead, the 'social' component of ESG issues is understood to cover human rights. Nonetheless, critics argue that 'it is possible to read the whole set of principles and actions to be without sanctions in the form of investor disinvestment no matter how [bad] a company's conduct may be'.[39] In other words, the PRI lacks sufficient enforcement mechanisms to ensure responsible investors properly influence their investee companies' behaviour, whether over human rights violations or other ethical transgressions.

An alternative framework, known as the Santiago Principles or the Generally Agreed Practices and Principles (GAPP), was developed *by* sovereign funds *for* sovereign funds specifically. Agreed in 2008, the 24 principles are endorsed by the 26 members of the International Forum of SWFs (IFSWF). As such, they offer a more ideal framework through which to interrogate norms for SWFs and human rights given the GAPP's exclusive focus on SWFs and its greater coverage of the investor class than the PRI. Like the PRI though, the GAPP has also been deemed inadequate when it comes to protecting human rights.[40] Only two Principles indirectly countenance the possibility of human rights considerations in SWF investing. Sub-Principle 19.1 requires funds to clearly state if their investments are on grounds other than 'financial and economic considerations', which may include 'social, ethical or religious reasons'.[41] But there is no requirement to *pursue* responsible investment, only to disclose where a fund does so. Similarly, in Principle 21 on the exercise of voting rights in investee companies, the only other GAPP principle to *indirectly* address human rights, the emphasis is again on the exercise of such rights so that it 'protects the financial value of [the fund's] investments'.[42] Other strategies besides exercising voting rights, such as informal engagement with the management of companies, is not countenanced and the only requirement upon SWFs is that they must disclose the exercise of such rights.

Beyond these specific principles, the overall thrust of the GAPP is that SWFs should restrict their investment decision making to economic and financial considerations only.[43]

[36] See UNPRI website www.unpri.org/signatories/signatories/, accessed 30 May 2013.

[37] ibid

[38] Introduction in Nystuen et al (n 22) 3.

[39] ibid, 4.

[40] Introduction in Nystuen et al (n 22) 2. For a less pessimistic assessment of the GAPP as 'agnostic/without prejudice to the applicability of notions of "socially responsible" investment to the realm of SWFs', see Demeyere (n 22) 184.

[41] International Working Group of Sovereign Wealth Funds, *Sovereign Wealth Funds: Generally Accepted Principles and Practices* (Santiago Principles) (2008) 22.

[42] Santiago Principles, 22.

[43] Introduction in Nystuen et al (n 22) 4–5.

The appropriateness of this investment approach was affirmed by the inaugural IFSWF Chairman in response to calls for SWFs to invest ethically:

> As SWFs are tools for preserving and augmenting wealth of their founding communities, any constraint on investment strategy impairs a fund's ability to generate an optimal return for their domestic beneficiaries. This deprives not only the fund, but most crucially its owning community of wealth, adversely impacting the living standards of both current and future generations.[44]

Whether a trade-off between virtuous and prosperous investing exists[45] is less relevant for our purposes than the presence of scepticism, in both the Santiago Principles and the IFSWF's leadership, regarding the *desirability* of ethical, and thus human rights-sensitive, investing for sovereign funds. Indeed, the overall impression made by the GAPP 'is that it would have been better if human rights issues were avoided altogether'.[46]

IV THE FIDUCIARY STATE AND CITIZEN-BENEFICIARY: RECONCEPTUALISING SWFS

On what basis might we counter this scepticism and demand that SWFs pursue ethical investment, including the protection and promotion of human rights? Scholars advance a range of utilitarian, prudential, moral and legal reasons for SWFs to pursue responsible investment, often justified by the funds' public character. Consider Richardson:

> SWFs share several characteristics which might lead them more than private sector financiers to invest in sustainable development. Their ownership or control by a state can enmesh them in the machinery of government, and thereby render them instruments of public policy. Further, because of their sheer size and government backing, SWFs tend to have higher risk tolerances and might therefore bear investment strategies eschewed by private financiers. Thirdly, SWFs tend to have longer-term financial considerations than the private sector, which may encourage investing that is mindful of threats such as climate change.[47]

For Richardson, sovereign funds' *state* ownership endows them with certain features (a public policy orientation, high-risk tolerance and long-term investment horizon) that make them suitable for ethical investment strategies like pursuing sustainability. Bugg-Levine also makes a utilitarian case for SWFs pursuing socially responsible investing on the basis of the funds' independence from (legal) fiduciary duties, long-term liabilities and unique governance arrangements, again all attributes associated with the public character of the funds.[48]

Others emphasise the moral significance of sovereign funds' state ownership when advocating ethically constrained investing. Kutz argues that as corporate agents, government

[44] D Murray, 'SWFs: Myths and Realities', *Keynote Address at Global Sovereign Roundtable* (London), 5 May 2011, www.ifswf.org/pst/london11.pdf, accessed 30 May 2013, 19.

[45] For a discussion on this, see Ghahramani (n 22) 92.

[46] Introduction in Nystuen et al (n 22) 2.

[47] B Richardson, 'Sovereign Wealth Funds and the Quest for Sustainability: Insights from Norway and New Zealand' (2011) 2 *Nordic Journal of Commercial Law* 2.

[48] A Bugg-Levine, 'Impact Investing: A New Asset Class and Its Implications for Sovereign Wealth Funds' in P Bolton, PF Samama and J Stiglitz (eds), *Sovereign Wealth Funds and Long-Term Investing* (New York, Columbia University Press, 2012)
110. See also Truman (n 3), 135.

investors are under a special obligation to protect the 'individual, personal complicity on the part of [their] Fund's beneficiaries', the citizens.[49] For Kutz, it is individuals' complicity and ethical agency that *matters*, morally speaking, and not that of the corporate fund since our 'system of moral responsibility functions, when it functions at all, through our individual consciences'.[50] On that basis, Kutz cautions that '[f]ocusing attention on the corporate or collective level can lead to dangerous . . . ethical mistakes' regarding culpability.[51] Reaching a similar conclusion but on a different moral basis, Backer has highlighted the unique coercive dilemma sovereign funds pose for their individual citizen-owners relative to private investors. Contrasting Norway's sovereign fund to real-life private equity fund TIAA CREF, which has similar social investment objectives to the GPFG, Backer isolates the moral quandary peculiar to government investors:

> The critical difference [between SWFs and private investors] is grounded in notions of coercion and in whether or not the ultimate investors have a choice in the manner in which they are represented and their funds are invested. In both the public and the private fund, individuals are the ultimate stakeholders and investors. It is for their benefit that these funds are created and it is their interests that they ultimately serve. [However] . . . [t]he Norwegian Fund's institutional holder is the state apparatus of Norway, but the ultimate beneficiaries are the citizens of Norway on whose behalf the government acts. The TIAA CREF funds are administered *directly* for the investors on whose behalf the fund managers operate. But TIAA CREF investors are free to exit the Social Choice Fund at will (or at least in accordance with procedures therefore agreed to when they first invested their funds). Norwegian citizens have *no such right*. They are bound by the choices made for them by the state apparatus. They are *at least one critical step removed* from the Fund. As a consequence, the TIAA CREF Fund has to be more careful and conscious of the wishes of its ultimate investors than does the Norwegian Fund. The Norwegian state is accountable to the people, but the Fund is accountable *only* to the state.[52]

Taking Kutz and Backer's observations together, a moral case exists for sovereign funds to be governed so that citizens, as ultimate, albeit indirect, owners of SWFs, can exert some control over their funds, including the exposure of their individual ethical agency through an SWF's investment activities.

How can we ensure citizens achieve control over their sovereign funds? For as Kutz observes, '[t]he individual ethical concern . . . which seeks to preserve the integrity of the individual beneficiaries of the Fund, must be consistent with the actual control individuals have over their lives'.[53] Yet, as Backer's analysis highlights, this is precisely the sort of control that citizens lack over government-sponsored funds. I submit that reconceptualising sovereign funds in fiduciary terms offers a basis for theorising a model of appropriate citizen control.

Fiduciary theory, where government is considered mere agent or trustee of the people whose interests it must loyally and solely promote, offers a powerful normative frame-

[49] C Kutz 'Responsibility Beyond the Law' in Nystuen et al (n 22) 71. Consider also Follesdal's more general moral claim that investors (whether public or private) are '*more* morally complicit in . . . wrongdoings than many other actors' involved in those wrongdoings, such as governments or corporations, since the investor directly profits from such harm (emphasis added). A Follesdal, 'Human Rights Investment Filters: a Defence', in Nystuen et al (n 22) 150.

[50] Kutz (n 49) 72.

[51] ibid, 72.

[52] L Cata Backer, 'Sovereign Wealth Funds as Regulatory Chameleons: The Norwegian Sovereign Wealth Funds and Public Global Governance Through Private Global Investment' (2009) 41 *Georgetown Journal of International Law* 101, 181–82 (emphasis added).

[53] Kutz (n 49) 76.

work for regulating the relationship between governments and citizens when it comes to sovereign funds. Such a theoretical move would not be unusual. The fiduciary conception of the citizen–state relationship has a long heritage stretching back to Lockean political thought.[54] Considered a 'common-place' means of understanding state power up until the earlier years of the twentieth century,[55] this conception has recently undergone a revival in international legal theory and even found its way into principles on sovereign borrowing.[56] However, the fiduciary conception does not enjoy similar visibility in frameworks governing sovereign investing such as the PRI or Santiago Principles discussed above.[57] While there is not space here to make the full case for the fiduciary conception of the state, a task ably undertaken elsewhere,[58] we can propose that in applying this conception to sovereign funds, we gain a normative framework for deriving obligations on the funds' state sponsors to their principals, the citizenry. I suggest one such obligation is that SWF investment activities must be conducted in a manner that protects the *ethical* interests of citizens. Specifically, a fiduciary conception of SWFs demands that ethical restrictions be placed on sovereign funds' investment behaviour so that individual citizens' ethical agency is shielded from complicity in morally objectionable acts.

V THE FORM AND CONTENT OF AN ETHICAL INVESTMENT OBLIGATION ON SWFS

How might such restrictions be imposed on SWFs? Since our goal is to enhance popular control over sovereign funds to ensure citizens are shielded from dirty hands complicity in unethical investment, a possible first step is to amend the Santiago Principles to require that all SWFs include a clause in their legal investment mandates to the following effect: 'The Fund must be invested in a manner consistent with the domestic and international ethical obligations of the owner state'. While deliberation over the content of ethical obligations within each state is likely to involve reasonable disagreement, this is not a justification for the fiduciary state to enjoy unfettered control over the ethical exposure of present and future citizens in the realm of sovereign investment. On the contrary, fiduciary theory demands that the government agent must be solely guided by the promotion of the principal's interests. We should therefore constrain these increasingly prolific and powerful investment entities to make it more likely that citizen interests are respected. Moreover, we have good reasons to think that the principal's interests in many communities would include a commitment to promote and protect human rights. Although not unanimously embraced, the almost 'universal acceptance' of the Universal Declaration of Human Rights, translated into over 250 languages and widely incorporated into the

[54] P Laslett (ed), *Locke's Two Treatises of Government* (Cambridge, Cambridge University Press, 1988) 367; J Gough, *John Locke's Political Philosophy* (Oxford, Clarendon Press, 1973).

[55] Gough (n 54); F Maitland in HLA Fischer (ed), *The Collected Papers of F.W. Maitland* (Cambridge, Cambridge University Press, 1911) 403 (vol III).

[56] See Principle 1 of the UNCTAD *Draft Principles on Promoting Responsible Sovereign Lending and Borrowing*: 'Lenders should recognize that government officials involved in sovereign lending and borrowing transactions owe a strict fiduciary duty to the State (including its citizens) for which they are acting as agents' UNCTAD (2011) at http://unctad.org/en/Docs/gdsddf2011misc1_en.pdf.

[57] The word 'fiduciary' or 'agent' does not appear at all in either set of principles when dealing with government investors.

[58] See n 6.

international law practice of many nations,[59] suggests human rights form a likely component of many communities' ethical orientation.[60] If true, such an obligation would at a minimum compel SWFs to *avoid* undermining human rights protections through investment decisions (the 'do no harm principle'), while also permitting funds to pursue the more ambitious goal of selecting investments that enhance human rights ends (the 'value added principle').[61]

VI ETHICAL SOVEREIGN FUND INVESTMENT IN PRACTICE

Turning from theory to practice, if our ethical prescription for compulsory responsible investment among SWFs is normatively persuasive, then the gap between ideal and reality is substantial. Of the more than 50 funds in existence today,[62] only two sovereign funds have an explicit legal obligation to invest ethically in their investment mandate. Norway's GPFG and New Zealand's Superannuation Fund have been investing according to ethical obligations for almost a decade and are considered world leaders in responsible investment.[63] As highlighted above, both are signatories to the PRI. A third SWF, not yet operational but legislatively created in early 2012 with a responsible investment mandate, is Papua New Guinea's Liquefied Natural Gas fund due to receive its first cash transfers in 2014.[64] At best then, a mere three funds in the current sovereign community are subject to an overarching legal obligation to invest ethically.

If we widen our focus beyond portfolio-wide legal mandates to targeted ethical obligations such as exclusions, positive screenings or active ownership through voting,[65] a further 18 sovereign funds potentially practise some limited form of ethically constrained investment.[66] This group of 'targeted' responsible investors lacks an overarching obliga-

[59] United Nations Declaration of Human Rights, 'A United Nations Priority', www.un.org/rights/HRToday/declar.htm, accessed 15 May 2013. Of course, not all communities embrace or support the idea of human rights, but the widespread adherence, both rhetorical and legal, to the concept of human rights in many states suggests it would be a likely component of such a mandate in many societies.

[60] Where communities do not ascribe to human rights as a concept or their principles, there is a much slimmer chance for their incorporation into an SWF's ethical investment mandate in accordance with the clause set out here. The task of defending a case for human rights-sensitive investing in these contexts is one for another project.

[61] This distinction is discussed in Dowell-Jones and Kinley (n 5) 204.

[62] See n 9 on number of SWFs.

[63] Richardson (n 47).

[64] In February 2012 Papua New Guinea's Parliament unanimously voted to create a sovereign wealth fund to manage its resource revenues from a major LNG project. The founding law sets out the investment mandate which requires the fund to develop ethical investment guidelines for 'avoiding prejudice to Papua New Guinea's reputation as a responsible member of the world community'. This wording is identical to that of the New Zealand Superannuation Fund's 'responsible investor' clause. See Section 7.2(c), 'Organic Law on the Sovereign Wealth Fund', *Papua New Guinea National Gazette*, No G306, 2 November 2011, 4.

[65] Exclusions and positive screenings require funds to either divest or actively seek out assets in certain sectors, countries or classes based on ethical grounds, while active ownership relates to the exercise of ownership rights by an investor such as an SWF over its investee companies. Typically, this involves the exercise of voting rights at shareholder meetings, direct engagement with management or other forms of influence.

[66] Rigorous data in this area is difficult to source. This estimate of ad hoc ethical investment obligations is based on the author's reconciliation of two different surveys of responsible investment among SWFs and institutional investors. As these studies cover distinct sample sets and do not fully disclose their methodology for what counts as a sovereign fund or ethical obligations, consistency across surveys is problematic. For example, the 2010 Truman Scoreboard finds that of 53 government investment funds surveyed, 14 SWFs had explicit ethical investment guidelines. In contrast, the 2012 Future Fund Senate Submission which reviewed 22 'select' sovereign wealth and pension funds identified the use of exclusions by 11 funds and human rights obligations

tion to take ethical considerations into account in *all* investment decisions. Instead, this approach singles out particular industries or companies whose products must be banned given characteristics of the industry or because such products violate norms the investors want to uphold. The 'industry' or 'product' approach to exclusions *may*, but not definitely, raise human rights considerations. Consider that assets most commonly banned under this targeted approach include tobacco, cluster munitions, landmine, nuclear and whaling industry products, some of which more readily raise human rights issues.[67] Interestingly, the majority of sovereign funds with targeted ethical obligations do not *explicitly* identify human rights obligations as considerations,[68] perhaps underscoring a general reluctance to adopt human rights concerns in the ethical investment discourse.

I set out above that sovereign funds must adopt a legal obligation to invest ethically as part of their investment mandate. A question then arises as to whether the targeted approach to ethical obligations is sufficient in light of this demand. The central difference between an *integrated* ethical investment mandate and *targeted* ethical obligations is that the former places funds under a 'thick' duty where ethical considerations assume equivalent status to other components of the investment mandate. This makes it more likely that funds will meet my normative demand to shield citizens' ethical exposure from complicity in immoral return seeking.

In contrast the larger group of funds with *isolated* ethical obligations are only subject to a 'thin' duty. Targeted requirements do not require a whole-of-portfolio outlook regarding ethical implications of investment decisions. Instead, the fulfilment of the ethically *un*constrained investment mandate is top priority, while compliance with ad hoc obligations is given separate consideration. In practice, this circumscribed approach to ethical investing means an SWF with *targeted* obligations is at higher risk of ethical transgressions in its wider portfolio not covered by the select ethical constraints. Accordingly, it is only through full incorporation of ethical obligations into the overarching investment mandate that sovereign funds are likely to meet my normative demands. From a human rights perspective, an SWF mandate that *explicitly* identifies the protection of human rights is necessary where a core objective is to shield citizen-owners from unintended complicity in human rights violations specifically.

VII NEW ZEALAND: A ROLE MODEL SOVEREIGN INVESTOR FOR HUMAN RIGHTS?

In closing, I consider the effectiveness of one of our 'role model' sovereign funds. Of the two funds that boast an integrated ethical investment mandate, I examine New Zealand.

in operational behaviour within 4 funds. Future Fund, 'Underlying Data for Senate Submission', private communication with author, December 2012. The figure of 18 funds here comes from reconciling these two surveys and accounting for overlap between funds.

[67] For instance, the morally objectionable aspects of landmine, nuclear or cluster munitions products are immediately intelligible in a human rights framework concerned with the right to life, security and freedom from war. In contrast, whaling products are morally objectionable insofar as they violate animal *contra* human rights.

[68] Again, comprehensive data is difficult to source. The Future Fund's survey of 22 SWFs identified 3 funds with explicit human rights obligations: Sweden's AP1-4 funds; Denmark's ATP and Norway's GPFG. Future Fund (n 66).

Not only is it the less studied of the two,[69] but some controversial divestments by the fund offer lessons for effective operationalisation of ethical investment practices that seek to protect citizen-owners' moral agency.

Since the NZSF's inception in 2003, the fund has been subject to a statutory responsible investment (RI) obligation. The overarching investment mandate requires the fund's Board, known as the Guardians,

> to invest the Fund on a prudent, commercial basis . . . in a manner consistent with:
>
> (a) best-practice portfolio management; and
> (b) maximising return without undue risk to the Fund as a whole; and
> (c) avoiding prejudice to New Zealand's reputation as a responsible member of the world community.[70]

From the citizen-owner perspective, the formulation of this 'responsible investment' obligation ground in 'reputational' concerns for the state is weak. It suggests the state should act ethically in investing only where it would be embarrassed not to do so. Moreover, the lack of clarity in the legislation about the hierarchical ordering[71] of these obligations leaves open the possibility that RI is treated as subservient to return-maximisation and best-practice management where these conflict. Promisingly, the Guardians interpreted the mandate to imply none of the three components has precedence over the other, so each must be taken in account when considering investment issues.[72]

Recent policy statements on the fund's RI approach also bode well from an ethical perspective, showing an evolution in the prioritisation of ethical considerations in the fund's investment strategy. The Board recently affirmed its belief in the importance of 'integrating consideration of environmental, social and governance (ESG) issues into the investment decision making process',[73] revealing an evolution from their initial interpretation of the RI obligation as requiring compliance 'with New Zealand Treaties and conventions such as those promulgated by the United Nations and International Labour Organization'.[74] Today, the Guardians espouse 'the belief that long-term financial performance can be affected by ESG issues' and have developed a Responsible Investment Framework that identifies 'investment, engagement, voting, exclusion and/or divestment from the Fund'[75] as relevant actions for management to take on RI issues.

Of these methods, the Guardians' preference is for active strategies of engagement rather than exclusion.[76] This involves directly communicating with investee companies or external managers, often collaboratively with other large investors, where there may be or is likely to be a breach of ESG standards, and trying to foster better corporate govern-

[69] This may be because the Norwegian GPFG has an explicit obligation to consider human rights violations, which allows the fund to exclude companies where 'there is an unacceptable risk that the company contributes to or is responsible for . . . serious or systematic human rights violations, such as murder, torture, deprivation of liberty, forced labour, the worst forms of child labour and other child exploitation'.

[70] New Zealand Superannuation and Retirement Income Act 2001, s 58(2)(c).

[71] Richardson (n 47) 18.

[72] NZSF, Responsible Investment Framework, September 2012, 3.

[73] NZSF, Statement of Investment Policies, Standards and Procedures , 1 July 2011.

[74] Mercer Consulting, *Review of the Guardians of New Zealand Superannuation*, 28 October 2009 (New Zealand, Mercer) 36.

[75] NZSF (n 73).

[76] The Guardians' SRI strategy focuses 'on acting as a responsible shareholder and fostering transparent corporate governance rather than necessarily excluding shares or securities'. See Controller and Auditor-General, *Guardians of New Zealand Superannuation: Governance and Management of the New Zealand Superannuation Fund* (New Zealand Government, May 2008), para 3.62.

ance. During 2011/12, the NZSF engaged with 37 companies on human rights and safety, 18 on severe environmental damage, 22 on bribery and corruption, 376 on meeting best reporting practices and three NZ companies on governance issues.[77] The majority of these engagements were part of collaborative efforts, with 16 companies in the portfolio approached directly by the Guardians.[78]

As part of this active approach, the Guardians have described exclusions as a measure of 'last resort',[79] and 'divestment as a form of failure',[80] although recent policy statements have toned down that language.[81] Despite the preference for engagement, the NZSF has an active exclusions policy that identifies five industries where entities directly involved in product manufacture will be automatically excluded or divested, including: (1) cluster munitions, (2) testing of nuclear explosive devices, (3) anti-personnel mines, (4) tobacco and (5) whale meat. Specialist screening companies are used to identify companies eligible for engagement, exclusion and divestment. As of August 2012, 115 companies have been excluded under these provisions, constituting a rapid escalation of this strategy from just 33 exclusions or divestments by June 2009.[82] This growth is largely being driven by tobacco-related entities, constituting almost 85 per cent of all exclusions.[83]

How effective is this RI approach in light of our demands for citizen-owners of SWFs to be properly shielded from complicity in unethical investment? Recent controversy over the NZSF's handling of some of its equity holdings that involved human rights violations offers some lessons for the operationalisation of responsible investing by sovereign funds where part of the objective is to respect the ethical interests of citizen-owners. The episode involved the NZSF's equity holdings in mining giants Freeport McMoRan Copper & Gold (Freeport) and Rio Tinto (Rio). In a scathing critique in 2011, freelance journalist Karen Abplanalp criticised the NZSF Guardians for their continued holding in Freeport given fresh evidence of human rights breaches, corruption and environmental harm at the Grasberg mine.[84] Abplanalp queried whether the NZSF's stated preference for engagement rather than exclusion was out of line with citizens' expectations of the fund's RI policy.

The NZSF defended its investment on engagement grounds with CEO Adrian Orr arguing that retaining the holding allowed the Guardians to continue influencing the company in an effort to improve the situation for West Papuans. In an official response to the article, the Guardians clarified that the holdings were passive investments gained

[77] NZSF, *Annual Report* (New Zealand, NZSF, 2012) 40.

[78] These direct engagements were primarily on human rights and safety issues, ibid.

[79] Richardson (n 47) 20, quoting the 2010 Annual Report.

[80] NZSF CEO Adrian Orr quoted in K Abplanalp, 'Blood Money', *Metro Magazine*, December 2011, www.pmc.aut.ac.nz/sites/default/files/file_bin/201111/Metro_Dec2011_FreeportSuperfund_pp43-49.pdf, accessed 15 May 2013.

[81] Interestingly, the 2012 Annual Report does not present these options in hierarchical order or indicate such a clear preference for engagement, possibly as a result of the fund's recent bending to public pressure over their reluctance to divest from several controversial holdings. Exclusions remain an important part of the Guardians overall RI process, although the bulk of RI activity was directed towards engagement. NZSF (n 72) 40.

[82] See the Guardians' Responsible Investment in Practice Reports, www.nzsuperfund.co.nz/index.asp?pageID=2145855970, accessed 15 May 2013.

[83] 97 of the 115 excluded companies were involved in tobacco manufacture. See NZSF, *Companies excluded from the New Zealand Superannuation Fund as at 31 August 2012*, www.nzsuperfund.co.nz/files/Responsible%20Investment%20documents/Exclusion_list_31_August_2012_for_web.pdf, accessed 15 May 2013.

[84] In October 2011 Indonesian police killed two unarmed, striking miners and strong evidence continued to emerge of corrupt payments to the Indonesian military to facilitate the mining project. See Abplanalp (n 80) 40.

through index investing, which meant they had not 'picked' the stock. They also challenged the equation of responsible investing with exclusion, arguing that their engagement approach fully recognised the failed ESG standards in Freeport and sought to address those by changing company behaviour, rather than walking away through divestment or exclusion. On the Guardians' view, their attempts to engage with Freeport management for the past five years would have the 'biggest impact on the affected people and environments'.[85]

Whether in the long term engagement could achieve more than exclusion is of less relevance than if the Guardians' approach endowed New Zealand citizen-owners with a sense of control over their ethical agency in relation to the fund's activities. As Abplanalp mused:

> Is the fund doing good, as [CEO Adrian] Orr believes, or simply helping to prop up activities that would be illegal in this country – activities that most New Zealanders would be horrified to support let alone make money from, if they were happening here? Do we want our pensions paid for in this way?[86]

In a worrying sign for democratic control of New Zealander citizens over NZSF investment, the Guardians' response to the article highlighted that 'responsible investment is not about making New Zealanders feel good about the Guardians' Investments'. The Guardians reiterated that investment decisions must make sense from an RI and a commercial perspective, underscoring that the 'Guardians cannot and do not invest to be popular'.[87]

While funds should avoid populist investment decisions, the case at hand represents a subtler dilemma in how best to give effect to citizens a sense of control over their sovereign wealth, particularly where embraced human rights values of the owning citizenry are at stake. Here, there was no question as to whether the company failed to meet the NZSF's ESG standards. The issue was whether this should be dealt with through engagement or exclusion. Significantly, the NZSF divested its NZ$1.28 million holding in Freeport in September 2012 on account of 'breaches of human rights standards by security forces around the Grasberg mine, and concerns over requirements for direct payments to government security forces'.[88] In defending the decision, the NZSF said it reached a conclusion that further engagement would not be successful and that such a consideration was a relevant factor in deciding which strategy to pursue. The final decision to divest suggests that there was a gap between popular expectations of New Zealand citizens and the Guardians' approach to ethical investment. If the New Zealand case is instructive, it suggests that where gross violations of human rights abuses are concerned, the preferable strategy for SWFs seeking to adequately protect citizen-owners from complicity is to exclude or divest, not engage.

[85] NZSF, *Guardians Respond to Metro Magazine Story, December 2011*, 28 November 2011, www.nzsuperfund.co.nz/files/FINAL%20VERSION%20Media_release_about_Metro_story.pdf, accessed 15 May 2013.

[86] Abplanalp (n 80) 39.

[87] NZSF (n 84) 2.

[88] NZSF, 'New Zealand Superannuation Fund excludes four companies on responsible investment grounds', Press Release, 26 September 2012, www.nzsuperfund.co.nz/news.asp?pageID=2145831983&RefID=2141742302, accessed 30 May 2013.

VIII CONCLUSION

Although sovereign funds continue to assume more influence as investors internationally, their embrace of ethical investment practices remains stagnant, making the case for ethical constraints on their investment more urgent. Unlike peer private investors, sovereigns coercively implicate their citizen-body in their investment activities. A fiduciary approach to these funds demands that the interests – and crucially the ethical interests – of their citizen-owners must always be foremost in the decision making of the sovereign fund. To this end, this chapter argued that sovereign funds should be subject to a legally entrenched RI obligation that governs the whole portfolio, not just limited exemptions. But such an obligation must be operationalised effectively if it is to truly endow citizen-owners with control over their government agent and their own ethical agency. The experience of New Zealand suggests that in the case of investments that involve egregious human rights violations, a strict exclusion approach rather than engagement with investee companies or governments is preferable since citizens cannot tolerate any complicity in, let alone profit from, such violations as occurs under engagement strategies.

12

Sovereign Financing and the Human Rights Responsibilities of Private Creditors

NICOLA JÄGERS

I INTRODUCTION

THE BURGEONING SUPPLY of sovereign debt is increasingly hampering the effective enjoyment of human rights in many countries. The international community of states has been occupied with addressing the adverse impact of unsustainable foreign debt on human rights for many years but so far has failed to come up with a durable solution despite the adoption of numerous resolutions and declarations.[1] States bear the prime responsibility for ensuring people can enjoy their human rights despite increasing debt stocks. Not only debtor states but also creditors share responsibility for preventing and resolving debt situations that have a negative impact on human rights.[2] There is no uniformity when it comes to lenders, which may consist of states, multilateral lenders (financial institutions) and commercial lenders. As will be discussed, private creditors, such as commercial banks and organised bondholders, also play an important role in the existing excessive debt burdens.

Parallel to the ongoing financial crisis and the ever-increasing sovereign debt is the evolving debate on responsibilities of corporations for human rights in general. However, as several authors have pointed out, the two developments only rarely meet.[3]

This chapter will analyse the emerging human rights responsibilities of corporations in relation to private creditors of sovereign financing. How and why is the emerging framework on corporate human rights responsibilities relevant in the context of adverse human rights effects of sovereign financing?

Since the start of the financial crisis in 2008, the supply of sovereign debt of many states has increased significantly.[4] The rise of sovereign debt has occurred both in developing and

[1] Such as the Millennium Development Goals and the Monterrey Consensus of the international Conference on Financing for Development.

[2] UN Doc A/HRC/20/23, 10 April 2011, *United Nations Guiding Principles on Foreign Debt and Human Rights* (UNGPs on foreign debt and human rights), para 23.

[3] As, inter alia, pointed out by M Dowell-Jones and D Kinley, 'large swaths of the financial system that have important consequences for human rights realisation have barely been touched on by human rights analysis': 'Minding the Gap: Global Finance and Human Rights' (2011) 25(2) *Ethics and International Affairs* 183. See also, by the same authors, 'The Monster under the Bed: Financial Services and the Ruggie Framework' in R Mares (ed), *The UN Guiding Principles on Business and Human Rights. Foundations and Implementation* (Leiden, Martinus Nijhoff Publishers, 2012) 193–216.

[4] C Primo Braga and G Vincelette (eds), *Sovereign Debt and The Financial Crisis. Will This Time Be Different?* (Washington DC, World Bank, 2011) 2.

developed countries. According to a 2011 study by the World Bank, the sovereign debt of industrialised countries has risen sharply. In 2008 the net sovereign borrowing by the United Kingdom and the United States was five times larger than the average of the preceding five years.[5] The IMF expects that in advanced economies government debt-to-GDP ratios will reach 110 per cent by 2015, an increase of almost 40 per cent compared to pre-crisis levels.[6] IMF statistics furthermore point out that many middle-income countries have also witnessed a deterioration of their debt positions (albeit less dramatic when compared to the developed countries). Forty per cent of low-income countries either are already in debt distress or are facing a high risk of this happening.[7] The total external debt of emerging and developing economies continues to rise, from US$2,678.4 billion in 2003 to US$5,414.6 billion in 2010 and it was projected to rise to US$6,446.3 billion in 2012.[8]

The sharp increase of sovereign debt is the result of radical measures states have taken to address the impact of the crises such as the bailout of corporate sectors, the overhaul of financial regulatory systems and the launching of fiscal stimulus packages. As will be discussed in the next section this high level of debt has a serious impact on the enjoyment of human rights.

This chapter addresses the emerging framework for corporate human rights responsibility in relation to the sovereign debt crisis. The first section will address the impact of sovereign debt on the enjoyment of human rights, specifically on economic, social and cultural rights. Then the chapter addresses the role of private creditors in sovereign financing. The last decades have seen a heightened interest in the responsibilities of corporations for human rights in general, an interest that has taken on a new dynamic with the work of the former UN Special Representative to the Secretary General on the issue of business and human rights, Professor John Ruggie (hereinafter UN Special Representative or SRSG).[9] The remaining sections of this chapter will address what the evolving debate on corporate responsibility implies in the context of sovereign lending. The third section will discuss what, if any, obligations international human rights law currently places on corporations in the context of sovereign financing. Subsequently, the chapter turns to the burgeoning body of soft law, standards and regulations in the field of business and human rights in general and in the context of financing in particular. In Section VI, some of the problems and pitfalls in operationalising the identified corporate responsibility in the field of sovereign financing will be addressed. Finally, the chapter concludes with a few observations concerning the way forward.

[5] ibid.

[6] ibid.

[7] Ibid.

[8] *UNGPs on Foreign Debt and Human Rights*, 10 April 2011 (n 2) para. 2.

[9] In 2005 the UN appointed Professor John Ruggie as the Special Representative to the Secretary General to further examine the relationship between human rights and business. He developed the three pillar policy framework (Protect, Respect, Remedy) consisting of the State obligation to protect human rights, the corporations' responsibility to respect human rights and, finally, the duty to ensure access to remedies. This PRR framework was adopted in 2008 by the Human Rights Council. The mandate of the SRSG was then extended to work on further clarifying the PRR Framework, which resulted in the Guiding Principles, which were unanimously adopted by the Human Rights Council in 2011.

II IMPACT OF FOREIGN DEBT ON THE ENJOYMENT OF HUMAN RIGHTS

Sovereign debt is connected to the enjoyment of human rights in various ways. The possibility for states to obtain credit is essential for the management of their financial affairs. Borrowing in times of revenue shortfall and repayment in times of surplus provide for the possibility of smoothing out spending without directly placing the burden on taxpayers. The possibility for states to borrow money has also become crucial to establish conditions to fulfil human rights obligations. The obligations in relation to economic, social and cultural rights require that states take steps 'to the maximum of their available resources' to progressively achieve the full realisation of these rights.[10] Moreover, states are under the obligation of non-retrogression.[11] Whether a state is living up to these rights is mostly measured by looking at its expenditure. Present-day reality is that most states can only live up to their human rights obligations by increasing their debt.

However, large burdens of debt significantly curtail the possibilities of states to fulfil their human rights obligations, especially concerning economic, social and cultural rights. Debt distress limits the possibility of states to provide social services that are necessary to ensure an adequate standard of living. The bodies supervising the international human rights treaties have time and again pointed out how external debts hamper the efforts of lender states to enhance the enjoyment of human rights.[12] The correlation between excessive sovereign debt and the enjoyment of human rights is clear when we see that states after debt relief have been able to scale up their social investment and spending on poverty reduction.[13]

As stated above, this problem is no longer only affecting the poor countries but increasingly developed countries are experiencing the problems of living up to their human rights obligations in the area of economic, social and cultural rights due to the unsustainable debt burden. Moreover, external debts will not only affect the fulfilment of economic, social and cultural rights but may also affect civil and political rights. High burdens of debt may, for example, affect issues such as legal aid limiting access to the courts. Ultimately, sovereign debt crises might even lead to escalating human rights violations given the negative impact that sovereign debt can have on peace and security. There is an intrinsic correlation between sovereign debt and the outbreak of civil war.[14] Overall,

[10] See Article 2 International Covenant on Economic, Social and Cultural Rights (ICESCR) and General Comment No 3.

[11] This refers to the obligation that states should not deliberately allow the existing protection of economic, social and cultural rights to deteriorate unless there are strong justifications for a retrogressive measure. General Comment No 3, para 9.

[12] For an overview of Concluding Observations in which treaty bodies have addressed issues relating to foreign debt see: www2.ohchr.org/english/issues/development/debt/docs/table_TB_on_foreign_debt.doc, accessed 13 February 2014.

[13] *UNGPs on Foreign Debt and Human Rights*, 10 April 2011, introduction.

[14] The correlation between unsustainable levels of sovereign debt and armed conflict has been addressed by informal arrangements that provide possibilities for conditional rescheduling such as the Heavily Indebted Poor Countries Initiative (HIPCI). These arrangements, however, exclusively address states. Private creditors are not addressed and remain free to sue a state disrupting any efforts the debtor state may undertake to restructure its debts and avoid the possible escalation into armed conflict. This chapter will focus on the adverse human rights impact of sovereign debt that follows from the restricting effect of such debt on the possibilities of states to live up to their human rights obligations before the situation actually aggravates into a situation of armed conflict. For more on the relation between sovereign debt and armed conflict, see M Goldmann, 'Sovereign Debt Crises

it is clear that high levels of sovereign debt have a serious negative impact on the enjoyment of human rights. The global financial and economic crises have made this issue even more pressing.[15]

Another link between sovereign financing and the enjoyment of human rights occurs when the money provided goes to a sovereign that violates human rights. It may be argued that the financial support enables the regime to violate human rights or to continue doing so.

Finally, sovereign financing may have an adverse impact on the enjoyment of human rights as a result of the conditions that notably the international institutional lenders such as the World Bank and the International Monetary Fund (IMF), attach to their loans. Over the past decades, programmes of structural adjustment and other loan conditionalities resulted in deep cuts in public sector spending with detrimental consequences for the enjoyment of human rights in certain debtor countries.[16]

III ROLE OF PRIVATE CREDITORS IN FINANCING SOVEREIGN DEBT

States owe money to a variety of creditors: other states, international financial institutions and private agents. In this chapter, the focus is on the role of the latter, the private sector. Private creditors are connected to sovereign debt in several ways. First, sovereign debt is owed to private creditors, either directly or by means of bonds.[17] Commercial banks may extend credit directly to sovereigns. However, since the 1980s, virtually all claims of private lenders have been passed on in the bond market.[18] As a result private creditors are no longer only banks but encompass a broad range of actors such as insurance companies, pension funds and individuals. By issuing bonds, which guarantee repayment of the sum including interest, states can acquire funds from all over the world. Dowell-Jones and Kinley state that sovereign bonds are 'intimately associated with the

as Triggers of Armed Conflict: Restructuring under Chapter VII of the UN Charter?'(2012) 4 *Goettingen Journal of International Law* 153–75, arguing that the UN Security Council should use its powers to order restructuring of sovereign debt before escalation into armed conflict.

[15] In response to the financial and economic crises states have implemented a range of austerity measures. There is increasing concern about the negative human rights impact of these measures, especially on the rights of the poor. See, inter alia, the reports and statements of the Special Rapporteur on Extreme Poverty and Human Rights, Ms Magdalena Sepulveda: www.ohchr.org/EN/Issues/Poverty/Pages/Impactofausteritymeasures ontheenjoymentHR.aspx, accessed 30 September 2013.

[16] The focus of this chapter is on private lenders, which are taken not to include the intergovernmental international financial institutions (IFIs). The impact of the conditionalities attached to loans provided by the IFIs and questions of their responsibility are therefore beyond the scope of this chapter. For more on the issue of the human rights obligations of the IFIs see, inter alia, M Darrow, *Between Light and Shadow, the World bank, the International Monetary Fund and International Human Rights Law* (Oxford, Hart Publishing, 2003).

[17] The author realises that there are many more, highly complex financial products provided by private creditors that may play a role in the context of sovereign financing. See for more information on such products, inter alia, the explanation of derivatives by Dowell-Jones and Kinley. However, as these authors point out, the relationship of these products to is even more opaque than is the case with bonds. Dowell-Jones and Kinley, 'Minding the Gap' (n 3) 193.

[18] C Barry, 'Sovereign Debt, Human Rights, and Policy Conditionality' (2011) 19(3) *The Journal of Political Philosophy* 284.The bond markets are now estimated to be worth over $90 trillion of which sovereign bonds are the largest segment ($34 trillion). For more on the development starting in the 1980s which resulted in large amounts of sovereign debt being in the hands of dispersed private bondholders, see Goldmann, (n 14), and the reference mentioned in footnote 36 See also, Dowell-Jones and Kinley, 'Minding the Gap' (n 3) 190 and the references mentioned there in fn 26.

realization of a state's human rights obligations, such as those relating to welfare, health and education'.[19] As these authors point out:

> the current sovereign debt problems in the Euro zone demonstrate, the relationship between sovereign spending, the enjoyment of human rights, and the bond markets is multi-facet; and there are far-reaching economic consequences of bond market dynamics that have a critical impact on human rights by influencing the capacity of states to deliver on their human rights obligations.[20]

A vicious circle exists where states are required to issue new bonds simply to pay the interest on existing debt and to pay off bonds that have matured. As Dowell-Jones and Kinley put it 'the bond markets can effectively hold states to ransom'.[21]

A particular group of private sovereign funders in this context is the category of creditors that is often referred to as 'vulture creditors'. This is a term applied to private institutions that purchase defaulted debt obligations of sovereign borrowers in the secondary market, typically for a small fraction of the face value of the instrument. Subsequently, 'vulture creditors' threaten or commence legal action to recover the full amount due.[22]

Besides private agents that lend to sovereigns directly or bondholders, private creditors are connected to sovereign debt in another, more indirect way. Excessive borrowing in the private sector is increasing the overall level of debt as unsustainable levels of private debt are increasingly forcing governments to take over private sector debts.[23] The inflation of private debt is threatening the achievements of development goals in developing countries.[24]

In sum, excessive levels of sovereign debt hamper the effective enjoyment of human rights and private agents belong to the group of creditors to whom the sovereign debt is owed. Attention will now turn to the question whether any human rights obligations for these private actors can be discerned. This will be discussed by looking at the issue of private sovereign financing and its negative impact on human rights from two perspectives.

First, the question arises whether a private creditor may actually be held legally complicit when lending money to regimes that commit egregious human rights violations. It can be stated that financing has enabled certain regimes to continue violating human rights even despite the existence of political boycotts. Secondly, it may be argued that private creditors indirectly contribute to the curtailing of a state's possibility of fulfilling its human rights obligations as was discussed above. Both perspectives will be addressed in the next section.

[19] Dowell-Jones and Kinley, 'Minding the Gap' (n 3) 190.

[20] ibid.

[21] ibid, 192.

[22] For more on the issue of vulture funds see: L Bucheit and M Gulati, 'Responsible Sovereign Lending and Borrowing', *Discussion Papers United Nations Conference on Trade and Development*, No 198, April 2010, 2.

[23] For example, in the Netherlands, two of the four major banks have been nationalised to avoid their collapse. The latest nationalisation occurred on 1 February 2013 when the Dutch government bailed out the bank and insurance company SNS Reaal for the amount of $14 billion. The same kind of bailout has been occurring across Europe since the 2008 financial crisis.

[24] After Mexico first defaulted in August 1982, the country faced another debt crisis in the 1990s, followed by East Asia, Russia, Brazil, Turkey and Argentina, due to excessive borrowing by the private sector. www.ohchr.org/EN/Issues/Development/IEDebt/Pages/HRightsAndForeignDebt.aspx, accessed 13 February 2014. Developing countries are facing unsustainable private debt burdens 12 years after a global campaign successfully advocated the cancellation of some of the world's poorest countries' public debt, www.ohchr.org/EN/Issues/Development/IEDebt/Pages/HRightsAndForeignDebt.aspx, accessed 30 September 2013.

IV HUMAN RIGHTS OBLIGATIONS OF PRIVATE CREDITORS

In the previous sections it has been demonstrated that burgeoning sovereign debt is a major impediment to the realisation of human rights. Furthermore, the role played by private creditors in sovereign financing was discussed. In this section, attention turns to the question whether human rights obligations and/or responsibilities can be discerned that are applicable to these private creditors. First, attention will be given to international human rights law in general. What does this body of law provide concerning obligations of corporations for human rights violations and how is this relevant in the context of sovereign financing?

The traditional perception of international human rights law is that it protects individuals against the excesses of state power and therefore only binds states. Indeed there is no international human rights regime that directly addresses corporations. Therefore, also in the context of sovereign debt, the human rights supervisory bodies focus on the state. These treaty bodies have repeatedly stressed the obligations of lending countries to live up to their human rights obligations. Moreover, the obligations of creditor countries in the field of international cooperation and assistance to facilitate the full realisation of economic social and cultural rights have been pointed out.[25] These obligations also imply that international measures aimed at debt relief take the realisation of economic, social and cultural rights into account.[26] In sum, obligations to address the human rights impacts of sovereign debt rest primarily on states.

Nevertheless, at the same time several developments are permeating the orthodox view that human rights law can exclusively only be applicable to states. First, peremptory norms, norms of *jus cogens*, such as the prohibition of genocide or slavery are directly applicable to corporations.[27] This is reflected at the national level where an increasing number of states have incorporated the provisions in the Rome Statute of the International Criminal Court into their national legislation to include the possibility of prosecuting legal entities for such crimes.[28] The fact that there is no international enforcement mechanism whereby corporations can be held directly accountable should not mistakenly be taken to imply that the prohibition on committing international crimes does not directly apply to corporations.[29] Moreover, there has been an explosion of soft law standards

[25] See, inter alia, General Comment No 2 (1990) para 9; General Comment No 3 (1990) paras 13, 14; General Comment No 11 (1999) para 9; General Comment No 18 (2005) para 30 of the Committee on Economic, Social and Cultural Rights. More in general on the obligations of states to refrain from conduct that will impair the ability of other states to live up to their economic, social and cultural rights, see the *Maastricht Principles on Extraterritorial Obligations of States in the Area of Economic, Social and Cultural Rights*, para 21.

[26] This, according to the Office of the High Commissioner of Human Rights, may point in the direction of major debt relief initiatives. http://www.ohchr.org/EN/Issues/Development/IEDebt/Pages/InternationalStandards.aspx#information, accessed 14 February 2014.

[27] See, inter alia, A Clapham, *Human Rights Obligations of Non-State Actors* (Oxford, Oxford University Press, 2006); A Ramasastry, 'Corporate Complicity: From Nuremberg to Rangoon: an Examination of Forced Labor Cases and Their Impact on the Liability of Multinational Corporations' (2002) 20(1) *Berkeley Journal of International Law* 95; S Ratner, 'Corporations and Human Rights: A Theory of Legal Responsibility' (2001) 111 *Yale Law Journal* 443–545.

[28] See the 2006 report *Commerce, Crime and Conflict* by the Norwegian research institute Fafo surveying the possibility of holding corporations accountable for grave human rights crimes across 16 jurisdictions. Available at: www.fafo.no/pub/rapp/536/536.pdf, accessed 14 February 2014). The SRSG also referred to this increasing web of corporate liability for international crimes. See Commentary to UNGP 23.

[29] As Ratner has observed this 'confuses the existence of responsibility with the mode of implementing it' (n 27) 395. However, for a diverging view see JH Knox, 'The Ruggie Rules: Applying Human Rights Rules to

articulating human rights norms that are directly applicable to corporations. A spillover effect of these soft law norms into hard, binding law can be witnessed, solidifying the expected behaviour of corporations in this field.[30] And, finally, there is an increasing body of domestic litigation where corporations are being held accountable for human rights violations abroad. The litigation that has developed under the Alien Tort Statute (ATS) is the most renowned example. However, also in other jurisdictions a growing number of so-called foreign direct liability cases are being brought before the domestic courts.[31]

In sum, the conclusion can be drawn that the orthodox view that international human rights law is exclusively applicable to states is being permeated by developments pointing towards the applicability of human rights norms to corporations. From these scattered developments the rudiments of a human rights framework that is applicable to corporations may be discerned.

What does this evolution of the applicability of human rights norms to private actors imply in the context of sovereign lending by private creditors? As discussed above, the link between private lenders and human rights can be discussed from two perspectives. First, the most direct link between private creditors and adverse human rights effects of sovereign financing exists where private funds go or have gone to criminal or corrupt regimes and as such may have been used to commit egregious human rights violations. Second, the impeding effects of excessive burdens of sovereign debt on the realisation of human rights by states are partly enabled by private funders. This points to a more indirect link between private creditors and adverse human rights effects of sovereign financing that are the result of sovereign decisions concerning the allocation of funds. The relevance of the developing discourse on corporate human rights responsibilities in this specific context will also be discussed.

A Corporate Human Rights Complicity

Writing on the complex relationship between foreign economic assistance and human rights, Cassese points out what he calls a closed circle of 'cause' and 'effect'.[32] Referring to the case of Chile, he argues that not only does foreign economic assistance permit the perpetuation of human rights violations, the occurrence of human rights violations may actually attract foreign enterprises to invest in a country because of the cheap labour, low costs of production and absence of social unrest.[33] The relationship between foreign economic assistance and human rights raises the question whether human rights obligations

Corporations' in R Mares (ed), *The UN Guiding Principles on Business and Human Rights* (Antwerp, Brill, 2012) 51–83.

[30] D Kinley and J Tadaki, 'From Talk to Walk: The Emergence of Human Rights Responsibilities for Corporations under International Law' (2004) 44(4) *Virginia Journal of International Law* 956–58. Moreover, elements of the non-binding UN Protect-Respect-Remedy Framework (which will be discussed below) are hardening into hard, binding law. Section 1503 of the Wall Street Reform Act (the Dodd-Frank Act), which mandates corporations to conduct human rights due diligence down their supply chain, is a prime example. For more on this act see JC Drimmer and NJ Phillips, 'Sunlight for the Heart of Darkness: Conflict Minerals and the First Wave of SEC Regulation of Social Issues' (2012) 6(1) *Human Rights and International Legal Discourse* 131–58.

[31] L Enneking, Foreign Direct Liability and Beyond: Exploring the Role of Tort Law in Promoting International Corporate Social Responsibility and Accountability (The Hague, Eleven International Publishing, 2012).

[32] A Cassese, 'Foreign Economic Assistance and Respect for Civil and Political Rights: Chile – A Case Study' (1979) 14 *Texas International Law Journal* 263.

[33] ibid.

for private creditors can be discerned where private funds have gone to criminal or corrupt regimes that have subsequently committed human rights violations. Such a situation may give rise to questions of corporate complicity.[34] Bohoslavsky and Opgenhaffen offer an example in their study on the role of foreign financial institutions in sponsoring the Argentinean dictatorship from 1976 to 1983.[35] They point out that the financial support offered by private creditors can be essential for upholding such an illegal regime. According to the authors, evidence suggests that 'particular banks were enabling the junta to continue to function in a world that had largely shut down previous channels of economic and political support'.[36] They come to the conclusion that the significance of the role of the private funders warrants examination of the question whether further civil legal action can be taken against them for complicity in crimes against humanity.[37]

Is it possible to state that a corporate creditor is complicit when providing credit to a regime committing mass human rights violations? As pointed out by the SRSG, the notion of complicity in the context of business and human rights has both a legal and non-legal meaning. In a non-legal meaning, corporations may be seen to be complicit in human rights violations if they are seen to benefit from the human rights abuses committed by that other party.[38] It is beyond the scope of this chapter to examine the many different aspects related to the development of the notion of corporate complicity.[39] Here, a few remarks will be made concerning the main elements of corporate complicity for gross human rights violations that can be discerned and the complexities involved in the context of private creditors and sovereign financing.

The legal notion of corporate complicity in human rights violations has evolved starting with the judgments of the Nuremburg Tribunal to the contemporary corporate complicity cases that have been brought before the US domestic courts, especially under the ATS. This body of litigation mostly concerns situations in which corporations have allegedly contributed to or benefited from human rights violations committed by others. Hence, the current understanding of corporate complicity for human rights violations stems from developments both in civil and in criminal law. In 2008 the International Commission of Jurists (ICJ) published a report on corporate complicity for human rights violations drawing on developments in civil and criminal law across a number of jurisdictions.[40] In this report, the ICJ broadly identifies the core elements of corporate complicity for human rights violations.[41] Complicity revolves around three main questions relating

[34] Besides the question whether the financial contribution of creditors to regimes that violate human rights might raise questions of complicity in these human rights violations, providing such loans also raises questions whether such loans are valid to start with. This relates to the debate on odious debt. For more on the issue of odious debt see, inter alia, S Michalowski and JP Bohoslavsky, 'Ius Cogens, Transtional Justice and Other Trends of the Debate on Odious Debts: A Response to the World Bank's Discussion Paper on Odious Debts', (2009) 48 *Columbia Journal of Transnational Law* 61–121.

[35] JP Bohoslavsky and V Opgenhaffen, 'The Past and Present of Corporate Complicity: Financing the Argentinian Dictatorship' (2010) 23 *Harvard Human Rights Journal* 157–203. See also: JP Bohoslavsky, 'Tracking Down the Missing Financial Link in Transitional Justice' (2012) 1 *International Human Rights Law Review* 1–39.

[36] Bohoslavsky and Opgenhaffen (n 35) 158.

[37] ibid.

[38] Commentary to UNGP, 17.

[39] See, for a detailed examination, Bohoslavsky and Opgenhaffen (n 35).

[40] See ICJ, *Corporate Complicity and Legal Accountability* (2008) vol I (a synthesis of studies in vols 2 and 3), II (dealing with complicity in national and international law) and III (addressing complicity in civil law).

[41] The ICJ notes that there are considerable differences in approach under criminal law and under civil law and across jurisdictions. However, the ICJ finds that the identified core elements are consistent with all these approaches.

to causation/contribution, knowledge and foreseeability, and proximity. The ICJ concludes that corporate complicity will arise when corporations contribute to 'enabling', 'exacerbating' or 'facilitating' the abuse.[42] Complicity will also arise if the corporation 'knew or should have known that their conduct will contribute to human rights abuses'.[43] Finally, the closer a company is to the abuse, either because of geographic proximity, or because of 'duration, frequency, intensity and/or the nature of the connection', the more likely it is that complicity will arise because the company knew or should have known.[44]

The UN Special Representative comes to the conclusion that the weight of international criminal law jurisprudence indicates that the relevant legal standard for aiding and abetting is 'knowingly providing practical assistance or encouragement that has a substantial effect on the commission of a crime'.[45] In relation to civil liability the ICJ states that '[i]n every jurisdiction intentional and negligent conduct that harms legally protected interests will be considered by the courts to fall short of the legitimate expectations of society, and therefore could potentially give rise to civil liability'.[46] Courts will examine whether the corporation knew about the likelihood that its conduct would cause harm (in the case of intention) or should have known (in the case of negligence).[47] In the case of providing goods or services (finance), the question will be asked whether the company knew or should have known how the funds would be used. In the case of banks, Bohoslavsky and Opgenhaffen, argue that this implies that it must be proven 'either that the lenders knew or could not have *not known* about the criminal activity of the government borrower'.[48] These authors state that in numerous legal systems liability will arise if a creditor fails to adequately assess the credit risk of the borrower and finances being provided facilitating an illegal activity such as international crimes.[49] They state, 'assessing the risks not only includes anticipating the financial capacity to repay the loan but also creates responsibilities around what the borrower presumably does with the money being lent'.[50] As will be discussed below, this line of reasoning is reflected in the soft law standards in the field of finance and human rights. Even though a strong case can be made[51] showing that the provision of loans has supported regimes that were committing gross violations, in practice it will nevertheless often prove difficult to establish corporate complicity in these crimes, inter alia, for reasons of intent and causality.[52] Concerning the element of intent, the ATS litigation presents a somewhat contradictory picture. There are cases where the courts have held that it is sufficient that the company knew or should have known of the illegal activity.[53] However, in the 2009 *Talisman* decision, the court of appeals held that to determine corporate liability under the ATS not only required

[42] ICJ (n 40), vol I, 9.

[43] ibid.

[44] ibid.

[45] Commentary to UNGP 17. There is some controversy concerning the degree of knowledge required for complicity to arise. For more on this see Bohoslavsky and Opgenhaffen (n 35) 168–70.

[46] ICJ (n 40) vol III, 12.

[47] ibid, vol III.

[48] Bohoslavsky and Opgenhaffen (n 35) 170.

[49] ibid, 166–67.

[50] ibid, 167.

[51] As is done by Bohoslavsky and Opgenhaffen (n 35) with regard to the situation in Argentina. See also the examples provided by them concerning the role of finance in relation to the Apartheid regime and the Nazi regime. See also Bohoslavsky (n 35).

[52] Another controversial issue related to the question of complicity is the degree of knowledge of the human rights abuses that is required for complicity to arise. See for more on this Bohoslavsky and Opgenhaffen (n 35).

[53] See, inter alia, *re S Afr Apartheid Litig* 617 F.Supp. . . 2d 228, 260–62 (SDNY 2009).

knowledge but also plaintiffs would have to prove that the corporation purposefully aided and abetted a violation of international law.[54]

For corporate complicity to arise, the intentional or negligent corporate conduct must have contributed to the harm caused. This causual connection, which is a factual question, must be sufficiently close to warrant liability. According to the ICJ, in the case of multi-purpose generic products/services – loans can be considered as such – the law will most likely not consider that the company providing these products or services ought to have foreseen that third parties would be victims of gross human rights abuses through the misuse of their products.[55] Even though the prohibition of international crimes is directly applicable to corporations and a development may be detected towards increasing acknowledgement of the notion of corporate complicity for human rights violations, this kind of complicity in the context of financing seems more contested. It has indeed proven an obstacle in domestic civil proceedings to establish the factual chain of causality between human rights suffered and the money provided by the private creditor.[56] As Bohoslavsky and Opgenhaffen show, the acceptance of sufficient causal link between finance and human rights violations by domestic courts present a mixed picture at best.[57]

If it is established that the company knew or should have known about the harm, the next questions is whether the company took sufficient measures to prevent the harm from materialising.[58] As a point of reference, courts across jurisdictions take 'a reasonable person' to be a responsible careful actor, a 'good member of society'. What this is evolves with evolving societal expectations.[59] As will be discussed below, soft law standards may help interpret such open norms.

In sum, whether or not civil or criminal liability for complicity in gross human rights violations arises depends on causation, knowledge and measures taken. Even if intent or negligence can be proven there are many factors of a factual, contextual nature that will often prevent liability from arising. As argued above, especially in the case of the provision of funds, it may prove difficult to establish sufficient causation. Nevertheless, this, arguably too restricted, notion of corporate complicity for human rights violations is constantly being tested and refined in the increasing litigation against corporate defendants.

B Corporate Human Rights Responsibility for Unsustainable Sovereign Debt

Notwithstanding the fact that this role where there may be a direct and intertwined relationship between the private creditors and criminal regimes is reprehensible, it should be acknowledged that this is only a small part of the human rights problems that arise in the context of sovereign borrowing. Much more widespread is the problem of unsustainable sovereign debt hampering a state in fulfilling its human rights obligations, in particular

[54] *Presbyterian Church of Sudan v Talisman Energy*, Court of Appeals, 2 October 2009.

[55] ICJ (n 40) vol III, 30.

[56] In one of the cases brought under the ATS against banks for financially supporting the Apartheid regime, the *Khulumani* case, the court held that the provided funds could never sufficiently be connected to the crimes because they are not lethal commodities, *In re South African Apartheid Litig*, 617 F. Supp. 2d 228, 257(SDNY 2009) 258.

[57] See, the cases mentioned by Bohoslavsky and Opgenhaffen, (n 35), which present a contradictory picture.

[58] ICJ (n 40) vol III, 16.

[59] ibid.

with regard to economic, social and cultural (ESC) rights. These human rights implications of sovereign lending are of a much more systemic nature. What can be said about the human rights obligations of private creditors in such situations?

As pointed out by several authors,[60] human rights law tends to take what they call a micro approach to human rights violations. This refers to the fact that human rights law is actor orientated, and fulfilling human rights obligations is about allocating responsibilities and accountability to specific actors. As discussed above, this narrow approach has hampered efforts to establish complicity on the side of private creditors lending to sovereigns that have committed gross human rights violations. This micro approach is even more problematic when it concerns the more indirect, systemic negative consequences of sovereign debt for human rights. Clearly the obligations of a state that is not able to ensure the fulfilment of its human rights obligations due to its obligations to repay its debt cannot simply be allocated to private funders of sovereign debt. Responsibility for allocating funds to meet their human rights obligations belongs to the obligations of the borrowing states. Nevertheless, as discussed above, private creditors play an important role in the ever increasing stocks of sovereign debt. Due to the micro approach often taken, international human rights law as applied in domestic proceedings does not offer viable avenues to address the more indirect contribution of private creditors.

The above may lead to the conclusion that international human rights law is of little use in holding private creditors accountable for the adverse human rights impacts of sovereign debt. At the international level there is no mechanism for holding corporations accountable for human rights violations. The translation of international human rights norms into domestic standards of civil and criminal law could go some way in providing for the possibility to hold private lenders liable for financially assisting illegal regimes that subsequently commit gross human rights violations (provided the above-mentioned requirements of knowledge, causality and proximity are met). But only for the small category of *jus cogens* norms does this avenue seem potentially viable (the graver the harm the more easily liability will arise). The human rights problems that arise in relation to private creditors providing sovereign financing encompass a much broader range of rights than only *jus cogens* norms. Furthermore, there will be significant difficulties in the factual assessment of whether the relationship between the private funder and the violations committed is sufficiently intertwined to reach the conclusion of complicity.

The problems caused by the micro approach to human rights implying a need to establish sufficient causality between financing and human rights violations in these highly complex processes might seem to render the human rights discourse largely irrelevant in the context of sovereign financing. Moreover, the micro approach to human rights accountability concerns addressing human rights violations *after* the fact, after the human rights violations have occurred. There is a need to place more emphasis on prevention. Given the scale and the complexities resulting in the negative aspects connected to sovereign financing, it is clear that allocating responsibilities to particular actors, be they a state or a private creditor alone, will not suffice. A much broader effort is necessary involving multiple actors.

The next section will turn to the emerging framework on corporate human rights responsibility. There is a burgeoning body of soft law regulations and principles giving further substance to societal expectations of the role of corporations in relation to human

[60] Dowell-Jones and Kinley (n 3); Bohoslavsky (n 35).

rights in general and in relation to finance in particular. Even though this emerging framework also reflects a micro approach to solving human rights problems, ie allocating human rights responsibilities to a particular actor, it is argued that an analysis of certain elements of this framework is useful for a number of reasons.

One the one hand this body of regulations may have a normative effect influencing what society expects from private creditors and hence may assist in filling open norms in domestic legal proceedings such as those concerning societal expectations.[61] And, on the other, there seems to be growing attention to the necessity of preventing human rights violations from occurring as part of the corporate responsibility to respect human rights. These preventive elements need to inform a broader approach involving multiple stakeholders addressing the issue of the responsibility of private creditors in the sovereign debt crisis.

The next section will address what *ex ante* guidance is provided by first looking at the general UN Guiding Principles on Business and Human Rights before turning to the specific UN Guiding Principles on Sovereign Financing and Human Rights.

V EVOLVING RESPONSIBILITIES

In the many initiatives that have been undertaken by the international community of states to address the adverse impact on human rights of the growing level of unsustainable debt, the responsibilities of private creditors have been acknowledged. For example, in the report following the International Conference on Financing for Development, it was stated 'creditors and debtors share responsibility for preventing and resolving unsustainable debt situations'.[62] Moreover, the general duty of a responsible lender to know his/her borrower has also been acknowledged when it concerns a sovereign borrower. As stated by UNCTAD:

> Once upon a time, it would have been though an act of great impertinence for a private creditor to demand the disclosure of financial and economic information from a sovereign borrower. This same view also mandated that private creditors refrain from inquiring too closely into how a sovereign borrower proposed to spend the proceeds of a loan. The borrowers were, after all, sovereign.[63]

This is no longer the case. Nowadays the view is that sovereign borrowers must be approached with even more solicitude than corporate debtors.[64] Thus, private creditors share an active responsibility to address the negative impact that their financing to sovereigns may have on the enjoyment of human rights. How has this been laid down in soft law standards?

As can be witnessed across practically all corporate sectors, the financial sector has seen a proliferation of codes and standards addressing responsibilities in the field of human rights. At the epicentre of all corporate human rights responsibility standards are the 2011 UN Guiding Principles on Business and Human Rights (UNGPs). As mentioned above, when discussing the relevance of the corporate human rights discourse in the light

[61] See above.

[62] Report of the International Conference on Financing for Development, Monterrey, Mexico, 18–22 March 2002.

[63] Bucheit and Gulati (n 22).

[64] ibid.

of complex global processes such as have occurred following the financial and economic crises and the continuing debt crisis, it is especially important to focus on the elements of prevention. What do the UNGPs provide on the corporate responsibility to prevent human rights violations from occurring?

At the heart of the corporate responsibility for human rights as described in the UNGPs lies the responsibility of corporations to conduct human rights due diligence (HRDD). According to Guiding Principle 17, the core elements of HRDD include the responsibility of corporations to (i) identify actual or potential human rights impacts; (ii) prevent and mitigate human rights impacts thus identified; and (iii) account for impacts and responses to them.[65] This Guiding Principle further provides that HRDD:

(a) should cover adverse human rights impacts that the business enterprise may cause or contribute to through its own activities, or which may be directly linked to its operations, products or services by its business relationships;
(b) will vary in complexity with the size of the business enterprise, the risk of severe human rights impacts, and the nature and context of its operations;
(c) should be ongoing, recognizing that the human rights risks may change over time as the business enterprise's operations and operating context evolve.

Thus, the UNGPs require that corporations have an ongoing, systematic and active procedure in place to seek information about the actual or potential negative impacts of their activities on human rights. Moreover, there is an important preventive element included in the responsibility to conduct HRDD. Corporations need to take appropriate action to prevent potential negative human rights impacts.

As pointed out by Dowell-Jones and Kinley, applying the UN Framework and Guiding Principles to the financial sector in general is fraught with difficulties.[66] Some clarity might be sought by looking at standards that have since been adopted dealing specifically with sovereign financing to identify what these general elements of the corporate responsibility to respect human rights imply in relation to this specific issue.

There is a growing body of soft law standards and guidelines that are particularly relevant for private creditors in the context of sovereign financing. Standards have been developed that elaborate upon the shared responsibility of lenders and borrowers such as the UNCTAD Principles on Responsible Sovereign Lending and Borrowing[67] and the Monterrey Consensus of the International Conference on Financing for Development[68] and the Principles on Responsible Investment.[69] Standards explicitly connecting human rights to financing have emerged most notably in the area of project financing, such as the Performance Standards of the World Bank[70] and the Equator Principles.[71]

Here the focus will be on the recently adopted UN Guiding Principles on Foreign Debt and Human Rights.[72] This standard, adopted by the UN Human Rights Council in 2012,

[65] UNGP 17.

[66] Dowell-Jones and Kinley (n 3).

[67] Adopted in Doha, April 2012. Principle 1 establishes a fiduciary relation between governments and their citizens and a corresponding duty of lenders.

[68] Report of the International Conference on Financing for Development, Monterrey, Mexico, 18–22 March 2002, UN Doc A/Conf.198/11.

[69] See www.unpri.org, accessed14 February 2014.

[70] See www.worldbank.org, accessed 14 February 2014 for the World Bank safeguard policies.

[71] See www.Equator-principles.com, accessed 14 February 2014.

[72] These Guiding Principles were adopted by the Human Rights Council on 18 July 2012, UN Doc HRC/Res/20/20. The text of the Guidelines is available in UN Doc A/HRC/20/23, 10 April 2011. The Guidelines are

is the most relevant standard for the topic at hand as it is the first to explicitly connect human rights obligations and responsibilities to the issue of sovereign financing. The UNGPs on foreign debt and human rights can be seen as complementary to the general UNGPs on business and human rights.[73]

The UNGPs on foreign debt and human rights confirm that private creditors have the responsibility to respect human rights, which 'implies a duty to refrain from formulating, adopting, funding and implementing policies and programmes which directly or indirectly contravene the enjoyment of human rights'.[74] Further, paragraph 16 provides that '[n]on-State lenders have an obligation to ensure that debt contracts to which they are party or any policies related thereto fully respect human rights'. Principle 23 of the UNGPs on foreign debt and human rights further explains the requirement of creditors to conduct due diligence:

> [F]or creditors, this includes the obligation to perform due diligence on the creditworthiness and ability to repay of the borrower as well as the duty to refrain from providing a loan in circumstances where the lender is aware that the funds will be used for non-public purposes or for a non-viable project.

Given the wording of this due diligence obligation, it would at first seem to refer mainly to a rather specific type of due diligence: financial due diligence. As has been made clear by the SRSG, however, due diligence in the context of business and human rights refers to a broader notion. Regarding private creditors this implies that they should not only examine the creditworthiness and ability to repay the provided funds but also have processes in place aimed at gathering information on the negative human rights impacts of funding and the adoption of measures to prevent and mitigate such adverse consequences. HRDD concerns a risk assessment, which is about human rights risk to others, to the community not to the corporation itself. The second part of Principle 23 refers to such measures when stating that creditors refrain from providing a loan if aware that funds will be spent on 'non-public purposes or for a non-viable project'. Principle 38 further operationalises what this obligation to conduct due diligence implies:

> All lenders should satisfy themselves that a Borrower State has made an informed decision to borrow and that the loan is to be used for a public purpose. They should conduct due diligence or obtain assurances from the Borrower State to ensure that the loan funds will not be wasted through official corruption, economic mismanagement or other unproductive uses in the Borrower State. If any such eventuality is reasonably foreseeable under the circumstances, lenders should not provide the loan or continue with the disbursement of the loan.

In any case it is clear that where a private creditor is aware that funding is supporting the execution of human rights violations, the UNGPs on foreign debt and human rights pro-

the outcome of a process started in 2004 when the (then) Commission on Human Rights adopted resolution 2004/18 requesting the independent expert on the effects of structural adjustment policies and foreign debt on the full enjoyment of human rights, particularly economic, social and cultural rights 'to draft general guidelines to be followed by States and by private and public, national and international financial institutions in the decision-making and execution of debt repayments and structural reform programmes, including those arising from foreign debt relief, to ensure that compliance with the commitments derived from foreign debt will not undermine the obligations for the realisation of fundamental economic, social and cultural rights, as provided for in the international human rights instruments'. After adopting the Guidelines, the Human Rights Council has requested the independent expert to provide a commentary to the Guidelines.

[73] The UNGPs on foreign debt and human rights explicitly refer to this in para 17.

[74] Para 9.

vide that private creditors must refrain from providing loans. According to Principle 40 '[l]enders should not finance activities or projects that violate, or would foreseeably violate, human rights in the Borrower States'.

The UNGPs on foreign debt and human rights expand the due diligence obligation of (private) lenders beyond the obligation to only investigate whether they may be financing human rights violations. According to Principle 39, lenders have the obligation

> to ensure that the proposed loan will not increase the Borrower State's external debt stock to an unsustainable level that will make debt repayment difficult and impede the creation of conditions for the realization of human rights. Lenders should satisfy themselves that, even with the new loan, the Borrower State is still capable of servicing its external debt without compromising its ability to perform its international human rights obligations . . ..[75]

As mentioned above, the general UNGPs on business and human rights, provide that the responsibility of corporations to conduct HRDD must be an ongoing process. What this implies for private creditors in the context of sovereign financing is elaborated upon in Principle 69 of the UNGPs on foreign debt and human rights. According to this Principle:

> Lenders should similarly conduct periodic public audits of their lending portfolios to assess compliance with the objectives of their foreign development cooperation or lending policies, the development priorities of Borrower States and universally recognised human rights standards. The findings of such audits should be publicly disclosed.

The reference to public disclosure is to be found in several places in the UNGPs on foreign debt and human rights. Besides transparency, the Guiding Principles also underline that other human rights principles should be guiding in any lending decision. Principle 28 provides that

> [t]ransparency, participation and accountability are core values that should be observed in the lending and borrowing decisions by States, international financial institutions and other actors as appropriate, the negotiation and execution of loan agreements or other debt instruments, the utilization of loan funds, making of debt repayments . . ..

What transparency means in this context is elaborated upon in Principle 35:

> Lender States, international financial institutions and private institutions should have a comprehensive legal and institutional framework that promotes and ensures transparency and accountability in the negotiation and contracting of loans.

Due to proportionality considerations the required HRDD will differ depending on the type of creditor and clearly more is expected from commercial banks or organised, institutionalised bondholders than is the case with individual bondholders. Bohoslavsky suggests that, as a minimum, lenders should read the fact-finding investigations of UN and regional human rights organisations.[76] According to Guiding Principle 40, in case of funding for specific activities or projects it is incumbent on lenders 'to conduct a credible Human Rights Impact Assessment (HRIA) as a prerequisite to providing a new loan. Alternatively, lenders may request the national human rights institution of the borrower State, if any, to conduct such assessment'. The exact content of the HRDD to be conducted by lenders needs, however, to be determined on a case-by-case basis.

[75] Principle 39 UNGPs on Foreign Debt and Human Rights.
[76] Bohoslavsky (n 35).

In sum, what can be concluded from this brief analysis of these two standards addressing the responsibility of private actors for the adverse impact on human rights generally and in relation to sovereign financing in particular? Private creditors must have ongoing procedures in place to gather information before issuing a loan. This implies not only seeking information about the financial health of the borrower state but also investigating whether there is the possibility that the loan will assist/support human rights violations. Moreover, the obligation to conduct HRDD is taken to imply that private lenders seek information concerning the relationship between the loan and the (in)ability of the borrowing state to fulfil its human rights obligations. The information gathered should subsequently lead to the private creditor taking measures to prevent or mitigate the adverse human rights impact. This may result in refraining from funding. Finally, the soft law standards discussed here place great emphasis on the role of human rights principles such as transparency, participation and accountability.

Notwithstanding the laudable nature of many of the responsibilities laid down in the soft law instruments outlined above, implementing these responsibilities in practice is fraught with difficulties. As mentioned earlier, large sums of sovereign debt are in the hands of often dispersed bondholders. Clearly, the quite far-reaching expectations concerning the responsibility to conduct HRDD cannot be applicable to individual bondholders. There will have to be a certain degree of organisation and capacity on the side of private creditors to be able to live up to these responsibilities.

Many institutional creditors have in place policies reflecting such responsibilities where specific project financing is concerned. The quite expansive notion of how lenders should assess the risks involved in funding will however be a lot more complex in case of loans and bonds which are not specifically attached to a certain project. Not only should financial risk be assessed but also the broader risk, which even includes investigating whether increasing debt will hamper the sovereign's ability to live up to its human rights obligations.

The discussed standards are non-binding. Nevertheless, their normative impact can be significant. Such standards may fill in the open norms that are applied in domestic proceedings such as 'the duty of care' or 'societal expectations'. For example, courts in the Netherlands have relied on non-binding international standards to establish the standards of duty of care under Dutch tort law.[77] For courts to rely on such international standards the norms will have to be sufficiently evolved before they will be accepted as publicly accepted standards though. It can be stated that the impact of soft standards will increase depending on the degree to which they reflect law. From that perspective it is to be expected that the emerging standard of behaviour of lenders will wield most influence where it concerns their impact on the responsibility of private creditors in the context of violations of *jus cogens* norms as it is accepted that these norms are directly applicable to all entities including corporations.[78]

[77] This first occurred in 1979 in the Netherlands in a case against the corporation BATCO where the court relied on the OECD Guidelines to determine the appropriate standard for the duty of care, Ondernemingskamer [Dutch companies and Business Court], 21 June 1979, NJ, 1980, 71. More recently, the Dutch Supreme Court ruled that non-binding guidelines on financial reporting had evolved into publicly accepted norms with which the defendant company had to comply. See Koninklijke KPN N.V./Stichting SOBI, Hoge Raad der Nederlanden [HR] [Supreme Court of the Netherlands], 10 February 2006, *LJN* AU7473 (Neth). See N Jägers and MJ van der Heijden, 'Corporate Human Rights Violations: The Feasibility of Civil Recourse in the Netherlands' (2008) 33(3) *Brooklyn Journal of International Law* 857–59.

[78] See above.

It is too early to conclude anything on the normative impact of the UNGPs on foreign debt and human rights as they were only adopted in 2012. The normative influence of the 2011 general UNGPs on business and human rights is, however, already proving to be significant. These UNGPs were unanimously adopted by the Human Rights Council and have been widely embraced by states, corporations and civil society. A process of redeployment is taking place where the UNGPs, in whole or with regard to certain elements, are being incorporated into corporate policies, transnational private regulation,[79] inter-state regulation[80] and even state legislation.[81] Hence, soft norms may assist states and regulators in shaping their policies aimed at regulating the adverse human rights impact of private creditors. This is important as a broader approach involving multiple stakeholders is needed to address the negative impact that private lending to sovereigns can have on human rights.

Notwithstanding the potential influence of the emerging framework on corporate responsibility for the adverse effects of sovereign financing, the operationalisation of this responsibility in practice faces significant hurdles, which will be discussed in the following section.

VI OPERATIONALISING CORPORATE HUMAN RIGHTS RESPONSIBILITY IN THE CONTEXT OF SOVEREIGN LENDING: PROBLEMS AND PITFALLS

This section will highlight some of the challenges that exist when operationalising the soft human rights standards discussed above in the field of sovereign financing.[82] A core element of corporate responsibility to respect human rights consists of the responsibility to conduct HRDD processes. According to the SRSG, corporations failing to live up to their responsibility to respect human rights 'can subject companies to the courts of public opinion – compromising employees, communities, consumers, civil society, as well as investors – and occasionally to charges in actual courts'.[83] Concerning the latter, it has already been demonstrated that a restricted approach taken by courts to issues such as causality and knowledge thereof will be a significant hurdle to overcome for plaintiffs trying to establish legal accountability of private creditors for human rights violations in domestic proceedings. The threat of litigation may therefore not constitute sufficient incentive for private creditors to adopt the quite expansive HRDD processes required by the soft law standards discussed above. There might in fact be a strong disincentive to conduct extensive HRDD as such an investigation might actually expose the lender to liability claims as it then may be more easy to prove that they had the required knowledge of the human rights abuses. They then enter a zone of legal risk.[84] Moreover, in the

[79] See, for one of the many possible examples, the International Code of Conduct for Private Security Providers (ICoC-PSP) which refers to and builds on the UNGPs, www.icoc-psp.org, accessed 14 February 2014.

[80] See, for example, the OECD Guidelines on Multinational Corporations, which were revised in 2011 and now include a whole chapter on business and human rights, which wholly integrates the UNGPs.

[81] The most famous example is the above-mentioned s 1503 of the Dodd-Frank Act.

[82] For more on the challenges in applying the Protect-Respect-Remedy Framework to finance in general, see Dowell-Jones and Kinley (n 3).

[83] Human Rights Council, 'Protect, Respect and Remedy: a Framework for Business and Human Rights: Report of the Special Representative of the Secretary General on the Issue of Human Rights and Transnational Corporations and Other Business Enterprises', A/HRC/8/5 (7 April 2008) para 54.

[84] Unless conducting a due proper due diligence investigation offers an accepted line of defence in legal proceedings. The UNGPs point out that 'conducting appropriate human rights due diligence should help

specific context of sovereign financing, there is another reason why incentive for private creditors to 'behave' is lacking. Contrary to 'ordinary' debtors, sovereigns are not subject to bankruptcy regimes. There is no international insolvency system with formal and fixed rules ranking creditors.[85] When it comes to default and debt restructuring, creditors will by and large be treated in the same manner, responsible and irresponsible lenders alike. Or rather, the defaulting sovereign enjoys a wide measure of discretion in determining who will be paid what.[86] A private creditor that has conducted agonising HRDD does not have a right to be treated any differently in an eventual restructuring compared to another creditor that did little to nothing. It has been argued that '[t]his neutralizes a central motivation for any lender to pursue responsible sovereign lending practices – namely the fear of being disadvantaged in any workout of the country's debts that may become necessary down the road'.[87]

Thus there would seem to be little incentive for private creditors to voluntarily take on the expected standard of behaviour. The SRSG has pointed out, by referring to 'the courts of public opinion', that the uptake of the corporate responsibility to respect human rights is not wholly voluntary despite its non-binding character. The UNGPs rely on stakeholders such as employees, communities and investors to exert pressure on corporations to do so. For this mechanism to work it is essential that stakeholders have access to sufficient and relevant information.[88] It is therefore vital that information concerning human rights risk assessments is available and transparent as is emphasised in the UNGPs on foreign debt and human rights.

Finally, it should be kept in mind that it makes little sense to require lenders to take up human rights responsibilities when there is no binary relationship between the lender and the borrower. In practice the responsibility may become very diluted when bonds are sold on the secondary market.[89] The private creditors may then be so remote from the lenders' human rights violations that it is simply impossible to attribute any human rights responsibility to those private creditors.

VII CONCLUSION

Excessive sovereign debt and the adverse impact on human rights have been on the international agenda for quite some time, especially in relation to developing countries. The

business enterprises address the risk of legal claims . . . However, business enterprises conducting such due diligence should not assume that, by itself, this will automatically and fully absolve them from liability for causing or contributing to human rights abuse', Commentary to UNGP 17.

85 For more on how losses are distributed among creditors in practice see JP Bohoslavsky, 'Lending and Sovereign Insolvency: A Fair and Efficient Criterion to Distribute Losses among Creditors' (2010) 2(1) *Goettingen Journal of International Law* 387–412.

86 ibid, 395.

87 Bucheit and Gulati (n 22) 17. To address this problem Bohoslavsky suggests that the principle of responsibility for granting abusive loans found in domestic insolvency proceedings, which results in creditors providing abusive loans collecting less money, should be applied at the international level: Bohoslavsky (n 85), 387.

88 For a discussion of the lack of attention to the need to secure access to information in the Guiding Principles see N Jägers, 'Will Transnational Regulation Close the Governance Gap?' in D Bilchitz and S Deva (eds), *Human Rights Obligations of Business: Beyond the Corporate Responsibility to Respect?* (Cambridge, Cambridge University Press, 2013), 295–329.

89 For a discussion of this issue in the context of the sub-prime process, see Dowell-Jones and Kinley (n 3), 199–206.

international community of states has so far nonetheless not been able to come up with a durable solution. The financial and economic crises starting in 2008 have brought the human rights problems that emanate from unsustainable levels of debt to the doorsteps of developed states as is particularly noticeable in the Eurozone.

This chapter has addressed the role that private creditors such as institutional investors or (organised) bondholders play in the sovereign debt crisis that is impairing the enjoyment of human rights. The rapidly evolving debate on the human rights responsibilities of corporations warrants a closer examination of this discourse in the light of the sovereign debt crisis. What human rights obligations and responsibilities of private creditors can be discerned? And how are they relevant in the context of sovereign financing?

Peremptory norms of international law, such as the prohibition of (contributing to) crimes against humanity are directly applicable to corporations. Even though it is clear that the support of private creditors often plays a crucial role in upholding regimes that violate such peremptory norms, translating the applicable international human rights standards into civil or criminal liability for private creditors is fraught with difficulties.

This can be explained by the micro approach often taken in human rights law, which refers to the fact that human rights law is actor orientated, and fulfilling human rights obligations is about allocating responsibilities and accountability to specific actors. This often results in a restrictive approach requiring a strict causality between the human rights violation and, in this case, the funds offered by private creditors. This approach is, however, constantly being tested and refined in the increasing litigation against corporate defendants in domestic proceedings.

The soft law instruments relating to corporate human rights responsibilities in general and in relation to sovereign financing in particular clarify the steps private creditors should take. This includes a far-reaching approach implying that a private creditor must also examine whether loans will exacerbate the level of debt to unsustainable levels, threatening the fulfilment of human rights obligations. Clearly, this responsibility will be proportional and differ in the case of large institutionalised private creditors or smaller creditors. Moreover, it is difficult to see how this responsibility can apply to private creditors that do not stand in a direct relation to the borrower. Nevertheless, the norm placing a responsibility of private creditors to conduct HRDD may assist in broadening the restricted approach taken so far regarding issues of causality and knowledge by pushing the boundaries of what is expected from private creditors. Such standards may colour the 'societal expectation' towards private creditors to do more to ascertain whether their funding is contributing in any way to human rights violations.

The chapter has shown that the operationalisation of the human rights responsibilities as laid down in soft law instruments in the context of sovereign financing faces some significant hurdles relating to the lack of incentives to push private creditors to take on their human rights responsibility. Moreover, the micro approach to issues of human rights and sovereign financing will fall short in providing a solution to the complex processes at hand. It is clear that certain adverse impacts on human rights are beyond the scope of private creditors to address. This necessitates a wider approach including states, regulators and private creditors. The emerging corporate human rights discourse also in the area of sovereign financing can assist such efforts.

Thus, the identified human rights responsibilities of private creditors may help fill in open norms in domestic proceedings. Moreover, importantly, given the need for a broader approach, the emerging framework can advise states and regulators in how to use their regulatory capacity to further explicate, encourage or mandate private creditors to engage in HRDD.

Notwithstanding the fact that the scale and complexity of the human rights violations that occur in the context of sovereign financing necessitate much wider efforts to address the negative human rights impact, this fact cannot be taken to permit private creditors to obviate the basic requirement of private creditors to investigate possible adverse human rights impact and to prevent and mitigate such impact.

13

Project Finance and Human Rights

SHELDON LEADER*

I INTRODUCTION TO THE ISSUES

AS SOVEREIGN STATES seek to accomplish public purposes while drawing on private finance, they often use the methods of project finance (PF). This collaboration takes various forms, under the generic label of public-private partnerships. These partnerships have in common the fact that governments aim to avoid some of the expense, risk and administrative headache involved in building and operating projects themselves, as happens in the complex infrastructure development that is often a feature of road systems, oil and gas pipelines, health care facilities and many other examples. Project Finance helps governments to reduce direct use of taxpayers' funds and also narrows and focuses the risks they face. As a lending technique designed to achieve these objectives, PF is both praised and feared. It is seen by some as an excellent tool for encouraging investment, since it provides a set of refined methods for the spreading and mitigating of risks between corporations, host governments, lenders and those contractors involved in building and operating a project. At the same time, a suspicious civil society is producing its own increasingly refined tools for measuring the potential gains and losses to the populations affected by this investment strategy. Project Finance has thereby become one of the most closely watched modes of international finance as various bodies – both public and private lenders – assess the risk to social and environmental standards by projects to which this form of lending is extended.

It is important to hold on to the positive and negative elements in the picture. Positively, the finance provided by this method has sometimes provided a bridge to large social gains, generating revenues that give host governments the space to fund major work in housing, health care and education. Negatively, praise is sometimes brought up short by those whose lives are overturned by a project because of its pollution; accidents during its construction or operation; seizure of lands; and many other impacts. In short, PF provides a prism through which pass many of the fundamental tensions characterising the relation between basic rights, sustainable development and foreign direct investment.

As civil society, both national and international, raises the pressure for meaningful social accountability of business, PF is often in its sights – either intentionally or without realising it. Demands made for protection of local populations sometimes place particular requirements on this financing technique, which it may not be well equipped to

* This chapter draws on S Leader, chs 1 and 5 in S Leader and D Ong (eds), *Global Project Finance, Human Rights, and Sustainable Development* (Cambridge, Cambridge University Press, 2011) with the kind permission of the Cambridge University Press.

handle. Because of certain structural features of PF, a company borrowing under such a scheme may not easily cede to civil society's demands because of its perception that there is little room for manoeuvre left by the conditions set by lenders. Of concern here are some of the largest projects in the world, many playing a central part in the politics and societies of those countries receiving the investment. A measure of this concern is to be seen in a special meeting which focused on the impact of PF called by the UN's Special Representative on Human Rights and Transnational Corporations, Professor John Ruggie.[1] It has also been the subject of a report by International Alert, an organisation interested in the links between PF and social conflict.[2]

The investment community has been taking its own initiatives towards meeting the demand for accountability. Lenders have been developing social and environmental standards that are the most elaborate criteria yet to have been deployed by the international financial community aimed at controlling the impact of what they do. Two leading examples of these standards are, in the public sector, the International Finance Corporation's (IFC) performance standards,[3] and in the private sector, major lending banks concerted with PF have banded together to formulate the Equator Principles (EP).[4]

Can the norms for a better environment, human rights and related concerns be adequately satisfied by an investment community aiming to hold on to the full commercial benefits offered by PF? The jury is still out. The aim in this chapter is to look at this issue via one of the central decisions PF calls on all parties to make: a decision about how to evaluate the risks one takes on a project.

It is important, first of all, to briefly describe the elements of PF and to sketch, in an introductory way, its main points of contact with key social and environmental issues.

II A DEFINITION

Project financing is a method of funding in which the lenders '. . . base credit appraisals on the projected revenues from the operation of the facility . . . and rely on the assets of the facility . . . as collateral for the debt'.[5] It is to be distinguished from those modes of finance in which the general assets of a sponsoring company, often owning several projects, are wholly or in part the subject of claims by the lender in the event of a failure to repay the loan.[6]

This relatively sparse definition needs to be placed within the corporate structure tailored for it. We can use here a classic model: a parent company or a group of compa-

[1] See report of the United Nations High Commissioner on Human Rights on the sectoral consultation entitled 'Human rights and the financial sector', 16 February 2007 A/HRC/4/99, 6 March 2007, http://198.170.85.29/UNHCHR-finance-sector-consultation-report-6-Mar-2007.pdf.

[2] The report was focused on the relationship between PF and social conflict. See International Alert, *Conflict and Project Finance: Exploring Options for Better Management of Conflict Risk*, by Corene Crossin and Jessie Banfield, January 2006.

[3] IFC Performance Standards, 2012 edition, www.ifc.org/wps/wcm/connect/Topics_Ext_Content/IFC_External_Corporate_Site/IFC+Sustainability/Sustainability+Framework/Sustainability+Framework+-+2012/Performance+Standards+and+Guidance+notes+2012/, accessed 30 September 2013.

[4] The most recent version of the Equator Principles came into force 4 June 2013, www.equator-principles.com/index.php/ep3, accessed 30 September 2013. In this chapter the IFC Project Standards and the Equator Principles will be referred to collectively as IFC/EP standards.

[5] SL Hoffman, *The Law and Business of International Project Finance*, 2nd edn (The Hague, Kluwer Law International, 2001) 4–5.

[6] ibid, 6–7.

nies in a consortium (project sponsors) typically set up a project company, or special purpose vehicle (SPV), the latter usually owning the land, machinery, operating funds and other assets directly connected to its owning and operating the pipeline, dam, hydroelectric plant, etc which is the target of the investment. The controlling equity in the SPV will be held by the project sponsor(s), sometimes accompanied by equity participation from the host state. A loan is then made to the SPV by private banks or public lenders, without – or with limited – recourse to the parent in the event of default on the loan. Instead, as the definition indicates, the lender's recourse will be to the assets of the SPV.[7]

This arrangement has several noteworthy characteristics:

- The project sponsor is protected from threats to its assets that would otherwise be posed by a venture's failure. The sponsor stands to lose the money it has already invested in the SPV, but its explicit understanding with the lender is that the latter will not have recourse against its other assets. This autonomy is buttressed by the fact that the SPV is a separate legal entity and its sponsors, as shareholders, enjoy limited liability.
- Emphasis is placed by the lender on predictable revenue flow. This concern, while also present in lending against general assets of a sponsor, is here heightened. Were the loan to have been made to the project sponsor, the latter would normally be obligated to pay the loan back from its general revenues, coming from all of the projects in which it is involved. In PF, however, the loan is repaid from one source only: a single project. This typically leads to a heightened emphasis on meeting target dates for construction and the start of the operation, together with a focus on the need to keep project costs as close as possible to their initial predicted amounts.

These two factors lead to certain intensified concerns on the part of both lenders and borrowers that can have social and environmental impacts. These concerns are also present in other modes of financing, but can be stronger here:

- *Regulatory stability*: Lenders, as well as other parties investing in the project, have a strong interest in discouraging the host state from introducing changes in law or regulation that will have a negative impact on project costs, and hence can put pressure on the ability of the project to meet its loan repayment targets.
- *Allocation of risk*: While such allocations are a concern in all projects, those financed by PF place particular emphasis on a spread of risks that will induce the relevant parties to help meet project deadlines and keep expenses within the expected limits.
- *Presumption in favour of meeting of costs from within project revenues*: Given the insulation of the project from its sponsor's own liabilities, there is a concern to avoid calling on further funds – beyond those initially set aside – from sponsors to meet unexpected problems with the project.

These concerns can generate both positive and negative effects on societies hosting a project:

- *Positive*: The needs for predictability of return on project investment may encourage a particularly careful calculation of environmental/social risks, given the impact these

[7] This non-recourse element functions primarily during the operational phase of the project. The earlier construction phase is often accompanied by some form of recourse the lender will have to the sponsor directly. There are many variants and qualifications to this picture, but it is a good starting point.

can have on steady cash flow. Where the lender has recourse against the project sponsor's assets, there can be less inducement to pay close attention to such factors. The assessment of these risks is called for by the performance standards set by several major public and private lenders, most notably by the IFC and commercial banks subscribing to the EP.

- *Negative*: On the other side, there is the possibility that risks of certain types of damage to local populations might be heightened by some of the pressures on project timing and performance, as well as techniques of risk management, in PF. This may be so, for example, when unrealistic completion deadlines for construction are set; stringent stabilisation requirements freezing regulatory change are placed on host governments; or the possibility exists for project sponsors to abandon a project that is underperforming, allowing the SPV to collapse with potential loss to third parties. The concern for stability might even be intense enough to pull against an investor's enthusiasm for democracy in the host country in favour of the more predictable environment that a strong non-democratic form of government can provide.[8]
- *Issues shared with other modes of finance*: Finally, there is a set of concerns that involve problems of projects financed by PF which would also be shared to the same extent by other modes of finance, such as complicity with human rights violations, and shortcomings in the due diligence processes conducted by the financial institutions.

III BASIC RIGHTS

'Basic' and 'human' rights and duties: the fundamental rights of concern to PF strategies fall into two overlapping categories. First, there are internationally recognised human rights that come from recognised sources. For these purposes such sources include the International Covenant on Civil and Political Rights and the International Covenant on Economic, Social and Cultural Rights as well as more narrowly focused human rights conventions. Secondly, at some points a wider, generic category, 'basic' rights, is used. They are the fundamental entitlements that are formulated in instruments such as the 1972 Stockholm Declaration of the United Nations Conference on the Human Environment, and the 1992 Rio Declaration on Environment and Development. Finally, within the class of basic rights and duties are those entitlements and obligations imposed on borrowers by the requirements of the IFC as well as Equator Principles Banks (hereafter IFC/EP standards), several of which coincide with the international norms mentioned.

How should one deploy human or basic rights as a critical tool for evaluating the impacts of private investment? How, in turn, should these critical standards be used in evaluating PF projects? There are several elements in an answer:

Comparing rights-based development and rights-based investment: Host states have obligations to respect, protect and fulfil human rights of their populations, and these in turn have been woven into the guidelines for rights-based development: guidelines developed by the UN High Commissioner for Human Rights.[9] Investors can come under an

[8] This is one possible explanation for the correlations between forms of government and the price of loans discussed in Leader and Ong (above, opening note asterisked) ch 8.

[9] For the UN's approach to rights-based development, see UN High Commissioner on Human Rights,

overlapping, but also diverging, set of obligations corresponding to the same rights. The difference between the two sets of duties is one of scope. This can be seen if we consider the example of the right of access to water.[10] Consider an investment in a pipeline project that uses water to such an extent that the supply to the local population falls below minimal standards set by international instruments. The host state could legitimately impose, in fulfilment of its obligation to protect this basic right, regulations requiring the pipeline not to block this access. At that point, the obligations (if not the interests) of the investor and those of the host state converge: both aim at a portion of the guarantees involved in rights-based development. Not only that, but were the host state to fail to enforce protection of this right in its own domestic rules, there would nevertheless be independent grounds on which the investor could be held responsible for the damage done to the water supply. It could, for example, be held to have broken a basic condition of its loan from an EP bank. The same would be true were the project company to violate fundamental labour rights as defined in certain ILO conventions. These are conventions that bind the host states, but which also form part of the lending conditions set by the Equator banks and the IFC.[11]

An investor's human rights obligations do not completely mirror the host state's responsibilities for rights-based development. Yet over a significant terrain those responsibilities coincide. It is in this domain and others like it that tensions can appear. Even though the private investor might acknowledge, at a general level, that it has to respect these rights, it may aim to determine their content and weight in a way that weakens their protective potential. This can happen as the web of contracts framing an investment are drawn up and given effect. It is important to see how the disciplines of PF might stand behind these problematic features of the legal framework, and then to see what changes to PF arrangements might be made in order to avoid the problem. These issues will be considered below.

Basic rights of populations on both sides of the fence: It is tempting to place the concern for basic rights on the side of a population that can be damaged by a project, and the concern for other goals, such as commercial objectives, on the side of the investor. Such a division does not work, however strongly one focuses on the welfare of those affected by a project. This is because there are situations in which the choice of PF as a technique can clearly help a host state to discharge its own human rights responsibilities. Water supplied by private sources might reach the neediest parts of the population; and schools or hospitals financed from tax revenues generated by a petroleum pipeline might do the same. Of course, they may not achieve these objectives as well – and often do not. These concerns about the need of a state to satisfy its core obligation to improve the *provision* of key social goods, such as access to better national health care financed partly

Rights-based approaches, www.unhchr.ch/development/approaches-04.html, accessed 30 September 2013. For a discussion of the conceptual framework of a rights-based approach to development, see J Kirkemann Hansen and H-O Sano, 'The Implications and Value-added of a Rights-Based Approach', in B Andreassen and S Marks (eds), *Development as a Human Right – Legal, Political and Economic Dimensions* (Boston, Intersentia, 2010) 36–56, 42. See also L VeneKlasen et al, 'Rights-based Approaches and Beyond: Challenges of Linking Rights and Participation' (Brighton, Institute of Development Studies, Working Paper 235, 2004).

[10] See 'Note: What Price for the Priceless? Implementing the Justiciability of the Right to Water' (2007) 120 *Harvard Law Review* 1067.

[11] For example, ILO Conventions no 182 on Worst Forms of Child Labour, no 176 on Health and Safety in Mines, no 167 on Health and Safety in Construction, or no 154 on Collective Bargaining, www.ilo.org/ilolex/english/convdisp1.htm, accessed 30 September 2013.

out of tax on project revenue, run alongside a distinct concern that the same projects may do significant *damage* as they operate: to people, to environments and to property. The real issue at that point might be better cast as a matter of choosing between or mixing two courses of action, each with their own distinct impacts on human rights. Is it, for example, better to take a step towards fulfilling a basic right to adequate medical care on a national level, but at the expense of allowing construction of a tax-paying project to move at a pace that destroys the health of some of a local population; or should the adjustment between the two sets of rights move in the opposite direction? Where does the drive for commercial profit legitimately fit into this picture? This clash of fundamental entitlements of different parts of the population stands in the background, and sometimes in the foreground, of these enquiries.

Basic rights of the investor: It is important to include in the mix of relevant basic rights a model in which the investor enjoys a right to protection of its property via internationally recognised human rights norms. It is tempting, as some do, to construct policy around the denial of this fundamental status to property rights, and in particular to the rights of the investor. The approach taken here admits the right to property fully into the picture, but the existence of a basic right is one thing, its relative weight is another. Focus then turns to the question of the appropriate adjustment between this entitlement and competing fundamental rights of those who are affected by any given investment project. It is here that the appropriate constraints on the operation of PF can be constructed. They are not built on the assumption that the property rights of the investor must automatically take second place, but also that those property rights are not automatically dominant. They must enter into a balanced adjustment against one another.

IV RISK TO BASIC RIGHTS AND RISK TO PROFIT

The cost, timing and other features of lending to a project under PF are themselves determined by principles of risk management. It is here that two agendas may clash: that of managing risk to the basic rights of those in society affected by a project, and that of managing risk to the objectives – and sometimes to the rights – of those investing in a project. PF is potentially a locus for negotiation over both types of risk. However, too often the parties to the bargain are those focused on the commercial variables, while those representing civil society are left to pick up the pieces: reacting to features of a project that have been set between banks and borrowers some time before the project takes shape on the ground. Those concerned about the project's social effects may try to intervene in order to avoid the worst damage to their environments, health or allied interests, via insisting on their rights to be consulted before land is expropriated, or a potentially polluting measure is implemented. While the obligations to consult on these matters are formally part of the agenda that the IFC and Equator Banks set when they lend, the logic of risk management in PF can get in the way of giving these social obligations their proper weight.

In order to see this, it is important to note three distinct parts of a risk management policy: avoidance, allocation and mitigation.

Risk avoidance: The policy of avoidance calls for measures to prevent or reduce the chance of damage happening. This may include technologies for better protecting, for example, health and safety or the environment, standards that the IFC or EP banks will insist be met as conditions attached to the loan.[12] It also includes protocols for the construction or operation of a project, such as indications of the appropriate speed at which it functions if health and safety is not to be jeopardised, or the way in which its sites or access routes are to be established.[13] This second set of avoidance protocols is important for our purposes, and one principle that is central can be called the 'avoidance over compensation' priority. The IFC, for example, in its formulation of project standards, says that:

> The measures and actions to address identified impacts and risks will favor the avoidance and prevention of impacts over minimization, mitigation, or compensation, wherever technically and financially feasible. Where risks and impacts cannot be avoided or prevented, mitigation measures and actions will be identified so that the project operates in compliance with applicable laws and regulations, and meets the requirements of Performance Standards 1 through 8.[14]

Risk allocation: Risk allocation is largely accomplished via negotiated agreements among project participants. The resulting rise or fall in risk to local populations affected by the project, which we will consider in a moment, are not here termed a risk 'allocation'. This is a piece of terminological legislation in order to allow us to distinguish the spread of risks among parties who negotiate over the distribution of responsibility for those risks, and who have to agree as parties to a contract before the allocation can be binding, as opposed to local populations which incur risks of damage to health, land or their environment as a result of the negotiation process, but do not, because they are not parties to the negotiated contracts allocating risk, have any say in the process.

Insofar as principles play a role in the process of negotiation over risk allocation, there are several such principles that are candidates, embraced with different degrees of enthusiasm by the various parties. The principles are: (a) allocate the risk to the party best able to control it (the dominant guideline); (b) allocate the risk to the party with resources adequate to address it (eg strong contractors sometimes assume liability for damage even though weaker sub-contractor is better placed to prevent the damage); (c) allocate the risk to the party which stands to profit most from the project (eg the reason host governments sometimes give for transferring risk for changes in law to project companies and accordingly to project sponsors by potentially decreasing the return on their equity in those companies).[15] Negotiation among project parties may refer to these principles, but negotiation is itself a process, not a principle. As such, parties to it may try to deploy one or more of the three principles mentioned, or none at all. In the latter case, they may be content to prevail or lose simply because the balance of bargaining power allows this to happen. The consequences of any particular outcome of this bargaining can be dramatic

[12] See for example the IFC's classification of projects, and definition of Category C projects which 'need not [comply with] any specific requirements', IFC Policy on Social and Environmental Sustainability, paras 18 and 28, www.ifc.org/ifcext/enviro.nsf/AttachmentsByTitle/pol_SocEnvSustainability2006/$FILE/Sustainability Policy.pdf, accessed 30 September 2013.

[13] This was an issue in, eg, the Chad–Cameroon pipeline project. See for a discussion below.

[14] International Finance Corporation, Performance Standard 1: Social and Environmental Assessment and Management Systems, April 2006, para 14, www.ifc.org/ifcext/enviro.nsf/AttachmentsByTitle/pol_Performance Standards2006_full/$FILE/IFC+Performance+Standards.pdf, accessed 30 September 2013.

[15] An example of the last principle would be a negotiating position according to which in case of a rise in market prices of oil, and as a result of a consequent increase in the share of profits of project sponsors from the project, the risk of change in environmental, social and even tax legislation could be shifted from a state (as a party best able to control that risk) to the parties that would be benefiting most from the project. The party advancing this argument should be ready to face counterclaims that increased profits of project sponsors would lead to increase in amount received as taxes on the realised profit, etc. This point is owed to Rasmiya Kazimova.

for those sitting on the sidelines: local populations. If, for example, risk is allocated to the party which stands to profit most from a project, such as the SPV, this might not be the party best placed to control that risk, which could be the contractor. The SPV might be much less able to *avoid* a given risk than is the contractor, given the latter's superior technical grip on the situations likely to arise in the construction phase of a project.

Risk mitigation: These are measures that do not distribute responsibility for risk, but instead reduce the overall risk for one or more of the project participants. Any given mitigating measure may or may not heighten risk to third parties in turn. The central form of mitigating device is project insurance. A further important form of mitigation is the reduction of certain types of legal liability. For example, clauses in investment contracts between companies involved in projects and host states have been known to restrict liability for the building or operation of the project to intentional damage, thus removing responsibility based on negligence and areas of strict liability otherwise introduced by standards for health and safety and environmental protection.[16] There is also the example of removals of certain financial risks that come from the creation of tax-free zones. Uruguay, for example, has done this for the two pulp mills. Both mills were granted Free Zone status. According to Article 19, Law NR 15.921: 'Users of the Free Zones shall be exempted from all national tax, created or to be created, including those requiring by law a specific exemption, as regards any activity carried out therein'.[17] By this provision, the project is insulated from tax changes which are understood as a regulatory risk. Finally, host governments may further mitigate risk of loss by making capital contributions from various parts of the community with the greatest stake in a particular project, be these local authorities, national authorities or regional sources. There may also be guarantees provided at these same levels designed to mitigate certain risks that the SPV would not be able to shoulder by itself.

THE PLACE OF CORPORATE SOCIAL RESPONSIBILITY IN THE MANAGEMENT OF RISK

For each of the participants in PF, it is important to locate the impact of principles of corporate social responsibility (CSR). While the detail of such an impact obviously varies, depending on features of the roles of lender, sponsor, SPV, or contractor, there are some shared aspects of responsibility that are important to identify. These concern the appropriate balance between two elements: on the one hand, the basic rights of those affected by a project and on the other the fact that the parties to the project have as their core objective the earning of adequate return on their investment. Principles of CSR can then take two forms: first, they might require the company to enlarge on its objectives so that it positively assists the host country to build capacity in various domains so as to render development sustainable.[18] On the other hand, CSR principles also demand that

[16] See, eg, Art 20.2 of the Azeri-Chirag-Guneshli Production Sharing Agreement of 20/9/1994, http://subsites.bp.com/caspian/ACG/Eng/agmt1/agmt1.pdf, accessed 30 September 2013.

[17] Art 19, Law NR 15.921, Republic of Uruguay, 'LEY DE ZONAS FRANCAS N°. 15921 del 17 de diciembre de 1987', www.zonafrancacolonia.com/ley.htm, accessed 30 September 2013.

[18] This accords with the IFC's definition of sustainable development and its view that the corporate role in such development calls for such positive contributions. See IFC, *Banking on Sustainability*, 2007, 13 ('Defining sustainability') http://riskybusiness.wordpress.com/2007/03/30/new-ifc-report-banking-on-sustainability-march-2007/, accessed 30 September 2013.

the company avoid certain types of damage to society, and it is here that risk management enters into the picture: CSR provides a set of tools for filtering out some methods of dealing with project risk that are dangerous to society and so needing careful control.

It seems at first glance to add nothing here to invoke the *social* responsibility for bodies engaged in risk management of this sort. If we know that a company should avoid certain levels of environmental damage or damage to health and safety, then this looks no different from what has happened for generations as companies are prevented from committing frauds, providing cover for enemy aliens etc. However, that ignores an important point. In the area of risk management there are issues of adjustment between competing interests to focus on, and principles of social responsibility can strongly affect the way in which this adjustment is carried out.[19] For example, when an SPV is under an obligation via the EP/IFC standards to avoid certain types of damage to the environment, this requirement is to be placed alongside the need to respect the EP/IFC principle, seen earlier, to the effect that avoidance of damage is to be favoured over compensation for it. Taken together, these two parts of the standards identify the types of damage of concern – be it to social or to environmental interests – and then they permit the company to cause that damage when this '. . . cannot be avoided . . . (in the light of what is) . . . financially feasible'.[20]

Much turns on the way in which these terms are to be understood, and it is here that the impact of CSR principles can be felt. Once the damage to society that a project risks causing is identified, a spectrum of solutions is opened up – with avoidance at one end and compensation for the damage caused at the other. There is a point on that spectrum at which a company decides that it should stop trying to achieve the former and instead opt for the latter. In deciding where that point is located, management is told by the EP/IFC principles that it cannot select the commercially most *convenient* stage at which to move to the compensation solution, but that it may move to it only when avoidance of the damage is not technically or financially feasible: it is a point beyond the *capacity* of the available technology or of the financial structure to accommodate extra costs.

This is where principles of CSR can make a difference. They call for an altered approach to identifying where the limits of that capacity lie. The change involves a different direction of adjustment between commercial and non-commercial concerns. That is, it makes a difference to know if one is searching for a version of the protection of basic environmental or social rights which, from among alternatives, does least damage to established commercial arrangements in PF; or that one is searching from among alternative means of carrying forward those commercial arrangements for the method that does least damage to the rights. The demand for CSR can be understood as inviting the banks and companies to switch from the former form of adjustment to the latter at certain key points.[21] Unless such an alteration happens, the promise behind the IFC's call to treat certain social damage as a priority, via its demand that avoidance of harm takes priority over its compensation, can turn out to be empty. The danger in turn is that the project can begin to make trade-offs which the wider society will find fundamentally unacceptable.

[19] See S Leader, 'Corporate Accountability' in M Bovens, RE Goodin and T Schillemans (eds), *The Oxford Handbook on Public Accountability*, (Oxford, Oxford University Press, forthcoming 2014).

[20] IFC Performance Standard 1.

[21] On directions of adjustment, see S Leader, 'Collateralism' in R Brownsword (ed), *Global Governance and the Search for Justice* (Oxford, Hart Publishing, 2005) 53–67; and S Leader, 'Two Ways of Linking Economic Activity to Human Rights' (2005) 185 *International Social Science Journal*, Blackwell/UNESCO, 541 ff.

The project company and contractors may, for example, knowingly run a higher level of risk to the environment by refusing the implementation of expensive measures that would call for stopping or slowing the project, since their calculations may show that it is better to run the risk of damage happening and then to compensate as and when it occurs.[22] Every measure that stops or slows down a project delays the flow of revenue. If the lender's and project sponsor's common priority in PF is to start that flow as soon as possible, and then to stabilise it, it can make more sense to pay for damage out of a reserve fund held by the SPV, and then to replenish the fund out of fresh project revenues, rather than stop the project in order to rectify the risk, and thereby temporarily cut off the revenue stream.[23] The alternative facing the project sponsor is to feed the reserve fund out of its own fresh equity contributions or operating funds, which it will be typically less happy about doing than it is to rely on project revenue. The boundary between the interruptions to project plans that are and are not 'financially feasible' is thus strongly affected by the disciplines of PF on the one hand, and by the centrality accorded to human and other basic rights by principles of CSR on the other.

AN EXAMPLE: THE CHAD–CAMEROON OIL PIPELINE AND THE HEALTH OF LOCAL POPULATIONS

The building of the Chad–Cameroon oil pipeline raised certain health problems for local populations, one of which was associated with dust control as heavy vehicles passed through populated areas along dirt roads.[24] This was a difficulty aggravated by the high speed with which operations had been carried out.[25] Equivalent problems, arising from the speed at which the completion of construction work has happened, have confronted other pipeline projects.[26] The drive for such speed makes sense in terms of the ground rules for PF. Analysts often point to the fact, mentioned above, that the lender wants to reach as quickly as possible the point at which the reimbursement of its loan begins, given that there is no revenue stream to service the loan coming from a company's several projects, but only this one.[27] As a prop to this objective, the project will often offer bonuses

[22] One consequence of following this logic too far is to be seen in a scandal that involved the Ford Motor Company. In producing the Ford Pinto it was discovered that the car had design faults that could aggravate fatalities in accidents. Ford was aware of this design flaw but allegedly decided it would be cheaper to pay off possible lawsuits for resulting deaths rather than engage in a costly recall of all Pintos. This decision led to substantial lawsuits and badly damaged the reputation of the company. For the decision see *Grimshaw v Ford Motor Co*, 174 Cal Rptr 348 (Ct App 1981). Research on this point has been carried out by Rajat Khosla.

[23] 'A reserve fund is an account mandated by the debt documentation for the purpose of setting aside funds designed for use to ameliorate the effects of a project risk. The account can be funded from the construction budget, equity contributions, a draw on a letter of credit, a call on a guarantee, from project cash flow, or any combination of these sources' SL Hoffman, *The Law and Business of International Project Finance*, 2nd edn (The Hague, Kluwer Law International, 2001) 664.

[24] The legal power to use the roads is granted by the Consortium-Chad Convention for the Development of Oil Fields Article 8.2. On the dust problem, see Report by the Bank Information Center 2003, 2.

[25] 'The speed of construction work stands in marked contrast to the substantial delays of measures intended to ensure the welfare of local people and protection of the environment, some of which may never see the light of day'. Report by the World Rainforest Movement January 2003, www.wrm.org.uy/countries/Cameroon/Horta.html, accessed 30 September 2013. Compare similar issues for the BTC pipeline, Baku-Ceyhan Campaign, BP's pipeline record, www.bakuceyhan.org.uk/more_info/bp_ pipeline.htm, accessed 30 September 2013.

[26] On the effects of the emphasis on speed in completing pipeline projects, see Baku Ceyhan Campaign, BP's pipeline record, www.bakuceyhan.org.uk/more_info/bp_pipeline.htm, accessed 30 September 2013.

[27] J Delmon, *Project Finance, BOT Projects and Risk* (The Hague, Kluwer Law International, 2005) 292.

to contractors for work that comes in ahead of schedule, the Chad–Cameroon project having been completed a year ahead of the deadline. Interviews among contractors have established that these bonuses can often make the difference between some profit or none for their work, given the highly competitive bidding environment that often accompanies projects. Pressure is thereby created that pushes the company more easily towards the post hoc compensation solution, so as to keep work going, and away from the proactive, avoidance solution which would slow the pace of work down. Were the consortium owning the project companies in Chad and Cameroon to have looked for a way of adjusting its commercial objectives so as to do least damage to health concerns, it could have held to the original schedule for project completion, thereby giving more time to make changes to the access roads, which would have reduced the impact of the dust generated considerably. The company and the lenders would have stayed within their initial commercial plans: they would have delayed reimbursement of the loan, but at a lesser social cost.

This is not to say that such pressures of timing arise solely from the constraints of PF. In any given situation, the pressures may well arise for other reasons. An oil pipeline may rush to completion in order to fit in with wells beginning to produce; or in order to meet market demand that will soon peak. The pressures arising from the terms of loan reimbursement are therefore only one factor among several potential ones. What can be aimed at, however, is the tempering of one of the pressure points in this combined picture: that which is contributed from this mode of finance.

What if it becomes clear that serious social and environmental damage is threatened even if a project remains within its planned constraints of price and timing for completion? Initial calculations of costs involved in *avoiding* that damage may have been inaccurate, and now turn out to be too high for the project to be viable. The project might then be able to survive only by using the less expensive compensation alternative after damage is done. In the circumstances of PF, this point can be reached more quickly than it is when lending is made against the full balance sheet of the project sponsor. An SPV usually operates with a large proportion of its income already spoken for by the lender. In addition, as has been said, it services that loan via a single income stream coming from a single project, not the multiple streams from several projects that feed into the servicing of a typical corporate loan. This will mean that the ability of an SPV to take the measures necessary to avoid damage by slowing or stopping a project will depend on how it can manage to do so while still giving the lender the comfort that its expectations about reimbursement will be met. That will depend on the reserves held by the SPV: reserves available both to make the changes necessary to the project in order to avoid the damage, and to meet the ongoing financial obligations.

This pushes calculations in a direction that PF planners do not find congenial. As several authors in the theory of finance argue, the SPV is intended to be an entity with relatively low reserves: both as a means to keep it under the tight control of the project sponsor and in order to make it less attractive for host governments as an object of expropriation.[28] If the SPV opts for compensation to third parties as and when damage happens, this will also make demands on its reserve funds, but it is likely to a lesser demand than that involved in stopping the flow of revenue, spending money on structural changes to the project to deal with the problem, and reimbursing the loan at the same time. As a

[28] C Hainz and S Kleimeier, 'Project Finance: Managing Risk in International Syndicated Lending' (Limburg, Limburg Institute of Financial Economics, 2006) www.fdewb.unimaas.nl/finance/workingpapers, accessed 30 September 2013.

result, the project can slip more easily into trading off health, safety and environmental concerns against commercial demands. Projects may do more social damage when financed this way.

It is in these points drawn from the example of the Chad–Cameroon project that a tension emerges between the social and environmental standards that certain lenders try to bring to bear on investment, and the constraints imposed by the terms of investment that they are in fact providing. If lenders and borrowers are to create projects able to give adequate place to the avoidance of damage, then it may be necessary at certain points to carve out exceptions to the classic non-recourse PF model. That is, if lenders and borrowers are to take seriously the priority accorded to the avoidance of damage by slowing or stopping projects, this might only be a realistic prospect if either the sponsor is required to help meet the project company's shortfall in funds, or the lender relaxes its reimbursement schedule to make room for such delays. Negotiation among the parties, reflecting the impact of CSR, would add this necessary element of flexibility to the positions, with important potential benefits to the surrounding society.

THE FUTURE

As was said at the outset, PF provides a prism through which pass many of the fundamental tensions arising in the attempt to link the welfare of populations and foreign direct investment. As the reach of the UN Guiding Principles on Business and Human Rights is steadily extended, so will be their potential conflict with some traditional principles that have structured investment and corporate law and practice. Several such sites of conflict are on the horizon. First, PF has been attractive to borrowers because it fits neatly with a model of corporate law that divides parent company and subsidiary into spheres of separate responsibility. The fact that responsibility for repayment of a PF loan lies solely with the subsidiary goes well with the doctrine that the parent company is, as a general matter, not responsible for the obligations of the other members of the corporate group – while at the same time it controls these member companies via shareholdings carrying limited liability. But where PF relies on fragmentation of corporate responsibility, the UN Guiding Principles are aiming at integration. The Principles call on companies to take responsibility for the formulation and implementation of human rights principles at the highest level of corporate authority. The subsidiary might be a separate legal person, and might take on the PF loan as a borrower separate from the parent, but the UN Principles point in the opposite direction: the parent might not have the obligation to repay the loan, but if damage is done by the subsidiary as it presses ahead recklessly in order to meet repayment schedules, the parent may well find itself condemned in light of the Principles for failure to supervise its subsidiary adequately. Indeed, the law in a major jurisdiction is not far behind, given that a duty of care for a parent company's negligent failure to oversee the implantation of a company-wide norm intended by the parent to govern a subsidiary's conduct has recently been imposed by the Court of Appeal for England and Wales.[29] So while a parent company may continue to be insulated from liability to repay a PF loan, this will not deliver it immunity from shared liability for the activity by the subsidiary, financed by that loan, which damages a local population.

[29] *Chandler v Cape Plc* [2012] EWCA Civ 525 (25 April 2012).

There is a second site of potential conflict between the demands of human rights and the practice of PF. The basic contours of a PF loan rely on key features of the project being agreed *in advance* between project sponsor and the lending institution. Enough detail has to be provided by the sponsor in order to give the lender confidence. This can mean that by the time a project reaches the attention of a local population with concerns about the impact on its lands and people, there is little space left for substantial alterations. There is, in the standards set by the public lenders such as the IFC as well as the Equator banks a broad duty that cuts in the opposite direction: to consult in advance those populations at risk of negative impacts, such as eviction from their homes and productive lands. However, there is a range of points along a spectrum here as well: ideally the consultation should be undertaken before final decisions are reached about the core features of the project so as to allow space for fundamental alterations to deal with well-founded objections. At the other end of the spectrum, the requirement of consultation can be delayed until well after most of the details of the project have been decided – with the populations affected being brought into the picture in order to know how to minimise impacts that it has already been decided will occur. Human rights norms want to place consultation in the first part of the spectrum, given the importance of the interests of local populations at stake, while the decisions relating to PF are more comfortable with the latter part of the spectrum. Where consultation is located on this spectrum is an important issue, and is a test of how seriously financial planners take human rights. It is also a test of how seriously sovereign governments take those rights, as legislation and other forms of regulation design the consultation requirements.

These sites of competition between commercial and social rights concerns stand on a platform of emerging basic agreement on all sides that finance and human rights are linked to one another. As the practices of PF work through these competing positions, there will be valuable lessons for other areas in which this new linkage is being developed.

14

*Enhancing the International Monetary Fund's Compliance with Human Rights – The Issue of Accountability**

GIUSEPPE BIANCO AND FILIPPO FONTANELLI

I THE INTERNATIONAL MONETARY FUND AT THE BAR

THE INTERNATIONAL MONETARY Fund (IMF) is under strict scrutiny. Its legitimacy is *questioned* so frequently and in so many ways that nobody, not even officers of the Fund, really doubts that its legitimacy is indeed *questionable*. This chapter examines two areas in which the legitimacy record of the IMF is perceived to be so unsatisfactory that an incisive reform seems the only available cure to avoid a possible decease by irrelevance, or the only potential safeguard from violent death. These *loci horridi* are the institutional governance of the Fund and the mechanism of conditionality, or the 'accountability within' and the 'accountability without'. The present analysis looks in particular at the instances in which the IMF's design and its action are likely to impinge on the interests of two kinds of stakeholders: its own member states and the population of the countries affected by conditionality requirements.

The IMF cannot overlook the importance of its obligations towards the respect of human rights in its members and in particular in the countries where its programmes are implemented. As clearly stated in the Tilburg Guiding Principles on World Bank, IMF and Human Rights:

> As international legal persons, the World Bank and the IMF have international legal obligations to take full responsibility for human rights respect in situations where the institutions' own projects, policies or programmes negatively impact or undermine the enjoyment of human rights.[1]

On the one hand, combative economic powerhouses are increasingly challenging the post-war design of the Fund and its Western-centric features. On the other hand, there

* Although this chapter is the result of both authors' work, Giuseppe Bianco wrote Sections II and IV, Filippo Fontanelli wrote Sections III and V.

[1] Principle no 5. The Tilburg Guiding Principles on World Bank, IMF and Human Rights have been drafted by a group of experts, meeting at Tilburg University, the Netherlands, in October 2001 and April 2002. They relate to human rights obligations for international financial institutions (such as the World Bank and the International Monetary Fund), link these legal obligations in the field of human rights to the economic and political realities the organisations are confronted with, and discuss the possible redress of adverse human rights impacts of the activities of the financial institutions. The Guiding Principles are published as part of W van Genugten, P Hunt and S Mathews (eds), *World Bank, IMF and Human Rights* (Nijmegen, Wolf Legal Publishers, 2003) 247–55.

are peoples vexed by the adverse effects of IMF-imposed policies, wondering whether such a price is worth paying in exchange for their governments' financial relief. The tension between the IMF's activity and the human rights of the populations affected does not need to be detailed here. Suffice it to remember that the IMF typically requires states to improve their economic policies through various measures that often include spending cuts, and that cuts in governmental spending are likely to prejudice the provision of public services, which are closely related to the minimum levels of protection of economic, social and cultural rights.[2]

In fact, these very different manifestations of discontent rely on a similar realisation. In both cases, the social contract has lost whatever balance it originally had, and one of the contractors is not happy to bear the burden of performance any longer. The other one, however, has relatively little incentive to abdicate a share of its power, until the moment where the situation reaches the snapping point. Rising powerful countries which fight to achieve more power within the institution, and the poorest countries of the world, which are subject to the draconian policies of the Fund, have something in common. Both feel that the difficulties that they endure are based on obligations which lack legitimacy, because they flow from acts or processes that are not representative. In such a scenario, the very viability of the IMF is put into doubt, like that of other global institutions whose far-reaching powers are not matched by democratic decision making. As put by Stutzer and Frei, 'delegation of competencies to international organizations and their policy-making under current forms of democracy do not meet adequate procedural conditions to ensure that people in member countries feel like empowered citizens with autonomy and influence'.[3] This short remark encapsulates the double problem that affects the IMF. The decision-making process of the IMF is so far removed from the will of the citizens of member states that no generous massaging of representative democracy will succeed to convince them that they are choosing their own destiny. In addition to this, there is another social milieu in which collective decisions are taken according to a procedure that unreasonably favours certain members over others. The institutional decisions of the Fund, based on a system of weighted voting powers that has not been properly put on any scale for more than 60 years, is seen as perpetuating the privileges of a little club of Western powers in egregious disregard of contemporary trends in the global economy. In short, the IMF is perceived to be using a non-democratic procedure to take decisions which affect the human rights of hundreds of millions of people, whose right to have their voices heard within the decision-making process is virtually non-existent.

The current debt crisis, which poses a direct threat to human rights protection all over the world,[4] is also bringing to light the legitimacy shortcomings of the Fund. European countries are increasingly the recalcitrant recipients of IMF-dictated instructions, after four decades in which the latter mainly addressed developing countries. This shift is indicative of another change that might multiply the concerns about the current institutional

[2] Just to provide a comprehensive overview, consider Art 25(1) of the Universal Declaration of Human Rights: 'Everyone has the right to a standard of living adequate for the health and well-being of himself and of his family, including food, clothing, housing and medical care and necessary social services, and the right to security in the event of unemployment, sickness, disability, widowhood, old age or other lack of livelihood in circumstances beyond his control'.

[3] A Stutzer and BS Frey, 'Making International Organizations More Democratic' (2005) 1(3) *Review of Law and Economics* 305, 306.

[4] For a general study, see I Saiz, 'Rights in Recession? Challenges for Economic and Social Rights Enforcement in Times of Crisis' (2009) 1(2) *Journal of Human Rights Practice* 277.

structure of the Fund. Now that long-time lenders of IMF's resources are turning into potential and actual borrowers, whatever governance legitimacy underpinned the quota system on the basis of a borrower–lender divide, is vanishing together with the latter.

It is not the first time that a change in the mandate of the Fund has led to structural changes in its setup and activity: already after 1971 it had lost most of its powers on monetary matters and slowly transformed into a global policymaker. By the 1980s it had virtually stopped lending to developed countries and mainly engaged in the business of assisting the poorest states, through an inextricable mix of policy recommendations and financing loans. The regulatory reach of the IMF's actions was novel and was designed to react to 'the change in the IMF's clientele',[5] which at that point consisted mainly of developing countries.

Nowadays the number of clients has grown hugely and the diversity of the clientele is striking: the European Union is a recurrent addressee of IMF policy suggestions and EU members seek its assistance.[6] The width and reach of the IMF's powers, magnified in times of financial instability, demands a rethinking of its practice and structure. The fact that the IMF has no magic formula to solve the crisis overnight is not surprising in itself,[7] but should conjure up a more realistic idea of what the Fund is: not a technocratic dispenser of effective solutions, but a forum for consultation and deliberation on global economic policies. As such, its actions should be subjected to certain safeguards of legitimacy and democracy that would render them acceptable even when they do not work.

II THE PROTECTION OF A GLOBAL PUBLIC GOOD AND THE QUEST FOR LEGITIMACY

The functions currently performed by the IMF have made it the principal arbiter of international financial stability. The latter can be seen as a global public good: as the Fund's Managing Director Michel Camdessus once simply put it, 'If it works well, all countries have the opportunity to benefit; if it works badly, all are likely to suffer'.[8]

Global public goods are public in the sense that they are non-exclusive and non-competitive. This means that 'there must be free access to the public good in question and everybody must be able to consume the good without it being used up'.[9] These goods are also global because their effects are positive for more than just a group of countries (some approaches also consider that this characteristic implies that benefits 'accrue to several, if not all, population groups; and extend to both current and future generations

[5] S Schlemmer-Schulte, 'International Monetary Fund' in *Max Planck Encyclopedia of Public International Law* (2011).

[6] On the challenges posed by the post-2007 crisis to the lending facilities of the Fund, see M Committeri and F Spadafora ,'You Never Give Me Your Money? Sovereign Debt Crises, Collective Action Problems, and IMF Lending', IMF Working Paper WP/13/20 (2013) 27–32.

[7] See discussion on the IMF's guidelines in April 2013, www.ft.com/cms/s/0/6244099c-a8d1-11e2-a096-00144feabdc0.html#axzz2RhwseSjw, accessed 30 September 2013.

[8] M Camdessus, 'International Financial and Monetary Stability: A Global Public Good?', Remarks by the Managing Director of the International Monetary Fund, IMF/Research Conference *Key Issues in Reform of the International Monetary and Financial System*, Washington, DC, 28 May 1999, www.imf.org/external/np/speeches/1999/052899.HTM, accessed 30 September 2013.

[9] EA Andersen and B Lindsnæs, 'Public Goods: Concept, Definition, and Method' in EA Andersen, and B Lindsnæs (eds), *Towards New Global Strategies: Public Goods and Human Rights* (Leiden, Martinus Nijhoff Publishers, 2007) 34.

of people'[10]). The protection of a global public good such as international financial stability requires a heightened degree of legitimacy for the IMF. The global character of the good calls for the involvement of a constituency which should be as close as possible to universal. The public trait, on the other hand, brings with it the need to aim at transparency, fairness and accountability.[11]

Yet, what does legitimacy means for a global governance institution? One cannot but begin with the indicators put forward by Buchanan and Keohane: an institution is legitimate in the normative sense when it has the 'right to rule', and in the sociological sense if it is 'widely believed to have the right to rule'.[12] Key to the definition of legitimacy is the degree of acceptance of its use of power delegated by its constituency.[13] Although legitimacy can often be at odds – and in need of a permanent trade-off – with efficacy, a lack of the former can ultimately endanger the latter.[14] As has been argued with respect to national and supranational organisations, also at the international level 'no regime, even the most autocratic ones, can survive without the support, implicit and/or explicit, of its citizens'.[15]

Accountability is a helpful tool to assess the legitimacy of an institution. Accountability here stands for the possibility to monitor whether the activities performed by the institution are fair, democratic and resulting from a deliberative process. This monitoring process has to be on an ongoing basis, since accountability needs to reflect the changes and developments of the institution itself and of the context in which it operates. This in turn requires the institution to have two further characteristics, transparency and flexibility.[16] Institutions have to be transparent about their 'terms of accountability' and allow for a public debate on the issue. External analysis of the institution's performance can bring about contestation, which can then make the case for a reform of the accountability of the institution.[17]

Accountability, in turn, is required if an institution is to guarantee its respect for human rights. The Tilburg Guiding Principles on World Bank, IMF and Human Rights assert that 'Rights and obligations demand accountability, [. . . accountability] mechanisms must be accessible, transparent and effective'.[18] Accountability is the means through which the Fund's human rights record can be made public, scrutinised and gradually

[10] B Choudhury, 'International Investment Law as a Global Public Good' (2013) 17(2) *Lewis & Clark Law Review* 481, 499.

[11] J Brassett and E Tsingou, 'The Politics of Legitimate Global Governance' (2011) 18(1) *Review of International Political Economy* 1–16; M Bukovansky, 'Liberal States, International Order, and Legitimacy: An Appeal for Persuasion over Prescription' (2011) 44 *International Politics* 175–93.

[12] A Buchanan and RO Keohane, 'The Legitimacy of Global Governance Institutions' (2006) 20(4) *Ethics & International Affairs* 405.

[13] C Cottarelli, 'Efficiency and Legitimacy: Trade-Offs in IMF Governance' (2005) IMF Working Paper WP/05/107, www.imf.org/external/pubs/ft/wp/2005/wp05107.pdf, accessed 30 September 2013, 3. On the importance for an institution to preserve an appearance of legitimacy which would make its community of reference ready to voluntarily abide by the instructions dictated by the institution, see I Hurd, 'Legitimacy, Power, and the Symbolic Life of the UN Security Council' (2002) 8 *Global Governance* 50–51.

[14] See M Kahler, 'Internal Governance and IMF Performance' in EM Truman (ed), *Reforming the IMF for the 21st Century* (Institute for International Economics, Special Report 19, 2006) 266–67.

[15] AA Svetlozar, 'The EU "Crisis of Legitimacy" Revisited: Concepts, Causes, and Possible Consequences for the European Politics and Citizens' (2007) 2(7) *Political Perspectives EPRU* 3.

[16] Even the official discourse of IMF papers is a testimony to the importance of transparency: 'The conversion of the IMF in the second half of the 1990s into a transparent institution was a major step in the right direction', L Van Houtven 'Governance of the IMF Decision Making, Institutional Oversight, Transparency, and Accountability' (2002), IMF Pamphlet series no 53, www.imf.org/external/pubs/ft/pam/pam53/pam53.pdf, accessed 30 September 2013, 60.

[17] Buchanan and Keohane (n 12) 429.

[18] Principle no 17.

improved. Human rights accountability is all the more necessary ('imperative'[19]) since the consequences of the actions of the Fund are capable of influencing directly the standards of living of millions of citizens and because it is generally agreed that the IMF is bound, as a legal person, by the obligations of public international law, which obviously encompass at the very least the responsibility to respect the standards of human rights protection set by customary law.[20]

To what extent does the IMF comply with these legitimacy standards? When compared with other international institutions such as the World Trade Organization,[21] a difference which becomes immediately apparent is that even the formal decision-making process is not based on equality of sovereign states.[22] Reflecting the 'fund' nature of the IMF, ever since its inception, the reality of economic and financial power has been at the heart of the institution's governance.[23] Instead of attributing one vote to each member and following the egalitarian paradigm, the Articles allocate voting powers proportionally to each country's quota – which, in turn, somehow represents its importance in the world economy (more on this below). Such a structure strongly resembles that of a corporation, with shareholders having a different weight in proportion to their shares.

From a corporate governance point of view this might make sense and might guarantee a high degree of efficiency,[24] at least so long as the relative power of the members is proportionate to their quotas, *quod non*. Nevertheless, this approach can hardly be reconciled with the protection of a global public good. Indeed, the public character of international financial stability has to be echoed in the structure of the Fund, in order to increase its legitimacy.

For an institution's legitimacy to be called into question, however, its power structure must first come to the point of colliding with its contextual actors. Contestation, which is the trigger for reform, arguably occurs when the actors which originally guaranteed the governance structure stop supporting it, or if these actors are overwhelmed by other ones. This is what happened with respect to the IMF.

At the beginning, when the Fund was conceived, the focus on the quota system was arguably justified. The IMF was envisaged as a mechanism through which several countries could intervene to support other members when the latter encountered problems with their balance of payments.[25] Although the technical arrangements employed would

[19] See for instance N Wahi, 'Human Rights Accountability of the IMF and the World Bank: A Critique of Existing Mechanisms and Articulation of a Theory of Horizontal Accountability' (2005) 12 *UC Davis Journal of International Law & Policy* 333, 334.

[20] S Skogly, *The Human Rights Obligations of the World Bank and the IMF* (London, Cavendish Publishing, 2001).

[21] PFJ Macrory, AF Appleton and MG Plummer (eds), *The World Trade Organization: Legal, Economic and Political Analysis* (New York, Springer, 2005).

[22] D Mügge, 'Limits of Legitimacy and the Primacy of Politics in Financial Governance' (2011) 18(1) *Review of International Political Economy* 52–74.

[23] L Martinez-Diaz, 'Executive Boards in International Organizations: Lessons for Strengthening IMF Governance' (2008) IEO Background Paper BP/08/08, www.ieo-imf.org/ieo/files/completedevaluations/05212008BP08_08.pdf, accessed 30 September 2013; A Mountford, 'The Formal Governance Structure of the International Monetary Fund', IEO Background Paper BP/08/01, www.ieo-imf.org/ieo/files/completedevaluations/05212008BP08_01.pdf, accessed 30 September 2013.

[24] The economic efficiency of the IMF's policies can, however, be called into question. See eg JW Head, *Losing the Global Development War: A Contemporary Critique of the IMF, the World Bank, and the WTO* (Leiden, Martinus Nijhoff, 2008).

[25] See MD Bordo, 'The Bretton Woods International Monetary System: A Historical Overview' in MD Bordo and B Eichengreen (eds), *A Retrospective on the Bretton Woods System: Lessons for International Monetary Reform* (Chicago, University of Chicago Press, 1993) 3–108.

not warrant such terminology, the countries in the first group are usually referred to as the lenders, and those in the second as the borrowers. Lenders were bound to coincide with the most developed countries, and borrowers with the low income ones. Such a state of affairs did in fact materialise, and accounts for most of the IMF's history. The current financial crisis blurred the distinction between the two groups. Even before the crisis, the global economic landscape had witnessed the growing importance of middle-income countries, whose interests were not taken into account by the lenders/borrowers equilibrium. Over the two past decades, the conditionality attached to the lending programmes became so demanding and intrusive that several countries 'opted out' of IMF lending altogether. In order to do so, these middle-income nations repaid their outstanding amounts due to the Fund and started stockpiling resources to draw from in case of future crises. This action, although probably not thoroughly coordinated by the IMF members involved, was capable of threatening the effectiveness, and potentially the very existence, of the Fund.

This change opened a channel for calling into question the legitimacy of the institution, and this contestation is what made the case for reforms of the quota system, inter alia.[26] The governance system of the IMF has thus been put under fire. Criticisms have come from sources as diverse as economists, human rights activists and emerging countries. Arguably the single most prominent critic has been Joseph Stiglitz, whose Nobel Prize for economics and career as the World Bank's Chief Economist have warranted worldwide visibility of his remarks.[27] Stiglitz's points on the IMF's choices in political economy were so fierce as to command a response directly from the IMF itself.[28]

Human rights lawyers have in particular pointed at the potentially disruptive consequences of imposing too heavy a burden through conditionality programmes. Indeed, some have invoked a shift from economic conditionality imposed on borrowing countries to human rights conditionality placed on the IMF itself: 'accountability to the full range of human rights obligations must be embedded within [the Fund's] mandate, and these must be asserted as having primacy over any other competing global policy considerations'.[29]

Such contestation, and the menace to the IMF's viability, made an impact and were reflected in the institution's decisions. Since 2006, an increasingly incisive reform has been carried out to change the system of governance of the Fund, with a particular focus on the quota system. Moreover, from 2000 to 2009 a series of measures progressively reduced the areas where conditionality was to be employed, and its coverage.[30] Although these innovations undoubtedly represent positive progress, there remains a wide margin for improving the human rights accountability and institutional legitimacy of the Fund. The following sections assess the internal and external accountability of the organisation, and reflect on potential future reforms.

[26] Amongst many others, see V Kelkar, PK Chaudhry, M Vanduser-Snow and V Bhasker, 'Reforming the IMF: Towards Enhanced Accountability and Legitimacy' in A Buria (ed), *Reforming the Governance of the IMF and the World Bank* (London, Anthem Press, 2005) 45–74.

[27] See eg J Stiglitz, *Globalization and Its Discontents* (New York, Norton & Company, 2003).

[28] TC Dawson, 'Stiglitz, the IMF and Globalization' (13 June 2002) A Speech to the MIT Club of Washington by Director, External Relations Department, IMF, www.imf.org/external/np/speeches/2002/061302.htm, accessed 30 September 2013.

[29] I Saiz, 'Rights in Recession? Challenges for Economic and Social Rights Enforcement in Times of Crisis' (2009) 1(2) *Journal of Human Rights Practice* 290.

[30] A Bloom 'The Power of the Borrower: IMF Responsiveness to Emerging Market Economies' (2011) 43 *International Law and Politics* 797 ff.

III ACCOUNTABILITY WITHIN

A The System of Quotas and Governance before the Reform

All members of the IMF have an assigned quota that reflects a percentage of the Fund's resources as well as their respective voting shares in the Fund's decision-making procedures.[31] It is expressed in SDR (Special Drawing Rights) and is proportional to the amount of the contribution the member owes to the Fund, as well as the amount it can borrow from its lines of credit.

The quota allocation shapes the decision-making process of the IMF and therefore has a direct bearing on the de facto ownership of the Fund's actions: as is briefly explained, a small number of countries are able to capture the agenda of the institution and secure the adoption of far-reaching policies that affect countries (and their citizens) who have little or no weight in the deliberation. This is a major concern for the human rights accountability of the Fund, and it is enough to quote an excerpt of the Tilburg Principles to appreciate how the lack of equal representation[32] translates inevitably into a legitimacy deficit in terms of human rights guarantees:

> 32. Concrete policies, programmes, projects and actions activate specific duties, including in particular with regard to people whose lives are affected by the decisions taken. In order to establish the nature and implications of such concrete duties, decision-making by the World Bank and the IMF should be open and transparent, so that the interests of all stakeholders be represented and acknowledged in the light of applicable international human rights standards.

From this short extract it is easy to understand that the optimal form of decision-making, as far as accountability and human rights protection are concerned, would envisage all stakeholders having a voice and a weight in the deliberative process that are somehow commensurate to the interests that might be affected by the decision. As was noted, the lack of transparency and the democratic deficit in the decision-making procedure, besides having an impact on the lives of those affected and their economic rights, determine at the outset a breach of human rights, as they violate 'the civil and political rights to information, representation and participation in the decision-making process'.[33]

In reality, the allocation of powers within the IMF is very far from this model. The magnitude of state quotas is vaguely reflective of their economic power, and a set of formulas have been devised[34] to calculate them on the basis of the member's GDP and the 'openness' of its economy, plus other secondary variables.[35] However, the initial allocation of quotas, designed in 1944, was largely dictated by a political and diplomatic

[31] IMF, 'Articles of Agreement', Art III(1).

[32] An element that is often quoted as a flaw of the institution's democratic governance. On the concept, see M Zurn, 'Democratic Governance Beyond the Nation-state: The EU and Other International Institutions' (2000) 6(2) *European Journal of International Relations* 183.

[33] See Wahi (n 19) 348.

[34] A Mirakhor and Z Iqbal, 'Rethinking the Governance of the International Monetary Fund', IMF Working Paper, WP/06/273 (December 2006).

[35] The current formula 'is a weighted average of GDP (weight of 50 percent), openness (30 percent), economic variability (15 percent), and international reserves (5 percent). For this purpose, GDP is measured through a blend of GDP – based on market exchange rates (weight of 60 percent) – and on PPP exchange rates (40 percent). The formula also includes a "compression factor" that reduces the dispersion in calculated quota shares across members'. See IMF Factsheet, *IMF Quotas*, 31 March 2013, www.imf.org/external/np/exr/facts/quotas.htm, accessed 30 September 2013.

balancing exercise.[36] Only thereafter were these formulas developed, *ex post facto*, and they were never used, since quotas are adjusted very seldom (when there is a routine quota review, the proportion between quotas is generally maintained).

Although initially quotas corresponded to the actual economic power held by each member, over time the distribution of economic power has shifted. Thus, a gulf has arisen between the picture implicated by the quota allocation and the real position of members in the global economy. In particular, dynamic economies with higher growth rates found themselves underrepresented in the Fund and have started pushing, during the last decade, for a reform of the quota system that could bring about a 'realignment' between quotas and real economic weight. This reform would necessarily include the adoption of a new formula, which takes GDP as the main element of the calculation, discarding other elements such as 'openness'.[37] In addition to those members advocating a genuine proportion between quotas and economic powers, there are many members that, conversely, protest the ineluctable effect that weighted membership has on small countries. In other words, those members whose economies are incommensurably smaller than those of the G20 will end up having virtually no voice in the Fund, precisely because their quota is fated to be irrelevant.[38] This problem is only modestly alleviated by the existence of basic voting rights, a minimum number of votes shared evenly among all members, which now adds up to an aggregate 5.5 per cent of the total voting rights.[39]

Along with the quota allocation, another governance aspect that has spurred growing discontent among members is the design of the Executive Board. In the Board of Governors, which manages all the Fund's powers, each member has a representative whose vote is weighted in accordance with its quota. The Executive Board, instead, manages the day-to-day activities of the IMF, and exercises all the powers conferred upon it by the Board of Governors. The Executive Board is comprised of 20 directors (now 24), and five seats are reserved by law to the five IMF members holding the highest quotas.[40] The other directors, currently 19 due to a temporary enlargement of the Board, are elected. The existence of a non-elected contingent and the institutional custom of reserving 10 seats to Western European countries have been increasingly pointed at as a symptom of reduced legitimacy and democratic accountability. This aggravates the position of those non-European countries that already experience underrepresentation because of the quota system.[41]

[36] See the accurate historical account of the 1944 arrangement in A Buira, 'The Governance of the International Monetary Fund' in I Kaul et al (eds), *Providing Global Public Goods* (Oxford, Oxford University Press, 2003) 227 ff and in M Skala, C Thimann and R Wölfinger (2007), 'The Search for Columbus' Egg: Finding a New Formula to Determine Quotas at the IMF', ECB Occasional Paper Series, no 70, August 2007, www.ecb.int/pub/pdf/scpops/ecbocp70.pdf, accessed 30 September 2013, 9.

[37] See RN Cooper and EM Truman 'The IMF Quota Formula: Linchpin of Fund Reform' (2007) PIIE Policy Brief 07-01, Washington: Peterson Institute for International Economics, www.piie.com/publications/interstitial.cfm?ResearchID=709, accessed 30 September 2013, 5 ff.

[38] N Woods and D Lombardi, 'Uneven Patterns of Governance: How Developing Countries are Represented in the IMF' (2006) 13(3) *Review of International Political Economy* 499.

[39] The current percentage is the result of a reform undertaken in 2008, which tripled them, after successive rounds of quota reviews had progressively watered down the relative weight of basic voting rights, which initially was up to 11%, see A Gaentzsch, 'IMF Quota Reform: The Prospects of Improving Governance and Voice Opportunities through Revised Voting Shares' (2009) 10 *The Journal of International Policy Solutions*, 6.

[40] IMF, 'Articles of Agreement', Art XII(3).

[41] For an overview and the reasons behind the calls for reform, see DP Rapkin and JR Strand, 'Voting Power Implications in a Double Majority Voting Procedure in the IMF's Executive Board' in A Buria (ed), *Reforming the Governance of the IMF and the World Bank* (London, Anthem Press, 2005) 235; EM Truman, 'Rearranging IMF Chairs and Shares: The Sine Qua Non of IMF Reform' in EM Truman, *Reforming the IMF for the 21st*

B Accomplished and Missing Steps

The state of the IMF's governance described above, which betrays its post-War origin, caused many members and observers to voice doubts about the Fund's overall record in legitimacy and accountability. Criticism from members and stakeholders permeated the debates inside the institution, and governance reform has become a fixed item on the Fund's agenda, so much so that the IMF established the Independent Evaluation Office (IEO), an internal watchdog body with the mandate of providing objective assessments on IMF operations.[42]

As highlighted by Torres, alongside with the Fund's effectiveness deficit, its action suffers from a legitimacy deficit that threatens its viability and existence, and is reflected in a list of recurring accusations, summarised as follows.[43] Failure to use a reasonable quota formula makes the IMF incapable of updating and adjusting its governance to reflect the current balance of power;[44] the practice of subjecting loans to strict conditions (see below) raises the suspicion that, in the absence of a transparent and democratic decision-making procedure, regulatory decisions will be captured by lending members' interests, to the detriment of borrowing countries' population; the oversight powers of the Fund, which transcend its role as a lending institution,[45] are hardly reconcilable with the wealth-based distribution of powers; the link between economic weight and borrowing caps, encapsulated in the use of quotas, makes it more difficult for small states to obtain enough funds in times of need (conversely, big economies can count on larger borrowing reserves even if they will hardly need to use them). For all these reasons, 'it does not seem functional for the Fund's purposes that the rich should have the right to integrate bigger quotas and, therefore, have greater access to the Fund's financing and the privilege of running the institution by themselves'.[46] The state of affairs had evolved to a point where the IMF's crisis of legitimacy, reflected in a steady decrease of the support from its constituency, made the 'recalibration' of its governance structure a forced passage.[47]

Century (Washington, Peterson Institute for International Economics, 2006) 201; L Martinez-Diaz, 'Executive Boards in International Organizations: Lessons for Strengthening IMF Governance' (2008) IEO Background Paper BP/08/08, www.ieo-imf.org/ieo/files/completedevaluations/05212008BP08_08.pdf, accessed 30 September 2013.

[42] See the rules of engagement of the IEO on the official website, www.ieo-imf.org/ieo/pages/ieohome.aspx, accessed 30 September 2013. Principle 41 of the Tilburg Principles calls for the IEO to include human rights protection among its competences.

[43] See HR Torres, 'Reforming the International Monetary Fund – Why Its Legitimacy is at Stake' (2007) 10(3) *Journal of International Economic Law* 448 ff.

[44] It is easy to appreciate the scenario of imbalances by taking a look at the table on the members' voting powers, www.imf.org/external/np/sec/memdir/members.aspx, accessed 30 September 2013.

[45] On the increased mandate of the IMF, which exceeds its function as lending centre and might stretch to areas that fall outside its powers under the Articles of Agreement, see B Eichengreen, 'A Blueprint of IMF Reform. More than Just a Lender' (2007) 10(2) *International Finance* 153 and R Hockett, 'From Macro to Micro to "Mission Creep": Defending the IMF's Emerging Concern with the Infrastructural Prerequisites to Global Financial Stability' (2002) 41(1) *Columbia Journal of Transnational Law* 153.

[46] Torres (n 43) 452.

[47] On the concept of legitimacy crisis and the causes leading to institutional reforms, see C Reus-Smit, 'International Crises of Legitimacy' (2007) 44 *International Politics* 168 ff. On the causes and the scope of the IMF's legitimacy deficit, see L Seabrooke, 'Legitimacy Gaps in the World Economy: Explaining the Sources of the IMF's Legitimacy Crisis' (2007) 44 *International Politics* 253 and passim. On the endemic contemporary challenges posed to international economic institutions, see JW Head, *Losing the Global Development War: A Contemporary Critique of the IMF, the World Bank, and the WTO* (Leiden, Martinus Nijhoff, 2008).

Starting in 2006, a comprehensive cycle of reforms has been embarked upon. It aimed at resolving the inequalities inherent in the governance design of the Fund, and specifically the shortcomings related to the quota allocation (also in connection with ordinary and basic voting rights), and the membership of the Executive Board. The first reform, in 2006,[48] allowed for a small ad hoc adjustment of the quotas of a handful of dynamic, underrepresented economies (China, Mexico, South Korea and Turkey), as well as for a doubling of basic voting rights, and the attribution of more resources to overcrowded constituencies in the Executive Board (that is, those elected directors representing a large number of members). In 2008 a second reform was approved, which entered into force in 2011.[49] A second ad hoc adjustment was undertaken, basic votes were tripled, and a rule was adopted to prevent their further dilution. Directors representing a high number of members were granted the power to appoint an additional Alternate Director.

These changes stopped short of eradicating the congenital governance defects: the two major advancements (a quota realignment based on a genuine formula and a more representative Executive Board) were still outstanding. This motivated members to enter the subsequent round of reforms, which is still under way. This plan[50] is premised on three major reforms:

- In the framework of a general quota review that would double the Fund's resources (up to approximately US$ 300 billion), quotas will be redistributed so as to cause a 5–7 per cent shift from the aggregate quotas of old powers to those of emerging economies. Through the incisive curtailment of the powers of few overrepresented countries, a legion of smaller countries will have their quotas increased, and all major distortions will be removed (ie the biggest economies will figure at the top of the quota chart, pushing down what now look like random outsiders, such as Belgium or Italy). The exact proportions of this revolutionary realignment depend on the quota formula adopted to guide the process, an element over which the struggle is still very much open.[51]
- The Executive Board will do away with appointed members, and include only elective ones. The democratic profile will benefit from the European countries' readiness to give up two of the 10 seats that had been customarily reserved to them, and from the increased organisational privileges of directors heading large constituencies.
- The relative weight of poorest countries' basic voting rights will be frozen to prevent further quota reviews from rendering them irrelevant.

These reforms have been approved on paper, but their entry into force is still under question. The reform of the Executive Board has not yet been accepted (ratified) by a sufficient number of members.[52] This stalemate is also blocking the implementation of the quota

[48] *IMF Board of Governors Approves Quota and Related Governance Reforms*, IMF Press Release no 06/205 (18 September 2006).

[49] *IMF Board of Governors Adopts Quota and Voice Reforms by Large Margin*, IMF Press Release no 08/93 (29 April 2008), www.imf.org/external/np/sec/pr/2008/pr0893.htm, accessed 30 September 2013.

[50] Aptly summarised in RM Nelson and MA Weiss, 'IMF Reforms: Issues for Congress Analyst in International Trade and Finance' (2012) CRS Report for Congress of 12 December 2012, www.fas.org/sgp/crs/misc/R42844.pdf, accessed 30 September 2013.

[51] IMF, *Quota Formula Review – Data Update and Further Considerations* (Washington, 28 June 2012) www.imf.org/external/np/pp/eng/2012/062812.pdf, accessed 30 September 2013.

[52] Since this reform would imply a change of the Articles, it requires approval by at least three-fifths of the members, representing at least 85% of the total quotas.

increase,[53] since the members agreed on an interlocking system aimed at securing the simultaneous entry into force of the two reforms: unless both are accepted, neither will enter into effect. The major suspect for the reform's failure to materialise, besides the objective difficulty of agreeing on a shared quota formula, is the initial reluctance of the US to submit the reform to Congress (during the 2012 presidential election campaign), as well as the recent refusal by both Houses to speed up the process of approval of the increase of US's contribution permanently allocated to the Fund (which would be required to maintain the quota after the doubling of the Fund's resources).[54] Since the US hold 17.69 per cent of the Fund's quotas, it is fair to say that they have the veto power over any change in the Articles, and that they are currently preventing the reform from coming into effect.

IV ACCOUNTABILITY WITHOUT: CONDITIONALITY

A The Origins of Conditionality

The accountability of the IMF also has to be analysed with respect to its external dimension: accountability 'without'. This aspect relates to the manner in which the organisation is involved in its programmes on balances of payments. In essence, the Fund grants its loans to countries in need on the basis of conditionality: only if the country implements the predetermined set of measures required, is it entitled to obtain the successive instalments from the IMF. The way conditionality is regulated and applied provides a good indicator to assess the external accountability of the IMF.

Conditionality is described by the IMF as 'the link between the approval or continuation of the Fund's financing and the implementation of specified elements of economic policy by the country receiving this financing',[55] or 'those features of a member country's program of economic reform whose successful implementation is expressly established by the IMF as a condition for the availability of IMF financial assistance'.[56] Another, more colourful definition of conditionality is that of a '*portmanteau* word that encompasses all the policies that the Fund wishes a member to follow so that it can resolve its problem consistently with the Articles'.[57]

Conditionality includes performance criteria, which originated in loans for Latin American members, and were subsequently extended to all requests.[58] Performance conditions determine specific targets to be met by a set deadline. If the objective, expressed in quantitative terms, is attained, then the country can obtain the instalment conceded by the IMF.

[53] The requisite majority had been attained (acceptance by members representing at least 70% of the total quotas), but the quota review has been made conditional upon the acceptance of the governance reform, so as to couple the two.

[54] See www.reuters.com/article/2013/03/06/us-imf-usa-idUSBRE92501M20130306, accessed 30 September 2013, on Obama's plans to gain Congress's approval.

[55] IMF, Conditionality in Fund-Supported Programs – Overview, www.imf.org, accessed 30 September 2013.

[56] RB Leckow, 'Conditionality in the International Monetary Fund' in IMF Legal Department, *Current Developments in Monetary and Financial Law*, vol 3 (IMF, 2005) 4.

[57] M Guitián, *Fund Conditionality: Evolution of Principles and Practices* (1981) IMF Pamphlet Series, no 38. See also RW Stone, 'The Political Economy of IMF Lending in Africa' (2004) 98(4) *American Political Science Review* 577–91.

[58] J Asherman, 'The International Monetary Fund: A History of Compromise' (1984) 16(2) *New York University Journal of International Law & Politics* 266.

Different studies have demonstrated that the level of human rights protection in a country borrowing from the IMF can be affected by conditionality. Conditionality requirements are translated into domestic policies, which tighten fiscal budgets, often operating horizontal cuts. National measures prioritise economic liberalisation and privatisation over other values, such as social welfare and the environment, and can unleash 'the destructive potential of the new "liberal" era'.[59]

This unintended outcome of the IMF's interventions runs counter to the obligation to respect human rights. Firstly, it might provoke a head-on collision with the basic right to self-determination of the people affected by the conditionality straitjacket: this essential right instantiates the people's entitlement to determine autonomously their political, economic and social agenda, and naturally includes the freedom to choose how to dispose of the country's wealth and resources.[60]

This unintended consequence, moreover, can be seen as breaching the Fund's Articles of Agreement, which acknowledge the need to respect domestic social and political policies of members (see Art IV(3)b).[61] As has been argued in the Tilburg Principles, these domestic 'policies include international commitments to human rights [and] the IMF [should not] impede the Borrower from honouring such legal obligations, or agree to measures depriving individuals of their rights under domestic and international law'.[62]

This is often due to the fact that the lower groups on the social ladder can suffer heavily from budget cutting and can resort to protest, which then provokes government repression.[63] Furthermore, since the protection of all human rights requires public spending, harder conditions included in the programme will entail higher chances for a poorer guarantee of human rights.[64]

The introduction of conditionality occurred a few years after the creation of the organisation at Bretton Woods, and was initially adopted by the means of decisions. In 1952 conditionality and standby arrangements were born, soon to be followed by disbursement in tranches (in 1956).[65] The practice of conditionality could find a thin ground in the original text of the Articles, whose Art I included amongst the purposes of the Fund that of 'making the Fund's resources available to them [IMF members] under adequate safeguards'.[66]

[59] M Kothari and A Kothari, 'Structural Adjustment vs Environment' (1993) 28(11) *Economic and Political Weekly* 474.

[60] See common Art 1 of the International Covenant on Civil and Political Rights and the International Covenant on Economic, Social and Cultural Rights.

[61] For an analysis of the legitimacy of the imposition of conditionality requirements, on the basis of the IMF's mandate set out in the Articles of Agreement, see C Pirzio-Biroli, 'Making Sense of the IMF Conditionality Debate' (1983) 17 *Journal of World Trade Law* 115.

[62] Principle no 25.

[63] MR Abouharb and DL Cingranelli, 'IMF Programs and Human Rights, 1981–2003' (2009) 47 *Review of International Organisations* 50.

[64] This is immediately clear for rights such as economic and social rights, but it is also true for rights such as the safeguard of physical integrity and life, since the latter's protection necessitates a properly functioning police and judicial system. See J Donnelly, Universal human rights in theory and practice, 2nd edn (Ithaca, NY, Cornell University Press, 2003)

[65] Y Akyüz, 'Reforming the IMF: Back to the Drawing Board' (2006) *Third World Network Global Economic Series*, no 7, 11.

[66] IMF, 'Articles of Agreement,' Art I (v), original text. It is open to debate whether conditionality was invented by IMF officials (eg S Dell, 'On Being Grandmotherly: The Evolution of IMF Conditionality', Essays in International Finance, Princeton University, no 144, Oct 1981, 4) or whether they merely expressed 'the underlying principle of conditionality that had been there all along' (E Wiesner, 'Discussion' of A Diz, 'The Conditions Attached to Adjustment Financing: Evolution of the IMF Practice' in *The International Monetary*

This innovation was 'constitutionalised' by the First Amendment of the Articles, enacted in 1969. On the one hand, Art I(v) was slightly modified: 'making the Fund's resources *temporarily* available to them under adequate safeguards' (emphasis added). On the other hand, in Article V 'Transactions with the Fund', a subsection (c) was added to section 3. This subsection elaborated on the language of Art I(v), and stipulated:

> A member's use of the resources of the Fund shall be in accordance with the purposes of the Fund. The Fund shall adopt policies on the use of its resources that will assist members to solve their balance of payments problems in a manner consistent with the purposes of the Fund and that will establish adequate safeguards for the temporary use of its resources.[67]

The entrenchment of conditionality provided a firmer basis for what had only been hinted at by the original text. This was used by IMF officials to rebut any doubts about the legitimacy of conditionality: 'The desirability of a concept of conditionality is usually accepted, and the legal necessity for it cannot be questioned at all since the date of the First Amendment'.[68]

A further innovation was introduced by the Second Amendment, which was approved by the Board of Governors on 24 March 1976, and entered into force on 1 April 1978. Although the Second Amendment is best known for the acknowledgment of the right of members to adopt exchange rate arrangements of their choice (after the US brought an end to par values and convertibility of the dollar on 15 August 1971), it must be recalled that it also intervened in the field of conditionality. The new Art V(3)(a) stipulated: 'The Fund shall adopt policies on the use of its general resources, including policies on stand-by or similar arrangements'. 'Stand-by arrangements' detail the conditions a country has to respect when it requests funds above the reserve tranche.[69] The reference to 'similar arrangements' was added 'mainly in recognition of extended arrangements but also to make room for further categories of arrangements if they should be found necessary'.[70] Subsections (b) and (c) further stipulated that the country had to abide by the IMF's policies on the use of its resources, and that the Fund must examine the compatibility of the member's request with such policies.

Consequently, by the entry into force of the Second Amendment in 1979, conditionality was well established as an essential part of the IMF's lending operations. Although not explicitly foreseen in the original Articles of Agreement, it does not appear unreasonable for the Fund to require certain conditions to grant its resources. The objective is to have a sort of 'security' for the repayment of its loans. At the same time, it would serve the country's interest to avoid a recurrence of its balance of payments problems, and thus contribute to global stability. However, the significant impact that conditionality can have, and has had, on IMF members calls for a closer look at the manner in which it has been implemented.

System: Forty Years after Bretton Woods, Conference Series no 28 (Boston, Federal Reserve Bank of Boston, 1984) 237). See also J Gold, 'Public International Law in the International Monetary System' (1984) 38(3) *Southwestern Law Journal* 799–852.

[67] Resolution no 22-8 of the Board of Governors of the IMF at its Twenty-Second Annual Meeting in Rio de Janeiro, 29 September 1967.

[68] J Gold, *Conditionality*, IMF Pamphlet Series (1979), no 31, 14.

[69] Asherman (n 58) 284.

[70] Gold (n 68) quoted in M Darrow, *Between Light and Shadow: The World Bank, the International Monetary Fund and International Human Rights Law* (Oxford, Hart Publishing, 2003) 47, fn 218.

The content of conditionality requirements must abide by certain rules: for instance, it cannot run against the IMF's purposes, nor impose the removal of restrictions on capital movements.[71] Furthermore, 'In helping members to devise economic and financial programs, the Fund will pay due regard to the domestic social and political objectives'.[72] This has been taken to imply that 'the IMF could not, for example, establish conditions that are related to the human rights record of a member'.[73]

The degree of conditionality varies according to the credit tranche concerned. As it has been nicely put, 'les conditions économiques imposées par le FMI seront d'autant plus contraignantes que les tirages demandés par un pays porteront sur les tranches de crédit élevées'.[74] Thus, the higher the loan relative to the requesting country's quota, the tougher the conditions imposed. For instance, in the 1960s, when the United Kingdom obtained a drawing corresponding to 5 per cent of its quota, it did not have to undertake a programme, whereas when Chile asked to borrow an amount equal to 16 per cent of its quota, it had to provide 'a clearer indication that appropriate fiscal and monetary measures were in prospect'.[75]

B The Shift Towards Structural Adjustment

The use of the IMF's general resources has significantly evolved over time. The initial focus on balance of payments crises has gradually shifted towards tackling developing countries' debt burden, especially with the debt crises of the 1980s. As a consequence, the Fund's therapy has moved from short-term arrangements to stabilisation programmes and structural adjustment programmes.[76] This in turn entailed that programmes detailed not only macroeconomic conditions, but also structural policies, which could be so broad as to include

> financial-sector policies; liberalization of trade, capital markets, and of the exchange rate system; privatization and public enterprise policies; tax and expenditure policies (apart from the overall fiscal stance); labor market policies; pricing and marketing policies; transparency and disclosure policies; poverty-reduction and social safety-net policies; pension policies; corporate governance policies (including anti-corruption measures); and environmental policies.[77]

This was reflected in the number of commitments (prior actions, structural benchmarks, conditions for programme reviews and performance criteria) required of the requesting country, which during the Asian crisis of 1997–98 went up to 104 structural policy undertakings in the case of Indonesia, for instance.[78]

[71] Since restricting capital movements is recognised as a right of IMF members, see Art VI, section 3.

[72] Decision no 12864-(02/102) 25 September 2002, *Selected Decisions*, at I.A.4.

[73] RB Leckow, 'Conditionality in the International Monetary Fund' in IMF Legal Department, *Current Developments in Monetary and Financial Law*, vol 3 (IMF, 2005) 59.

[74] D Carreau and P Juillard, *Droit international économique* (Paris, Dalloz, 2010) 638.

[75] Asherman (n 58) 265.

[76] Darrow (n 70) 49–50.

[77] M Goldstein, 'IMF Structural Conditionality: How Much Is Too Much?' (2000) *Institute for International Economics* 4, petersoninstitute.org/publications/wp/01-4.pdf, accessed 30 September 2013. See also R Swaminathan, 'Regulating Development: Structural Adjustment and the Case for National Enforcement of Economic and Social Rights' (1998) 37(1) *Columbia Journal of International Law* 161.

[78] A Buira, *An Analysis of IMF Conditionality* (2003) G-24 Discussion Paper no 22, Washington DC, 9.

The depth and breadth of the structural policies included in the IMF conditionality have had a strong impact, and not always a positive one, especially on developing countries.[79] This has spurred analyses and overt criticisms of the Fund's policies: 'The Fund approach to adjustment has had severe economic costs for many of these [developing] countries in terms of declines in the levels of output and growth rates, reductions in employment and adverse effects on income distribution'.[80] The proliferation of structural policy conditions has had negative consequences in terms of accountability. It has led to a lack of transparency in the level of compliance by the country involved. Moreover, it has been more and more difficult for national 'authorities [to feel] a strong commitment to and ownership of' the adjustment programme.[81]

The human rights record of structural conditionality is highly controversial. The social impact – at least in the short run – of policies intended to favour growth and prosperity in the long term, has often been dim: 'the privatisation of public services [. . .], as well as other measures required in the context of structural adjustment, frequently meant that the poorest parts of the population lost free access to water, health care, education, and other public services'.[82]

The negative impact of structural adjustment conditionality on development has also been emphasised by international organisations. In particular, the UN Commission on human rights has argued that 'structural adjustment policies have serious implications for the ability of the developing countries to abide by the Declaration on the Right to Development and to formulate national development policies that aim to improve the economic, social and cultural rights of their citizens'.[83]

In order to assess the external accountability of the IMF, attention must also be drawn to the legal nature of the arrangements between the Fund and the requesting member, and to the process followed. The Guidelines on Conditionality of the IMF unambiguously stipulate that

> a Fund arrangement is a decision of the Executive Board by which a member is assured that it will be able to make purchases or receive disbursements from the Fund in accordance with the terms of the decision during a specified period and up to a specified amount. Fund arrangements are not international agreements and therefore language having a contractual connotation will be avoided in arrangements and in program documents.[84]

Therefore, from a legal point of view, the unilateral decision of the Executive Board[85] is followed by a letter of intent of the requesting country, and no common agreement simultaneously binds the international organisation and the state.

[79] IEO, An IEO Evaluation of Structural Conditionality in IMF-Supported Programs (2008) www.ieo-imf.org/eval/complete/eval_01032008.html, accessed 30 September 2013.

[80] Group of Twenty-Four (1987), *The Role of the IMF in Adjustment with Growth*, Intergovernmental Group of Twenty-Four on International Monetary Affairs, Washington DC, 9.

[81] A Buira, *An Analysis of IMF Conditionality* (2003) G-24 Discussion Paper no 22, Washington DC, 9.

[82] S Michalowski, 'Sovereign Debt and Social Rights – Legal Reflections on a Difficult Relationship' (2008) 8(1) *Human Rights Law Review* 43.

[83] UN Commission on Human Rights Res 1999/22, Effects of the full enjoyment of human rights of the economic adjustment policies arising from foreign debt and, in particular, on the implementation of the Declaration on the Right to Development, 23 April 1999, E/CN.4/RES/1999/22.

[84] Decision no 12864-(02/102) September 25, 2002, as amended by Decision no 13814-(06/98), November 15, 2006, Guideline no 9.

[85] Leckow (n 73) 58.

As regards the process, when the need for an IMF intervention arises, negotiations take place between the authorities of the country concerned and the staff of the Fund. The procedure does not contemplate the possibility of the country presenting the programme directly before the Board. Instead, it is only the IMF's staff who attend this crucial meeting. This does not allow the Board to be aware of the degree of acceptance of the plan by the state which will undertake it. Thus, even Executive Directors designated by developing countries – who could theoretically form a majority against the programme – fail to do so.[86]

This state of affairs does not ensure a high level of external accountability. The intrusiveness of structural performance criteria and the process and legal nature of the arrangement fail to guarantee national ownership of the stabilisation programmes. In the more recent period, several reforms have been adopted, and other ones have been suggested, in order to increase the IMF's legitimacy in its external relations.

C Recent Reforms and the Way Forward

The IMF has become aware of the significance and relevance of several of the criticisms which had been voiced. Consequently, it has taken some actions to react. First, it decided that structural performance criteria shall no longer be established as a modality for monitoring performance under any type of Fund arrangement.[87] This decision is of paramount importance, in that it does away with the most problematic trait of IMF conditionality. It thus represents a decisive step towards greater external accountability. Countries will retain higher ownership over their policies, and this will make popular protest (and government repression) less likely. Consequently, this reform can potentially have a positive effect on the level of the protection of human rights, especially in light of the disruptive impact of structural conditionality on the enjoyment of economic and social rights.[88]

For the sake of completeness, it must be highlighted that structural reforms have not completely disappeared from the IMF's radar. If structural reform programmes recommended by the Fund no longer constitute conditions for obtaining instalments, their implementation is however monitored under a review-based approach.[89] Thus, their role has muted, and the consequence of non-compliance is not a stop to funding, but rather a negative feedback in the report at the end of the review.

A further novelty brought about by the global financial crisis was the introduction of the Flexible Credit Line in 2009. This new lending facility has the unprecedented characteristic of not having conditions attached to it, which works towards the objective of

[86] Akyüz (n 65) 54–55.

[87] Decision no 14280-(09/29), 24 March 2009.

[88] MR Abouharb and D Cingranelli, *Human Rights and Structural Adjustment: The Impact of the IMF and World Bank* (Cambridge, Cambridge University Press, 2007); G Bird and T Willett, 'IMF Conditionality, Implementation and the New Political Economy of Ownership' (2004) 46(3) *Comparative Economic Studies* 423–50; P Policzer, 'How Organizations Shape Human Rights Violations' in SC Carey and SC Poe (eds), *Understanding Human Rights Violations* (Aldershot, Ashgate, 2004) 221–38.

[89] The Acting Chair's Summing Up – GRA Lending Toolkit and Conditionality – Reform Proposals, Executive Board Meeting 09/29, 24 March 2009, BUFF/09/50, 27 March 2009, www.imf.org/external/pubs/ft/sd/index.asp?decision=EBM/09/29, accessed 30 September 2013. See also IMF, *IMF Overhauls Nonconcessional Lending Facilities and Conditionality*, Press Release (3 April 2009), www.imf.org/external/np/sec/pn/2009/pn0940.htm, accessed 30 September 2013.

'reduc[ing] the perceived stigma of borrowing from the IMF'.[90] This is a welcome development, since it diminishes the possibilities of the IMF's interference with sovereign countries' policies, and thus eliminates a major source of criticism in terms of external accountability of the Fund. On the other hand, the Flexible Credit Line is open exclusively to countries with very strong economic fundamentals and a track record of compliance with strong policies; therefore, it will not be available to developing countries. Thus far, only Poland, Mexico and Colombia have accessed this new facility.[91]

Although these recent reforms do represent a progress towards increased accountability, much more could be done. An important reform would be to allow the country seeking assistance to present the programme directly before the Board.[92] This would ensure that the Executive Directors have a clear picture of the country's needs and openness to accepting certain conditions. The current procedure, which only allows IMF staff to attend this meeting, does not guarantee against the inclusion in the programme of clauses which the member was compelled to accept. This innovation would clearly increase the degree of legitimacy of the lending agreement, in terms of both its normative and sociological senses.

As regards the legal nature of the arrangement between the Fund and the country requesting a loan, it could take the form of an agreement anchored in international law. In this respect, the IMF could follow the example of the European Stability Mechanism (ESM). Article 13 of the ESM Treaty stipulates that

> the Board of Governors shall entrust the European Commission [. . .] with the task of negotiating, with the ESM Member concerned, a memorandum of understanding (an 'MoU') detailing the conditionality attached to the financial assistance facility. The content of the MoU shall reflect the severity of the weaknesses to be addressed and the financial assistance instrument chosen.[93]

The Memorandum of Understanding is then signed by the European Commission on behalf of the ESM.[94] Thus, an act of international law simultaneously binds the international financial institution and the state receiving the funds. If followed by the IMF, this method would improve transparency and fairness, since it would increase the accountability of the organisation vis-à-vis the country.

Accountability and transparency, however, cannot suffice when at risk is the very implementation of rights, and in particular the preservation of the minimum standard of protection. It is important here to remember the nature of the state obligations to implement economic, social and cultural (ESC) rights. Whereas it is true that countries are only obliged to ensure the progressive realisation of these rights (that is, they are not bound to ensure their full implementation), the Committee for Economic Social and Cultural Rights has long established a powerful corollary of the principle of progressive realisation, that is, the presumption against retrogressive policies.[95] The impact of the sovereign

[90] *The IMF's Flexible Credit Line (FCL)*, Factsheet, 3 April 2012, www.imf.org/external/np/exr/facts/fcl.htm, accessed 13 January 2014.

[91] ibid.

[92] Akyüz (n 65) 54–55.

[93] Art 13(3).

[94] Art 13(4).

[95] See Committee on Economic, Social and Cultural Rights, General Comment 3, The nature of States parties' obligations (Fifth session, 1990), UN Doc E/1991/23. For a recent study on the link between this non-retrogressive obligation and the budgetary policies of the states, see A Nolan and M Dutschke, 'Article 2(1) ICESCR and States Parties' Obligations: Whither the Budget?' (2010) 3 *European Human Rights Law Review* 280.

debt crisis and the austerity policies on the progressive realisation of human rights is clear, and the chair of the Committee has reminded all state parties to comply with their obligations and minimise the adoption of regressive policies.[96] An echo of this concern is reflected in the Committee's recommendation to Spain in response to the country's 2012 periodic report on the implementation of ESC rights,[97] or in the European Committee of Social Rights' decisions finding that Greece had violated several provisions of the European Social Charter by implementing the austerity measures.[98]

In the light of the foregoing, it is fair to maintain that the IMF should take into account borrowing countries' obligations – especially human rights obligations – when concluding this type of agreements. In this perspective, the Tilburg Principles recall that 'the IFIs shall respect the obligations of the members according to Article 103 of the UN Charter, including giving priority to respect for human rights'.[99] The Fund should strive to respect developing countries' efforts towards greater human rights compliance and not constitute an obstacle in this path, or the decisive factor for the adoption of regressive policies. In other words, Fund-recommended policies should be carefully designed so as to allow states 'to meet their duty to protect [economic and social rights and not] hinder business enterprises from respecting human rights', in particular in situations where the crisis itself is a major obstacle to the full enjoyment of those rights by citizens who are in a vulnerable position, such as in scenarios characterised by burgeoning unemployment rates and severe welfare cuts.[100]

V CONCLUSIONS

In sum, it can be stressed that the IMF is now under fire because its undemocratic setup, long tolerated in favour of a supposedly higher-performance-driven potential, is no longer seen as an asset, in a time of global financial distress that prejudices the minimum implementation of human rights. In other words, the neoliberalist drive, which since World War II has favoured the rise of apparently technocratic international institutions entrusted with the task of dealing with those matters that democratic states are inherently unable to cope with,[101] is now over. As a consequence, the IMF's power to manage and redistribute public goods is now subject to closer scrutiny and must meet several standards that are routinely required of public authorities within the state. The lack of

[96] Open letter of the Chair of the Committee on Economic, Social and Cultural Rights to States parties to the ICESCR, dated 16 May 2012; CESCR/48th/SP/MAB/SW, www2.ohchr.org/english/bodies/cescr/docs/LetterCESCRtoSP16.05.12.pdf, accessed 30 September 2013.

[97] See Committee on Economic, Social and Cultural Rights, 6 June 2012, Consideration of reports submitted by States parties under articles 16 and 17 of the Covenant, Spain, E/C.12/ESP/CO/5, para 8: 'The Committee recommends that the State party ensure that all the austerity measures adopted reflect the minimum core content of all the Covenant rights and that it take all appropriate measures to protect that core content under any circumstances, especially for disadvantaged and marginalized individuals and groups'.

[98] European Committee of Social Rights, Collective Complaints nos 65/2011 and 66/2011, decisions on the merits of 23 May 2012. See also Complaints 72 and 76 to 80/2011.

[99] Principle no 26.

[100] See Report of the Special Representative of the Secretary-General on the issue of human rights and transnational corporations and other business enterprises, J Ruggie: *Guiding Principles on Business and Human Rights: Implementing the United Nations 'Protect, Respect and Remedy' Framework*, A/HRC/17/31 (2011), endorsed in Res 17/4 adopted by the Human Rights Council, A/HRC/RES/17/4 (2011), in particular Principles 3, 8 and 10.

[101] Bukovansky (n 11), see in particular the discussion at pp 178 ff.

proper internal and external accountability is harmful to human rights compliance by the Fund itself, by its members, and also by countries receiving its financial support. Criticisms of such a state of affairs are an expression of the quintessential vindication of those theories that signal the emergence of a framework of global administrative law[102] whereby the rule of law of global institutions is primarily channelled through compliance with public law guarantees.[103]

To borrow Klabbers' words, organisations that exercise public authority lend themselves, for this very reason, to an assessment as to whether they are doing it in the most appropriate and opportune manner.[104] They 'operate, so to speak, on the market of legitimacy, and legitimacy, however precisely conceptualized, is a scarce resource. And when this happens, the organization loses its character as organization and becomes something else – whatever the "something else" may be'.[105] This 'something else', in the case of the IMF, is something akin to a democratic polity. It is not easy to assess whether this incidental 'statification' of the Fund is a sign of maturity (the Fund wants to get rid of its bad governance practices) or of weakness (the Fund has lost its technocratic immunity because of poor performance, and must now abide by the standards of good governance that states have had to respect for decades). In either case, greater accountability is a welcome step towards enhancing the Fund's human rights compliance, as the IMF's record in this field will be opened to public scrutiny, and hopefully improved. Although very gradually and possibly very late, the IMF is trying to meet the demands 'that human rights be considered in the making of foreign policy and in the IMF's policy of good governance', in the attempt 'to ensure that the dangers [of globalisation] are diminished and the opportunities are taken'.[106]

The result is encouraging. Through the governance reforms and the softening of conditionality requirements, part of the IMF's legitimacy deficit is starting to be paid off. The process might still be long before it reaches a point of equilibrium, but its direction is clear: to minimise the very concrete possibility that the actions of the Fund might have human rights-adverse externalities, the IMF is internalising the basic standards of human rights protection. The devastations brought by the global economic crisis in terms of living standards, rise in poverty rates and human rights violations are widely observable.[107] The IMF, like any policymaker, is largely unaccountable for the *results* achieved through its actions. At times, policies formulated to alleviate financial crises might cause unintended effects that are adverse to human rights protection, due to the inherent uncertainty

[102] *Ex multis*, see B Kingsbury et al, 'The Emergence of Global Administrative Law' (2005) 68 *Law and Contemporary Problems* 15; S Cassese, 'Administrative Law without the State? The Challenge of Global Regulation' (2005) 37 *New York University Journal of International Law and Politics* 663.

[103] In an interesting (or ironic) twist, the principles of good governance of GAL are the same as those of which the IMF itself, as well as the World Bank, recommends the implementation whenever it couples financial assistance with instructions towards structural reforms, see for instance part 4 of C Harlow, 'Global Administrative Law: The Quest for Principles and Values' (2006) 17(1) *European Journal of International Law* 187–214.

[104] See RP Delonis, 'International Financial Standards and Codes: Mandatory Regulation without Representation', (2004) *New York University Journal of International Law and Politics*, vol 36, 563.

[105] See J Klabbers, 'The Paradox of International Institutional Law' (2008) 5 *International Organizations Law Review* 151, quoted in B Kingsbury and L Casini, 'Global Administrative Law Dimensions of International Organizations Law' (2009) 6 *International Organizations Law Review* 328–29.

[106] R McCorquodale and R Fairbrother 'Globalization and Human Rights' (1999) 21 *Human Rights Quarterly* 735, 766.

[107] For an incisive overview, see M Dowell-Jones and D Kinley 'Minding the Gap: Global Finance and Human Rights' (2011) 25 (2) *Ethics & International Affairs* 183, in particular 185 ff.

that divides policy implementation and actual outcomes.[108] However, the internalisation of human rights obligations within the structure of the institution and the design of its decisions is a guarantee that the *process* will be mindful of basic obligations.

This much can be demanded, to avoid that the IMF's management of a common good ends up threatening the implementation of the most important of all, that is the minimum protection of fundamental human rights. Arguably, the constitutionalisation of human rights obligations within political decision-making is a powerful catalyst for achieving better results in economic rights protection.[109] The IMF's subscription to this process of internalisation and the abandonment of the previous 'denial mode'[110] cannot but foster the convergence between the profile of its structure and activity and the purposes of its actions: the clinical isolation of the IMF from the human rights discourse, once saluted as a healthy practice of non-interference,[111] is not tenable, in light of its international obligations and of the effectiveness boost that is attached to increased institutional legitimacy.[112]

[108] M Monshipouri and CE Welch, 'The Search for International Human Rights and Justice: Coming to Terms with the New Global Realities' (2001) 23(2) *Human Rights Quarterly* 370, see 375 ff.

[109] L Minkler, 'Economic Rights and Political Decision Making' (2009) 31(2) *Human Rights Quarterly* 368.

[110] See Wahi (n 19) 356.

[111] DD Bradlow, 'The World Bank, the IMF, and Human Rights' (1996) 6 *Transnational Law and Contemporary Problems* 47.

[112] See, generally, DD Bradlow, and C Grossman, 'Limited Mandates and Intertwined Problems: A New Challenge for the World Bank and the IMF' (1995) 17 *Human Rights Quarterly* 411; K De Feyter, 'The International Financial Institutions and Human Rights: Law and Practice' (2004) 6 *Human Rights Review* 56.

15

Extraterritorial Human Rights Violations and Irresponsible Sovereign Financing

FOZIA NAZIR LONE

I INTRODUCTION

IT IS WELL known that the protection of fundamental human rights was the grand norm for establishing the United Nations in 1945. The human rights conventions and treaties focus on the respect, protection and guarantee by states of the human rights of their residents, as embodied in the Universal Declaration of Human Rights, ICCPR, ICESCR and other conventions.[1] The idea was that guarantee of human rights assists to secure the peace and prevents humanitarian catastrophes.

In July 2012 the Human Rights Council considered the effects of foreign debt and other related international financial obligations of states on the full enjoyment of all human rights, particularly economic, social and cultural rights.[2] The aim of this resolution is to encourage all governments and other agencies to take into consideration the Guiding Principles on Business and Human Rights: Implementing the United Nations 'Protect, Respect and Remedy' Framework (Guiding Principles)[3] when designing their policies and programmes.[4] In the contemporary world we are faced with a growing problem of human rights violations caused by sovereign financing. There are two sides to sovereign debt/lending, ie the borrower and the lender. Both borrower and lender should be accountable for their own conduct in these transactions. If a corporation is lender and a state is borrower each side needs to be responsible for their misconduct. The state as an actor in sovereign financing cannot shift the economic, legal and monitoring liability to a corporation that is investing abroad. This is supported by the 'Principles on Responsible Sovereign Lending and Borrowing' (PRSLB) as drafted by UNCTAD, which not only

[1] The Universal Declaration of Human Rights, www.un.org/en/documents/udhr/index.shtml, accessed 23 September 2013; International Covenant on Civil and Political Rights 1966,www2.ohchr.org/english/law/ccpr.htm, accessed 23 September 2013; International Covenant on Economic, Social and Cultural Rights 1966, www2.ohchr.org/english/law/cescr.htm, accessed 23 September 2013; Convention on the Prevention and Punishment of the Crime of Genocide 1948; International Convention on the Elimination of All Forms of Racial Discrimination 1966; Convention on the Elimination of All Forms of Discrimination against Women 1979; Convention against Torture and Other Cruel, Inhuman or Degrading Treatment or Punishment 1984; Convention on the Rights of the Child, New York, 20 November 1989.

[2] Promotion and protection of all human rights, civil, political, economic, social and cultural rights, including the right to development, Human Rights Council, Twentieth session, Agenda item 3, UN GA Resolution A/HRC/20/L.17, 2 July 2012.

[3] A/HRC/17/31.

[4] ibid, para 3.

recommends investigation in financial matters[5] but also declares among other things that any form of peculation by government officials is wrongful.[6]

It is argued that mother[7] states of corporations should hence be responsible for lack of monitoring regulations and exercising control over its corporations abroad. This chapter proposes to use the concept of state responsibility to make mother states' liability vivid. This approach is adopted because rules laid down in the Guiding Principles and PRSLB do not unambiguously declare that states can be held liable for corporations' misconduct. Further under the current system of sovereign debt, the role of corporations and states is not well delineated. For example UNCTAD, through voluntary implementation of the PRSLB, proposes to stop irresponsible financing, which can have harmful human consequences for the debtor country, its citizens, its creditors, its neighbours and its trading partners. However, in this recommendation it does not lay out the role of the corporation or the mother state. For the extraterritorial protection of human rights under sovereign financing we are left to draw an inference that the mother state of the corporation can be held liable if funds are invested irresponsibly, but it is not unequivocally affirmed.

The current international framework for corporate human rights responsibility is inadequate.[8] This includes the instances of human rights violations caused by sovereign financing. This chapter intends to elaborate on extraterritorial human rights violations in the context of sovereign debt. This responsibility is based on the regulation and monitoring that the state should perform over its corporations abroad. The contention is that exterritorial human rights violations are worsened due to corruption/bribery, controversial understanding of human rights from a cultural perspective and lack of due diligence and complicity as required under social corporate responsibility. In this regard it is argued that if government officials are corrupt and willing to accept bribes then it will affect monitoring as well as implementation of any rules abroad. This delicate balance of regulation, monitoring, human rights protection, anti-corruption, anti-bribery and social corporate responsibility are inherently linked and need to be analysed closely.

At this point it is to be recognised that the OECD Anti-Bribery Convention and the Convention's 2009 Anti-Bribery Recommendation[9] fights bribery in international business to strengthen development, reduce poverty and bolster confidence in markets. In 2009 a report was prepared by International Council on Human Rights Policy and Transparency International which discussed a link between corruption and human rights.[10] This report believed that discussing such a link may encourage states to combat corruption and respect human rights in situations where they are connected.[11] It asserted that a human rights approach may make it more likely that those who are corrupt are sanctioned appropriately and will make sanctioning possible even in countries where reference to human rights is sensitive, hence obliging a state to act.[12]

[5] Principles on Responsible Sovereign Lending and Borrowing', UNCTAD (amended and restated as of 10 January 2012). See Principles 5 and 12.

[6] ibid, Principle 8 (Agency).

[7] This term has been coined by the author to be used in the context of sovereign lending and borrowing. It is intended to use this term to refer to a state where a corporation originated.

[8] See generally, S Deva, 'Human Rights Violations by Multinational Corporations and International Law: Where From Here?' (2003) 19 *Connecticut Journal of International Law* 1–57.

[9] See www.oecd.org/corruption/anti-bribery/, accessed 23 September 2013.

[10] Report by International Council on Human Rights Policy and Transparency International, *Corruption and Human Rights: Making the Connection*, 2009, 3.

[11] ibid, 6.

[12] ibid, 5.

Adopting this approach to human rights protection in the context of sovereign debt at an international level would allow us to experience optimal results in the fight against exterritorial human rights violations in the area of sovereign financing. Finding this missing connection and discussing these factors holistically would assist in structuring an ideal solution for the growing problem of human rights violations caused by sovereign financing. It is believed that a state, when monitoring its corporations abroad, should take these factors into account. Where a state fails to effectively monitor its corporations, it cannot escape its liability and can be held accountable using the principle of state responsibility. It is arguable under these circumstances that not only corporations but also states can incur civil liability for failing to effectively monitor their corporations abroad.

Confusion in the area of sovereign debt is hindered to a large extend by the fact that in contemporary international law concepts such as human rights abuse, corporate social responsibility, corruption, bribery, sovereign financing and state responsibility are compartmentalised and the link between them is not formally recognised. This chapter intends to critically evaluate this connection and use of the extraterritoriality principle to assert that states are obliged to respect human rights standards by regulating the activities of companies registered in their territories[13] that may incur liability if this responsibility is not fulfilled by states. Courts also play a significant role in this complicated puzzle. At present courts are unreasonably making it difficult to hold corporations liable for human rights violations in borrowing states by adopting a harsh purpose test, which puts a higher burden of proof on the plaintiff than required in civil litigation. This burden is higher than that required in criminal litigation. Extending this approach to sovereign financing, if a corporation is not found liable then its mother state will not incur any liability either. The mother state would be seen as having tacitly fulfilled its monitoring duties under the Guiding Principles and PRSLB. Hence a legal approach to finding corporate liability is significant and would eventually affect implementation of rules and regulations adopted for tackling sovereign lending and borrowing.

II HOW ARE CORPORATE VIOLATIONS OF HUMAN RIGHTS LINKED TO STATES?

A State Responsibility

The concept of state responsibility makes states directly liable for acts of a private person either authorising or failing to stop wrongful acts. While this liability is vicarious in nature where the unauthorised act in question is performed by officials of a state, Oppenheim noted:

> a state's responsibility for the acts of a private person is not vicarious responsibility stricto sensu. The state is in international law not legally responsible for the act itself, but for its own failure to comply with obligations incumbent upon it in relation to the acts of the private person: those acts are the occasion for the state's responsibility for its own wrongful acts, not the basis of its responsibility.[14]

[13] N Bernaz, 'Enhancing Corporate Accountability for Human Rights Violations: Is Extraterritoriality the Magic Potion?' (2013) 17(3) *Journal of Business Ethics*.

[14] R Jennings and A Watts (eds), *Oppenheim's International Law* (London, Longman, 1992) vol 1, 501.

A state is hence required to make appropriate reparation for failure to comply with the obligations and also to punish the private person for any wrongful act committed. When extending state responsibility to financial corporations, a state may be held liable for violating its obligation for not preventing and punishing human rights violations within its jurisdiction. For a state to be held liable it firstly needs to be established that a wrongful act was committed and secondly that there was a link between the state and a corporation. Under Article 2 of Draft Articles on Responsibility of States for Internationally Wrongful Acts (2001) an internationally wrongful act exists when conduct consists of an action or omission: (a) which is attributable to the state under international law; and (b) which constitutes a breach of an international obligation of the state. This breach of an international obligation is determined by international law and not by domestic law.[15]

The principle of attribution is applicable if the state has some degree of fault, culpability, negligence or lack of due diligence. For example in the *Corfu Channel* case, the ICJ held Albania liable based on the fact *that it knew, or must have known*, of the presence of mines in its territorial waters and it did nothing to warn third states about it.[16] Likewise in the *United States Diplomatic and Consular Staff in Tehran* case, the Court concluded that the responsibility of the Islamic Republic of Iran was entailed by the 'inaction' of its authorities which 'failed to take appropriate steps', in circumstances where such steps were evidently called for.[17] In recent years the concept of attribution has been extended to international organisations.[18] In the *Behrami* and *Saramati* cases the European Court of Human Rights (ECHR) sat as Grand Chamber and joined its examination of both applications pursuant to Rule 42 § 1 of the Rules of Court. On 2 May 2007 the ECHR concluded that the 'Kosovo Force' was exercising lawfully delegated Chapter VII powers of the UN Security Council so that the 'impugned action', ie violations of applicants' human rights, was, in principle, 'attributable' to the UN. The Court noted that the 'United Nations Interim Administration Mission in Kosovo' was a subsidiary organ of the UN created under Chapter VII of the Charter so the impugned inaction (omission) was, in principle, 'attributable' to the UN in the same sense.[19] In these circumstances, the Court concluded that the applicants' complaints were incompatible *ratione personae* with the provisions of the Convention.[20] Applying the reasoning of these judgments it is possible to argue that under state responsibility concept a state might be held liable for corporate violations of human rights if there is a breach of an international legal obligation or inaction on the part of a state.

B Social Corporate Responsibility

All corporations owe a social responsibility to protect the rights of their human resources as well the rights of the society in which they operate.[21] It is a requirement for businesses

[15] *Rainbow Warrior Case (New Zealand v France)* 1990 RIAA, vol XX, 317.

[16] *Corfu Channel*, Merits, Judgment, ICJ Reports 1949, 4, 22–23.

[17] *United States Diplomatic and Consular Staff in Tehran*, Judgment, ICJ Reports 1980, 3, 31–32, paras 63 and 67.

[18] See Grand Chamber Decision as to the Admissibility of *Behrami and Behrami v France*, ECHR, App no 71412/01 and *Saramati v France, Germany and Norway*, ECHR App no 78166/01, 2007.

[19] ibid, para 151.

[20] ibid, para 152.

[21] See n 3.

to have an action plan to accommodate this aspect of globalisation.[22] Globalisation impacts on business firms as they expand markets. In this connection Shelton argues that:

> with the shift in sovereignty accompanying globalization has meant that non-state actors are more involved than ever in issues relating to human rights. This development poses challenges to international human rights law. . . [and] has enhanced the ability of civil society to function across borders and promote human rights, other actors have gained the power to violate human rights in unforeseen ways.[23]

It is argued that this cross-border operation may potentially have negative impacts on human rights, which are magnified with foreign governments' varying commitment to human rights protection. This connection between both the legal nexus (employer–employee relationship) and the corporeal closeness to society within which a company operates may result in corporations' liability for human rights violations. This equation is complicated where human rights violations are related to sovereign debt.

Corporate responsibility to respect human rights means that business enterprises as lenders should act with *due diligence*, avoid infringing the rights of others and address adverse impacts in which they are involved.[24] The origins of the concept of due diligence are connected with the US Securities Act of 1933, which provided for a 'due diligence' defence for broker-dealers when accused of inadequate disclosure of material information to investors.[25] The Act protected against legal liability if the broker-dealer could demonstrate that the lost information could not be found despite having conducted good faith due diligence on the issuer of securities. The main feature of this process is that an investigative process must be undertaken for the purpose of preventing harm. For this reason due diligence has become a key element of risk control. The due diligence process means investigation of facts and their evaluation by taking into consideration the relevant standard of care. So conducting due diligence is not an automatic process and requires exercise of informed judgement by the observer.

In order to fulfil the responsibility to respect human rights, financial corporations can conduct due diligence to assess the human rights risks that may be associated with their activities, operations and relationships.[26] Due diligence can play a key role in helping to identify both the dilemmas companies face in practice as well as ways in which companies can overcome these and meet their responsibility to respect human rights. These companies need to analyse their activities that affect people and chart out the risks of company participation in human rights violations, both directly in their operations and indirectly through their relationships.[27] Human rights risk assessments are not mechanical processes and each company needs to identify, understand and manage risks through dialogue processes, with its stakeholders. The information contained in a risk assessment should be made available to company managers, both in-country and at headquarters, so that steps towards preventing or solving the problem can be taken. This process would

[22] T Friedman, *The World is Flat: A Brief History of the Twenty-First Century* (New York, Farrar, Straus and Giroux, 2005).

[23] D Shelton, 'Protecting Human Rights in a Globalized World', (2002) 25(2) *Boston College International & Comparative Law Review*, 273–322.

[24] See n 3.

[25] See 15 USC 77a ff, s 11.

[26] MB Taylor, L Zandvliet and M Forouhar, 'Due Diligence for Human rights: A Risk-Based Approach', Working Paper No 53, Harvard University and John F Kennedy School of Government, 2009, 3, www.hks.harvard.edu/m-rcbg/CSRI/publications/workingpaper_53_taylor_etal.pdf, accessed 23 September 2013.

[27] ibid.

allow the company to assess the risks of possible violation of human rights by its activities while engaging in conflict regions, while at the same time helping a company and its stakeholders understand better the limits of those responsibilities within the universe of rights.[28]

Due diligence can help a company function beyond making economic gains from a society. Hence due diligence and good faith human rights risk mitigation is likely to provide the company with crucial elements in a defence against allegations that it is involved in human rights violations. Conducting an assessment becomes a necessary basis for taking the practical steps towards managing the risks of harm to people and ensuring that the company respects human rights.

However, the specific features of sovereign financing pose difficulties for the corporation to conduct a thorough due diligence investigation. This is because in sovereign financing government officials act as agents to the financing. In such circumstances it would be difficult for a foreign corporation from a lending state to get an authentic investigation result if the borrowing state is corrupted, ie it will be highly likely that they will hide the human rights violation. Hence, practising due diligence by lending institutions can assist them in conducting thorough investigations which in turn could prevent them from financing human rights violation in the borrowing states.

III SOVEREIGN DEBT: GUIDING PRINCIPLES AND PRINCIPLES ON RESPONSIBLE SOVEREIGN LENDING AND BORROWING

In a limited sense sovereign debt is the bonds that are issued by a national government in a foreign currency to finance the issuing country's growth. If a state defaults on its sovereign debt it will have difficulty in obtaining a loan in the future. In recent years it has been recognised that the debt burden of developing states contributes to extreme poverty and is an obstacle to sustainable human development, which in turn seriously impedes the realisation of all human rights.[29] In sovereign debt crises the less explored aspect of corporate liability is the potential human rights abuse caused by the corporation while investing in the borrowing state. In recent years, recommendations such as the Guiding Principles[30] and PRSLB[31] have been proposed to inhibit ill-effects on human rights by improving business values of corporations and irresponsible sovereign financing.

In March 2011 the Report of the Special Representative of the Secretary General, John Ruggie, on the issue of human rights and transnational corporations and other business enterprises was put to the Human Rights Council in the form of the Guiding Principles.[32] These principles are meant to enhance business standards and practices to promote and protect human rights so as to achieve tangible results for affected individuals and communities. They took into account the existing human rights activism and integrated it as a coherent template by elaborating on the implications of existing standards and prac-

[28] ibid.

[29] Promotion and protection of all human rights, civil, political, economic, social and cultural rights, including the right to development, Human Rights Council, Twentieth session, Agenda item 3, UN GA Resolution A/HRC/20/L.17, 2 July 2012.

[30] See n 3.

[31] See n 5.

[32] See n 3.

tices for states and businesses and possible consequences for breaching them.[33] Under the Guiding Principles there is an affirmative duty for a state to investigate and punish violations of human rights by companies. States are also encouraged to have effective policies, legislation, regulations and adjudication to prevent human rights abuse. The state also has a duty to assist companies to avoid getting drawn into human rights abuse that might occur in a conflict situation.[34]

In 2009 UNCTAD launched an initiative to promote responsible sovereign lending and borrowing after the global financial and economic crisis. In 2012 this resulted in the drafting of principles and practices relating to sovereign debt. The PRSLB explicitly mentioned that sovereign borrowers have a responsibility to conduct a thorough *ex ante* investigation into the financial, operational, civil, social, cultural and environmental implications of the project and its funding.[35] This risk management proposed that ill-designed or underfunded projects must be taken over by the state to avoid public sector liabilities which may result in human rights violations. The UNSLB propose to stop irresponsible financing, which can have harmful human consequences for the debtor country, its citizens, its creditors, its neighbours and its trading partners. Under these principles each side of a sovereign lending transaction, ie the borrower and the lender, is accountable for its own conduct in these transactions. Hence it is not possible for state as an actor in sovereign financing to shift the economic, legal and monitoring liability to a corporation.[36]

The Guiding Principles, as well as the PRSLB, are therefore intended to provide informed guidance that is backed by actual practice aiming to avoid human and economic collateral damage to people. Among other things the common effect of these recommendations seems to be that the impact on human rights due to unmanageable debt situations, such as lack of social awareness of businesses, can be assessed. In other words these principles assist in classifying, coordinating and standardising the basic principles and best practices applied to sovereign financing and transnational corporations. However, these principles in no way prejudice application of international rules concerning the action of lenders, borrowers and transnational corporations.[37] Hence the general principles of international law will continue to apply and absence of effective regulations to prevent human rights violations by companies may not exonerate a state from its liability under state responsibility if an 'effective link' exists between a mother state and the human rights violations committed in the borrowing state. Although it is not spelled out clearly by these recommendations it should be possible to hold governments accountable for not fulfilling their obligations to protect their residents from human rights abuses by corporations if effective steps are not taken. Having said this, the major drawback of these frameworks is that they do not provide any implementation mechanism unless states are willing to adopt them. In this context, the only way to go beyond voluntarism is for domestic law to step in.[38]

[33] S Deva, *Regulating Corporate Human Rights Violations: Humanizing Business* (London, Routledge, 2012). The author analyses the Bhopal gas disaster and argues that no robust regulatory mechanism exists to compensate victims of corporate human rights abuses.

[34] See n 3, para 11.

[35] PRSLB Principles 5 and 12.

[36] UNSLB, Preamble.

[37] PRSLB, Preamble; UN Human Rights Council, UN Doc A/HRC/17/31, 21 March 2011.

[38] See n 13.

IV FACTORS EXACERBATING EXTRATERRITORIAL HUMAN RIGHTS VIOLATIONS RELATED TO SOVEREIGN FINANCING

In recent years there has been extensive awareness of corporate violations of human rights and it has been argued that lenders providing financial assistance to authoritarian regimes should be held responsible for complicity if they knew or should have known that they would facilitate human rights abuses. In this connection Bohoslavsky argues that when interpreting the missing financial link in such instances a macro approach and dynamics of sovereign financing should be applied which could be integrated into the domain of transitional justice.[39] In the Argentinean context Bohoslavsky and Opgenhaffen argue complicity of foreign financial institutions in supporting the Junta regime (1976–1983), which committed mass human rights violations such as torture, murder and enforced disappearance in Argentina. The authors argue that during the Argentinean dictatorship, the US government recognised that the most 'serious' human rights violations, or those that infringe peremptory norms (*jus cogens*) should be discouraged through the use of severe restrictions on financial and military aid.[40]

In order to alleviate sovereign financing practices, factors such as corruption/bribery, which exacerbate the corporate human rights violations, needs to be stamped down. It is also significant to adhere to the human rights practices of the borrowing state. It is believed that taking an advanced approach to corporate violations in relation to sovereign debt would assist the mother state to better monitor its corporations abroad.

A Corruption and Bribery

In 2004 the corporate social responsibility (CSR) programmes initiative of the UN, the Global Compact, incorporated anti-corruption as its tenth principle in the following words: 'Business should work against corruption in all its forms, including extortion and bribery.'[41] Likewise in 2005 the United Nations Convention against Corruption recognised a treacherous pandemic of corruption.[42] This convention, among other things, recognised that corruption corrodes societies, undermines human rights, distorts markets and threatens human security.[43] The Guiding Principles imposed on companies similar human rights duties as states to 'promote, respect, and protect human rights'.[44] Based on these legal principles and the principle of state responsibility, it is then possible that corporations could be seen as accomplices in human rights violations and as supporting a corrupt regime.

[39] JP Bohoslavsky, 'Tracking Down the Missing Financial Link in Transitional Justice' (2012) 1 *International Human Rights Law Review* 1–39.

[40] JP Bohoslavsky and V Opgenhaffen, 'The Past and Present of Corporate Complicity: Financing the Argentinean Dictatorship' (2010) 23 *Harvard Human Rights Journal* 245–46.

[41] This principle became the Compact's 'tenth principle' in 2004. For the 10 principles see the Global Compact, www.unglobalcompact.org/AboutTheGC/TheTenPrinciples/index.html, accessed 23 September 2013.

[42] For text see, www.unodc.org/documents/treaties/UNCAC/Publications/Convention/08-50026_E.pdf, accessed 23 September 2013.

[43] ibid.

[44] See n 3.

The accountability for corruption and human rights violations intersects and is mutually reinforcing forms of abuse. Carranza argues that the field of transitional justice should therefore approach economic crimes in the same way as it approaches civil and political rights violations. The author suggests that traditional transitional justice mechanisms would be strengthened by an engagement with corruption and economic crimes.[45] Human rights scholars argue that international human rights law imposes direct duties on corporations and other private actors. Without question, the position of multinational corporations (MNCs) in international law has been a subject of interesting debates and intense disputation.[46]

Further the Convention on Combating Bribery of Foreign Public Officials in International Business Transactions 1997 (Convention on Combating Bribery),[47] imposes obligations on corporations but the subject matter of this treaty is silent about corporate liability for violations of human rights and whether it is a universally accepted norm of customary international law. On the other hand Article 1 of the Convention on Bribery,[48] states that:

> Each party shall take such measures as may be necessary to establish that it is a criminal offence under its law for any person intentionally to offer, promise or give any undue pecuniary or other advantage, whether directly or through intermediaries to a foreign public official, for that official or for a third party, in order that the official act or refrain from acting in relation to the performance of official duties, in order to obtain or retain business or other improper advantage in the conduct of international business.

Further under Article 3 it will be possible to impose 'non-criminal sanctions' (civil liability) on a corporation if under the legal system of a party, criminal responsibility is not applicable to legal persons.[49]

In United States the Foreign Corrupt Practices Act 1977 (FCPA) prohibits a payment or offer of payment that is made 'corruptly' and with 'evil motive or purpose, intent to wrongfully influence the recipient' to misuse a foreign official position. For incurring liability under this act the focus is not on whether a corrupt intent of a recipient of the payment actually has the ability to influence an official decision.[50] There is a liability for sponsoring human rights violations directly or indirectly.[51] This statute focuses on corrupt intent; it is irrelevant whether the intended recipient of the payment actually has the ability to influence an official decision. Further, as long as the inducer has corrupt intent, an FCPA violation occurs where the inducer offers or promises a payment; it is irrelevant whether the payment is actually made.[52] In cases of sovereign financing states should advise companies to be on the look out for unusual payment patterns or financial arrangements, a refusal by

[45] R Carranza, 'Plunder and Pain: Should Transitional Justice Engage with Corruption and Economic Crimes?' (2008) 2 *The International Journal of Transitional Justice* 310.

[46] E Duruigbo, 'Corporate Accountability and Liability for International Human Rights Abuses: Recent Changes and Recurring Challenges' (2008) 6(2) *Northwestern Journal of International Human Rights* 262.

[47] Entered into force 15 February 1999. Also see Convention Against Transnational Organized Crime, Art 10(1), adopted 15 November 15 2000.

[48] See www.oecd.org/investment/briberyininternationalbusiness/anti-briberyconvention/38028044.pdf, accessed 23 September 2013.

[49] ibid.

[50] S Rep no 114, 95th Cong 1st Sess 10 (1977).

[51] See *Titan Corporation case* www.nytimes.com/2005/03/02/business/02titan.html, accessed 23 September 2013.

[52] R Blume and J Taylor McConkie, 'Navigating the Foreign Corrupt Practices Act: The Increasing Cost of Overseas Bribery' (2007) 36 *The Colorado Lawyer* 92.

the intermediary to provide a certification that it will not take any action in furtherance of an unlawful bribe, unusually high commissions, lack of transparency in expenses and accounting records, apparent lack of qualifications or resources on the part of the intermediary to perform the services offered, and whether the intermediary has been recommended by an official of the potential governmental customer.[53]

The OECD Convention on Combating Bribery of Foreign Public Officials in International Business Transactions (OECD Convention)[54] defines foreign public official as 'any person holding a legislative, administrative or judicial office of a foreign country', or exercising a public function.[55] It also prohibits any person from giving undue pecuniary or other advantage to a foreign public official for the retention of business or other improper advantage.[56] Small facilitation payments are excluded as an offence under Article 1(1) of the OECD Convention.[57] States can refuse mutual legal assistance (MLA) where the evidence is related to a political offence.[58] OECD Guidelines on Multinational Enterprises (MNE) are of a supplementary nature to the domestic law, implying the supreme nature of domestic laws.[59] In *US v Kay*, the Court of Appeals for the Fifth Circuit stated that the test is whether the bribery has assisted in the obtaining of business.[60] Further, the FCPA[61] suggests that if the payment is not written under the law, it is not a valid defence. Further, it is an offence 'irrespective of . . . [the] perceptions of local custom, the tolerance of such payments by local authorities . . . in order to obtain or retain business or other improper advantage'.[62]

The MNE Guidelines apply to 'multinational enterprises' which have an 'investment nexus' with their business partners.[63] Cases with an 'investment nexus'[64] require enterprises to have 'investment like activities'.[65] In accessing the presence of an 'investment nexus', all factors relevant to the nature of the relationship and the practical ability of the multinational enterprise to influence its business partner with investment-like relationships should be considered.[66] Chapter VI of the MNE Guidelines provides that enterprises should not 'demand a bribe or other undue advantage to obtain or retain business or other improper advantage'. Enterprises 'should not use subcontracts . . . as means of channeling payments to public officials, to employees of business partners or to their relatives. . .'.[67] In this context Deva argues that regulation of MNCs by the home state through a specific extraterritorial law is a relatively recent addition to the measures under consideration in the ongoing search for an effective and efficient model for MNCs'

[53] ibid, 93–94.

[54] Adopted by the Negotiating Conference on 21 November 1997.

[55] OECD Convention on Combating Bribery of Foreign Public Officials in International Business Transactions (adopted by the Negotiating Conference on 21 November 1997) Art 1(4)(a).

[56] OECD Convention, Art 1(1).

[57] Official Commentary, para 9.

[58] Model Treaty on Mutual Assistance in Criminal Matters (adopted by General Assembly Resolution 45/117) (subsequently amended by General Assembly Resolution 53/112) Art 4(1)(b); European Convention on Mutual Assistance in Criminal Matters, Art 2(a).

[59] Commentary on the MNE Guidelines, para. 2.

[60] *US v Kay*, 359 F.3d 738, 756 (5th Cir. 2004).

[61] FCPA 15 USC §§ 78dd-1(c)(1), 78dd-2(c)(1), 78dd-3(c)(1).

[62] See n 57, para 7.

[63] Commentary on the Implementation Procedures, n 164, Preface para 1; OECD, Annual Report on the OECD Guidelines for Multinational Enterprise 2003, 22.

[64] OECD (n 63) 42.

[65] MNE Guidelines, ch 1, para 10

[66] MNE Guidelines Annual Report 2003, 42.

[67] MNE Guidelines, Ch VI, para 1.

accountability for human rights violations.[68] The author also argues that it is legitimate for a state to enforce internationally recognised human rights obligations on corporations' overseas activities and its overseas subsidiaries by enacting an extraterritorial law. Secondly, it is the home states of MNCs which should enforce law as this model is more effective.[69]

Keeping in view the current law which may be applicable to corporate financing it is argued that it is not sufficient and using the state responsibility principle alongside it can make a robust framework to hold the mother state of a corporation accountable for human rights violations related to bribery. The state could be held liable for the failure to enact appropriate legislation to prevent or punish corruption committed by private corporations but also for ignoring corrupt behaviour of government officials who systematically accept bribes from corporations. To some extent, support could also be gained under principle 8 of the PRSLB, which states: 'Governments are agents of the State and, as such, when they contract debt obligations, they have a responsibility to protect the interests of their citizens. Where applicable, borrowers should also consider the responsibility of lenders' agents toward their organizations'. The implication of this principle is that any form of peculation by government officials is wrongful.[70] It shows a preliminary intention that this status makes wrongful any form of self-interest or peculation on the part of government officials involved in the borrowing. National laws as well as international and regional conventions against corruption are relevant in assessing the legality of this behaviour.[71]

It is also argued that in the case of transnational corporations, both mother state and borrowing state may have responsibility for not preventing (punishing) human rights abuse related to corruption. However, it is the mother state that is better equipped to ensure that a company comply with human rights standards[72] because of its prescriptive and enforcement jurisdiction. Further the world we live in is highly privatised and even the public services (such as health, transport or telecommunications) are run by private companies. This further multiplies the possibilities for corruption and may infringe the economic, political and cultural human rights of people. Even in privatisation cases the state may retain direct responsibility for the service in question but in others the state may simply transfer authority to private companies. In the latter case a state may be still responsible for human rights abuse and failure to prevent exposure to corruption. Further privatisation for major infrastructure projects involving public money and private investment is a particularly high-risk situation. In such projects public officials work closely with corporations, creating opportunities for corruption and compromising the integrity of government institutions. The public officials may be involved in securing tenders for corporations and simplify official procedures, concealing corporations' mismanagements of funds and protecting wrongdoers from investigation or prosecution. This

[68] S Deva, 'Acting Extraterritorially to Tame Multinational Corporations for Human Rights Violations: Who Should "Bell the Cat"?' (2004) 5 *Melbourne Journal of International Law* 37–65.

[69] See R Emerick, 'The Extraterritorial Application of United States Law and the Protection of Human Rights: Holding Multinational Corporations to Domestic and International Standards' (1996) 10 *Temple International and Comparative Law Journal* 123, 144.

[70] Principle 8, Principles on Promoting Responsible Sovereign Lending and Borrowing, United Nations General Assembly, www.unctad.info/upload/Debt%20Portal/Principles%20drafts/SLB_Principles_English_Doha_22-04-2012.pdf, accessed 10 October 2013.

[71] Commentary on Principle 8.

[72] ibid.

situation creates the conditions for human rights abuse and amplifies its effect by depriving local communities of the opportunity for seeking compensation.

B Cultural Expectations and Human Rights Protection

Under Principles 5 and 12 PRSLB liability is imposed on sovereign lenders and borrowers respectively to perform their own *ex ante investigation* and monitor its financial, operational, civil, social, cultural, and environmental implications. Under these circumstances it is problematic for corporations to follow such principles because human rights expectations are understood in a relative manner by member states. For example the 'Bangkok Declaration'[73] states: '. . .*while human rights are universal in nature, they must be considered in the context of a dynamic and evolving process of international norm-setting, bearing in mind the significance of national and regional particularities and various historical, cultural and religious backgrounds.*' On the other hand the Vienna Declaration states:

> All human rights are universal, indivisible and interdependent and interrelated The international community must treat human rights globally in a fair and equal manner on the same footing, and with the same emphasis . . . it is the duty of States, regardless of their political, economic and cultural systems, to promote and protect all human rights and fundamental freedoms.[74]

Hence there is a controversy and a cultural clash in the understanding of human rights. From the corporate responsibility and corporate financing perspective it is 'a question of navigating between two extremes'[75] and in practice it is not easy to implement such standards across the board because of cultural expectations. There is a problem if member states' legislation does not conform to international standards. Under these circumstances states need to influence the businesses and take appropriate steps to prevent, investigate and redress human rights abuse through effective policies, legislation, regulations and adjudication. It is argued in such cases the expectations of all the parties – host state, home state, lenders and the community in question – should be taken into consideration to find liability.

V THE ROLE OF COURTS IN FINDING CORPORAL ACCOUNTABILITY FOR HUMAN RIGHTS VIOLATIONS IN RELATION TO SOVEREIGN DEBT? – 'CONSTRUCTIVE KNOWLEDGE TEST' VS 'PURPOSE TEST'

Accountability is always linked to enforceability and hence the role of courts is pertinent to determine the meaning of 'aiding and abetting' to hold the corporation liable. In the United States there is an increasing use of the domestic legislation, the Alien Tort Claims Act (ATCA), to bring civil litigation against corporations who are alleged to have com-

[73] Report of Regional Meeting for Asia for the World Conference on Human Rights, 29 March–2 April 1993 www.law.hku.hk/conlawhk/conlaw/outline/Outline8/Bangkok%20Declaration.htm, accessed 10 October 2013.

[74] Vienna Declaration and Programme of Action (World Conference on Human Rights, Vienna, 14–25 June 1993).

[75] J Cramer, *Corporate Social Responsibility and Globalization – An Action Plan for Business* (Sheffield, Greenleaf Publishing, 2006) 42.

mitted violations of customary international law. Even though ATCA may be used to file a lawsuit, nonetheless the procedural obstacles in the civil litigation makes it hard to succeed in such a claim unless less strict principles are used to establish liability. This problem is illustrated by the *Khulumani*,[76] *Talisman*[77] and Amicus Banks litigation, which will be discussed later. This approach puts a higher burden of proof on the plaintiff than that required in civil litigation, with the result that corporations are escaping liability. This also affects indirectly sovereign financing situations because if a corporation is not found liable then arguably the mother state cannot be held liable for not exercising effective control on its corporations abroad. The mother state would be seen to have tacitly fulfilled its monitoring duties under the Guiding Principles and PRSLB.

During the Nuremberg Trials individual responsibility was recognised for violations of international law and for involvement in war crimes. Further the Allied prosecutors also sought to hold corporate executives liable for their role as accomplices.[78] For determining the requisite mental state or *mens rea* knowledge that the acts in question assisted in the abuses is required[79] or alternatively that a reasonable person should have known it. For the *mens rea* of 'aiding and abetting', the ICTY held that actual or constructive (ie 'reasonable') 'knowledge that the accomplice's actions will assist the perpetrator in the commission of the crime' is required.[80] Hence to incur liability on the accomplice/abettor it is not required to know exact *mens rea* of the actual perpetrator as long as the accused is aware that the crime committed is in fact one of the crimes that he intended to facilitate. [81] In *Prosecutor v Vasiljevic*,[82] knowledge was accepted by the ICTY as the established *mens rea* for aiding and abetting the commission of the crime. The accused was found guilty as a co-perpetrator of the Milan Luki Serbian paramilitary unit, which shot seven Muslims, killing five of them.[83]

Hence under this test corporations could be held liable for human rights abuses if 'they knew or should have known' that their conduct would substantially assist or encourage a government to commit certain human rights abuses.[84] For sovereign debt liability it is also arguable that a state could be responsible for breach of international law for not legislating and enforcing laws for controlling corporations' conduct abroad. Where the perpetrator remains unknown it should be possible to claim compensation.

The loss of civil cases against corporations is mainly due to the fact that it seems hard for courts to recognise exterritorial human rights violations by corporations. This is clear from the case of *Esther Kiobel, et al v Royal Dutch Petroleum Company et al*[85] in which Barinem Kiobel, an Ogoni activist who opposed the environmental disaster caused by Shell's extractive activities in the Niger Delta in Nigeria, was arbitrarily detained, tried

[76] *Khulumani v Barclay National Bank*, 504 F.3d 254 (2d Cir 2007).

[77] US District Court for the Southern District of New York, 01 Civ. 9882 (DLC), 453 F. Supp. 2d 633.

[78] KR Jacobson, 'Doing Business with the Devil: The Challenges of Prosecuting Corporate Officials Whose Business Transactions Facilitate War Crimes and Crimes Against Humanity' (2005) 56 *Air Force Law Review* 174–75. Also see the Case No 9, Zyklon B Trial in which three ex-officials of the German chemical company Tesch & Stabenow were convicted for selling poison gas used to kill prisoners in concentration camps and were held accountable as accomplices, www.ess.uwe.ac.uk/wcc/zyklonb.htm, accessed 23 September 2013.

[79] *Doe v Unocal Corp*, 395 F.3d 932, 949 (9th Cir. 2002) at 951.

[80] *Prosecutor v Furundzija*, ICTY case no IT-95-17/1-A, 21 July 2000 at para 245.

[81] See n 79.

[82] *Prosecutor v Vasiljevic*, case no IT-98-32-A, Judgment of Appeals Chamber (25 February 2004).

[83] ibid, at 1.

[84] *Mehinovic v Vuckovic*, 198 F. Supp. 2d 1322, 1355–56 (ND Ga 2002) at 1355.

[85] There are various cases in different US Courts on this matter from 2009 to 2012. Finally the matter was accepted for rehearing in the US Supreme Court in 2012.

by a special court established by the military government, convicted of murder and finally executed.[86] In 1996, based on ATCA, Esther Kiobel sued Royal Dutch Petroleum in the US courts for involvement with the Nigerian military in acts of torture and murder committed against the Ogoni community.[87] It was alleged that Shell, through its Nigerian subsidiary Shell Petroleum Development Company of Nigeria (SPDC), provided transport to Nigerian troops and allowed company property to be used to attack the Ogoni community. In 2010 the US District Court dismissed this case on the basis that the plaintiffs had not shown that a direct business relationship existed between the US and SPDC. On 17 September 2010 a majority opinion in the Appeals Court stated that ATCA could not be used to sue corporations for violations of international law. In a separate opinion, Leval, third Circuit Judge, disagreed with the majority's reasoning and asserted that the majority's opinion was a 'substantial blow to international law and its undertaking to protect fundamental human rights'. Criticising the majority opinion, he said:

> According to the rule my colleagues have created, one who earns profits by commercial exploitation of abuse of fundamental human rights can successfully shield those profits from victims' claims for compensation simply by taking the precaution of conducting the heinous operation in the corporate form . . . So long as they incorporate . . ., businesses will now be free to trade in or exploit slaves, employ mercenary armies to do dirty work for despots, perform genocides . . . all without civil liability to victims. By adopting the corporate form, such an enterprise could have hired itself out to operate Nazi extermination camps or the torture chambers of Argentina's dirty war, immune from civil liability to its victims. By protecting profits earned through abuse of fundamental human rights protected by international law, the rule my colleagues have created operates in opposition to the objective of international law to protect those rights.[88]

The Majority view hence discounted liability of corporations and possibly private military corporations under international law.

As a specific case of sovereign financing, *Khulumani v Barclay National Bank*[89] placed a significant emphasis on how domestic legislation can be used to regulate international human rights violations committed by financial institutions. In 2002 a group of South Africans, represented by the Khulumani Support Group, sued 20 banks and corporations in US federal court for doing business in South Africa during the apartheid regime. It was alleged by the plaintiffs that the participation of the defendant companies encouraged furthering abuses against black Africans during apartheid. The abuses, such as extrajudicial killings, torture and rape, ensued because of alleged activities of the defendants during the apartheid era in South Africa, making them complicit in the commission of such abuses. Over the objection by the State Department of the United States, the 2nd Circuit agreed that banks and companies that included the automotive, computer and energy industries could be sued under the Act for aiding and abetting torts in violation of customary international law.[90]

[86] C Kaufmann, 'Case Profile: Shell Lawsuit (re Nigeria)', Business & Human Rights Resource Centre, University of Zurich. www.ivr.uzh.ch/institutsmitglieder/kaufmann/archives/hs11/humanrights/24_Case_Profile_Shell_Lawsuit_Nigeria.pdf, accessed 23 September 2013.

[87] L Choukroune, 'Foreign Direct Investment and Corporate Liability for Human Rights Abuses', City University of Hong Kong, School of Law, 2012.

[88] *Kiobel v Royal Dutch Petroleum*, United States Court Of Appeals for The Second Circuit, Docket Nos 06-4800-cv, 06-4876-cv, 17 September 2010. http://online.wsj.com/public/resources/documents/091710atsruling.pdf, accessed 23 September 2013.

[89] See n 76.

[90] ibid; see also www.law.com/jsp/article.jsp?id=1202429769165&slreturn=20130211115029, accessed 23 September 2013.

The peculiar facts of *Khulumani* made it hard for plaintiffs to win, however it is predicted that the *per curiam* opinion, and the three individual opinions of the judges will have a great impact on future attempts to hold corporations responsible for violations of international law outside the United States.[91] Although this case is in itself a positive step, nonetheless it was decided in the case that to find a corporate liable for aiding and abetting the human rights violation, there should be 'knowledge' that the corporation substantially assisted in the human rights violation.

The *Talisman*[92] case was heard by the US court in 2001 under ATCA. The First Presbyterian Church of Sudan filed a lawsuit against the Canadian oil and gas producer, Talisman Energy. It was claimed that Talisman committed genocide, war crimes and crimes against humanity in collaboration with the government of Sudan. It was alleged that Talisman created buffer zones around certain oilfields and secured the Sudanese regime's access to oil, which also effectively assisted it in the perpetration of international crimes. On 3 October 2009, the US Court of Appeals affirming the decision of the Second Circuit, held that the claimants had failed to establish that Talisman 'acted with the purpose to support the Government's offences'. On the procurement of arms issue, the Court upheld the decision of the Second Circuit finding that there was insufficient evidence to prove that Talisman directed its royalty payments to the Sudanese government's procurement of arms, despite a jury finding that Talisman was aware that such payments could be directed to that purpose. The Court concluded that 'the mens rea standard for aiding and abetting liability in ATCA actions is purpose rather than knowledge'.[93] On 4 October 2010, the US Supreme Court declined to hear the case.[94]

It is now clear that the *Khulumani*[95] and *Talisman*[96] litigation imposes the higher standard to hold a corporation liable. Such a high standard of 'purpose' in civil litigation, which is higher than knowledge test as imposed in criminal litigation,[97] seems rather unreasonable.[98] In this connection Bhashyam argued that if knowledge is a sufficient standard for criminal aiding and abetting liability then neither should it be problematic for civil liability under the ATCA nor should standards be made higher.[99]

In a lawsuit in Buenos Aires in an Amicus Curiae[100] against allegedly complicit banks that supported the military Junta, it was suggested that a reasonable – both international and domestic – standard is required to prove the liability of financial institutions. It was alleged that the banks provided substantial contribution to the Argentinian military during the dictatorship era, which caused massive human rights violations, and that the lenders should have known this fact. It was argued that the capital made available to the

[91] T Nemeroff, 'Untying the Khulumani Knot: Corporate Aiding and Abetting Liability under the Alien Tort Claims Act after Sosa', www3.law.columbia.edu/hrlr/hrlr_journal/40.1/Nemeroff.pdf, accessed 23 September 2013.

[92] US District Court for the Southern District of New York, 01 Civ 9882 (DLC), 453 F. Supp. 2d 633.

[93] *Presbyterian Church of Sudan v Talisman Energy, Inc*, 582 F.3d 244, 258–59 (2d Cir 2009) at 259.

[94] See n 92.

[95] See n 76.

[96] US District Court for the Southern District of New York, 01 Civ 9882 (DLC), 453 F. Supp. 2d 633.

[97] M Drumbl, 'Sands: From Nuremberg to The Hague: The Future of International Criminal Justice' (book rev) (2005) 103 *Michigan Law Review* 1295, 1313–14.

[98] See generally J Morrissey, 'Presbyterian Church of Sudan v. Talisman Energy, Inc.: Aiding and Abetting Liability Under the Alien Tort Statute' (2011) 20 *Minnesota Journal of International Law* 144.

[99] S Bhashyam, 'Knowledge or Purpose – The Khulumani Litigation and the Standard for Aiding and Abetting Liability under the Alien Tort Claims Act' (2008) 30 *Cardozo Law Review* 274.

[100] *Ibanez Manuel Leandro and others*: Preliminary measures against undetermined financial institutions, per Judge Dr Omar Cancela, para 65.

military government allowed it to increase the military operations that led directly to the harms caused to the plaintiffs/victims.[101]

VI CONCLUSION

The concept of sovereign financing and possible violations of human rights is an incredibly complex subject. The complexity is due to lack of clarity on the causal link between sovereign financing and human rights violations, corruption, social corporate responsibility, due diligence and state responsibility. It was argued that under state responsibility principle both lenders and mother states can be held liable for irresponsible lending/borrowing of finances that result in human rights violations. Such a conclusion was drawn by taking into account the contemporary laws and rules on sovereign financing such as PRSLB, Guiding Principles, corruption, due diligence and corporate social responsibility.

A case was made that corruption is interrelated with extraterritorial human rights violations because it is the former that may become a source for exploitation, injustice and human rights violations. Cobus de Swardt rightly asserts that 'the fight against corruption is central to the struggle for human rights . . . From violent ethnic cleansing to institutionalised racism, political actors have abused their entrusted powers to focus on gains for the few at great cost for the many'.[102] It was argued that the link between corruption and extraterritorial human rights obliges both the mother state and host state of financial corporations to protect their nationals from human rights violations emanating from the corrupt and irresponsible sovereign financial practices.

It was demonstrated that the nature of international law was keyed to the actualities of past centuries in which international relations were inter-state relations. The actualities have changed; the law is changing.[103] In 2012 UNCTAD proposed that the responsibility of sovereign borrowing and lending be strengthened and that:

> Lenders financing a project in the debtor country have a responsibility to perform their own ex ante investigation into and, when applicable, post-disbursement monitoring of, the likely effects of the project, including its financial, operational, civil, social, cultural, and environmental implications.[104]

It has thus imposed a responsibility on the lenders to conduct investigations on projects. It is also arguable that similar responsibility could be imposed on mother states to conduct investigations with an aim to improve and prevent human rights violations in the borrowing state.

It was argued that state responsibility should be used as a complementary mechanism for holding corporations responsible for human rights violations. This process should not

[101] ibid.

[102] See, Foreword of Cobus de Swardt (Managing Director, Transparency International) in Report by International Council on Human Rights Policy and Transparency International, *Corruption and Human Rights: Making the Connection*, 2009, 3.

[103] P Jessup, 'The Subjects of a Modern Law of Nations' (1947) 45 *Michigan Law Review* 383, 384; see also M McDougal and G Leighton, 'The Rights of Man in the World Community: Constitutional Illusions Versus Rational Action' (1949) 59 *Yale Law Journal* 84.

[104] Principle 5 Project Financing, Principles on Promoting Responsible Sovereign Lending and Borrowing, United Nations General Assembly, www.unctad.info/upload/Debt%20Portal/Principles%20drafts/SLB_Principles_English_Doha_22-04-2012.pdf, accessed 23 September 2013.

be seen by the host state as an infringement of their state sovereignty.[105] Today mother and host states are under a duty of due diligence to prevent violations of human rights by corporations. Where such violations occur, states should investigate, punish and provide effective remedies to victims. Finally both home and host state should have responsibility to draft laws locally that can clearly require the observance of international rules of conduct for corporate responsibility.

It was argued that for liability under state responsibility to be incurred, victims are not required to demonstrate that the mother government was negligent in restraining its officials; rather, the acts of such officials are attributed to the state and the state is liable for the violation because of the effective link between the state and its officials.[106] Likewise for a business to be held liable it should be per se responsible for all its components/officials acting under its corporate authority without any separate requirement of fault on the part of the business independent of its components.[107] The *Khulumani* litigation and *Presbyterian Church of Sudan v Talisman Energy, Inc*[108] suggested that it is possible to bring litigation against financial corporations. However, courts seek to apply more stringent tests such as the 'purpose test' to hold companies liable for aiding and abetting human rights violations rather than using the knowledge test that is used in criminal litigation. By adopting stringent tests courts are unnecessarily raising the bar for holding the financial corporations liable. It also needs to be proved that the company was providing substantial assistance to further human rights abuse.

It is recommended that by applying the state responsibility concept mother states could also be held liable for extraterritorial human rights violations caused by irresponsible financing of a corporation. Mother states could be held liable based on not preventing, investigating, punishing and redressing abuse through effective policies, legislation and adjudication. It is believed that a fear of litigation may encourage states and corporations equally to take reasonable steps to implement monitoring as described under the Guiding Principles as well as the UNSLB and to avoid potential extraterritorial human rights violations committed by their financial operation.

[105] DM Chirwa, 'The Doctrine of State Responsibility as a Potential Means of Holding Private Actors Accountable for Human Rights' (2004) 5 *Melbourne Journal of International Law* 35.

[106] International Law Commission, Draft Articles on Responsibility of States for Internationally Wrongful Acts, November 2001, www.unhcr.org/refworld/docid/3ddb8f804.html, accessed 23 September 2013; *Velásquez Rodríguez v Honduras*, Inter-American Court of Human Rights, Series C, no 4, para 170 (1988).

[107] B Fisse and J Braithwaite, *Corporations, Crime and Accountability* (Cambridge, Cambridge University Press, 1993) 483–88.

[108] US District Court for the Southern District of New York, 01 Civ 9882 (DLC), 453 F. Supp. 2d 633.

16

Sovereign Debt and Human Rights: The United Nations Approach

CEPHAS LUMINA*

I INTRODUCTION

DEPENDING ON A variety of factors, such as responsible lending and borrowing, the financing conditions and prudent use of funds, external financing (including loans) can contribute to countries' development. Despite the plethora of international commitments and efforts to address the problem and the fact that the issue has been on the international agenda for more than four decades, however, excessive debt burdens continue to constrain the development prospects of many low- and middle-income countries and to undermine the capacity of such countries to create the conditions for the realisation of human rights, particularly economic, social and cultural rights and the right to development.[1] Indeed, the available evidence indicates that in many countries, especially the poorest, debt servicing is often undertaken at the expense of the country's population's fundamental rights, including the rights to food, health, education, adequate housing and work. In addition, harmful policy conditions linked to loans and debt relief often limit investment in, and undermine the provision of, accessible public services, as well as national ownership of development strategies.

In circumstances where debt has been cancelled, some countries have been able to invest more in public services, such as healthcare, education, water and sanitation, and to abolish user fees for some of these services (such as healthcare and primary education previously introduced as part of austerity measures imposed by the international financial institutions) thereby enhancing the enjoyment of the rights to healthcare, education, water and sanitation.

This chapter discusses how the United Nations human rights bodies have addressed the question of sovereign debt and its impact on the realisation of human rights. The chapter is organised as follows. Section II briefly discusses the impact of debt and related policies on the realisation of human rights, particularly economic, social and cultural rights and the right to development. Section III discusses the treatment of the debt problem by the various United Nations human rights bodies. Section IV is the conclusion.

* United Nations Independent Expert on the effects of foreign debt and other related international financial obligations of States on the full enjoyment of all human rights, particularly economic, social and cultural rights; Extra-Ordinary Professor, Centre for Human Rights, University of Pretoria.

[1] See United Nations, Human Rights Council, Consolidation of findings of the high-level task force on the implementation of the right to development, 25 March 2010, A/HRC/15/WG.2/TF/2/Add.1, para 52.

II SOVEREIGN DEBT AND ITS IMPACT ON HUMAN RIGHTS

There is extensive evidence that excessive external debt burdens and related policy reform measures adopted by States to address them have an adverse impact on the realisation of human rights and development in debtor countries. In order to service their debt, governments are often constrained to redirect scarce national financial resources from essential investments in human, social and physical infrastructure including schools, health services, agriculture, roads and other areas that provide the foundation for sustainable and equitable development.[2] The diversion of resources significantly reduces the capacity of countries to establish the conditions for the realisation of human rights and also undermines national development.[3] In these circumstances several human rights, including the rights to education, food, health, adequate housing, work and development, are placed under threat or violated and millions face poorer living conditions.[4]

In addition to undermining States' human rights obligations, excessive debt burdens create considerable obstacles for some countries in achieving their development strategies, including internationally agreed goals.[5] For example, in a report issued in 2010, covering 68 countries where more than 95 per cent of all maternal and child deaths occur, the World Health Organization and UNICEF noted the inadequate progress towards the Millennium Development Goals (MDGs). The report indicated that 49 of the countries surveyed were off track for achieving Goals 4 (reduce child mortality) and 5 (improve maternal health).[6] It is interesting to note that, while the report does not explicitly attribute this lack of progress to the countries' external debt burden,[7] 33 of the countries surveyed are classified by the World Bank and IMF as heavily indebted poor

[2] For example, between 1992 and 1997, the portion of the national budget devoted to basic social services and debt service for some African countries was: Cameroon – 4 per cent on social services and 36 per cent on debt service; Cote d'Ivoire – 11.4 per cent on social services and 35 per cent on debt service; Kenya – 12.6 per cent on social services and 40 per cent on debt service; Zambia – 6.7 per cent on social services and 40 per cent on debt service; and Tanzania – 15 per cent on social services and 46 per cent on debt service. See D Millet and E Toussaint, 'Figures Relating to the Debt for 2009' (Brussels, CADTM, 2009). According to a study by the New Economics Foundation, in 2005, 20 countries spent more than 20 per cent of their budget on debt service. That year, Lebanon spent 52 per cent of its budget on debt service as compared with 23.1 per cent on education and health; Jamaica spent 27.9 per cent on debt service and 16.1 per cent on education and health; and Bulgaria spent 23 per cent on debt service and 11.6 per cent on education and health. See Lucie Stephens, *Debt Relief As If Justice Mattered* (London, New Economics Foundation, 2008) 11. Other independent studies have confirmed the high level of spending on debt servicing relative to expenditure on basic social services such as education and healthcare. See, for example, Christian Barry, Barry Herman and Lydia Tomitova (eds), *Dealing Fairly with Developing Country Debt* (Oxford, Blackwell Publishing, 2007) 2; Jubilee Debt Campaign, 'Debt and Public Services,' Briefing, October 2007 <old.jubileedebtcampaign.org.uk/Debt3720and3720Public3720Services+3704.twl> accessed 30 September 2013; Alcino Ferreira Camara Neto and Matias Vernengo, 'Lula's Social Policies: New Wine in Old Bottles?', Working Paper, Department of Economics, University of Utah (2006–2007) 11.

[3] See A/HRC/12/WG.2/TF/2, para 87. See also Isabella Bunn, 'The Right to Development: Implications for International Economic Law' (2000) 15 *American University International Law Review* 1452–67.

[4] See Jubilee Debt Campaign, 'Debt and Health', Briefing, December 2007 <old.jubileedebtcampaign.org.uk/Debt3720and3720Health+3795.twl> accessed 30 September 2013; Jubilee Debt Campaign, 'Debt and Education', Briefing, April 2007 <old.jubileedebtcampaign.org.uk/Debt3720and3720Education+3198.twl> accessed 30 September 2013; Jubilee Debt Campaign, 'Debt and Public Services' (n 2 above).

[5] See A/HRC/15/WG.2/TF/2/Add.1 (n 1), paras 54 and 87. See also Bunn (n 3).

[6] World Health Organization and United Nations Children's Fund, *Countdown to 2015 Decade Report (2000–2010): Tracking Progress in Maternal, Newborn and Child Survival* (New York and Geneva, WHO and UNICEF, 2010) 1.

[7] The report identifies user fees and inadequate levels of official development assistance as the key financial barriers. See ibid, 2.

countries and include 27 that have completed the Heavily Indebted Poor Countries (HIPC) Initiative.

Similarly, in 2011, the World Bank and IMF, while reporting that HIPCs had increased their poverty-reducing expenditure as a result of debt relief under the HIPC Initiative, noted that 'HIPCs have made uneven, and in some cases, limited, progress towards achieving the MDGs'.[8] Only a quarter of completion point HIPCs were on track to achieving Goal 1 (to eradicate extreme poverty and hunger), with progress towards Goal 5 (to improve maternal health) less certain.[9]

Furthermore, policy conditions linked to the provision of new loans and relief on old debts by international financial institutions,[10] as well as drastic austerity policies which indebted countries are constrained to implement in an attempt to address their debt problems, have jeopardised the realisation of many basic rights by compelling reductions in government spending or limiting investment in social services such as education and health, and undermined country ownership of national development strategies.

These policy conditions include measures such as privatisation of State-owned enterprises (such as electricity generation and distribution, water utilities and telecommunications); reduction of government expenditures for public services; wage ceilings; redundancies from the public service (the main employer in many countries); introduction of user fees for basic services like health and education; trade liberalisation (involving removal or reduction of subsidies and import tariffs and promotion of exports); deregulating investment; financial sector liberalisation; fiscal and monetary reforms (strict inflation targeting, accumulation of international reserves, currency devaluation and expansion of domestic credits); taxation reforms (such as introduction of value added tax and other regressive taxes, tax holidays for foreign corporations and improvement of customs collection); and land reform (ie changes in laws governing ownership of land by foreigners).

The ostensible aim of these conditions is to promote economic growth and prosperity,

[8] International Development Association and International Monetary Fund, 'Heavily Indebted Poor Countries (HIPC) Initiative and Multilateral Debt Relief Initiative (MDRI) – Status of Implementation and Proposals for the Future of the HIPC Initiative', 8 November 2011, 4.

[9] ibid.

[10] For a discussion of typical policy conditions, see N Molina and J Pereira, *Critical Conditions: The IMF Maintains Its Grip on Low-income Governments* (Brussels, Eurodad, April 2008) www.eurodad.org/uploadedfiles/whats_new/reports/critical_conditions.pdf> accessed 23 September 2013; JR Vreeland, *The International Monetary Fund: Politics of Conditional Lending* (London, Routledge, 2007) 23–25; RA King and MD Robinson, 'Assessing Structural Adjustment Programs: A Summary of State Experience' in JF Weeks (ed), *Debt Disaster? Banks, Governments, Multilaterals Confront the Crisis* (New York, New York University Press,1989) 103; and NG Villaroman, 'A Fate Worse Than Debt: An Alternative View of the Right to Development and its Relevance in the External Debt Problem of Developing Countries' (LLM Thesis, Monash University, Australia 2010) 115–16. It has been estimated that the IMF imposes an average of 13 conditions per low-income country loan. See Molina and Pereira, *Critical Conditions*, 4. Although the international financial institutions claim that there has been a shift in their policies from conditionalities in the form of Structural Adjustment Programmes to 'country-owned' Poverty Reduction Strategy Papers (see, for example, IMF, 'Poverty Reduction Strategy Papers (PRSP): A Factsheet', September 2005, www.imf.org/external/np/exr/facts/prshtml, accessed 30 September 2013; and World Bank, 'From Adjustment Lending to Development Policy Lending: Update of the World Bank Policy', August 2004) independent analyses show that there is very little difference, if any, in terms of substance. For example, a 2001 UNDP Review of PRSP concluded that: 'A review of the macroeconomic policies in different countries' PRSP indicates that they are not significantly different from earlier stabilisation and structural adjustment lending'. UNDP Review of the Poverty Reduction Strategy Paper (PRSP), December 2001, www.bb.undorg/uploads/file/pdfs/poverty/Library/PRSP%20Library/UNDP%20%20Review%20of%20thePRSpdf, accessed 23 September 2013.

as well as to restore the debt repayment capacity of recipient countries.[11] However, the available evidence shows that they do in fact have an adverse impact on the realisation of human rights in the longer term and they have contributed to increasing poverty in many debtor countries and the marginalisation of the poor.[12] To illustrate, the privatisation of public enterprises often results in large-scale retrenchments, thereby depriving many individuals of a livelihood; and the reduction of government expenditures for public services (such as education, health and housing) and/or the introduction of user fees for these services, limits access to these services for many sectors of the population, especially the poorest; and the removal of food subsidies has resulted in declining nutritional levels, especially among poorer segments of the population.[13] The change in agricultural policies from food production for local consumption to production of export crops such as coffee, tobacco or cotton for the purposes of generating foreign exchange, has also resulted in a decline in food production and in reduced nutritional levels and malnutrition; and a decrease of tax revenues arising from the general impoverishment of the population and from tax incentives offered to transnational corporations leaves governments with little income for social investment. In 2002 the United Nations Conference on Trade and Development (UNCTAD) reported that the rapid and extensive trade liberalisation undertaken by the least developed countries during the 1990s failed to benefit the poor and in fact resulted in increased unemployment, wage inequality and poverty.[14]

Thus, while conditionalities can be beneficial,[15] the overwhelming view is that they have destroyed livelihoods, increased poverty and inequality and left many poor countries ensnared in externally prescribed or approved policy frameworks that not only make it difficult for them to comply with their human rights obligations but also undermine their development.

It is generally accepted that country ownership of national development strategies is the foundation of development effectiveness.[16] The Declaration on the Right to Development recognises this by proclaiming that:

[11] See International Monetary Fund, *Factsheet: IMF Conditionality*, www.imf.org/external/np/exr/facts/conditio.htm, accessed 30 September 2013. See also, Independent Evaluation Office, Evaluation of Structural Conditionality in IMF-Supported Programs, IMF Background Document I, para 2 (2009) www.ieo-imf-org/eval/complete/eval_010322008.html, accessed 30 September 2013.

[12] See, for example, JD Sachs, *The End of Poverty: Economic Possibilities for Our Time* (New York, Penguin, 2005) 81–88, 280–81, 342; M Dent and B Peters, *The Crisis of Poverty and Debt in the Third World* (Aldershot, Ashgate Publishing, 1999) 73–79. For concerns expressed by the UN human rights mechanisms on the adverse impacts of conditionalities, see the Concluding Observations cited in n 70 below. See also United Nations, Commission on Human Rights, Report of the Special Rapporteur on adequate housing as a component of the right to an adequate standard of living, Miloon Kothari, submitted pursuant to Commission resolution 2000/9, E/CN.4/2001/51, 25 January 2001; United Nations, Commission on Human Rights, Report of the Special Rapporteur on adequate housing as a component of the right to an adequate standard of living, Miloon Kothari, E/CN.4/2002/59, 1 March 2002; and Commission on Human Rights, Annual Report of the Special Rapporteur on the right to education, Katarina Tomasevski, submitted in accordance with Commission resolution 2000/9, E/CN.4/2001/52, 11 January 2001.

[13] Report by the Independent Expert, Mr Fantu Cheru, submitted in accordance with Commission decisions 1998/102 and 1997/103, E/CN.4/1999/50, 24 February 1999, para 65.

[14] United Nations Conference on Trade and Development (UNCTAD), *Least Developed Countries' Report 2002: Escaping the Poverty Trap* (New York and Geneva, United Nations, 2002).

[15] For example, trade liberalisation may lead to more competition and lower prices of commodities.

[16] According to UNCTAD, country ownership does not mean 'some form of national commitment (or buy-in) to the policy reforms advocated by the IFIs', as it is often understood: it 'implies that national Governments should have the ability to freely choose the strategies which they design and implement, and take the lead in both policy formulation and implementation.' UNCTAD, *The Least Developed Countries Report 2010: Towards a New International Development Architecture for LDCs* (New York and Geneva, United Nations, 2010) 162.

> States have the right and duty to formulate appropriate national development policies that aim at the constant improvement of the well-being of the entire population and of all individuals, on the basis of their active, free and meaningful participation in development and in the fair distribution of the benefits resulting therefrom'[17]

and that 'States have the primary responsibility for the creation of national and international conditions favourable to the realization of the right to development'.[18]

Nevertheless, as UNCTAD has observed, it is extremely difficult for a country to achieve ownership of national development strategies in a situation of continuing dependence on aid and even more so where the country concerned is heavily indebted. Indeed, severe indebtedness leaves debtor countries subject to the control of international financial institutions and other creditors,[19] thereby eroding the ability of these countries to freely determine and pursue policies favourable to their development in line with the right to development. The situation was aptly summarised more than a decade ago by the then Independent Expert on the effects of structural adjustment policies on the full enjoyment of human rights, Fantu Cheru, in his report to the Commission on Human Rights:

> The countries of sub-Saharan Africa, with their poor credit rating, have largely been turned into an IMF 'macroeconomic guinea pig' since they depend largely on resources from the multilateral institutions . . . Since most of these countries have very weak political structures, an IMF-World Bank condominium has been imposed on them under the guise of providing aid. As a result, these countries have pretty much ceded their sovereignty to the IMF and the World Bank. Consequently, their responsibility to abide by the Declaration on the Right to Development and to formulate national development policies that aim to improve the economic, social and cultural rights of their citizens is severely undermined.[20]

In short, the available evidence indicates that excessive debt burdens and policy conditions meant to address them have undermined prospects for development in many countries as well as the capacity of governments to fulfil their human rights obligations, particularly those relating to economic, social and cultural rights.

III THE UNITED NATIONS AND THE PROBLEM OF SOVEREIGN DEBT

The issue of sovereign debt and its impact on the realisation of human rights and development has been on the agenda of various United Nations bodies for several decades. The discussion in this section focuses on how the various United Nations human rights bodies have addressed the problem.

[17] Article 2(3).

[18] Article 3(1).

[19] See Jubilee Debt Campaign, 'Debt and Women', Briefing, March 2007 <old.jubileedebtcampaign.org.uk/Debt3720and3720Women+3973.twl> accessed 30 September 2013.

[20] Cheru Report (n 13) para 30. See also Joint Report of the Special Rapporteur on the effects of foreign debt on the full enjoyment of economic, social and cultural rights, Reinaldo Figuerado and the Independent Expert on structural adjustment policies, Fantu Cheru, E/CN.4/2000/51, where the experts conclude: 'Put simply, HIPC/ESAF is a back-door way for both IMF and the World Bank to maintain control over the national development priorities of poor and indebted countries' (para 6).

A The Sub-Commission on the Promotion and Protection of Human Rights

Early efforts by the United Nations human rights mechanisms to address the question of debt and its impact on human rights and development can be traced to the Sub-Commission on the Promotion and Protection of Human Rights (before 1999 known as the Sub-Commission on Prevention of Discrimination and Protection of Minorities).[21] In 1983 the Sub-Commission's Special Rapporteur on the new international economic order and the promotion of human rights observed that the 'situation regarding the external debt of the developing countries [was] extremely serious'.[22]

In 1991 the Special Rapporteur of the Sub-Commission on the realisation of economic social and cultural rights, Danilo Türk, examined the effects of structural adjustment programmes on the enjoyment of economic, social and cultural rights and the role of the international financial institutions.[23] The Special Rapporteur concluded that structural adjustment programmes continued to 'have a significant impact upon the overall realisation of economic, social and cultural rights, both in terms of the ability of people to exercise these rights, and of the capability of Governments to fulfil and implement them'.[24]

In response to the Special Rapporteur's recommendations, the Sub-Commission and the Commission on Human Rights requested the Secretary General to prepare guidelines on structural adjustment policies and economic, social and cultural rights which could serve as a basis for a continued dialogue between the human rights bodies and the international financial institutions.[25] The Sub-Commission approved the guidelines by consensus through its resolution 1995/32 in which it also recommended that the Commission establish a working group 'to elaborate, on the basis of the preliminary set of basic policy guidelines on structural adjustment policies and economic, social and cultural rights . . . policy guidelines on the subject matter'.

The Sub-Commission also conducted a number of studies on the subject of structural adjustment policies, including one prepared by its Special Rapporteurs, J Oloka-Onyango and D Udagama, which was critical of the macroeconomic reform policies prescribed by the World Bank and IMF, and recommended reform of international trade, investment and finance rules, taking into account respect for, and promotion of, human rights by the key actors in the global economy. The report also reasserted the primacy of human rights over all other considerations of international law.[26]

[21] The Sub-Commission was a subsidiary body of the Commission on Human Rights. It was abolished following the replacement of the Commission by the Human Rights Council in March 2006. In 2008 it was replaced by a consultative committee of experts with a more limited mandate.

[22] The New International Economic Order and the Promotion of Human Rights, study prepared by Raul Ferrero, E/CN.4/sub.2/1983 24/Rev.1 para 112.

[23] Sub-Commission on Prevention of Discrimination and Protection of Minorities, Realization of economic, social and cultural rights: second progress report prepared by Mr Danilo Turk, Special Rapporteur, E/CN.4/Sub.2/1991/17, 18 July 1991.

[24] ibid, para 67.

[25] See Sub-Commission resolutions 1991/27 and 1992/29; Commission resolutions 1993/14, 1994/37 and 1997/20.

[26] See Sub-Commission resolution 1999/8, 25 August 1999 and Preliminary and final reports on globalisation and its impact on the full enjoyment of human rights, E/CN.4/Sub.2/2000/13, 15 June 2000.

B The Human Rights Council

Since the 1990s, the Commission on Human Rights and, its successor, the Human Rights Council,[27] have in numerous decisions and resolutions referred to the challenges that excessive external debt burdens and economic reform policies (particularly structural adjustment policies) present for the realisation of human rights, in the developing countries.[28] In many of its resolutions, the Commission emphasised that:

> The permanent solution to the foreign debt problem lies in the establishment of a just and equitable international economic order which guarantees the developing countries, inter alia, better market access, stabilization of exchange rates and interest rates, access to financial and capital markets, adequate flows of financial resources and better access to the technology of the developed countries.[29]

The Commission also affirmed and the Council reiterated that 'the exercise of the basic rights of the people of the debtor countries to food, housing, clothing, employment, education, health services and a healthy environment cannot be subordinated to the implementation of structural adjustment policies, and economic reforms arising from the debt'.[30]

In 1995 the Commission requested the United Nations Secretary General to recommend a way of establishing 'a political dialogue between creditor and debtor countries in the United Nations system, based on the principle of shared responsibility'.[31] In the Commission's estimation, such a dialogue would contribute to the creation of a process designed to restructure the international economic order with 'the objective of achieving more equitable and fair relations among all nations'.

It should be noted that the consideration by the Commission and Council of the question of the impact of sovereign debt burdens on the realisation of human rights has not been without controversy. The decisions and resolutions of both bodies reflect strong differences of opinion between the developed and developing countries on whether foreign debt should be treated as a human rights issue.[32] The developed (mainly creditor)

[27] The Council is an inter-governmental body within the UN system consisting of 47 Member States elected by the majority of the members of the UN General Assembly through direct and secret ballot, taking into account the candidate State's contribution to the promotion and protection of human rights, as well as their voluntary pledges and commitments in this connection. It was established by the General Assembly on 15 March 2006 by resolution 60/251 to replace the Commission on Human Rights.

[28] See Commission resolutions 1998/24 of 17 April 1998, 1999/22 of 23 April 1999, 2000/82 of 26 April 2000, 2001/27 of 20 April 2001, 2002/29 of 22 April 2002, 2003/21 of 22 April 2003, 2004/18 of 16 April 2004, 2005/19 of 14 April 2005; and Council decision 2/109 of 27 November 2006.

[29] See, eg, Commission on Human Rights resolutions 1998/24, 17 April 1998, para 3 and 1999/22 of 23 April 1999, para 3.

[30] See, eg, Commission on Human Rights resolutions 1998/24, of 17 April 1998, para 5 and 1999/22 of 23 April 1999, para 5; Human Rights Council resolution 20/10, para 24. See also Council resolution 23/11 of 13 June 2013 in which the Council reaffirmed all resolutions and decisions adopted by the Commission and the Council on the effects of structural adjustment and economic reform policies and foreign debt on the full enjoyment of all human rights, particularly economic, social and cultural rights.

[31] See Commission on Human Rights resolution 1995/13.

[32] See, eg, Commission on Human Rights resolution 2004/18 of 16 April 2004, adopted by a vote of 29 in favour (Argentina, Bhutan, Brazil, Burkina Faso, China, Cuba, Dominican Republic, Egypt, Eritrea, Ethiopia, Gabon, Guatemala, Honduras, India, Indonesia, Mauritania, Nepal, Nigeria, Pakistan, Philippines, Republic of the Congo, Sierra Leone, South Africa, Sri Lanka, Sudan, Swaziland, Togo, Uganda and Zimbabwe), 14 against (Australia, Austria, Croatia, France, Germany, Hungary, Ireland, Italy, Japan, Netherlands, South Korea, Sweden, United Kingdom and United States) and 10 abstentions (Armenia, Bahrain, Chile, Costa Rica,

countries have strongly opposed addressing the issue within the two bodies, contending that these bodies were not the 'appropriate' ones to address the debt problem. For example, during the March 2011 session of the Council, the US delegation, while claiming that the United States 'has long recognized the potentially harmful effects that excessive debt burdens can have on developing countries, especially Heavily Indebted Poor Countries', argued:

> [W]e continue to believe that it is incorrect to treat the issue of foreign debt as a human rights problem to be addressed by this Council. Rules other than human rights law are most relevant to the contractual arrangements between States and lenders. There are other international fora which are much better equipped to deal with the questions of foreign debt and debt forgiveness, which are principally economic and technical in nature. Unfortunately, continuing the mandate of the independent expert does not simply further the inappropriate treatment of this important issue as a human rights problem. It also diverts the focus and finances of this Council away from serious human rights issues that more urgently require our attention. We must therefore vote against this resolution.[33]

Similarly, in March 2013, Ireland, speaking on behalf of the European Union, in relation to a draft resolution of the Council (A/HRC/22/L.24) concerning the negative impact of the non-repatriation of funds of illicit origin to the countries of origin on the enjoyment of human rights and the importance of improving international cooperation, claimed that the resolution covered issues that exceeded the mandate and expertise of the Human Rights Council.[34] It went on to argue that while it accepted that corruption affected the enjoyment of human rights, its effective elimination lay rather in the area of criminal law, including at the international level and that the European Union did not agree that a human rights approach to these issues should always be the primary objective. For these reasons, the European Union would abstain on the vote.[35]

The arguments advanced by the United States and other developed countries reflect a misunderstanding of international human rights law. They are also inconsistent with the spirit and purport of resolution 60/251 establishing the Council and the commitments which candidate States for membership of the Council make. In this regard, it is important to note that in resolution 60/251, the General Assembly recognised 'the importance

Mexico, Paraguay, Peru, Qatar, Saudi Arabia and Ukraine); Human Rights Council decision A/HRC/DEC/12/119, adopted on 12 October 2009 by a vote of 31 in favour (Angola, Argentina, Bahrain, Bangladesh, Bolivia [Plurinational State of], Brazil, Burkina Faso, Cameroon, Chile, China, Cuba, Djibouti, Egypt, Gabon, Ghana, India, Indonesia, Jordan, Kyrgyzstan, Madagascar, Mauritius, Nicaragua, Nigeria, Pakistan, Philippines, Qatar, Russian Federation, Saudi Arabia, Senegal, South Africa and Uruguay), 13 against (Belgium, Bosnia and Herzegovina, France, Hungary, Italy, Japan, Netherlands, Republic of Korea, Slovakia, Slovenia, Ukraine, United Kingdom and United States), and 2 abstentions (Mexico and Norway).

[33] See *US EOV on Foreign Debt as a Human Rights Problem*, Explanation of Vote by the United States of America, Mandate of the independent expert on the effects of foreign debt and other related international financial obligations of States on the full enjoyment of all human rights, particularly economic, social and cultural rights, UN Human Rights Council, 16th Session, 23 March 2011, geneva.usmission.gov/2011/03/23/eov-foreign-debt/, accessed 22 June 2011.

[34] See Summary Records of the Human Rights Council, 21 March 2013.

[35] ibid. The resolution was adopted by a vote of 32 in favour (Angola, Argentina, Benin, Botswana, Brazil, Burkina Faso, Chile, Congo, Costa Rica, Cote d'Ivoire, Ecuador, Ethiopia, Gabon, Guatemala, India, Indonesia, Kazakhstan, Kenya, Kuwait, Libya, Malaysia, Maldives, Mauritania, Pakistan, Peru, Philippines, Qatar, Sierra Leone, Thailand, Uganda, United Arab Emirates and Venezuela), 2 against (Japan and United States) and 13 abstentions (Austria, Czech Republic, Estonia, Germany, Ireland, Italy, Montenegro, Poland, Republic of Korea, Republic of Moldova, Romania, Spain and Switzerland). See A/HRC/RES/22/12. It is interesting to note that while Switzerland abstained on the vote, it participated in the consultation organised by the Independent Expert on this issue and submitted comments.

of ensuring universality, objectivity and non-selectivity in the consideration of human rights issues, and the elimination of double standards and politicization'[36] and decided that the work of the Council should 'be guided by principles of universality, impartiality, objectivity and non-selectivity, constructive international dialogue and cooperation, with a view to enhancing the promotion and protection of all human rights, civil, political, economic, social and cultural rights, including the right to development'.[37] It should also be noted that members of the Council are obliged to 'fully cooperate with the Council'.[38] Thus, the position of the United States and other developed countries regarding the issue of debt and human rights is inconsistent with the obligation of Member States to cooperate with the Council and is indicative of selectivity in the consideration of human rights issues, contrary to resolution 60/251.

The contentions by the developed countries within the Council are also untenable for a number of reasons. First, with specific reference to the claims by the United States, it should be noted that the 'rules other than human rights law' and 'other international fora which are much better equipped to deal with the questions of foreign debt and debt forgiveness' (presumably, the international financial institutions and the Paris Club) have thus far failed to deliver an equitable and lasting solution to the sovereign debt problem. As creditors, these institutions cannot realistically be expected to focus on finding a solution to the debt crisis that prioritises social and economic justice over debt repayment.[39] It is also worth noting that these institutions do not have the expertise to properly factor human rights into their policies and strategies. Moreover, the 'rules other than human rights law' provide no protection for States that experience debt repayment difficulties as is the case for similarly situated individuals and entities under domestic insolvency laws,[40] nor do they acknowledge or address the unjust circumstances in which some of the debt was incurred.[41]

Second, the claims are inconsistent with the holistic approach to the promotion and protection of human rights that is envisaged in paragraph 13 of the Vienna Declaration and Programme of Action which calls upon States to 'eliminate all violations of human rights and their *causes*, as well as *obstacles* to the enjoyment of these rights' (emphasis added).[42]

[36] A/RES/60/251, preamble, para 9.

[37] A/RES/60/251, para 4.

[38] See A/RES/60/251, para 9.

[39] It has been asserted that the Bretton Woods Institutions 'helped create the very situation of indebtedness that they themselves had responsibility for fixing'. See Jubilee Australia, 'Alternatives to Debtors' Prison: Developing a framework for international insolvency', Policy Paper, October 2011, 19–22 <www.acfid.asn.au/resources_publications/publications/acfid-research-in-development-series/alternatives-to-debtors-prison-developing-a-framework-for-international-insolvency> accessed 30 September 2013.

[40] See, for example, K Raffer, 'Internationalizing US Municipal Insolvency: A Fair, Equitable and Efficient Way to Overcome a Debt Overhang' (2005) 6 *Chicago Journal of International Law* 361.

[41] The Office of the High Commissioner for Human Rights has stressed the need, from a human rights perspective, for developed countries and international financial institutions to 'acknowledge that a significant portion of the debt was not acquired fairly'. See United Nations, Office of the High Commissioner for Human Rights, *Claiming the Millennium Development Goals: A Human Rights Approach* (New York and Geneva, United Nations, 2008) 47.

[42] Although the Declaration does not create binding obligations for States, it provides an indication of global opinion on the issues that it covers. It is notable that Resolution 60/251 establishing the Human Rights Council reaffirms the Vienna Declaration and Programme of Action. See A/RES/60/251, preamble, para 2.

Third, in line with the provisions of article 22 of the International Covenant on Economic, Social and Cultural Rights (ICESCR), it is competent for the United Nations human rights bodies (including the Council) to address this issue and to bring the recommendations made by its independent experts to the attention of, inter alia, the international financial institutions dealing with foreign debt and debt relief.[43] Thus, for example, the Committee on Economic, Social and Cultural Rights (ESCR Committee) and other treaty bodies have often urged international financial institutions to pay greater attention to the protection of human rights in their lending policies, credit agreements and debt relief initiatives.

Finally, it is interesting to note that these same States have never questioned the competence of the various United Nations human rights treaty bodies to address the impact of foreign debt and related policies on the realisation of human rights. Significantly, as the Independent Expert on structural adjustment policies observed more than a decade ago, no single institution has a monopoly on how to establish a just and sustainable world order.[44]

C The Independent Expert on the Effects of Foreign Debt

The Human Rights Council and the former Commission on Human Rights have also attempted to address the issue of sovereign debt and human rights by establishing thematic special procedures[45] mandates to monitor, report and advise on the effects of foreign debt on the enjoyment of all human rights, particularly economic, social and cultural rights. These mandates have undergone several changes over the years in response to the evolution of the policies of the international financial institutions.

i Overview of the Mandate

Initially, two different mandates were established by the Commission on Human Rights: the Independent Expert on structural adjustment policies in 1997 and the Special Rapporteur on the effects of foreign debt on the full enjoyment of economic, social and cultural rights in 1998. Those two mandates were merged in 2000 with the creation of the mandate of the Independent Expert on the effects of structural adjustment policies and foreign debt on the full enjoyment of all human rights, particularly economic, social and cultural rights. In 2005 the Commission decided to rename the mandate, 'Independent Expert on the effects of economic reform policies and foreign debt on the full enjoyment of all human rights, particularly economic, social and cultural rights'. The Independent Expert was requested to report annually to the Commission.

[43] See General Comment no 2.

[44] See E/CN.4/2000/51, para 92.

[45] The special procedures of the Human Rights Council are independent human rights experts with mandates to report and advise on human rights from a thematic or country-specific perspective. Their tasks are defined in the resolutions establishing or extending their mandates. In general, the experts undertake country visits; act on individual cases and concerns of a broader, structural nature by sending communications to States and other relevant actors; undertake thematic studies and convene expert consultations, engage in human rights advocacy, raise public awareness and provide advice and support for technical cooperation. Special procedures report annually to the Human Rights Council; most also report to the Third Committee of the General Assembly. As of 1 January 2013, there were 36 thematic and 12 country mandates. For more information about special procedures, see www.ohchr.org/EN/HRBodies/SP/Pages/Welcomepage.aspx, accessed 30 September 2013.

In 2008, by resolution 7/4, the Human Rights Council redefined and renamed the mandate 'Independent Expert on the effects of foreign debt and other related international financial obligations of States on the full enjoyment of all human rights, particularly economic, social and cultural rights'. The Council mandated the Independent Expert to, inter alia, study in consultation with all relevant stakeholders (including governments, relevant international organisations and civil society organisations) the effects of foreign debt and the policies adopted to address them on the full enjoyment of all human rights, in particular, economic, social and cultural rights in developing countries; the impact of foreign debt and other related international financial obligations on the capacity of States to design and implement policies and programmes, including national budgets, that respond to vital requirements for the promotion of the realisation of social rights; measures taken by governments, the private sector and international financial institutions to alleviate such effects in developing countries, especially the poorest and heavily indebted countries; new developments, actions and initiatives being taken by international financial institutions, other United Nations bodies and intergovernmental and non-governmental organisations with respect to economic reform policies and human rights; and quantification of minimum standards to support the realisation of the MDGs.[46]

The Council also requested the Independent Expert to explore, through his annual analytical reports, the interlinkages with trade and other issues, including HIV/AIDS, when examining the effects of foreign debt and other related international financial obligations of States on the full enjoyment of all human rights and to contribute, as appropriate, to the follow-up to the International Conference on Financing for Development, with a view to highlighting the broad scope of his mandate. The Independent Expert reports annually to the Council and to the General Assembly. The mandate was extended in 2011 for a further three years.

ii Contribution of the Mandate

In common with other thematic special procedures, the Independent Expert contributes to the progressive development of international human rights law, notably through studies, consultations and the elaboration of guiding principles within the remit of the mandate. As part of his mandate, the Independent Expert carries out country missions to study the effects of foreign debt and other international financial obligations of States on the realisation of human rights and to engage in dialogue with governments, international financial institutions, United Nations agencies and civil society as a part of his global analysis of the subject as well as to develop practical recommendations and suggestions to the countries concerned. Reports on these country missions are submitted to the Human Rights Council.

The Independent Expert has conducted several thematic studies which have highlighted topical aspects of the issue of debt and human rights. In 1999, for example, the Independent Expert on the effects of structural adjustment policies on the full enjoyment of human rights highlighted the negative impact of structural adjustment policies on the rights to food, education, housing and health, noting that the 'failure of the IMF and World Bank to protect health, nutrition and education budgets from general fiscal retrenchment in the design of structural adjustment programmes (was) a grave policy error'.[47]

[46] See Human Rights Council resolution 7/4.

[47] Cheru report (n 13) para 65.

Since his appointment in 2008, the current Independent Expert has conducted several studies and presented his findings and recommendations to the Council and General Assembly addressing the following issues: the human rights impact of international debt relief initiatives;[48] the negative impact of the non-repatriation of funds of illicit origin on human rights in the countries of origin;[49] the impact of sovereign debt and related economic reform policies (such as austerity) on women's human rights;[50] export credit agencies and human rights;[51] the need for policy coherence in the areas of international trade, finance and human rights;[52] the impact of 'vulture fund' litigation on debt relief and human rights;[53] the shared responsibility of creditors and debtors for 'illegitimate debt';[54] and an assessment of the human rights impact of the international debt relief initiatives.[55]

The Independent Expert has also issued numerous news releases and public statements, either alone[56] or with other special procedures[57] on issues of interest to the mandate. These have been used by various stakeholders, including governments and civil society organisations, in their advocacy efforts. For example, during the second reading of the Debt Relief (Developing Countries) Bill in the UK House of Lords, Baroness Quin, who sponsored the Bill, referred to a press release issued by the Independent Expert on a case against Liberia, in which the Independent Expert had stated that it was 'illogical to cancel poor country debt and at the same time allow unconscionable "vulture fund" claims'.[58] Similarly, the States of Jersey Green Paper consultation on debt relief for poor countries referred to a statement issued by the Independent Expert in which he urged the government of Jersey to enact legislation to restrict the ability of vulture funds to use the British Crown dependency's courts to sue heavily indebted poor countries.[59]

[48] A/HRC/23/37.

[49] A/HRC/22/42.

[50] A/67/304.

[51] A/66/271.

[52] A/65/260 and A/65/260/Corr.1.

[53] A/HRC/14/21.

[54] A/64/289.

[55] A/HRC/23/37.

[56] See, eg, '"Greece: Troika bailout conditions are undermining human rights," warns UN expert on debt and human rights', 1 May 2013; 'United Nations human rights expert to assess impact of EU/IMF stabilisation programme in Latvia', 10 May 2012; 'United Nations expert on foreign debt tells Latvia that any measure for economic growth and stabilisation must benefit all', 18 May 2012; 'Argentina/Ghana: vulture funds should not be allowed to paralyze debt relief, says UN expert on the eve of key ruling', 13 December 2012. See generally www.ohchr.org/EN/NewsEvents/Pages/DisplayNews.aspx?.

[57] In 2012 special procedures issued 334 news releases and public statements, including 53 statements issued jointly with other special procedures and/or mandate holders from other mechanisms. See United Nations Special Procedures – Facts and Figures 2012. See, eg, 'Equality or bust for post-2015 development goals – UN rights experts', 21 May 2013; 'A call on States to ratify new instrument to enhance protection of economic, social and cultural rights', 8 May 2013; '"World Bank-led privatization of Burundian coffee industry must not repeat errors of the past" – UN experts warn', 18 April 2013; 'UN experts urge World Bank to adopt human rights standards on the eve of key gathering in Washington', 18 April 2013; 'Rio+20: "No global goals without accountability" say over 20 United Nations experts', 19 March 2012; 'G-8/EU: A global financial transaction tax a human rights imperative now more than ever', 14 May 2012; 'United Nations experts call for European Union banking sector reform in line with States' human rights obligations', 5 October 2012. See generally www.ohchr.org/EN/NewsEvents/Pages/DisplayNews.aspx?.

[58] See House of Lords Official Reports, Parliamentary Debates (Hansard), vol 718, no 68, 8 April 2010, 1696. The Bill was passed into law on 8 April 2010 as the Debt Relief (Developing Countries) Act 2010. See also 'UN expert sounds alarm over court order for Liberia to pay back "vulture funds"' www.un.org/apps/news/story.asp?NewsID=33289, accessed 30 September 2013.

[59] See States of Jersey, Debt Relief for Poorer Countries: Green Paper Consultation – September 2011, presented by the Chief Minister on 15 September 2011, R114/2011. See also 'UN expert urges Jersey to curb vulture

In Australia, various organisations have used the Independent Expert's public statements in their campaign for the country's Parliament to enact similar legislation on vulture funds.[60]

iii The Guiding Principles on Foreign Debt and Human Rights

One of the key achievements of the Independent Expert has been the elaboration of international standards on sovereign debt and human rights.[61] In its resolution 2004/18, the then Commission on Human Rights requested the Independent Expert on economic reform policies

> to draft voluntary general guidelines to be followed by States and by private and public, national and international financial institutions in the decision-making and execution of debt repayments and structural reform programmes, including those arising from foreign debt relief, to ensure that compliance with the commitments derived from foreign debt will not undermine the obligations for the realisation of fundamental economic, social and cultural rights, as provided for in the international human rights instruments and to present a preliminary draft on (the) matter to the Commission at its sixty-first session and a final draft at the sixty-second session of the Commission.

In November 2006 the Human Rights Council requested the Office of the High Commissioner for Human Rights (OHCHR) to convene an expert consultation to contribute to the process of preparing the draft general guidelines and to invite the international financial institutions, notably the World Bank and IMF, as well as regional development banks, relevant United Nations agencies and national experts and stakeholders to contribute to the consultations.[62] The expert consultation was held in July 2007 and, in March 2008, the then Independent Expert presented a preliminary draft of the guidelines to the Council.

In subsequent resolutions and decisions (7/4, 11/5 and 12/119), the Human Rights Council requested the Independent Expert on the effects of foreign debt and other related international financial obligations of States on the full enjoyment of all human rights, particularly economic, social and cultural rights, to continue consultations on the draft general guidelines with States, international organisations, United Nations agencies, funds and programmes, regional economic commissions, international and regional financial institutions and non-governmental organisations and to conduct a series of regional consultations, an expert meeting and a public consultation. These consultations were held between June 2010 and February 2012. The Independent Expert also invited

funds' ability to sue poor countries', 13 December 2011, www.un.org/apps/news/story.asp?NewsID=40718&Cr=debt&Cr, accessed 30 September 2013. The Independent Expert made an official submission to the government on the need for anti-vulture fund legislation. Subsequently, the government of Jersey passed the Debt Relief (Developing Countries) (Jersey) Law 2013, which came into force on 1 March 2013.

[60] See Jubilee Australia, 'Preying on the Poor: Vulture Funds', Briefing Paper, June 2011<www.jubileeaustralia.org/literature87200/BriefingPaper-Preyingonthepoor(2011)> accessed 23 September 2013; Uniting Church in Australia, Synod of Victoria and Tasmania, 'Stopping Debt Vultures from Preying on the Poor', August 2011 <wr,victas.uca.org.au/assets/3469/Letter-writingactiononDebtVulturesAug2011.pdf> accessed 23 September 2013..

[61] The thematic Special Procedures contribute to the progressive development of international human rights law, notably through studies, consultations and elaboration of standards within the scope of their mandates.

[62] Decision 2/109 of 27 November 2006, adopted by a recorded vote of 33 to 13 with 1 abstention.

public submissions on the draft of the Guiding Principles which had been placed on the mandate's website.[63]

The final text of the renamed United Nations Guiding Principles on Foreign Debt and Human Rights, the outcome of the broad and inclusive process of consultation mentioned above, was endorsed by the Human Rights Council in June 2012 through resolution 20/10.[64]

The Guiding Principles are designed to assist States and all relevant actors (including private and public, national and international financial institutions, bilateral lenders and organised groups of bondholders) in the conduct of their respective activities and pursuit of their respect interests relating to external debt.[65] The overall aim of the Principles is to balance States' contractual obligations arising from external debt and both debtors' and creditors' international human rights obligations.

The Principles recommend various measures to ensure that debt obligations do not undermine human rights, including:

- the holding of periodic, transparent and participatory debt audits to inform future decisions on borrowing and lending;
- moratoriums on debt payments when a profound change in circumstances beyond the control of the borrower State arises;
- limiting payments to all creditors to be in line with debt relief agreed as part of any debt relief mechanism in order to prevent vulture funds claiming extortionate profits from heavily indebted countries;
- ensuring that debt sustainability assessments take into account the impact of debt on the realisation of human rights and development goals;
- indexing loan repayments to rates of economic or export growth in order to help balance the risk of loans more fairly between lenders and borrowers;
- State monitoring and regulation of external lending and borrowing by the private sector in order to prevent private debt burdens being created which bring financial instability;
- the avoidance of linking conditions (such as privatisation and trade liberalisation) to loans and debt relief; and
- establishment of an independent international debt workout mechanism.

The Principles have been invoked in discussions on global governance issues. For example, at the Special High Level Meeting of ECOSOC on 'External Debt Sustainability and Development', the Group of 77 and China called upon States to adopt legislation consistent with the Principles to prevent vulture funds from pursuing excessive claims against heavily indebted countries before their national courts.[66]

In his approach to the issue of sovereign debt, the Independent Expert has always emphasised the primacy of human rights obligations. Thus, the Expert has favoured a

[63] For a discussion of the background to the Guiding Principles, see A/HRC/20/23.

[64] The Guiding Principles on Foreign Debt and Human Rights, www.ohchr.org/EN/Issues/Development/IEDebt/Pages/GuidingPrinciples.aspx, accessed 30 September 2013.

[65] See A/HRC/20/23, para, 1.

[66] See, eg, Statement on behalf of the Group of 77 and China by HE Mr JV Bainimarama, Prime Minister of the Republic of Fiji, Chairman of the Group of 77, at the Special High Level meeting of ECOSOC on 'External Debt Sustainability and Development: Lessons Learned from the debt crisis and on-going work on sovereign debt restructuring and debt resolution mechanisms', New York, 23 April 2013, para 13, www.g77.org/statement/getstatement.php?id=130423, accessed 30 September 2013.

human rights-based approach, arguing that such an approach offers specific value through its emphasis on non-discrimination, participation, transparency and accountability, as well as the universality, interdependence and indivisibility of all human rights, to ensure that the goals of development in general and debt service obligations and debt relief measures in particular are consistent with international human rights standards.

D The Treaty Bodies

The various United Nations human rights treaty bodies have also recognised the adverse impacts of high debt burdens and related economic reform policies (such as austerity measures) on the realisation of human rights, particularly economic, social and cultural rights. For example, in its concluding observations on Algeria's State party report, the ESCR Committee took note of 'the adverse effects of the *high foreign debt burden*, the requirements of *structural adjustment programmes* and the recurring droughts, on the ability of the State party to implement its obligations under the Covenant'[67] (emphasis added). The Committee therefore recommended that Algeria should take into account its obligations under the Covenant in all its negotiations with international financial institutions, such as the IMF, World Bank and World Trade Organization, to ensure that economic, social and cultural rights were not compromised.[68]

More recently, the Committee expressed concern that the levels of effective protection for the rights enshrined in the Covenant had been lowered as a result of the austerity measures adopted by Spain, which had disproportionately curtailed the enjoyment of rights by disadvantaged and marginalised individuals and groups, especially the poor, women, children, persons with disabilities, unemployed adults and young persons, older persons, gypsies, migrants and asylum seekers.[69]

Other treaty bodies have made similar observations on reports submitted by States parties. For example, in 2003, the Committee on the Rights of the Child acknowledged that 'the external debt, the structural adjustment programme and the limited availability of financial and skilled human resources [have] had a negative impact on social welfare and on the situation of children and have impeded the full implementation of the Convention' in Madagascar.[70] In 2001 the Committee on the Elimination of all forms of Discrimination against Women expressed concern about the widespread nature of

[67] E/C.12/1/Add.71, para 9.

[68] ibid, para 43.

[69] E/C.12/ESP/CO/5, 6 June 2012, para 8.

[70] CRC/C/15/Add.218, para 4. See also the following concluding observations, Committee on Economic, Social and Cultural Rights: E/C.12/1/Add.106 (Zambia); E/C.12/1/Add.78 (Benin); E/C.12/Add.71 (Algeria); E/C.12/1/Add.66 (Nepal); E/C.12/1/Add.63 (Syrian Arab Republic); E/C.12/1/Add.62 (Senegal); E/C.12/1/Add.60 (Bolivia, Plurinational State of); E/C.12/1/Add.57 (Honduras); E/C.12/1/Add.55 (Morocco); E/C.12/1/Add.49 (Kyrgyzstan); and E/C.12/1/Add.48 (Sudan); Committee on the Rights of the Child: CRC/C/15/Add.218 (Madagascar); CRC/C/15/Add.204 (Eritrea); CRC/C/Add.207 (Sri Lanka); CRC/C/15/Add.197 (Republic of Korea); CRC/C/15/Add.193 (Burkina Faso); CRC/C/15/Add.190 (Sudan); CRC/C/15/Add.186 (Netherlands/Netherlands Antilles); CRC/C/15/Add.179 (Niger); CRC/C/15/Add.174 (Malawi); CRC/C/15/Add.172 (Mozambique); CRC/C/15/Add.160 (Kenya); CRC/C/15/Add.152 (Turkey); CRC/C/15/Add.138 (Central African Republic); CRC/C/15/Add.130 (Suriname); CRC/C/Add.124 (Georgia); and CRC/C/15/Add.115 (India); Committee on the Elimination of Discrimination against Women, *Official Records of the General Assembly, Fifty-seventh Session, Supplement no 38* (Trinidad and Tobago); ibid, *Fifty-sixth Session, Supplement no 38* (A/56/38), part one, para 227 (Jamaica) and part two, paras 161 (Guyana) and 227 (Netherlands); ibid, *Fifty-fifth Session, Supplement no 38* (A/55/38), para 44 (Cameroon).

poverty among women in Uganda as a consequence, inter alia, of 'gender-insensitive privatization and the implementation of structural adjustment policies'.[71]

In its General Comment 2, the ESCR Committee stresses that while Article 2 of the ICESCR allows for 'progressive realization of economic, social and cultural rights with due regard to the "available" resources', there are minimum core obligations which every State must fulfil. Thus, in its concluding observations on Spain, the Committee recommended that Spain should

> ensure that all the austerity measures adopted reflect the minimum core content of all the Covenant rights and that it take all appropriate measures to protect that core content under any circumstances, especially for disadvantaged and marginalized individuals and groups.[72]

The Committee also drew the attention of Spain to its open letter of 16 May 2012 to States parties on economic, cultural and social rights in the context of the economic and financial crisis.

The treaty bodies have also underscored that the human rights obligations of States are relevant in the context of their external debt arrangements. Thus, for example, the ESCR Committee has often urged borrower States to take into account their obligations under the Covenant in all aspects of their negotiations with international financial institutions in order to ensure that economic, social and cultural rights, particularly of the most vulnerable sectors of society, are not undermined.[73]

It has also encouraged creditor countries to do all they can to ensure that the policies and decisions of the international financial institutions of which they are members are consistent with the obligations of States parties to the Covenant. In 2001, for example, the ESCR Committee urged Germany,

> as a member of international organizations, in particular the International Monetary Fund and the World Bank, to do all it can to ensure that the policies and decisions of those organizations are in conformity with the obligations of States parties to the Covenant, in particular the obligations contained in articles 2(1), 11, 15, 22 and 23 concerning international assistance and cooperation.[74]

It is notable, however, that while these States have supported international debt relief efforts, there is little evidence that they have done 'all they can' to ensure that the policies of the international financial institutions do not undermine States' obligations under the Covenant. This is regrettable, particularly in view of the fact that it is well established that States must adhere to their international law obligations when they act through international organisations.[75] Thus, for example, the European Court of Human Rights has held

[71] Committee on the Elimination of Discrimination against Women, *Official Records of the General Assembly, Fifty-seventh Session, Supplement no 38* (A/57/38), para 149.

[72] E/C.12/ESP/CO/5, 6 June 2012, para 8.

[73] See, eg, E/C.12/1/Add.71, para 43 (Algeria); E/C.12/1/Add.44, para 28 (Egypt); E/C.12/1/Add.55, para 38 (Morocco); and E/C.12/1/Add.57, para 10 (Honduras).

[74] E/C.12/1/Add.68 (Germany). See also E/C.12/1/Add.54, para 31 (Belgium); E/C.12/1/Add.43, para 20 (Italy); E/C.12/1/Add.70, para 24 (Sweden); E/C.12/1/Add.72, para 32 (France); E/C.12/1/Add.77, para 37 (Ireland); and E/C.12/1/Add.79, para 26 (United Kingdom). It is also notable that the Maastricht Guidelines on Violations of Economic, Social and Cultural Rights deem a human rights violation of omission, '[t]he failure of a State to take into account its international legal obligations in the field of economic, social and cultural rights when entering into bilateral or multilateral agreements with other States, international organizations or multinational corporations' (Para. 15(j)).

[75] The Maastricht Guidelines on Violations of Economic, Social and Cultural Rights provide that 'the obligations of States to protect economic, social and cultural rights extend also to their participation in international organizations, where they act collectively' (para 19).

that the human rights obligations of Member States continue even after the transfer of competences to international organisations.[76]

Furthermore, the treaty bodies have often urged international financial institutions to pay greater attention to the protection of human rights in their lending policies, credit agreements and debt relief initiatives. Thus, for example, in General Comment No 2, the ESCR Committee has recommended that 'international measures to deal with the debt crisis should take full account of the need to protect economic, social and cultural rights through, inter alia, international cooperation'.[77] The Committee has further emphasised that international agencies 'should scrupulously avoid involvement in projects' that infringe human rights and they should promote projects and approaches that contribute not only to economic growth and other defined objectives, but also to enhanced enjoyment of all human rights. In a similar vein, the Committee on the Rights of the Child has recommended that the World Bank Group, the IMF and the World Trade Organization should ensure that their activities related to international cooperation and economic development promote the full implementation of the Convention on the Rights of the Child.[78]

E Other United Nations Bodies

The link between sovereign debt, human rights and development has also been confirmed in the declarations, resolutions and decisions of major United Nations conferences and bodies. These include the Universal Declaration on the Eradication of Hunger and Malnutrition, which acknowledges that hunger and malnutrition are exacerbated by the 'heavy burdens imposed by external debt on the balance of payments of many developing countries';[79] the Rio Declaration on Environment and Development, which acknowledged the importance of reducing foreign debt, particularly where it was aggravated by the net transfer of resources for the benefit of developed countries;[80] the Vienna Declaration and Programme of Action, which called upon the international community to make all efforts to help alleviate the external debt burden of developing countries in order to supplement the efforts of governments of such countries to attain the full realization of the economic, social and cultural rights of their people';[81] and the

[76] See *Mathews v United Kingdom*, ECtHR Application no 24833/94, Grand Chamber judgment of 18 February 1999, paras 29, 32 and 34; *Waite and Kennedy v Germany*, ECtHR Application no 26083/94, Grand Chamber judgment of 18 February 1999, para 67; *Bosphorous Airways v Ireland*, ECtHR Application no 45036/98, Grand Chamber judgment of 20 June 2005, paras 152–156.

[77] See also General Comment no 4, on the right to adequate housing, para 19; General Comment no 12, on the right to adequate food, para 41; General Comment no 13, on the right to education, para 60; and General Comment no 14, on the right to the highest attainable standard of health, para 64. The Relationship Agreements between the United Nations and the two institutions provide that these institutions should 'consider' the decisions and recommendations of the United Nations. See the Agreement between the United Nations and the World Bank, UN Treaty Series, vol 16, 346 and the Agreement between the United Nations and the IMF, UN Treaty Series, vol 16, 328.

[78] Committee on the Rights of the Child, General Comment no 5, para 64, CRC/GC/2003/5.

[79] Adopted on 16 November 1974 by the World Food Conference, in accordance with General Assembly Resolution 3347 (XXIX), 17 December 1974, para 1 d.

[80] Report of the UN Conference on Sustainable Development, A/CONF. 216/16, 20–22 June 2012, Rio de Janeiro, para 19.

[81] Paragraph 13 of the Vienna Declaration underscored the 'need for States and international organizations, in cooperation with non-governmental organizations to create favourable conditions at the national, regional and international levels to ensure the full and effective enjoyment of human rights'.

Millennium Declaration, adopted by the General Assembly in September 2000, which expressed a determination by United Nations Member States 'to deal comprehensively and effectively with the debt problems of low- and middle-income developing countries, through various national and international measures designed to make their debt sustainable in the long term'.[82]

All of these resolutions and decisions have highlighted the adverse impact of foreign debt and economic policy reforms pushed by the international financial institutions on the realisation of human rights.

IV CONCLUSION

Although the issue of sovereign debt has been on the agenda of various United Nations bodies for more than four decades, progress on the issue has been modest. Heavy debt burdens continue to contribute to extreme poverty and to undermine the capacity of governments, particularly in developing countries, to create the conditions necessary for the achievement of sustainable human development and the realisation of human rights,

This situation is attributable to the position of the developed countries, which, while acknowledging the adverse effects of excessive debt burdens, are reluctant to accept that excessive debt burdens constitute an obstacle to the full realisation of human rights in highly indebted countries and to cooperate in the efforts of the Human Rights Council, which has primary responsibility for the promotion and protection of human rights throughout the world, to address the issue.

If a durable and equitable solution to the sovereign debt problem is to be found, it is important that developed countries accept its human rights ramifications and the competence of United Nations human rights mechanisms, including the Council, to address it.

[82] Millennium Declaration, paras 13 and 28. See also the Programme for the Further Implementation of Agenda 21, adopted by the General Assembly at the Earth Summit +5 during its 19th session, 23–28 June 1997, paras 20 and 82; Copenhagen Declaration on Social Development, adopted at the World Summit for Social Development, Copenhagen, 6–12 March 1995 (commitments 1.k and 7.c); the Vienna Declaration and Programme of Action, adopted by the World Conference on Human Rights, Vienna, 14–25 June 1993, para 12; the Declaration and Platform of Action of Beijing, adopted at the Fourth World Conference on Women, Beijing, 4–15 September 1995, para 13; the Millennium Declaration, adopted by the UN General Assembly, 8 September 2000, A/RES/55/2, paras 15 and 28; Report of the World Summit on Sustainable Development, A/CONF.199/20 & A/CONF.199/20/Corr.1, Johannesburg, 26 August –4 September 2002, para 89.

Part IV

Case Studies

17

Bloody Bucks? – Foreign Finance and Armed Conflicts in Africa

DAN KUWALI*

I INTRODUCTION

ALTHOUGH AFRICA IS a continent endowed with diverse and abundant natural resources, these are more of a curse than a blessing, given the scramble for these resources in African conflicts.[1] Aside from loss of human life, armed conflicts on the continent cost Africa around US$18 billion annually, with adverse repercussions of derailing vital resources that could be employed for social and economic development.[2] One of the common features in these armed conflicts is the existence of warlords who tend to exercise territorial control of resources and the employment of mercenaries who fight for money. Rebel organisations need manpower and military materiel for them to be viable and survive militarily against government forces. In turn, the need for sustenance and survival creates the need for finance.[3]

Weapons are either sold to warring factions or bartered with warlords in exchange for natural resources. In the war in the Darfur region of Sudan, for example, the floodgate of cheap Avtomat Kalashnikova 47 (AK-47) rifles into Darfur has driven fighters to cherish their rifles: that 'the Kalash brings cash' and 'without a Kalash you're trash'.[4] While most of these warlords are protégés of foreign barons and corporations, mercenaries by definition, are foreigners fighting for financial gain. Also, the bulk of the arms and 'their ammunition – perhaps 95 per cent – come from outside Africa'.[5] It is therefore easy to see that armed conflicts largely border on financial gain in that they are caused or exacerbated by financial motive.

Belligerents and entrepreneurs reap profits from the devastation that is concomitant with armed conflict. Armed conflicts generate financial strain not only in the country, but

* The author wrote this chapter while pursuing a post-doctoral fellowship at the Centre for Human Rights, Faculty of Law, University of Pretoria.

[1] United Nations Environmental Programme [UNEP], 'Armed conflict: a threat to regional cooperation,' Africa environmental outlook 2, www.unep.org/dewa/Africa/publications/AEO-2/content/035.htm, accessed 12 February 2013 [UNEP Report].

[2] Oxfam, 'Africa's missing billions international arms flows and the cost of conflict', www.oxfam.org/sites/www.oxfam.org/files/africas%20missing%20bils.pdf, 20 January 2013 [Oxfam Report].

[3] P Collier and A Hoeffler, 'Military Expenditure in Post-conflict Societies' (2006) 7 *Economics of Governance* 89–107.

[4] National Geographic, http://ngm.nationalgeographic.com/2008/04/sahel/paul-salopek-text/3, accessed 11 March 2013.

[5] Oxfam (n 2).

also in the region. The availability of external and internal finance determines the length and outcome of armed conflicts.[6] Conflict generates financial strains, particularly if it is associated with an increase in military expenditure and arms imports, where elites seek to protect their interests and quash protest using violent techniques.[7]

On the one hand, armed conflicts occasion unfathomable harm to innocent civilians and civilian objects. On the other hand, however, armed conflicts are a profitable business for politicians (the political elites such as Charles Taylor in the Sierra Leonean civil war), civilian contactors (such as the diamond dealers in Democratic Republic of the Congo (DRC)), military contractors (such as Executive Outcome in the Angolan civil war), commodity dealers and black marketeers (for example, the cocoa entrepreneurs in Côte d'Ivoire), and lenders who may provide loans, including foreign debt, to a party to the conflict to finance the war, optimistic that it will be paid back at the end of the hostilities.

A distinction can be drawn between war profiteers who benefit by fuelling the war and those who gain by supporting the warring parties. While general profiteering usually occurs in peacetime, war profiteering occurs where a person or organisation makes profits from warfare or by selling weapons and other goods to parties in an armed conflict, taking advantage of the breakdown of law and order in the violence. The financial motivation of the belligerents has led Grossman to conclude that 'the insurgents are indistinguishable from bandits or pirates'.[8]

An assessment of the armed conflicts in Africa shows that insurgents often finance their armed groups using the illegal export of precious natural resources such as diamonds and other gemstones, oil, timber, cocoa and similar commodities.[9] War profiteering has fuelled deadly armed conflicts in countries such as Angola, the DRC and Sierra Leone where blood (also called conflict or converted) diamonds were mined in a war zone and sold to buy arms and ammunition, as well as financing the insurgency. This chapter, therefore, discusses the impact of finance in armed conflicts, with a special focus on Africa. It does so by looking at the role of finance on causing and exacerbating conflicts in Africa and also investigates the source of finance of insurgents and examines the financial implications of these armed conflicts. This contribution further assesses the phenomenon of sovereign debt on countries in armed conflicts and concludes by recommending a robust framework to curtail war profiteering in Africa.

II THE FINANCIAL INTEREST IN ARMED CONFLICTS

Armed conflicts in the form of civil wars are now far more common than interstate wars, particularly in Africa. Although interstate violence has declined, internal conflicts such as civil wars, separatist tensions and terrorism have increased exponentially. In all cases, conflict is inversely correlated with per capita incomes, and low-income countries are

[6] Collier and Hoeffler (n 3); T Addison, P Le Billon and SM Murshed, 'Finance in Conflict and Reconstruction', *World Institute for Development Economics Research (WIDER)* DP 2001/44, UN University, August 2001, 3.

[7] MC Baddeley, 'Poverty, Armed Conflict and Financial Instability', available at: www.econ.cam.ac.uk/dae/repec/cam/pdf/cwpe0857.pdf, accessed 1 December 2012, 7.

[8] HI Grossman, 'Kleptrocracy and Revolutions' (1999) 51 *Oxford Economic Papers* 267–83, 269. See also Multilateral Investment Guarantee Agency (MIGA) WIPR Report, 2010, 30.

[9] JD Fearon, 'Primary Commodity Exports and Civil War' 49(2) *Journal of Conflict Resolution* 483–507, 484; P Collier and A Hoeffler, 'Greed and Grievance in Civil War' *World Bank Working Paper Series* 2000-18, Washington DC, 2.

more at risk of violence.[10] Most of the contemporary armed conflicts in Africa and globally are civil wars that have taken place within national boundaries. Civil war is defined as 'an internal conflict with at least 1,000 combat-related deaths, with both an identifiable rebel organization and government forces suffering at least five percent of these casualties'.[11]

Although grievances are often seen as the main causes of rebellion, factors which determine the financial and military viability of a rebellion are more important than objective grounds for grievance.[12] In order to create and maintain a rebel organisation the rebels have to be paid and military equipment has to be purchased.[13] Collier and Hoeffler, who examined the causes of armed conflicts, found that greed considerably outperforms grievance.[14] They dwell on the 'greed' theory, which focuses on the ability to finance rebellion, against a 'grievance' theory focusing on ethnic and religious divisions, political repression and inequality.[15] For these reasons, armed conflicts are far more likely to be caused by economic opportunities than by grievance.[16] Armed conflicts that are motivated or influenced by the incentive of natural resource exploitation tend to reflect strong economic interests of belligerents and an underlying war economy dominated by private political and economic agendas.[17]

III FINANCIAL IMPLICATIONS OF ARMED CONFLICTS

There is no doubt that armed conflicts bring about adverse financial implications, including the diversion of resources that could have been invested in development projects that benefit the economy and population in a country.[18] By stalling development and as a result of the humanitarian tragedy associated with them, armed conflicts, including their financing, exacerbate economic, political and social problems in a country.[19] Actually, the availability of external and internal finance determines length and outcome of armed conflicts.[20]

Civil conflict has far-reaching effects on underdeveloped economies. Whilst military expenditure may be diverted into projects that encourage human capital accumulation and the construction of essential infrastructure, conflict destroys institutions and infrastructure, generating financial instability and exacerbating stagnation and underdevelopment. Baddeley states that 'Vicious circles emerge as socioeconomic instability contributes to ongoing civil unrest and financial instability, in turn increasing the risk of future conflicts'.[21] Thus, generally, the economic costs of armed conflicts can be grouped into three:

[10] MIGA WIPR Report (n 8).

[11] Collier and Hoeffler (2000) (n 9) 2.

[12] ibid, 1.

[13] Collier and Hoeffler (n 9) 1.

[14] ibid.

[15] ibid.

[16] Fearon (n 9)

[17] N Brunnschweiler and EH Bulte, 'Natural Resource Abundance and Violent Conflict: Resource Abundance, Dependence and the Onset of Civil Wars', *Working paper no 08/78*, Zurich: CER-ETH Center of Economic Research, January 2008, 3; P Le Billon, 'The Political Ecology of War: Natural Resources and Armed Conflicts' (2001) 20(5) *Political Geography* 564–65.

[18] Oxfam (n 2).

[19] Baddeley (n 7) 10.

[20] Addison et al (n 6).

[21] Baddeley (n 7).

direct costs, expenditure costs and indirect costs. In this sense, direct costs arise directly from violence and involve actual expenditure, whereas indirect costs represent lost resources and opportunities. Likewise, intangible costs are immeasurable but fundamentally affect people's lives, their livelihood and their capacity for development.[22]

Conflicts destroy public and social services in country.[23] Armed conflicts also occasion indirect human and humanitarian costs such as actual physical violence and the loss of opportunities for economic progress and development.[24] Further, armed conflicts generate inequality across different income groups.[25] Activities such as corruption, military expenditure, financial instability and ineffective financial regulation further contribute to economic loss of a country in armed conflict.

A Ineffective Regulation of Financial Institutions

Weak financial regulation in underdeveloped economies promotes wealth accumulation through fraud and corruption, thereby destroying savings and living standards and sparking widespread conflict. The pessimism and uncertainty that emerge in times of armed conflict also contribute to financial instability. Financial instability is exacerbated by corruption and cronyism, given that financial instability invariably generates financial shocks in the banking system. Baddeley states that 'Resolving financial shocks in conflict prone countries can involve large fiscal costs, taking money away from reconstruction and destabilising already fragile societies and economies'.[26] As the political elite and warlords seek to protect their own political interests in the face of financial instability, this crisis exacerbates the conflict.

Problems of regulatory capture are common in conflict-ridden countries due to the absence of democratic institutions needed to protect impartial financial regulation. Usually, state control of financial systems in conflict-prone countries has been poor. As was seen in Angola and Mozambique, the financial system is usually used by influential politicians, entrepreneurs, criminal syndicates and warlords to leverage existing wealth. In the wars in Angola and Mozambique, controls on financial systems, such as ceilings on interest rates, operated to favour the protagonists in the armed conflicts.

In Liberia, Charles Taylor also owned a private bank under the style of the Bong Bank. In this way, loan facilities could be directed towards enterprises run by political elites occasioning an increased risk of bad debts. Such private banks may also be conduits for criminal transactions bordering on money laundering and war profiteering. Such an ineffective system is fertile ground for money laundering and other rent-seeking activities in armed conflicts, for instance inclusion of dubious fees and fines associated with the licensing of a bank.[27]

[22] Oxfam (n 2).

[23] P Collier, and JW Gunning, 'War, Peace and Private Portfolios' (1995) 23(2) *World Development* 233–41.

[24] Baddeley (n 7) 4.

[25] F Stewart and EVK Fitzgerald, 'Introduction: Assessing the Economic Costs of War' in F Stewart and EVK Fitzgerald (eds), *War and Underdevelopment*, Queen Elizabeth House Series in Development Studies (Oxford, Oxford University Press, 2000) 6–7.

[26] Baddeley (n 7) 8.

[27] ibid, 8.

B High Military Expenditure

Baddeley has noted that 'Conflict generates financial strains particularly if it is associated with an increase in military expenditure and arms imports'.[28] Military spending for personal gain is often financed by sale of public assets. Financing of military expenditure has negative socio-economic impacts in conflict-prone economies. The use of violent techniques to protect vested interests requires military spending, particularly on arms imports and this has implications for foreign exchange reserves in a country. Military expenditure may also divert social expenditures that could be deployed to promote broad-based development.[29] Thus, increased military expenditure usually diverts finances meant for social services, thereby promoting dualism and narrow development rather than broad-based development.[30]

Political institutions and policies put in place in a country also play a key role regarding the influence of finance and armed conflicts. It is usually the political elites that make policies for increased military spending in cases of armed conflicts.[31] It is easy to imagine that financial reforms are more likely to be effective in democratised systems than in conflict-affected and fragile (CAF) countries.[32]

Military expenditure also drains foreign currency exchange reserves especially resulting from arms and ammunition imports. The result is that there is less foreign exchange available to finance the imports needed for economic investment and infrastructure development projects.[33] While high military expenditure diverts resources for social and infrastructure, it also contributes to the destruction of existing infrastructure, thereby exacerbating the ongoing conflict.[34]

Normally, in a democracy there are set rules of funds that can be allocated to the defence budget in proportion to the gross domestic product (GDP) of a country. In this way, 'Democratic institutions are a pre-commitment mechanism reducing the severity of conflicts and releasing resources for consumption'.[35] The proportion of military expenditure to GDP tends to be lower in democracies than in war-torn countries.[36] According to Addison et al, the 'political competition that characterises democracies introduces a negative bias into nations' military spending patterns and, given a strategic approach to military policy, this reduces other nations' incentives to arm as well'.[37]

Military expenditure can be used as a signal by government or a screen by insurgents to indicate a commitment to peace agreements.[38] In this sense, a low level of post-conflict military spending tends to signal intentions to honour peace agreements whereas a high level of post-conflict military spending signals intentions to renege on peace agreements.[39]

[28] M Baddeley, 'Civil War and Human Development: Impacts of Finance and Financial Infrastructure,' CWPE 1127, February 2011, 3.

[29] Baddeley (n 7) 9.

[30] Addison et al (n 6) 3.

[31] P Collier and A Hoeffler, 'Greed and Grievance in Civil War' (2004) 56(4) *Oxford Economic Papers* 563–95.

[32] Baddeley (n 28) 4.

[33] ibid, 4.

[34] ibid.

[35] ibid.

[36] Collier and Hoeffler (n 31).

[37] Addison et al (n 6).

[38] Collier and Hoeffler (n 3) 89–107.

[39] ibid.

This is because governments have incentives to renege on peace agreements owing to the fact that the military capability and, therefore, the bargaining power of rebel groups erodes during peacetime.[40] The selection of strategies is determined by the relative benefits and costs of reversion to conflict.[41] It should also be noted that high levels of military spending are associated with increased risk of renewed conflict.[42]

C Uncertainty of Financial [In]stability in Armed Conflicts

A country where there is an armed conflict, weak, or no rule of law, is unlikely to be able to attract much-needed foreign investment and hence such a country would depend more heavily on resource exports and in certain instances foreign debt.[43] The result could be dependence on resource exports and foreign debt to sustain the war effort.[44] In such cases, government liabilities become difficult to sell during armed conflicts and liquidity preference shifts and becomes unstable, reflecting changes in the precautionary motives for holding money.[45] The climate of financial instability and speculation during armed conflicts impels investors to take precautionary measures to hold hard cash and to prefer to save profits in liquid form during armed conflicts, which may be converted to investment during peacetime.[46]

Keynes also notes that armed conflict leads to changes in the distribution of wealth in that it 'raises the discount rate reflecting shifts in people's inter-temporal preferences'.[47] For example, in a situation of armed conflict there may be a sale of real assets to finance a war effort because government liabilities become problematic to sell, thereby shifting liquidity preferences and creating financial instability.[48] Armed conflicts also usually lead to a shortage in the supply of commodities, which results in higher prices and higher revenues. The instability of market forces has adverse repercussions on monetary policy as it is difficult to target money supply when money demand is erratic. Armed conflicts also have 'negative impacts on business confidence and pessimism and uncertainty will be magnified within a highly liquid financial sector'.[49]

This notwithstanding, however, it should also be noted that armed conflicts may inspire financial innovation.[50] This is particularly true as the need to finance wars may bring about institutional reforms when states increase control over banking in order to generate funds for war efforts. For instance, in the Angolan war, there were compulsory purchases of sovereign debt and nationalisation of financial institutions, thereby creating periods of financial innovation.[51] However, such financial innovations may only be applicable

[40] Collier and Hoeffler (n 3).

[41] Collier and Hoeffler (n 31) 8–10.

[42] ibid.

[43] M Ross, 'A Closer Look at Oil, Diamonds and Civil War' (2006) 9 *Annual Review of Political Science* 265–300, 266.

[44] Baddeley (n 8) 3–4.

[45] Collier and Gunning (n 23).

[46] JM Keynes, 'War and the Financial System' (1914) 24(95) *Economic Journal* 460–86 (cited in Baddeley, n 8).

[47] ibid, 486.

[48] Baddeley (n 7) 5.

[49] ibid.

[50] ibid, 4–7.

[51] Addison et al (n 6) 3.

where domestic infrastructure is weak. As globalisation tends to expand the catchment area for war financing, it may be difficult to track financial flows in such situations.[52]

D Financial Implications for Neighbouring States

Invariably, armed conflicts have spill-over effects, including humanitarian and economic implications. Severe economic costs to a whole region can be caused by the disruption of trade and loss of investor confidence, which translates into lost business potential and lower GDP.[53] Apart from being susceptible to conflict and instability at home, fragile countries and those in armed conflicts can also destabilise entire regions through refugee flows and barriers to trade and investment.[54] A civil war in one country reduces the growth rate of neighbouring countries by around 0.9 per cent; thus the combined growth loss to neighbours can exceed the loss to the country itself.[55] Effects of the conflicts are exacerbated as the conflict intensity increases. The spill-over effects of armed conflict, and the perceived or real fear of violence spreading across the border, also translate into increased military spending by neighbours.[56]

E The Impact of Finance on the Duration of Armed Conflicts

Natural resources may also affect the duration of armed conflicts in several ways. For example, revenue from mineral resources may provide funding to the weaker side to acquire firepower, thereby equalising the balance of power between the belligerents. This in turn may protract the conflict. This was clear in the Angolan war where the governing MPLA was enriched by oil revenues and the opposition UNITA was unable to compete with its much smaller income from diamonds. As a result, the MPLA was able to garner Western diplomatic support to remain in power.[57] Alternatively, where mineral wealth is more readily available to the stronger side, it may enhance the military capacity needed for a quicker victory, thereby shortening the conflict.

Further, funding from natural resources could prolong conflicts by providing combatants with economic opportunities that may not be available in peacetime, thereby providing an incentive to prolong the conflict.[58] For example, the instability within the Angolan diamond fields benefited both the MPLA and UNITA since it provided a conducive environment for 'cohabitation and the extraction of profits that would not be possible during peace'.[59] It is also reasonable to imagine that resource wealth could shorten conflicts where there are possibilities of economic opportunities which can only be realised in peacetime. Furthermore, mineral resources could make 'separatist civil wars last

[52] ibid.
[53] Oxfam (n 2).
[54] MIGA WIPR Report (n 8) 30.
[55] ibid.
[56] ibid.
[57] A McIntyre and T Weiss, 'Weak Governments in Search of Strength: Africa's Experience of Mercenaries and Private Military Companies' in S Chesterman and C Lehnardt (eds), *From Mercenaries to Market: The Rise and Regulation of Private Military Companies* (Oxford, Oxford University Press, 2007) 67–81.
[58] Addison et al (n 6).
[59] V Brittain, *Death of Dignity: Angola's Civil War* (London, Pluto Press, 1988) 7.

longer by reducing the credibility of any government commitments to regional autonomy'.[60]

It is usually argued that an abundance of natural resources can prolong conflict because they provide a reliable source of finance with which warlords and armed groups are able to sustain combat engagement over a long period of time.[61] In situations where factions involved in a conflict have a mutual interest in abundant natural resources, their preoccupation with the exploitation of such resources could contribute to the emergence of a mutually beneficial stalemate. As was the case in Somalia, the different factions are not interested in the prospect of peace since the chaos associated with conflict becomes an avenue for economic gain and profiteering. This makes the resolution of the conflict difficult and also contributes to its protraction.[62]

IV SOURCES OF FINANCE FOR ARMED CONFLICTS

As noted above, finance or funding plays a central role in sparking or escalating an armed conflict. There are several sources of finance which are widely used by insurgents in armed conflicts. The common ones are revenue from natural resources, extortion, donations from diasporas, and subventions from hostile governments. Some of these sources of funding for armed conflicts are discussed below.

A Financing from Natural Resources

Generally speaking, the link between armed conflict and natural resources is not that straightforward. However, it is not contested that natural resources, whether abundant or scarce, have the propensity to foment conflict and also play a crucial role in the prolongation and resolution of conflicts.[63] Countries with abundant natural resources have a higher risk of conflict.[64] Among the CAF countries, 18 are considered economically dependent on natural resources.[65]

Natural resources especially play a crucial role when internal sources of war finance are limited.[66] Since conflict commodities are attractive they instil competition among political elites over access and control of the natural resource.[67] Thus, natural resources or conflict commodities may serve as a source of funding for disgruntled groups and can influence the motivation, incentive and opportunity for insurgents to employ violence as a means of settling political scores and grievances, and their determination to continue fighting.[68] This is especially true for armed conflicts in Africa, in which the struggle for access and control of precious natural resources has resulted in, or exacerbated, conflicts. A clear illustration is the Angolan conflict, which was increasingly determined by strug-

[60] Fearon (n 10).
[61] Brunnschweiler and Bult (n 17) 3.
[62] ibid.
[63] ibid, 1.
[64] Collier and Hoeffler (n 3) 1.
[65] MIGA WIPR Report (n 8) 29.
[66] Fearon (n 9) 484.
[67] Brunnschweiler and Bulte (n 17) 2.
[68] ibid.

gles for diamonds, oil and other precious resources. Ironically, diamonds have been said to be 'the guerrilla's best friend'.[69]

Revenue from cocoa, which is used as a main ingredient in chocolate, has been responsible for the internecine conflict in Côte d'Ivoire, which is the largest producer of cocoa. Both sides to the conflict in Côte d'Ivoire funded their armies with the tacit acceptance of cocoa companies. Armed conflicts financed or sustained through the harvest and sale of timber are also emerging as a serious problem in many countries in Africa.[70]

As stated earlier, UNITA in Angola financed its war largely through taxes on the illicit trade in diamonds, particularly between the mid-1990s and 2002.[71] From 1999 to 2002 alone, UNITA is reported to have earned about US$300 million per year from illicit diamond sales.[72] In Sierra Leone, the Revolutionary United Front (RUF) financed its war by trading in illicit diamonds. This is why in the case against Charles Taylor, the supermodel Naomi Campbell was summoned to testify in court how she was given 'blood diamonds' that were at the centre of the conflict in Sierra Leone, which was financed by Taylor.[73]

In DRC, struggles over the control of diamonds, coltan and timber have prolonged civil war, especially in the eastern part of the country.[74] Apart from diamonds, other precious minerals which have protracted the conflict in DRC are tin, tantalum, tungsten, gold and coltan, which are largely destined for the global electronics industry to be used in mobile phones and laptops.[75] The same is the case with the conflict in the Darfur region of Sudan, which has strong links to environmental and natural resources.[76] The government of Sudan was fighting a civil war in the south, and oil development was both a source of conflict and a source of military finance.[77]

Conflict commodities that cannot be easily hidden, like timber, are generally exploited with the overt connivance of actors connected to the state.[78] This creates clear opportunities for state actors to extort funds from illicit trade for personal gains. Warlords have clearly used conflict commodities to finance military operations. Such commodities are either sold directly or exchanged with arms and ammunitions for the war effort.[79]

However, it is 'unlikely that oil exports (or cash crops) predict higher civil war risk because oil provides better financing opportunities for would-be rebels'. According to Fearon, 'high oil exports indicate a weaker state given the level of per capita income and possibly a greater "prize" for state or secessionist capture, both of which might favour civil war'. The same applies to conflict commodities other than oil.[80]

[69] Fearon (n 9) 484.

[70] *The Economic Times*, 'Conflict commodities: illicit trades fuel armed conflicts in Africa, Asia, http://articles.economictimes.indiatimes.com/2011-09-30/news/30228929_1_cocoa-trade-conflict-commodities, accessed 20 December 2012.

[71] A Ganesan and A Vines, 'Engine Of War: Resources, Greed, And The Predatory State' in *World Report 2004* (Human Rights Watch, 2004).

[72] ibid.

[73] Global Policy Forum, 'Naomi Campbell said Taylor sent diamond', www.globalpolicy.org/security-council/dark-side-of-natural-resources/diamonds-in-conflict/debates-and-articles-on-diamonds-in-conflict/49387.html, accessed 1 March 2013.

[74] Ganesan and Vines (n 71).

[75] *The Economic Times* (n 70).

[76] UNEP (n 1).

[77] Ross (n 43) 295.

[78] *The Economic Times* (n 70).

[79] ibid.

[80] Fearon (n 9).

It has been observed that a 'given resource has a higher chance of fuelling conflict when it has characteristics that require less specialized skills to exploit and refine it, has high liquidity, and is highly portable and therefore "smugglable"'.[81] This means that commodities that can be seized and transported easily are more likely to be used to fuel conflicts. For example, the commodity that is actually fuelling the armed conflict in DRC is gold, which is less traceable than diamonds.[82]

B Sovereign Debt and Armed Conflicts

Natural resources may also be used for commercial borrowing, where future returns from resource wealth are mortgaged by insurgents thereby tapping into influential international private interests.[83] For example, the armed conflict in Angola was funded on the basis of oil reserves and diamonds, which led to 95 per cent of Angola's oil share being used in debt servicing of loans to finance arms and mercenaries.[84] Similar patterns can be seen in the armed conflict in Somalia and eastern DRC. According to Baddeley, 'This sort of expenditure deflects finances away from social uses, promoting dualism and narrow development rather than broad based development'.[85]

Foreign capital can be realised through foreign direct investment (FDI) or through sovereign loans. The importance of foreign capital is that it can contribute to economic growth and development and, therefore, ease fragility and the risk of conflict.[86] Yet armed conflicts have negative effects on the number of FDI projects and their value. FDI accounts for most of private capital flows to CAF countries because private debt and portfolio investment flows are minimal. FDI in CAF countries is heavily concentrated in a handful of economies, which are either middle income or rich in natural resources.[87]

In the context of an armed conflict, decisions whether or not to invest in a country seem to be largely influenced 'by the risk of asset destruction, of unavailability of local inputs and infrastructure, and of abrupt declines in domestic demand. Investors' relative vulnerability to each of these channels helps explain the sector composition of FDI flows to CAF countries'. [88] This reasoning entails that other considerations for investment 'such as geological constraints, the potential for high returns on investment, payback periods, and the ability to mitigate political risk, also weigh heavily on investment decisions'.[89] The risk of non-honouring of sovereign guarantees and breach of contract is certainly high in countries in conflict situations.[90]

Countries considered fragile and prone to conflict present unique challenges, caused not only by heightened risks of new or recurring political violence, but also by structural and institutional weaknesses. As a result, the volume and composition of foreign capital flows to these countries is significantly different from patterns observed in developing

[81] Brunnschweiler and Bulte (n 17) 1.
[82] *The Economic Times* (n 70).
[83] Baddeley (n 28) 6.
[84] ibid.
[85] Baddeley (n 7) 6.
[86] MIGA WIPR Report (n 8) 30.
[87] ibid, 29.
[88] ibid, 29.
[89] ibid.
[90] ibid.

countries in general.[91] This explains why lenders have a responsibility to examine and monitor the likely effects of the project for which the debt is incurred.[92] Lenders are 'responsible to make a realistic assessment of the sovereign borrower's capacity to service a loan based on the best available information and following objective and agreed technical rules on due diligence and national accounts'.[93] Arguably, lenders are required to conduct an assessment on funding to prevent support to irresponsible sovereigns and atrocious projects.

C Extortion by Insurgents

As civilians are regarded as soft targets to be menaced, insurgents find it easy to finance themselves by extortion of primary commodities from them. Where opportunities exist, insurgents indulge in extortion for financial viability, thereby escalating the armed conflict. According to Collier and Hoeffler, 'the endowment of unskilled labor and guns which characterizes rebel organizations is particularly suited to raise finance through the extortion of primary commodity exports'.[94] This view is supported by extortion of commodities such as diamonds and other gemstones in Angola, DRC, Sierra Leone; timber in DRC; and other cash crops such as cocoa in Côte d'Ivoire.[95] Extortion of primary commodity exports occurs where it is profitable, and perpetrators of extortion organise themselves into a rebellion in order to achieve this end.[96]

However, as has been noticed in eastern DRC, extortion can also be perpetrated by government forces for their personal gain or survival. At one point, it was said that the greatest threat to civilians in DRC was the members of the Congolese army.[97] This claim is validated by AngloGold Ashanti, a multinational mining company, which has revealed that they provided cash and transport to the militia in DRC under duress and threats from the militia.[98]

In the Liberian conflict, Charles Taylor invited investment from a Liberian Timber association located in the neighbouring Côte d'Ivoire, which paid 'taxes' of the order of a quarter of a million dollars each during 1991–92.[99] Taylor and his followers also took over state-like functions, visibly directing 'tax' payments to local officials in order to finance the National Patriotic Front of Liberia.[100] The extortion in an armed conflict is different from common criminal extortion in that the former targets the production or

[91] ibid.

[92] United Nations Conference on Trade and Development (UNCTAD), Principles on Promoting Responsible Sovereign Lending and Borrowing [Principles on Promoting Responsible Sovereign Lending and Borrowing]. Principle 5, www.unctad.info/upload/Debt%20Portal/Principles%20drafts/SLB_Principles_English_Doha_22-04-2012.pdf, accessed 6 March 2013.

[93] ibid, Principle 4.

[94] Collier and Hoeffler (n 3) 6.

[95] ibid.

[96] ibid.

[97] VK Holt and TC Berkman, 'The Impossible Mandate? – Military Preparedness, the Responsibility to Protect and Modern Military Operations', Henry L Stimson Centre, Protecting Civilians on the Ground: MONUC and the Democratic Republic of the Congo', www.stimson.org/images/uploads/research-pdfs/Chap_8-The_Impossible_Mandate-Holt_Berkman.pdf, accessed 27 February 2013, 157.

[98] MIGA WIPR Report (n 8) 41.

[99] W Reno, 'Humanitarian Emergencies and Warlord Economies in Liberia and Sierra Leone', United Nations University, *Working Paper no 140*, August 1997, 12.

[100] ibid.

transportation of primary commodities exports, which is usually in rural areas, whereas the latter targets urban-based commerce.[101]

As with other common crimes, the returns on extortion can be decreased by defensive measures.[102] Faced with a military defence, a viable extortion racket itself needs considerable defensive power to be able to survive in confrontation with resistance. As extortion gives insurgents both an incentive and a means to collect revenue in order to buy equipment for defence, the resulting greater scale economies of violence eventually escalate the armed conflict.[103]

D Remittances from the Diasporas

Another potential source of funding for insurgents are remittances from diasporas living in developed countries.[104] Diasporas are usually more financially comfortable than the population in their country of origin and better placed for collective action to fund their causes in their native countries. As diasporas may harbour historical anguish and grievances against a party to the armed conflict in their country of origin, they are impelled to provide finance to support a party in an armed conflict.[105] This has been witnessed in the civil war in Somalia, which has been sustained by money sent by Somali diasporas.[106]

Diasporas transmit funding through legitimate as well as illegal means. In this respect, money laundering is a common means of funding wars where there are external capital inflows in the form of legitimate diasporas, which are systematically moved internationally by circumventing exchange controls on international transfers. The 'dependence upon primary commodity exports and a large diaspora substantially increase the risk of conflict'.[107] Countries with a large diaspora abroad experience higher conflict risks because diasporas often have the ability to use large financial resources and publicity to keep combatants active in their native countries.[108]

E Financial Support from Hostile Governments

Another potential source of finance for an armed conflict is funding from hostile governments. A clear example would be the role of the government of Zimbabwe (then Southern Rhodesia) in financing the Renamo rebellion in Mozambique.[109] Another example is the involvement of South Africa in the Angolan war. South Africa was giving UNITA aid 'of a material, humanitarian and moral nature'.[110] The most significant African player in the Angolan war was the DRC (then Zaïre), which was allegedly a key conduit for the US action in Angola. Other participating countries were Gabon and Congo (Brazzaville),

[101] Collier and Hoeffler (n 3) 6.
[102] ibid.
[103] ibid, 7.
[104] Addison et al (n 6). MIGA WIPR Report (n 8) 32.
[105] Collier and Hoeffler (n 3) 8.
[106] AA Ismail, 'Diaspora and Post-war Political Leadership in Somalia' (2011) 20(1) *Nordic Journal of African Studies* 28–47.
[107] ibid.
[108] ibid.
[109] ibid.
[110] Brittain (n 59) 27, quoting the then South Africa Defence Minister, Magnus Malan.

including Côte d'Ivoire and Morocco, because of their leaderships' ties with Jonas Savimbi.[111]

Foreign countries may support the war effort for different reasons. For example, coupled with oil and mineral interests, both sides to the 'Diamond War' in Angola were also supported by foreign armed forces. Portugal, the United States and Russia were allegedly the greatest war instigators in Angola by dumping in it weapons, goods, money and everything that was necessary to protract the war.[112] Aside from the support from other countries, foreign assistance also constitutes a significant source of external financing for CAF countries in the form of sovereign debt, among other things.[113]

V PROFITEERING FROM ARMED CONFLICTS

A war profiteer is any person or organisation that profits from warfare or by selling weapons and other goods to parties at war. The term has strong negative connotations. While general profiteering may also occur in peacetime, war profiteering occurs in armed conflicts. War profiteering has been rampant in recent years in the armed conflicts in Africa. Recently, there has been a proliferation of corporations in wartime activities, especially private contractors that have been driven by profit.[114] The phenomenon of private military companies is regarded as an example of sanctioned war profiteering.[115] Others make their money by cooperating with the authorities by selling weapons to all the parties involved in the armed conflict.[116]

Political figures taking bribes and favours from corporations involved with war production have been called war profiteers.[117] A Canadian company, Talisman, came under intense public pressure regarding its involvement in an oil development project in Sudan.[118] The same was the case with AngloGold Ashanti, which was accused by Human Rights Watch of providing financial and logistical assistance to armed militia responsible for atrocities in the north-eastern region of DRC.[119]

States should make an effort to prohibit excessive war profiteering by, for example, the imposition of an excess profits tax in wartime and ensure transparency and responsible revenue management.[120] Global Witness, an NGO whose key goal is 'breaking the links between natural resources, conflict and corruption', has scrutinised and exposed payments made by oil and mining companies to host governments.[121]

[111] AJ Venter, *War Dog: Fighting Other People's Wars: The Modern Mercenary in Combat* (Philadelphia, Casemate, 2006) 350.

[112] J Cilliers, 'Resource Wars – New Type of Insurgency' in J Cilliers and C Dietrich (eds), *Angola's War Economy: The Role of Oil and Diamonds* (Pretoria, International Security Studies, 2000) 1–20.

[113] MIGA WIPR Report (n 8) 32.

[114] United States Government, 110th Congress, 1st Session, War Profiteering Prevention Act of 2007, available at: www.gpo.gov/fdsys/pkg/CRPT-110srpt66/pdf/CRPT-110srpt66.pdf, last accessed 4 March 2013.

[115] J Scahill, 'Bush's Rent-an-Army', *The Los Angeles Times*, 25 January 2007, available at: http://articles.latimes.com/2007/jan/25/opinion/oe-scahill25, accessed 4 March 2013.

[116] Brittain (n 59).

[117] Senator Patrick Leahy, available at: http://web.archive.org/web/20080626080712/http://leahy.senate.gov/press/200703/032007.html, accessed 4 March 2013.

[118] V Haufler, 'Governing Corporations in Zones of Conflict: Issues, Actors and Institutions', University of Maryland, College Park, available at: www2.gwu.edu/~igis/assets/docs/who_rules../Haufler_IGIS.doc, accessed 4 March 2013, 19.

[119] MIGA WIPR Report (n 8) 40.

[120] ibid.

[121] Haufler (n 118) 19.

In this respect, the United Kingdom has taken the lead by establishing a Corporate Citizenship Unit in the Foreign Office, and through the Department for International Development, which supports research in this area by organisations such as International Alert.[122] Through the Extractive Industries Transparency Initiative (EITI), the United Kingdom seeks to promote transparency in revenue payments by corporations, especially those operating in conflict zones. The EITI targets host governments 'to persuade them to be more transparent about natural resource revenues, and where the money goes'.[123] However, unlike the Kimberly Process Certification Scheme, the EITI relies more on voluntary action by governments and does not directly target the industry.[124]

VI DO NOT FEED THE GREED – CURBING WAR PROFITEERING IN AFRICA

One of the reasons why violent conflicts are difficult to resolve is that armed conflicts are often supported from somewhere else, either from neighbouring countries, which might share certain affinities to parties in the conflict, or from outside.[125] While the bulk of arms and ammunition used in conflicts in Africa is foreign, the ultimate victims of these weapons are mainly found in Africa.[126] The rich mineral and oil deposits and the cash crops in Africa have proven to be a curse rather than a blessing, as they have spurred protracted internecine wars with extensive foreign involvement. The illicit trade in gemstones has been a major obstacle to a peaceful solution to the conflicts in Africa. Both rebels and government have used natural resources to sustain wars.[127] The formal (institutionalised) and informal (not institutionalised) sectors were blurred, and this enhanced the difficulty of regulating trade in resources.

Mercenaries, with no altruistic interest or concern for the countries in which they fight, rarely have an incentive to end the conflict and they not only prolong, but also intensify conflicts. Furthermore, with an avaricious eye on African gemstones, mercenaries have an interest in developing local bases and effectively colonising the country that is in conflict. Yet they invest nothing and have no roots or ties in the regions, so for them too, peace and orderly governance is not an option as it curtails their economic opportunities.[128]

In theory, the UN Security Council-mandated sanctions have the potential to convey international disapproval for unacceptable behaviour, encourage political dialogue, and diminish the military means that sustains fighting. In practice, however, the success of sanctions as a primary coercive means to secure compliance with UN resolutions is limited for several reasons. One reason is the lack of commitment by important international and regional players. The Security Council often employs sanctions as a political statement without the accompanying commitment to enforce them, thereby rendering sanctions to be violated with impunity.[129]

[122] ibid.

[123] ibid.

[124] See also the Kimberly Process was endorsed by the UN and begun in May 2000.

[125] DANIDA, Report from the Maputo Conference, 28–29 June 2001, Danish Ministry of Foreign Affairs, DANIDA [The Maputo Conference Report] 20.

[126] K Rupersinghe, *Civil Wars, Civil Peace: An Introduction to Conflict Resolution* (International Alert, 1998) 14.

[127] The Maputo Conference Report (n 125) 48.

[128] Rupersinghe (n 126) 55.

[129] International Peace Academy, *IPA Training Seminar Report*, International Peace Academy, Hotel Thayer, West Point 8–11 May 2000, 4.

Another reason is that the UN has not taken deterrent action against sanctions busters. It should be noted that the UN's capacity to monitor and review sanctions regimes is central to their effectiveness. In order for an arms embargo to be effective, it has to be applied early in the conflict, but the UN has had little success in this regard. The proliferation of private arms brokers further negates UN attempts to starve a conflict zone of weapons. Also, sanctions on their own are unlikely to prevent the outbreak of armed conflicts; they need to be integrated into a wider strategy of conflict management and resolution.[130] The UNCTAD Principles on Promoting Responsible Sovereign Lending and Borrowing succinctly posit that 'All lenders have a duty to comply with United Nations sanctions imposed against a governmental regime',[131] the rationale being that UN sanctions are imposed in order to maintain or restore international peace and security.[132]

While eliminating the negative effects of sanctions, the UN Security Council should impose sanctions that are 'targeted' and 'smart' in order to effectively stave off war profiteers.[133] Given the problems of sanctions, Africa needs to complement the UN to enforce sanctions in order to contain violence. Due to proliferation of war profiteering on the continent, African states need a regional capacity to monitor borders and enforce sanctions. The UN, the African Union and humanitarian agencies should go beyond naming and shaming sanctions busters and take a bold step to deter them. Moreover, financial 'lenders should not participate in financial transactions that violate, evade or hamper such sanctions'.[134] More importantly, there is need to ensure proper use and management of the resources in countries, especially those that are prone to conflict.

It is greed not grievance that causes or exacerbates conflict.[135] Given the centrality of economic incentives in armed conflicts, it is crucial to cut off the economic incentives for conflict.[136] Making unreasonable profits from war is generally considered unethical and selfish. This is clear from the outcry that led to the folding of a mercenary firm, Executive Outcomes, which terrorised Angola and other countries in Africa. Private corporations engaged in the business of supplying the coalition forces in the Iraq War also came under fire for allegedly overcharging for their services.[137] Hence, there have been attempts to prohibit excessive war profiteering, through such means as imposition of an excess profits tax. However, defining 'excessive' accurately is difficult and such legislation frequently allows some instances of profiteering to go unchecked while reducing the income of other war-related business to loss-making levels. Given the centrality of finance in causing and prolongation of armed conflict, countries with resources should pay serious attention to addressing the primary drivers of conflict and their underlying vulnerabilities by way of conflict prevention.[138]

While the wars in Angola and Sierra Leone are now over and fighting in DRC has decreased, the problem of conflict commodities is not over yet in those countries. There have been several legal and policy strategies that have been employed to prevent war

130 ibid.

131 UNCTAD Principles on Promoting Responsible Sovereign Lending and Borrowing (n 124) 7.

132 ibid.

133 F Mabilangan (Philippines) in a Press Release, United Nations, General Assembly, UN Doc GA/9782.

134 UNCTAD Principles on Promoting Responsible Sovereign Lending and Borrowing (n 124) 7.

135 Baddeley (n 8) 7.

136 Dr Leonardo Santos Simão, then Mozambican Minister of Foreign Affairs and Cooperation, in his opening address to the Maputo Conference, Maputo Conference Report (n 125) 16.

137 R Greenwald, 'Iraq for Sale', available at: http://iraqforsale.org/profiteers.php, accessed 4 March 2013.

138 Brunnschweiler and Bulte (n 17) 7.

profiteering. Multinational corporations operating in conflict zones are undergoing rigorous scrutiny and are asked to be transparent in their dealings.[139] To reduce the occurrence of armed conflicts, countries should diversify their economies and channel commodity income into social service programmes to undermine support for rebels.[140] For these reasons, policymakers should dissuade insurgents from fighting and persuade them to lay down their arms by finding ways to cut off their financial benefit or support in the armed conflict.[141] For its part, the Security Council has time and again imposed sanctions and arms embargoes on warring factions. Although in some cases these measures have not been effective, sanctions and embargoes have driven insurgents out of business or forced them to the negotiating table.[142]

The Kimberley Process Certification Scheme is an important policy initiative that was introduced to stem the flow of 'conflict diamonds' and requires participants to certify that shipments of rough diamonds are conflict free.[143] However, diamonds are not the only natural resources that fuel armed conflicts; revenue from other equally valuable minerals such as coltan, tin, tantalum, tungsten and gold, as well as cocoa, cocaine and timber, among others, has sparked and sustained armed conflicts.[144] As a continent entangled in internecine conflicts, Africa needs to take the lead to implement the Kimberly Process religiously and also ensure that insurgents do not benefit from natural resource wealth on the continent.

The 2007 US War Profiteering Prevention Act, which intends to create criminal penalties for war profiteers, is an appropriate model for legislation to curtail war profiteering.[145] The War Profiteering Prevention Act seeks to prohibit profiteering and fraud relating to military action, relief, and reconstruction efforts, and for other purposes.[146] However, there are no internal armed conflicts in the United States but rather in Africa. Yet, there is no continental-wide criminal law specifically targeted at prohibiting contracting fraud during times of war, military action, or relief or reconstruction activities in Africa.

The current regime of fraud and money laundering legislation does not provide an offence for those who take advantage of the exigent circumstances created by armed conflicts let alone providing extra-territorial jurisdiction for such offences. The numerous wars in Africa point to the need for a continental instrument that may be domesticated by its member states in order to suffocate the insurgents and force them out of the business of waging war for profit on the continent. Corporations also have a responsibility to suffocate insurgents by preventing conflict resources from making their way to their businesses.[147]

[139] MIGA WIPR Report (n 8) 41.
[140] Collier and Hoeffler (n 3) 2.
[141] Brunnschweiler and Bulte (n 17) 7.
[142] ibid.
[143] The Kimberly Process (n 124); Fearon (n 9) 484; Collier and Hoeffler (n 3) 2.
[144] *The Economic Times* (n 70).
[145] US Government (n 114).
[146] ibid.
[147] ibid.

VII CONCLUSION

Although armed conflicts occasion unfathomable harm on innocent civilians and civilian objects, armed conflicts are a profitable business for politicians, civilian as well as military contractors, commodity dealers and black marketeers. Where a party to the conflict takes out a foreign loan to finance the war, the sovereign or foreign debt is a risky investment which the lender takes as the payment of the loan largely depends on the outcome of the conflict. In either case, the debt contributes to the devastation that is concomitant with war. While general profiteering usually occurs in peacetime, war profiteering occurs where a person or organisation makes profits from the armed conflict or by selling weapons and other goods to parties at war, taking advantage of the breakdown of law and order in the violence. One of the common causes of armed conflicts is a country's economic dependence on natural resources and export commodities. The profit incentive from revenue from gemstones and other valuable cash crops fuels violence and determines the duration of such conflicts.[148]

Conflict commodities that cannot be easily hidden, such as timber, are generally exploited with the overt connivance of actors connected to the state.[149] This creates clear opportunities for state actors to extort funds from illicit trade for personal gains. Warlords have clearly used conflict commodities to finance military operations. Commodities are bartered with trading partners either directly or in exchange for the arms and ammunition needed to sustain an armed conflict.[150] It should be noted that 'natural resources not only represent a source of rebel finance but also of government revenue'.[151] War profiteering has fuelled deadly armed conflicts in countries such as Angola, DRC and Sierra Leone, where blood diamonds have been mined in a war zone and sold to buy arms and ammunition as well as financing the insurgency. There are war profiteers who benefit by fuelling the war and those who gain by supporting the warring parties.

Considering that greed and economic incentives are central to the outbreak and sustainability of armed conflicts, there should be a concerted effort to curtail the economic incentives for conflict. Since Africa is a continent that is host to many countries at war, the African Union (AU) should take the initiative to cut off the lifeline of insurgents that benefit from conflict commodities.[152] The AU needs to implement the Kimberly Process to the letter and even expand the scope of commodities beyond diamonds and include all possible conflict commodities. Just as it adopted a regional instrument to eliminate mercenary activities in Africa, the AU should also adopt a continental-wide instrument of the kind of the US War Profiteering Prevention Act to curtail war profiteering. However, given the proliferation of war profiteering in Africa, it is clear that Africa needs such an instrument more than the United States.

For their part, countries should also diversify their economies and direct resource wealth into developmental programmes that benefit the population, to dissuade rebellion. African countries should also domesticate the UN Convention Against Illicit Traffic

[148] Fearon (n 9) 484.
[149] *The Economic Times* (n 70)
[150] ibid.
[151] Collier and Hoeffler (n 3) 1–2.
[152] Baddeley (n 7) 7.

in Narcotic Drugs and Psychotropic Substances and Convention against Transnational Organized Crime in order to combat money laundering.[153] States and corporations, too, should cut businesses that finance the killing of innocent civilians in Africa.[154]

[153] UN Convention Against Illicit Traffic in Narcotic Drugs and Psychotropic Substances of 1988, available at: http://en.wikisource.org/wiki/United_Nations_Convention_Against_Illicit_Traffic_in_Narcotic_Drugs_and_Psychotropic_Substances, accessed 28 February 2013.

[154] Collier and Hoeffler (n 3) 2.

18

Development, Sovereign Support to Finance and Human Rights: Lessons from India

SURYA DEVA*

I INTRODUCTION

ECONOMIC DEVELOPMENT REQUIRES funds. States, both developed and developing ones, are increasingly relying on the private sector to finance their developmental needs.[1] Such financing can take several forms: foreign direct investment (FDI), corporate finance or project finance.[2] This model of economic development has direct implications for the human rights project. Although both developed and developing states' access to economic resources and achieving a certain level of economic development are critical to realise human rights,[3] the *process* by which finance is secured and the development goals are accomplished can impact adversely on human rights.[4]

This chapter seeks to explore this potential adverse dimension of the investment/finance-driven model of development. Against the background of an analytical rights-compatible framework proposed in the next section, the exploration is done with reference to two case studies from India. The first case study concerns Enron's power project in Dabhol in the state of Maharashtra.[5] Apart from allegations of corruption and lack of transparency, the project attracted criticism for resulting in the suppression of the human rights of people who opposed the project. The second case study is about the

* I would like to thank Mr Calvin Chun-ngai Ho for providing excellent research assistance.

[1] Scannella notes that due to limited bank lending capacity, 'it is necessary to attract an increasing amount of private capital to finance long-term investments'. E Scannella, 'Project Finance in the Energy Industry: New Debt-based Financing Models' (2012) 5(2) *International Business Research* 83.

[2] While project finance is not a dominant model of finance, its role is still crucial in large investment projects. S Leader and R Kazimova, 'Overview and Recommendations' in S Leader and D Ong (eds), *Global Project Finance, Human Rights and Sustainable Development* (Cambridge, Cambridge University Press, 2011) 490, 491.

[3] Cephas Lumina, the independent expert on the effects of foreign debt and other related international financial obligations of States on the full enjoyment of all human rights, notes that 'the full enjoyment of all human rights requires that adequate resources are allocated to this goal by States'. Human Rights Council, 'Guiding Principles on Foreign Debt and Human Rights', A/HRC/20/23 (10 April 2011), Introduction (p 9).

[4] As an analogy, Dufey and Grieg-Gran rightly note that 'the effects of FDI on sustainable development – whether positive or negative – are *context dependent*'. A Dufey and M Grieg-Gran, 'The Linkages between Project Finance and Sustainable Development' in Leader and Ong (eds) (n 2) 12, 28 (emphasis added).

[5] See Part III.A below, and Human Rights Watch (HRW), *The Enron Corporation: Corporate Complicity in Human Rights Violations* (New York, HRW, 1999).

refinery-cum-mining operations of Vedanta, a British company, in the state of Orissa.[6] In this case too, Vedanta has faced constant criticism for polluting the environment and disregarding the human rights of local tribal people.

The financial support for Enron's project was in the form of guarantees provided by both the central and state governments that the Maharashtra State Electricity Board (MSEB) would make payment to Dabhol Power Company (DPC), an Indian subsidiary of Enron, for buying the generated electricity. As we will see below, the state government also provided security to DPC against continuous public protests. Sovereign support in the case of Vedanta was of a different nature. In addition to a public sector company holding 26 per cent equity in the joint venture company, the state government also promised to make bauxite available to Vedanta.

One may note that the case studies selected in this chapter deal with sovereign support to finance in both direct and indirect ways, rather than being strictly related to sovereign financing in the strict sense. There are two reasons for this. First, project finance by its very nature depends on the potential benefits and risks of a given project. An evaluation of such benefits and risks has to take into account not only financial aspects (eg, cash flow) but also non-financial aspects (eg, the availability and supply of raw materials; licence approvals). Second, having a wider canvas of inquiry is also useful because the distinction between 'financial' and 'non-financial' aspects might not always be very clear. For example, if the government of a country guarantees to acquire land and transfer it to a company to complete its proposed project or offers to provide it security and electricity, such apparently non-financial support by the sovereign will have positive financial implications for the company in question.

Analysing these cases from India offers a distinct advantage because India possesses many attributes considered necessary to safeguard human rights: democracy, the rule of law, an independent judiciary and a robust civil society. If sovereign support to financing can adversely affect human rights even in such settings, then there is more likelihood of negative outcomes in states with authoritative or repressive regimes.

For the sake of convenience as well as linkages, I will use the term 'human rights' in this chapter in a broad sense so as to include both labour rights and environmental rights.

This chapter, in short, will demonstrate that sovereign support to private financing of development projects can result in serious human rights abuses if the process is not rights compatible. As the Indian experience shows, the underlying assumption of the state being the guardian of people's human rights might not come true, because it may not represent interests of all sections of society equally. It might, therefore, be necessary to rely also on non-state actors such as non-governmental organisation (NGOs) and the media to ensure that the state does not pursue policies of economic development of 'some' at the cost of undermining human rights of 'others'. In other words, the state should not be allowed to exert a monopoly over this politics of inclusion and exclusion vis-à-vis both development and human rights, which has a direct bearing on the right to equality and the principle of non-discrimination.

[6] See Part III.B below, and Amnesty International, *Don't Mine Us Out of Existence: Bauxite Mine and Refinery Devastate Lives in India*, ASA 20/001/2010 (London, Amnesty International, 2010).

II GETTING THE 'PROCESS' RIGHT: AN ANALYTICAL FRAMEWORK

In my view, the quest for economic development and sovereign support for financing of development projects is not inherently antagonistic to the realisation of human rights. In fact, their support is vital to the success of the human rights project. What is, however, crucial is that the *process* of achieving these goals does not undermine human rights. This requires that the process should be rights compatible. Some key aspects that will make the process rights compatible are proposed below.

A Negotiating under the Shadow of Human Rights

Memorandums of understanding (MoUs) and/or agreements concerning investment and financing of development projects should be negotiated under the 'shadow' of international human rights law. Ignoring the relevance of human rights is one main reason why development-cum-financing projects tend to result in an abridgement of human rights.[7]

The 'shadow' analogy has three vital elements. First, human rights concerns should be an integral part of project negotiations, rather than a post-approval afterthought.[8] Moreover, similar to how the shadow of an object moves with it, human rights screening should follow the entire life of the project instead of being a requirement to be satisfied in the beginning at the pre-approval stage.

Second, the normative hierarchy of human rights over other public goods (including development) and of human rights law over investment/financial law should be maintained. In other words, the human rights impact assessment or other due diligence processes should not merely be used as tools to confer legitimacy on, and secure approval for, financing of development projects.[9] Rather, these tools should be able to justify, in appropriate cases, denying approval to projects or rolling back approved projects.[10] The recognition of such a normative hierarchy will be similarly useful even when 'integrated analysis' of investment or financial projects is done to judge potential risks and rewards,[11] because this approach does not mean that human rights considerations will automatically prevail over financial considerations.

Third, since states alone might not be able to counter-balance the economic power as well as the profit-maximisation drive of companies, which are key players in financing

[7] For the relevance of human rights to project finance, see OC Kahale, 'Project Finance and Relevant Human Rights' in Leader and Ong (eds) (n 2) 37.

[8] Leader and Kazimova, for example, propose taking into account 'human rights and environmental protection as separately identifiable concerns from the very inception of the project'. Leader and Kazimova (n 2) 498.

[9] To illustrate, ANZ, a member of the Equator Principles, has financed 4 out of 5 Category A projects – the 'projects with potential significant adverse social or environmental impacts that are diverse, irreversible or unprecedented' – between 2009 and 2012. ANZ, 'Equator Principles, www.anz.com/about-us/corporate-responsibility/customers/responsible-business-lending/equator-principles/ (accessed 20 February 2013).

[10] The Guiding Principles on Foreign Debt and Human Rights, for example provide: 'Lenders should not finance activities or projects that violate, or would foreseeably violate, human rights in the Borrower States. To avoid this eventuality, *it is incumbent upon lenders intending to finance specific activities or projects in Borrower States to conduct a credible Human Rights Impact Assessment (HRIA) as a prerequisite to providing a new loan*' Guiding Principles on Foreign Debt and Human Rights (n 3) para 40 (emphasis added).

[11] 'Integrated analysis' implies combining financial considerations with non-financial considerations such as human rights and the environment. See PRI Association, *Integrated Analysis: How Investors are Addressing Environmental, Social and Governance Factors in Fundamental Equity Valuation* (February 2013).

development projects, non-state actors should be given a role to play in ensuring that project negotiations continue to take place under the shadow of human rights. I elaborate this point further under 'Tripartite Negotiations' and 'Developing Development through Participatory Consultations'.

The idea of negotiating investment or financing projects under the shadow of human rights can be supported with reference to a number of recent developments. One may refer to the Equator Principles launched in 2003,[12] and the 2006 Principles of Responsible Investment (PRI), which encourage investors to put into practice six principles.[13] The PRI, a voluntary initiative of investors, has grown significantly: as of April 2012, over 1,000 signatories with assets of over USD30 trillion under their management have pledged to follow the six principles,[14] including taking into account the environmental, social and corporate governance (ESG) issues. Almost parallel to this initiative, the bilateral investment agreements (BITs) signed in recent years have also not remained oblivious to the human rights implications of agreements enabling investment.[15] Several Model BITs[16] contain explicit provisions recognising the power of states to take appropriate steps to safeguard labour rights, human rights and the environment.[17] I will stress that states do not merely have such power, they in fact have a *duty* to ensure that investment by business does not undermine human rights.

More recently, UNCTAD's Principles on Promoting Responsible Sovereign Lending and Borrowing expect both lenders and sovereign borrowers to investigate and assess 'financial, operational, civil, social, cultural and environmental implications' of projects.[18] Similarly, the UN Guiding Principles on Business and Human Rights[19] rightly remind states not to ignore their role as the guardian of human rights while supporting business activities or negotiating commercial deals with companies.[20] In particular, states should ensure that government departments/agencies/institutions responsible for investment, export credit, insurance and trade observe states' human rights obligations when fulfilling their respective mandates.[21] Similar care should be taken at the time of contracting with companies to provide public services that may impact upon the enjoyment of human rights.[22] States should also maintain adequate 'policy space' to discharge their

[12] 'About the Equator Principles', www.equator-principles.com/index.php/about, (accessed 20 February 2013).

[13] UNPRI, 'The Six Principles', www.unpri.org/about-pri/the-six-principles/ (accessed 20 February 2013). Apart from this institutionalised initiative, the idea of socially responsible investment (SRI) has also grown over the years.

[14] UNPRI, 'About the PRI Initiative', www.unpri.org/about-pri/about-pri/ (accessed 20 February 2013).

[15] In relation to the integration of the environment into investment and free trade agreements, see JE Viñuales, *Foreign Investment and the Environment in International Law* (Cambridge, Cambridge University Press, 2012) 14–17. Viñuales also notes that environmental issues are breaking into investment disputes most significantly post-2000, ibid 17–23.

[16] Canadian Model BIT (2004) art 11; US Model BIT (2012) arts 12 and 13; IISD Model International Agreement on Investment for Sustainable Development (2005) arts 20 and 21.

[17] See R Moloo and J Jacinto, 'Environmental and Health Regulation: Assessing Liability Under Investment Treaties' (2011) 29 *Berkeley Journal of International Law* 1; AA Ghouri, 'Positing for Balancing: Investment Treaty Rights and the Rights of Citizens' (2011) 4(1) *Contemporary Asia Arbitration Journal* 95.

[18] United Nations Conference on Trade and Development (UNCTAD), 'Principles on Promoting Responsible Sovereign Lending and Borrowing' (January 2012) Principles 5 and 12.

[19] Human Rights Council, 'Guiding Principles on Business and Human Rights: Implementing the United Nations "Protect, Respect and Remedy" Framework', A/HRC/17/31 (21 March 2011) (HRC, 'Guiding Principles').

[20] See also the Guiding Principles on Foreign Debt and Human Rights (n 3) para 6.

[21] HRC, 'Guiding Principles' (n 19) Principle 8 (including Commentary).

[22] ibid, Principle 5 (including Commentary).

human rights obligations when pursuing other business-related goals with business enterprises or acting as members of multilateral institutions concerning trade, investment and finance.[23]

B Tripartite Negotiations

In most of the cases, two sets of parties negotiate and sign deals to finance development projects. The first set comprises the government and/or its public institutions. Various private actors (such as the project company, the parent company, output consumers, lenders, banks and financial institutions) constitute the second set of parties. In some instances, international financial institutions – eg, the World Bank, the International Monetary Fund (IMF), the Asian Development Bank and International Finance Corporation – may also be involved in financing projects. But these can be clubbed with either of the two categories depending upon the nature of the institution.

For our purposes, it is crucial to note that whereas the second set of parties is primarily driven by economic gains, the first set tries to juggle and perform multiple goals – ranging from fostering economic development to creating jobs, building infrastructure, protecting the environment, promoting human rights and satisfying a given political constituency – at the same time. In this juggling exercise, the government might end up, as the case studies discussed in the next section will illustrate, not giving enough weight to the protection of human rights. To overcome the problem of non-human rights considerations triumphing over human rights, I propose to introduce a third party – human rights groups (HRGs)[24] – and in turn make the model of negotiations to be 'tripartite'. The HRGs should be able to ensure that human rights are not lost sight of when financing of development projects is being negotiated and approved.

The tripartite model is required because sole reliance on the state as the guardian of human rights is proving to be problematic in view of the multiple hats that the state has to wear. The other related factor is the investment dependency of states on companies, contributing to a deficit of political will to act against companies. Then there are instances in which states are unable to act because of low governance capacity or being run by a repressive or authoritarian regime.[25] Therefore, we need to develop a governance model that harnesses the power of non-state actors to fill the gaps in the regulatory role of states in protecting human rights. It will also be desirable that the law and policy guidelines concerning FDI as well as project financing should provide for such a consultative role of HRGs.

The justification for the tripartite model of negotiations can be grounded on two interrelated principles. The first is the importance of ensuring the independence and autonomy of states to take appropriate decisions concerning their investment, development and financing goals.[26] The presence of HRGs should also guard against the problem of

[23] ibid, Principles 9 and 10 (including Commentary).

[24] Apart from NGOs, research centres, media organisations, trade unions, student bodies and the associations of lawyers and academics espousing the cause of human rights can be regarded as HRGs.

[25] See JP Bohoslavsky, 'Tracking Down the Missing Financial Link in Transnational Justice' (2012) 1 *International Human Rights Review* 10–18.

[26] See, for example, the following articulation of this principle: 'Every State has the sovereign and inalienable right to implement a process of national development independently and free from pressure, influence or interference from external actors, including other States and international financial institutions' Guiding Principles on Foreign Debt and Human Rights (n 3) para 27.

state capture by certain sections of society or external private actors. The second principle is that people should be consulted about key decisions that affect them. One dimension of this principle, which is underpinned by notions of both democracy and fairness, is elaborated further below.

C Developing 'Development' through Participatory Consultations

Although the idea of tripartite negotiations should be able to offer some guarantee against state capture, HRGs themselves might be open to capture. More importantly, HRGs' role as envisaged above cannot influence the *conception* of 'development' pursued by the state. Developmental projects generally benefit some people more than others, even if they are presented as creating a 'win-win' situation for all.[27] Moreover, some people might disagree with the concept of development rooted in the construction of large dams, townships, a network of highways and bridges, and mega-factories at the cost of damaging forests or taking over agricultural land.

Therefore, the scope of consultations should not be limited to pre-defined development parameters imposed on people from the top. Rather, the nature and contours of development as well as the means adopted to achieve it should evolve through bottom-up participatory consultations. This kind of consultation will be especially critical for vulnerable or marginalised sections of society, whose interests may not be adequately represented within the state's institutions that make decisions about finance, investment and development. As the case studies in Section III will show, one of the paradoxes of the current model of development is that the people most severely affected or displaced by development projects gain least from them. Giving people a voice in deciding whether they want a particular development project in their locality should counter-balance, at least partially, the power currently enjoyed by potential beneficiaries over the decision-making process.

D Transparency

Finally, it is vital that there is transparency in how the state invites tenders and grants necessary licences to the selected private actors to commence a project. Similar transparency is desirable in financing of projects.[28] Lack of adequate information about projects' human rights impacts – both to lenders/borrowers and affected communities – does not allow a fair assessment of the financial viability of development projects as well as their adverse social impacts.[29] As Enron's Dabhol power project shows, secrecy breeds corrup-

[27] Leader poses a pertinent question in a related context: 'Is it, for example, better to take a step towards fulfilling a basic right to adequate medical care on a national level via tax revenues from a project, but at the expense of allowing construction to move at a pace that destroys the health of some of a local population, or should the adjustment between the two sets of rights move in the opposite direction?' S Leader, 'An Introduction to the Issues' in Leader and Ong (eds) (n 2) 3, 10.

[28] 'Transparency requires the full disclosure of all relevant information regarding loan agreements, debt repayments, debt management, outcomes of public debt audits and other related matters' Guiding Principles on Foreign Debt and Human Rights (n 3) para 29.

[29] See Leader and Kazimova (n 2) 492–93.

tion and suspicion that the project was not beneficial to the general public.[30] In this case, neither the MoU that Enron had signed with the state of Maharashtra nor the contents of the power purchase agreement were open to the public. Even the report of the Munde Committee, which was constituted to review Enron's Dabhol project, was not published.[31] The lack of competitive bidding made the matter worse.

It would be apt here to quote Human Rights Watch's recommendation that private as well as public financial institutions that financed the Dabhol power project should:

> . . . adopt explicit policies in support of human rights and establish procedures to ensure that financing of projects does not contribute to or result in human rights abuses. At a minimum, implement a policy to conduct a 'human rights impact assessment.' Such procedures should involve governmental and nongovernmental actors and should be fully transparent.[32]

Although the above recommendation – which embodies some of the key elements canvassed above – was made specifically in the context of the Dabhol project, it is clearly relevant in all situations of financing of development projects.

III APPLYING THE FRAMEWORK: TWO CASE STUDIES

This section analyses two case studies from India in light of the analytical framework proposed above. The basic objective of this analysis is to investigate factors that led to human rights abuses in these instances.

A Enron's Dabhol Power Project

In 1993 a contract was signed between DPC – an Indian subsidiary of Enron, a US company – and the MSEB.[33] This was the first major investment project after India opened up its economy in the early 1990s. The Maharashtra state government guaranteed the payment obligations of the MSEB to DPC and the central government issued a counter-guarantee.[34] One commentator notes that India 'provided every imaginable sort of guaranty that the terms of the relevant contracts would be honored'.[35]

The project was financed from various sources, including Indian government-owned banks.[36] The Overseas Private Investment Corporation (OPIC), a US government agency that provides assistance to US companies in the form of loans, guarantees and political

[30] See HRW (n 5).

[31] F Pretorius et al, *Project Finance for Construction and Infrastructure: Principles and Case Studies* (Oxford, Blackwell Publishing, 2008) 316. This report is though produced as Appendix B in HRW (n 5) 133–54.

[32] HRW (n 5) 8.

[33] W Ahmed, *Spaces of Power: Foreign Direct Investment in India* (PhD Dissertation, Clark University, Worcester, 2007) 9.

[34] JW Salacuse, *The Three Laws of International Investment: National, Contractual and International Frameworks for Foreign Capital* (Oxford, Oxford University Press, 2013) 238. 'Dabhol was the first of the eight fast-tracked energy projects for which central government offered guarantees in order to attract private sector involvement' Pretorius et al (n 31) 315.

[35] RJ Bettauer, 'India and International Arbitration: The Dabhol Experience' (2009) 41 *George Washington International Law Review* 381, 385.

[36] Salacuse (n 34) 238; Pretorius et al (n 31) 315.

risk insurance, had also provided a US$160 million loan.[37] The power purchase agreement – under which the MSEB had agreed to buy the electricity generated by DPC – was central to the viability of the project.[38] Salacuse explains:

> An essential requirement for the financial success of the proposed Dabhol project was the existence of a credible, long-term purchaser of the electricity it would generate. A commitment from such a buyer was necessary to enable the project company to secure long-term debt financing and to assure the equity investors an adequate return on their investment. For the Dabhol Project to become a reality, it was therefore necessary for the Maharashtra State Electricity Board, the only potential buyer in the state, to enter into a long-term power purchase agreement with the Dabhol Power Project Company.[39]

The 'revenue stream',[40] which was used by the project company (DPC in this case) to pay the debt and equity capital, was soon drained because in 2000 the MSEB defaulted on its payment obligations to DPC.[41] It seems that the power purchase agreement heavily favoured Enron and DPC: it protected their economic interests by imposing most of the risk on the central and state governments.[42]

As Sawant explains, one main reason why MNCs invest in infrastructure through the mode of 'project finance' rather than using 'corporate finance' is because the latter cannot fully mitigate threats of creeping expropriation from host governments.[43]

> Project finance is a debt finance technique used for the development of a public infrastructure project where lenders rely primarily on the cash flow produced by the project to service their loan rather than on other sources of payment such as government guarantees or project sponsors' assets or credit.[44]

So Enron's Dabhol power project was a classic example of project finance that did not materialize as per the expectations of either party.

The Dabhol power project proved to be controversial from its very inception[45] and resulted in multiple legal and arbitration proceedings.[46] The government neither conducted a financial appraisal of the project nor invited any competitive bidding.[47] It is also

[37] See 'Settlement of Disputes: US Initiatives Arbitration Against India over OPIC Claims for the Dabhol Power Project' (2005) 99 *American Journal of International Law* 271–72.

[38] Salacuse (n 34) 236.

[39] JW Salacuse, 'Renegotiating International Project Agreements' (2001) 24 *Fordham International Law Journal* 1319, 1347.

[40] Scannella (n 1) 84.

[41] D Mathavan, 'From Dabhol to Ratnagiri: The Electricity Act of 2003 and Reform of India's Power Sector' (2009) 47 *Columbia Journal of Transnational Law* 387, 394.

[42] B Choudhary and P Kulkarni, 'Re-crafting Bilateral Investment Treaties in a Development Framework: A Comparative Regional Perspective' in A Deshpande (ed), *Capital without Borders: Challenges to Development* (New Delhi, Anthem Press India, 2011) 209, 221.

[43] RJ Sawant, 'The Economics of Large-Scale Infrastructure FDI: The Case of Project Finance' (2010) 41(6) *Journal of International Business Studies* 1036.

[44] DD Banani, 'International Arbitration and Project Finance in Developing Countries: Blurring the Public/Private Distinction' (2003) 26 *Boston College International and Comparative Law Review* 355, 355–56. See also A Loke, 'Risk Management and Credit Support in Project Finance' (1998) *Singapore Journal of International and Comparative Law* 37, 37–38.

[45] F Pretorius et al (n 31) 312; HRW (n 5) 125.

[46] See Bettauer (n 35); Z Mody and S Jacob, 'India: Interim Injunction' (2004) 7(6) *International Arbitration Law Review* 74.

[47] A state government committee, which reviewed the project, commented that 'in a matter of less than three days, a MoU was signed between Enron and MSEB in a matter involving a project of the value of 10,000 crore rupees [US$2.5 billion] at the time' (quoted in Pretorius et al (n 31), 312).

worth noting that the World Bank had rejected the loan for the project on the ground that it was 'not economically viable'.[48] It also became a subject of football between political parties. At the time of negotiations for this project, Congress was the ruling party at both federal and state levels.[49] However, after the Bhartiya Janata Party (BJP), which had opposed the Dabhol project on the ground of corruption and higher cost of electricity,[50] came into power in the state of Maharashtra in 2005, it cancelled the project on the recommendation of a review committee.[51] This prompted DPC to commence arbitration proceedings against the MSEB and the state government.[52] Later the parties renegotiated the agreement terms.[53] Even the revised power purchase agreement was given a counter-guarantee by the central government.[54] The disputes between parties – mostly for non-payment under the power purchase agreement – continued until 2005 when the Indian government reached a final agreement with companies that had bought Enron's stake in DPC.[55]

Apart from these financial and governance concerns, the Dabhol project also raised human rights issues, as documented at length in the 1999 report of Human Rights Watch.[56] In short, it was alleged that the state government had:

> engaged in a systematic pattern of suppression of freedom of expression and peaceful assembly coupled with arbitrary detentions, excessive use of force, and threats . . . The police have also misused preventative detention laws to detain people for the peaceful expression of their views. The state has also tolerated the failure of the police to investigate or prosecute perpetrators of attacks on opponents of the Dabhol Power project.[57]

The report also highlighted the potential complicity of Enron and DPC in these human rights violations. It was alleged that DPC 'paid the abusive state forces for the security they provided to the company', provided other material support to police, and failed to act on credible allegations that its own contractors intimidated or harassed people protesting against the project.[58] There were also reports of improper land acquisition and environmental degradation caused by the project[59] – which were the root cause of local people opposing the project in the first place.

It is apparent from the above analysis that both the central and state governments had offered diverse kinds of support to the Dabhol project. They not only provided guarantees but also issued necessary licences and provided necessary security. The MSEB also agreed to buy the generated electricity at a premium price for 20 years, which was vital for the success of the project. This sovereign support to the project was driven by a desire to secure electricity to sustain economic development. But human rights considerations were hardly on the radar of either government. In other words, the Dabhol project was

[48] Pretorius et al (n 31) 313–14.
[49] Mathavan (n 41) 394.
[50] Bettauer (n 35) 383.
[51] Pretorius et al (n 31) 316.
[52] Bettauer (n 35) 383.
[53] Mathavan (n 41) 394; Salacuse (n 39) 1350–54.
[54] Pretorius et al (n 31) 317. But the central government did not give any guarantee for the second phase of the project, ibid, 318.
[55] Pretorius et al (n 31) 320–21; Bettauer (n 35) 383–85.
[56] HRW (n 5) 38–99.
[57] ibid, 3.
[58] ibid, 3 and 106.
[59] ibid, 38–50.

not negotiated under the shadow of human rights. Nor did HRGs have any role to play in negotiations; in fact, the government tried to suppress NGOs protesting against the project. Even the BJP's opposition to the project was seemingly superficial and more like a political stunt, because it ended up renegotiating the contract terms with Enron. The project lacked transparency as no competitive bidding was invited by the government. In short, the Dabhol project was not rights compatible as per the analytical framework proposed above.

B Vedanta's Refinery-cum-Mining Operations in Orissa

The second case study concerns the refinery-cum-mining operations of Sterlite Industries India Limited (Sterlite) and Vedanta Alumina Ltd, subsidiaries of the UK-based Vedanta Resources plc, in the Indian state of Orissa. In 2003 Vedanta signed an MoU with the state of Orissa to build an aluminium refinery.[60] The refinery depended on bauxite mining in the Niyamgiri hills,[61] which was to be carried out by a joint venture company of Sterlite and the state-owned Orissa Mining Corporation (OMC).[62] In addition to OMC transferring a bauxite mining lease to Vedanta, the state government's support was in the form of OMC, a public sector company, holding 26 per cent shares in the joint venture company.[63] OMC's support to Vedanta is also clear from its decision to challenge in the Supreme Court the decision of the central government's Ministry of Environment and Forest (MoEF) to revoke environmental clearance of the project's second stage.[64]

The grant of mining rights in the Niyamgiri hills became controversial because these hills have religious and cultural significance for the Dongria Kondh tribe who have lived there for generations.[65] They

> consider the Niyamgiri Hills as sacred and do not cut trees or practice cultivation on top of the Hill as they worship *Niyam Raja Penu*, [a male deity] who they believe lives on top of the Niyamgiri Hills. Their identity is closely tied to the Niyamgiri Hills, which they believe are essential to their culture, traditions, and physical and economic survival.[66]

Moreover, it seems that the environmental impact assessment and public consultation with the affected people as per the relevant laws were not properly carried out.[67] The OECD national contact point too found that Vedanta had 'failed to engage the Dongria

[60] MoEF, Government of India, 'Report of the Four Member Committee for Investigation into the Proposal Submitted by the Orissa Mining Company for Bauxite Mining in Niyamgiri' (August 2010) 11.

[61] A Margolis, 'Prioritising Profit Over People: Multinational Corporations Operate Seamlessly Across National Borders, But Insufficient Regulations Have Led to Disastrous Consequences for Human Life' (2010) 64(1) *International Bar News* 23, 28.

[62] Amnesty International (n 6) 4.

[63] See 'Agreement of OMC with M/s Vedanta Alumina Limited in the Best Interest of the State' (Press Release of OMC dated 19 October 2004), http://orissa.gov.in/news/archive/2004/october/191004/191004.pdf (accessed 15 March 2013).

[64] 'OMC Opposes Government's Decision to revoke Sterlite's Mining License', *Economic Times* (13 October 2012), http://articles.economictimes.indiatimes.com/2012-10-13/news/34431340_1_niyamgiri-hills-omc-sterlite-india (accessed 15 March 2013).

[65] Margolis (n 61) 28.

[66] Amnesty International (n 6) 17 and generally 18–25.

[67] ibid 25–31. See also DM Conway, 'Promoting Indigenous Innovation, Enterprise and Entrepreneurship through the Licensing of Article 31 Indigenous Assets and Resources' (2011) 64 *SMU Law Review* 1095, 1114–15.

Kondh in adequate and timely consultations about the construction of the mine'.[68] Vedanta though has rejected all these allegations and has claimed the company's 'processes, planning and consultation have been in line with all Indian national laws'.[69] This perspective of Vedanta has been strongly rebutted by Amnesty International, including on account of Vedanta 'misusing the concept of sustainable development to ignore human rights abuses'.[70] Amnesty's 2012 report notes:

> In human rights terms the Dongria Kondh are being asked to accept violations of their rights as Indigenous peoples in order to access their rights to education and health. This view represents a serious misunderstanding of international human rights law and standards. Human rights are indivisible and should not be traded against each other . . . Although corporate initiatives such as assisting with local medical care can be beneficial, they do not give licence to continue with other practices that cause harm to human health and well-being.[71]

Despite these concerns, which were raised from the very beginning, the MoEF granted environmental clearance for Vedanta's refinery in 2004 and 'in principle' environmental clearance for the mining project in 2009.[72] It is worth noting that Vedanta had tried to abuse the judicial process in that it attempted to bypass the statutory process of seeking approval from the government and approached the Supreme Court directly for approval.[73] This strategy partly succeeded in that the Court granted Vedanta the requested clearance in an August 2008 order.[74] However, since Vedanta did not comply with the conditions for environmental clearance, the central government issued a show-cause notice to Vedanta in August 2010. On 20 October 2010 the MoEF directed Vedanta to take several additional steps such as continuous monitoring of air quality, conserving energy, and raising green belts.[75] On the same day, it withdrew the permission granted to Vedanta to expand its Alumina refinery and directed it not to carry out any further construction in relation to the expansion project.[76] The latter decision was taken based on the report submitted by the Saxena Committee, which had concluded that Vedanta began construction activity without obtaining environmental clearance and had violated various laws.[77]

This case study again reveals the development dynamic of state collusion with companies resulting in human rights abuses. The Saxena Committee alluded to the 'deliberate

[68] UK National Contact Point, 'Final Statement by the UK National Contact Point for the OECD Guidelines for Multinational Enterprises: Complaint from Survival international against Vedanta Resource plc' (25 September 2009).

[69] Vedanta Resources, 'The Lanjigarh Development Story: Vedanta's Perspective' (August 2012) 11.

[70] Amnesty International, *Vedanta's Perspective Uncovered: Policies cannot Mask Practices in Orissa*, ASA 20/029/2012 (London, Amnesty International, 2012) 18.

[71] ibid.

[72] Amnesty International (n 6) 11.

[73] See International Commission of Jurist (ICJ), *Access to Justice: Human Rights Abuses Involving Corporations – India* (Geneva, ICJ, 2011) 45–46.

[74] *T N Godavaraman Thirumulpad v Union of India* (2008) 9 SCC 222 (para 9).

[75] Ministry of Environment and Forests (MoEF), 'Direction under Section 5 of the Environment (Protection) Act, 1986 regarding 1MTPA Alumina Refinery and 75 MW Captive Power Plant at Lanjigarh in Dist. Kalahandi in Orissa by M/s Vedanta Aluminum Limited' (20 October 2010), http://moef.nic.in/downloads/publicinformation/Vedanta-direction-sec5.pdf (accessed 3 February 2011).

[76] MoEF, 'Direction under Section 5 of the Environment (Protection) Act, 1986, regarding withdrawal of ToRs, Cancellation of Public Hearing and action under Provision of the Environment (Protection) Act, 1986' (20 October 2010), http://moef.nic.in/downloads/public-information/letter-vedanta-sec5.pdf (accessed 3 February 2011).

[77] MoEF, 'Report of the four member committee for investigation into the proposal submitted by the Orissa mining company for bauxite mining in Niyamgiri' (16 August 2010) 84–87, http://moef.nic.in/downloads/public-information/Saxena_Vedanta.pdf (accessed 3 February 2011).

non-cooperation' of the state government in providing information to the Committee.[78] The Committee further observed:

> If the state government illegally prioritizes the short-term interests of a private company by sacrificing a sensitive ecological and hydrological area that is rich in biodiversity, and an ecosystem that supports the livelihood and culture of the [. . .] Tribal Groups, it will be violating the rights of forest-dwelling Scheduled Tribes under the [Forest Rights Act] as well as the Environment Protection Act and the Forest Conservation Act.[79]

The state government is also accused of suppressing opposition to the project by tribal people and NGOs.[80]

In December 2012 Vedanta had to shut down its Orissa refinery because of inadequate supply of bauxite directly linked to the MoEF's decision to withdraw permission for stage II mining in the Niyamgiri hills.[81] OMC's appeal against this decision of the MoEF,[82] was dismissed by the Indian Supreme Court in April 2013, wherein the Court held that local indigenous people decide whether to allow Vedanta to extract bauxite from the Niyamgiri hills.[83] After all tribal villages voted against the proposed mining, in January 2014 the MoEF decided not to allow Vedanta to mine the Niyamgiri hills for bauxite.[84] Although this amounts to victory (at least for the time being) for the Dongria Kondh tribe living in the Niyamgiri Hills, it is worth noting that the state government as well as its public sector company (OMC) had tried to do everything they could to serve the economic interests of Vedanta, a company that invested in the state of Orissa to fulfil the government's agenda of economic development. The only silver lining was the continuous advocacy and opposition marshalled by the civil society, which also compelled the central government to reverse its initial decision to grant 'in principle' environmental clearance for mining.

IV COMMON LESSONS

Analysing these two case studies against the backdrop of the analytical framework proposed at the beginning of this chapter, we can draw some common lessons which should be useful not only for India but also all other developing countries in Asia and elsewhere. First of all, the distinction between financial and non-financial support offered by the state to companies pursuing a project may not always be very clear cut. The sovereign's financial support is often not enough to take the project forward. Conversely, non-financial support provided by the state may have financial implications for investors.

[78] NC Saxena, 'Letter to Minister' (23 August 2010) http://moef.nic.in/downloads/public-information/Letter_to_Minister_23_Aug.pdf (accessed 3 February 2011).

[79] ibid.

[80] Amnesty International (n 70) 19–22.

[81] 'Vedanta to Close Orissa Refinery', *Indian Express* (5 December 2012), www.indianexpress.com/news/vedanta-to-close-orissa-refinery/1040510 (accessed 3 March 2013).

[82] PM Thomas, 'All Eyes on Govt vs Vedanta Case' *Forbes India* (22 January 2013), http://forbesindia.com/article/special/all-eyes-on-govt-vs-vedanta-case/34539/1 (accessed 3 March 2013).

[83] 'India Court Says Locals to have Say on Vedanta Mine' (18 April 2013), *BBC News*, http://www.bbc.co.uk/news/world-asia-india-22196355 (accessed 16 February 2014).

[84] 'Environment Ministry Rejects Vedanta's Mining Proposal in Niyamgiri' (11 January 2014), *The Economic Times*, http://articles.economictimes.indiatimes.com/2014-01-11/news/46067729_1_mining-proposal-niyamgiri-hills-source-bauxite (accessed 16 February 2014).

Second, one main reason why project finance can harm human rights is the failure to give (adequate) attention to human rights and human rights law while negotiating and approving projects. Even in those cases where human rights impact assessment is conducted, it is driven by a 'tick box' mindset to seek approval of the project. In relation to the role of impact assessment, a radical change in orientation is needed so that the normative hierarchy of human rights over developmental goals could be preserved.

Third, the rights-compatible framework to negotiate financing of development projects is required to protect not only human rights but also the economic interests of private actors who invest in (or finance) such projects.[85] The case studies reviewed in this chapter demonstrate that sovereign support for development projects is necessary but not enough. Projects can be delayed or have to be rolled back if the local community do not lend their support to projects. In other words, the state's approval and support may bestow a given project only with legality and not necessarily legitimacy.

Fourth, it is quite clear that states – even those that are democratic, are wedded to the rule of law and have an independent judiciary as well as a robust civil society – cannot be trusted always as custodians of human rights. They may act in concert with private economic actors or sacrifice human rights in trying to strike a balance while juggling between multiple goals. In some cases, their ability to safeguard human rights may be hampered by governance deficits or the 'race to the bottom'. To augment states' capacity to protect human rights, I have proposed to give HRGs a role in the process of negotiating financial projects.

Finally, one fundamental issue that is often ignored is the nature of the very purpose for which finance is secured, that is, economic development. In most cases, people who are directly affected adversely by development projects have no say in deciding whether they want that kind of development or not. Rather their participation, whether symbolic or real, is limited to softening of adverse consequences of development projects. This conceptual orientation should be remedied by developing the notion of 'development' through participatory consultations.

V CONCLUSION

The availability of finance is crucial to both economic development and the realisation of human rights. The process through which states secure finance to fund development projects has a direct bearing on whether financing of projects will promote human rights or abridge them. One common method adopted by states to secure finance is by offering financial and/or non-financial support to corporate investors and lenders. However, as human rights law does not often feature prominently during financing negotiations, potential adverse human rights implications of development projects do not take centre stage. Nor do states always show an unflinching commitment to protect the human rights of their populace against assault by profit-driven companies.

In short, the current process of financing of development projects is not rights compatible. It is not rights compatible because financial considerations are determinative of projects' viability and approval. Even in those instances where human rights considerations

[85] See TW Fernandez, 'Human Rights Impact Assessments and Project Finance' in Leader and Ong (eds) (n 2) 174.

are taken into account, it is done mostly for financial reasons. An analysis of two case studies from India – Enron's Dabhol power project and Vedanta's refinery-cum-mining operations in Orissa – shows this clearly.

We therefore require a more holistic regulation of financing, which combines both financial and non-financial aspects. This chapter has proposed four aspects that will go a long way in making sovereign support to financing rights compatible: negotiating under the shadow of human rights, tripartite negotiations, developing development through participatory consultations, and transparency. These aspects were apparently missing, to a different degree, in both case studies analysed here. Were they followed, the outcome would have been very different, not merely for human rights but also for the bottom line of the concerned companies.

19

Contemporary Lessons from Carter's Incorporation of Human Rights into the Financing of Southern Cone Dictatorships

ROBERT BEJESKY AND JUAN PABLO BOHOSLAVSKY*

I INTRODUCTION

FOLLOWING HIS VICTORY in the US presidential election of 1976, Jimmy Carter set out to institutionalise human rights in US foreign policy. Building on a growing body of congressional legislation aimed at curtailing US military and financial (bilateral and multilateral) aid to states engaged in patterns of gross violations of human rights, the Carter administration attempted to design a robust legal framework that would integrate financial policies with the promotion of human rights. In his inauguration address, Carter famously asserted that 'our commitment to human rights must be absolute', and he quickly affixed Latin America as the regional focal point of the administration's human rights policy.[1] Dominated by repressive right-wing dictatorships with strong Cold War ties to the United States, Latin America was also characterised by high financial vulnerability and dependence on external capital, providing US policymakers with economic leverage to advance the human rights agenda.

The Carter administration placed special emphasis on human rights in the formulation and implementation of policy towards the nations of Latin America's Southern Cone. In the 1970s, military dictatorships in Argentina, Chile and Uruguay engaged in ferocious campaigns of repression against perceived subversives.[2] Operating under national security doctrine that extended the military's purview deep into the realms of social and economic policy, Southern Cone military leaders' expansive notions of counter-terror also facilitated the systematic use of kidnapping, torture and disappearance of tens of thousands of perceived subversives. Entering the White House in January 1977, Carter faced multiple human rights crises in the Southern Cone; spearheaded by the tireless

* The authors wish to extend their gratitude for the comments on the drafts of this chapter and the research material received from Alejandro Avenburg, Eduardo Basualdo, Margaret Crahan, Roberta Cohen, John Dinges, Jo Marie Griesgraber, Kunibert Raffer, Dustin Sharp and Lars Schoultz. The views and conclusions reflected in this chapter are solely those of the authors and are in no way intended to reflect the views of any of the institutions with which the authors are affiliated.

[1] J Carter, Inaugural Address, 20 January 1977, www.jimmycarterlibrary.gov/documents/speeches/inaugadd.phtml, accessed 1 March 2013.

[2] W Heinz and H Frühling, Determinants of Gross Human Rights Violations by State and State-Sponsored Actors in Brazil, Uruguay, Chile, and Argentina (1960–1990) (The Hague, Kluwer Law International, 1999).

advocacy of Assistant Secretary of State for Human Rights and Humanitarian Affairs Patricia Derian, the administration focused its efforts on using financial policies to prevent human rights violations in Argentina, Chile and Uruguay, among other countries in the world.

This chapter examines the Carter administration's efforts to elicit human rights improvements from the authoritarian governments in Uruguay, Chile and Argentina. Then it studies whether and how these historical experiences help to better understand the connection between sovereign financing and human rights abuses perpetrated by criminal regimes as well as the legal analysis of this same link. Although the US policy towards the Southern Cone during the late Cold War has been broadly studied in the fields of history and international relations, these case studies and their important implications for the current debate on responsibility for financial complicity have been largely absent in scholarship on international law, human rights law and especially financial law. This lacuna is all the more surprising since the Carter administration's effort to elicit human rights improvements in the Southern Cone offers significant empirical evidence on the impact of lenders and donors on the consolidation (or weakening) of criminal regimes. While Bohoslavsky and Escribà-Folch in this volume present a quantitative empirical study on financial complicity, this chapter uses a qualitative approach to analyse the causal link between sovereign financing and human rights promotion.

This chapter commences in Section II with the geopolitical and economic context that prevailed during the Nixon and Ford administrations as the military juntas came to power in Uruguay, Chile and Argentina. Section III discusses President Carter's drastic reversal in US foreign policy in support of human rights in the Southern Cone and attempts to enforce those policies by cutting financial assistance through bilateral, multilateral and – to a much lesser extent – private means. Section IV considers competing international obligations, identifies fundamentals, and draws lessons from these historical facts that might be meaningful in the current debates on financial complicity. Section V presents some concluding remarks.

II THE SOCIAL, ECONOMIC AND POLITICAL CONTEXT IN THE EARLY 1970S AND SOUTHERN CONE COUPS

A Geopolitical Economic Conditions

During US Congressional hearings in January 1974, Senator Church pointed out that the seven US- and British-owned multinational oil companies, which largely controlled global oil production and distribution, were all in the top 15 largest corporations in the world and had 'many of the characteristics of nations'.[3] A US Department of Commerce report estimated that net assets of the oil companies in the Middle East were $1.5 billion and annual profits were $1.2 billion for an annual return on investment of 79 per cent.[4]

In the early 1970s OPEC viewed concession agreements with the multinationals as extortion, and ire was further sparked by President Nixon's breach of the gold-par value

[3] A Sampson, *The Seven Sisters* (Toronto, Bantam Books, 1975) 273.
[4] ibid, 232.

currency exchange agreement and devaluation of the US dollar.[5] Devaluations reduced revenues for OPEC countries[6] and this led to a series of agreements with the multinationals starting in early 1971 to counter devaluations by increasing the price of oil.[7] Due to price increases and supply reductions during disputes, the price of oil tripled from 1970 to 1973, causing oil rationing; price increases in early 1974[8] led to a global recession;[9] and another oil shock tripled prices in 1978–79 and crippled Latin America.[10]

Inflation was a significant problem for advanced economies in the 1970s.[11] A substantial cause of the transnational spread of inflation was the combination of economic integration and US monetary policies and mechanisms to pay for the Vietnam War and other increases in public spending.[12] In the Southern Cone, Argentina experienced a 21 per cent annual average inflation rate over the 1960s, but 142 per cent over the 1970s; Uruguay faced a 50 per cent annual inflation rate during the 1960s and 64 per cent over the 1970s;[13] and Chile confronted a 27 per cent annual inflation rate over the 1960s and 175 per cent over the 1970s.[14] There was a fivefold increase in gasoline prices to $2.50 per gallon between 1970 and May 1974 in the Southern Cone.[15]

Higher energy prices brought cost-of-living and government budgetary increases for consuming nations to the benefit of oil-rich country interests.[16] Significant profits were deposited in Western multinational banks that sought to earn high returns[17] by lending substantial sums to developing countries, but increased government expenditures (not necessarily benefiting the public interest) and lower revenues caused large-scale structural deficits and sired the developing world debt crisis.

[5] See A Meltzer, *Report of the International Financial Institution Advisory Commission (IFIAC)*, 2000, www.house.gov/jec/imf/meltzer.pdf, accessed 1 March 2013 (providing that President Nixon failed to convert dollars into gold under the IMF agreement).

[6] Sampson (n 3) ix–x, 6, 28, 32–37, 58, 162, 175, 248, 252–55, 268.

[7] ibid, 210–13, 226–27.

[8] ibid, x.

[9] D Harvey, 'Political and Economic Dimensions of Free Trade: Neoliberalism as Creative Destruction' (2007) 610 *Annals* 22, 27.

[10] M de Paiv-Abreu, 'The External Context' in V Bulmer-Thomas et al (eds), *The Cambridge Economic History of Latin America* (Cambridge, Cambridge University Press, 2006) 128.

[11] P Hall and D Soskice, 'An Introduction to Varieties of Capitalism' in P Hall and D Soskice (eds), *Varieties of Capitalism: The Institutional Foundations of Comparative Advantage* (Oxford, Oxford University Press, 2001) 3.

[12] R Franzese, Jr, *Macroeconomic Policies of Developed Democracies* (Cambridge, Cambridge University Press, 2002) 2, 35 (indicating that in 21 economically advanced democracies, inflation was 13% in 1974, 13% in 1980, and 3% on average in the 1990s).

[13] The World Bank, World DataBank: World Development Indicators (using 'Inflation, consumer prices (annual %)'), available at http://databank.worldbank.org/data/views/variableselection/selectvariables.aspx?source=world-development-indicators, accessed 1 March 2013.

[14] C Végh, 'Stopping High Inflation: An Analytical Overview' (1992) 39(3) *IMF Staff Papers* 632–33.

[15] W Davis, Warnings From the Far South: Democracy versus Dictatorship in Uruguay, Argentina, and Chile (Westport CT, Praeger, 1995) 53 (citing Uruguay).

[16] Federal Deposit Insurance Corporation, vol 1, *An Examination of the Banking Crises of the 1980s and Early 1990s*, 1999, 191–93, available at www.fdic.gov/bank/historical/history/191_210.pdf, accessed 1 March 2013.

[17] A Lowenfeld, 'Political Economy for the 1980's: Global Banks and National Governments' (1988) 101 *Harvard Law Review* 1069; M Hulbert, 'The Causes and Risks of Excessive Foreign Lending' (1983) 23 *Cato Institute Policy Analysis*, www.cato.org/pubs/pas/ pa023.html, accessed 1 March 2013 ('the banks' profits from Third World lending are windfall profits, to the extent that public resources have been committed to assure that the banks' loans do not go sour. The banks have not internalized all the risks of lending to the Third World yet continue to earn all the profits from their loans').

In the context of the cyclical deterioration in terms of trade,[18] Southern Cone dictatorships had poor growth rates[19] and escalating debt over the period of military rule. Chile held $3.7 billion in external debt in 1972, but this grew to $19.3 billion in 1990, Argentina held $7.9 billion in 1975 and $46 billion in 1983, and Uruguay $477 million in 1972 and $4 billion in 1985.[20] In fact, the US government encouraged the banks pursuant to the belief that the foreign loans would stimulate American exports and the US job market, while banks furthered the financial problems by engaging in irresponsible 'loan pushing' on the countries[21] and by setting aside almost no credit reserves to address debt difficulties of imperilled countries that were caused by the overlending.[22]

The adverse economic conditions preceding the emergence of military rule in the Southern Cone would foster socio-economic discontent and might be expected to cause citizens to place more demands on government, particularly if the percentage of the economically disenfranchised population grows and becomes more irritated and perceives that the detrimental conditions might significantly be due to exogenous influences and economic integration.[23] With a coup, the military and national elites could impose and enforce an economic ordering that appeases external financial interests but this may severely clash with the will of the populace and the position of the previously elected regime. If external financial assistance to the military regime funds instruments of repression, corruption benefiting the dictatorship and national elites, or other assistance that keeps the regime in power, the will of the populace and human rights may likely be continuously undermined by financing that perpetuates the regime. This external patronage and societal strife unfolded in the Southern Cone countries.

B Uruguay

Unlike in Chile and Argentina, where military coups entirely displaced elected regimes, in Uruguay, Juan Maria Bordaberry won the presidency in November 1971 with 18 per cent of the vote, but his elected government evolved into a dictatorship after civil unrest, violence directed at the government,[24] and exhaustion of treasury funds. By 1973 the military had fully seized power and Bordaberry dissolved the legislature, ruled by decree,

[18] K Raffer and HW Singer, *The Economic North–South Divide. Six Decades of Unequal Development* (Cheltenham, Edward Elgar, 2001).

[19] The World Bank, World DataBank (n 13) (using 'GDP Growth (Annual Percentage)) (calculating that Argentina and Uruguay averaged 1% and Chile 3.4% annual growth over the period of military rule).

[20] ibid (using 'External Debt Stocks, total (DOD, current, US$)').

[21] R Bejesky, 'Currency Cooperation and Sovereign Financial Obligations' (2012) 24 *Florida Journal of International Law* 109–10.

[22] WR Cline, *International Debt and the Stability of the World Economy* (Washington DC, Institute for International Economics, 1983) 98 (noting that the credit reserves of the nine largest banks in the US were only $614 million, or 1.7% of the value of the total loans granted to countries that had previously undergone debt repayment difficulties).

[23] H O'Shaughnessy, *Pinochet: The Politics of Torture* (New York, New York University Press, 2000) 37 ('Chilean working people were frustrated by the constant flux in their conditions brought about by the influence of powerful foreign interests').

[24] J Linz and A Stepan, *Problems of Democratic Transition and Consolidation* (Baltimore, Johns Hopkins University Press, 1996) 153, 155 (noting that the Tupamaros in Uruguay were a puissant insurgent force in Uruguay from 1968 to 1973, but at the time that the military took power in 1973, the group did not have a significant presence in Uruguay).

and banned the National Convention of Workers (who called for strikes across the country) and other leftist, socialist and Marxist groups.[25]

As in other Latin American countries,[26] as a geopolitical implication of the Cold War and the fight against communism, the United States contributed to the development of an authoritarian regime in Uruguay[27] by assisting the Uruguayan military and government before the coup in 1973. United States aid translated into military training, the sale of weapons and police equipment, intelligence capacity building, and economic aid.[28] Uruguay's military regime vowed to continue a policy of furthering neoliberal economic foreign relations. After the coup, Uruguay received mixed signals from the United States due to disagreements between the US Congress and the executive branch.[29]

C Chile

Consistent with other strong leftist movements in Chile that had supported the poor over the previous decade,[30] in September 1970 Chileans elected Salvador Allende, a candidate who made campaign promises to nationalise industries dominated by foreign ownership, such as mining.[31] After Allende's victory, the Nixon administration sought to persuade the Chilean Congress from confirming Allende, promoted an unsuccessful military coup prior to Allende taking office,[32] and planned to take actions that would 'hurt him and bring him down' while 'retain[ing] an outward posture that is correct'.[33] United States officials recognised that Allende was democratically elected, but Secretary of State Kissinger stated: 'I don't see why we should let a country go Marxist because its people are irresponsible'.[34] In fact, there was a populist participation explosion that demanded more government representation, favoured more economic benefits and equality, and questioned the effectiveness of capitalist development.[35] Under Allende, nationalisation laws were passed with overwhelming legislative consent.[36]

[25] Davis (n 15) 45–47, 50–53.

[26] M Esparza et al, State Violence and Genocide in Latin America: the Cold War Years (Oxford, Routledge 2009).

[27] C Aldrighi, El caso Mitrione. La intervención de EEUU en Uruguay, 1965–1973 (Montevideo, Trilce, 2007).

[28] Heinz and Frühling (n 2) 313, 357.

[29] K Sikkink, *Mixed Signals. US Human Rights Policy and Latin America* (New York, Cornell University Press, 2004) 127.

[30] S Huntington and J Nelson, *No Easy Choice: Political Participation in Developing Countries* (Cambridge MA, Harvard University Press, 1976) 154–55.

[31] O'Shaughnessy (n 23) 38.

[32] S Huntington, *American Politics: The Promise of Disharmony* (Cambridge MA, Harvard University Press, 1981) 252–53; *Schneider v Kissinger*, 310 F. Supp. 2d 251, 265–66 (DDC 2004) (regarding an assassination during a coup attempt in Chile during 1970 and an allegation of US government involvement, the court accepted Kissinger's *respondeat superior* defence, 'The Court finds that Dr Kissinger was acting within the scope of his employment as National Security Advisor to President Nixon when he allegedly conspired to kidnap General Schneider. The establishment of a Socialist government in Chile would have had a substantial impact on US foreign policy') *aff'd*, 412 F.3d 190 (DC Ctr 2005).

[33] White House, *Memorandum of Conversation – NSC Meeting – Chile (NSSM 97)* at 2, dated 6 November 1970, declassified in 2000, available at www.gwu.edu/~nsarchiv/news/20001113/701106.pdf, accessed 1 March 2013 (referencing Secretary of Defense Melvin Laird).

[34] G Grandin, Empire's Workshop: Latin America, The United States, and the Rise of the New Imperialism (New York, Henry Holt and Company, 2006) 59–60; W Bello, Dilemmas of Domination: The Unmaking of the American Empire (New York, Metropolitan Books, 2005) 16.

[35] Huntington and Nelson (n 30) 23, 25–26.

[36] O'Shaughnessy (n 23) 38 (stating that there was substantial political support across the political spectrum for nationalising Chilean copper mines in July 1971); Davis (n 15) 175 (noting that 100% of the Chilean

In September 1973 the Chilean military bombed the presidential palace and killed scores of occupants, and General Pinochet assumed control, declared martial law, vowed to exterminate Marxism, formed a 13-member military cabinet, progressively tightened controls over society,[37] and followed a strict free market approach[38] to reverse Allende's programmes. Soon after the coup, the military government started receiving financial aid from several countries, especially the United States, and multilateral financial institutions,[39] which was a drastic turnabout because the Nixon administration went on a 'campaign to starve Allende of foreign loans'.[40] Thus, there was US support for the Pinochet regime, purportedly grounded in geopolitical reasons on the fight against communism,[41] as happened with other Latin America countries.[42]

D Argentina

During the early 1970s Argentina faced protests, riots, kidnappings, insurgent attacks on businesses, and government instability.[43] In October 1973 Juan D Perón, who had previously led governments that favoured economic redistribution policies, became president for the third time with 62 per cent of the vote and there was an assumption that his presence would quell unrest, but he died of a heart attack less than a year after taking office.[44] With left-wing and right-wing violence and dire economic conditions, on 24 March 24 1976 a military junta banned political parties, took control over the mass media, dismissed Congress, and appointed military officers as legislative and judicial officials, and eventually opened Argentina's oil reserves to foreign investment[45] and implemented capitalist economic ordering by force.[46]

United States officials were privy to the events leading to the coup in Argentina and recognised the danger of human rights abuses. Six weeks before the coup, the US Ambassador to Argentina reported to the Secretary of State that 'the Military Planning Group' in Argentina was asked 'to prepare a study and make recommendations as to how the future military government can avoid or minimize the sort of problems the Chilean and Uruguayan gov[ernments] are having with the United States over the human rights

Congress approved nationalisation of mining and they passed a general nationalisation and indemnification law on 31 December 1970).

[37] Davis (n 15) 184, 186, 196; N Roht-Arriaza and L Gibson, 'The Developing Jurisprudence on Amnesty' (1998) 20 *Human Rights Quarterly* 846–47.

[38] L Baldez and J Carey, 'Budget Procedure and Fiscal Restraint in Posttransition Chile' in S Haggard and M McCubbins (eds), *Presidents, Parliaments, and Policy* (Cambridge, Cambridge University Press, 2001) 115.

[39] A Cassese, 'Study of the Impact of Foreign Economic Aid and Assistance on Respect for Human Rights in Chile', E/CN.4/Sub.2/412 (1978) vol III, 5.

[40] O'Shaughnessy (n 23) 137.

[41] Heinz and Frühling (n 2) 585.

[42] J Dinges, 'Green Light-Red Light: Henry Kissinger's Two-Track Approach to Human Rights During the "Condor Years" in Chile and Argentina' in C Arnson (ed), *Argentina–United States Bilateral Relations: An Historical Perspective and Future Challenges* (Washington DC, Woodrow Wilson International Center for Scholars, 2003) 59–76.

[43] Roht-Arriaza and Gibson (n 37) 856.

[44] Davis (n 15) 113–15.

[45] ibid, 113–19.

[46] See generally H Verbitsky and JP Bohoslavsky (eds), *Cuentas pendientes. Los cómplices económicos de la dictadura* (Buenos Aires, Siglo XXI, 2013).

issue'.[47] United States Department of State transcripts, dated two days before the coup, quote officials discussing that the coup would be in the US interest, that it would make Argentina 'governable,' and that months earlier the officials had 'worked out as intermediaries a sensible program for international assistance, using private banks and monetary institutions'.[48] Kissinger explained: 'Whatever chance they have, they will need a little encouragement from us'.[49]

E Generalisations on the US Administrations

In August 1976 the US Department of State discussed regional trends and stated that the regimes in Argentina, Brazil, Bolivia, Chile, Paraguay and Uruguay felt that they were embattled by international Marxism and terrorism and that the military suppression across these countries was united in eradicating subversion.[50] United States officials did not cease providing financial support to the neoliberal military regimes[51] and officials affirmed that the United States was a beneficiary of right-wing generals who were reportedly battling those who would tilt towards the Soviets and Cubans, while also expressing concern about the human rights abuses.[52]

Congress also intensified regard for human rights shortly after military regimes displaced democracy in Uruguay and Chile. Congress stipulated in the US Foreign Assistance Act of 1974, that, except in 'extraordinary circumstances', military aid to governments that were involved in 'consistent patterns of gross violations of internationally recognized human rights' had to be reduced and eventually extinguished.[53] This was reaffirmed in 1976.[54] Congress recognised the problems and there was fierce political conflict over issues involving US alliances with dictatorships, but significant change required a turnover in the executive branch.

[47] US Dept of State, 'Memo from Ambassador Hill for ARA/Acting Assistant Secretary, Subject: Military Take Cognizance of Human Rights Issue', 16 February 1976, at www.gwu.edu/~nsarchiv/NSAEBB/NSAEBB185/19760216%20Military%20Take%20Cognizance%20of%20Human%20Rights%20Issue%2000009FF0.pdf, accessed 1 March 2013.

[48] US Dept of State, 'Secretary of State Henry Kissinger Staff Meeting Transcripts,' 26 March 1976, 20–21, at www.gwu.edu/~nsarchiv/NSAEBB/NSAEBB185/19760326%20Secretary%20of%20Stet%20Kissinger%20Chariman%20apgesl%201-39%20-%20fullpdf, accessed 1 March 2013.

[49] ibid.

[50] US Dept of State, 'Harry W. Shlaudeman memo to the Secretary,' ARA Monthly Report (July) 3 August 1976, 1, 3, www.gwu.edu/~nsarchiv/NSAEBB/NSAEBB133/19760610%20Memorandum%20of%20Conversation%20clean.pdf, accessed 1 March 2013.

[51] S Kaufman, *Plans Unraveled: The Foreign Policy of the Carter Administration* (DeKalb, Northern Illinois University Press, 2008) 29; D Sheinin, *Argentina and the United States* (Athens, University of Georgia Press, 2006) 161–63.

[52] US Dept of State (n 50) 11 ('The use of bloody counter-terrorism by these regimes threatens their increasing isolation from the West and the opening of deep ideological divisions among the countries of the hemisphere').

[53] Foreign Assistance Act of 1974, Pub L No 93-559, § 46, 88 Stat 1795, 1815–16 (adding § 502B to the Foreign Assistance Act of 1961).

[54] International Security Assistance and Arms Exports Act of 1976, Pub L No 94-329, § 301(a) 90 Stat 729, 748–50 (amending § 502B of the Foreign Assistance Act of 1961).

III CARTER'S INITIATIVES: POLITICAL AND FINANCIAL MESSAGES TO LATIN AMERICAN DICTATORSHIPS

A American Values

If events fester in the American political landscape and generate a gulf between reality and American cultural values relating to democracy, liberty, equality, checks on government, and legitimate rule of law, there can be inherent disharmony, backlash, conflict, credibility gaps and demand for political change.[55] From the early- to mid-1970s, Americans were outraged over a prolonged war in Vietnam that cost upwards of $150 billion and economic adversity with the oil crisis. The public was also shocked over President Nixon's progressing impeachment proceedings and resignation after the Watergate scandal, misuse of executive secrecy, and spying on and harassment of innocent Americans. Americans were abruptly awakened to events in US foreign policy with the publication of Congress's Church Committee investigations in 1975–76, which exposed CIA involvement in assassinations, controversial global covert operations, ties to abusive foreign regimes, and attempts to weaken unfriendly governments; and the Rockefeller Commission Report in 1975, which reported more CIA scandal.

Polls revealed that between 1966 and 1976, American confidence in the executive branch dropped from 41 per cent to 11 per cent, for Congress from 42 per cent to 9 per cent, for the US military from 62 per cent to 23 per cent, and for companies from 55 per cent to 16 per cent.[56] The moral outrage led to a general precipitous decline in respect for authority[57] and set the milieu for the election of Democrat Jimmy Carter. Carter apparently believed that reversing this climate of American cynicism and controversial foreign policy required sustaining democratic values and human rights against abuse of power.

The public and open work of numerous non-governmental organisations and international efforts successfully raised awareness of human rights violations in several Latin American countries.[58] Human rights were strongly incorporated into US foreign policy. President Carter delivered an address to the Organization of American States within three months of taking office and announced that he would be departing from the previous administrations and affixing

> a high regard for the individuality and the sovereignty of each Latin American and Caribbean nation, . . . our respect for human rights, . . . [and] our desire to press forward on the great issues which affect the relations between the developed and the developing nations.[59]

[55] Huntington (n 32) 11–14, 34, 36–41. Drastic changes may be demanded in the electoral system. W Burnham, 'American Politics in the 1970s: Beyond Party?' in W Chambers and W Burnham (eds), *The American Party Systems: Stages of Political Development* (Oxford, Oxford University Press, 1975) 316–17 (noting that a 'critical realignment' has been called 'a major change rooted in the behavior of critically large minorities of American voters which durably alters electoral coalitions, the shape of election outcomes, and the flow of public policy').

[56] Huntington (n 32) 175.

[57] ibid, 174, 181–84.

[58] See L Schoultz, *Human Rights and United States Policy Toward Latin America* (Princeton, Princeton University Press, 1981) 311.

[59] R Fagan, 'The Carter Administration and Latin America: Business as Usual?' (1978) *Foreign Policy*, www.foreignaffairs.com/articles/31971/richard-r-fagen/the-carter-administration-and-latin-america-business-as-usual#, accessed 1 March 2013.

Following the US Department of State's official acknowledgment that human rights violations were occurring in other nations (with special attention given to Argentina),[60] and after instituting a policy for dealing with human rights violations that differed significantly from that of the Ford administration,[61] the US government and Congress[62] adopted several financial measures seeking to prevent these abuses. However, there are difficulties in implementing restrictions on financial assistance to change policy due to the three general dimensions of lending. There are direct official loans and guarantees from US government and quasi-public entities (Overseas Private Investment Corporation (OPIC) and the Export-Import Bank of the United States (Ex-Im Bank)), multilateral institutions, and private entities. As they are not under the total control of the government, the latter two actors can be (and actually were) more difficult to curtail.

B Direct Leverage: Official Loans[63]

The Carter administration promoted an aggressive foreign policy towards Latin American regimes with the specific objective of using diplomatic pressure and conditional assistance to reduce human rights violations.[64] This led to a policy of explicit refusal to grant financial and military aid to the Argentinean dictatorship, which arguably had the goal of provoking political embarrassment and some economic and financial drawbacks in order to force the military government to improve its performance in the human rights field.

The US Congress stated that it was mandatory to deny security assistance to any country with a government that engages in a consistent pattern of gross violations of internationally recognised human rights. On 24 February 1977 the US Secretary of State, Cyrus Vance, announced to the Subcommittee on Foreign Operations of the Senate Appropriations Committee that the government was going to reduce its aid to Argentina,[65] Ethiopia and Uruguay on the basis that gross violations of human rights were being committed in these countries.[66] In 1977 the US Congress prohibited any additional military

[60] US Dept of State, Report to H Comm on Int'l Relations, 94th Cong, 'Human Rights and US Policy: Argentina, Haiti, Indonesia, Iran, Peru, and The Philippines' 5 (Comm Print 1976) 5; US Dept of State, Report to Subcomm on Foreign Assistance of the S Comm on Foreign Relations, 95th Cong, Human Rights Reports (Comm Print 1977) 106–08.

[61] US Dept of State, Memorandum of Conversation: US–Argentine Relations (6 October 1976) (on file with authors).

[62] With the change of the political composition of the US Congress, in 1974 members of Congress had already started focusing on human rights issues. See R Johnson, *Congress and the Cold War* (Cambridge, Cambridge University Press, 2005).

[63] This section draws on previous case studies carried out by Juan Pablo Bohoslavsky and other researchers published in S Michalowski (ed), *Corporate Accountability in the Context of Transitional Justice* (London, Routledge, 2013) 189–207; (2010) 8 *Journal of International Criminal Justice* 829–50; and (2010) 23 *Harvard Human Rights* Journal 157–203.

[64] C Vance, 'Human Rights and Foreign Policy' (1977) 7 *Georgia Journal of International and Comparative Law Quarterly* 223.

[65] On the role of Carter's foreign policy in Argentina, see generally A Avenburg, 'Entre la presión y el apoyo a los *moderados*. La política de derechos humanos de Carter y el régimen militar argentino (1976–1978)', Masters thesis, FLACSO/Argentina, Universidad de San Andrés, Universidad de Barcelona, 2009, available at www.flacso.org.ar/uploaded_files/Publicaciones/Disertacion_Alejandro.Avenburg-05-06.pdf, accessed 1 March 2013.

[66] Foreign Assistance and Related Programs Appropriations for Fiscal Year 1978: Hearing Before the Subcomm on Foreign Operations of the S Comm on Appropriations, 95th Cong 9 (1977) (testimony of Cyrus Vance, US Secretary of State).

aid to Argentina in the way of donations, credits, guaranteed loans, sales and export licences, effective from 30 September 1978 onwards.[67] The need to incorporate human rights as a condition for military aid was stated more clearly in the International Security Assistance Act of 1978.[68] It appears that pressure did correlate with a reduction in human rights violations in Argentina by 1978–79, but the vicious treatment of the many thousands who were killed, disappeared and imprisoned was so appalling[69] and efficient during the first years,[70] that it is difficult to fathom that numbers could worsen.[71]

At the end of 1978 OPIC had decided to not grant insurance coverage to those companies that wanted to invest in Argentina and Uruguay, precisely because of the serious violations of human rights known to be taking place there.[72] By August 1978 the US State Department had withheld an estimated US$1.25 billion in non-military exports to Argentina based on human rights violations, including eleven Ex-Im Bank transactions valued at nearly US$600 million.[73]

The aforementioned regulations tying economic aid to human rights, coupled with widespread knowledge of Uruguay's human rights abuses,[74] led the Secretary of State to announce reductions in US military assistance to Uruguay in 1977.[75] The United States channelled its financial assistance to Uruguay exclusively through projects that directly benefited the poor.[76] By 1978 the Ex-Im Bank regularly refused to consider loan applications from Uruguay, informing the government that the refusals were based on human rights grounds.[77] OPIC had also adopted the policy of refusing to consider insurance

[67] Act of 4 August 1977, Pub L No 95-92, § 11, 91 Stat 614, 619–20; see also Schoultz (n 58) 260; Cong Research Serv, Report to S Comm. on Foreign Relations, 96th Cong, 'Human Rights and US Foreign Assistance: Experiences and Issues in Policy Implementation' (1977–1978) 106 (Comm Print 1979).

[68] International Security Assistance Act of 1978, Pub L No 95–384, § 6, 92 Stat 730, 731–32 (amending § 502B of the Foreign Assistance Act of 1961).

[69] While human rights organisations estimate that there were 30,000 disappeared during the dictatorship in Argentina, official records and the report 'Nunca Más' elaborated by the National Commission on the Disappearance of Persons in 1984 estimate there were between 9,000 and 13,000 disappeared.

[70] In June 1976, Argentine Foreign Minister Admiral Cesar Augusto Guzzetti defended the use of military rule to suppress terrorism and subversion and Secretary of State Henry Kissinger warned of international condemnation and using military rule but noted: *'If there are things that have to be done, you should do them quickly. But you should get back quickly to normal procedures'* Memorandum of conversation, Santiago de Chile, 6 June 1976, 9–10, available at www2.gwu.edu/~nsarchiv/NSAEBB/NSAEBB133/19760610%20 Memorandum%20of%20Conversation%20clean.pdf, accessed 1 March 2013.

[71] US Dept of State, 'Memo Re: Disappearance Numbers' 27 December 1978, at www.gwu.edu/~nsarchiv/ NSAEBB/NSAEBB185/19781227%20Disappearance%20Numbers%200000A8B1.pdf, accessed 1 March 2013; Luis Felipe Alemparte Díaz to DINA Intelligence Official Enrique Arancibia Clavel, 'Re: Actividades de Massera: Massara en Londres, Londres 3/4 de Julío de 1978', A-8, www.gwu.edu/~nsarchiv/NSAEBB/ NSAEBB185/full%20%5BReport%20on%20Argentina%20disappeared%5D.pdf, accessed 1 March 2013 (Argentine military estimating that the number killed or disappeared between 1975 and July 1978 was approximately 22,000). Davis (n 15) 122–23.

[72] Schoultz (n 58) 311, 320.

[73] Memorandum from Robert Pastor to Zbigniew Brzezinski, US Nat'l Sec Advisor, 31 August 1978, reprinted in Declassified Documents Reference System (Doc No CK3100116847).

[74] Between 1973 and 1984, there were at least 172 cases of detained-disappeared, 4,933 people were arrested and imprisoned for political reasons and subjected to legal processes, while 3,700 were arrested and imprisoned without any legal process. See Universidad de la República, 'Investigación histórica sobre la dictadura y el terrorismo de Estado en el Uruguay (1973–1985)' (Montevideo, Ed Cruz del Sur-Tradinco-CEIU, 2008); and Uruguay's Commission for Peace (COMPAZ) 'Informe Final' (Montevideo, 10 April 2003).

[75] T Phelps, 'US Cuts Foreign Aid in Rights Violations; South Korea Exempt', *New York Times*, 25 February 1977.

[76] International Development and Food Assistance Act of 1975, Pub L No 94-161, Sec 310, 89 Stat 849 (codified at 22 USC Sec 215n 1976).

[77] Schoultz (n 58) 311, 320.

applications for investments in countries engaged in egregious human rights violations, including Uruguay.[78]

Under condemnation by human rights organisations and institutions, Uruguay did ostensibly improve its human rights record, the number of political prisoners dropped significantly and the United States restored some financial aid.[79] The role played by American representatives and senators, US Assistant Secretary of State for Human Rights Patricia Derian,[80] and private organisations operating in the United States and Europe were key not only to publicising the human rights abuses perpetrated in Uruguay, but also to implementing governmental actions in order to stop these crimes.

Over the duration of the Chilean dictatorship, there were about 3,200 deaths and disappearances and more than 27,000 political prisoners and victims of torture.[81] As international and US congressional concerns over human rights violations grew from 1976 onwards, official financial and military aid decreased dramatically.[82] The United States opposed granting loans to Chile because of its already disastrous record on human rights.[83] Following a similar position adopted by the Federal Republic of Germany,[84] the Netherlands,[85] Italy,[86] and Norway,[87] the US government suspended most forms of bilateral economic aid to Chile, expressing disapproval of human rights abuses by the Pinochet government.[88] These measures taken by the United States reflect an understanding that there was a crucial relationship between financial support and the (economic and political) capacities of the Chilean dictatorship to not only survive as a regime, but to actually execute its now famous campaign of mass human rights abuses against its own population.

However, Chile and Argentina turned to Western European suppliers and Israel when the United States imposed arms embargoes.[89] Also, some countries continued to grant aid to Chile, saying it was for concrete humanitarian or developmental goals, but the ways in which the government spent these funds did not, in fact, benefit the needy.[90] Assistance

[78] ibid.

[79] I Morris, 'Torture in Uruguay' (18 March 1976) *New York Review of Books*, www.nybooks.com/articles/archives/1976/mar/18/torture-in-uruguay/?pagination=false, accessed 1 March 2013; Davis (n 15) 57–58.

[80] See US Dept of State, 'Country Reports on Human Rights Practices for 1979 and 1980', submitted to the Committee on Foreign Relations, US Senate, and Committee of Foreign Affairs, US House of Representatives, 4 February 1980 and 2 February 1980.

[81] See Informe Rettig, 'Comisión Nacional de la Verdad y la Reconciliacion', Ministerio del Interior, 1991, available at www.ddhh.gov.cl/ddhh_rettig.html, accessed 1 March 2013; and Informe de la Comisión Nacional sobre Política y Tortura, 'Comisión Asesora para la Calificación de Detenidos Desaparecidos, Ejecutados Políticos y Victimas de Prisión Política y Tortura', created by law N8 20.405, 2011, available online at www.indh.cl/informacion-comision-valech, accessed 1 March 2013.

[82] Heinz and Frühling (n 3) 520.

[83] A detail of US negative votes and abstentions on multilateral development banks loans for human rights reasons, in JM Griesgraber, 'Implementation by the Carter Administration of Human Rights Legislation Affecting Latin America' (unpublished PhD dissertation, Georgetown University, 1983) (on file with authors) 368.

[84] Report of the Economic and Social Council: Protection of Human Rights in Chile, Report of the Secretary General, 32 UN GAOR (Agenda Item 12) 9, UN Doc A/32/234 (1977).

[85] ibid, 12–13.

[86] Cassese (n 39) 407.

[87] ibid, 409.

[88] Center for International Policy, 'Chile: An Analysis of Human Rights Violations and United States Security Assistance and Economic Programmes', 1–2 July 1978.

[89] R Cohen, 'Human Rights Diplomacy: The Carter Administration and the Southern Cone' (1982) 4 *Human Rights Quarterly* 233.

[90] Cassese (n 40) Vol III, 11; Vol IV, 15.

was often used by the government to replace national resources, which were diverted to other ends, including that of financing the apparatus of repression.[91]

C Multilateral Financial Diplomacy

Congress expanded its original Harkin initiative[92] and ordered US representatives in multilateral and development banks to vote against the provision of loans for countries known to be violating the fundamental human rights of their citizens.[93] This initiative appears to have been the primary motivation for the US government to take such a strong stance against the violations occurring in Latin American countries and also explains why the government abstained or voted against the numerous multilateral loans requested by these military regimes.[94]

In 1977 the United States raised the human rights issue in discussions within multilateral financial institutions when these institutions were faced with deciding whether to grant loans to Southern Cone authoritarian governments. This policy of rejecting multilateral loans for political and legal reasons was explained in the following terms: the United States felt it had to use its voice and voting power in the six multilateral development banks to which it belonged at the time in order to protect human rights. This policy included a decision to open channels of assistance to those countries whose governments were not involved in consistent patterns of gross violations of human rights.[95] The United States repeatedly voted against such credits out of human rights concerns.[96] Nevertheless, the United States was outvoted, and these loans went forward.[97]

D Private Banks

From 1976 onwards, official creditors were replaced by private multinational banks, which started lending enormous sums to Latin American dictatorships with no stated regard for the potential impact of these loans.[98] In 1973 the Chilean public external debt was US$2.86 billion, US$6.27 billion in 1979, and US$14.34 billion in 1983. In Argentina

[91] Cassese (n 39) vol IV, 24.

[92] International Development and Food Assistance Act of 1975, Pub L No 94-161, § 310, 89 Stat 849, 860. This legislation added Section 116 to the Foreign Assistance Act 1961, prohibiting economic aid to countries in which gross human rights violations were committed, unless this aid directly benefited the needy people, ibid; see also Schoultz (n 58) note 123, 195.

[93] Act of May 31, 1976, Pub L No 94-302, § 211, 90 Stat 591, 595; Act of October 3, 1977, Pub L No 95-118, § 701, 91 Stat 1067, 1069–71.

[94] Schoultz (n 58) 296–98.

[95] Act of October 3, 1977, Pub L No 95-118, § 701, 91 Stat 1067, 1069–71; see also International Development Institutions Authorizations-1977: Hearing on HR 5262 Before the Subcomm on Int'l Development Institutions and Finance of the H Comm on Banking, Finance and Urban Affairs, 95th Cong 2 (1977).

[96] The United States opposed 12 of 13 loan requests made by Uruguay to international financial institutions during 1977–80. Schoultz (n 58) 297–98.

[97] Cohen (n 89) 227.

[98] Cassese (note 39) vol III, 67. As the article 'How Chile Reappeared on the Tombstones' by C Meynell said in *Euromoney* in its edition of June 1977, 101–5, 'Both countries [Chile and Argentina] have arguably staged an economic turnaround which appears to have impressed the international banking fraternity. Although the Carter tirade against those countries infringing Human Rights gave somewhat sticky start to the development of the two countries as a much needed sink-hole for excess banking liquidity, it is plain that doubts over the wisdom of lending to countries that contravene Human Rights are fast being dismissed'.

the same type of debt was US$4.021 billion in 1975, US$9.960 billion in 1979 and US$26.341 billion in 1982. And in Uruguay the public external debt was US$469 million in 1973, US$1.416 billion in 1979 and US$3.287 billion in 1985. In the cases of Argentina and Chile private external debt also grew considerably, but in the three cases most of the increasing debt was borrowed from private banks.[99] This indebtedness allowed these countries not only to avoid the embarrassing process of renegotiation of their external debts but also to buy key loyalties and support from their domestic elites and maintain an effective and expensive repressive apparatus. For a certain period, these monies contributed to the consolidation of these regimes.

More concretely, in the case of Chile, the Institute for Policy Studies submitted a report for the Congressional Record in 1978 and explained,

> Without continual inflow of credit from private banks, Chile will either be forced to return to the Paris Club to seek renegotiation – where it will certainly be held accountable for its massive human rights violations – or to swallow a new dose of austerity like the one Pinochet and Cauas introduced in April, 1975. But with the Pinochet regime under attack from both the right and the left, and with the political division within the military junta. . .greater than ever, it would be political suicide for Pinochet to ask a country wracked by poverty and economic austerity to endure another severe depression.[100]

The American government expressly warned banks that lending money to Chile was eroding US foreign policy, which considered human rights to be a crucial factor when deciding whether to financially support a regime.[101] The Chairman of the US House Banking Committee officially told six of the main multinational banks lending to Chile that their actions appeared inconsistent with standards intended to prevent banking practices from interfering with public interest and thus that he hoped they would make public a full explanation.[102] Leaders of the banking community argued that financial institutions should not be impeded from doing their 'normal business' regardless of the governments they were engaged with.[103]

This stubborn reluctance by private multinational banks to be held in the least bit accountable for the consequences of their loans helped to prompt an unusual step by the United States. In 1978 Senator Edward Kennedy introduced the Foreign Bank Loans Disclosure Act[104] requiring disclosure of bank loans made to known human rights

[99] On data from IMF, BAI, WB and Banco Central de Chile.

[100] S 3631-Foreign Loans Disclosure Act of 1978, 124 Cong Rec 37677 1978.

[101] 'Reuss: Rights Policy Not Helped by Loans To Chile From Banks', *The Washington Post*, 13 April 1978, at A19.

[102] 'Several US banks Accused of Undercutting Policy on Chile', *The Washington Post*, 12 April 1978.

[103] For example, during his trip to Argentina in March 1979, David Rockefeller – then chair of US bank Chase Manhattan – made a public speech criticising President Carter's human rights policy and stressing that 'it is not fair to use trade as an instrument to force other nations to do things in the way we think they must be done, because this does not benefit the human rights policy and, in addition, is detrimental to our economy and the one of other countries', 'Rockefeller opinó sobre el plan económico', *Clarín*, 9 March 1979. He went even further by explaining that limiting or curtailing trade as the penalty for non-conformance with human rights standards was not only a wrong-minded approach, but also, at base, antidemocratic as it tried to impose American values on other countries, see D Rockefeller, 'America's Future: A Question of Strength and Will', *The Atlantic Community Quarterly*, Spring 1979, 14–19; and D Rockefeller, 'In Pursuit of a Consistent Foreign Policy: The Trilateral Commission', *Vital Speeches of the Day*, 15 June 15, 517–20. In 1978, the chairman of Lloyds Bank in London responded to criticism for granting loans to the Chilean dictatorship, admitting that this regime was repressive, but also alleging that lending money to Chile was not banned. See 'Lloyds bounces Chile protest', *The Guardian*, 31 March 1978.

[104] S 3631-Foreign Loans Disclosure Act of 1978, (n 100) 37676.

violators. In proposing this act, Senator Kennedy affirmed the fact that 'one of the guiding principles of [US] foreign policy is that except in cases of humanitarian assistance, we shall give no aid to gross violators of human rights'.[105] It also led to discussion on the Senate floor about the capacity of various Latin American dictatorships to retain their stronghold, with his colleague, Senator Church, commenting that 'massive funding such as [what Hanover Trust provided to Chile's Pinochet] may be what enabled five Latin American governments . . . to continue their anti-democratic practices and violations of human rights'.[106] Nonetheless, massive private funds were poured into Latin American dictatorships.

IV CARTER'S CONTRIBUTION TO THE CURRENT DEBATE ON FINANCIAL COMPLICITY

From the perspective of international law, President Carter's initiatives contributed to the current debate on financial complicity by showing that it is politically, economically and legally possible to promote human rights in international relations through financial means. The linking of lending policies to human rights in the cases of the dictatorships in Argentina, Chile and Uruguay – particularly the Carter administration's effort to ensure that aid had a positive impact by endeavouring to abate widespread human rights violations – demonstrated that financial aid can have a positive or negative impact on the human rights situation on recipient countries, depending on the concrete circumstances.[107] Carter's approach involved navigating the interpretable worldview and philosophical inclinations of the previous administrations and elevating human rights principles that may have already been binding law, but because Carter and Congress did not impose penalties or restrictions on banks, market considerations prevailed over human rights.

With respect to loosening the fixated philosophical worldview of the previous administrations, Carter reoriented US foreign policy away from *realism* and its assumptions of high risk from potential adversaries[108] and neglect of international law[109] to a more *liberalist* view of international relations that supports cooperation, the efficacy of international law,[110] and respect for human rights, which are positions that are also characteristic of the collective endeavours of international institutions with their high regard for international law, diversification of member interest, and relatively high level of transparency. Consistent with heightening the priority of international human rights law, President Carter did not believe that US foreign policy should finance or promote financing to sustain illegitimate regimes.[111] Nonetheless, if financial assistance is not made contingent

[105] ibid.

[106] ibid.

[107] Cassese (n 39) vol I, 3, 18.

[108] J Mearsheimer, *The Tragedy of Great Power Politics* (New York, WW Norton, 2001) 30–36; K Waltz, *Theory of International Politics* (New York, Random House, 1979) (constructing balance of power theory in which states pursue power-increasing strategies).

[109] C Joyner, *International Law in the 21st Century: Rules for Global Governance* (Lanham MD, Rowman & Littlefield, 2005) 5; O Schachter, 'In Defense of International Rules on the Use of Force' (1986) 53 *University of Chicago Law Review* 119.

[110] J Owen, IV, 'International Law and the "Liberal Peace"' in G Fox and B Roth (eds), *Democratic Governance and International Law* (Cambridge, Cambridge University Press, 2000) 343–44.

[111] Anthony Lake to Cyrus Vance, 'The Human rights Policy: An Interim Assessment', 16 January 1978, I, 10, White House Central Files, Human Rights, Box HU-I-JCL.

on elevating the rule of law, illegitimate regimes can be strengthened and perpetuated, making domestic[112] and international actors complicit in the violation of human rights and undermining democratic choices of the populace. Consequently, the Carter administration and Congress did impose restrictions and cut official aid, and utilised diplomacy to punish human rights violations, but bilateral (from other governments), multilateral and private financial assistance was still provided to authoritarian governments. Why did private funding in particular, since it was the source of most aid, recklessly flow into Southern Cone dictatorships during the Carter administration, even impairing US foreign policy and endangering the American banking industry?[113]

Multinational commercial banks played a leading role in sovereign financing due to the phenomenal development of the Eurodollar market, the recycling of petrodollars, and a market-based American legal system that facilitated loans to the countries in the southern hemisphere, including dictatorships.[114] From a purely financial point of view, banks needed to lend their petrodollars deposits, and the loans were lucrative: banks lent massive amounts at variable interest rates pegged to the three- or six-month London Interbank Offer Rate (LIBOR) to regimes that considered *pacta sunt servanda* an absolute commitment, whatever the future cost to the debtor populations.[115] Even as knowledge of illegitimacy of the regimes aggregated from the work of the media, human rights groups and the US Congress, many private financial institutions were involved in providing loans to military dictators that resulted in multiplying Argentina's total national debt by six in eight years, Chile's debt by nearly five in 18 years, and Uruguay's debt by over eight in 13 years, when an average annual growth rate for a healthy developing economy might be 4 per cent.[116] In turn, these same debts consolidated these regimes, with all the human suffering that this meant. It was neither the people's choice in the Southern Cone to be subjected to egregious crimes, nor to be subjected to mounting debt that helped their executioners.

There was even interest advocacy inside the United States to use Latin American buying power and demand to stimulate the domestic economy and exports.[117] Foreign investors and lenders may be attracted to countries with vicious human rights violations if suppression lowers risk by ensuring the stability and enforcement of investment rules and an amenable political environment. At a time when the dictatorships were still in power, Cassese remarked that 'Foreign economic assistance to a great extent serves to prop up

[112] In 2013, the Argentinean Ministry of Defense discovered a 359-page document in its archives that was submitted by the Argentinean Banks Association (ADEBA) to the military government in 1978. The document recognizes the depth and degree of abuse and offered social, economic and political recommendations that would probably not pass any respectable basic human rights test, then or now. The report is ADEBA, 'Presentación atinente a los antecedentes, fundamentos y alcances para un esquema de proyecto nacional', 3 April 1978, Buenos Aires. See R Montes, 'El documento doctrinario que la cámara de banqueros entregó a la Junta Militar', *La Capital*, 11 November 2013. The document ostensibly acknowledges, in significant detail, the importance of using financial resources to sustain the regime and its desired economic policies.

[113] C Lichtenstein, 'The US Response to the International Debt Crisis: The International Lending Supervision Act of 1983' (1985 25(2) *Virginia Journal of International Law* 401–35.

[114] W Darity and B Horn, *The Loan Pushers. The Role of Commercial Banks in the International Debt Crisis* (Cambridge MA, Ballinger Publishing Co, 1988).

[115] 'The Chilean pay their bills', said an official of the US Bureau for Latin America, Agency for International Development, during the course of a favourable report on the Pinochet government, Subcommittee on International Organizations, 'Chile: The Status of Human Rights', 94th Cong, 2d Sess, April–May 1976, 36.

[116] World Bank, 'IV. Economic Growth Rates', see www.worldbank.org/depweb/english/beyond/global/chapter4.html, accessed 1 March 2013 (placing the average annual GDP growth rates for low-income and middle-income countries at between 3.8% and 4.2% over the 1965–99 period).

[117] See Schoultz (n 58) 301–43.

the government authorities in Chile' and the 'economic policy fosters repression of basic human rights because implementation is only possible without dissent'.[118] As private funds helped to consolidate the regimes, social demands were repressed and there were more favourable conditions to attract additional funding and investments. Funding and aiding dictatorships that are not beholden to the people but maintain power by violating human rights may promote the security of investments and assure more profit from aggregating loans, but banks and investors should not make decisions solely out of self-interest even if penalties and punishment seem improbable.[119] It is further possible that cutting aid and loans can potentially destabilise the regime and increase repression,[120] which would certainly be unfavourable, but continued support for short-term stabilisation should not justify the existence of the dictatorship or its criminal acts and may not be in the long-term interest of the population.

It is not clear that profitability considerations should necessarily have prevailed over human rights, even in the 1970s. The Southern Cone military regimes were violating virtually every provision in the Universal Declaration of Human Rights, including prohibitions against torture, deprivation of life and liberty, arbitrary arrest and detention, denial of the right of conscience and political rights, and the right to choose government.[121] The United Nations Charter guarantees the right to self-determination and prohibits illegal interference in the political sovereignty of the nation.[122] Did external financial and military support to the military regimes embody a form of outside intervention and assistance that violated these binding principles at the time the regimes came to power and terminated democracy, or were they transgressed later to the extent that support continued to subdue public will and facilitate severe human rights oppression, imposition of lasting debt obligations on entire countries, and other abominable repercussions? The Nixon and Ford administrations, prior to Carter, did financially support the regimes and did not oppose multilateral and private bank lending to these dictatorships,[123] pursuant to the assumption that they were sustaining regimes that suppressed communism. Carter dropped the previous worldview inclination and sought to halt official aid and warned about the injurious impact of financing regimes that arguably were not entitled to assistance that could be used to continue oppression. This shift indirectly ennobled the self-determination rights of the people against regimes imposing their own will.

While the Nixon and Ford administrations did not intricately incorporate human rights into foreign policy, there are reasons to believe that elevating and respecting human rights could be a necessary underlying condition to ascertain the legitimate governing authority under the United Nations Charter's right to self-determination. After all, the United Nations Charter presumably became binding international law upon adoption[124]

[118] A Cassese, 'Foreign Economic Assistance and Respect for Civil and Political Rights: Chile – A Case Study' (1979 14 *Texas International Law Review* 261.

[119] ibid, 261.

[120] I Nixon, 'Economic Sanctions and Autocratic Repression', Masters thesis, Georgetown University, Washington DC, 12 April 2012, available at http://repository.library.georgetown.edu/bitstream/handle/10822/557778/Nixon_georgetown_0076M_11634.pdf?sequence=1, accessed 1 March 2013.

[121] Universal Declaration of Human Rights, GA Res 217A (III) UN GAOR, 3d Sess, arts 3, 5, 9, 18–19, UN Doc A/810 (1948).

[122] UN Charter arts 1(2), 2(4).

[123] US Dept of State (n 49) 20–21; Heinz and Frühling (n 2) 313, 357; Cassese (n 39) 5.

[124] UN Charter art 4(1) (stating that UN membership is open to all 'peace-loving states which accept the obligations contained in the present Charter and . . . are able and willing to carry out these obligations'); B Fassbender, *The United Nations Charter as the Constitution of the International Community* (Leiden, Brill

and *jus cogens* norms permit no derogation.[125] If this line of reasoning is compelling, perhaps Carter was merely recognising what was already mandatory. Patricia Derian, then Carter's Assistant Secretary for Human Rights and Humanitarian Affairs at the Department of State, publicly argued that the human rights situation of any given country must be evaluated when deciding whether to grant economic assistance.[126] In her public statement to representatives of the US government at the time, Derian explained the implications that *jus cogens* norms would have on foreign policy:

> The rights about which we are concerned . . . are recognized in the Charter of the United Nations, the UN Universal Declaration of Human Rights and other international agreements and covenants as being universal and applicable throughout the world. The countries of the Western hemisphere have also acknowledged basic human rights in the Charter of the OAS and are now according additional attention to them in the American Convention of Human Rights, which is now ratified by 12 countries and has recently entered into force . . . . [T]he promotion of internationally recognized human rights is in fulfillment of obligations imposed upon us by the international agreements and covenants described above.

The fact that *jus cogens* norms are obligatory should apprise government and non-government actors[127] that are substantially involved with pernicious non-democratic regimes of the reasonableness of financial, commercial and related interactions. Inherent to the self-interested choices of private-sector entities in free market economies and their quest to achieve pecuniary prosperity and diversify risk on behalf of owners of institutions is that it seems unreasonable to have international financial institutions absorbed in contractual relations that bankroll and strengthen regimes involved in assassinations, torture, disappearances and other human rights violations. An integral component to the fundamental discussion on whether there should be responsibility for financial complicity is whether there is a real causal link between (financial) action and damage.[128] The expectation of the causal link should be more conspicuous if there is substantial and general harm deriving from an environment where *jus cogens* violations are regularly occurring. Perhaps glaring human rights violations make it more evident that the US administrations before Carter that promoted loans because of their extra-sensitive threat perceptions should have been ignored; and that the Carter administration's explicit warning that disfavoured aiding the regimes should have been heeded.

Without placing punitive restrictions on the private sector for conducting business relations with the military regimes in Argentina, Chile and Uruguay, the Carter administration

Academic Publishers Inc, 2009) 3, 32–34 (citing authorities that regard the UN Charter as rights and duties consummated by the people of the world, rather than a treaty consummated by states, and as a constitution of binding principles).

[125] Vienna Convention on the Law of Treaties, art 53, 23 May 1969, 1155 UNTS (calling *jus cogens* a 'peremptory norm of general international law . . . accepted and recognized by the international community of States as a whole as a norm from which no derogation is permitted and which can be modified only by a subsequent norm of general international law having the same character'); see also International Law Commission, Study Group, *Fragmentation of International Law: Difficulties Arising From the Diversification and Expansion of International Law*, 189, UN Doc A/CN.4/L682 (13 April 2006) (finalised by Martti Koskenniemi).

[126] Arms Trade in the Western Hemisphere: Hearing Before the Subcomm on Inter-American Affairs of the H Comm on International Relations, 95th Cong (1978) (statement of Patricia M Derian, Assistant Secretary of State for Human Rights and Humanitarian Affairs).

[127] *Paquete Habana* 175 US 677 (1900); *Ware v Hylton* 3 US (3 Dall) 199 (1796); *Kadic v Karadzic*, 70 F.3d 232, 246 (2d Cir 1995).

[128] On the micro and macro causal link between sovereign financing and human rights, see the Introduction in this volume.

asked the banks to reduce their loans to regimes.[129] Even the Congress took a step in this same direction.[130] The hitch is that attempting to enjoin economic decisions *ex ante* or placing punitive restrictions on the private sector could have been regarded as an extreme regulation anathema to free market American values and an initiative that would have imposed significant political costs on the government (in addition to the ones already afforded for the fact of cutting official aid grounded on human rights considerations).[131] Government officials may have surmised that the political messages delivered through the rejection of bilateral and multilateral financial aid would have been sufficient to catalyse positive human rights improvements in the countries. This did place private financial institutions on elevated notice, ostensibly requiring them to conduct heightened due diligence, which was an admonition in addition to the common knowledge of abuse that should already have been possessed even before Carter entered office. Perhaps the question is whether financial institutions should have been cognisant that disbursements would be providing varying degrees of assistance to the crimes of a regime, depending on the terms of the loans, actual or implied knowledge, and the use of the loans.

The Carter presidency provided guidance in another way because US regulations governing lending to authoritarian regimes were passed under the assumption that if aid or loans were granted with the precise objective of building houses for the poorest, for example, that aid would be less likely to adversely impact human rights than loans granted for general spending.[132] This suggests there was a requirement to pay close attention to the specific contractual terms of the financial agreements and the actual use of the funds, so while they avoid consolidating the regime, they seek to reach and actually help the needy people.

Consequently, the Carter administration's human rights policy could have been stronger,[133] and this fact seems to indicate that holistic and broadly agreed responses are needed in order to effectively hamper the financing of authoritarian governments. Carter's foreign policy exclusively focused on political and civil human rights abuses (excluding social and economic rights from its consideration), and this approach ostensibly impaired the effectiveness of the policy. In particular, as social contestation was fed precisely by low incomes and deep inequality, the economic policies of the regimes and their socio-economic implications should also have been seen as a meaningful variable when making diagnoses and deciding whether to grant aid and loans and support or oppose private-sector funding.

V CONCLUDING REMARKS

The impact of Carter's foreign policy on Latin American dictatorships is not easily assessable. To what extent did this policy improve the overall human rights situation in

[129] See nn 101 and 102.

[130] See nn 104–06.

[131] See, for example, the opposition from organised labour to incorporate human rights considerations into the OPIC procedures because the activities of this agency encouraged the export of jobs, Schoultz (n 58) 315.

[132] J Walczak, 'New Directions in US Food Aid: Human Rights and Economic Development' in V Nanda et al (eds), *Global Human Rights: Public Policies, Comparative Measures and NGO Strategies* (Boulder, Westview Press, 1981) 29–57.

[133] K DeYoung and C Krause, 'Our Mixed Signals On Human Rights In Argentina; Our Mixed Signal On Human Rights', *Washington Post*, 29 October 1978, C1.

these countries? To what extent did it prevent the situation from getting worse? While it is obvious that the financial sanctions did not completely stop the human rights abuses, the international scandal that the US financial policy provoked in international fora and media probably drew attention to what the Latin American regimes were doing to their own populations, hence more monitoring of the situation.[134] Also, there were specific cases in which the US bargaining (financial and political) power facilitated some specific and concrete human rights improvements, such as the case in which the Argentinean military junta agreed to submit to a formal visit from the Inter American Human Rights Commission in order to elaborate a report about the human rights situation, in exchange for US approval of an Ex-Im Bank credit to build a dam.[135]

President Carter endeavoured to drastically alter US policies towards the Southern Cone dictatorships, but the non-holistic approach did not deter private lenders from a number of industrialised countries.[136] The cases in this chapter illustrated that even when a powerful state decides to use bilateral and multilateral aid as an incentive to promote human rights, a broad consensus of the international community is needed in order for the initiatives to be effective. The use of sanctions (or withholding of previously granted aid) to modify the actions of foreign regimes proves more difficult to the extent that financial assistance moves from official loans – over which the government has direct control – to multilateral institutions, – over which effective diplomacy must be used to persuade other states – and to private financial institutions, for which domestic regulations and penalties should be adopted and enforced on parent, subsidiary, and branch financial institutions in lending countries. However, domestic financial regulations – as seen in the case of the United States during the Carter administration – face the problem of competition with other legal jurisdictions. Why would one country prohibit private lending to criminal regimes when its neighbour is making fortunes by allowing its financial institutions to do business with these same regimes? At this point, it would seem desirable to have global standards that could be applied to both official and private lenders in order to prevent loans from consolidating criminal regimes.[137]

Yet invoking international law to design and implement a foreign policy that fortifies human rights makes the idea that there is already a universal principle prohibiting financial contributions to criminal regimes very persuasive, particularly when *jus cogens* norms are involved.[138] In this case, non-state actors are bound by these fundamental rules.[139] Actually, there has been a growing foundation to indicate that these international law obligations do impose requirements on transnational, non-governmental actors.[140] This thesis is reinforced by the fact that most legal orders establish responsibility for

[134] D Schmitz and V Walker, 'Jimmy Carter and the Foreign Policy of Human Rights. The Development of a Post-Cold War Policy' (2004) 28(1) *Diplomatic History* 113–43.

[135] M Novaro and A Avenburg, 'La CIDH en Argentina: Entre la democratización y los derechos humanos' (2009) 49(193) *Desarrollo Económico* 61–90.

[136] B Cohen, 'International Debt and Linkage Strategies: Some Foreign-Policy Implications for the United States' (1985) 39(4) *International Organization* 699–727.

[137] In this regard see Lumina's chapter in this volume.

[138] See S Michalowski and JP Bohoslavsky, 'Ius Cogens, Transitional Justice and other Trends of the Debate on Odious Debts. A Response to the World Bank Discussion Paper on Odious Debts' (2010) 48(1) *Columbia Journal of Transnational Law* 62–120.

[139] See generally C Tomuschat and J-M Thouvenin (eds), *The Fundamental Rules of International Legal Order. Jus Cogens and Obligations Erga Omnes* (Leiden, Martinus Nijhoff, 2008).

[140] See Jägers's and Černič's chapters in this volume, and JP Bohoslavsky, 'Tracking Down the Missing Financial Link in Transitional Justice' (2012) 1 *International Human Rights Law Review* 54–92.

complicity.[141] These legal foundations have been a basis for international political initiatives, discussions, negotiations and implementation of economic sanctions by the UN Security Council, and could be a prime focus for more inclusive fora, such as the UN Human Rights Council. Alternatively if the international community fails to implement *ex ante* financial measures to curtail human rights violations, courts will still be open to punish those lenders that did not fulfil basic due diligence human rights standards before disbursing funds to a criminal regime.

The non-existence of explicit prohibitions or punitive measures does not preclude foreign financial entities and multinational corporations from being obliged to make reasonable decisions that respect the populations in which they operate. To the extent that domestic or foreign regimes urge transactions that transgress the rights of the populace, financial institutions should consider those choices cautiously. Private financial firms are not acting 'under color of law' and they do not have sovereign immunity, and even states should not have sovereign immunity to the extent that official acts rise to the level of a *jus cogens* violation.[142]

Carter's foreign financial and human rights policy towards Southern Cone dictatorships substantially contributed to a better understanding of the causal link between sovereign financing and gross human rights violations. This observation has notable implications on whether and how bilateral, multilateral and private lenders should grant aid and loans to authoritarian regimes.

[141] A Ramasastry and R Thompson, 'Commerce, Crime and Conflict: Legal Remedies for Private Sector Liability for Grave Breaches of International Law. A Survey of 16 Countries' (2006) FAFO Institute of Applied International Studies.

[142] On this see A Colangelo, 'Jurisdiction, Immunity, Legality, and *Jus Cogens*' (2013) 14(1) *Chicago Journal of International Law* 54–92.

20

*Engagement, Divestment or Both? Conflicts and Interactions: The Case of the Norwegian Pension Fund**

ANDREAS FOLLESDAL

I INTRODUCTION

IN 2011 MONITOR Group named the Norwegian Government Pension Fund the largest sovereign wealth fund in the world. The Fund merits international attention not only because of its size, but also in terms of its complex mission with regard to responsible investment and the mechanisms it employs in pursuit of this mission. The market value of the Government Pension Fund – Global at the end of 2012 – was 3816 billion kroner (approximately 670 billion USD/514 billion EUR). In 2012 it yielded a total return of 13.42 per cent.[1]

The Norwegian Parliament adopted an Act relating to the Fund in 2005 as a continuation of the Petroleum Fund, which was established in 1990. On the one hand, the Fund is meant to facilitate long-term fiscal policies and help carry the future economic burdens caused by demographic changes combined with declining future oil revenues. The Fund must thus ensure that a reasonable portion of the country's petroleum wealth benefits future generations. It must therefore generate a sound return in the long term.

The Fund has three sources of income: the return on the Fund's assets, the cash flow from petroleum activities that is transferred from the central government budget, and net financial transactions associated with petroleum activities. The transfer of capital from the Fund to the central government budget must be approved by the Norwegian Parliament. The Ministry of Finance delegates responsibility for the operational management of the Fund's international assets to Norges Bank Investment Management (NBIM). This capital is invested in non-Norwegian financial instruments (bonds, equities, money market

* These arguments were first presented at a Conference hosted by the Norwegian Ministry of Finance: 'Investing for the Future' January 16, 2008. I am grateful for comments received at that occasion. I also draw on material published in Cecilia Bailliet and Katja Franko (eds), *Cosmopolitan justice and its discontents* (Milton Park, Routledge, 2011); M Micheletti, A Follesdal, and D Stolle (eds), *Politics, Products, and Markets: Exploring Political Consumerism Past and Present* (New Brunswick, NJ, Transaction Publishers, 2006); and G Nystuen, A Follesdal and O Mestad (eds), *Human Rights, Corporate Complicity and Disinvestment* (Cambridge, Cambridge University Press, 2011).

[1] Norges Bank Investment Management, NBIM, 'Annual Report of the Norwegian Government Pension Fund Global 2012', 2013, www.nbim.no/Global/Reports/2012/Annual%20report/Annual%20report%2012.pdf.

instruments and derivatives) in developed and emerging equity markets and in several currencies for fixed-income investments.

At the same time, the Norwegian Parliament does not want the Fund to contribute to unethical acts or omissions, such as violations of fundamental humanitarian principles, serious violations of human rights, gross corruption or severe environmental damage. It has established two main mechanisms to avoid such complicity. These mechanisms ensure that the Fund is involved in 'Socially Responsible Investing' (SRI) of two distinct kinds:[2] An *activist* approach and a *negative* approach.

The following sections explore these mechanisms and discusses tensions among them, against a historic and current background.

II SHAREHOLDER ENGAGEMENT: HISTORICAL AND RECENT CONTRIBUTIONS

The Fund must exercise its ownership rights by means of active shareholder engagement. The NBIM should thus reflect the UN's Global Compact and the OECD's principles of corporate governance and guidelines for multinational companies. Before turning to these recent initiatives, it is worth recalling that shareholder engagement is not new.

The term 'Socially Responsible Investing' may be new, but moral qualms about investment, and indeed divestment as a response, are old. Appeals to divest from multinational corporations go back to the seventeenth century, against one of the earliest forms of economic globalisation: the international slave trade. Such morally questionable practices have been part of corporations since they began. The first corporation ever to issue shares was the Dutch East India Company, established in 1602. One important source of its profits was slave trade across oceans. In 1696 and 1698 the Philadelphia Yearly Meetings of Friends – Quakers – warned against the slave trade as an investment venture. [3] Their protests in America and Britain served to blacklist some multinational corporations at the time. As the Quakers saw it, the corporations that maintained the slave trade should be shunned for multiple reasons: such trade was inconsistent with the will of God, against minimal standards of justice, and in violation of the golden rule. Even though many Quakers kept slaves, they objected to investment in the slave trade. They eventually came to also condemn the holding of slaves. They employed what social sanctions they could against their fellow believers. The Philadelphia Yearly Meeting in 1758 called on slave-holding Friends to change their ways. They even urged the exclusion of 'anyone who bought or sold slaves from participation in the business affairs of the church'.[4]

The challenges of this early case of socially responsible investing remain to this day: how are we to respond to practices that make us as morally complicit in immoral actions? Furthermore, the slave trade illustrates the coordination problems in the absence of a common authority: the Quakers realised that other traders moved into the market 'over whom we have no gospel authority'.[5]

[2] S Vallentin: 'Socially Responsible Investing: Approaches and Perspectives' in J D Rendtorff (ed), *Værdier, Etik og Socialt Ansvar i Virksomheder - Brudflader og Konvergens* (Roskilde, Center for Værdier i Virksomheder, Institut for samfundsvidenskab og erhvervsøkonomi, RoskildeUniversitetscentrum 2003), 114–21, 117.

[3] T E Drake, *Quakers and Slavery in America* (Gloucester, MA, Peter Smith, 1965) 4.

[4] ibid, 61.

[5] ibid, 65.

Moving to the present practices of the NBIM, its active shareholder engagement is perhaps best understood against the background of political, legal and economic globalisation, and some of the initiatives in response: the UN Global Compact,[6] the UNEP Finance Initiative,[7] and the Principles for Responsible Investment (PRI), developed by institutional investors on the basis of the Global Compact and the UNEP Finance Initiative.[8]

What is new with 'globalisation'? Under globalisation, individuals' opportunities, life plans and choices are influenced by the political decisions of their own national governments, but also by other governments and various non-state actors. They include regional and international organisations set up by states themselves, but also powerful private actors – in particular transnational corporations – who affect the opportunity space and choices of individuals directly. Some of these actors, such as multinational corporations, also have great indirect effects. They influence the scope of decisions available to national governments, the expected results, and thus the strategies that states pursue – with major consequences for citizens. Those who are invested in these corporations thus benefit from – and are morally complicit in – some of these effects, for better and worse.

Globalisation affect the *value* of even well-functioning democracies. Many states find that they can no longer buffer their own citizens from the effects of actors outside their territorial borders – if they ever could.[9] Many are thus concerned about the 'basic global structure'[10] that frame the opportunities and choices of individuals. Such rules and practices specify the actors and the scope of decisions they may take, and influence their choices. Some actors, such as states and interstate organisations, are legally authorised to make binding decisions, at various territorial levels that often overlap, such as the European Union and UN bodies. Other actors – such as transnational organisations, corporations and/or regulatory networks – are evidence of more diffuse forms of 'governance'. They have de facto power to get things done, albeit without legal competence to command compliance.[11]

We now witness some efforts to make some such governance actors – specifically, corporations – more accountable. The UN Global Compact is a voluntary platform for private companies that are committed to sustainability and responsible business practices outlined in 10 principles covering human rights, labour, environment and anti-corruption. The Global Compact seeks to incorporate the principles among corporations, as well as to promote collective action, eg the Millennium Development Goals. Human rights, for instance, is covered in two principles:

Principle 1: Businesses should support and respect the protection of internationally proclaimed human rights; and

[6] United Nations Global Compact, www.unglobalcompact.org, accessed 2 September 2013.

[7] The United Nations Environment Programme Finance Initiative, www.unepfi.org, accessed 2 September 2013.

[8] Principles for Responsible Investment, www.unpri.org, accessed 2 September 2013.

[9] JG Ruggie, 'International Regimes, Transactions, and Change: Embedded Liberalism in the Postwar Economic Order' (1982) 36(2) *International Regimes* 379–415.

[10] A Follesdal, 'The Distributive Justice of a Global Basic Structure: A Category Mistake?' (2011) 10(1) *Politics, Philosophy and Economics* 46–65.

[11] JN Rosenau, 'Governance, Order, and Change in World Politics' in JN Rosenau and EO Czempiel (eds), *Governance without Government: Order and Change in World Politics* (Cambridge, Cambridge University Press, 1992) 1–29.

Principle 2: Businesses should make sure that they are not complicit in human rights abuses

The UN Global Compact is a voluntary initiative, the world's largest in corporate sustainability. As a voluntary association, its principles and impact may be criticised as too weak; on the other hand the number of corporations and the UN backing may impact on the reputation even of non-signatories. And signatory companies are subject to an annual review to determine how they are implementing the 10 principles. A central weakness of the review is that it is self-reporting. Again, some may say in defence of such a weak measure that such statements at least make it possible for civil society groups to criticise corporations for self-acknowledged weaknesses in their practices.

The UNEP Finance Initiative is a collaboration between the UN Environmental Programme and more than 200 financial institutions who have agreed to the UNEP Financial Initiative statements. The objective is to promote best environmental practices within financial institutions. Critics may question their definition of 'sustainable development' and the best means thereto, namely

> . . . development that meets the needs of the present without compromising the ability of future generations to meet their own needs . . .

> . . . best achieved by allowing markets to work within an appropriate framework of cost efficient regulations and economic instruments (Commitments 1.1 and 1.2).

Again, as a voluntary initiative it should not be surprising that they focus on the 'business case' for such environmental policies, and on establishing guidelines and build capacity, rather than monitoring and sanctioning non-compliance. As long as such initiatives do not prevent or hinder other activities in furtherance of environmentally sound policies, such supplements should arguably be welcomed as part of consciousness raising and standard setting.

One example of such longer-term effects of the Global Compact and the UNEP Finance Initiative is the 'PRI Initiative', which the Norwegian Pension Fund Global has signed. The PRI Initiative[12] is investor led, in partnership with the UNEP Finance Initiative and UN Global Compact. It includes six principles concerning environmental, social and corporate governance (ESC) issues, each of which mentions several possible actions. The central principles are:

(1) We will incorporate ESG issues into investment analysis and decision-making processes
(2) We will be active owners and incorporate ESG issues into our ownership policies and practices
(3) We will seek appropriate disclosure on ESG issues by the entities in which we invest

Note that the principles and suggested actions do not include divestment, nor is there mention of other responses to corporations that fail to comply with the requests of investors.

These initiatives, which the NBIM has supported, help shape the mandate and objectives of the management of the Fund. It is helpful to consider parts of these texts extensively.

[12] ibid.

III EXERCISE OF OWNERSHIP RIGHTS: SHAREHOLDER ENGAGEMENT

The Management mandate laid down by the Ministry of Finance 2010 states inter alia:[13]

> Chapter 2. Responsible investment
>
> *Section 2-1 The Bank's work with responsible management*
>
> (1) The management of the investment portfolio shall be based on the goal of achieving the highest possible return, cf. section 1-2, third paragraph. A good return in the long term is regarded as being dependent upon sustainable development in economic, environmental and social terms, as well as well-functioning, legitimate and effective markets.
> (2) The Bank shall have internal guidelines for integrating considerations of good corporate governance and environmental and social issues in investment activities, in line with internationally recognised principles for responsible investment. . . .
>
> *Section 2-2 Active ownership*
>
> (1) The Bank's primary goal in its active ownership is to safeguard the financial interests stipulated for the investment portfolio, cf. section 1-2, third paragraph.
> (2) Active ownership shall be based on the UN Global Compact, the OECD's Principles of Corporate Governance and the OECD's Guidelines for Multinational Enterprises. The Bank shall have internal guidelines for its exercise of ownership rights that state how these principles are integrated

In the NBIM Policy concerning responsible investment, the NBIM defines central terms and lays out its policies thus:

> **Corporate Governance** is the system by which companies are directed and controlled
>
> **Environmental and social factors** are concerns which may affect portfolio performance in the long term . . .
>
> Ownership activities shall promote the fund's interests and take into consideration internationally recognised principles such as the UN Global Compact, the OECD Principles for Corporate Governance, the OECD Guidelines for Multinational Enterprises and the UN PRI . . .
>
> Through investment analysis, company contact and voting at the company's general meeting, NBIM will work to maximize the long term value of the portfolio.[14]

These citations suggest at least two central topics that may create tensions. First, the definitions of environmental and social aspects are specified in ways that may seem to limit them to those that reduce the long-term value of the portfolio. Other environmental or social aspects may thus not register as such with the NBIM investors. Secondly, precisely *how* the NBIM shall 'take into consideration' the various principles remains open ended. One way NBIM specifies this is as quoted, that NBIM will always work as an active investor to 'maximize the long term value of the portfolio'. Again, there is a risk that initiatives to respect or promote environmental and social factors will not be pursued

[13] Norges Bank Investment Managment, Management mandate for the Government Pension Fund Global, www.nbim.no/en/About-us/governance-model/management-mandate/, accessed 2 September 2013.

[14] Norges Bank Investment Managment, NBIM Policy – Responsible investor, www.nbim.no/Global/Documents/Governance/Policies/NBIM%20Policy%20RI.pdf, accessed 2 September 2013.

insofar as such initiatives will be negative for the long-term value. For instance, the policy document states that NBIM will vote in favour of:

> 27. Proposals that request the company to perform and disclose a social or environmental impact assessment of specific project or operations when the current information publicly available is insufficient *and such disclosure will benefit shareholders*,
>
> 28. Proposals that request adoption or implementation of a code of conduct based on human rights and international labour standards covering a company's operations and supply chain when the actions suggested in the proposals are considered to be reasonable with regard to what the company can be held accountable for *and will benefit shareholders* (my emphasis).

How NBIM addresses some of these tensions becomes evident in relation to the other main mechanisms of ethical investment of the Norwegian Pension Fund Global.

IV AVOIDING MORAL COMPLICITY IN CERTAIN UNETHICAL INVESTMENTS

In addition to shareholder engagement, Parliament established a Council on Ethics ('the Council'). It assists the Ministry of Finance and the Fund, to avoid running the risk of moral complicity in particularly problematic cases. By the end of 2011, 55 companies had been excluded on such grounds.[15]

It is relevant for the later discussion in this chapter to consider how the Council implements these filters. The mandate of the Council specifies two central tasks. It shall first screen companies that produce certain products, namely weapons that violate fundamental humanitarian principles, and companies that produce tobacco. The weapons of concern are those that 'through normal use may violate fundamental humanitarian principles'. The relevant principles as the Council sees it are 'the principle of distinction' – between civilians and military targets – and 'the principle of proportionality' – to avoid unnecessary suffering or injury. Among such weapons are weapons of mass destruction, anti-personnel mines and cluster weapons. All companies involved in the production of such weapons are excluded from the Fund. To illustrate: Parliament made clear that cluster weapons are to be excluded One reason may be that these weapons do not distinguish sufficiently between military and civilian goals during – and especially after – an attack, in violation of fundamental humanitarian principles. The Council recommended the exclusion of companies that produce key components, such as the canisters and guide mechanisms, and the 'bomblets' themselves. Similar arguments lie behind exclusion of companies involved in production of some other weapons, such as anti-personnel mines.

The Council can also recommend that the Minister of Finance exclude certain corporations from the portfolio of the Fund. The Council should recommend exclusion of companies that entail an unacceptable risk, through acts or omissions, that the Fund contributes to certain unethical acts:

- serious or systematic human rights violations, such as murder, torture, deprivation of liberty, forced labour, the worst forms of child labour and other forms of child exploitation
- serious violations of individuals' rights in situations of war or conflict

[15] Etikkrådet. 2011. 'Årsrapport 2011', 9, www.regjeringen.no/pages/1957930/Arsmelding2011.pdf, accessed 2 September 2013.

- severe environmental damages
- gross corruption
- other particularly serious violations of fundamental ethical norms

The Council shall act on its own initiative or as requested by the Ministry of Finance.

How does the process of excluding specific companies work? The Council, assisted by a Secretariat, gathers information to document claims concerning the corporation in question. Sources in the past have included a wide range of voices: the companies' own websites, the Norwegian People's Aid landmine division, Human Rights Watch's Arms Division, Jane's Information Group, the International Campaign to Ban Landmines (ICBL) and the Norwegian Ministry of Foreign Affairs.

There is also an adversarial element, in that companies seriously considered for exclusion are invited to comment and correct the proposed recommendation before the Council's final recommendation.

The Council submits its recommendations to exclude a company to the Ministry of Finance. If it chooses to heed the advice, the Ministry will instruct the Norwegian Central Bank to sell the company, typically within a window of two months. To analyse the impact of such exclusions, note that the Ministry then makes its decision public. The mandate, the recommendations and their grounds are publicly available – in Norwegian and English – at the Council website (www.etikkradet.no).

Every month the Secretariat's in-house and subcontracted searches reveal approximately 30 companies as possible violators. Of these, typically five to eight are considered with greater care by the Council. Often the process is stopped. Thus during 2011, five companies were recommended for exclusion.

V REMARKS ON MORAL COMPLICITY

Among important and complex issues to be resolved is the relevant kind of *moral complicity* in human rights violations. Relevant sources include international case law on companies' complicity in war crimes, including the Nuremberg tribunal that sentenced senior executives of Zyklon B gas producers that supplied the gas to the Nazi regime. Note that such assessments are complex. John Ruggie, UN Special Representative of the Secretary-General on the issue of human rights and transnational corporations and other business enterprises, briefly addressed this issue. He noted that

> 'Moral support' can establish individual liability under international law, and the tribunals have extended it to include silent presence coupled with authority. But a company trying in good faith to avoid involvement in human rights abuses might have difficulty knowing what counts as moral support for legal purposes. Mere presence in a country and paying taxes are unlikely to create liability. But deriving indirect economic benefit from the wrongful conduct of others may do so, depending on such facts as the closeness of the company's association with those actors. Greater clarity currently does not exist. However, it is established that even where a corporation does not intend for the crime to occur, and regrets its commission, it will not be absolved of liability if it knew, or should have known, that it was providing assistance, and that the assistance would contribute to the commission of a crime.[16]

[16] JG Ruggie, Report of the Special Representative of the Secretary-General on the issue of human rights and transnational corporations and other business enterprises, Business and human rights: mapping international standards of responsibility and accountability for corporate acts, A/HRC/4/35, 19 February 2007, para 42.

How should one operationalise such complex theoretical concepts? The Council has laid out several conditions that must be satisfied for a company to be held morally complicit in present human rights violations:

- There must be a linkage between the company's activities and the relevant human rights violations.
- The violations must be perpetrated in order to secure the company's interests.
- The company must have contributed to the violations, or be aware of the violations yet refrain from attempts to prevent them.
- The violations must be ongoing, or there must be an unacceptable risk that they will occur in the future, as for instance established by past conduct.

To illustrate: in 2005 the Council recommended divestment from Kerr-McGee Corporation, due to its contract with the Moroccan government oil company ONAREP to explore for oil offshore Western Sahara.[17] The concern was whether investment in the company would put the Fund at risk: would it contribute to future acts or omissions that would violate fundamental ethical norms?

I submit that these assessments may be guided by a general approach to moral complicity in human rights violations along the following lines.[18]

The normative perspective is based on what we may think of as a principle of respect for vital interests: each agent must respect others' vital interests at least in the 'mild' sense that their own actions and projects do not impose threats to the vital interests of others. The guiding idea is that corporations' profit-seeking projects should not violate the vital interests of those who contribute to the project or those of third parties. When corporations rely on subcontractors to increase their profits, the actions of the subcontractors become part of the project.

Corporations are more morally complicit when the violations of vital interests are part of the project. That is, when these violations

- are integral and foreseeable parts of the corporation's strategy to maximise returns, rather than unintended or unforeseen consequences;
- could be prevented by requiring subcontractors to respect vital interests of workers and third parties, and monitoring such promises.

A central test question to determine whether moral complicity of corporations – and of investors – is at stake is to ask: Would this risk be taken if it did not benefit the bottom line?

A final note concerning assessment of moral complicity in this context. In the judicial system it is better to err in favour of the guilty. However, for exclusions by the Norwegian Pension Fund, arguments may be stronger for a risk assessment that is as accurate as possible: moral obligations are in favour both of maximising yield and avoiding complicity in wrongdoing. And for such decisions regarding exclusion it may be more important to avoid 'false positives' than to avoid 'false negatives'. That is, it might be better to exclude too many corporations rather than too few – from the moral if not from the financial point of view. We now turn to some of the dilemmas that arise from conflicts between these two perspectives.

[17] Details are in the 2005 Annual Report, at www.regjeringen.no/pages/1957930/Årsmelding%202005%20eng.pdf, accessed 2 September 2013.

[18] For a more elaborate account, from which I draw, cf C Kutz, *Complicity: Ethics and Law for a Collective Age* (Cambridge, Cambridge University Press, 2001).

VI THREE NORMATIVELY VALUABLE OBJECTIVES AND STANDARDS FOR INVESTORS

This sketch of the Norwegian case illustrates how socially responsible investment practices must handle three distinct normative objectives in defensible ways. In no particular order – and most decidedly not in order of moral priority! – these three are:

(1) to secure returns, even arguably to *maximise* returns for shareholders, within limits, eg those set by the two other normative objectives.

The two other objectives express respect for the fundamental interests of all parties affected by the investment, in two distinct ways:

(2) Improve on the wrongs that there are in the world. In particular, it does not seem unreasonable that investors should consider to some extent those wrongs perpetrated within the global economy by corporations in which they invest. One central means for this objective is by *active shareholder engagement*. The NBIM engages in such practices. Such actions may aim at preventing wrongs from occurring, or seek to change unacceptable practices in each corporation, or seek to overcome collective action problems – such as those that give rise to environmental problems. Which corporations should be targeted for such engagement? Presumably those that would maximise the expected marginal impact of this particular shareholder's involvement. On this line of argument shareholder engagement can *not* just be limited to issues that maximise return in the long run.
(3) Avoid moral complicity in the wrong acts that still do occur. The main mechanism of concern here is to *divest*, especially where gross violations of certain fundamental norms are likely to continue. This will typically be when the violations are part of the business strategy and essential to the comparative advantage of the corporation. The irony which is sometimes pointed out is that where moral investors divest, other investors rush in. We should also keep in mind that other investors may well continue to urge change from within. And those investors who divest are free to pursue *other* means to influence those businesses.

VII POTENTIAL CONFLICTS

There are some ways that engagement and divestment may come into *conflict*.

One problem arises if engagement is limited to addressing those normative objectives that are also instrumental to maximise long-term return, such as corporate governance issues. Secondly, alas, some normative violations, such as the worst forms of child labour or violations of labour rights, may be *sustainable* by some corporations – and even crucial if the company is to secure maximal return over time. In these cases, we might expect that prudent shareholder engagement will not be pursued, since the company will have strong objections to change its procedures towards normative standards that will reduce returns. Thirdly, bodies in charge of *engagement* but generally set to maximise long-term profit alone may want to prevent divestment since divestment from the presumably most profitable companies will tend to reduce profits, however slightly.

Another kind of tension arises if involvement is focused not on those corporations that are most likely to reduce evil in the world, but instead mainly to *prevent divestment*. This creates a risk that the investor remains morally complicit in wrongdoing, and that ills in the world remain which would otherwise have been addressed by active engagement.

A further tension occurs if the mere possibility of divestment *reduces* the impact of engagement. Consider two alternative scenarios. The management of such 'problematic' corporations may decide to ignore the engagement attempts, knowing full well that sooner or later the noisy, morally concerned investors will pull out. Alternatively, if the criteria for disinvestment are too vague, even managers of 'good will' will not know what to do and perhaps ignore engagement attempts since they risk divestment anyway.

VIII OPPORTUNITIES FOR BETTER INTERACTION

There are several ways that divestment and engagement may benefit from such a two-fold strategy.

First, a credible divestment policy can strengthen the objective and impact of shareholder engagement. The real, predictable threat of divestment can increase the influence of attempts at dialogue engagement. This may be even more the case when there is a division of responsibilities so that decisions about divestment are taken by another body than the body involved in the dialogues with management. Such a division of responsibility, as in the Norwegian case, can have the following effects: (a) it can boost the credibility of those engaged in dialogues when they warn of divestment, since this is out of their hands; (b) the quality of information from management may increase, and the risk of 'capture' of the engaged agent by the corporation may be reduced, since an independent body will monitor the information and the process as part of the risk assessment; (c) the division of responsibility may help reduce public suspicion of moral corruption: that the investor has sacrificed moral principles for the sake of maximal yield. Such suspicion is not unreasonable, particularly when the sacrifice has entailed moral complicity in order to do good: to achieve some marginal changes in the corporation – or in order to not reduce profits.

Such opportunities for better interaction might best arise under certain conditions:

When divestment imposes reputational costs

This is not always the case: some funds, such as the Vice Fund (VICEX), may regard exclusion as a 'buy' signal. Reputational costs may also vary across sectors, and depend crucially on whether the normative triggers are broadly shared This is a reason to use divestment only for certain violations that are likely to command broad agreement.

Publicity of reasoned divestment

Publicity and argued decisions are necessary to maximise shaming effects, to facilitate copying by other investors, to strengthen NGOs and other concerned parties, and to facilitate the corporation's strategies for improvement.

Trustworthy: predictable threats

The divestment threat must be credible. This requires publicity, including about failed attempts at shareholder involvement.

Procedures for re-inclusion in the investment universe
Once excluded, there should be real, predictable prospects of lifting a divestment decision, to increase the corporation's willingness to engage in dialogues with 'future shareholders' – without conveying a stamp of 'high ethics'.

Procedures for dialogue with excluded companies
There should be ways to engage with the corporation to prompt its speedy re-inclusion into the investment universe. I submit that such dialogues might be best handled by the body in charge of shareholder engagement, if that body is more likely to have the requisite competence and knowledge about the situation on the ground.

The second way that interaction between these two mechanisms may be beneficial is that shareholder engagement itself may boost the objectives of divestment. Recall that the objective of divestment mechanisms – such as the Council – is to avoid moral complicity in violations of certain norms. The aim is *not* to maximise the number of divested companies. Rather, if corporations can credibly commit to internal changes to avoid risks of future complicity, this is excellent. Shareholder engagement may contribute to such changes.

However, there is sometimes a risk that such changes will reduce the profitability and the comparative advantages of the corporation, with the result that the fund nevertheless moves its investments elsewhere, but for financial reasons alone.

Several conditions make such contributions more likely:

- Visible changes. The changes must be visible for those deciding on divestment. However, it is not necessary that these changes are seen as resulting from the engagement process itself; that may be too difficult to discern.
- The corporation's changes must be credible.
- The corporation's changes must be done with all due speed. Otherwise, the morally best strategy may be to divest, and let other investors be involved. Investments may again be permitted if the risks have been reduced

IX IMPLICATIONS AND FURTHER RESEARCH

In conclusion, I first summarise some of the central implications for the Norwegian system of two bodies authorised to pursue engagement and divestment, respectively, and then indicate some topics for further research.

A Implications

i The Role of Transparency

I have argued that there is in general a strong case that many of the processes should be as transparent as possible. This case is even stronger since the Fund manages *public* funds. This feature strengthens the argument of democratic accountability for these mechanisms. It will also be important in the dialogues that corporations *know* that certain of their responses will be made public if they are excluded from the investment universe.

ii Clearer Standards and Indicators

What seems urgent is to develop clearer standards and indicators, to measure the shareholder impact, to determine when exclusion should occur, and – not least – standards for re-inclusion. The standards must be such that they are reasonably robust against abuse – be it by companies avoiding taking on costly burdens, or by attention-seeking NGOs eager to criticise companies for high media impact.

iii Routines for Re-inclusion into the Investment Universe

I have suggested that there are good reasons to establish procedures for re-including corporations that so desire into the investment universe. We have seen that some excluded corporations are eager to have such well-publicised divestment decisions reversed. The procedures and the competence to deliberate with management might be best placed with the body in charge of engagement, rather than with the body in charge of divestment.

B Topics for Future Research

i The Impact of Transparency on Effective Engagement

It is striking that different stakeholders make conflicting claims about the need for and impact of secrecy or transparency at various stages of the engagement process: in advance of dialogues, during engagement, and afterwards. Some claims might emerge from NGOs that have other reasons to seek publicity, others from investors who have other reasons to keep a low profile. *These are empirical issues that I recommend should be subject to careful, comparative research.*

ii The Extent of Confluence and of Conflict between Investment Performance and Broader Environmental and Social Objectives.

Some actors in the field of socially responsible investing hold that there is a positive correlation – and perhaps even complete congruence – between the fiduciary obligations of institutional investors to promote the best long-term economic interests of their beneficiaries, and the other normative societal concerns such as environmental sustainability, respect for human rights etc. Thus the Investors' initiative 'Principles for Responsible Investment' rests on the belief that:

> There is a growing view among investment professionals that environmental, social and corporate governance (ESG) issues can affect the performance of investment portfolios. Investors fulfilling their fiduciary (or equivalent) duty *therefore* need to give appropriate consideration to these issues (UNEP Finance Initiative 2006, my emphasis).

They hold:

> [W]e believe that environmental, social, and corporate governance (ESG) issues can affect the performance of investment portfolios (to varying degrees across companies, sectors, regions, asset classes and through time). We also recognise that applying these Principles may better align

> investors with broader objectives of society. Therefore, *where consistent with our fiduciary responsibilities*, we commit to the following . . .[19] (my emphasis).

Two important research topics seem obvious in this regard. First, in which sectors, regions and asset classes are such arguments of convergence between profit maximisation and normative concerns correct, and how can these objectives best be strengthened? Secondly, in which areas must we expect conflicts to remain – and how can we best prevent investors from violating ethical constraints in such cases?. The challenge may be particularly difficult if the efforts of the investor community lead to the public perception that those concerns that are not in the long-term fiduciary interest of the funds are not 'properly' regarded as ethical.

iii The Longer-term Impact of Engagement and Exclusion Mechanisms on 'Hard' and 'Soft' Regimes for Multinational Corporations

If ethical standards for engagement and exclusion are carefully expressed and employed, they may contribute to securing that corporations respect these standards. Even such efforts that are neither legally binding nor tied to costly sanctions may help move corporations to comply with higher standards concerning respect for human rights and the environment. John Ruggie, Special Representative of the Secretary-General on the issue of human rights and transnational corporations, has explored some such paths.[20] Further research should seek to determine the conditions for such efforts to contribute to these longer-term effects.

X CONCLUSIONS

What are the opportunities for constructive interaction between two relatively independent mechanisms for socially responsible investment, aimed at engagement and divestment, respectively?

In this chapter I provided a sketch of the procedures of the Norwegian Government Pension Fund Global, drawn against a background ranging from the Quakers to the United Nations initiatives. I then offered some comments on the three moral objectives of the Fund. By sketching some possibilities for conflict between engagement and divestment and turning to the opportunities and conditions for better interaction between these two mechanisms, I pointed finally to three important areas that require further research: the impact of transparency on effective engagement; the extent of confluence and conflict between investment performance and broader environmental and social objectives; and the longer-term impact of engagement and exclusion mechanisms on 'hard' and 'soft' regimes for multinational corporations. The practices of the Norwegian Government Pension Fund Global may be read as a response to the historic challenges of the Quakers' efforts to avoid complicity in slavery: how to respond to practices that make us morally complicit in immoral actions. The slave trade illustrated some of the coordination problems in the absence of a common authority; the Norwegian case illustrates that

[19] UNEP Finance Initiative 2006. Principles for Responsible Investment (PRI), www.unpri.org, accessed 2 September 2013.

[20] JG Ruggie, 'Business and Human Rights: The Evolving International Agenda' (2007) *KSG Faculty Research Working Paper Series 07/029*.

sometimes such coordination problems do not arise. The long fight to outlaw the slave trade may also suggest that divestment by single actors is not irrelevant to help end condemnable practices – through standard setting, active ownership and monitoring.

21

Towards Making Blood Money Visible: Lessons Drawn from the Apartheid Litigation

INGRID GUBBAY*

I INTRODUCTION

MUCH HAS BEEN written and said about the conceptual challenges raised in the two cases comprising the Apartheid litigation[1] ('*Re Apartheid*'). Of the 100 cases or so run under the Alien Tort Claims Act[2] (ATCA) since its reinvigoration in 1980, *Re Apartheid* is unique in that it has spotlighted the high level of 'collaboration/integration between non South African sectors of the business community and the State, in extending, maintaining, and profiteering from the Apartheid regime'.[3] First filed under the ATCA in the Southern District Court in 2002, the South African plaintiffs have sought to publicly interrogate banks and other major corporations for their key role in allegedly supporting the crimes against humanity committed by the regime during the period of its operation between 1948 until the election of Nelson Mandela in 1994.

The case narrative, told first through the reports to the Truth and Reconciliation Commission of South Africa[4] (TRC), and later in the US courts, establishes unequivocally that the financial and operational support provided by certain corporations maintained

* The author is the European head of human rights and environmental law at Hausfeld & Co LLP, based in London. Her role in the litigation is to assist on areas of international law, and liaise with members of the Khulumani group. She worked in South Africa taking depositions from the named plaintiffs in the Khulumani case. The author would like to thank the Khulumani litigation team in *Re Apartheid*, for their contribution to this chapter. They are currently Michael Hausfeld, Jeannine Kenney and Kristen Ward Broz, based in the Washington DC office of Hausfeld LLP.

[1] *In Re South African Apartheid*, 617F. Supp.2d 228 (S.D.N.Y. 2009) now addresses the complaints of the two cases formerly known as *Khulumani v Barclays Nat'l Bank Ltd* 504F 3d254 (2nd Cir 2007) and *Ntzebeza v Daimler AG*. The *Khulumani* complaint, www.khulumani.net/khulumani/documents/category/5-us-lawsuit.html, accessed 30 August 2013. Note, Khulumani means 'speak out' in Zulu.

[2] *Alien Tort Claims Act* (ATCA), 28 U.S.C. § 1350 (2006).

[3] For example, the Statement of Owen Horwood, South African Minister for Finance, in 1983, 'The story of the economic development of this country is intimately bound up with Foreign capital, technology, and expertise. Significant investments usually bring all three. It allows us to do what we want rather more quickly It allows us to do some things better than we would otherwise do' in South African Restrictions, Hearing before the Subcommittee on Financial Institutions, Supervision, Regulation and Insurance of the House Committee on Banking, Finance and Urban Affairs, 98th Cong, 1st Sess, 8 June 1983, 102.

[4] The Promotion of National Unity and Reconciliation Act (SA) 1995, is the founding Act of the Truth Commission.

and lengthened the duration of apartheid, and the suffering of its victims, who now seek to bring them to account. Scholars following developments in lenders' liability have written on the importance of the contribution made in the *Re Apartheid* case to this emerging legal area. Michalowski noted that:

> Given the scarcity of legal analysis and authority on the problem of complicity for financing gross human rights violations committed by regimes, it is likely that the arguments on this point, will prove influential far beyond litigation against banks under the ATCA. South African Apartheid Litigation is thus significant not only for future complicity cases under ATCA, but also for advancing the debate on lender liability for complicity in gross human rights violations generally.[5]

Other courts adjudicating under the ATCA have since adopted the reasoning in the Apartheid litigation.[6]

Re Apartheid, however, has become illustrative of the nuanced approach the US Court took in filleting out any legal links between the banks (lenders), who provided the commercial loans and the atrocities committed by the Special Forces, despite the existence of specific international and domestic trade and investment prohibitions, sanctions and embargoes in place during this period. Conversely, the remaining case defendants who held direct contracts with the apartheid regime in the key identified sectors of technology, weapons and the automotive industries met the requisite causative standard in the central case.

The chapter begins by outlining recent developments in the US case law and the scope of the ATCA in so far as it impacts on the Apartheid litigation and the future access of foreign plaintiffs to the US courts. The background to the key role of foreign finance in supporting the apartheid regime, which led up to the decision of South African organisations to file the case in the United States, includes an exposition of the reports commissioned by the TRC at the business hearings. The submissions to the TRC demonstrate how the evidence gathered for this purpose can be produced later in a judicial context and thus align and inform the objectives of the litigation with the aims of transitional justice.

The key challenge in reaching the requisite *actus reas* standard to establish lenders' liability is reflected in the decision to narrow the original complaint and drop the defendant banks from the action, because the Court's formulation of the 'neutrality' and 'fungibility'[7] of money rendered commercial loans too far removed in this context, and so there was a real risk the banks' inclusion would weaken the case.

Ultimately, the purpose here is first to elucidate the constraints of legal theory with its abstract approach to analysing the causative links between the provision of commercial loans which substantially enabled the atrocities committed by state agents, and second to draw upon some of the recent discussion on alternative approaches to establishing these hitherto elusive links.

[5] For a contrasting view of the approach taken in the Apartheid litigation with US case law on funding on terrorism see generally, S Michalowski, 'No Complicity Liability for Funding Gross Human Rights Violations?' (2012) 30 *Berkeley Journal of International Law* 451.

[6] ibid, 37, eg *Doe v Nestle, SA et al*, 748F Supp.2d at 1096.

[7] The Oxford Dictionary: 'A fungible good can replace or be replaced by another identical item mutually interchangeable – money is fungible, it can be raised for one purpose and used for another'.

II ALIEN TORTS CLAIMS ACT (ATCA)

The ATCA of 1789, is part of the United States Judiciary Act, and thus is a jurisdictional statute only. The relevant text for these purposes states:

> The District Courts shall have original jurisdiction of any civil action by an alien for a tort only, committed in violation of the law of Nations or Treaty of the United States.

The text itself does not place any limitations on who can be a defendant. Conversely, it does limit who can be a plaintiff ('alien'), the type of action ('tort only') and norm violated ('law of Nations or Treaty of the United States'). It removes all common law actions for violations of international law from state courts. ATCA cases are in essence federal common law actions claims.

In 1980 the ATCA was reinvigorated in the case of *Filartiga v Pena Irala*[8] in which the Second Circuit Court of Appeals then held the ATCA allowed claims to sue in US courts for serious violations of international law. What followed was a string of ATCA cases, first against individuals associated with authoritarian regimes, and then later against transnational corporations for aiding and abetting them. The scope of the violations allowed under the ATCA was clarified in 2004 in the case of *Sosa v Alvarez – Machain (Sosa)*. The Court in *Sosa* held that the ATCA provided a limited cause of action for foreign plaintiffs for violations of international norms that are 'specific' universal and obligatory'[9] in character, consistent with the norms of the eighteenth century prohibiting 'violations of safe conduct' 'infringements of ambassadors' and 'acts of piracy'.

Accordingly, the US courts have recognised that cases alleging crimes against humanity, genocide, extra-judicial killing, torture, arbitrary detention, and cruel and inhuman treatment are such violations of international law consistent with these norms, albeit subject to the statute being interpreted narrowly. Thus,

> the main litigation issues for corporate complicity under the ACTA are, how to define what falls under the law of nations, whether cases can be brought against corporations, whether the ACTA encompasses liability for aiding and abetting and if so, what standard should apply to determine the actus reus and mens rea of such liability.[10]

III RECENT ATCA DEVELOPMENTS

The ATCA has proved highly controversial with respect to its application by foreign plaintiffs against corporate defendants. The resultant pressure from political and industry interests has led to intense judicial scrutiny as to the extent of its extraterritorial application, evidenced recently in the Supreme Court's decision in the *Kiobel v Royal Dutch Petroleum*[11] (*Kiobel*) case. Nigerian petitioners residing in the United States filed suit under the ATCA against Royal Dutch Shell alleging certain Dutch, British and Nigerian corporations aided and abetted the Nigerian government in committing

[8] *Filartiga v Pena-Irala* 630F.2D876,880 (2nd Cir 1980).

[9] *Sosa v Alvarez–Machain* 542 US 692, 724 (2004).

[10] Michalowski (n 5) 2.

[11] *Kiobel v Royal Dutch Petroleum No 10-1491*, April 10 2013, Chief Justice Roberts delivered the opinion of the Court.

violations. In brief, the decision against the petitioners introduced a new presumption with respect to the reach of the ATCA's extraterritorial application, which now requires that claims brought by foreign plaintiffs must 'touch and concern the United States with sufficient force to displace the presumption against extraterritorial application'.[12] The decision itself appears narrowly confined to the particular facts in the case, applying only in the context of a paradigmatic 'foreign-cubed' case, ie foreign defendant, foreign plaintiff and exclusively foreign conduct, lacking any connection to the United States beyond 'mere corporate presence' of the defendants. It has explicitly left unresolved how other claims may 'touch and concern' the United States with sufficient force to displace the presumption in other factual contexts.

In the month following the *Kiobel* decision, lawyers for the plaintiffs in *Re Apartheid*, submitted a supplemental briefing[13] to the Court of Appeals for the Second Circuit, at the Court's request, on the impact of the US Supreme Court decision in *Kiobel* on *Re Apartheid*. The supplemental briefing, among other reasons concerning jurisdiction, argues that the Apartheid litigation should be referred back to the District Court where the plaintiffs will be afforded the opportunity to amend the complaints to plead appropriate facts in light of *Kiobel*, specifically, because here, unlike in *Kiobel*, several of the corporate defendants are citizens of the United States. Standing alone, this is sufficient to displace the presumption. The Supreme Court decision marks the most significant challenge to the scope of the ATCA in the entire history of the statute.

Much hangs in the balance, not least the very real possibility of shutting out foreign plaintiffs from continuing to seek redress in the US courts under the ATCA. This chapter, however, will not feature the *Kiobel* case which, while it may have profound and lasting socio/legal consequences, will be fully explored over coming months and years, as the scope and impacts of the decision become clearer, and are fully debated in many eminent circles. Instead, this chapter surveys some of the key ideas and observations emerging from the growing body of literature around lenders' liability, some of which have been generated from the central case in *Re Apartheid*.

IV FOREIGN FINANCE AND THE MAINTENANCE OF THE APARTHEID ERA

Apartheid[14] was instituted in South Africa beginning in 1948. Apartheid was a system that concentrated economic and political power in the hands of the white minority. It depended on systemic violence, routinely perpetrating gross crimes against humanity. It also set up institutional methods of segregation and exploitation for its maintenance and enforcement, which paralleled the Nuremberg laws passed by Nazi Germany. Apartheid-era laws classified all South Africans according to one of four races – white, Asiatic (Indian), 'Coloured' and Native (African) – and then designated specific residential and business areas for the sole use of particular racial groups.[15]

[12] ibid, 14.

[13] Plaintiffs' supplemental brief, US Court of Appeals for the 2nd Cir, *Balintulo, et al v Daimler AG, et al*, No 09-2778-cv (lead), May 24 (2013).

[14] *In Re South African Apartheid* (n 1), Complaint (2009) 'Definitions', para 8, the word apartheid means 'separateness'.

[15] The Population Registration Act (1950).

The government required all blacks[16] over the age of 16 to carry 'passbooks',[17] which included their population registry identity card, their fingerprints, and pages for any history of government opposition, labour control and employer signatures. Without proper documentation, no black person could legally enter or remain in an urban area. Relations between races were banned.[18] Laws were passed to suppress dissent. Between 1960 and 1970, almost two million people were forcibly moved into 'Bantustans' and their South African citizenship was forcibly revoked.[19]

Beginning in 1950, the world community condemned apartheid as a crime against humanity[20] and instituted various sanctions against South Africa. The UN Security Council adopted numerous resolutions condemning apartheid and collaboration with the apartheid regime. Collaboration by transnational corporations was repeatedly denounced and embargoes put in place and states were called upon to take measures to ensure that corporations complied with the embargo. The General Assembly called upon the Security Council to enforce mandatory sanctions against South Africa and adopted a resolution outlining a voluntary set of sanctions based on the International Convention on the Suppression and Punishment of the Crime of Apartheid, adopted in 1976.[21] In 1979 the Chairman of the UN Special Committee Against Apartheid released a report on bank loans to South Africa which specified that:

> At a time when the international community through the General Assembly has repeatedly condemned collaboration with South Africa, we learn today that more than $5.4 billion has been loaned in a six year period to bolster the regime which is responsible for some of the most heinous crimes ever committed against humanity.[22]

The Security Council responded by adopting a resolution 'urging State members of the UN to suspend all new investment in South Africa, prohibit the sale of Kugerrands and all coins minted in South Africa' and 'all sales of computer equipment that may be used by the police or security forces'.[23] In 1986 the United States passed the Comprehensive Anti-Apartheid Act (CAAA).The immediate effect of the Act was to prohibit all loans and credit by lenders, and supply of arms and software to supporters of the regime. It excluded South Africa from holding accounts in US financial institutions, and voided the tax treaty between the two nations.

Clearly the links between corporate support with respect to these key sectors and the maintenance of the regime were recognised through the advent of the CAAA. Further, the actions of the international community over more than 40 years placed businesses involved in the financial and economic support of the apartheid security forces' abuses on notice that their collaboration violated international law. Following a particularly

[16] 'Black' is used to refer to the Native (African) in this chapter, consistent with the term used in the apartheid era.

[17] The Natives (Abolition of passes and Coordination of Documents) Act (1952) required Africans of both sexes to carry passes in a single book together with a population registration identity card pasted in the front.

[18] The Immorality Amendment Act barred intercourse between the races.

[19] *In Re South African Apartheid* (n 1) (2009) para 177, 'Farming, 1866–1966' in M Wilson and L Thompson (eds), *The Oxford History of South Africa* (Oxford, Oxford University Press, 1971).

[20] For example, UN General Assembly, Resolution 32/105 of 14 December 1977 and the Comprehensive Anti-Apartheid Act, pub L No 99-440, 100 Stat 1086 (1986).

[21] The Programme of Action adopted by the International Conference of Experts for the Support of Victims of Colonisation and Apartheid in South Africa (Oslo, 9–14 April 1973) A/9061, 7 May 1973.

[22] Bank Loans to South Africa, 1972–1978, Corporate Data Exchange for United Nations centre Against Apartheid at p 1 (statement by Mr Leslie Harriman, Chairman of the Special Committee Against Apartheid).

[23] Security Council Resolution, S/RES/569, 26 July 1985.

bloody period between 1990 and 1993, negotiations led to an agreement on a date for democratic elections. Apartheid ended in 1994 with the election of Nelson Mandela.

The TRC, under the leadership of Archbishop Desmond Tutu, was established by the Government of National Unity, to begin to heal the damage inflicted by the regime. The TRC commenced hearings in 1996 and issued its final report in March 2003. Significantly, the TRC found that certain businesses were involved in helping to design and implement apartheid policies.[24] The TRC also found that businesses failed in hearings to take responsibility for their involvement in state security initiatives specifically designed to sustain apartheid rule.[25]

What became strikingly clear from the findings in the TRC process, and later from further archived documents which came to light, is that the maintenance of apartheid in South Africa was a hugely expensive business, more so because the oppressors were a minority desperately clinging to power over a vast majority. In fact, it was an impossible task without wooing and enlisting the support of willing private actors, which the apartheid government managed to do through the auspices of their Total Strategy[26] plan. As the original Complaint in *Re Apartheid* set out in some detail:

> International banks were integrally involved in providing foreign capital in the form of trade loans, large international bonds and credits, direct loans from banks to South African borrowers, and project financing supported the apartheid regime. German and Swiss banks along with the South African Reserve bank, were also involved in the gold trade.[27]
>
> From the early 1960's to the early 1970's, foreign investment accounted for approximately eight percent of South Africa's gross domestic investment, providing the margin for economic growth.[28]

According to the former apartheid Prime Minister John Vorster, 'each bank loan, and each new investment was another brick in the wall of our continued existence'.[29]

In 1997 the Centre for Conflict Resolution ('CCR') based in Cape Town, made a comprehensive submission to the Business Sector Hearing of the TRC which set out in depth the history of the close 'integration' of the public–private relationship with a focus on the local 'military–industrial complex'[30]. The submission concluded that:

> The apartheid state had a systematic strategy of enticing the private sector into the defence of apartheid. The private sector did not articulate a clear response to this, and many sections of the [business] community increasingly collaborated with the state by supporting the development of the local arms industry, exploiting loopholes in the embargo regulations and embarking on sanctions busting activities. This led to the development of a military–industrial complex, an arrangement from which certain private sector businesses benefited enormously.[31]

[24] Truth and Reconciliation Commission of South Africa Report vol 4, ch 2, 58 (1998).

[25] ibid, 58.

[26] Centre for Conflict Resolution (CCR) University of Capetown, compiled by Nathan, Batchelor, and Lamb, *Submission to the Truth and Reconciliation Commission, Business hearing*, Oct 1997. The 'Total Strategy Plan' was a system devised by the State to coerce business into supporting it. Many sections of the business community willingly accepted this, www.ccrweb.ccr.uct.ac.za/archive/staff_papers/guy_trc.html.

[27] M Madorin and G Wellmer, 'Apartheid-Caused Debt: The Role of German and Swiss Finance', Jubilee 2000, 1999, 33.

[28] *In Re South African Apartheid* (n 1), paras 392 and 393 of the complaint (2009): W Raiford, Analyst, Congressional Research Service, *International Credit and South Africa*, The Library of Congress, 12 August 1977.

[29] B Klein, 'Bricks in the Wall: An Update on Foreign Bank Involvement in South Africa' (World Council of Churches Report, March 1981).

[30] No 25 of the (CCR) 2: '"military–industrial complex" functions on the basis of structural pairing of business and the military'.

[31] ibid, 10.

Finally, the loans came under intense scrutiny after the Sharpeville massacre in 1960 when a consortium of 10 banks led by Chase Manhattan provided South Africa with rescue loans, 'thus making available funds to compensate for capital leaving the country because of police brutality'.[32]

The CCR submission predicated the request made in the same year by 'The South African Coalition against Apartheid Debt' to the TRC in which it requested an investigation into the financing of apartheid by foreign banks. The focus on foreign debt accrued through the apartheid era and reparations for its victims fostered two important organisations around the issue of the role of finance to the state. The first, the International Apartheid Debt and Reparations Campaign, specifically deals with cancelling apartheid-caused foreign debt.[33] The second is a much broader movement originally founded in the UK, which included the faith-based organisation Jubilee 2000 along with a coalition of individuals, unions, council of churches, NGO coalitions and the Khulumani Support Group (Khulumani).[34] The Khulumani remit is around social reconstruction, including individual compensation to victims and corporate responsibility of international companies that had backed and profited from the crime of apartheid.

The failure of the business community to appear, and engage with the TRC process, resulted in a forfeit to the right to an amnesty for business and financial institutions, thus later opening the way to legitimately instituting legal proceedings against them, exposing the full story of their alleged participation in open court for the world to witness.

Meanwhile,

> It was left to individual countries to take steps to bring the role of business in Apartheid to light. The Swiss Government, for example, commissioned a study in the late 1990's[35] to determine the role that nationals and businesses played in supporting Apartheid. It found that amongst other things, Swiss corporations routinely helped the Apartheid regime circumvent UN embargoes and that certain companies provided the enforcement agencies of the regime with the moral, financial and material support needed to sustain itself.[36]

Despite these findings,

> in 2003 the Swiss Federal Council whilst research was still underway, shut down access to official archival files documenting links to the apartheid regime. It argued that keeping access to archives open would disadvantage Swiss banks in relation to the defendants named in the case in other countries. Against detailed research findings, the Swiss authorities took the view they must protect the Swiss and foreign defendants such as UBS named on the case docket, under the Swiss formulation of '*Equality before the Law*' '*Rechtsgleichheit*'.[37]

[32] *In Re South African Apartheid* (n 1), Complaint (2009) para 405, source J Davis, 'Squeezing Apartheid', [1993] *The Bulletin of the Atomic Scientist*.

[33] Michalowski (n 5) 1: 'to the extent that funding gross human rights violations voids a loan, the consequence of a violation would be to relieve the debtor from its repayment obligation'.

[34] R Kesselring, 'Research Note: Corporate Apartheid-era Human Rights Violations before US Courts: Political and Legal Controversies around Victimhood in Today's South Africa' (2012) 23(12) *Stichproben. Wiener Zeitschrift Fur Kritische Afrikastudien* 82.

[35] Study carried out by Bern University historian Peter Hug for the Swiss National Science Foundation, focused on military, arms industry and nuclear relations between the two countries. According to the study, Switzerland continued illegal exports after the UN embargo of 1963, some of which were uncovered during the trial of arms trader D Buhrie in 1970, www.swissinfo.ch/eng/news_digest/Study-reveals_illegal_ties_to_apartheid_regime 17/11/2009, accessed 1 June 2013.

[36] *In Re South African Apartheid* (n 1), complaint (2009).

[37] Kesselring (n 34) 90.

Some six years after the conclusion of the TRC hearings, the Mbeki government announced that the South African government would only very partially institute the recommendations of the Reparation and Rehabilitation Committee of the TRC.

> The State rejected the Committee's recommendation that a one off wealth tax be imposed on business, and announced that each of the 22,000 victims who testified at the TRC hearings would receive a one off payment of R30,000 instead of the R17,000 to 23,000 for a period of 6 years each, which had also been recommended by the Committee.[38]

There were many compelling reasons why only such a small number of victims testified: fear, regime fatigue, and in many cases people simply did not know the TRC existed. These reasons along with the narrow definition of victim[39] in the TRC frame of reference, conspired against victims coming forward.

Many felt that the companies who profited from their suffering should be made accountable and that a result of any legal proceedings in the plaintiffs' favour should lead to the establishment of a foundation,[40] which would create funds that would provide relief for the crimes supported materially by business.[41] These might follow the examples of other settlement funds in the slave labour and Holocaust litigation providing, for example, programmatic relief and direct payment to victims.

V *RE APARTHEID*

A The Original Complaint

The culmination of these events, together with the perceived shortcomings in the outcome of the final reparations scheme, led to a search elsewhere for a remedy. In 2001 the Apartheid Debt and Reparations Campaign took the decision to institute legal proceedings against non-South African, multinational companies following the example of the action taken in Switzerland for the billions of dollars of accrued assets unclaimed by the descendants of former Jewish victims of the Nazis. The lawsuit should be understood in that context as an alternate means to holding corporations liable for complicity with the apartheid regime.

Michael Hausfeld of the US law firm Hausfeld LLP,[42] who had led the highly successful Swiss bank Holocaust cases,[43] was instructed, with the South African attorney Charles Abrahams advising. The original proceedings began as over a dozen distinct cases filed under the ATCA in 2002. The complaints were broad, *Khulumani et al v Barclays National*

[38] ibid, 87.

[39] ibid, 80. Many submissions about individual torture and disappearances, were not accepted by the statement takers because they fell through the TRC's narrow and legalistic categories of 'gross' human rights violations hence most victims did not testify at all. See definition in the Founding Act of Truth Commission, The Promotion of National Unity and Reconciliation Act 1995 (ch 1, s 1).

[40] Above note 34, 84. The National Unity and Reconciliation Act 1995, which established the TRC, provided for the creation of a fund to pay financial reparations, ie compensation to victims. Such a fund, for example, was established as a result of the *Holocaust litigation* see n 43.

[41] E Daly, 'Reparations in South Africa: A Cautionary Tale' (2003) 33 *University of Memphis Law Review*, 367, 383–87.

[42] Khulumani: at that time Michael Hausfeld was a partner with Cohen Milstein Hausfeld and Toll until 2008 when he set up Hausfeld & Co LLP in London.

[43] *In re Austrian and German Holocaust Litigation*, 250 F.3d 156 (2nd Cir 2001).

Bank et al[44] ('*Khulumani*'), sued 50 multinationals and banks spanning six countries (Switzerland, Germany , France, the Netherlands, the UK and the US) and involving six key industries (arms and ammunition, oil, transportation, banking, computer technology and mining). These also included South African corporations.

A few months before the Khulumani litigation was filed with the Eastern District Court of New York, another US personal injury attorney filed the case of *Lungisile Ntsebeza at al v Daimler Chrysler Corporation et al* ('*Ntsebeza*') against UBS, Credit Suisse Group and Citicorp in the Southern District Court of New York. In an amended version of the case, Anglo American, de Beers, Sasol and Fluor Corporations, Barclays, Deutsche Bank, Dresdner Bank, Commerzbank, Credit Lyonnais, Banque Indo Suez, IBM, Novartis Sulzer and the South Africa government were added. That attorney's South African partners were Advocate Dumisa Ntsebeza, head of the TRC's Investigative Unit, and attorney John Ngcebetsha of Nagel Rice and Madlanga Inc in South Africa.

Paul Hoffman, a partner with Schonbrun, De Simone, Seplow, Harris and Hoffman LLP took over the running of the *Ntsebeza* case and together counsel for the two separate cases agreed that prospects of success would be greatly enhanced if they removed the South African companies, and the South African government from the complaint, which they did in December 2002. As a result, The Multi District Litigation Panel (MDLP) decided that the apartheid cases should be consolidated and heard by the Southern District Court of New York.[45]

The original complaints not only requested damages but also sought broad equitable relief, for example an historic commission and the institution of affirmative action education and training programmes. After the *Khulumani* case was filed in 2002, the Court requested *amicus* briefs from all parties.

What followed is a matter of public record. The South African government submitted its concerns about the litigation stating, 'it would make little sense for the government to support litigation, which sought to impose liability and damages on corporate South Africa', and that the litigation would undermine the reconciliation process. The US government filed a statement supporting South Africa's position.

Meanwhile, South Africans, individuals and organisations wrote letters of support to the plaintiffs. Twelve of the former TRC Commissioners including its Chairman and former Archbishop of Cape Town, Sir Desmond Tutu, wrote a letter of support in response to the South African government's statement. He wrote;

> There was nothing in the TRC process its goals, or the pursuit of the overarching goal of reconciliation, linked with truth, that would be impeded by this litigation. To the contrary, such litigation is entirely consistent with these policies and with the findings of the TRC. The TRC never contemplated that victims would be precluded from seeking compensatory damages from those liable for abuses, unless the TRC had granted the perpetrator Amnesty[46].

[44] *In Re South African Apartheid* (n 1), *Khulumani* (2007).

[45] Kesselring (n 34) 84.

[46] *The Brief of Amici Curiae Commissioners And Committee Members of South Africa's Truth and Reconciliation Commission In Support of Appellant's*: On Appeal from the US District Court for the Southern District of New York (Case No Civ 4524 and MDL No 1499) *In Support Of Reversal* 01/23/2009.

Other supporters included Joe Stiglitz,[47] Nobel Economy Prize winner 2001, and other high-profile organisations. Meanwhile objections were raised by the governments of Switzerland, Germany, the UK and Australia. All officially spoke up in favour of those companies headquartered in their territories, and duly filed *amicus curiae* briefs in support. The foreign policy questions raised in those briefs during the first years until 2009 were almost successful in getting the case struck out. The level of state intervention, in any case as far as the plaintiffs' lawyers are aware up until that time, was unprecedented.

In light of the above it was hardly surprising that in November 2004 Judge Sprizzo of the Southern District Court of New York did dismiss the original complaints in their entirety,[48] on the grounds that he did not regard aiding and abetting international law violations as a universally accepted standard of international law and that the plaintiffs' theory of liability was too broad – merely doing business in South Africa was too tenuous a connection. He also referred to foreign policy considerations. The judge did, however, grant a right of appeal and the plaintiffs appealed to the Second Circuit Court of Appeals, which reversed in part, and reinstated the plaintiffs' ATCA claims. The Appeal Court centrally held that 'a plaintiff may plead a theory of aiding and abetting' under the ATCA and referred the cases back to the lower court, which allowed for the plaintiffs to submit amended complaints.[49]

There followed an immediate appeal by the defendants to the Supreme Court for *Certiorari*.[50] Had this been granted, the case could ultimately have been dismissed. The Court, however, was unable to pass judgment for lack of a quorum as the plaintiffs raised conflict issues. As a result, four justices recused themselves as they owned stock in some of the defendants. Thus, the case survived, and in October 2008 the plaintiffs filed two amended consolidated complaints, which now reflect the entirety of the litigation.

On 8 April 2009 the District Court rejected the lender liability claims and held that the plaintiffs' significantly narrowed amended complaints filed in 2008 could proceed against the current defendants as they had addressed the broad scope of the claims that the South African government highlighted in 2002.[51] In narrowing the complaints, the banks and South African corporations were off the hook[52] as the plaintiffs made it clear to the Court they were not alleging liability for merely doing business in South Africa during apartheid. The reasons for this are further elaborated below.

Accordingly, at the hearing the *Khulumani* case had considerably narrowed down its defendants to only those corporations that held direct and exclusive contracts with the apartheid state and had full knowledge of the implications of their activities in supporting the apartheid policies.

Broad equitable and programmatic relief was also dropped from the amended complaint, which now simply states that injury will be evaluated on a category basis,

[47] J Stiglitz, Letter in support of Plaintiffs, to Judge Sprizzo, Southern District Court, *Re Khulumani, et al v Barclays National Bank, et al*, 6 August 2003, www.khulumani.net/khulumani/documents/category/5-us-lawsuit.html, accessed 30 August 2013.

[48] *In Re South African Apartheid Litigation*, 346F, Supp.2d538,550 (S.D.N.Y) 2004.

[49] Kesselring (n 34).

[50] Most decisions of the Circuit courts are not appealable to the Supreme Court (SC). A party can apply for a *Writ of Certiorari* when it wishes to have a lower court decision reviewed. The SC will decide whether the case is of sufficient legal or constitutional gravitas before deciding to accept the *Writ*.

[51] The Zuma Government of South Africa wrote a letter to the Court reversing its previous position in 2010 on the basis that the complaint had been narrowed and did not include South African businesses or the government.

[52] This is further elaborated in the next section.

individualised for exceptional circumstances. Aggregate recovery is unknown at this time and there is no demand for a sum.[53]

B The Current Complaint

In Re South African Apartheid Litigation now addresses the concerns of the two cases in the consolidated complaint amended in 2009, which alleges a specific nexus between defendants' conduct and gross human rights violations. The first complaint is now known as *Balintulo et al v Daimler AG, Ford Motor Company, General Motors Corporation, International Business Machines Corporation, and Rhienmetall Group AG* (informally known as the *Khulumani* case).[54]

The plaintiff organisation (Khulumani) has 44,000 victims on its database with a list of their harms, and contact with many more. Represented by 13 individuals,[55] they allege specific violations of extra-judicial killing, torture, detention and cruel treatment, all of which took place between 1960 and 1994 and which were enabled with corporate support.

> Khulumani is a South African organisation that works to assist victims of apartheid violence and individuals who suffered segregation, arbitrary arrest and detention, rape, torture, and the extra judicial killing of family member, run by Hausfeld LLP assisted by Abrahams Kiewitz Attorneys who are located in South Africa.[56]

The second case is *Ntsebeza v Daimler AG*, in which discriminatory employment practices are alleged on behalf of the plaintiffs and all black citizens (and their heirs and beneficiaries) who, during the period 1973 to 1994, suffered injuries as a result of defendants direct and secondary violations of law of nations run by Nagel Rice and Ngcebetsha Madlanga Inc, who are based in South Africa.

The remaining defendants in *Re Apartheid* post 2009 are:

- The technology company IBM, which is alleged to have aided and abetted the South African government's denationalisation of black South Africans through the provision of computers, software training, and technical support for that express purpose. It provided the Department of Interior with a computerised population registry 'specifically designed' to assist the government to enforce racial pass laws and other structural underpinnings of the apartheid state.
- Automotive companies Daimler and GM Ford Motors, which are alleged to have aided and abetted apartheid and extra-judicial killing by supplying specially designed and manufactured military vehicles for the purpose of violently suppressing anti-apartheid activities. The special purpose vehicles were directly used to patrol and carry out attacks on black townships.
- GM Ford Motors, which settled the claim against them in 2012, and which has now been dropped from the docket.

[53] *Khulumani v Barclays Nat'l Bank Ltd* 504F 3d254 (2nd Cir 2007).

[54] ibid.

[55] The named plaintiffs are Sakwe Balintulo, Dennis Brutus, Mark Fransch, Elsie Gishi, Lesiba Kekana, Archington Madondo, Mpho Masemola, Michael Mbele, Catherine Mleangeni, Reuben Mphela, Thulani Nunu, Thandiwe Shezi and Thobile Sikani.

[56] Kesselring (n 34).

- Weapon supplier Rheinmettal, which is alleged to have 'ensured that the security forces of the apartheid regime acquired the armaments and military equipment it needed to suppress dissent and control the population despite international arms embargoes. Their support included exporting a complete ammunition factory to South Africa in spite of international sanctions in force at that moment, training the South African security forces, supplying weapons that would be used in connection with extra-judicial killing, torture and cruel and inhumane degrading treatment'.

The grounds of the action are that the corporate defendants (formerly including banks) are accomplices in civil liability in line with international law. It is a general principle of law recognised by civilised nations within the meaning of Article 38(1)(d) of the International Court of justice (ICJ) Statute,[57] and has been widely recognised by US courts in the context of civil law suits brought against corporations for complicity in gross human rights violations.[58] Moreover, states are 'required to take appropriate steps to investigate, punish and redress corporate-related abuse of the rights of individuals within their territory and/or jurisdiction through judicial, administrative or other appropriate means'.[59]

C Money for Bullets – The Weakest Link

The original complaint in the litigation set out the allegations made against the banks in their role of funding the regime. In particular the plaintiffs alleged:[60]

- The banking companies directly financed the South African security forces, which carried out apartheid's most brutal acts.[61]
- Any transfer of capital to South Africa had military implications: loans to the railways and harbours systems assisted in the mobilisation of the armed forces; trade financing provided the computers and telecommunications equipment necessary to the efficient functioning of a modern army; and financing for housing projects perpetuated the segregated housing of apartheid.
- Both UBS and Barclays provided substantial financing for the South African security forces, Barclays, inter alia by acquiring large amounts of SA Defence Bonds, which directly financed the South Africa armed forces, UBS by holding billions of dollars in funds for the South African reserve bank that were destined for the armament industry. At the same time, Barclays worked closely with the apartheid regime to advise its armed forces. In May 1980 South African Prime Minister PW Botha appointed one of Barclays' directors, Basil Hersov, to a Defence Advisory Board created to advise the armed forces on the 'best business methods and other matters' including relating to the

[57] Brief of international law professors in support of Plaintiffs/Appellees, submitted to the US Court of Appeals for the 2nd Cir. in *Balintulo et al v Daimler AG et al*, 22 December 2009, 14–19, www.khulumani.net/khulumani/documents/category/5-us-lawsuit.html.

[58] For example *Unical v Doe* 395 F3d 932 (9th Cir 2002) The plaintiffs sued Unical for complicity in forced labour, rape, and a murder carried out by soldiers along a natural gas pipeline route in Myanmar. A confidential settlement was reached in 2005.

[59] Report of the Special Representative of the Secretary General on the issue of human rights and transnational corporations and other business enterprises, John Ruggie, A/HRC/11/13, 22 April 2009, para 87.

[60] *In Re South African Apartheid* (n 1), variously sourced from the 'Banking' section of the Complaint (2009) 103 to 125, www.khulumani.net/khulumani/documents/category/5-us-lawsuit.html, accessed 30 August 2013.

[61] *In Re South African Apartheid* (n 1), Complaint (2009), see variously 'Banking' section, 103–25.

manufacture of arms. By joining the Board, Hersov assured Barclays a prominent role assisting the security forces.

- UBS participated in secret funds for loans to the South African government made to finance military and security expenditures.
- Both banks also made vast loans to the South African regime, a significant portion of which went to the security forces. Plaintiffs argued that without the financing provided by those two banks, the regime could neither have maintained nor expanded its security forces to the same degree.

The two cases, having been previously consolidated, came before Judge Sheindlin based on both direct and complicity theories. 'The Court however, excluded all legal bases other than liability for aiding and abetting established both in customary international law and in the US domestic law. Accordingly, the Court's analysis is primarily focused on this discussion'.[62]

The Nuremberg Trials first confirmed that those who aid and abet crimes in violation of customary international law are liable for those acts. For example, the Military Tribunal convicted Emil Puhl,[63] one of the leading officials of the Reichsbank, for participating as a banker in the disposal of looted assets. Similarly, Friedrich Flick, the head of a large group of industrial enterprises, was convicted of slave labour based on his employer's decision to increase company production quotas knowing that forced labour would be required to meet the increase.[64] The application of aiding and abetting liability was more recently reaffirmed by the International Criminal Tribunal for the Former Yugoslavia (ICTY).[65]

D *Actus Reus*

In examining the question of the degree of *actus reus*[66] by the banks in this context, Judge Sheindlin cited with approval the statement of the ICTY later adopted in the US Court of Appeals Ninth Circuit's decision in *Doe v Unical*,[67] holding that:

- '[T]he *actus reus* of aiding and abetting in international criminal law requires practical assistance, encouragement, or moral support which has a *substantial effect* on the perpetration of the crime.'
- On the other hand, assistance having a substantial effect 'need not constitute an indispensable element, that is, a *condition sine qua non* for the acts of the principal'. An accessory may be found liable even if the crimes could have been carried out through different means or with the assistance of another.

[62] Michalowski (n 5) 4.

[63] *In Re South African Apartheid* (n 1), Complaint (2009) *Ministries case*, vol XIV, para 661.

[64] *In Re South African Apartheid* (n 1), Complaint (2009) *United States of America v Friedrich Flick*, 6 Trials of War Criminals Before the Nuremberg Military Tribunals Under Control Council law No 10 (1952) para 662.

[65] *Prosecutor v Furundzija*, IT-95-17/1-T (10 Dec 1998) the Tribunal first set out the *actus reus* and *mens rea* formulation followed in the US Court in *Doe v Unical,* and adopted by Judge Sheindlin. The Tribunal also held liability is appropriate where '*the criminal act most probably would not have occurred in the same way* '*without the acts of the aider and abettor*' in *Prosecutor v Tadic*, ICTY-941 (7 May 1997).

[66] *Actus reus* (criminal act or omission); *mens rea* (criminal intention).

[67] *Doe v Unical* 395 F3d 932 (9th Cir 2002).

- It is (or should be) undisputed that simply doing business with a state or individual who violates the law of nations is insufficient to create liability under customary international law. International law does not impose liability for declining to boycott a pariah state or to shun a war criminal. Aiding a criminal 'is not the same thing as aiding and abetting [his or her] alleged human rights abuses'.

Based on the evidence in the complaint, increased foreign lending was accompanied by a significant increase in military expenditures as well as a drop in social spending. The in-depth study underpinning the CCR submission to the TRC business sector hearings made the obvious inference that the difference in social spending went into military equipment and thereby had a substantial effect on the crimes committed by the regime. While the plaintiffs were able to show the large enabling role in the crimes of the regime, it was not possible to show a direct nexus between the contributions made by individual banks and the increase in the military budget in the overall economic and financial context. In the same way a direct linkage could be made between the special purpose vehicles and technological services which were manufactured and supplied by the other defendants in the litigation. Accordingly, this case determined that what were described as 'mere' commercial activities cannot give rise to complicity, unless the object of the contract is the direct means by which the violations of international law will be carried out.[68]

The argument led by the plaintiffs which reflected the 'substantial effect' standard, drawn from international law, that without the loans the regime could neither have maintained nor expanded its security forces to the same degree, was therefore unsuccessful. The approach taken by Judge Sheindlin is clarified thus:

> The actus reus of complicity liability for the provision of commercial goods and services depended upon first, whether the goods were inherently dangerous or neutral, and secondly, whether they were direct means through which the crimes were committed. The Court excluded as too remote from the commission of the principal offence the provision of goods, such as money, that are inherently neutral, and which cannot, by their nature be the instrument with which violations are carried out. On the other hand, supply goods that are specifically designed for harmful purposes or that provide the direct means for carrying out gross human rights violations does amount to the actus reus of complicity liability. In those cases, defendants can only avoid complicity liability if they show that they thought the goods would be used for legitimate purposes. With inherently harmful goods, an examination of the corporation's mens rea is therefore important to filter out those cases in which liability arises. For neutral goods however no mens rea was necessary as proof of liability already fails at the actus reus stage. Therefore mens rea is irrelevant to goods such as money. Liability for other goods decisively depends on whether the company had the requisite means rea.[69]

The Court's approach to *actus reus* and causation in the context of commercial loans relied heavily on its understanding of the Nuremberg Military Tribunal's decision against Karl Rasche in the *Ministries* case, which set a precedent that commercial lending does not give rise to such liability.[70] Doubts as to the US Apartheid Court's interpretation of the case, and Nuremberg case law generally, suggest that there may have been considerably more room to distinguish the facts in the apartheid litigation had Judge Sheindlin

[68] For the full 'critical reflection' on the fungibility and neutrality (or non-directness of money), see generally, Michalowski (n 5) 7.

[69] ibid, 10.

[70] For a full critique of the relevant Nuremberg case law, see generally, ibid.

been minded to do so, and fuels the argument that each case involving lender liability in this context should be decided on a case-by-case basis, in particular, 'the actus reus of aiding and abetting should not depend on the nature of the corporate activity, but rather on its effect on the commission of the offense'[71] in each individual case.

Consistent with this reasoning, recent critiques of the Apartheid litigation Court's traditional 'micro'[72] analysis suggest that courts could take a 'macro' approach to 'understanding the links between finance and human rights and the breach of due diligence duties, when applied to the specific case of the lender's responsibility in a context of gross and massive atrocities'. This would require taking a more holistic view on a case-by-case basis,

> '. . . collecting and interpreting information about structures, processes and dynamics of the criminal regime, that borrowed the funds. In carrying out this exercise, a number of variables should be assessed, amongst others, the internal and external political context, specifically the political role of the military forces; the seriousness and volume of the human rights abuses, public knowledge about them, denunciations by international organisations, other States and NGO's, features and performance of the national economy monetary trade and financial policies adopted by the Government and other contractual conditions of the loans budgets in relations to national security.[73]

Examples of this methodology being applied are cited in South American dictatorship cases including Argentina, Brazil, Chile and Uruguay.[74]

The structure of political architecture of the apartheid regime and the dictatorship situations may be relevant as regards the accessibility of data supporting claims in lender liability actions. Evidence of specific transactions retrieved in the South American cases demonstrated the 'economically decisive role played by lenders'[75] centrally, because of the 'accessible data on the massive capital inflows received through public debt and on increasing military expenditure'.[76] In these cases, commercial loans were perhaps more easily traceable to source and, by inference, purpose, than those loans to the apartheid regime with its semblance of 'elected government' and concomitant diverse capital inflows to various departmental administrations and the security forces. Conversely, while a massive amount of 'macro' research was gathered on the business sector activities, and made available through the TRC process to the plaintiffs in the litigation, tracing specific loans proved elusive given the confidential nature of the transactions, the fungibility of the money, and the decision by the Swiss government to close down access to the data of its resident banks.

Accordingly, the macro approach may be more easily deployed in civil and transitional justice procedures, where the tribunals of fact take a wider, more active role. Generally, in adversarial systems, the costs associated with 'macro' discovery beyond the public domain, combined with discovery applications for specific commercial transactions,

[71] ibid, 10.

[72] JP Bohoslavsky, 'Tracking Down the Missing Financial Link in Transitional Justice' (2012) 1 *International Human Rights Law Review* 54–92, 58: 'legal theory focuses almost exclusively on human rights as individual legal entitlement' 'which usually entails a rigid and narrow view of the causal link between financial contribution and its consequence' ('micro approach').

[73] For a full in-depth discussion of how the traditional view is being challenged though the lens of the 'macro' approach, see generally, ibid, 81.

[74] ibid.

[75] ibid.

[76] ibid.

would be prohibitive, and likely subject to frequent interlocutory applications regarding confidentiality of sensitive information which is legally protected, and various other delaying tactics from defendants.

Working with civil society partners for example, NGOs and university networks, regulators with investigatory powers or such credible public institutions as United Nations agencies and state bodies, who have responsibility for investigating and producing reports on the conduct of finance in this context, and are seized with the specific legal power to look behind transactions, could greatly assist in establishing the vital linkages. The barrier of legal confidentiality surrounding specific commercial transactions is one that could be identified for further research in the transitional justice context.

One attempt to widen the courts' approach in establishing lenders' liability is the argument submitted in 2009 in an *amicus curiae*, based on domestic tort law principles, to the Federal Court in (Argentina):

> In the context of domestic litigation, it is not uncommon to depart from the normal causal link analysis in favour of an approach which would avoid unfair results, in cases where, because of the particular nature of the contribution, it is extremely difficult to determine a direct link between the action in question and the subsequent harm. The responsibility of the actor is nevertheless established where it is possible to show that on balance of probabilities, his act materially increased the risk of a known source of harm to which the claimants had been exposed. To demand a provable link in such case would be over exclusionary, this principle is pertinent in the context of loans, given that the fungibility of money makes it in most cases impossible to trace back the harm to the specific contribution made by any individual lender, while it is exactly this quality of money that turns it into a highly dangerous commodity.[77]

It remains to be seen whether the Federal Court of Argentina will be persuaded to adopt this established principle in this context. If it does, it may open the way in certain circumstances for a less strict approach to at least establishing *actus reus* in lender liability.

E *Mens Rea*

While the Apartheid litigation Court's formulation on *actus rea* meant the banks were already absolved with regard to liability for financing gross human rights violations,[78] the Court continued to examine the *mens rea* liability standard with respect to both the lenders and the other defendant companies in whose case the question of whether they met the requisite *mens rea* was decisive.[79]

> The Court relied on the Rome Statute to support its view that whether goods provided constitute the means through which the crime is committed is relevant for deciding aiding and abetting liability. Article 25 (3) (c) of the Statute makes an accessory to a crime liable if 'he/she' aids and abets in the commission of a crime or otherwise assists in its commission or its attempted commission, including providing the means to its commission[80].

[77] Essex Transitional Justice Network (ETJN) and the Essex Business and Human Rights project (EBHRP) of the University of Essex United Kingdom, *Amicus Curiae*, Ibanez Manuel Leandro and others/Preliminary measures against undetermined financial institutions.

[78] Michalowski (n 5) 7.

[79] ibid, 7.

[80] ibid, 8.

However, the amicus briefs of the legal scholars submitted amongst other arguments that Article 25(3)(c) of the Rome Statute does not exist in isolation. Article 30 entitled 'Mental State' provides that:

> A person has intent where (a) In relation to conduct, that person means to engage in the conduct: and (b) in relation to the consequence, that person means to cause that consequence, or is aware that it will occur in the ordinary course of events. Even assuming that for the 'purpose of' facilitating commission of such a crime in Article 25(3)(c) carries an 'intent' requirement, within the context of the Rome Statute 'intent' does not require that an aider and abettor share the primary actor's purpose.[81]

The Court concluded that customary international law requires that an aider and abettor only *know* that its actions will substantially assist the perpetrator in the commission of a crime or tort in violation of the law of nations. Accordingly, citing these legal scholars, Judge Sheindlin accepted the lower threshold constructive knowledge test pronounced by the International Commission of Jurists that 'liability of a financier will depend on what he or she knows about his or her services, how those loans will be utilised, and the degree to which these services actually affect the commission of a crime' and that purpose might be inferred from 'facts and circumstances'. She concluded that there was enough international consensus and other sources of customary international law which supported a mere knowledge standard and accordingly, in the cases of the automotive and technology companies, the plaintiffs had adequately pled the *mens rea* standard.

This ruling from a judge well versed in international law principles was a significant breakthrough for the plaintiffs despite its undesirable consequences for lenders' liability, but it was not to last long. Shortly before this decision, the Second Circuit Appeal Court in *Talisman*[82] had reversed the lower court's decision which held that aiding and abetting, or secondary liability, is actionable under the ATCA. The Appeal Court also rejected the proposition that corporations could be held liable under international law, and drawing upon the wording of the Rome Statute,[83] they categorically rejected the knowledge standard applied by Judge Sheindlin. The *Talisman* appeal decision almost seems to suggest that the aider and abettor must be 'partisan in the hostilities'.[84]

VI CONCLUSION

Re Apartheid, is best viewed as a continuum, from the first detailed submissions on the key role of business in supporting the regime presented to the TRC, pausing at the central judgment in 2009, where lenders' loans failed to meet the requisite *actus reas* standard, to the *Kiobe*l judgment in 2013, with its likely profound effect on the final outcome of the litigation. It is allegorical both of the 'lack of visibility around how the monetary system

[81] ibid, 9.

[82] *Presbyterian Church of Sudan v Talisman Energy Inc* 582F.3d244 (2nd Cir 2009) (Plaintiff sued Talisman Energy for aiding and abetting genocide and other violations committed by the Sudanese government in the context of development of oil concessions in Southern Sudan). The Court first decided there was 'no corporate complicity' under the ATCA.

[83] *Rome Statute* Article 25(3)(d)(ii) 'be made in the knowledge of the intention of the *group* to commit the crime'.

[84] *Presbyterian Church of Sudan v Talisman Energy Inc.* (n 82).

influences domestic and social conditions around the world',[85] and of the extent of global integration and reliance on private actors by governments worldwide. The number of high-level interventions in the case by the executive branch is clearly indicative of the special relations and protection major financial and other corporations enjoy with their respective governments.

Moreover, the growing body of literature and initiatives on finance and human rights in recent years highlights the underlying problem which is illustrated here, that the 'integration of the two spheres has so far been shallow and narrowly focussed around a few key areas that are most easily comprehensible to those without specialist financial knowledge'.[86] 'The high profile initiatives, for example, the *Equator Principles*[87] and the *UN Environment Programme Finance Initiative*,[88] which have so many adherents among leading financial firms', many of which have corporate human rights policies in place, may lead to perceptions that there is a 'comprehensive embedding of human rights principles in the global financial system taking place'.[89] A recent report[90] suggests otherwise:

> While there has been a tendency to focus on large project finance and corporate investment, making inroads into other type of finance such as investment banking, and structured products has not been well addressed. Corporate codes of conduct may prove useful where defined corporate action impinges on human rights in a reasonably direct way – for example, labour policies, equality, and discrimination, but they are patently inadequate in addressing the underlying processes that are not visible in human rights analysis – for example, derivatives, risk management, global liquidity, leverage levels across institutions, and algorithmic trading now estimated to account for 50 percent of trading volume on the New York stock exchange.

Other broader initiatives, include the Ruggie[91] Guiding Principles (GPs) and the Multinational Enterprises OECD Procedure, which sets up a national complaint mechanism where complaints against companies can be investigated at OECD Member States National Contact Points (NCPs).

The GPs are directed at transnational companies operating often in conflict zones in host states abroad. UN Special Representative Professor John Ruggie, who has responsibility for implementing the GPs, originally set out international norms binding on corporations during his first term[92] in office. These, however, failed to be adopted, and were replaced by a mandate to 'operationalise' a set of voluntary guiding principles under the

[85] M Dowell-Jones and D Kinley, 'Minding The Gap: Global Finance and Human Rights' (2011) 25(2) *Ethics and International Affairs* 183.

[86] ibid, 183.

[87] ibid. Note the Equator Principles (EPs) are a risk management framework, adopted by financial institutions for assessing and managing environmental and social risk. See www.equator-principles.com, accessed 30 August 2013.

[88] Dowell-Jones and Kinley (n 85) 183, note UNEP (FI) is a public–private partnership established between UNEP and the financial sector. It has 200 members including leading banks, investment firms and insurance companies.

[89] ibid, 186.

[90] ibid, 183, R Roca and F Manta, 'Values Added: The Challenge of integrating Human Rights into the Financial Sector' Danish Institute of Human Rights, 2010.

[91] Professor John Ruggie is the UN *Special Representative* for Business and Human Rights.

[92] Sub-Commission on the Promotion and Protection of Human Rights, 'The Norms on the Responsibilities of Transnational Corporations and other Business Enterprises with Regard to Human Rights', E/CN.4/Sub.2/2003/12/Rev.2, 26 August 2003. See also, J Ruggie, 'The Evolving International Agenda' (2007) 101 *American Journal of International Law* 825. 'The Draft Norms on the Responsibilities of Transnational Corporations and other Business Enterprises with regard to Human rights (UN Draft Norms)', which were presented to the UN in 2003, were initially meant to be binding rules.

three pillars of 'Respect', 'Protect' and 'Remedy'. While they possess some moral force and provide guidance for companies and others, they still fall short of creating judicial obligations on financiers and other corporations, or delivering any new remedial avenues to victims. The Guiding Principles have been endorsed by state parties and will be implemented domestically in accordance with state priorities.

Recently the European Centre for Constitutional and Human Rights (ECCHR) concluded its evaluation of the functioning of the NCPs in four European Countries.[93] The NCPs were set up under the OECD Guidelines for Multinational Enterprises, as points where complaints about companies, including banks, infringing human rights standards can be lodged to a committee in each OECD member state. It is a mediation process in which companies volunteer to participate. Significantly, while the ECCHR found the OECD complaint mechanism lacking in a number of areas, and recommended a strengthening of the Guidelines, they reported a 'very positive response from a number of financial institutions'[94] with investments in Uzbekistan projects. The institutions 'have shown interest'[95] in the forced child labour violations reported by the ECCHR and they have been 'monitoring'[96] the situation with updates from the ECCHR with a view 'to abandoning direct contractual relations' and 'not to accept products from the supply chain, take a public and uncompromising stand, and call on home Governments to take a stand on forced labour in Uzbekhistan'.[97]

If, indeed, such action goes ahead there may be some measurable outcomes on changing rogue state behaviour through pressure from lenders. These lofty aspirations, however, will need to be reviewed regularly to determine if such action has taken place, and whether it was effective.

In conclusion it is clear that courts are not always the best means of adjudicating these cases, and legal theory with regard to financial complicity is still under development. Ideally, cases of this nature would be run in the country where the applicants are domiciled, removing extraterritorial complications, and where victims can more easily attend the hearings and feel connected to the process, if that is possible and desirable. In many cases, however, it remains the situation that many jurisdictions have either inadequate legal remedies , lack credible judicial processes, or do not have the funding or expertise, or local lawyers who will bring these daunting cases on their own.

Recourse to the courts is generally an avenue of last resort for victims, where other remedial mechanisms of accountability have fallen away, broken down, simply do not deliver, or do not yet exist. Carefully explaining to victims in these cases that they will never be put in the place they were before the harm occurred, and the realities of the litigation route, is essential from the outset.

Despite the setbacks to the judicial route outlined in this chapter, the incremental development of the law in lenders' liability in some jurisdictions, and exposure to reputational risk through disclosure of revealing evidence, in the author's experience, increasingly offer a sure-fire way to get lenders to respond and engage with the victims directly.

[93] European Centre for Constitutional and Human Rights, ECCHR policy paper, 'A Comparison of National Contact points – Best Practices in OECD Complaints Procedures', Berlin, November 2011.

[94] European Centre for Constitutional and Human Rights, 'How Effective Is the OECD Procedure?', May 2013, 4.

[95] ibid, 4.

[96] ibid.

[97] ibid.

Finally, *Re Apartheid* brings a dark history into the full light of day. The courage and tenacity of the plaintiffs in the case, and the broader group of victims that they represent, cannot be overstated. Many of the named plaintiffs live in the same houses and streets where the atrocities took place.

The rusting beacon towers where the armed security forces kept watch over the townships still stand nearby, a reminder of how recently the trappings of apartheid were dismantled. Sitting with Elsie Gishi,[98] now 88 years old, in the house where her husband was killed, and where she suffered bullet wounds for which she is on daily medication, it is difficult to conceive how such a repugnant regime could have come to power in the same year as the Universal Declaration of Human Rights[99] came into force. Elsie, like other survivors of such regimes, is trying to find answers from those financial institutions and companies which materially support extreme oppression and division in armed-conflict zones, either through specific commercial activities or the supply of goods and services which maintain and enable gross abuse.

Accordingly, the issue of corporate complicity has not yet been legally resolved. This was not the issue in *Kiobel*, despite the *Talisman*[100] ruling. Judicial avenues will continue to be sought to secure legal accountability of rogue lenders in this context.

[98] *In Re South African Apartheid* (n 1) 26. Elsie Gishi is one of the named plaintiffs, she was shot by South African Police (SAP), on 26 December 1976, when officers kicked in the door of her house during a demonstration in the township. She was shot six times in the back. The bullets lodged in her throat, chest and arms. The entire left side of her body is lame and the bullets cause her respiratory dysfunction and kidney problems all as a result of the shooting.

[99] The Universal Declaration of Human Rights was proclaimed and adopted by the UN General Assembly on 10 December 1948 (South Africa abstained).

[100] *Presbyterian Church of Sudan v Talisman Energy Inc* (n 82).

Index

www.ingramcontent.com/pod-product-compliance
Lightning Source LLC
LaVergne TN
LVHW080015210926
848481LV00011B/3029
* 9 7 8 1 5 0 9 9 0 9 2 4 7 *